Kids were given to us
to teach
not someone else.

THE BIG BOOK OF HOME LEARNING

THE
BIG
BOOK
OF HOME
LEARNING

Mary Pride

Crossway Books • Westchester, Illinois
A Division of Good News Publishers

Interior Design and Cover by Karen L. Mulder
Illustration by Guy Wolek

First printing, 1986.

Printed in the United States of America.

Library of Congress Catalog Card Number 85-72919

ISBN 0-89107-374-4

TABLE OF CONTENTS

INTRODUCTION

What is my excuse for writing this book? That I love reading books on education? Weak. That I am actually teaching my own children at home? Unimpressive. That I am interested enough in finding the best educational products to spend thousands of hours checking them out, and fritter away hundreds of dollars on phone calls and letters? Unconvincing. After all, shouldn't the job have been left to a committee of PhDs? They would have given the book a dignified title, like *Strategies for Obtaining Optimal Educational Outcomes in a Domestically-Oriented Environment.* Then you'd have something *really* worth writing domestically-oriented letters about!

No, this is not another dreary tome by an "educational expert" trying to awe you with her supposedly superior knowledge. We have experts enough already, scattered here and there like land mines in the field of education. The results of their expertise? Just look at the shattered lives of millions of schooled, yet uneducated, Americans. Each new crisis brings the experts out in swarms, recommending solutions that bring them more power and prestige—though they are the very people who caused the crisis in the first place!

This book is not by experts or for experts. It's for *anybody* who wants to learn at home or to help a child learn. You might be a home schooler, a would-be "afterschooler," a grandparent, neighbor, friend, or just an average American who wants to finally learn what the schools failed to teach you. Maybe you're an independent-minded teacher or administrator looking for ways to help your students. Whoever you are, I wrote this book for you!

We, the people, need to become our own educational experts. We can't afford to stay dependent on education that doesn't educate, but rather produces an unending (and unnecessary) stream of woeful, self-doubting "failures," among whom may be our own children and grandchildren, or even ourselves.

What's more, we, the people, *can* become experts.

How? By *discovering* what's out there, *comparing* the different programs, philosophies, and resources, and then *choosing* the best for our own particular needs. That's how anyone becomes an expert in any field. First, he learns what exists in that field. Second, he compares the different options. Finally, he forms his personal opinion based on knowledge and puts it into practice.

In order for you to do this, obviously the first step is *finding out what's out there.* I've done my best to help you with this.

We then go on to the next step, *comparing the options.* Having a legitimate book contract, I was able to persuade hundreds of companies to let me see samples of their products. My motive? Not only to *review* them, but to *compare* them. Very few people have the means to try ten different reading programs, say, or five different language courses. Your problem is not so much finding a program, but finding the *best.* If I have been successful in explaining the features that make different products different, so that you can confidently choose the one that's right for you, I will feel amply rewarded.

All you have to do is to find the subjects that interest you, read the reviews, and make your choices. And since each chapter discusses the educational philosophies *behind* different products and programs, you will be able to intelligently evaluate any new products or programs you come across. Addresses for all these are given in the Index of Suppliers at the end of the book.

Something you should know: it is my general policy to leave out products that expend more effort on indoctrination than on the actual skills they purport to teach. Standard school texts are the worst offenders in this category. I therefore see no need to showcase them in a book about home learning. Another thing you should know: Most products included are reviewed favorably, not because I am uncritical, but because it seemed more helpful to rip up bad *ideas* rather than individual *products*. Thus, in the introductions to each section you are warned away from whole classes of products, but the really awful products are mostly left in kind obscurity (often by the producer's request). Is this a great loss? I think not. After all, you want products you can *use*, not lots of negative reviews.

You will also notice that this book stresses learning as much as teaching. That is because, while teaching is very important at the start, *learning* is the goal of education. If learning does not occur, all the teaching in the world is wasted. Moreover, we should expect the student to eventually become his *own* teacher. When he has mastered the tools of learning, he is free and the world is at his feet. More on this later.

Finally, you may be interested in what experience yours truly has with all these subjects about which I write so enthusiastically. Fair enough. I was favored with a home education myself. Not everyone is blessed with a father who is a professor of philosophy and who is hooked on the Socratic method of instruction. As the firstborn, I got the benefit of all Dad's educational theories. Dad taught me to read when I was five ("Nothing to it!" he said). Graduating from Dr. Seuss (who I still think writes the best books for beginning readers), very soon Dad and I were toting home four brown shopping bags full of library books a week.

Learning to read before first grade *does* have its drawbacks. The first-grade teacher caught me reading *Jane Eyre* in the back of the classroom, and I was promptly double-promoted.

Now Dad was on a roll. The summer before I entered second grade, he got hold of an experimental math series one of his colleagues had dreamed up, and mercilessly stood over me until I'd done the whole thing up to eighth-grade level, which was as far as it went.

"I don't know why everyone says teaching math is so hard," Dad said, and lay back on his laurels. I was doing some laurel-laying myself, since at the age of seven I had already learned everything the schools would be trying to teach me for the next six years. And so on to high school, where I skipped another grade, college ditto, a year and a half of grad school, and out! At that point I finally realized I didn't need school at all, and haven't gone back since.

I don't want to bore you with my academic history, and I especially don't want you to get the idea that I am a "brain." That's what my teachers always told me—"Mary, you're so smart!"—and it kept me from seeing the truth about education for years. *I* wasn't special. My father's teaching was special. Learning at home was special. Access to interesting educational products was special. Reading, instead of watching TV, was special. You can have the same, or better, results by following the simple methods outlined in this book.

Bill and I are now teaching our own children, all of whom perform well above "grade level." Ted, at age five, can and does read the Bible and solves third-grade arithmetic problems, for instance. He also writes his own little books, which he illustrates himself and then binds. Joseph, age four, can read Beginner Books fast and our Psalter pslowly. All by himself Joe has figured out several songs on the piano, which he insists on playing in almost harmonious four-part harmony. Sarah, age two, is learning her ABC's and can do puzzles designed for eight-year-olds. This is not unusual for home schooled children, by the way! *Most* children are geniuses . . . *if* they are given a chance to learn the way God intended.

And that is what this book is about!

HOW TO USE THIS BOOK

You know how to read a resource book. Just turn to the section that interests you and browse through the reviews until something pops out at you from the text. Well, guess what?

You can do the same thing with this book!

The editors and I have, however, incorporated a few innovative features that, we hope, will make *The Big Book of Home Learning* more useful than the average resource book.

If you'll flip to the Index of Suppliers you can see that it is more than just names with addresses attached. We've added all sorts of helpful information: toll-free telephone numbers for ordering, best times of day to call, methods of payment allowed, refund policy, whether or not the supplier has a free brochure or catalog and what it costs if it *isn't* free, plus a brief description of the supplier's product line. Underneath all this you'll notice a little code that tells you in which chapters the supplier's products are mentioned.

Because the addresses, telephone numbers and all the rest of it are in the index, not in the text, we were able to include much more information about each supplier, as well as giving you a cross-index to *other* products that might interest you. For example, say you're looking for math manipulatives. In the Math chapter you see the Firm ABC sells these. The catalog sounds good. In the index you see that Firm ABC also carries hands-on language arts and science materials. You're interested in all of these, so you look up those reviews too. Now you have a much fuller picture of the company.

This way it is also easier to find the address of any given company. Instead of searching through a chapter to find the company, as you have to when full addresses are given in the text, just flip to the index.

What all this means is that you can relax and enjoy *The Big Book of Home Learning* without having to write down reams of information about every product that interests you. Just jot down the name of the supplier and the name of the item on a handy index card or whatever. If you think you will want to order it right away, you might also jot down the price. When you get your whole list together, then you can turn to the index and highlight or underline the companies you intend to contact. Stick the card you were taking notes on in the index and go your merry way. When you are ready to order, all the addresses are in one convenient location and you have all the item names and prices handy, too.

The information in *The Big Book of Home Learning* is as current and up to date as we could possibly make it. After the reviews were written, both they and the index infomation were sent back to the suppliers for verification. The prices listed should be good at least through 1986 and into 1987, and the ordering information is current.

Lastly, this book would not have been possible without the active cooperation of many of the companies listed. Those who supplied me with samples and free catalogs bravely ran the risk of review, and I have not hesitated to point out their products' warts. I would like them to feel they gained something besides a critical going-over by their largesse. Both the publisher and I would be grateful if you would mention *The Big Book of Home Learning* if you write to a supplier whose product is mentioned here.

SMARTER EDUCATION NOW!

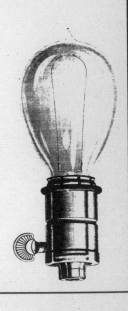

CHAPTER ONE

HOME IS WHERE THE SMART IS

Are you one of those people who was *not* in the 99th percentile on every test? Have you learned to think of yourself as an "average" person, or perhaps even "slow"? Are you one of the millions who entered kindergarten with bright-eyed enthusiasm, but who lost their love of learning along the way? If you are, then this book is for you.

Or perhaps you *were* in the 99th percentile. You soared gracefully through school while others waddled. You know you don't really need a classroom in which to learn, but you do need to locate some sources for instruction in the subjects that interest you. This book is for you too.

Or perhaps your child is a labeled child. He or she is "learning disabled" or "dyslexic" or "retarded" (or even "gifted"), and you have gone around and around with the school trying to find out what the label means and what the school plans to do about it. Are you looking for a sensible way to help your child, one that doesn't depend on federal funding or special programs? Would you like to see *dramatic* improvement in your child's academic progress? The sources that can help you are right here.

Maybe you have already decided to teach your children at home. You look at the schools near you and are not thrilled at the prospect of incarcerating your children in them for thirteen years. You have precious values that you want to pass on, and you are determined to fight for your children's souls and minds. This book is *especially* for you!

Learning at home is the magic key that millions of people have used to unlock the educational treasure-chest. No longer must you or your children climb the academic beanstalk in competition with a hundred other Jacks, each of whom can only succeed by knocking his fellows off into the depths. No longer must you spend a fortune on college credits for knowledge that is sold elsewhere for a pittance. No longer must you watch your

child shrivel up under the burden of a "label" that some trendy educrat has stuck on him or her. In the comfort and privacy of your own home you can learn whatever you want to, whenever you want to—and so can your children.

We are privileged to live in an age when recording technology makes knowledge more accessible than ever before. Not only can we easily obtain information through books and other printed matter, we also can readily acquire a vast array of audio and visual recordings. In the old days, home learning meant book learning only. Now in many cases you can purchase a "teacher on cassette," thereby eliminating most of the remaining distinction between the classroom and the living room.

This technology works to the advantage of both students and teachers. The student has access to an enormous number of options at very reasonable cost. The teacher can, conversely, reach a much wider audience with his method and message. And since home education is as close to a free market as we still experience in this over-regulated republic of ours, dud products quickly sink to the bottom of the pile, there to remain buried in nameless obscurity.

The advantages of learning at home are *price, options,* and *freedom.* Home educational products come wrapped in Kraft paper and delivered by the mailman. Classroom products come wrapped in classrooms (very expensive) and delivered by the school administration (likewise, very expensive). Home learning can be done at your convenience, and in most cases there are no deadlines at all. You cannot, however, *physically* attend a class and take a bubble bath or groom the dog at the same time. At home, you have thousands of choices at your fingertips through this book alone. Away from home, you either are limited to whatever options are offered in your geographical area—or forced to pay exorbitant sums for transportation in order to get to that great seminar in San Diego or that workshop in Bangor, Maine. At home nobody nags you or grades you unless you want them to. Schools, however, *run* on grades, and you must do the work *they* require when *they* want you to do it and in the way *they* want you to do it, or you come away empty-handed.

Let's look at how you can reap the advantages of price, option, and freedom by learning at home.

PRICE

What do you think you'd pay for a private lesson in country guitar from Merle Watson? $100 per hour? $200? Homespun Tapes will sell you one solid hour of the master on cassette, teaching you all his tricks for just $12.95. This amounts to actually three hours' worth of lessons, as in person you would be taking a considerable amount of lesson time practicing the techniques. Further, you can rewind the tapes and hear Merle over and over again. No real-life teacher is *that* patient! When you count these latter factors in, the price of a lesson from a musical master comes to less than the price your next-door neighbor would charge.

What would it cost for you to send your child to one of the top private schools in the country? The going rate is now over $5,000 per year for these elite schools, and even those who have money are often turned away because there are fewer places than would-be students. You can, however, get the entire Calvert School program, including teacher grading and counseling, for just a tad over $400. Calvert's home-taught graduates consistently demonstrate the same achievement as its classroom students. You have thus purchased virtually all the benefits of one of the nation's most exclusive schools at a fraction of the in-person price.

OPTIONS

Lovers of the offbeat and unusual are sure to be delighted with the educational offerings available at home. From make-your-own-globe kits to authentic pioneer stories to a kid's magazine featuring Greek and Roman classics (talk about Golden Hits!) to prereading with rebuses, the home market is popping with surprises. Buy a "noncoloring book" for your granddaughter. Find out how to make reproductions of ancient instruments. Dance about the room to folk songs. Cut out and assemble a covered wagon, complete with horses. Play a computer game where you twirl disks about on the screen to practice your spatial skills.

On the serious side, some items you need are available only at home. Very few churches show their members how to teach their children about God. But at home you can get a complete Through the Bible curriculum. You can get a wide variety of flannelgraphs, felts, and picture stories to present Bible stories attractively and interestingly to your little learners. You can get a beautiful wall chart showing all the important Bible genealogies.

You can get Bible memory helps and even some excellent Christian newspapers for kids.

In the same way, although very few schools have truly excellent literature programs nowadays, you can obtain the finest literature from all ages and all countries by simply mailing a check to the appropriate address. On reading instruction, are you stuck with whatever method the local school uses, no matter how poorly your children respond? Not at all! There are dozens of excellent programs, and although most public schools and even a goodly number of private schools pass them by (witness our national illiteracy), that doesn't mean *you* can't rescue *your* children by reaching for *Play 'n Talk* or *Sing, Spell, Read and Write*.

FREEDOM

In the spring a young man's fancy lightly turns to thoughts of . . . final exams. If you have ever fallen in love while enrolled in school, you will remember how very inconvenient that was. There you were, struggling with papers and reports and deadlines when your heart was emphatically elsewhere.

School, like time and Amtrak, waits for no man. The oldest grandfather in graduate school has no more freedom than the youngest preschooler when it comes to deciding *when* he wants to learn. The whole class must lurch forward at once, and laggards are left holding a lonely "F."

Under our present "credentialing" system, which focuses more on classroom attendance than actual knowledge and experience, education becomes a form of involuntary servitude. You give up control of your own life in order to (you hope) gain that coveted credential. You are not allowed to proceed at your own pace, or select the educational content or method. This applies equally to children and adults, with the major difference being that adults can switch from one institution to another or walk away from the whole thing if they are totally disgusted, whereas children usually have no choices at all.

At home, you are in control. You can pick and choose from a variety of sources instead of being tied to whatever is physically available in your area. You can do the work when it is convenient for you. If you are looking for knowledge, not credentials, you can skip the whole stupefying mass of busywork and tests, and concentrate only on what interests you. Learning becomes a pleasant adventure rather than a burden.

Browse through this book. See the vast array of educational products all begging for your attention. The people behind these products are all eager to please you. They are not interested in making you jump through hoops, but in meeting *your* needs, since they know that if they don't, you will turn to someone else who does. See how clever, unusual, helpful, and inexpensive many of their products are. Then you will know why the smart learn at home!

CHAPTER TWO

SIMPLE STEPS TO SMARTER LEARNING

I f I had a hammer . . . I'd probably use it to knock nails into wood. If school bureaucrats had a hammer . . . they'd probably hold it by the wrong end, punch feebly at one or two nails, and then call it "nailing disabled" and throw it away. Even more likely, some educrat would announce a "Nailing Crisis" and call for a few billion bucks to buy hammers with heads on *both* ends.

The more the schools fail, the less they learn. Educrats have become experts in blaming their students for the educrats' failures. We now have a bumper crop of "learning disabled" children and "functionally illiterate" adults. Blame the educrats? Never! Yet it is a tiny bit suspicious that a nation which had achieved *99 percent literacy* in 1910 all of a sudden is supposedly bursting with mental cripples![1]

Is learning *really* mysterious and difficult? Do we really *need* hordes of federally-funded educational experts? Let's put a pin to this bubble and see how ridiculously simple learning can be—once we understand a few very simple facts.

USING YOUR BRAIN

Take a look at the brain. It's that roundish mass inside your skull that looks like the Green Giant's leftover chewing gum. Understand how the brain operates and you will know why some educational methods work and others don't.

Oversimplifying grossly, we see that thinking involves two main operations: storage and retrieval. You store everything that comes in through your senses in infinitesimal brain cells. If you could remember all of this, you'd probably go crazy; but you *can't* remember it, since you lose track of what is stored there quite easily.

Learning is the art of connecting your memories in a way

that makes enough sense for you to be able to retrieve them rapidly. *Thinking is the act of making new connections* between your memories. In the brain, thinking causes physical connections to grow between the brain cells. The more connections you have, the better your thinking powers. The brains of geniuses are convoluted and heavy with all the connections they have made. Newborn babies, on the other hand, have smooth brains with almost no connections.

Let us, then, develop a very simple theory of education based on these two observable truths: (1) You can't connect what isn't there. And (2) you can't find what is there without a logical connection. Thus, it is vital to expose the student, whatever his age, to a lot of raw data *before* trying to "teach" him anything concerning that data. After he has soaked up hundreds of facts and experiences, then it is equally vital to supply him with a means of connecting them all. You could call this the "Data Connection Theory," but since there is actually nothing original about it, call it anything you like. It works like this:

Say you want to teach a child to read. You do not shove a book in front of his face and start teaching. First, you expose him to a lot of print. Big print, little print. Newsprint. Books. Cereal boxes. Meanwhile, you read to him. Snuggled in your lap, he is both cozy and unafraid—ideal conditions for learning. Slowly he will get the idea: those black marks are letters, letters make words, and words are what Mommy is reading to me. Once he understands what reading is all about, he will probably ask you to teach him to read. Your task, then, is to provide the logical patterns (phonics) which translate all those letters into sounds.

True, reading is a complex subject, and we haven't discussed the idea of physical readiness (i.e., brain maturation) or methods of teaching yet. But I want you to understand that there are really only four basic approaches to teaching, three of which are wrong.

Number One is to begin laying a logical framework *without* first supplying any individual data. You can actually feel the strain on your brain when trying to learn this way. You see, you are not only trying to connect your brain cells, but to fill them at the same time! It's easy to see that a lot gets lost in the shuffle this way.

Number Two is to supply the original data, but fail to show how the individual facts hang together. This is what the schools do when they load a kid up with "Readiness" activities and then spring sight-word reading on him. He is stuck trying to memorize zillions of seemingly unconnected facts. Some kids do manage to invent their own phonics patterns and survive, but it's in spite of, not because of, the way they are taught. This rote memorization approach is used all over: in history, in math, in spelling, in my college engineering courses. Learners are handed hundreds of little "rules" or "facts" without any reasonable way of hanging them all in order. The brain does not want to work this way, and so although individual students can stuff the facts down for a test, they promptly forget it all in a week. This is not real learning.

Number Three is to provide *neither* initial experiences *nor* a framework. Fluffhead professors with no communication abilities are the chief perpetrators of this style of "teaching." Others are deluded into thinking the profs are brilliant because nobody understands them. But flunking all your students is *not* a sign of genius. If a teacher gets garbage out, it's probably because he put garbage in.

The only way that works consistently, because it is based on the way the brain operates, is Number Four: providing the learner with raw data and, after he's had time to digest it, with a permanent framework for storing the data. New data can then be connected to the old with minimal effort.

In history, the framework would be a time line. In geography, the framework is a globe. The learner must have some way of getting a panoramic view of the field he is studying or he will be, as he puts it, "lost." Once he has that panoramic view, he can fill in the details as long as he lives. This is why our forefathers taught their children the Catechism; they wanted their offspring to have a total view of theology, to see how all the pieces hung together.

Some educational products provide data (which, as you remember, includes experiences). Others provide a learning framework, such as a good phonics program. Some provide both. As we learn to discern which product does what, we can educate ourselves and our children much more efficiently.

THE FIVE STEPS OF EFFICIENT LEARNING

What I am going to say now is even less original. Since the beginning of time, mothers and fathers have mastered these five simple steps of learning. Only in our science-worshiping age have we tried to bypass the wisdom of our grandparents—with the dismal results you now see. *Their* generation was 99 percent literate, remember?

THE FIRST STEP—PLAYING

Let kids be kids. That's step one. *Play* is the first step of learning. Earth-shaking, isn't it? Any kindergarten teacher could tell you

that! Ah, but do we *act* on this knowledge? How many times do we or Johnny's teachers try to rush him into "mastering" some new skill without giving him any chance to play around with it first?

Play is not just for babies. Play is the stage where you fool around with something before settling down to get serious about it. When you riffle through a book before starting to read, you are playing. When your husband plugs in his new circular saw and makes passes in the air, he is playing. When your wife tries on a new dress that she doesn't intend to actually wear anywhere today, she is playing. Play turns the strange into the comfortable, the unknown into the familiar. Dad hefts his new saw because he wants to know how heavy it feels before he risks his fingers using it on a piece of wood. Mom tries on her dress because she needs to feel comfortable about how she looks in it before appearing in public. In the very same way, children need to get comfortable with new words, new objects, and new ideas before they can be reasonably expected to do anything serious with them.

Several writers on education have noticed that children who are allowed to play with learning equipment before being put through any exercises with the equipment do much better than those who are immediately forced to put the equipment to its "proper" use.[2]

If you're going to open up unfamiliar new territory in your brain, your best move is to send out some scouts. Survey the terrain. Get to know what it looks like. Then you'll feel confident about building a town out there. Play is the brain's scouting expedition.

How does this apply in real life? Here are some examples:

- Children should *see* print and *hear* it read before trying to learn to read. If possible, they should also *manipulate* letters (like alphabet puzzle pieces) and *write* letters before beginning their reading lessons.

- Children should be allowed to scribble freely before you try to help them make specific marks on the paper. Allow them to use any color they want, and to color outside the lines in the coloring book. So far, three of my children have gone through the scribble stage and the color-it-any-color-but-the-right-one stage, and *without any help from me* all three have gone on to neat, accurate coloring.

- Words like *noun* and *verb* should be used well in advance of any grammar lessons. Ditto for all terminology and every subject. Making a student of any age learn both unfamiliar words *and* unfamiliar concepts at the same time is cruel and unusual punishment.

- Grabbiness is part of learning. See how quickly a baby explores the box his Christmas present came in! He is not satisfied until he has gone thoroughly over it with eyes, ears, nose, fingers, and mouth. Babies, more than the rest of us, are determined to make the unfamiliar familiar. They *know* they don't know, and are trying to catch up. (Incidentally, knowing we don't know and unself-consciously humbling ourselves to learn may be part of what Jesus had in mind when He said we must become like little children.)

THE SECOND STEP— SETTING UP YOUR FRAMEWORK

A child learning to read and an adult studying aeronautical engineering both need the same thing: a framework to help them organize their data. This framework is like a filing cabinet. It provides slots in which to fit the ever-accumulating new data. In history, the time line; in geography, the globe; in reading, the alphabet; in language, the web of grammar; these are frameworks under which myriads of new facts can be filed.

A good framework answers the question, "What in all tarnation is *this?*" History is about people and movements and dates; hence the time line. Geography is about where things are; hence the globe. Engineering is about putting little pieces together to make a building (or airplane, or circuit board). Grammar is about putting words together to make a sentence. Handwriting is about making marks on paper that people can read.

A framework is the big picture, the panoramic view of your subject. Your framework is what's going to glue together all the thousands of facts and ideas you are going to learn.

One big reason kids flounder in school is because the teachers are so wrapped up in skills and subskills and testing and grades that their students forgot what they are trying to accomplish. If a student can't see the relationship between filling out fourteen workbook pages on beginning consonants, and beginning to read (and believe me, the connection is pretty tenuous), his mind will not be storing the new information under the right headings. Reading will seem a succession of unrelated hoops the teacher is trying to make him jump through, and it won't "come together" for him. This is also why students shy away from those fuzzy graduate courses where the teacher wanders all over the landscape without ever making it clear what the course is *about.*

It's not hard to set up a learning framework. All classical instruction included frameworks. Just giving a subject a *name,* like oceanography or weaving or Renaissance art, is the beginning of a framework. If you know what you're trying to learn— whether TV repairing or gourmet cookery or the story of Ethelred the Unready—you're on your way!

THE THIRD STEP—CATEGORIES

Think of your filing cabinet, if you have one. Can you easily find papers you have filed away, or do you have to grumble your way through umpteen folders every time you need a paper? Those of us who have expanded into several filing cabinets quickly find that we need a system to keep it all straight. Some use colored folders, some use colored dots, some use each drawer for a special purpose—it doesn't matter. The main thing is that without organization our bulging files are as useless as if they were in Timbuktu.

You see, a framework is only half the story. You can have a filing cabinet (framework) without an organized arrangement of files. Without organization, though you can happily file new facts by the ton, you can't find them except by accident.

Efficient learners make it their practice to break every new subject down into manageable categories. They don't study the American Revolution all at once, for instance. They study Famous Loyalists, Famous Generals, Spies and Traitors, Naval Battles, the Continental Congress, or whatever categories give them most insight into what they are trying to learn.

It invariably happens that as you go deeper into a subject, your original categories become too broad and you have to make subcategories. In our example above, the Continental Congress quickly becomes too wide a field for the serious student. So he might break it down further into Congressional Leaders, Congressional Committees, Southern Congressmen, or other subcategories, each of which in turn can be further divided.

Let's take another example: reading. Why do phonics courses always spend so much time talking about Vowels and Consonants and Short Vowels and Long Vowels and Blends and Digraphs and Dipthongs? Those are *categories,* that's why! Anyone can remember five Short Vowels and twenty-one Consonants. These little boxes make the data much more findable. Contrast this with the sight-word method used in 85 percent of public schools, where Junior is trying to memorize the individual shapes of all the words in the English language, and you'll have a clue as to why we have a national reading problem.

The difference in learning efficiency between a product or course that organizes the data for you into categories, and one that doesn't, is immense. Although the latter may contain gobs of useful knowledge, you'll have a real struggle walking away with any of it. Keep this in mind as you shop.

THE FOURTH STEP—ORDERING YOUR DATA

Once you've become comfortable with your object of study, the next step is to pick up more information about it. You can do this by memorizing categories of facts, but your task will be *much* easier if you can sort the information into patterns.

Patterns are your method for filing new facts into a category. Going back to our example of the file cabinet, let's say you have organized your file cabinet by categories. The top drawer is for family records and the bottom one is for your home business. Within each drawer you have file folders (subcategories), also organized by topic. You have, for example, one file folder exclusively for Personal Correspondence. All is well and good so far. But if you want to quickly find the letter your Aunt Theresa wrote you six months ago, you'd better have a method for filing letters inside that folder.

You could have filed your letters with the most recent to the front of the folder and the oldest correspondence to the back. You could have filed letters by the names of the people writing to you, or by the topics on which they wrote. Although some of these schemes would be more efficient than others, *any* of them would be more efficient than simply shoving each letter helter-skelter into the folder.

In the same way, you will hold on to new facts much better if you can arrange them in order using a systematic pattern.

What do I mean by a "pattern"? As I said, *patterns are your organizing method.* When you have a category of related facts (such as, in phonics, words ending with "at"), the systematic way you file them (in this case, alphabetic order) is your pattern. Let's look at the pattern for our example of "at" words (alphabetically, by diagraphs, by dipthongs):

at	pat	flat
cat	rat	spat
fat	sat	sprat
hat	vat	splat
mat	brat	chat
Nat	drat	that

Once a child gets used to writing out families of words in alphabetic order, he has a tool for generating dozens of new words from *every* word ending or category he learns.

Some facts need to be sorted alphabetically, as in our example above. Others have a natural chronological pattern (as when studying the battles in a war). Still others sort out numerically, starting with the smallest and ascending to the largest. Arithmetic is full of these kinds of patterns, e.g.:

$$1+1=2$$
$$2+1=3$$
$$3+1=4$$
$$4+1=5$$
$$\cdots\cdots\cdots\cdots\cdots\cdots\cdots\cdots\cdots\cdots\cdots\cdots\cdots$$
$$10+1=11$$

Learning the "one-pluses" by this pattern is much easier than trying to memorize individual "math facts" out of order.

Matter can be organized by its physical layout. You will notice that this book you are now reading follows a definite pattern. Each chapter begins with text that discusses the issues in an educational field. The text is followed by reviews, sorted in alphabetical order. Each review has similar information in its heading. This makes the book easier to use than if all the information were jumbled together.

Why are we spending so much time talking about patterns? Because patterns are what make or break many educational products. If data is not patterned, or ordered according to the wrong pattern, it becomes much harder to use. Try this simple example. Which of the following foreign language programs would be easier to use? The first categorizes phrases together that deal with, say, table manners, and leaves it at that (this one has categories, but no patterns). The second categorizes the phrases and lists them in alphabetical order (category plus pattern). The third categorizes phrases, and lists them in *grammatical* order (e.g., "I like the meal. You like the meal. He likes the meal. She likes the meal . . ."). The third program sorts the data into *the*

form in which you need it, since you talk in terms of I or he or she, not in alphabet lists.

Similarly, it is easy to learn the days of the week in chronological order, which is the way we use them, whereas if you memorized them in random order, or alphabetical order, it would be extremely difficult to use them quickly.

Not every individual fact can be sorted into a pattern. You've just got to memorize the value of pi, for instance. But the vast majority of useful data does follow systematic patterns. It's the scientist's job to find these patterns, and the teacher's job to use them.

If you want to learn effortlessly, and remember what you learn, insist on products that provide both categories and patterns.

THE FIFTH STEP—FUSION

Have you ever had a brainstorm? Suddenly you could almost hear the clicking as light turned on inside your head. Misty ideas suddenly coalesced. Hundreds of previously unrelated facts joined arms and marched along singing.

That marvelous experience was what some writers call "synthesis" and I prefer to call "fusion." Fusion is when frameworks link. All at once, electrical impulses can take the express from Point A to Point B, when they used to have to make detours and swim muddy streams of consciousness to make the trip.

Fusion *feels* good. It unclogs your brain, and lets you spend the energy that used to be wasted hacking through jungles of confusion on more edifying pursuits.

Fusion is the opposite of *con*fusion, which is what happens when our carefully built frameworks turn out to be all wrong and we have to start rebuilding them from scratch. This confusion is the eternal lot of those who are heedless about looking for answers to the deep questions of life.

We live in an age when people are being taught that there *are* no answers, so one might as well not bother asking the questions. The only consistent responses if this is true are despair or ruthless hedonism. And these are the lifestyles we are seeing today.

Although the antiphilosophy of relativism—that there is no right and wrong—has had great success, it is not correct. The human brain was not constructed to be open to *everything.* People have a built-in need for right and wrong, for security, for an integrating philosophy of life. Perhaps the best books ever written on this subject, that describe our present confusion and the timeless solution, are *Escape from Reason* by Dr. Francis Schaeffer (published by InterVarsity Press) and *L'Abri* by Edith Schaeffer (published by Tyndale House). Puritan-Reformed Discount Book Service sells both these books, which between them cost less than $10.

We don't need to understand the meaning of our lives in order to eat, sleep, and park the car. But human beings are not worms in the mud; the more we learn about the world and the joys and injustices of life, the more every thinking person asks, "What is this all for?" How tragic if we, and our children, have been taught to strangle these questions before they can even be spoken. Tragic because there *is* Someone home in the universe; God is not dead; and everyone who seeks, shall find.

CHAPTER THREE

SIX TRICKS FOR LEARNING SMARTER AND LOVING IT

Every trade has its tricks. A blacksmith knows how to make a horse stand still while he hammers on a new horseshoe. Fly fishermen know how to snap the rod and make the line float out over the water. Knowing these tricks makes work a sport, and sport more enjoyable.

Learning can also be a sport. The difference between the duffers and the champions is that the champions know the tricks of the sport, and care enough to put them into practice.

I would now like to share with you some very simple tricks that can make a huge difference in how much you and your children *enjoy* learning.

MODALITIES—YOUR SPECIAL LEARNING STYLE

Jack Sprat could learn by chat,
His wife could learn by sight.
Their son, named Neil, could learn by feel.
They were a funny sight!

Everyone is born with a special learning style. Some, like Jack Sprat in the ditty above, learn best by listening. Others, like his wife, learn best by seeing. Still others are sensuous types who need to have real objects to handle. If you are taught through the channel that suits you, fantastic! If you're not, it's frustration time.

Educators, in their slow grappling with reality, have recently rediscovered learning styles and christened them "modalities." Don't expect any sudden changes in the schools from this discovery, though. Mass-produced education and individualized learning styles do not mesh. The best you can hope for is that *after* your child has been labeled "dyslexic" or "hyperactive" or "learning disabled" some up-to-date remedial teacher will discover that Johnny really just has a learning style that his classroom did not accommodate.

Now let's discover *your* learning style.[1]

Are you easily distracted by new sights? Do you remember where you put things? Are you good at catching typos and doing puzzles? Are you very aware of visual details in drawings? Do you remember names better when you see them on a nametag? If you answered "yes" to these questions, you are a *visual* learner.

Visual learners need to *see* what they are supposed to do. The effective teacher will write out a model, or demonstrate visually the skill to be learned. Some materials that are good for visual learners are:

a. flash cards

b. matching games

c. puzzles

d. instruction books

e. charts

f. pictures, posters, wall strips, desk tapes

Do you like to talk a lot? Do you talk to yourself? As a child, were you a "babbler?" Do you remember names easily? Can you carry a tune? Do you like to "keep that beat" along with the music? Do you read out loud or subvocalize during reading? Can you follow oral directions more easily than written directions? When taking tests, do you frequently know the answer, but have trouble expressing it on paper? Then you are an *auditory* learner.

Auditory learners learn best by hearing. They need to be *told* what to do. Auditory learners will listen to you reading for hours, but you may not think they are paying attention because they don't look at you. They like to memorize by ear and can easily develop a good sense of rhythm. Naturally, auditory learners have a head start when it comes to learning music. Good materials for auditory learners are:

    a. cassette tapes

    b. educational songs and rhymes (like the ABC song)

    c. rhythm instruments

Now for the physical types! Here are your so-called "hyperactives." As a child, did you have difficulty sitting still? Were you always grabbing for things? Did you always run your fingers across the boards when walking past a fence? Do you move around a lot, and use animated gestures and facial expressions when talking? Can you walk along the curb without losing your balance? Do you prefer hugs from your spouse rather than verbal praise? Do you like to take things apart? Are you always fooling with paper or something on your desk when you're on the phone? If so, then you're a *kinesthetic* learner.

Hands-on learning is a must for kinesthetic learners. They need to mold or sculpt or whittle or bend, fold, and mutilate in order to express themselves. Kinesthetic learners learn to read best by learning to write. They like math manipulatives and sandpaper letters. Kinesthetic learners do *not* like sitting at a desk for hours staring at the blackboard—it's like blindfolding a visual learner to do this to a kinesthetic learner.

For kinesthetic learners, try:

    a. long nature walks

    b. model kits

    c. yard work and gardening

    d. textured puzzles

    e. typing instead of writing (it's faster and less frustrating)

Be sure to have kinesthetic learners write BIG when they are first learning. Large muscle action zips through to the brain more easily than small, fine movements. Manipulative materials and a good phonics program cure reversals in kinesthetic learners, who are the group most frequently labeled "dyslexic."

You *can* be all three: visual, auditory, and kinesthetic. God designed people to learn through *all* their senses. But since most of us lean more to one learning style, you can increase your learning enjoyment by adapting the input to fit your style.

MASTERY—A FINITE TASK

I would now like to offer one simple thought that can greatly reduce stress in learning. *You can master any new skill in a reasonable amount of time.* Again, this idea does not *sound* earthshaking. But when you compare it to the way schools usually teach, you'll see how revolutionary it is.

Say Johnny wants to learn to read. Does his teacher say, "O.K., Johnny, I'll teach you to read. It should take about twenty hours total, and then with practice you will be able to read

anything you want"? No way! Johnny is facing up to *eight years* of reading instruction. No matter *how* well he can read, every year he will be reviewing his sight words, writing out spelling lists, filling out endless "reading comprehension" tests, and on and on and on. Would this discourage *you*? Of course it would! And it discourages Johnny too. The task seems endless. Nothing he does will make it shorter.

For *dramatic* results in your home program, just make it clear to the student that this task will *not* go on forever. If he applies himself, he *can* finish it more quickly. Promise *not* to review him constantly on his skills. Instead, immediately put those skills to work.

How do you do this? Well, let's say you are teaching your daughter arithmetic. Once she has learned addition, throw a party. Buy her a present. Treat her to a yogurt popsicle. Do *something* to celebrate. Any ceremony you come up with will help cement the fact that an era is over. Addition study is over. (Celebrating will also make her more anxious to finish the *next* step.) Now you are not going to study addition any more. Rather, you are going to *use* addition. Let her help you tally up the checks when you balance your checkbook. Have her keep running tabs on the cost of your shopping trip. Addition is used in multiplication and division, which she will be studying next, so if you don't do anything special at all she will still be using it.

If you teach your child something that he never gets any practice using in daily life, you probably didn't need to teach it in the first place.

ACCELERATION—GETTING UP TO SPEED

Another reason school seems like such a hopeless burden to many children is that it goes on so *long*. Thirteen years is a longer sentence than most murderers get nowadays. Yet we toss kids into school and lock the door on them for thirteen years and expect them to be *enthusiastic* about it!

Nobody needs thirteen years to learn what the schools have to teach. At the most, you need three or four.

Let me explain why I said that. It's really pretty obvious when you see how our forebears handled education. In those olden golden days, kids didn't start school until age eight or nine. They attended classes for, at the most, three six-week sessions a year, six hours a day, and by the time they were sixteen they could read, write, and cipher rings around modern children. Nor was their instruction confined to the Three R's. American children of the 1700s through the early 1900s learned history, theology, geography, practical science, and hundreds of practical skills that are now only tackled in college, if at all. When you add up the total time in school, it comes out to eight years of eighteen weeks each. Modern children go to school thirty-six weeks a year; so by simple arithmetic four years of old-time instruction should be all it takes for similar results.

In actual fact, it has been shown again and again that twenty hours of phonics instruction is all that children need in order to read. As for math, you may recall that my father taught me eight years of math in three months, two hours per day. That amounts to 120 hours for *all* basic math, as opposed to the 1,440 the schools now spend. Surely I am not twelve times smarter than everyone else! Similar reasoning applies to the other subjects: history, geography, handwriting, composition, and so forth.

Every child who attends school, public or private, is retarded. "Retarded" means "held back." Schools are in the business of keeping children off the street and out of the job market for twelve years. So they drag out learning needlessly for years, and fill up the time with mindless, boring exercises.

You may wonder what to do with a child who flashes through the standard school subjects. Don't worry. *He'll* know what to do! The whole point of learning the basics is to get to the good stuff—other languages, literature, serious writing, theological studies, designing and inventing, art, music, and on and on. By the time your children finish their basic education, it should be clear what subjects interest them enough to qualify for further study. Let Junior start a business. Send his articles to magazines. Patent his amazing arcade game. Give him a one-man show and invite the artistic community in to admire his work and suggest improvements. With the whole wide world out there, who wants to spend eight years with reading comprehension worksheets!

Some states, in an attempt to save high school dollars, are letting teenagers take the GED at sixteen. But why stop at sixteen? Any wide-awake ten-year-old who is home-taught ought to be able to pass it. And wouldn't *that* be a motivator!

INDEPENDENCE—GETTING ON WITH THE JOB

John Holt has become famous for suggesting that kids can teach themselves *without* adult interference. Although this idea can be carried to extremes, it is undoubtedly easier to learn without

someone hovering over you and babbling in your ear while you are trying to work.

Anyone who has a fine crop of youngsters to teach at home quickly discovers the importance of letting students do as much as they possibly can by themselves. One of my favorite lines is, "Try it. If you have trouble, come and ask for help."

Only children, and adults, who are allowed to work through a problem on their own ever discover the thrill of accomplishment. Throw away those crutches!

The koala may carry her baby until he is as big as she is, but this does not work well for humans.

INCREMENTAL LEARNING— THE HITS JUST KEEP ON COMING

I am indebted for this next suggestion to John Saxon, the developer of the world's greatest algebra series (read all about it in the Math chapter). Saxon's idea is brilliantly simple. Teach one skill at a time, and then *let students keep using that skill.* He calls this "incremental learning"—learning one little thing at a time and then building on it.

Obvious, you say? Not in *practice.* In *practice,* once a student learns a new skill, do we ever reward him again for his achievement? Isn't that standard response a sigh of relief and "Now let's get on to the *next* subject"? Johnny and Sally soon learn that nobody cares about all the things they've already learned.

Whether in kindergarten or college, students spend their whole lives constantly struggling with the unfamiliar, only to be rewarded for their successes by *more* hoops to jump through. The constant pressure to learn *new* things never relaxes; old accomplishments get no praise.

Math instruction has been an arid field when it comes to praising the student. Children are taught new skills, and then the skills are abandoned until final exam time, when they spring from the shadows on hapless test-takers. Saxon, seeing the fruitlessness of this "method," decided to *not* jump from skill to skill, but to include questions on previously learned concepts in *every* lesson. This is *not* the same thing as teaching the same old tired idea over and over again, that odious practice of unnecessary review. Saxon's students get to *use* their learning, and to be praised for it.

How does this apply to other subjects? Here are some suggestions:

- *Every* multisyllable word decoded is cause for rejoicing, not just the first one, until the student gets so good at reading that it would be insulting to praise him. (At this point, accepting his reading as just as good as yours, and asking him to read things for you, is praise enough.)

- Can Johnny color inside the lines? That doesn't mean he has just graduated from coloring books, and never gets to color again. It *does* mean he can experiment with hard and soft coloring, with density, with different kinds of crayons and markers and coloring pencils, meanwhile being praised for his fine coloring.

- Just because Suzy is now in Book 3 of Suzuki piano, she shouldn't think she can never play her old Book 1 pieces again. Rather, encourage her to give them a whirl every now and then. She'll be able to see how much her expression and dynamics have improved, and see her progress.

Seeing how much you have improved is always great encouragement. So is feeling really competent at a task. Incremental learning makes learning *fun!*

THE TEACHER'S ROLE—TEACHING AS PUTTING IN

Lastly, here is how to make *teaching* more enjoyable.

You know, teachers are the most overworked and harassed bunch of people around. Why is that? In large part, it's because so much of their assigned job is *pulling facts out of people.*

I've never plowed with a mule, but I do believe that it's no harder to get an ornery mule to pull that plow than it is to get an ornery kid to divulge what's in his mind. Especially if *nothing* is in his mind. You can't pull out what isn't there. Yet 90 percent of schooltime is spent on tests, quizzes, seatwork assignments, and verbal cross-examinations ("Who can tell us when Charlemagne was crowned Holy Roman Emperor?"), instead of on giving children information and giving them a chance to ask their *own* questions.

These demands for feedback are not teaching. Teaching is *telling or showing people what they don't know.* And it is *so* much easier to concentrate on input (telling) than on output (dragging feedback out of students)!

To make the most of your teaching time, and to make it easier on yourself, *tell your children what they need to know.* Don't be afraid to repeat yourself. Increase the proportion of input to output. A few simple oral questions will tell you whether your offspring are on track. Forget those piles of workbook exercises!

Read history to your children. *Read* science books together. *Read* the Bible at meals. Whatever the knowledge you want to impart, put it *in!* Don't wear yourself out checking whether they are learning. *After* they've received ample instruction is the time for a little low-pressured feedback.

Nobody tests your children on TV commercials. But if you still have a TV, you can see they have learned the ads. TV taught them. Unless your children are actively hostile, or so lazy that they won't even bother to listen, or so illiterate that they never read anything, you should be able to do at least as well as a TV set.

Robert Doman, head of the National Academy of Child Development, has said that the average child gets only *three minutes* of individualized instruction daily in school. Three minutes! I don't know where Mr. Doman gets his figures, but my own school experience sure validates them. Do you think you can beat this at home? Even fifteen minutes a day is five times more than your children get in school!

You *can* help your children educationally, in the few fragmented minutes they have left after school. But you can do even more. The next section will tell you what home schooling is, and why so many of your neighbors are doing it.

PART II

FOR HOME SCHOOLERS: HOME SCHOOL MADE SIMPLE

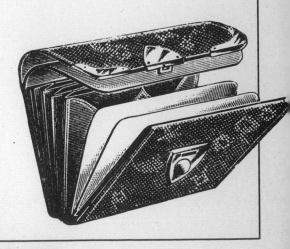

CHAPTER FOUR

INTRODUCTION TO HOME SCHOOLING

"When they saw the courage of Peter and John and realized that they were unschooled, ordinary men, they were astonished . . ." (Acts 4:13).

Nothing is new under the sun. Two thousand years ago the Sanhedrin was flabbergasted to see men preaching confidently who hadn't been to their approved schools, and today Americans are astonished at the idea of children learning at home. After the first shock passes, though, most people are sensible enough to judge the movement by its results. After all, what can you say about:

- An eleven-year-old girl who entered Oxford University, and two years later received her mathematics degree. Ruth Lawrence was one of only two math students to receive special commendation for her work. Ruth had never been to school. Her father taught her at home.[1]

- Ishmael Wallace, a boy who the public school considered "not musically gifted," and who they were in the process of labeling "slow" when his parents withdrew him. Ishmael is now nationally recognized as a talented musician, and is the author of an award-winning musical.[2]

- Grant Colfax, a totally home-schooled lad, made national news by getting accepted at college. Of course, Grant didn't apply to just *any* old college—he sent in his forms to Yale and Harvard, and was accepted at *both*.[3]

All throughout human history, children have been educated at home. Virtually none of the signers of the Declaration of Independence had formal schooling. Thomas Edison was taught at home (the school said he was "addled," and his mother disagreed). Until compulsory attendance laws were passed, which is a fairly recent development in our history, children were normally taught to read at home *before* attending school, and many well-educated people never went to school at all.[4]

As I said, home school is nothing new. What *is* new is the mass movement out of public school and back to private education, including home-based private education—e.g., home school. These are your three choices: public school, private school, and home school.

WHAT ABOUT PUBLIC SCHOOL?

This section is not about what is wrong with public education. Heck, *you* know what's wrong with public education! Any contestant on "Family Feud" could quickly list Ten Things That Appall Me About Public School: crime, drugs, illiteracy, lack of discipline, antireligious curriculum, plummeting standards, busing, lack of respect for authority . . . You see how easy it is? The question is not so much, "What is wrong with the public schools?" as, "What should we do about it?"

Many people see the problems public school bureaucrats have brought upon themselves and, with virtuous zeal, are crusading to "reform the schools." I have never considered this as an option, for the following reasons:

(1) As a Bible-believing Christian, I do not believe that education is a function God has granted to the government. We have never needed public schools, and we don't need them now.[1]

(2) As an American citizen, I do not believe that bureaucrats have the right to force their values on other people's children. The Bible says we can try to persuade others "with gentleness and respect." Civil government may punish evildoers for their crimes, but under God it has no right to prevent parents from passing on their morals and beliefs, whether Christian or non-Christian, to their children. This does not mean that public schools, as long as they exist, should outlaw *voluntary* Bible

reading and prayer. It does mean that school should not be a vehicle of compulsory religious indoctrination. Which it is.

(3) As a very concerned mother, I am not about to make my children into guinea pigs for my, or anyone else's, social experiments. Crusaders for school reform generally feel they must put their kids into public school in order to be taken seriously. Bill and I would never subject our children to a bad environment in order to legitimize a "cause."

WHAT ABOUT PRIVATE SCHOOLS?

You probably agree with me that public school is not exactly what it should be. You might be considering home schooling. If you are not home schooling already, you are wondering about whether perhaps private school would be a better choice.

Private education differs from public education in the following ways:

(1) It costs money. Sometimes lots of money. This is reason enough for many lower- and middle-class families, or large families, to seriously consider home education.

(2) It is more parent-controlled. This is more significant in a small school than in a large one. Some of the large parochial schools are every bit as hard for parents to deal with as the public schools.

(3) It may offer an alternative approach to education. I say "may" because many private schools are merely public schools in disguise. Their teachers have been taught in the same schools as public school teachers, they have the same mania for "educating the whole child" (a euphemism for forcing their values on children instead of teaching them skills), they use the same offensive methods and the same curricula. Do not assume that because the school is "private" it is different.

Private school is certainly a valid choice, once children are mature enough to know what they believe and defend it from their peers. But because parents cannot always find a private school that supports their educational philosophy and values without totally draining their pocketbook, for many the choice comes down to simply public school or home school.

WHAT ABOUT HOME SCHOOL?

Every mother and father is a teacher. The question really is, "How much of what my children need to know should I help them learn?"—not "Should I try to teach them?"

This section is designed to help you make that decision. The more you know about your options, the clearer the choices become. This chapter gives you a simple introduction to the major people and methods in the home school movement. The next chapter covers how to set up your program. I've also included a section with books that you might want to read, and resources especially for home schoolers, with reviews to help you pick the ones that can help you most. Finally, the Curriculum Buyer's Guide gives you a complete overview of the correspondence programs that your fellow parents are using. Or, if you have educational expertise and a hefty hunk of confidence, the reviews in the rest of the book will give you plenty of options from which you can fashion your own program.

Let's take a look now at some of the leading thinkers in the area of home education. By becoming familiar with their ideas, you will not only sound much more erudite ("they laughed when I stood up to talk about education—but when I mentioned John Holt . . ."), but you will be able to make informed decisions about whether and how you'd like to do it.

BIG NAMES IN HOME SCHOOLING

Little kids are people. That is the message of two of the most respected names in home education, John Holt and Maria Montessori. Both Holt, whose career as a teacher spanned several decades and who was the founder of *Growing Without Schooling*, and Montessori, whose work began early in this century in Rome and who has since passed away, agree that children *want* to learn. Further, the things children want to learn are *adult* things: how to take care of themselves, how to cook, how to drive a car, how to read the newspaper.

Maria Montessori and the "Normalized" Child

Looking at Montessori first, we find a great devotion to the inner goodness of children. So intense was this devotion that interviewers spoke of her as establishing a "new religion," and she in fact spoke this way herself. In those days, a lot of people talked like that. Socialism was relatively new, and heady in its insistence that people were naturally good and only society was bad. Unhappily, some Christian preachers had laid it on a bit thick about our carnal nature, to the point where the church seemed to be saying that children were nothing but bad. Montessori's experience did not bear this out, and neither does the Bible, for it teaches that all people, saved or unsaved, are made in the image of God and therefore children do have the ability to love others and enjoy obedience.

Theology aside, we find Montessori, a medical doctor, carefully observing children and making notes about what they liked and disliked. Asked to take over the education of some Italian slum children, she put her theories into practice and stunned the world by turning these children into adept scholars.

What did she do? She gave the children pieces of equipment carefully designed to help them learn adult skills: wooden frames with canvas attached and string for practicing lacing, frames for buttoning, frames for using the button-hook devices of that day. She gave them materials they could feel with their hands: textured blocks, letter stencils, number stencils. She gave them grown-up tools scaled down to child's size: pots and pans, brooms and mops. She gave them responsibility for doing as adult a job as possible. Children in Montessori's own school served themselves lunch and cleaned up afterwards, although they were only three to five years old.

Having prepared the environment as carefully as she could to be free of distractions, Montessori and her teachers sat back and watched. They might show a child how to use a piece of apparatus; then they would withdraw and let the children learn as much as they could totally unaided. The data was there—hands-on experiences by the roomful. The framework was there—careful graduated exercises led the children almost imperceptibly to reading, writing, and figuring. The children learned.

Awed by Montessori's success, teachers all over the world descended on her. She was less than delighted by their attention, since she was very busy and most of her callers did not speak Italian, a prerequisite for intelligent conversation with this Italian-speaking doctor. In time she ended up writing several books and teaching others to carry on her work. The "Montessori method" is now taught by several different societies and in hundreds of schools and preschools, as well as home schools.

Many Montessori schools use her special equipment, but do not follow her spiritual ideals. The two *are* separable; using Montessori's materials need not compromise your religious beliefs.

The three fundamental Montessori principles are:

(1) "Observation." According to Montessori, "the teacher must refrain from interfering directly."[5]

"The child educates himself, and when the control and correction of error is yielded of the didactic material [she means when the stuff you hand the kid doesn't confuse him], there remains for the teacher nothing but to observe . . . the teacher teaches little and observes much."[6]

In "true" Montessori education, adults do not teach at all. Instead, they closely watch the children in order to see how the environment should be changed to meet their needs. The closest an adult comes to "teaching" a child is in showing him how to use Montessori's materials.[7]

(2) "Individual Liberty." Children are turned loose and allowed to do whatever suits their fancy. This does not result in random play, however, because of the next principle.

(3) "Peparation of the Environment." In Montessori's thought, it is very important to "control for error" by only presenting materials that logically relate to one another. Shapes must fit neatly into their allotted slots, graduated cylinders must go up by uniform sizes, color-coded items must logically follow the code, and so on. Thus children are not confused.

The point of all this, as is obvious, is to build a framework for the child. Montessori provides many experiences, and by concentrating deeply on the work provided, the child is able to build his own framework. Montessori called this process "normalization" and attributed mystical significance to it. A "normalized" child learns, in time, to build frameworks for himself even when he is not provided with a perfect environment. He learns to look for patterns on his own and to try to fit reality into categories.

Much of what Montessori recommends makes a lot of sense, once you realize that "normalization" is just framework-building and the concentration required is merely the brain making lots of little connections. As God made us, children and adults do have that ability to learn without being "taught," and it is marvelous.

John Holt and "Invited Learning"

If Maria Montessori is the high priestess of "prepared environment," John Holt is the Josiah to knock down those altars. For years Mr. Holt quietly but insistently taught that children can learn *all by themselves,* without any well-intentioned adult interference. He sees the idea of programmed learning as positively evil. As he so tellingly put it,

> The difference between fond and delighted parents playing "This Little Piggy Went to Market" with their laughing baby's toes and two anxious home-based would-be clinicians giving "tactile stimulation" to those same toes, so that the child will one day be smarter than other children and thus get into the best colleges, may not on the face of it seem to be very much. But in fact it is the difference between night and day. Of two ways of looking at children now growing in fashion—seeing them as monsters of evil who must be beaten into submission, or as little two-legged walking computers whom we can program into geniuses, it is hard to know which is worse. . . .[8]

John Holt did not reject all of Montessori's thought, but he fiercely defended the right of children to tackle the *real* environment. Where Montessori would carefully create a lacing frame for children to practice on, Holt would let them mess with Daddy's shoes. Where Montessori would carefully exclude from her prepared environment all randomness and chance, Holt would be happier in the mess of normal living.

In this area of disagreement, I would follow Holt, as God certainly didn't create children to need a special, isolated world of their own. In fact, Montessori's apparatus is, if you examine it, just a child-centered copy of what every normal home contains: pots and pans, buttons and laces, round things and square things, soft things and prickly things. Her genius is in letting children actually handle these things, rather than forbidding them to touch or try to use adult possessions.

John Holt's motto was "Trust Children." Based on his own observations of children learning and not learning, garnered in real-life situations, Holt believed children really want to learn and that they will learn what they need to know if left entirely to themselves. In actual practice, Holt advocated involving children in our adult activities rather than begging them constantly, "What do *you* want to do today?" Still, his theory almost eliminates "teaching" as a profession, other than a master/apprentice type of relationship where the apprentice is eager to learn a particular difficult skill. What a person can learn on his own, Holt says, he should learn on his own. Our teachers are not there to tyrannize us, but to offer the help we need.

Raymond Moore: Let Children Be Children

Based on his own experience as an educator and on analysis of more than eight thousand early childhood studies, Dr. Raymond Moore and his associates at Hewitt Research Foundation came to the following conclusions:

Readiness for Learning. Despite early excitement for school, most early entrants (ages 4, 5, 6 etc.) are tired of school before they are out of the third or fourth grades . . . They are far better off *wherever possible* waiting until ages 8 to 10 to start formal studies (at home or school). . . . They then quickly pass early entrants in learning, behavior and sociability. . . .

The eyes of most children are permanently damaged before age 12. Neither the maturity of their delicate central nervous systems nor the "balancing" of the hemisphere of their brains, nor yet the insulation of their nerve pathways provide a basis for thoughtful learning before 8 or 9. The *integration* of these *maturity levels* (IML) comes for most before 8 and 10.

This coincides with the well-established findings of Jean Piaget and others that children cannot handle cause-and-effect reasoning in any consistent way before late 7's to middle 11's. *And the bright child is no exception.*

Socialization. We later become convinced that little children are . . . better socialized by parental example and sharing than by other little children. . . . Contrary to common beliefs, little children are not best socialized by other kids; the more persons around them, the fewer meaningful contacts.[9]

For these reasons, the Moores have been writing, lecturing, appearing on radio and TV, organizing seminars, and otherwise getting out the word that *little children don't belong in school.* Parents who are convinced by their arguments must de facto elect home schooling for their younger children, since even a private school means formal education.

The Moores don't believe that young children should even be taught formally at home—unless the child himself or herself requests it. Instead, they advocate an unschooling approach to the early years: "more loving firmness, less indulgence; more work *with you,* fewer toys; more service for others—the old, poor, infirm—and less sports and amusements; more self-control, patriotism, productiveness and responsibility—which lead to, and follow, self-worth as children of God." Through a rich relationship with their parents and a rich exposure to real life, children will then approach their formal school studies unwearied, with minds ready to learn and sufficient abilities to master learning quickly.

For a deeper look at delayed formal education, see the Moores' books, described in chapter 6.

Dorothy Sayers: Bring Back the Tools of Learning

Another woman whose ideas about education are becoming increasingly popular is Dorothy Sayers. An associate of J. R. R. Tolkien and C. S. Lewis, and herself the writer of witty and erudite murder mysteries featuring the unflappable Lord Peter Wimsey, Miss Sayers was an Anglican Christian of no mean intellectual powers. Like Lewis and Tolkien, she was very concerned about the lack of thought that seemed to characterize the rising pre-World War II generation. Unlike them, she wrote about it.

Do you ever find that young people, when they have left school, not only forget most of what they have learnt (that is only to be expected) but forget also, or betray that they have never really known, how to tackle a new subject for themselves? . . .

Is not the great defect of our education to-day . . . that although we often succeed in teaching our pupils "subjects," we fail lamentably, on the whole, in teaching them how to think? They learn everything, except the art of learning.

What answer does Dorothy Sayers propose? Hang on to your hats, folks—she wants to bring back the Middle Ages! This is not as flaky as it sounds. Miss Sayers is primarily interested in the first half of the medieval syllabus, called (believe it or not) the Trivium. As Miss Sayers points out,

The whole of the Trivium was, in fact, intended to teach the pupil the proper use of the tools of learning, before he began to apply them to "subjects" at all. First, he learned a language; not just how to order a meal in a foreign language, but the structure of language—a language, and hence of language itself—what it was, how it was put together and how it worked. Secondly, he learned how to use language: how to define his terms and make accurate statements: how to construct an argument and how to detect fallacies in argument (his own arguments and other people's). Thirdly, he learned to express himself in language: how to say what he had to say elegantly and persuasively. . . . At the end of his course, he was required to compose a thesis upon some theme set by his masters or chosen by himself, and afterwards to defend his thesis against the criticism of the faculty. By this time he would have learned—or woe betide him—not merely to write an essay on paper, but to speak audibly and intelligently from a platform, and to use his wits quickly when heckled. . . .

The great difference of emphasis between the two conceptions holds good: modern education concentrates on *teaching subjects,* leaving the method of thinking, arguing and expressing one's conclusions to be picked up by the scholar as he goes along; mediaeval education concentrated on first *forging and learning to handle the tools of learning.*

Miss Sayers then proceeds to lay out her ideal course of study. She recommends beginning with Latin grammar,

. . . not because Latin is traditional and mediaeval, but simply because even a rudimentary knowledge of Latin cuts down the labour and pains of learning almost any other subject by at least fifty percent. It is the key to the vocabulary and structure of all the Romance languages and to the structure of all the Teutonic languages, as well as to the technical vocabulary of all the sciences and to the literature of the entire Mediterranean civilization, together with all the historical documents.

She prefers the livelier postclassical, medieval Latin to the Augustan style.

Recognizing that the healthy child is capable of absorbing an astounding number of facts before he or she can yet connect them with adult logic (here is our Data again!), Dorothy Sayers suggests beginning foreign languages in the early years, as well as memorizing stories and poems, historical dates and facts, geographical facts, the identifying and naming of specimens (science), and the multiplication table, geometric shapes, and the grouping of numbers (math). This she called the Grammar stage. Any amount of memory work may be done: memorizing Scripture in outline form, the Catechism, the Psalms, the Ten Commandments. "At this stage, it does not matter nearly so much that these things should be fully understood as that they should be known and remembered. Remember, it is material that we are collecting."

Now the child moves on to Formal Logic. When? "When she shows herself disposed to Pertness and interminable argument" (i.e., "when the capacity for abstract thought begins to manifest itself"). In Language, we examine the logical construction of speech. In Reading, we move to "essay, argument and criticism, and the pupil will learn to try his own hand at writing this kind of thing." Mathematics—algebra, geometry, and so on—comes into its own as "a subdepartment of Logic." History will now be examined in the light of Theology. Theology itself now blossoms into Systematic Theology. Miss Sayers, as a devout Christian, is concerned that the pupil learn to analyze all that is presented to him according to the teaching of the Bible. "Criticism must not be merely destructive; though at the same time both teacher and pupils must be ready to detect fallacy, slipshod reasoning, ambiguity, irrelevance and redundancy, and to pounce on them like rats."

What of the "subjects?" "The 'subjects' supply material; but they are all to be regarded as mere grist for the mental mill to work upon."

At last the child advances to the Rhetoric stage of full mental maturity. At this point, he chooses and develops his own style of writing and speech. Aptitude for a particular branch of knowledge now leads naturally into training for real work in that branch.

Is the Trivium, then, a sufficient education for life? Properly taught, I believe that it should be. . . . For the tools of learning are the same, in any and every subject; and the person who knows how to use them will, at any age, get the mastery of a new subject in half the time and with a quarter of the effort expended by the person who has not the tools at his command. . . .

For the sole true end of education is simply this: to teach men how to learn for themselves: and whatever instruction fails to do this is effort spent in vain.[10]

The essay from which the above quoted fragments have been extracted is entitled "The Lost Tools of Learning" and is contained in a book by the title of *A Matter of Eternity*, published by William B. Eerdmans Publishing Company, a Christian publishing firm in Grand Rapids, Michigan. If you find Miss Sayers' ideas intriguing, go ahead and read the whole article.

I have no criticisms of Miss Sayers' educational theory at all, except to note that although geniuses may be more readily produced by teaching Latin, still our children can do quite well even without it. We all need the tools of learning, man, woman, and child, and let not fear of Roman grammar deter us!

Socrates: Make the Student Think

Going back even beyond the Middle Ages, we find an enduring educational theory taught by an ancient Greek philosopher.

Was Socrates the first Rogerian counselor? He liked to ask questions rather than give his students any answers. Unlike Carl Rogers, though, Socrates had a definite end in mind. The teacher was not just an echo to bounce the student's ball back into the student's court a la Rogers. ("Why does $E = MC^2$, Professor?" "Hm. I see you have some questions about relativity.") Socrates would nudge his students along in the right direction. ("Well, what does E stand for, Jim? And M, and C? Have you read the text pages on quantum theory?")

You need to know what you're doing to mess around with the Socratic method. You also need patient students, since a teacher's constant refusal to give his students a direct answer can quickly become infuriating. For this reason, I suggest that you mix Socratic nudging with occasional merciful answers, following Jesus' example with His disciples.

John Dewey: Progressive Education

No discussion of educational theory would be complete without a nod to John Dewey, generally regarded as the father of Progressive Education. Progressive Education is distinguished by its emphasis on socialization (the "affective domain") rather than on academics (the "intellectual domain"). Thus the goal of Progressive Education is to produce "well-adjusted citizens," that is, compliant followers, rather than to impart any particular skills.

It is fair to say that the majority of home learners are seeking rather to escape Progressive Education than to implement it.

CHAPTER FIVE

SETTING UP YOUR PROGRAM

As the ocean swarms with fish, so the home school market is swarming with ideas. The richness and diversity of home schoolers' imaginations make it impossible to list *every* possible home schooling setup. However, the field breaks down into several general categories, and by looking them over quickly you can see which format fits your family's particular personality. Thus you can avoid "reinventing the wheel" as well as feeling comfortably certain that your choice is based on knowledge.

HOME SCHOOLING STYLES

School at Home

The first commonly used method of home schooling is to make home into a school. Mom becomes Teacher, the kids pupils. A room is set up complete with desks, wall maps, ticking clock (to record when one "period" ends and another begins), storage cabinets, and bookcases. Each subject is handled in one-hour chunks.

Following the typical classroom method, Teacher lectures all subjects. Pupils must raise their hands for permission to speak. Teacher decides what is to be learned and when and enforces her will on the students.

People who strictly follow this method rarely last long as home schoolers. They burn out from trying to imitate, for the sake of maybe four students, a ritual designed to cope with hundreds. The children also become dissatisfied, finding that the home environment is not much freer than their old classrooms.

Many families find it convenient to adopt the physical layout of a schoolroom and to keep records in a professional way while abandoning the "school" mentality. They reason that there is nothing sacred about one-hour-per-subject and schedule their

time in a multitude of creative ways. Teacher also gets tired of trying to do it all for the children, and finds it is usually simpler to let them take more initiative for their own scheduling.

In some cases, where children have been brought home to cure their severe discipline problems, parents find that the strict "school at home" method is necessary in order to give some structure. As problems subside, generally so does the strictness.

Traditional Schooling, or "Back to Basics"

The cry of "Back to Basics!" has been ringing throughout our land for lo, these fifteen years, without any glorious results. Except at home. The public school establishment is unable to implement the much-desired basics because, as one principal put it, "We're too busy teaching the kids other things." Home schoolers aren't all wrapped up in sex ed, death ed, drugs ed, values clarification, nuclear ed, and all the other far-left programs of the NEA, and thus they do have time to teach the basics.

At home, getting back to basics means a lot of teacher-led drill. The very discipline required to do a lot of drill is praised by many as character-building. Also, by stressing the academic "survival skills" of reading, writing, and arithmetic, parents insure that their children's academic foundation is solid before trying to build anything gaudy atop it.

Basics, then, means first things first and drill, drill, drill. This need not be boring. You can play games with flash cards (see Margwen Product's Match-A-Fact math series, for example). You can learn the facts in song. Problems arise, however, when believers in basics try to jam the facts down without first allowing the learner to handle them and become comfortable with them.

When teaching arithmetic, for example, it is easy to get most children to parrot the "addition facts." This is the way the public schools teach them. First kids are taught the "facts" for combinations up to 5—e.g., 1+1=2, 1+2=3, 1+3=4, 1+4=5, 2+3=5, 3+2=5, etc. After they have struggled with these for a year, they get to learn combinations to ten. Sooner or later they learn combinations to twenty. Somewhere along the line the "subtraction facts" are also introduced. But if kids *never actually add and subtract,* handling actual apples and oranges and pieces of gum and pencils, the "facts" mean nothing to them at all. Moreover, this is an awful lot of headwork to do when so many "facts" are really repetitions of each other. 1+4=5 is the same as 4+1=5 is the same as 5−4=1 is the same as 5−1=4. A rose is a rose is a rose.

Kids should get to mess around with math. After they are comfortable with numbers, they should be told the various principles that describe the same operation. The commutative principle means that 1+4 is the same as 4+1. This eliminates 50 percent of addition memorization. The inverse principle means that 5−1=4 is the same fact as 4+1=5. This eliminates another 50 percent. Once they know how to derive the answer, then it makes sense to drill them so the answer comes swiftly. This is reinforcing the framework, not replacing it.

As this thinking applies to math, so it applies to all areas. Rigorous repetition and drill are useful when used correctly. Our country's past experience of this form of traditional schooling bears this out. But drill without understanding produces parrots, not thinkers.

Most Christian home school correspondence programs emphasize basics. Among these are A Beka Video School and its sister A Beka Christian Correspondence School; American Christian Academy and Living Heritage Academy, both carrying Basic Education's Accelerated Christian Education series; Associated Christian Schools, with a Baptist flavor; and with an eclectic selection of Christian materials, Christian Liberty Academy. For Catholics, Our Lady of Victory has a strong basics approach.

Both A Beka Books and Bob Jones University Press offer complete "basics" materials for home schoolers. Both also allow you to order as little or as much of their program as you wish. Bob Jones is especially friendly to home schoolers, offering a toll-free number for information as well as for orders.

The Classical School

Following the teachings of Dorothy Sayers (discussed in the last chapter), a number of families are resurrecting the "classical" or "medieval" style of education. In the early years they fill their children up with reams of facts: poetry, foreign languages, history, geography, classification of all kinds of animals-vegetables-minerals, and arithmetic facts. Christian families do a lot of Bible memory work in this stage, and some learn the Catechism. Some, following Miss Sayers exactly, pursue the study of Latin, as well as the fine arts (music, painting, and literature).

This first stage is a lot of fun for both parents and students. Most of us adults have never had an extended pleasurable learning experience, and it is a treat to finally learn French or to take up the classical guitar after years of longing to do so. Parents and children thus often end up learning together.

The second stage becomes much more rigorous. Miss Sayers calls it the "Formal Logic" or "Dialectic" stage, because formal analysis (frameworks) are introduced at this point. In language,

the student learns grammar. In math, logic. In reading, criticism. In writing, essays and arguments. Theology now becomes Systematic Theology, and history is examined (for Christians) in the light of God's providence. This is the time for asking "Why?" about everything and discovering and testing truth. For the learner this is a very heady stage, as the world begins to blossom before him, and care must be taken to prevent the beginnings of arrogance.

The last stage, "Rhetoric," is where the learner develops his own particular style of writing and speech, and launches into learning his actual calling. For some, this will mean apprenticeship (discussed later in this chapter).

It is possible to go at this medieval thing with a lot of flair: to not only use the classical method, but read the classical writers; to learn calligraphy and other gentle arts of the Middle Ages. One family we know is doing just that. By tenderly admiring what was great in the past, you get a real standard by which to judge the arts in the present.

Classical schooling is not for all, of course. A kid who is a genius with tools, whose fondest wish is to be an auto mechanic, might find it hard to settle down in front of a ripe passage from Virgil. But families with an intellectual bent should definitely consider it. As Miss Sayers so pungently points out,

> The truth is that for the last 300 years or so we have been living on our educational capital. . . . But one cannot live on capital forever. A tradition, however firmly rooted, if it is never watered, though it dies hard, yet in the end it dies. And to-day a great number—perhaps the majority—of the men and women who handle our affairs, write our books and our newspapers, carry out research, present our plays and our films, speak from our platforms and pulpits—yes, and who educate our young people, have never, even in a lingering traditional memory, undergone the scholastic discipline.[1]

If you are upset by soup cans masquerading as art and pornography posturing as great fiction, perhaps you and your youngsters would like to produce something better. This book's Literature, Music, and Art chapters can help put you in touch with the masters.

Calvert School (secular, Christian flavor) and Seton Home Study Program (Catholic) are about as close to a classical program as is offered today in training method. Our Lady of Victory (Catholic) gets deeply into Catholic classics with a "basics" emphasis. Nobody anywhere has a full program that covers Greek, Latin, and the gamut of classical writings. Even Christian programs don't deeply study the Christian classics, leaving that to seminary. Mistake! Will someone out there meet this need?

Unschooling

Along with traditional and classic schooling, "unschooling" is one of the most popular home school formats. To avoid confusion, I should mention that the word "unschooling" is used for two separate things. Some people refer to the act of removing one's children from the schools, or refusing to enroll them, as "unschooling." But "unschooling" also describes a very popular home schooling philosophy: that children learn better from doing real things than made-up exercises.

One might, for example, teach writing by assigning essays, poems, etc. which are then graded and filed away in a little folder. Alternatively, a child might learn to write by writing actual letters to Grandma, writing shopping lists, writing stories to be submitted to a children's magazine, and so on. On the one hand, a child can learn to read by following a strictly tracked "primer" series; on the other hand, he might prefer to begin by reading books he picks out himself from the library.

Unschooling is a far more radical approach to education than enrolling in a traditional home correspondence course or following a planned curriculum. It requires more creativity and flexibility. (Some say this is also one of its rewards!) Some people find unschooling more stressful, as they are constantly worrying whether Johnny really is learning *all* the math he needs to know, or whether some day they will discover that he is eighteen years old and still has never heard of George Washington! Others, more confident, think unschooling is the most relaxing, friendly way for children to learn.

All unschoolers are not created equal. Since unschooling is actually an apprenticeship to the parents, the parents must be *doing* something in order for the children to learn. Parents also must enjoy answering questions and taking the time to patiently show children how to do things they could do much more quickly themselves. Since unschooling follows the interests of the family, a family that is very deficient in some major area (all extremely poor readers or totally ignorant of math, say) must resort to outside help in order to overcome their own lacks.

No law says that children can learn *only* from their parents, and many unschoolers rely heavily on relatives, friends, and community resources to supply opportunities for their children to learn.

Unschoolers are generally shy of tests—not that their children don't know anything, but because testing is one of the "school" things they dislike. To show the children are making progress, unschoolers often rely on journals of learning experiences and/or folders of "work" completed.

Experienced home school parents, even those who use curricula, often incorporate unschooling into part of their program. "Total" unschoolers, those who use no set structure at all, seem to be a minority (this is my guess based on what I see home schoolers writing about themselves). Parents generally feel less nervous about unschooling "skills" (e.g., carpentry, cooking, sewing) than academic subjects.

In some cases, children who did not respond to any kind of formal learning have demonstrated amazing abilities when unschooled. I don't, offhand, know of any cases where the reverse is true.

Waldorf Education

A small number of parents are home schooling according to the principles of Rudolf Steiner, an Austrian educator, now deceased. Steiner's Waldorf School stressed imagination in the learning process. Children learned their letters and numbers by hearing fanciful stories about each symbol. (The number "1", for example, looks like the letter "1" because there is only one of me.) Math follows the adventures of little gnomes who add, subtract, multiply, and divide the king's treasures. Much attention is given to storytelling and delighting the children, rather than to rote learning. This translates into a heavy emphasis on artistic creativity; children learn to play the recorder and do a wide variety of crafts.

Steiner's philosophy was rather mystical, and New Age people seem especially fond of it. Now that there is so much attention being brought to "right-brain" (i.e., creative thinking) as opposed to "left-brain" (i.e., logical thinking), Steiner's work is undergoing a mild revival.

Oak Meadow School in Ojai, California offers a Waldorf home schooling curriculum.

The "Project" or "Integrated" Approach

Followers of Dr. Raymond Moore (see the previous chapter) adopt an "unschooling" method for their youngest children, followed by a "project" or "integrated" approach for those they consider old enough for more formal learning. By learning to cook, for example, children deal with fractions (one-half cup, one-quarter teaspoon), measurements, multiplication and division (doubling or halving recipes), some properties of chemistry, neatness, and so on. This is an excellent way to collect data, but it does not create a framework. Thus the more enlightened believers in projects also teach reading and arithmetic as separate disciplines and use history time lines.

For Christians, Dr. Moore's Hewitt-Moore Curriculum provides planned projects. The Konos Character Curriculum, also for Christians, is a year's K-6 activities correlated with a history time line (you have to buy your own math and phonics programs). Bill Gothard's Advanced Training Institute also has a project approach (again, for Christians).

Apprenticeship

A strange new thing is happening in our day. Families are looking at the universities and colleges and saying, "We should spend ten thousand a year on *this*?" Think it over. Is it smarter to spend thousands of dollars on a credential that will get you a job, or to get the same education on the job for free? Is it better to spend thousands of dollars training to be another man's servant (that is what corporate-industrial careers actually are), or to save that money as capital for your own business?

Not so long ago, it was normal for a man to train his sons to carry on his business. They would start with both experience and capital. If the son in question had no aptitude for the family work, he would be apprenticed to the craft he desired. This is the way the world ran for thousands of years, and it worked. All forms of education described above flow neatly into apprenticeship: classical education, basics, unschooling, project/integrated, and even Waldorf education. Children who learn by doing are ideal apprentices, and all forms of home education in some degree prepared children for this responsibility.

Hewitt-Moore Child Development Center has a list of several hundred home businesses that the young learner can tackle while at home, thus apprenticing himself to a craft under the guidance of his parents or another community member. Bill Gothard has taken this a step farther, and is even now working with Christian businessmen to set up apprenticeship opportunities for the graduates from his Advanced Training Institute home-study program. Further, the Economics section of this book will give you some guidelines for thinking through the question of apprenticeship and independent home business.

OPTIONS IN HOME SCHOOLING

I don't want to give you the impression that most home school families sit down, consciously pick out an educational approach, and then stay with it forever afterward. Nor do all home school families necessarily think of themselves as home schooling. My father, for example, didn't think he was home schooling me when he taught me reading and math. It was just a fun thing we did together.

Some of the options in home schooling, beyond choices of educational method, are:

Total home schooling. Parents take full responsibility for the children's instruction until they are grown.

Transitional home schooling. The children's early school years are spent at home, with the understanding that later on they will make the transition to formal school (whether college, high school, or third grade).

Supplemental home schooling. The children are enrolled in school, but Mom and Dad realize they need more, or different, instruction than they receive there. So on evenings, weekends,

vacations, or special days off from school, parents and children study together.

The first two options are generally well understood. Most families fall into category two, the transitional home schoolers. The third option, supplemental home schooling, is still valid for many situations, although it does not receive as much attention because it does not conflict with public officials' perception of the compulsory attendance statutes.

Some parents have found it possible to make creative use of their school districts' truancy laws to partially home school their children. If a child is not considered "absent" if he leaves at 1:30, then a parent could conceivably remove him at that time every day without infringing on the school's attendance policy. If departure after 10:30 is considered only half of an absence, and parents are allowed up to twenty-five parent-caused absences a year, that can add up to an awful lot of days mostly spent at home. And then there are long family trips (which are not illegal). Some families (not many) live a nomad life precisely to be able to home school without hassles.

When the parents have no fundamental quarrel with the school's policies, but merely feel that their children need additional help in a particular subject area, supplemental home schooling makes a lot of sense.

The subject reviews in this book were designed to help home schoolers *and* those attempting supplemental home schooling.

Beyond total, transitional, or supplemental home schooling, there are other options for parents and children. *Directed* home schooling is making an appearance. The children are enrolled in a "satellite" program of an existing school, or are otherwise taught under the supervision of a tutor. The tutor, or satellite program administrator, is not there to teach the children but the parents. He or she handles the satellite program records, orders curriculum, organizes support groups and field trips, helps the parents when educational problems arise, and in general provides both legal shelter and direction.

Finally, you have the *self-study* option. Young people and adults can obtain accredited or unaccredited degrees from a wide variety of sources, studying at home on their own. (See the chapter on Adult Education.) Resourceful people can also learn quite a bit at the library, from "picking the brains" of other people, or by attending some of the numerous workshops, seminars, etc. that are constantly being given on any imaginable subject. This is a good way to learn how to cook or build a house. Self-study can work equally well in academic areas, for those who have mastered the "tools of learning."

HELP FOR HOME SCHOOLERS

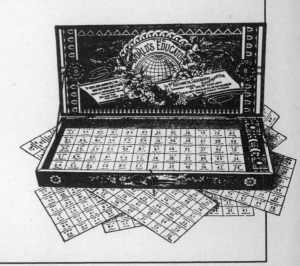

CHAPTER SIX

BASIC BOOKS ABOUT SCHOOL AND HOME SCHOOL

Winnie-the-Pooh and Piglet had an exciting experience one day. Pooh was out walking around a grove of trees when he noticed tracks. Following those tracks, he was joined by Piglet. As they circled the grove speculating whether the tracks were made by Woozles or Wizzles, Pooh and Piglet noticed that the whatever-they-weres had been joined by more whatever-they-weres, since there were now *more* pairs of tracks! After Piglet left, fearing that the animals they were tracking might "be of Hostile Intent," Christopher Robin enlightened Pooh: the animal he had been tracking around and around the grove was himself. Nobody had really been there before him.

This, I am glad to say, is not the case with home education. Many have been there before us. When Bill and I realized we were expecting our first child, in fear and trembling we determined to teach him or her at home. Neither of us had ever heard of the home schooling movement. We thought (I blush to say it) that we were going to be pioneers. Surprise! Before our first son was even three, I was invited to my first home school seminar. And as we delved more deeply into home schooling, we were delighted to find that all the really hard work had already been done. Court cases had been fought and won. Books had been written. Curricula had been developed. We owe a lot to the true pioneers of home schooling, who braved prejudice and adversity to pave the way for us.

Yes, much remains to be done. But today's home schoolers are in the position of those who took the train out West, after pioneers had marked out the way with their covered wagons and gangs of working men had laid the tracks. The train ride had its difficulties, but compared to the first dangerous wagon caravan over the mountains, it was comfortable and safe.

Because those who blazed the way have worked so hard, we have a flood of books and magazines to read, seminars to attend, and other teaching aids. I can't review all of them here, but it is still possible to cover 80 percent of the field, a feat that will be impossible two years from now in a space this small. You are looking for the best, so I will concentrate on those, leaving the strictly amateur productions aside.

This section, then, contains reviews of the materials that will help *you* grow as a teacher. If the student is not above his master, the master had better take care to stay ahead of his student. With the help of these resources, you can keep learning even while you teach.

BOOKS FOR BEGINNERS

Virginia Birt Baker. *Teaching Your Children At Home*. Self-published. Updated three times since 1981. 54 8½ x 11″ pages. $8.75 postpaid. Make check out to Virginia Birt Baker, P.O. Box 1237, Quitman, TX 75783.

Mrs. Baker has the honor of having home schooled longer than the authors of any other home schooling books. Her book, which contains legislative information, is updated often.

Unique features of Mrs. Baker's book are the sections on compulsory attendance statutes and constitutional law, and her very specific advice on how to set up a home school program. Mrs. Baker goes so far as to produce a sample weekly schedule and share her choice of curriculum materials with us. I found this overwhelming when, as a novice home schooler, I first read her book, but was afterwards grateful for the introduction to so many fine products.

For *detailed* procedural how-to's, this is the book.

Samuel Blumenfeld. *How to Tutor.* Currently published by Mott Media. $5.95 plus shipping. Available from Christian Life Workshops or Educators Publishing Services, among other sources.

How to Tutor is a book I longed to get my hands on. Other books talk grandly about the theory of education; but what do you do face to face with a child who is supposed to be learning math or reading? Having used Mr. Blumenfeld's *Alphaphonics* method successfully, I had faith that his tutoring book would be of similarly excellent quality. He did not disappoint me.

Beyond excellent advice on the basics of tutoring, *How to Tutor* has sections for teaching the basics of reading, writing, and arithmetic. These consist of step-by-step instructions, with explanations of *why* Mr. Blumenfeld has such success with his approach. This last feature, the reasoned explanations of why you should follow classic methods of instruction, sets *How to Tutor* apart. It would be quite possible to take your child from zero to Grade 6 in the three R's armed with this book alone.

Ingeborg U. V. Kendall. *School at Home: Teach Your Own Child.* ICER Press. 1982. 173 pages. Appendix. Index. Softcover. $6.95.

School at Home is a decent beginner's book. The author, a home schooling mother, has done her research, as the copious footnotes show. The book deals with nitty-gritty areas such as motivation and scheduling, as well as educational philosophy and legalities. Mrs. Kendall is enthusiastic about correspondence programs, in contrast to others who prefer to completely develop their own curriculum. Her book discusses the advantages and disadvantages of both the programmed curriculum approach and the self-designed program.

Susan Schaeffer Macaulay. *For the Children's Sake: Foundations of Education for Home and School.* Crossway Books. 1984. 161 pages. $6.95 plus shipping. Sold in Christian bookstores and some home school catalogs.

I have never read a book that was more full of joy. Addressing the relationship of Christianity and education, Susan

Macaulay shares with us the insights of Charlotte Mason, a teacher extraordinaire from the last century. The sweeping freedom that a child raised God's way can know, and the depth of beauty he or she can enjoy, shines through on every page. The author includes many of her personal experiences as a home schooled child, and the experiences of her own family as they searched for appropriate education for their children.

For the Children's Sake is not a "how to" book as much as a beautiful "why to" and "in what manner."

Raymond and Dorothy Moore. *School Can Wait,* qpb, $9. *Home-Style Teaching,* hardback, $12. *Home-Spun Schools,* qpb, $7. *Better Late Than Early,* qpb, $7. *Home Grown Kids,* qpb, $8. Shipping 4 percent; $2.50 minimum. Hewitt Research Foundation sells all these books.

Dr. Raymond Moore has assembled a formidable corpus of work bearing out his hypothesis that little children belong at home. With the help of the Hewitt Research Foundation staff, and with wife Dorothy coauthoring in some cases, Dr. Moore has branched out into home schooling "how to's."

Better Late Than Early lays down the thesis that delayed formal education makes the best academic sense. *School Can Wait* is the same argument, this time with impressive footnotes and written in the educational jargon that school folk love.

Home Grown Kids contains a short case for home education, followed by the Moores' views on child-rearing and teaching, from birth to age ten.

Home-Spun Schools has inspiring examples of families who have successfully home schooled, interspersed with the Moores' suggestions and philosophy.

Home-Style Teaching, the latest entry, is the Moores' how-to-book. Engagingly written, with lots of common-sense arguments and wisdom distilled from experience, *Home-Style Teaching* is a book well worth owning.

Of these books, I would first get *Better Late than Early* and *Home-Style Teaching.* The former could be obtained at the library, but you'll probably want to keep the latter for reference.

Mario Pagnoni. *The Complete Home Educator.* Larson Publications. 248 pages. $10.95 postpaid.

No, this book is not complete. It is, however, very funny, and does contain more info per square inch about the use of a personal computer in home school than any other book. Also helpful are the suggestions on how to teach the Three R's in a *relaxed* way. (Mr. Pagnoni, a schoolteacher by trade, has had plenty of experience with the other way!)

The book is brash and irreverent, covering such topics as Christmas gift sexism and why the Lawrence-Haverhill,

Massachusetts area, where Mr. Pagnoni teaches, was rated the worst in the USA. As one of Mr. Pagnoni's students so aptly remarked, "What do we need that cultcha stuff for anyhow?"

John Holt wrote the introduction, and unschoolers everywhere like this book.

Mary Pecci. *How to Discpline Your Class for Joyful Teaching.* Pecci Educational Publishers. 32 pages. $2.95.

This may not sound like a home schooling book, and in all honesty it isn't. It *is* the shortest, most helpful book on motivation that I've ever seen. Written for classroom teachers, the book is just as helpful for home schoolers. *How To Discipline . . .* is a guide to help children *want* to please you. Mary Pecci realistically faces the question of what you should do when you've *already* blown your stack, and other vital questions that most books blithely ignore. A book with "soul."

Ted Wade and eight others. *The Home School Manual,* second edition. Gazelle Publications. Revised edition, 1986, $16.50 postpaid. 350 pages. Hardcover. Twenty-five chapters, seven appendices, index.

Thoroughly Christian in content, *The Home School Manual* tries to establish a Christian approach to home schooling in general and each school subject in particular. This is a lofty objective, and the book makes a good beginning. The wealth of suggestions had me gasping for breath (count on at least two readings to master this book).

Non-Christians can also gain a lot from the *Manual.* The teaching tips and ideas are useful in any home.

The *Manual* contains all state statutes regarding home schooling as of 1985, and a small index of schools and resources. Written by many contributors, the *Manual* nonetheless is readable and even entertaining in spots.

If you like to have a reason for what you are doing, and if you're looking for *lots* of teaching ideas, *The Home School Manual* is worth the money.

Nancy Wallace. *Better Than School.* Larson Publications. 1983. $14.95 postpaid. 256 pages. Hardbound. Introduction by John Holt.

Another beautiful book about home schooling, this one is entirely personal. The author's son, Ishmael, was having a terrible time in school until his parents decided to pull him out. Their struggles in doing so were amply rewarded, as Ishmael first blossomed emotionally, then academically, and finally musically. The family's love of learning and life comes through, and we are delighted but not surprised when Ishmael becomes an accomplished musician and when a play he writes gets performed by serious (well, in the case of this play, humorous) actors. All this from a child the school considered very ordinary musically, and below average academically.

The Wallaces' daughter, Vita, is likewise home schooled and likewise musical. Holt Associates sells a tape of the Wallace family playing music together.

What is amazing about this book is how a whole family can thrive when they stop accepting artificial limits. Nancy wants to learn to play the piano, so she starts taking lessons. Ishmael wants to write a musical, so he does. Vita wants to do everything, so *she* does!

Better Than School reads like a novel and is better than a fairy tale. Bring home the boy the school considers an "ugly duckling," and he turns out to be a swan. What hath God wrought?

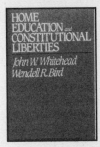

John Whitehead and Wendell Bird. *Home Education and Constitutional Liberties.* Crossway Books. 1984. $5.95 plus shipping, or discounted from Puritan-Reformed. Everyone sells it. Quality paperback, 144 pages. Appendices.

Every home school list contains this book, and with good reason. John Whitehead, a Constitutional lawyer, summarizes all the major court decisions affecting home schooling and shares his reasons for believing that home schooling is inherently Constitutional. In this day of activist judges, Whitehead's arguments, although sound, are not completely sufficient. However, he has done us a great service by showing we are *not* antiestablishment rebels, but are actually within the American legal tradition. The book is worth reading for your own peace of mind, and "must" reading for your lawyer (or, better, the school board) if you are challenged.

BOOKS ON "FREE" OR "INVITED" LEARNING

John Holt. *How Children Learn, How Children Fail, The Underachieving School,* and *Teach Your Own* are available through Holt Associates. Try your library for the others.

How Children Learn. 1983 revised edition, $7.95, qpb. 303 pages. *How Children Fail,* 1982 revised edition, $5.95, qpb. 298 pages. *The Underachieving School.* 1969. $4.50. *Teach Your Own.* 1981. $8.95 qpb. *Escape from Childhood.* 1974. $4.50. *Instead of Education,* a 1976 work, will be available in a reprint edition in 1986.

How Children Fail and *How Children Learn* are Mr. Holt's firsthand observations of children doing both, along with some very penetrating analysis of the causes.

Teach Your Own is his book about home schooling: why and how to do it. It is an excellent introduction to the subject. Holt's chapter answering objections against home schooling is particularly valuable.

Instead of Education, The Underachieving School, and *What Do I Do Monday?* come from a period when Mr. Holt was still trying to reform the public school system. All contain brilliant insights, and *What Do I Do Monday?* also has long sections of suggestions on how to teach some difficult subjects, with the thoughts on math being especially helpful.

Holt's book on children's rights, *Escape from Childhood,* while provocative, is utopian in tone and therefore not as valuable. Holt's basic thesis is that children are people just like adults, only smaller, and should be allowed the privileges and responsibilities of adults, including sex, drugs, employment, and property ownership. About the latter two I agree. But what about the sex and drugs, you may ask? Holt is not a maniacal pervert: he is reasoning coldly and logically from our society's current beliefs in these areas. If, as so many seem to believe, sex is primarily for "fun" and procreation merely a sorry afterthought, then we have no good reason to protect children from it. Disgusting, but true. Similarly, if society permits adults to drug themselves (not that Holt approves of this), then it is hypocritical to forbid tobacco, booze, and marijuana to children. Similar arguments apply to child-parent "divorce" and all the other shocking suggestions in the book. If you are unhappy with Holt's conclusions in these areas, you might want to look over my book *The Way Home*

(Crossway Books, 1985, $7.95), which sets forth a different set of initial premises, based on the Bible. *Escape from Childhood* at least raises all the right questions, and if we are not willing to look for God's answers we'd better be prepared to live with Holt's.

Ivan Illich. *Deschooling Society.* Available from Holt Associates for $4.95.

In flighty intellectual prose, Illich points out the deficiencies of our present school-oriented pedagogy, and how inconsistent it is to exalt individual potential while slaying it in the classroom. Illich is strongly biased against Christianity, and very much a believer in evolutionary progress. The book is well documented and inflammatory.

A. T. Neill, *Summerhill.*

Summerhill has become a minor cult classic. A. T. Neill, a British educator of the early to mid-1900s, thought that children could learn just as well if adults never made them do a thing, and he founded his school Summerhill to prove it (also to make himself a living). Classroom teaching was available for those who wanted it, and sooner or later almost everybody did. Neill was more than a bit of an eccentric: he preached the virtues of masturbation (actually, he would have liked to be more consistent and let his students copulate, but that would have killed the school at the time in England) and believed that understanding how babies were born would cure a variety of childish mental problems. Nudity was encouraged in this co-ed school, and when a faculty member decided to play tennis in the nude nobody objected. Swearing was likewise allowed, except in town, where the "natives" might object. The book is full of real-life examples from daily life in Summerhill, and is as fascinating to read as an anthropological document of some strange tribe might be. What *are* the limits between liberty and license, if God and His laws are presumed not to exist? For Neill, the peer group conveniently solved most of these problems, since as long as the students coerced each other into good behavior that was O.K.

Summerhill is not an accurate example of how "free children" might live, since it occurred in an ethically Christian England, and the unseen rules of good behavior and fair play were thus understood by all. Neill, for example, could not let the children copulate like animals because of what society would have thought. Neither could some bully be allowed to continue terrorizing the school for long, though it is not clear in Neill's philosophy why this might be wrong from an *ethical* viewpoint. Interesting reading, again more for the questions it raises than for the answers it provides.

BOOKS ON THE HISTORY OF SCHOOLING

Samuel Blumenfeld. *Is Public Education Necessary?* and *The NEA: Trojan Horse in American Education.* Order both from Christian Life Workshops or directly from Research Publications via a toll-free number. Each book $9.95 plus $1.50 U.P.S. delivery. 1985. Appendices, index, fantastic documentation.

Is Public Education Necessary? is a great book, not so much for its readability as for its thorough documentation of why we even have public education and who put it there.

The NEA: Trojan Horse in American Education shows how the schools have been turned into a political football and why our declining national intellectualism is no accident. Written in a lively, intelligent style, this is undoubtedly Blumenfeld's most important book, and essential reading for anyone concerned about curing America's educational inferiority. (The solutions are surprisingly simple.)

David Nasaw. *Schooled to Order: A Social History of Public Schooling in the United States.* Oxford University Press, 1979. Look for it at your library.

Find out how, from the very beginning, public school has been first and foremost a vehicle for social propaganda and secondarily a device for producing submissive employees. Find out how the elite control the poor by means of schooling. Though not an entertaining book, *Schooled to Order* is eye-opening.

BOOKS WITH THE FACTS ABOUT PUBLIC SCHOOL TODAY AND REASONS FOR HOME SCHOOLING

Mel and Norma Gabler with James C. Hefley. *What Are They Teaching Our Children?* Victor Books/Scripture Press. $5.95, qpb. 192 pages. Sold at Christian bookstores, or order from Mel and Norma Gabler, Educational Research Analysts.

The next time you hear some far-left group screaming about how right-wingers are trying to censor America's textbooks, you ought to pick up a copy of this book and thumb through it. Laced throughout with lurid little quotes from actual classroom texts, *What Are They Teaching Our Children?* is the story of one couple's fight against the arrogant elite who is determined to instill their peculiar antivalues into America's children. *Your* children may be learning the details of gang rape, cannabalism, and suicide from "approved" schooltexts. *Your* tax money is paying to indoctrinate children in antireligious values, bureaucratic dependence, antipatriotism, and psychopathic hedonism. Meanwhile, occupations such as motherhood and fatherhood are systematically weeded out of texts by the very groups which scream the loudest against "censorship"! I'm not making this up—all this stuff is in current textbooks, and you can read the quotes for yourself.

Barbara Morris. *Change Agents in the Schools.* Barbara Morris Report publication. $9.95. Also available from Puritan-Reformed.

A shocker. Relentless documentation of how humanists (in the worst sense of the word) are forcing their peculiar doctrines on our children under the guise of "educating them for the real world." Drug education that teaches kids to use drugs. Sex ed that promotes fornication and incest. "Values clarification" designed to unfreeze kids from their parents' values. The use of questionnaires as the first step in invading a child's mind. How "Back to Basics" is a phony cover-up for presenting mere survival skills (label-reading, simple addition) to secondary students while taking the heat off the schools. All of this in the educators' own words. *They* said it!

Bruce Mosier, *32 Reasons Why Christian Parents Should Teach Their Own Children at Home.* Jeanette Mosier, *Scriptural Reasons Why Christian Parents Should Teach Their Own Children at Home.* $4 each, plus 10 percent shipping. Self-published under the company name Food For Thot.

If you're a Christian thinking about home schooling, or if you have Christian relatives who are nagging you about your home schooling decision (unhappy thought, but it does happen), these two books would be a wise investment. While the other books in this section strongly point out the negative aspects of public education, the Mosiers' books also dwell on the advantages of home schooling. No wordiness here; no footnotes except Scripture references. Simple, clean, logical reasons for doing what your own heart knows is best.

Phyllis Schlafly. *Child Abuse in the Classroom.* Crossway Books. 1984. $4.95. 434 pages, mass market paperback. Appendices, index.

A bombshell, this time lobbed by the victims. So many parents were complaining about what was going on in their children's classrooms that the Protection of Pupil Rights

Amendment (commonly known as the Hatch Amendment) actually passed Congress. The Department of Education, loath to implement it, finally got around to holding hearings six years later. These all-day hearings were held in seven locations around the country.

Seeing that the Department of Education was equally slow to disseminate the transcript of the hearings, noted conservative activist Phyllis Schlafly dove in and published her own book, consisting entirely of testimony given at the hearings. (There are two appendices, "How Parents Can Evaluate Curricula" and "What's Happened to Spelling?") Every charge Barbara Morris made in her book is here documented by the experiences of those victimized by antihuman religion masquerading as "education." Teachers, parents, and students testified. Common complaints were that the public school was teaching: witchcraft, fornication, homosexuality, unisexism, antifamilialism, suicide, drug use, barbarianism (kill the old, the young, the infirm, anyone weaker than you), socialism, one-world government, psychological prying and manipulation, peer group dependence, and values teaching *in place of education*. (The classic example was a sermon on abortion rights in math class.) Parents also objected to the way school staff tried to brand them as troublemakers when they started asking questions or making their wishes known. Teachers objected to the way humanistic content and methodology were forcefully jammed down their throats. (One of the saddest testimonies is that of a teacher who tried to hold out against "Mastery Learning" in her school until the administration drove her to the brink of a breakdown. It seems that teacher

manipulation is part of the Mastery Learning program.) Some former students gave testimonies about the way they'd been encouraged to destroy themselves in school. One young lady, living with her boyfriend without benefit of clergy and undergoing multiple abortions, was held up as an example to her Marriage and Family Living class. She now has changed and doesn't want *her* children exposed to this.

If you, or any of your friends, think public school isn't *really* that bad, please get this book.

Peter Schrag and Diane Divoky. *The Myth of the Hyperactive Child and Other Means of Child Control*. Pantheon Books. 1975. $10, hardback (as of 1975). 229 pages plus appendix, bibliographical note, 33 pages of footnotes, and index. Your library should have it.

This terrifying book details how millions of normal American children are being labeled as suffering from a *physically unidentifiable* condition, and then tracked into educational dead-ends, treated like potential criminals, and even drugged—all for the convenience of their teachers and (in some cases) their parents. If you have been taught to believe in the nondiseases of "hyperactivity" or "learning disability," please read this book. Learn why diagnostic screening is *not* helpful, and how the schools are increasingly usurping the role of mental hospitals.

The authors are serious journalists and their charges are thoroughly documented. Read it and weep. Then pull your kids out of school.

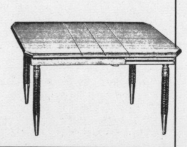

CHAPTER SEVEN

MAGAZINES AND JOURNALS

Magazines are the lifeblood of the home school movement. You can teach your children at home all alone. You can join a local support group or a state organization. But national magazines and newsletters keep you in touch with the movement—its excitement, its political unity and educational diversity.

The Christian Educator. Free. Quarterly. Published by Christian Liberty Academy.

If you like sassy cartoons, success stories, and newspaper articles with provocative headlines like "Teachers Oppose Drug Test" (Long Island public school teachers would have been tested for drug use like major league baseball players, but they were "violently opposed"), you'll love *The Christian Educator.* With a newspaper format and mainstream newspaper articles, *TCE* manages to cull article after article showing the shortcomings of government education and prints them alongside its own articles on home education. Who's being persecuted today, and what does the judge think about it? What teachers' union is opposing testing for its members? What percent of teachers just flunked their skills test? Why aren't public school students good at thinking? How many signers of the Declaration of Independence were educated at home? Stay on top of the struggle and get a few laughs.

Family-Centered Learning. $12/year. Quarterly.

Newspaper-style home school magazine put out by Eric and Debra Stewart. Interesting articles and ads, with a somewhat local flavor (Washington State). Pluralistic. Four times yearly.

Growing Without Schooling. $15/year (six issues), $27/twelve issues, $36/eighteen issues. Group subscriptions and back issues available. Single issue, $2.50. *For subscribers only:* Back issues are 75 cents/issue, plus $2 postage. Example: ten back issues are $7.50 plus $2.00 postage. Published by Holt Associates.

Indispensable. *GWS* is the only true home school forum. Most of the tabloid is given over to readers' comments, which makes a nice change from columns written by "experts." Although the *GWS* staff are staunch believers in "invited" learning, the philosophy of *GWS*'s late founder John Holt, they allow other points of view. Many articles are chronicles of home schoolers' actual experience; reading *GWS* is inspirational as well as informative. More: up-to-date legislative news and court decisions from every state. Plus reviews of books and products of use to home schoolers. *GWS* is *the* source for ideas and the stuff to make them happen.

New home schoolers should seriously consider buying all the *GWS* back issues. Together they contain as much material as several books, and cover every home schooling viewpoint. The teaching suggestions alone, all of which have been "field-tested" by the contributors, normal parents like you and me, are worth the price.

Home Education Magazine. $20/year (twelve issues). Sample issue, $2.

Articles by home school leaders: Ginny Baker, Donn Reed, Ingeborg Kendall, Ted Wade, John Holt. Excerpts from home school books (many of those reviewed above).

Home School Journal. Warren Rushton, editor. Free. Donations are requested; $18/year meets printing costs.

Coming at you directly from the People's Republic of Nebraska, this "Magazine of Christian Conviction" is a folksy, grass-roots effort. Much of the magazine is legal news from the various states; the rest is articles, success stories, and a "Kid's Page." Written by real, live home schoolers, it's a cut above the usual state newsletter, but not on a par (professionally) with the best national magazines except for the legal reporting, which is the best I've seen. Straight from the trenches, the *Journal* is a *war* journal of little folk against the Establishment, of Christians versus lions, full of fighting spirit, and thus not as spiffy and manicured as a peacetime production.

Instructor and Teacher. $20/year (nine issues). $27 Canada and other countries.

This schoolteachers' magazine, whose executive staff consists almost entirely of women, is a great resource for home schoolers. Why? Because:
(1) It gives us a look at education from "the other side." The March 1985 issue, for example, had a feature article entitled, "Do Public Schools Face Extinction?" What a new perspective this gives, for one accustomed to thinking of the "all-powerful public schools."

(2) Some of the teaching hints are cumbersome, and some wouldn't work at home, but many are useful.
(3) As a "use" magazine for elementary teachers, *Instructor* reports on model projects and promising innovations, as well as including reproducible teaching aids such as a monthly calendar, a science poster, puzzles, and "Mind Winders" for increasing thinking skills. You'll be up-to-date and competent to talk about what's new in the public school.
(4) The ads. The ads! THE ADS! Half the magazine is ads for educational products, and many companies offer *free* samples to teachers. If you have a named home school, you are a teacher and eligible for these offers. Stay in touch with the huge school products market through *Instructor's* ads.

On Teaching. Published by the American Reformation Movement. Donation. $5 a year is good; more is gladly accepted.

Provocative, quality newsletter that explores education from a Christian viewpoint. Philosophical. Reconstructionist. Witty.

The Parent Educator and Family Report. Hewitt Research Foundation. Donation. $10/year suggested.

A Hewitt Research Foundation production, the *Family Report* has good home schooling news coverage, reader letters, articles written by the Raymond Moores and the Hewitt staff, and a list of educational items for sale enclosed in every issue. Professionally laid-out, the *Family Report* is short (eight pages on average) and inspirational. The *Family Report* goes to people of all religious backgrounds. Most are evangelical or fundamentalist Christians. Dr. Moore, himself a Seventh-Day Adventist, strives to maintain a broadly evangelical stance.

The Stay-Homish Trading Post. $7.50/year (six issues). Classifieds, 20¢/word, $3 minimum. Print copy legibly on 3 x 5" file cards; indicate classification.

Here's a new idea in home school magazines, and an indicator of how fast the home school market is growing. *The Stay-Homish Trading Post,* apart from its squirmingly cute name, is a serious free-enterprise operation dedicated to getting home schoolers and home school products together. The format is convenient: 8½ x 11", three-hole punched for notebook use, linear layout for easy reading. The *S-H.T.P.* carries both display and classified advertising, and nothing else. Categories include:

Academic Equipment and Supplies
Announcements

Companies (advertisers listed alphabetically)
Cottage Industries
Curriculum, New
Curriculum, Used
Home School Support Group Information (listed by state, town)
Miscellaneous
Publications
Teaching Services
Wanted

The "Curriculum, Used" section alone is a chance to save a bunch of boodle—*if* anyone's selling the curriculum you want to buy! You can forget about getting Calvert or International Institute curriculum secondhand, since they require customers to return the instruction manuals upon course completion. You *might*, however, get some Calvert *books* secondhand. And then there are a few *other* curricula out there, too, you know!

The Teaching Home. $10/year (six issues). Back issues available. Published by Christian Home Schools.

The Teaching Home seems destined to become *the* national Christian home school magazine. The editors have a great idea: co-publish your state newsletter with *The Teaching Home!* Then, instead of having to publish (or pay for) two magazines, local and national news are covered at once. Presently thirteen editions of *The Teaching Home* are published: Arizona, California, Indiana, Illinois, Montana, National, Nevada, New England, Ohio, Oklahoma, Oregon, Tennessee, and Washington. Check with your state newsletter editor about doing this in your state.

The magazine has almost everything: philosophical articles, news, theme sections, success stories, reviews, and ads. Not only legal news, but news of workshops, conventions, and other services is carried. The ads are directed to Christian readers, so

you are aware of the products' theological content in advance. All it needs to be perfect is more reader input.

CHAPTER EIGHT

CATALOGS AND PARAPHERNALIA

Truckers, it is said, know the best places to eat. On that theory some people automatically start looking out their car windows for parked trucks when they're on a long trip and mealtime approaches. I don't know that much about truckers' gastronomical expertise, but I do know that a very similar theory applies when you're trying to track down educational bargains. Follow the home schoolers!

This chapter is a potpourri of companies cherished by home schoolers or created especially for home schoolers. Even if you are not contemplating home schooling, it won't hurt to browse through it. Lots of these resources are handy in any family, or for single people, or for classroom teachers. Here are such goodies as a catalog of catalogs (for dedicated mail order shoppers), discount book clubs, and a daily activity calendar. Spark up a blah day with some of these ideas.

DISCOUNT BOOKSELLERS AND BOOK CATALOGS

Barnes and Noble Booksellers

Huge discounts on books, records and tapes, videos, and kits. "Soft" porn is freely mixed in with the other items. If your fingers can do the walking while your eyes avoid the trash, you can nab yourself some bargains.

Conservative Book Club

Great discounts on conservative books. All areas: economics, politics, education, literature. I bought Sam Blumenfeld's *Alphaphonics* here for a song and a dance. See the ads plastered on the back pages of conservative magazines for a chance to join and get a free book or set of books. We got the *McGuffey Readers* (hardback) for $10 when we joined—all seven volumes.

Dover Publications

Everything Dover sells is a bargain, since Dover only sells reprints. The vast selection includes something in every educational category, plus far-out stuff that doesn't fit in *any* category!

Literary Guild

Most of Lit Guild's stock is current best-sellers, and most of these are trash—tired romance novels with a splash of porn. They do, however, offer free books to new enrollees, and they do also stock some nonfiction and children's books. Unlike Barnes & Noble and Publishers Central Bureau, the iffy stuff is sequestered by itself and labeled as to content (e.g., "Violence. Explicit sex"). You have to stay on top of their catalogs and send in your little cards faithfully or you get stuck with the wretched Featured Selection.

Publishers Central Bureau

Similar to Barnes & Noble. If you get one catalog, you might as well get them both and compare prices. Both carry publishers' closeouts, best-sellers, and arcane stuff for history buffs, military fans, art lovers, and the like.

Puritan-Reformed Discount Book Service

Upgrade your spiritual life by joining P-R! Five dollars will enroll you for your first year's membership, paying for your catalogs. With P-R's generous discounts, you can easily save many times that amount. Shekel-scrimping is not the real reason for joining, though. P-R carries the best in Christian books both modern *and* ancient, unlike so many bookstores that seem to have nothing but trendy testimonies and religious jewelry. Disconnect the TV, and feast on the writings of the giants of the past—Augustine, Calvin, Luther, Spurgeon, Jonathan Edwards, Dr. Martyn Lloyd-Jones, to name just a few of the thousands of illustrious Christians whose works P-R stocks. This is meat, not baby formula, and it works wonders.

Quality Paperback Book Club

We joined because of this priceless line in the advertising circular: "Just because books come from trees doesn't mean their leaves should turn yellow and drop to the ground." Also, we wanted the three free books. QPB is one of these we-send-you-our-brochure-every-six-weeks, selection-sent-automatically-unless-you-tell-us-differently jobbies. If you stay right on top of your mail, this should pose no problem. If not, watch out! You may end up buying Madame Mao Tse-tung's biography.

QPB carries books beloved by the Northeast literary elite. We, therefore, scorn their fiction, but sometimes can pick up instructive books. Examples: a book on recognizing architectural styles, another on the history of mathematics, a collection of Greek mythology. These are never the Featured Selections, so we make sure the little card gets sent back *promptly*.

You can easily rack up Bonus Points and earn free books and all that fun stuff. And yes, they sell *only* quality paperbacks.

ALL-PURPOSE CATALOGS AND TEACHING AIDS

Brainstorms

Nice little catalog of hands-on materials. Includes Cuisenaire rods, cooperative games, books, Wff 'n Proof Games (this is just a sampling). Strongest emphasis is creative play and math/science. For those areas, this is not a bad place to start.

Brook Farm Books. *The First Home-School Catalogue.* $10.50 U.S. or $12.50 Canadian.

240 pages of what to get and where to get it, plus scores of pages of fascinating information about home schooling. You can order many items direct from Brook Farm Books. Some of the nifty stuff: 137 sources of free educational materials. A book on home school teaching aids ($8.70 U.S. postage-paid). *High School Subjects Self-Taught* (four volumes in one, secular). Super selection of children's books. Madrigals's *Magic Key to Spanish* (a method using cognates). Science equipment.

The *Catalogue* is not a compare-and-review book like this one. It *is* a home school beginners' book and a good place to begin your shopping once you have a fair idea of what you want.

Builder Books and Home Grown Kids

Another good little catalog, this time for Christians. Creative materials for all subjects, including the Hewitt Research Foundation programs (Math-It, Winston Grammar, Moore-McGuffey readers, etc.), quality Christian kid's literature—discounted (!), creation science, workbooks, and most of the Bible-compatible books I reviewed at the beginning of this section. Don't expect anything fancy: the catalog is mimeoed on blue paper.

Creation's Child

A catalog just for home schoolers. Paula Carlson carries a selection of phonics materials. She also sells her own *Comments on Curriculum,* a very classy time line, the McGuffey primers, and more. Inventory changes, so write for a brochure.

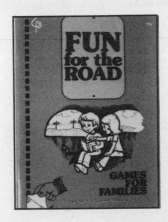

Gazelle Publications

Aside from *The Home School Manual* (reviewed above), Gazelle also sells its own *Fun for the Road* travel book (95¢) and *Science Activities for Christian Children* ($5.95). You can also get a poetry book for children (all new contributions), a natural cooking cookbook, and miscellaneous publishers' closeouts dramatically discounted.

Gazelle stresses character building and good prices. The present selection is small, but will grow if enough people are interested.

Hearth Song

"A Catalog for Families." Everything is natural and beautiful, from the wool-stuffed dolls to the holiday specialties (real hollow goose eggs and Ukranian egg coloring kits for Easter, for example). Books (for children and adults), music instruments, arts and crafts, herbal soaps and toiletries, and more. The catalog should appeal to those who read *Mothering* magazine, as it has that same post-Christian yet profamily flavor.

Holt Associates

John Holt's Book and Music Store catalog is a source of creative inspiration. John Holt was a lover of good literature and fine music, and Holt Associates is carrying on the tradition. Brevity is the soul of wit, and Holt Associates reviews are both pungent *and* brief. The book list, of course, includes many books about children and/or learning. You can also order some art supplies and musical instruments through this catalog. I've obtained many of these items and have never been disappointed.

Instructor Magazine

Instructor, a popular magazine for elementary teachers, also carries its own line of fun, inexpensive activity books, and workbooks. Most are designed to be useful in the home. Areas include art, science, drama, reading aloud, holidays from a secular standpoint, computer activities, poetry, and much, much more! *Instructor* is friendly to parents, so don't be afraid to write for their catalog. Or subscribe to *Instructor* magazine (it's a good investment) and use the enclosed order form. (Just leave the little blank on the form that says "Grade Taught" empty.)

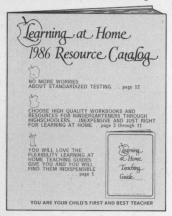

Learning at Home

You'll find reviews of Learning at Home's home school teaching guides and test prep series elsewhere. This Hawaiian-based company is now launching forth as a distributor of K-12 books and workbooks. Write for their sixteen-page 1986 Resource Catalog. Great oaks from little acorns grow; it'll be interesting to see how their line continues to expand.

Learning Every Day
Unifix Math Home Helper, $19.95. *Workjobs,* $14.60. *Mathematics Their Way,* $28.55. Shipping extra.

Another little catalog just for home schoolers. Learning Every Day has a small but fine selection of math manipulatives and activity books, all sized and priced for the home. See sample prices above. Also science, crafts, and home school resource books (like this one!)

Pinkerton Marketing. *The Great Book of Catalogs.* 192 pages. $12.95 postpaid.

Oh, boy! What a joy! For once, here is a book with an honest subtitle. Pinkerton's *The Great Book of Catalogs* really is "All You Need to Know to Shop by Mail." I've wasted hours, and more money than I care to admit, tracking down a good catalog for mail-order shoppers. All the others I've seen are too yuppy ("Honestly, darling, you can't find a *better* source for Dior seconds") or too strange ("Get a great buy on Latvian air-whistles here!"). *The Great Book of Catalogs* shares none of these defects. Perhaps that's because a real, live American couple, Steve and Betsy Pinkerton, put it out instead of a committee of jaded journalists.

TGBOC is updated frequently. The fourth edition for 1985/86 lists more than 2,600 U.S. consumer mail-order catalogs, all tidily sorted into eighty logical sections and traceable through the excellent index.

TGBOC does *not* contain educational items (or why would I be writing this book?). It *does* have a good cross-section of everything else, from Animals and Art to Toys and Travel. Crafts! Gifts! Hardware! Sports! Music! Business Supplies! You can overdose your VISA just by browsing here.

The book is available only by mail. Order directly from Pinkerton.

Pratte Religious Supplies

Books and booklets for home schoolers. Materials for those considering home schooling. Lots of documentation of what's going on in public school. For a couple of bucks you can pick up quite a bit of information here.

Indiana residents, note *Indiana Law and Home Education,* $3 postpaid from Pratte.

Sycamore Tree
Catalog costs $2, refunded with first order.

One-stop shopping with this super catalog of educational products, all of which you can obtain through Sycamore Tree. Great choices in every subject area—over 2,500 items in 1986! The reviews are terse but informative. Very few products are pictured. Exception: the "Felts" brochure shows all Betty Lukens' marvelous felts in gorgeous color. (You have to order the Betty Lukens brochure separately.)

HOME SCHOOL PARAPHERNALIA

Christian Life Workshops, Inc.
The Home School Family's Complete Household Organizer by Gregg and Sono Harris. 250 pages, with divider tabs in three-ring binder. $29.50 postpaid.

You know you want to be more organized. You don't want your little old home school to be buried in little old piles of paper, do you? CLW thinks they have the answer to your perpetual clutter machine: an organizer designed with the Christian home schooling family in mind. It's got field trip planning sheets, a loan library tracking system, home school lesson plans, grades, attendance and health records, hospitality records, profamily activism planning sheets, weekly menu planners, and lots of other stuff that doesn't come in your standard office or school supply versions.

A feature I like: the organizer is designed so you won't have to juggle info back and forth. Because of a clever system of major and minor planning keys, you jot only the key references on the month-at-a-glance or weekly planner sections. Details are recorded only once, on the Planning/Record sheets.

The organizer comes in a three-ring binder, complete with a full year's worth of materials. And you can use it practically forever, because every buyer has permission to reproduce the entire organizer for personal use only for the rest of his life. At the end of each year, just pop the entire year's organizer in an envelope and there are your school records for the year in easy-to-find order. Use your Copy Masters to reproduce the new year's sheets, click them into your three-ring binder, and you're ready to roll again.

Sounds good, doesn't it? CLW promises you will like it or you get your money back.

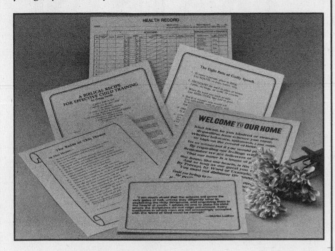

Christian Life Workshops
The Home School Refrigerator Door Packet by Gregg and Sono Harris, 50¢ each or $2.25 for complete set, postage paid.

What good is a naked refrigerator? You can cover up those unsightly acres of enamel-clad steel with kid art and Snoopy magnets—or how about these six *bona fide* home school resources? (For those who like their refrigerators *au naturel*, the packet contents do just as well on a convenient wall.)

What do you get? First, *The Eight Parts of Godly Speech*, a poem to help memorize the parts of speech and Biblical principles at the same time. E.g., "PREPOSITIONS show a clear relation: *By* grace *in* Christ *without* condemnation." *A Biblical Recipe for Effective Child Training* contains lighthearted directions like "Add one teaspoon of clarified instruction and whip lightly to remove any lumps of disobedience." *The 21 Rules of This House* sets realistic boundaries for your family that take the place of inconsistency and nagging—e.g., "If you take it out, put it back!" From the Harrises' historical studies comes *Welcome to Our Home*, a poem posted in colonial American homes to announce the balance between hospitality and a household's standards of behavior. Next, in case you're looking for something in good taste to nail to your local public school door on Reformation Sunday, you might consider Martin Luther's warning about schools, also included. Finally for your files, the packet includes a Health Record to keep track of your children's checkups and medical histories. These come on high-quality Sundance Text paper in autumn shades, for those of you who are interested in such things, and look nice in a frame.

Every Day Is Special.
Activity calendar, $15/twelve months, $2 sample month. U.S. funds only.

Tender loving care went into this home schooling calendar, the product of a home school mother. *Every Day Is Special* has twelve months of daily activities and neat historical facts in a calendar format. Did you know June 1 was Roquefort Cheese Day? (The day's activity suggestion: "Have a cheese-tasting party!") June 3 is likewise honored: it's Chicken Bone Day, a chance to perform a few experiments on ye olde dry bones.

Activities include discussion and writing sparkers, puzzles and riddles of all kinds, activities with food (have a "rainbow lunch!"), arts and crafts, and on and on. The author is widely read, knowledgeable about many fields, and incredibly creative. Families that like discovery learning will find *EDIS* a great resource for project ideas. Everyone will find it brightens up the day. Who can be dull anticipating a Rainbow Lunch, or a cheese-tasting party, or a chicken-bone cracking spree, or . . . ?

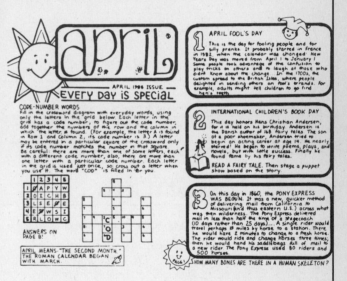

Free Ed Guide. $14/year (four issues).

Descriptions, addresses, and reviews of free educational materials. They include posters, games, records, toys, video cassettes, films, and more. The *Guide* also gives suggestions for how you might use each free item in your educational program, adding significantly to the *Guide's* value. If you believe in integrated learning, you can construct a whole year's wide-ranging program with free materials with the help of the *Free Ed Guide*. And even if you are following a more standard format, it's really fun to browse through this treasure trove of freebies and idea sparkers geared toward ages five to fifteen.

CHAPTER NINE

PARENT AND LEADERSHIP TRAINING

Training for home schoolers comes divided neatly into two categories: Christian and "other." Since at least 90 percent of home schoolers are Christians, this is not too surprising. We will consider the categories one by one.

CHRISTIAN TRAINING

Aletheia Publishers (a division of Alpha Omega Publications).
Child Training, $5.95.

What the Bible Says About . . . Child Training comes with endorsements by Dr. Paul Kienel of Association of Christian Schools International and Jerry Falwell. It is Scriptural reasoning on this difficult subject, and in combination with Gregg Harris's workshop tape on discipline (see Christian Family Workshops below) can be a real boon to your family.

Subjects include: the need for controlling young children; how and when to use chastisement; devices children use to avoid obeying, and how to respond; and developing self-controlled teenagers.

Aletheia Publishers also has a seminar based on this book, available on both cassette and video tapes. Write for a free brochure.

American Christian History Institute

One- to ten-day seminars on American Christian Education. James B. Rose, American Christian History Institute's president, is writing a book to be published in the spring of 1986, entitled *A Guide to American Christian Education for the Home and School: The Principle Approach.*

You're going to run into the Principle Approach now and again, so you might as well know what it is. Briefly stated, it is the belief that God has given us principles that govern *every* area of life: politics, education, business, and even such mundane things as dress and fashion. Followers of the Principle Approach also believe that America, being founded by users of this approach, has a unique opportunity in history to bring the gospel to the world. Their concentration so far (in writing) is on "the relation between Christianity and America and its form of government." Now bear with me, because I'm trying to explain something that has confused many people. *Although the Principle Approach as it now stands involves much study of American history, it is NOT a history course.* Rather, the history is shared in order to give us an example of how to apply the "seven minimal Biblical principles" to *all* areas of our lives, since many of America's founders strove to do so.

As it applies to education, the Principle Approach is basically a blueprint for raising Christian leaders.

Now that I've been carefully objective for a few paragraphs, let me tell you that I willingly bought everything the Foundation for American Christian Education has on the Principle Approach (see their review below) and intend, God willing, to acquire one of the first copies of Mr. Rose's book when it comes off the presses. *A Guide to American Christian Education* has three sections that I am particularly anxious to see. The Home section explains how to apply the "seven principles" to your family life. The Home-School section first tells parents how to educate themselves in the Principle Approach, and then how to teach their children. The School section "explains how to master 'the four R's' to teaching and learning and how to think governmentally." These "four R's" are: *researching* God's Word to find out what it says about a subject; *reasoning* from Biblical principles; *relating* Biblical principles to each student (making it relevant); and *recording* the application. This strongly resembles Bill Gothard's approach (see the Advanced Training Institute of America curriculum mentioned in the Curriculum Buyers Guide section). The School section also includes many real-life experiences of teachers and parents who have been using the Principle Approach over the last few years. You will know if this excites you or not.

Bible Truth for School Subjects. Dr. Ruth Haycock. Four volumes, $34.50 postpaid. Order from Christian Life Workshops.

Would you like to turn your encyclopedia into a dynamite Christian curriculum? Here's how to do it. Either look up all Scripture references for every subject in a concordance, study them, and create a framework for approaching each subject; or buy *Bible Truth for School Subjects.* It's a four-volume set of books that organizes all the passages of Scripture related to over thirty subjects of school study. For each subject you get a concept summary and Scriptural overview. By looking through the concept summary you can identify the places in your encyclopedia or regular text where passages of Scripture will be illuminating.

Ranging from Art to Zoology, Dr. Haycock gives the complete verse or passage (or a synopsis of a lengthy passage) along with historical information concerning the Bible's accuracy in areas under study. You'll be amazed at the amount of revelation the Bible offers on subjects like biology, mathematics, and athletics, subjects that most people think it doesn't address at all!

Volume I, *Social Studies,* covers history, geography, economics, government, leadership and administration, social relationships, the family, the church, and social problems. Volume II, *Language Arts/English,* gets into reading, writing, literature, speech, listening, and foreign languages. Volume III, *Science/ Mathematics,* looks at astronomy, earth science, physics and chemistry, zoology, botany, human biology, and mathematics. The final volume, *Fine Arts and Health,* has creativity, arts and crafts, music, health, sex education, physical education, athletics, and death education—all from a point of view you'll never hear in public school.

Each volume of *Bible Truth for School Subjects* also includes a vast list of resources for further study, including books for students and teachers, tapes, curriculum guides, textbooks,

resource units, supplementary materials, audiovisual materials, and periodicals. Each volume has its own index.

It's hard to see how anyone could go wrong with books like these; it's easy to see how someone might go wrong without them. This is the classic on integrating the Bible into school studies, whether at home or in the classroom.

Christian Family Educational Services.

Information clearinghouse about home schooling. Consultations for families and churches in Arizona only.

Christian Homesteading Movement

Come to New York State and attend a Home Education Workshop on the property of Richard and Anne Marie Fahey. The bio says, "Richard was one of the earliest advocates of home education. His experience in teaching children goes back 25 years. In 1963 he founded the Christian Homesteading School and in 1970 Anna Marie joined him. Together with guest instructors they have influenced many families to successfully begin home-teaching." The Faheys have eight children, who according to the testimonies I received are an advertisement for the workshops.

Workshops come in two sizes. Intensive three-day courses cover all the needful. You also can sign up for a personal, half-day Home Education Course that covers the bare essentials, to be given at your convenience.

Christian Life Workshops, Inc.
The Home Schooling Workshop. Twelve-cassette tape set by Gregg Harris, with notes and three-ring binder, $69.50 postpaid.

How true it is that "Pride goeth before a fall." I was only mildly interested in sending away for these tapes. After all, we've taught our children at home for a while now, and what could Gregg Harris tell me that I didn't already know?

Well, the week after the tapes arrived, the Pride family was listening to those tapes during breakfast, lunch, and supper. Gregg Harris told us how to help our children develop an enduring taste for righteousness by giving them a taste of it, "touching their young palates" with the best of our own experience and study. He shared with us *practical* principles of child discipline and instruction that help our children in the long run rather than just providing us with temporary relief. He taught us how to use casual family storytelling to pass on our values and national heritage to our children without even having to take time out from our household work. Gregg went on to discuss how to achieve financial independence and give children needed work experience through a home business and how to develop a ministry of hospitality (he calls this "the original Bed and Breakfast plan"). An extra: the tapes include insights on home evangelism, one of the modern church's most neglected areas.

The Home Schooling Workshop includes all this, plus the info you'd expect on the advantages of home schooling, the dangers of age-segregated peer dependency, how to begin a home study program, how to choose a curriculum, legal considerations, and instructional methods.

Though Christian Life Workshops is in fact a household ministry of the Harris family with very little additional staff, it is a thoroughly professional and ethical organization, charging no hidden fees and covering completely the normal costs of hosting the workshop. CLW Inc. has helped to establish Christian home education associations from coast to coast and has glowing recommendations from former hosts.

Although Gregg spends at least four days every week at home with his family, he manages to conduct nearly thirty workshops each year in major cities across the USA. You might be interested in attending one of these workshops (write to CLW Inc. for Gregg's schedule). At the workshop you not only get Gregg's constantly revised and up-to-date message, but you can also roam around the large exhibit hall of curriculum in which nearly every major Christian publisher has a display. There's also the thrill of meeting hundreds of other home schooling parents, all walking around in a daze saying, "I thought I was the only one!" Workshop alumni may attend free of charge each year; so the $30 per couple or $20 per individual is a one-time investment. Or if you buy the tapes, you'll get Gregg recorded live before an audience of four hundred. The set includes twelve cassettes plus a substantial packet of notes and resources in a nice three-ring binder.

This is *the* home schooling tape set to buy. And if your Christian home school support group or co-op is considering hosting a home schooling seminar, this is the one.

Christian Life Workshops, Inc.
The Family Storytelling Workshop. Six-tape set by Gregg Harris with notes and three-ring binder. $32.50 postpaid.

Roots. How can you help your children find them and grow them? You can share your past and your values with your children by learning the art of family storytelling.

The Family Storytelling Workshop shows how you can use casual storytelling in character education, child discipline, holiday celebrations, and Sunday school lessons. You can be as tongue-tied as the Rock of Gibraltar—it doesn't matter. All you need is to be willing to talk to your children while you're working together around the house.

I warn you, your children are going to like this! Ours now clamor for their favorite stories. "Tell me my birth story!" "Tell us the story of the Red Ink!" Storytelling is also great for developing your dramatic talents. Fathers would find it more fun to be around their families if they were the center of excited attention more often as the family storyteller. And storytelling mothers get more respect!

This six-tape set may do more good for your family life than any other one thing (besides maybe getting rid of your TV set).

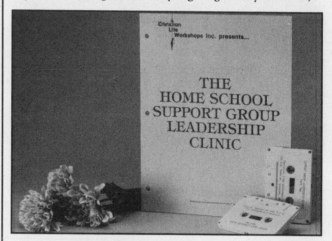

Christian Life Workshops
Support Group Leadership Clinic. $12.50 with notes and two cassette tapes. Tapes alone $10, notes alone $3.50. Bulk rates for notes, $3 each in lots of ten or more.

Gregg Harris has drawn on the experiences of dozens of home school support groups across the nation to produce this home school leadership training kit. In the live recording of a clinic presented in Indianapolis, Gregg shares tips and strategies for avoiding burnout while building your organization, plus ideas from California's "Park Days" to the Texas "Curriculum Fairs." Get your leaders this set before they're buried by success!

Family Restoration International
The Family Restoration Strategy, two-tape set by Gregg Harris. With notes. $8.50 postpaid.

If you like *The Home Schooling Workshop,* you'll love *The Family Restoration Strategy* tape set. Family Restoration International (FRI) is the association of Christian Life Workshops alumni and friends working with Gregg and Sono Harris. It's for Christian families and singles across the U.S.A. and Canada who want to make a positive difference in their homes, churches, and communities. All FRI-related activities (education, Biblical estate building, Christian activism, hospitality, and civil influence) grow out of weekly hospitality groups within local churches. These groups include all ages and encourage their members to practice hospitality and grow into other home-centered ministries. The groups operate under the oversight and with the approval of a local church's pastoral leadership. If you're interested, get the tapes or send for a free brochure.

Foundation for American Christian Education (FACE). *Christian History,* $7.50. *Teaching and Learning,* $7.50. *Rudiments,* $3. *Christian Self-Government,* $11. *Consider and Ponder,* $14. All prices postpaid.

Beautiful materials on the Principle Approach. (For a description of this approach, see above under American Christian History Institute.) Everything FACE sells is worth at least three times as much, for the materials alone. Home schoolers get hefty discounts off the already-low price. Prices quoted above are for home schoolers.

All FACE materials are designed for adults or mature teenagers. You soak up the Principle Approach, and then teach it to your children. These are not "textbooks," but teacher training materials.

The Christian History of the Constitution documents that America is a Christian nation (that is, it *was* once dedicated to Christ) with a Christian Constitution (that is, one based on Christian principles). The "Chain of Christianity" is traced westward to America, as the gospel spread from Israel to the Roman Empire and thence to the uncouth white tribespeople who, once Christianized, spread it over the world. A large book, 8½ x 11″, hardbound in red cloth, beautifully gold-stamped, almost five hundred pages, consisting almost entirely of quotes from source documents. Fascinating browsing; a historical education in itself; an argument impossible to resist.

Teaching and Learning America's Christian History is the original "how to" manual of the Principle Approach. Each principle is coolly spelled out, precept on precept, line on line. Likewise beautifully bound and gold-stamped, likewise large, likewise red. Under four hundred pages.

Rudiments of America's Christian History and Government is a workbook for students filled with source quotes from distinguished American Christian leaders of the past. Like all workbooks, it contains questions for which the student must fill in answers. Unlike other workbooks, the questions are designed to develop both Christian thinking and an awareness of our Christian heritage. Example:

What is the basic distinction between: MORAL law, RITUAL law, and CIVIL law? Write a brief description of each. Use the 1828 WEBSTER Dictionary [which FACE also sells—see review in Literature] to look up moral, rite, ritual, and civil.

And,

Why are qualities present in pagan nations present in America today?

Christian Self-Government with Union is red vellum, gold-stamped, eagle-embossed, illustrated, indexed, and 640 pages.

More Christian history from source documents, emphasizing the colonist's voluntary Christian union that led to self-government. *Consider and Ponder* is the first volume of a projected

series on the Christian history of the American Revolution. Covering the Constitutional Debate period of 1765-1775, it's another gorgeous heavy, its 736 pages nestling between blue vellum covers.

Heritage Education and Research Organization (HERO) Newsletter subscription $15.

Power corrupts, and absolute power corrupts absolutely. So does the desire for absolute power, or in more self-righteous terms the desire to be a Great Beneficent Friend of the People. Seems some of our leaders, real or self-appointed, now know what is best for our children. More, they don't want us plebian parents passing on our outmoded values to same.

HERO exists to warn us against those who would, ever so kindly, alienate our children from us or physically take them away. They have tons of evidence that this antifamily movement exists, and in some surprising places. The Anointed's bottom line: Parents simply aren't capable of taking care of their children, and citizens aren't capable of taking care of themselves. We need one-world government to keep the citizens in line, and a combination of compulsory "parenting" programs and state child institutionalization to keep families submerged. Their method: Create a crisis or exaggerate a problem (like child abuse). Once the hysteria is high enough, rob the people of their civil rights (they won't notice anyway). This "Crisis/Change" sting has been worked on America for the past thirty years with great success. The best part is that, once perpetrated, you never have to prove that your changes have made the situation better. In fact, the worse you make it, the more you can scream for *more* power and *more* federal funding. Witness what Planned Parenthood has done for teenage pregnancies, or what our Washington-inspired child abuse laws are doing for child abuse.

You can read about this movement every day in the paper, if you know what you're looking for. It has two weak points: God (who's against it); and Christians, especially home schoolers who don't let their kids get brainwashed in the public schools.

In Tolkien's *Lord of the Rings* trilogy, Saruman the sorcerer had things all going his way until the Ents, treelike giants, held a council and decided to attack him. *Saruman had forgotten the Ents.* Our would-be rulers likewise have forgotten God and aren't really prepared to face Christians who will stand for what is right instead of loafing in an armchair soaking up fluffheaded situation comedies.

HERO has seminars, tapes, and books. If these don't arouse your sleeping church, nothing will.

Home School Headquarters. *Resource Guide for Home Education* by Don Hubbs. Updated yearly. $10 postpaid.

Are you looking for a home school speaker? Would you like the addresses of a hundred groups that help the handicapped? How about some leads for a home business, or a list of educational research organizations? Guess what—they aren't in my book. The reason is that these, and many other areas of interest to serious home schoolers, are covered so well in Don Hubb's handy *Resource Guide for Home Education*.

The book is a browser's delight. There are scads of leads for curriculum design and student testing, legal information, resource lists, magazines and library services, and lots of other stuff that home schoolers find fascinating. Those who are dedicated to home schooling, especially home school leaders, will get some mileage out of the *Resource Guide*.

OTHER TRAINING

International Montessori Society
IMS membership of $15 for individuals includes subscription to all Society publications and discounts on books.
Home-study course, $800. Price increases to $1,200 May 1, 1986. Includes materials, tuition, and registration.

The IMS is working to implement Maria Montessori's educational ideals. They offer several Montessori certification programs, and an elementary Montessori home-study course. This is twenty-two lessons covering observation of children (including four required field trips to a Montessori environment), nine lessons on Montessori principles, and four lessons each on child development (including managing misbehavior), and use of the Montessori primary materials.

If you want the home-study course, you have to fill out an application form and send it in along with a $50 registration fee. If you are accepted, IMS will send you an enrollment form and the course catalog.

Home schoolers will be interested to know that Romalda Spaulding, author of *The Writing Road to Reading*, is a member of the IMS Advisory Board.

IMS also publishes a Montessori newspaper, a journal, and runs a mail-order bookstore that sells (naturally) books by and about Montessori and her methods.

Interpersonal Communications.

A newsletter, *For Parents*, and books and resources for liberal churchfolk. Materials are geared toward parents who would like their children to manifest old-fashioned morality (respect for elders, self-control, family togetherness), but feel uncomfortable with the "old-time religion." Many public school themes are echoed here: free expression of negative feelings (IC sells *The Hating Book*), nuclear disarmament, values clarification.
Interpersonal Communications materials stress relationships (natch). Their view is based on an egalitarian model. Techniques advocated include yoga and the communication measures made popular by Parent Effectiveness Training (P.E.T.). (Dr. Thomas Gordon, P.E.T.'s founder, endorses IC, by the way.) They have weekly meetings, all-day seminars, and retreats.

Open Connections
Open Connections, $12.50 ppd. *Spaces for Children,* $6 ppd. Annotated list, $1.50 and SASE.

Home schoolers may have heard of Susan Shilcock and Peter Bergson's work in the area of "flexible thinking." Susan is the president and Peter the executive director of Open Connections, "a family resource center specializing in the support of flexible thinking and self-directed learning in children." Open Connections offers on-site programs for parents and children together; workshops with slide presentations, held both on-site and away; and two books for parents.
Open Connections: The Other Basics features two hundred photos plus chapters on the value of flexible thinking and how to promote it. The book also gets into real work and real tools for children, plus activities and physical work/play structures to encourage creativity.
Spaces for Children is a manual for designing and building your own in-home work/play structure for children. *Spaces* is complete with photos and line drawings of the contraptions, which require only minimal money and wood-working skills to assemble.

Open Connections also has an annotated list of thirty books supporting creative problem-solving for children aged three to nine, which shows they are not alone in this interest.

CHAPTER TEN

LEGAL HELPS

What do you do when Mrs. Busybody reports you on the child abuse hotline for "educational neglect"? What do you say to an irate truant officer or an officious schoolperson? Most home school families never face these problems. Still, it's good to know what to do if the bureaucracy catches you by the shirt in its grinding gears.

First step, of course, is to join a home school group. There's safety in numbers, and more than one court case has been dropped when sympathetic friends packed the courtroom or picketed the courthouse. These groups are also well-informed about the current laws and in touch with legislators and other leaders.

Remember, you don't need any defense against school laws if your children are under the minimum compulsory attendance age, which varies from five to seven.

Following is a brief list of other legal resources that will help you be confident in your program.

Christian Liberty Academy. *National Guide,* **$5.** *Legal Manual,* **$5.**

The *National Guide to Home School Attorneys and Organizations* is a 115-page directory of names, addresses, and phone numbers, with over three hundred listings. CLASS also has a Legal Manual, which introduces you to the law and includes such things as a sample affidavit with step by step directions for dealing with school officials.

Home School Legal Defense Association. $100 per year, per family. Single payment on enrollment or two installments: **$60 upon enrollment and $50 thirty days later.**

Send SASE for application. Do not send money with your application request.

The purpose of the Home School Legal Defense Association is to establish the fact that responsible home schooling is legally permissible in every state. They will provide experienced legal counsel and representation by qualified attorneys to every member family who is challenged in the area of home schooling. The attorneys' fees will be paid in full by the Association.

Run by Concerned Women for America's general legal counsel Michael Farris, this appears to be a reputable organization. Knowing you can obtain quality legal counsel is enough to dissuade potential prosecutors in some cases.

National Association for Legal Support of Alternative Schools. Membership, $20/year.

See the review under "Alternative Schools" in the Curriculum Buyers' Guide. NALSAS offers help to nonreligious home school programs.

Rutherford Institute. *Home Education Reporter.* **$10/state (includes updates); $250 complete package.**

A state-by-state analysis of compulsory education laws and relevant court rulings. Each segment includes a synopsis of the state's law; a straightforward explanation of the requirements; and the consequences of violating the law. Updated quarterly. Order info on just your state, or any combination of states. If you are home schooling and thinking about moving, the packet on your target state may be a wise investment.

The Rutherford Institute newsletter tells you about the court cases Rutherford is currently fighting, many of which involve home school rights. Free, but donations are welcome (and needed).

Rutherford Institute also has a series of books and publications on your civil and religious rights, most written by noted constitutional lawyer John Whitehead.

CHAPTER ELEVEN

HOME SCHOOL ORGANIZATIONS COAST-TO-COAST

It was a dramatic moment in American history. The Declaration of Independence had just been signed, committing America to a war against the greatest empire on earth. Benjamin Franklin rose in his chair. "Gentlemen," he said solemnly, "we must hang together, or we shall all hang separately."

Now is not the time for home schoolers to hunker at home, fearfully avoiding the association of others. In numbers there is strength, as well as help and good fellowship. Your local and state home school groups do more than take your $10 or $20 and mail you a newsletter. The lobby legislators, sit in on court trials if necessary, set up conventions and educational fairs, organize field trips, present media events, and act as your resource network. Home schoolers who fail to tap into this rich source are not only denying themselves many wonderful opportunities, but are failing to support the sacrificial efforts of those who are working to make home schooling thoroughly legal and respectable. Obviously, the more numbers a state group can claim, the more impact it can have on legislators and the media. Stand up and be counted!

On the following page is a listing of *state* home school groups. I have spared no effort to try to locate at least one such group for every state, sending out hundreds of letters and making long-distance phone calls.

Addresses sometimes shift as leaders move, old groups disband, and new groups form. Home schoolers are in an organizing period, setting up organizations and networks coast-to-coast. When this period ends, we'll probably have one or two acknowledged home school organizations in every state.

Where there is no generally acknowledged state group, I have included several regional groups. Also, some states have more than one "state" group, dividing perhaps along religious or geographical boundaries from the others.

If you can't find your state listed here, don't despair. Try contacting the group in the *next* state, or write to a newsmagazine such as *The Teaching Home* or *Growing Without Schooling*. If you write for info, please enclose a dollar or two to pay for the time spent answering your letter, and an SASE. And if you call, remember that you are likely to be answered by a private individual working out of his or her private home; so time your calls accordingly. These little courtesies are what keep the overworked home school leaders from grinding to a halt.

HOME SCHOOL ORGANIZATIONS BY STATE

It would be nice to get this book printed and into the hands of its readers two seconds after writing it. Nice, but at the moment impossible. So the information you are reading *was* correct in November 1985, but is already partially out-of-date.

I expect most of the addresses will still be relevant by the time you read this, and of course the founding dates are the same. But expect big changes in the *membership* numbers! Home schooling is an *exploding* movement; so a group that had one hundred members when I wrote this may have five hundred by the time you read it. Also, as home schoolers gain political savvy, a uniform type of state group is springing up, equipped with newsletter, phone tree, support groups, media chairmen, field trips, state convention, and so on. This is the kind of group that works, and it's a joy to belong to. If your state doesn't have this kind of group, see if you can make contact with a state that *does* have one, and copy their format.

MOST FAVORED STATE STATUS

as of Jan. 1986

Alabama	15
*Alaska	15
Arizona	8
Arkansas	6
California	13
*Colorado	21
*Connecticut	18
*Delaware	17
Florida	7
Georgia	7
*Hawaii	15
*Idaho	19
Illinois	1
Indiana	1
#Iowa	24
Kansas	19
Kentucky	1
Louisiana	8
*Maine	17
*Maryland	22
*Massachusetts	18
#Michigan	24
@Minnesota	2
Mississippi	2
@Missouri	2
Montana	2
Nebraska	4
Nevada	4
*New Hampshire	17
*New Jersey	17
New Mexico	10
New York	17
North Carolina	1
*#North Dakota	24
*Ohio	23
Oklahoma	1
Oregon	2
*Pennsylvania	23
*Rhode Island	16
*South Carolina	17
South Dakota	7
Tennessee	9
Texas	25
Utah	5
Virginia	14
Washington	7
Wisconsin	3
*Vermont	11
West Virginia	12
Wyoming	2

This chart designates the most favorable states toward home schooling, starting with #1 to the least favorable states ending with #25. Each state's designation is based on 3 factors: (1) The maximum amount of freedom given to home schoolers versus the amount of state involvement (2) the vagueness of the compulsory attendance statute and (3) the number of legal conflicts occurring between home schoolers and the state at present.

(*) Designates states that require specific "approval" of each home school by the local school district or school board.

(#) Designates states that require home schools to have certified teachers.

(@) Designates that the compulsory attendance law was ruled void for vagueness, leaving present law unenforceable.

Reprinted from the *Home School Journal.* Used by permission. Chris Klicka's "Most Favored State Status" column is a regular feature in the *Home School Journal.* State laws do change, so you may want to subscribe to the *Journal* to keep on top of the news and your state's ratings! The *Journal* is reviewed in the "Books and Magazines" chapter.

Christopher J. Klicka is a lawyer with extensive home schooling research experience, both for the Rutherford Institute and the Home School Legal Defense Association.

ALABAMA

Alabama Citizens for Home Education
Rt. 3, Box 360-D
Montgomery, AL 36110
(205) 265-1221

Founded March 1984. Estimated five hundred members. Functions: lobbying, support groups, legislative watchdog, community events, media appearances, and "to reeducate the general public as to the many ways children learn." No membership dues. ACHE is looking for volunteers to be contact points for other home schoolers in their area.

Newsletter: *The Voice* is quarterly. A nice little mimeoed bulletin, it includes a calendar of home schooling events. $5/ year.

ALASKA

Alaska Home-Schoolers Association
P.O. Box 15000 #724
Wasilla, AK 99687

As far as I know, this group exists, but they did not reply to my questionnaire. Alaska is unusual in that it allows home schooling under state auspices (they supply texts, etc.). If this kind of situation meets your needs, contact the State Department of Education.

ARIZONA

Arizona Families for Home Education
639 E. Kino
Mesa, AZ 85203
(602) 964-7435

Founded 1982. Membership: 230. Functions: support groups, legislative watchdog, yearly convention. No membership dues.
Newsletter: *Arizona Families for Home Education,* ten monthly issues/year, $5 for subscription. Homey, mimeoed lists of home schooling events and resources.

ARKANSAS

Arkansas Christian Home Educators Association
P.O. Box 18057
Little Rock, AR 72115
(501) 224-2445

Founded 1981. 350 paid subscribers to the newsletter. Functions: lobbying, support groups, legislative watchdog, community events, media appearances. Membership dues: $20/year, which includes the newsletter. ACHEA could use at-home volunteer help—give them a call.
Newsletter: *Update* is available separately for $10/six monthly issues.

CALIFORNIA

Christian Home Educators Association of California
P.O. Box 2182
Westminster, CA 92684
(714) 963-8904

Founded Fall of 1982. General mailing list of 1,500. Functions: support groups, legislative watchdog, community events, media appearances, speakers bureau, statewide/regional convention, helpful materials for California home schoolers. No membership dues.

Newsletter: Co-published with *The Teaching Home,* bimonthly, $15/year.

Send for CHEAC's free brochure.

Affiliated Home School Ministries of Southern California

An incorporated network of home school programs, designed to provide activities, support, and credibility for home school families. For further information, contact Michele Robinson at (714) 751-7767.

Keys to Learning Association
2650 W. Trojan Place
Anaheim, CA 92804
(714) 995-6059

Founded 1981. Functions: support groups, community events, media appearances. Events: seminars, conferences, miniseminars, workshops, consultations, help starting home learning centers, help with school district difficulties. Home school materials, how-to manual.

Now pay attention, because this gets complicated. Keys to Learning is the parents' group. They have four professional staff members, but are grateful for extra help. To wit: "office help, plus tutors, teachers, assistants to teach others how to start their own home learning centers . . . attorneys who understand the laws about home education . . . most of all research specialists for good books and materials."

KTL is loosely associated with Abilities Research Associates, whose home school curriculum is reviewed under the Smattering section in the Curriculum Buyers Guide. To make this all more confusing, they are also loosely associated with the National Home Education Guild (est. 1985), and send the NHEG newsletter to their members. Subscription rate to NHEG is $10/year. The magazine

is presently bimonthly, but will soon be quarterly in a standard magazine format. If you want information about these groups, send a legal size SASE and a check for $3 made out to NHEG. This will get you information and a sample copy of the magazine. Send to:

National Home Education Guild
515 N.E. 8th St.
Grants Pass, OR 97526
(503) 474-1826

COLORADO

Colorado Association of Christian Schools
P.O. Box 26268
Denver, CO 80226

I have no info on this group, besides the address.

Colorado Home Schooling Network
c/o Judy Gelner
7490 W. Apache
Sedalia, CO 80135

Founded April 1981. One hundred members. Functions: support groups, legislative watchdog, community events, media appearances, monthly meetings, workshops for children. No membership dues.

Newsletter: *Colorado Homeschooling Network Newsletter,* $8/year, irregular. Address for subscriptions: CHSN, c/o Nancy McGuire, 365 Hooker, Denver, CO 80129.

Legal packet, *Homeschooling in Colorado,* $6.25 from Judy Gelner.

Send SASE for free brochure.

CONNECTICUT

Connecticut Home Schoolers Association
c/o Nancy Williams
Box 464
Chester, CT 06412
(203) 526-5005

Founded 1983. Over one hundred on mailing list. Functions: lobbying, support groups, legislative watchdog, media appearances, group field trips, guest speakers. Membership dues: $12/year if you can afford it, less if you can't.

At-home volunteer help is gratefully accepted.

Newsletter: *Hearth Notes,* bimonthly, free with membership.

Home Education League of Parents
P.O. Box 203
Abington, CT 06230
(203) 974-2415

Address and phone number reported in *The Teaching Home* of July 1985.

Nancy Eisele
Rt. 1, Box 180-D
Pomfret Center, CT 06259
(203) 928-9212

Christian home schooling support group founded 1985. Newsletter copublished with *The Teaching Home.*

DELAWARE

Delaware Home Education Association
Box 55
Dover, DE 19903
(302) 674-5234

Founded 1985. Informal support group structure seeking to develop into full-service state organization. One hundred member families and friends.

DISTRICT OF COLUMBIA

John and Sue Seel
116 11th St., N.E.
Washington, DC 20002

It's a small world; the Seels were friends of our next-door neighbors as it turned out! Contact them to find out what's cooking in D.C.

FLORIDA

Florida is the state for oranges, hurricanes, and home school organizations run by men with Ph.Ds. Sidney Mordes, head of FLASH, is an adjunct professor, and his wife has a degree in social welfare. Dr. Larry Walker, head of Florida Parent-Educator Association, is a professor of political science. Now all we need is a few groups run by lawyers (I hear there is one in Illinois) . . . or even better, *judges.*

Florida Association for Schooling at Home (FLASH)
Rt. 3, Box 215
Marianna, FL 32446
(904) 482-2568

Founded 1981. 225 names on the mailing list. Support groups, community events, clearinghouse for news and resources. No membership dues.

Newsletter: $2 or free. (Be generous and pay for it!) It comes out three or four times a year.

Florida Parent Educators Association
9245 Woodrun Road
Pensacola, FL 32514
(904) 477-9642

Founded June 1984. Rapidly growing membership, had 150 families in less than a year from inception. Functions: lobbying, legislative watchdog, media appearances, helps start new groups. Membership dues: $29/year. FPEA could use some amateur lobbyists (writing and calling legislators), and needs district directors and county coordinators.

Newsletter: *FPEA News,* included in subscription, published as needed (four issues in eight months thus far).

Send SASE for free brochure.

GEORGIA

Georgians for Freedom in Education
4818 Joy Lane
Lilburn, GA 30247
(404) 923-9932

Founded January 1983. Twelve hundred families are on the mailing list. Functions: lobbying, support groups, legislative watchdog, community events, media appearances, monthly lecture series during school year, weekly field trips, consultation services.

Membership dues in this classy, professional group are $10/year and include the bimonthly newsletter, entitled *Georgians for Freedom in Education.* The group has over twenty professional

advisers, but can use volunteer help with its office work.

Send an SASE for the most impressive free home school brochure in the USA. The group's seal features an eagle instructing its eaglet; both have a "don't-tread-on-me" look. Frankly, I'm glad I'm on the right side and don't have to tangle with this group!

HAWAII

If the fragments of information I pick up from here and there are correct, Hawaii has a fairly fierce State Department of Education. Nonetheless, groups of home schoolers are forming on each of the islands.

Hawaii Home Schoolers Association
c/o Bill and Barbara Hussey
P.O. Box 591
Hanalei, Kauai, HI 96714
(808) 826-9222

Recently founded. Mostly support and information.

Hawaii Home School Support Group
c/o Milton and Kathy Yamada
45-681 Kauhulu Place
Kaneohe, HI 96744

Recently founded. Fifty families are involved in a loose affiliation. Major functions are field trips and parents' meetings.

Mrs. Judith Wilson
P.O. Box 469
Mt. View, HI 96771

CLASS coordinator. Another loosely affiliated group using Christian Liberty Academy's curriculum.

IDAHO

Idaho Family Education Association
1821 Gallup St.
Idaho Falls, ID 83401

Newsletter inactive as of 8/85. Support groups, information on curriculum and legal information. Loosely organized; mobilizes for specific needs.

ILLINOIS

Illinois Christian Home Educators
P.O. Box 261
Zion, IL 60099

Founded January 1984. Functions: support groups, legislative watchdog, media appearances, seminars. No membership dues. ICHE is anxious to find home educators who can swing a pen to write for their newsletter, copublished with *The Teaching Home.* Subscription to same is $15/year.

ICHE support groups meet monthly and also provide resource centers and current news, as well as monthly field trips for the children.

Free brochure with SASE.

INDIANA

Indiana Association of Home Educators
4914 Derby Lane
Indianapolis, IN 46226
(317) 253-0058

Founded 1983. Membership of 175 families. Functions: lobbying, support groups, legislative watchdog, community events, media appearances. Dues are $15/year and include a legal packet, a field trip workbook, a membership certificate, and ongoing training opportunities for member parents.

Newsletter is copublished with *The Teaching Home.*

IOWA

What's going on in Iowa, the part of America that Christian humorist Mike Warnke calls "the state of Perfect Nothing"?

Iowa Families for Christian Education
c/o Ron Duncan
R.R. 3, Box 143
Missouri Valley, IA 51555

Loose association of Christian home schoolers who share the Biblical view of

Christian education. Founded 1985. Reported in *Home School Journal,* September 1985.

KANSAS

Kansans for Alternative Education
19985 Renner Rd.
Spring Hill, KS 66083

Founded April 1984, KAE already boasts 250 member families. Its functions: lobbying, linkage between support groups, legislative watchdog, media appearances, and a state conference.

Membership dues are $10/year and include the newsletter and access to the group's educational, legal, and legislative resources.

Newsletter: *Kansans for Alternative Education* is sent to members eight times a year (monthly January-April, bimonthly otherwise).

National Council of Parent Educators of Kansas
P.O. Box 3366
Shawnee Mission, KS 66217

Betty Jones, the state coordinator of NCPE-KS, called me long distance from Washington and spent an hour filling me in on what they are up to. NCPE-KS works with the legislature and helps those starting support groups.

KENTUCKY

Kentucky Home Schoolers
Rt. 1, Box 96-C
Dover, KY 40134

Founded in 1984, KHS then had fifty member families. Functions: support groups and community events only. Dues: $5/year, which entitles you to the two biannual issues of the newsletter, *The Exchange.* The newsletter is short but spicy, including book reviews, lists of things to do and see around the Bluegrass State, and homey contributions by home schoolers young and old. I can't resist including this snippet from the Fall 1984 issue:

Howwwddddddyyyyyy!! I'm just so paa-roud to write this: And hello out there all you fellow Home-schoolers. I am awritin this because my dear ole mammy suckered me into it; and for no other reason. And if you think it's too liberally dotted with semi-colons, that there is your problem. Let me correct that previous statement; I am also writing this because Alison won't and if neither of us do it Mother would mope around for a couple months. Ahem! Now to commence on a vivid description of the joys of being an older Home-schooler: I am so glad that I am a home-schooler, and have been so, for coming on 6 years now, that I could just faint. But honestly, it is soooooo wonderful. You can sleep to 8 or 9 o'clock. (If your brain doesn't get persnickity and wake you up at 5:30, that is.) But also, of course, you don't have to aso-see-ate with your peers. Let me see, what else is nice about home-schooling, ah yes, of course, you can read all day without interruption, you can visit your pets at anytime of the day, and you can work at volunteer jobs any time of the year and not just summer. (Sister Alison is much better qualified to tell you about that subject, seeing as I've never volunteered and she has.) . . .

Rebekah, the thirteen-year-old who penned these deathless words, has stated that she plans to move into the main branch of the Louisville Free Public Library or at least spend one day a week there. Isn't it *awful* how home school stifles children? How can she possibly *learn* anything, studying all day in the library? She should be in *school!* (Pardon my heavy irony.) As the editor said, "I certainly want to meet this girl."

LOUISIANA

Citizens for Home Education
3404 Van Buren
Baker, LA 70714

I take it on faith that this group exists, since the Post Office doesn't return my letters to me and neither do they.

MAINE

Maine Home Study Association
R.D. 4, Box 5500
Farmington, ME 04938

Founded in 1985, this group claims two hundred members, which isn't bad in a state where the lobsters outnumber the citizens. Functions: lobbying, support groups, legislative watchdog, community events, media appearances.

Membership dues are a suggested (but not required) $15. Benefits include the newsletter, information, and general support and friendliness (you *need* some friends to survive the Maine winters!).

Newsletter: *Maine Home Study Association,* bimonthly, $5 for subscription if you aren't a member.

MARYLAND

Maryland Home Education Association
9085 Flamepool Way
Columbia, MD 21045
(301) 730-0073

Founded 1980. The mailing list includes four hundred addresses, of which MHEA estimates about one hundred and fifty to two hundred can be counted as current home schoolers. No membership dues, but if you want the newsletter you'd better chip in $12. Functions: conferences, networking, resource clearinghouse.

MASSACHUSETTS

Growing Without Schooling, that resourceful home schooling magazine, is located in Boston. Ergo, the staff must know some Massachusetts home schoolers. Try contacting them *(briefly)* if you're having no success locating likeminded friends.

Home Education League of Parents
Box 175
Norfolk, MA 02056

Another I-wrote-and-they-didn't address. You'll recall that there is an organization by this name in Connecticut—perhaps they're connected.

MICHIGAN

Michigan has no home school law, as of Fall 1985, and thus you live at the whim of your local school superintendent. Bill Martin of Bronson, Michigan spent fifteen days in jail "because he did not have a certified teacher or approved curriculum for his home school," as reported in *The Teaching Home* of July 1985. Tyranny! As if certified teachers and approved materials weren't producing illiterates by the busload. Happily, both judges and the media are beginning to wake up to this glaring inconsistency.

National Coalition of Alternative Community Schools
1289 Jewett
Ann Arbor, MI 48104

Dr. Pat Montgomery, founder and director of Clonlara School, is the current president of this organization, which includes many home schools.

Information Network for Christian Homes
4150 Ambrose N.E.
Grand Rapids, MI 49505

All I know about this group is (1) they exist and (2) they are concerned about home schooling. See what kind of information you can pry out of them about home school groups in Michigan. And don't forget the SASE.

MINNESOTA

Minnesota Association of Christian Home Educators
Box 14326
Minneapolis, MN 55414
(612) 434-9004

Founded October 1983, this group has a membership of five hundred. Functions: support groups, educational field trips, annual picnic, media appearances, seminars. Dues are $10/year and include the newsletter, discounts on seminars, and a membership certificate. Unlike most home school organizations, MACHE has a professional staff of five. However, they will be happy to accept volunteer help with their mailings, especially computer-assisted addressing.

Newsletter: *Paper MACHE* (cute) comes out quarterly. Subscription rate is $10 for nonmembers. Although it's small, it's typeset on fancy paper, betokening good things to come from this group.

Send SASE for MACHE's free brochure.

Minnesota Home School Network
9669 East 123rd
Hastings, MN 55033
(612) 437-3049

Founded in 1982, this group now has fifty plus members. Functions: lobbying, support groups, legislative watchdog, community events, media appearances, speakers bureau. Membership dues of $7/year provide the bimonthly, mimeoed newssheet. An excerpt from same:

"Little Red Home School;" That's me. I am a former public school teacher with an expired teaching certificate and a thousand sheets of letter-head stationery. That's all it has taken for me to get the school records for families from four school districts, to act as a paid consultant/tutor to two families and to have a full time student in addition to my own two sons. Next year I hope to be able to work with more families.

The purpose of the above descriptions is to show that there is a market for the free-lance teacher. So dust off that teaching degree and get yourself a job.

The reason I quoted the above excerpt is to show that public school teachers are not all opposed to home schooling. In fact, some of the best homeschoolers *are* public school teachers (present or ex-).

MHSN is a "linkage" group, putting people in touch with each other and providing informal help.

MISSISSIPPI

Mississippi Home Schoolers Support Group
c/o Doug and Connie Ball
Route 4, Box 436
Pass Christian, MS 39571
(601) 452-9637

Founded in September 1983, this group says, "We don't have membership per se." Being translated, that means they are friendly but not superorganized. MHSSG's main function is, as its name suggests, support and encouragement. The quarterly newsletter is available for the minute sum of $4/year.

MHSSG is working on producing an introductory packet. No free brochure had emerged when I sent around my questionnaire, but you may have better success by the time you read this.

MISSOURI

It's all in how you pronounce it. Am I living in the state of Missouri or the state of Misery? We ask ourselves these questions in the hot, humid, miserable summers and the cold, cruel, miserable winters. Situated in the Mississippi River Valley, my hometown of St. Louis gets its share of both Northern winters and Southern summers. (And don't forget the tornadoes!) As one lady wrote to our local paper during a period of tourist boosterism, "You've got to be kidding. No way is Missouri ever going to become a tourist haven. The only way a tourist will ever see Missouri is while his family is heading through it on their way to Florida or Colorado."

One big reason for sweating it out in the home of the heat wave (well, St. Louis is not Texas, but we make up for the few degrees difference by building our entire town out of sun-soaking red brick) is the good people in Families for Home Education. Any group of people who can spend six hours jammed together in a schoolbus, to- and fro-ing it on a field trip to Amish Country, and still smile at each other, is worth knowing. I may be just lucky, but so far I have never met a Missouri home schooler I haven't liked. (Come to think of it, I've never met *any* home schoolers I haven't liked!)

Families for Home Education
Box 18252
Raytown, MO 64133
(314) 442-7608

This is it, folks: the one and only Missouri state home school group. At last count, we had over five hundred member families, but I can personally attest that there are many times that many home schoolers in this state, since four out of five of my home schooling friends haven't yet joined FHE, the rascals! Dues are a piddling $20 a year, which entitle the happy member to support groups, legislative watchdogging, a yearly conference and regional conferences, media representation, and earnest lobbying on his behalf. We also are blessed with some very fine regional newsletters (available separately).

Believe it or not, FHE doesn't have a free brochure. But you don't need one now, right?

MONTANA

Home Schoolers of Montana
Box 40
Billings, MT 59101

According to the *Parent Educator and Family Report* of November/December 1985, Montana has the "probably most unrestricted home education law in the U.S." ever to be achieved without a state home school organization. Montanans are not smug, though, and realize that these liberties will be maintained most effectively by revving up a state group as soon as possible. Home Schoolers of Montana is that brand-new group.

NEBRASKA

Yes, Virginia, there *is* a home school group operating in the People's Republic of Nebraska. The very state that jailed Reverend Everett Sileven and seven fathers from his church for daring to operate a nonstate-approved Christian day school still has home schoolers in its very midst! The state where law officers forcibly disrupted a Wednesday night prayer meeting and carried the worshipers out bodily (in order to show their disapproval of nonstate-approved Christian schooling, one surmises) is host to a Christian home school organization. Curiouser and curiouser! And all this in spite of the fact that a large majority of the Nebraska state legislators were elected with NEA money.

I'm not gloating, just amazed. It takes a special kind of person to home school in Nebraska—something like Harriet Tubman returning down South for another group of slaves, when her own freedom was in jeopardy. Embarrassed by the publicity surrounding Nebraska's stomping all over the Constitution, the legislature has since passed laws facilitating home schooling. However, the Nebraska NEA has been used to owning the state for a good long time now, and they aren't about to give up easily. They don't *like* home schoolers, or Christians, or

Orthodox Jews, or stay-at-home wives, or faithful spouses, etc., etc., etc. Why, children raised in those kinds of homes *won't fit into* the one-world government they're planning! (A Nebraska state rep actually said this on cable TV.)

Meanwhile, the University of Nebraska at Lincoln goes merrily along, selling its excellent courses by mail to all and sundry, including home schooling families. Life is full of contradictions.

Nebraska Christian Home School Association
Box 1245
Columbus, NE 68601
(402) 563-2747

This is the organization whose newsletter is the *Home School Journal,* that peerless piece of battle reporting. Founded in October 1983, they currently report two hundred plus members and five hundred plus subscribers to the newsletter. NCHSA offers support groups, serves as a legislative watchdog, and strews information around to them as wants it. Membership dues of $20 a year get you encouragement, and the *Journal.*

Warren Rushton, the *Journal's* editor, modestly says that the *Journal* is available for a "freewill" offering. I, being a Presbyterian and not believing in free will, suggest that you send in the $10 it deserves if you decide you like the first issue.

NEVADA

Nevada home schooling is divided up along geographic lines, as follows.

Nevada Home Schools—Northern Division
Box 21323
Reno, NV 89515
(702) 786-2428

Newsletter is copublished with *The Teaching Home.*

Home Schools United—Vegas Valley
2375 E. Tropicana, Suite 173
Las Vegas, NV 89109

Phone numbers to contact: 458-6427, 870-5658, 645-1875.
Newsletter: *Home Schools United.* It's a monthly.

NEW HAMPSHIRE

"Live free or die" has been New Hampshire's motto for longer than I can

remember. For some reason the state has had trouble applying this libertarian spirit to home schooling—perhaps because they're so proud of their schools being Number One in the U.S.A. (although they spend *less* money per pupil on education than twenty-eight other states). New Englanders are notorious for being slow to embrace new ideas, but New Hampshire has had enough time to catch on by now (especially since the nationally famous Wallace family first home schooled in New Hampshire). So perhaps you *will* get to "live free" without hassle.

New Hampshire Home Educators Association
9 Mizoras Drive
Nashua, NH 03062

Founded in 1983, this tiny group consists of about ten core families. Functions: support groups, community events, and home schooling information. $4 membership donation includes a subscription to the bimonthly *N. H. Home Schools Newsletter.*

NHHEA sells two info packets. Send them an SASE for their free brochure and information on these packets.

NEW JERSEY

New Jersey Unschoolers Network
2 Smith Street
Farmingdale, NJ 07727
(201) 938-2473

Founded in 1977. Nancy Plent, the director, points out that "strictly speaking, a network doesn't have 'members.'" The mailing list has over two thousand addresses.

Functions: support groups, community events, media appearances, workshops, statewide gatherings, resource clearinghouse, and general help and goodwill. No membership dues. The Unschoolers Network could use volunteers at times to answer letters from students. Volunteers produce the monthly bulletin. NJUN is seeking articles from New Jersey residents about favorite places for family outings.

Newsletter: *Unschoolers Network* costs $5/year for three issues. It's a pretty hefty tome as these things go, and contains advertising and articles with a *Growing Without Schooling* flavor. Everyone shares; nobody puts anyone down.

NEW MEXICO

As of Fall 1985, New Mexico had one of those odd laws that puts home schooling (a private schooling situation if there ever was one) under the jurisdiction of the public school state superintendent. One parent must have a Bachelor's degree or be granted a waiver, and you have to report to your local superintendent, have the children tested annually public school-wise, give the superintendent immunization and attendance records, etc. We hope this law has been mercifully put out of its misery since then.

New Mexico Family Educators
P.O. Box 13383
Albuquerque, NM 87192
(505) 293-2117 or (505) 265-3019

Founded in September 1983, NMFE has seventy-five member families. Functions: support groups, community events, media appearances, and general clearinghouse and contact point for people interested in the joys of home schooling. Suggested membership dues are $5. This gets you the newsletter and a slot on the phone tree. NMFE could use volunteer help with the newsletter and mailings, plus office help filing things and dynamic go-getters to organize some fun activities.

Newsletter: *NMFE Gazette* is given out free at monthly meetings, or mailed to paid members if so desired.

NMFE graciously gave me the names of several other New Mexico organizations:

Southern New Mexico Home Educators Association
3120 Good Shepherd Rd.
Las Cruces, NM 88005

Support groups and lobbying for better legislation.

New Mexico Coalition for Home Education
P.O. Box 40051
Albuquerque, NM 87196.

Another activist group.

New Mexico Christian Home Education, Inc.
c/o Larry Simpson
7417 Santa Fe Trail, N.W.
Albuquerque, NM 87120

Founded 1985. New organization reported in the *Home School Journal.*

NEW YORK

I was disappointed to find no home school group operating in my birthplace, New York City. With absenteeism of over 50 percent in some areas, you'd think the schools wouldn't even notice a few home schoolers here or there. However, one local group is operating in beautiful rural New York.

Home Schoolers Exchange
18 Washington Ave.
Chatham, NY 12037
(518) 392-4277

Founded in the freezing month of February 1984, HSE has twenty-five member families. Functions: support group, community events, and an information exchange. Dues are an insignificant $5/year and includes the bimonthly newsletter. Meetings are open to the public (hear ye!).

NORTH CAROLINA

North Carolinians for Home Education
P.O. Box 5182
Emerywood Station
High Point, NC 27262-9998

This is a brand-new group, as you can see by the jazzy zip code. Right off the bat they have a fancy brochure and a newsletter that goes for $12/year. NCHE is organizing local support groups across the state. They also serve as a legislative watchdog and do media work. As yet, they are not equipped to handle workshops, open houses, state conventions, and all that other high-flying stuff.

Newsletter: *The Greenhouse Report,* bimonthly.

I expect good things from anyone organized enough to typeset a brochure. Send an SASE if you're interested.

NORTH DAKOTA

North Dakota is a tough state for home schoolers. Legislation regarding home schooling is slated to be introduced in 1987; at the moment, home schoolers seem to be pretty much at the mercy of the local school superintendent.

North Dakota Home School Association
721 North 14th Street
Fargo, ND 58102
(701) 663-8959 or (701) 448-2646

Founded in 1984, NDHSA operates more as a network than as a membership organization. Functions: lobbying, support groups, legislative watchdog (there is an interim committee of legislators studying home schooling), plus advice and encouragement to those who need it. No membership dues are required, but gifts are gratefully accepted. Benefits of membership include the newsletter, legal counsel, and support and encouragement. NDHSA has some professional staff members, but could also use volunteer help. The newsletter, untitled, comes out irregularly.

OKLAHOMA

O-O-O-Oklahoma! Here's the place for home schooling! Our annual convention is held here, on the grounds of Oral Roberts University in Tulsa.

The Oklahoma State Constitution allows home schooling, so the NEA gnashes its teeth in vain.

Christian Home Educators Fellowship (CHEF)
P.O. Box 1694
Broken Arrow, OK 74013

CHEF takes their Christianity seriously. Their brochure includes not only their constitution, but a statement of faith. Membership dues are $20/year, and include a monthly newsletter (the *CHEF Report*), a 25 percent discount on books from over one hundred publishers, discounts on workshops sponsored by CHEF, free State Fair tickets, special book offers, discounts on home school-related classified ads in the *CHEF Report,* field trips, and recreational opportunities at group rates.

Oklahoma Christian Home Educators Association
2008 Meadowbrook
Ponca City, OK 74604
(405) 762-9806

Founded in March 1984, OCHEA has one hundred plus families. Functions: support groups, legislative watchdog, community events, media work, statewide workshops and seminars. Dues of $15/year include a subscription to *The Teaching Home,* in which OCHEA's state newsletter is inserted.

Send SASE for free brochure.

OREGON

Oregon is one of the more lenient states, and it is also blessed with a very strong home school network.

Christian Home Schools
8731 N.E. Everett
Portland, OR 97220

Publisher of *The Teaching Home,* a national Christian home school magazine copublished with many state newsletters. CHS also offers an array of home school books and resources for sale by mail. Not affiliated with CHS, but working closely with them, is Christian Life Workshops, the all-around best home school seminar provider in the country (in my opinion). The whole operation is humming along smoothly and growing by leaps and bounds.

National Home Education Guild
515 N.E. Eighth Street
Grants Pass, OR 97526

I don't know too much about this group, except that Keys to Learning is affiliated with it (see the California listings).

PENNSYLVANIA

Western Pennsylvania Homeschoolers
c/o Susan Richman
R.D. 2
Kittanning, PA 16201
(412) 783-6512

Two hundred and fifty families subscribe to the newsletter. Functions: lobbying, support groups, legislative watchdog, community events, media work, outings, and field trips. No membership dues.

Newsletter: *Western PA Homeschoolers,* $6/year; $1.50/sample issue. This quarterly newsletter is sixteen or more pages long, and includes a children's writing section! (Neat idea—it's *their* education, after all!)

RHODE ISLAND

Home school project: Take the people who designed the Rhode Island license plate slogan seriously and try to "discover Rhode Island." It's less than one-thirtieth the size of Texas and in the Northeast. Rhode Island is worth finding; some very nice people come from there (like my husband). Happy hunting!

Parent Educators of Rhode Island
P.O. Box 546
Coventry, RI 02816

A new group, or so I gather. I'm rather short on information about them.

SOUTH CAROLINA

Piedmont Home Educators Association
P.O. Box 2502
Greenville, SC 29602
(803) 288-3769

Founded in 1983, this group consists of seventy-five families. Functions: support groups, legislative watchdog, and community events. At-home volunteers help with the phone chain, newsletter, field trips, quarterly meetings, workshops, and book orders.

Newsletter: *Home Schooler's Digest* comes out monthly. Subscriptions are $10. It's a friendly little thing, with news, teaching tips, ads, a "Swap Shop," and people requesting help and others giving it.

SOUTH DAKOTA

South Dakota just finished knocking the compulsory attendance age down to six from its old setting of seven. A silly move for all but bureaucrats: almost everyone puts their five-year-old children in without any coercion. Still, it would look rather extreme to lower the age at which children are removed from the home for the majority of their day from seven to two, or to six months, all at once. When you see the hue and cry for "mandatory kindergarten" or "early childhood education" or "developmental screening," remember it means just one thing: more clients for the bureaucrats.

South Dakota Home Association
1616 S. 4th Ave.
Sioux Falls, SD 57105
(605) 334-2213

Founded September 1983. Functions: support groups, legislative watchdog, media work. Dues are $10/year and include the newsletter and voting privileges.

Newsletter: *SDHSA Newsletter.* Monthly.

Western Dakota Christian Home Schools
Box 9132
Rapid City, SD 57709
(605) 342-2911

Address and other info reported in *The Teaching Home.*

TENNESSEE

Home Education Association of Tennessee
3677 Richbriar Court
Nashville, TN 37211
(615) 834-3529

Founded January 1984, this group has seven hundred and fifty members. Functions: lobbying, support groups, legislative watchdog, community events, media work, curriculum fairs, statewide and area conferences.

Dues are $10 and do *not* include the newsletter. You must subscribe for this separately.

Newsletter: *Parent Educator* is an information bulletin, lacking the chattiness of some others. Subscriptions are $10 for a member, $12 for a nonmember.

ASSIST
P.O. Box 1321
Knoxville, TN 37901

I don't know if this group still exists. They no longer can be located at this address.

TEXAS

Texas Family Schools Co-op (Inactive)
P.O. Box 466
Elgin, TX 78621

TFSC is inactive, but its members are not. If you see a particular organization cease operations, that's no cause for alarm. It usually means either that the founders got tired of doing it all, or that another group has developed that serves the people better, or both.

National Council of Parent-Educators/TX
P.O. Box 821752
Dallas, TX 75382

I couldn't say if this group exists or not. They don't answer my letters, but neither does the Post Office return them with discouraging words printed all over them. It's a mystery.

Hearth and Home Ministries, Inc.
(formerly Texas Association for Home Education)
c/o Mrs. Beverly McCord
P.O. Box 835105
Richardson, TX 75083

At least one Texas home school group is alive and doing very well, and this is it. Over fourteen hundred people attended their First Annual Home School Book Fair. Their newsletter (called *Texas Home Educators Newsletter*) goes for $10/year or $18/two years. It is nicely done, with colored ink on fancy stock, and has all the needful, from classified ads to news of seminars and meetings.

Hearth and Home Ministries has no membership dues, but gladly acepts donations, which are tax-exempt. Functions: support groups, legislative watchdog, community events, media work, legal information on home schooling, guidance, and encouragement.

They publish a yearly edition of the *Handbook for Texas Home Schoolers,* and you can get it for a donation of $5 or more.

When you see the names Kirk and Beverly McCord popping up in home school magazines, you'll know this is where they come from.

Texans for Educating a Child at Home
c/o Mrs. Ruth Canon
9403 Winding Ridge
Dallas, TX 75238

Another I-wrote-and-they-didn't group.

UTAH

Utah Home Education Association
P.O. Box 6338
Salt Lake City, UT 84106

Founded in October 1981, UHEA has approximately five hundred "associated families." Functions: lobbying, support groups, legislative watchdog, media work, annual convention, community events.

UHEA strives to maintain a "diplomatic relationship" with state and local officials. They are not antipublic school as much as prochoice.

No membership dues; however, your tax-free donations keep UHEA going. Associated families can get SAT tests on request.

Newsletter: *UHEA Bulletin.* When I wrote, they weren't quite sure what the *Bulletin's* new format would be, having just changed editors. Best guess was that it would be quarterly at about $12/year.

Yes, UHEA has a free brochure. Send them an SASE and hear all about it!

VIRGINIA

Home Educators Association of Virginia
P.O. Box 1810
Front Royal, VA 22630-1810
(703) 636-1704, (703) 368-3659

Founded in December 1983, HEAV has a whopping one thousand members already. Functions: lobbying, support groups, legislative watchdog, media work, and an annual Home Education Convention held in June.

Dues are $12/year and include the newsletter, support, legislative updates, tests and testing service, and membership in a regional group. HEAV has twelve professional staff members, but can still use home volunteers to help with phoning, letter-writing, and research.

Interesting sidelight: Mary Kay Clark, the director of the Seton Home Study Program for Catholics (reviewed in the Biggies section of the Curriculum Buyers Guide) was HEAV's secretary, the last I heard.

Newsletter: *HEAV Newsletter* goes only to members. It comes out monthly.

HEAV has a free brochure. You can get one by sending an SASE.

VERMONT

Vermont Alternative Educational Network
188 S. Winooski
Burlington, VT 05401

I sendee, they no returnee.

WASHINGTON

Washington is beautiful, when Mt. St. Helen isn't dumping ash all over it. It is also one of the better home schooling states.

Teaching Parents Association
8821 N.E. 118th Place
Kirkland, WA 98034

Founded in 1984, this group has seventy member families. Functions: lobbying, support groups, legislative watchdog, and media work. Membership dues of $12/year entitle you to the monthly newsletter and activity sheet, and discount admission to area programs. In Seattle, for example, TPA has aquarium classes.

Volunteers are needed for phone-calling and letter-writing.

Newsletter: *TPA Newsletter* costs $5/ year.

TPA is a nonprofit organization. Send SASE for their free brochure.

Washington Association of Home Educators
P.O. Box 7256
Spokane, WA 99207-0256
(509) 467-2552

Founded 1983, WAHE serves a constituency of approximately six hundred. Functions: lobbying, support groups, legislative watchdog, community events, media work. Dues are $18/year and include the newsletter, meetings, field trips, seminars, and affiliated membership in the WAHE.

Newsletter: *Family Learning Exchange* (FLEX), P.O. Box 7256, Spokane, WA 99207-0256.

WEST VIRGINIA

West Virginia Homeschool Education Association
Rt. 1, Box 352
Alderson, WV 24910
(304) 445-7105

Founded in 1982, this organization stresses the positive: support groups and community events. No dues, no newsletter, no professional staff. WVHEA provides: curriculum resources and planning, parenting skills workshops,

specialized tutoring by certified teachers, legal referrals and information, and family interaction and enrichment events. Additional services are available on an "as-needed" basis. Fees for services vary.

WVHEA's free brochure has an "alternative schooling" feel to it, a la John Holt and others.

WISCONSIN

Wisconsin Home Oriented Meaningful Education (HOME)
W. 8229 Tower St.
Onalaska, WI 54650
(608) 783-7779

Founded 1983, seventy-five families. Functions: lobbying, support groups, legislative watchdog, media work. Dues are $12/year and include the bimonthly newsletter.

Newsletter: *Network News.*

Wisconsin Parents' Association
P.O. Box 2502
Madison, WI 53701
(414) 593-8176

Founded in 1983; three hundred member families. Functions: lobbying, support groups, legislative watchdog, media work, yearly conference, regional coordination, phone tree.

Dues are $15/year and include the newsletter, access to the regional coordinators, slot on the phone tree, and discount on printed materials. Write if you're interested in helping out as a volunteer.

Newsletter: *W.P.A. Newsletter* comes out quarterly. Bulletins are sent out as needed.

WYOMING

Wyoming Home Educators Network reports, "We have a new state statute specifically recognizing home education as legitimate. We thank God for it."

Wyoming Home Educators Network
158 W. Harney
Laramie, WY 82070
(307) 742-9243

Founded in 1983. One hundred families on the mailing list. Functions: support groups, legislative watchdog, community events, media work. No membership dues. Volunteers are solicited for letter-writing and phone-calling.

Newsletter: *Wyoming Home Educators Newsletter* is monthly. At present it is free.

CANADA

Canadian Alliance of Home Schoolers
195 Markville Road
Unionville, Ontario L3R 4V8
CANADA

Also:

2267 Kings Ave.
W. Vancouver, British Columbia V7V 2C1
CANADA

Founded in 1979, this is a networking group, not a membership organization. Function: lobbying, support groups, media work. No membership dues or newsletter.

PART IV

MORE FOR HOME SCHOOLERS: THE CURRICULUM BUYERS' GUIDE

CHAPTER TWELVE

CHOOSING A HOME SCHOOL PROVIDER: THE BIGGIES

I have good news and bad news. First, the good news. If you are in the market for a home school curriculum or want to buy parts of a curriculum to supplement your child's education, there is *plenty* to choose from. You can find suppliers who follow the traditional public school plan as well as those who emphasize projects and creative thinking. Some programs are back-to-basics (A Beka, Basic Education, Associated Christian Schools, Christian Liberty Academy, Our Lady of Victory). Some are classical (Calvert and Seton). Some are in-between (the various Alpha Omega programs, for instance). And some programs are just completely different from anything else (Abilities Research Associates and Oak Meadow). There are big programs and small programs, old programs and new programs, time-tested programs and innovative programs, programs for elementary-age kids only and programs for high-school students. Everything you could possibly desire in a home school program is out there . . . somewhere.

And that's the bad news. *It's almost impossible to keep on top of it all!* How do you get a handle on which program does what and for how much when there are so many of them? The secret, I found, is to group them according to their characteristics, just like you learned to do in biology class. That way you can compare them all without going crazy.

Now you know that those fellows who invented the classification schemes for plants and animals were pretty arbitrary. If they'd chosen to group animals by similar eyes, for example, humans would have wound up next door to the octopi instead of the apes. No man-made method of classification can divide up reality that neatly. In just the same way, the categories I came up with aren't the last word, either. But they give you a place to start.

So . . . you will find these reviews divided into three major sections: big programs, small and alternative programs, and just curriculum.

"Big" programs have either been around for a while or have an enrollment of over two hundred or both. "Small" programs are mostly new, with enrollments of less than two hundred. "Alternative" programs have grown out of "alternative" or "free" schools and partake of the child-centered, nontraditional philosophy. The "just curriculum" section has reviews of some curricula that aren't connected to any school, plus a list of all the programs that will let you buy their curriculum without enrolling.

Here we are in the Biggies chapter, and we find it hard to divide programs any more finely than that. Seton is Catholic and also classical. Do we put it with our Lady of Victory (Catholic) or Calvert (classical)? A Beka Video School is evangelical. Do we put it with the other evangelical Christian schools, or by itself as the only video home school program? Evading all such classifications, I decided to list all the big programs alphabetically, followed by a Comparison Chart that lists their major characteristics. Thus, if you are looking for a project-oriented program, you check out all the schools that are billed as such under the Program Type heading, and so on.

Please keep in mind that programs are not totally uniform; they vary from grade to grade, and often the supplier will upgrade his product (which may be a change for the better or the worse). However, you can expect that the basic educational philosophy will usually remain constant. Keeping all this in mind, I have looked at a cross-section of grades for each program, with particular attention to the "entry" grades (kindergarten and first grade), the "middle" grades (fourth through eighth), and the final grades. Unless stated otherwise, the reviews are based on actual inspection of those courses.

You would be wise to send for a current brochure and application form for the curricula you find interesting and make your final choice on that basis. Some suppliers also have sample packets, and you might want to spend a few dollars on one of those before investing in the entire program. Although prices listed were checked out as being valid for the 1986-87 season, this guide is not intended as an order form. Its main purpose is to alert you to what's out there and also help you narrow down your choices.

Good hunting!

A Beka Christian Correspondence School
(formerly known as Pensacola Christian Correspondence School)
$160 Nursery (two and three-year-olds), $175 K4 (four-year-olds), $350 K5, $425 1-6, $420 grade 7, $435 grade 8, $485 grades 9-10 (full program), $370-$445 grades 11-12 (depending on electives). Additional $75 deposit grades Nursery-6. $10 testing fee. Book deposit for some upper-grade texts. Reuse discount, $50 less than the normal tuition.

Any program whose trademark is a cartoon owl in an academic cap can't be all bad! An offshoot of "America's Largest Christian Day School," A Beka's correspondence program was established in 1973. As a ministry of Pensacola College, it uses the popular "A Beka Book" series of Christian texts that the college publishes. These texts, featuring the studious A Beka owl, are used in more than eighteen thousand Christian schools. The Day School itself is recognized by both the State of Florida and the Florida Association of Christian Schools. (See also the entry under A Beka Video School, for A Beka's new home video program.)

Grades offered are nursery (for two- and three-year olds) through 12.

A Beka's rules are strict: no discounts, no payment plans, no refunds, no course alterations allowed. A Beka may terminate students at their discretion. Noncompliance with A Beka guidelines spells automatic termination.

A Beka provides a teacher's manual identical to that used in Christian classrooms. *This manual is only leased and must be returned at the end of the course.* A Beka also supplies all needed textbooks and materials; periodic grade reports; permanent school records; and advice and counseling as requested.

A Beka's approach is traditional and textbook-oriented. Curriculum is based on a classroom model. If followed exactly, it would be a whole school day's work for both parents and students. Count on spending some time adapting the lessons to your home situation.

Handwriting starts with manuscript. Cursive writing begins in grade 2. Writing and reading are taught together in Kindergarten, which is a serious academic program also including fun stuff like art, music, and poetry.

Expect to find a lot of questions with one right answer and not too many open-ended questions. A Beka uses a programmed approach, with the child drilled in correct responses, rather than a discovery approach. These books thus frequently use "I"

sentences. Example: "I must ask God to help my hands do what is right."

A Beka is evangelical, patriotic, creationist, and profree enterprise.

Lessons follow one another logically, so students should not become frustrated through lack of understanding. Though there is a lot of repetitive drill, the exercises are fairly interesting.

No record-keeping is required for nursery and K4. Beyond these grades the amount of record-keeping is average (returning work to school, grading daily work, keeping attendance records).

This entire program is available on video for grades K-5. See the A Beka Video School review in this section.

Home schooling parents may now purchase individual subject area curricula, textbooks, tests, and teacher aids in all subjects for grades 1-12 without enrolling in A Beka's Correspondence School. Send for the free A Beka Books catalog.

A Beka's products are colorful and generally professional-looking. Some illustrations in some books are amateurish—this only bothered me in the early Science series, where realistic art is a plus.

The teacher's manuals are cumbersome in the home situation (although the course of study is well laid out). I hope that in time A Beka will produce its own Home Study manuals like many other suppliers have done.

Subjects we liked the least were lower-grades Language Arts and upper-grades Literature. Subjects we liked the best: Math, History, and Geography.

If you enroll in the Correspondence Program, prepare to move along at a brisk pace. A Beka expects you to administer weekly tests and keep right on top of things. Some people like being held to a schedule like this. But if you're the mellow type who dislikes tight schedules, you'd be better off bypassing enrollment services and just buying the A Beka books you need direct from the catalog.

A Beka Video School

$600 plus $75 deposit. $10 for optional placement test. Everything included. No discounts. Tapes must be rewound every two weeks and returned UPS prepaid and insured.

You knew it was inevitable. We have video cooking classes, video rock, and now . . . video home school! A Beka's brand new program has generated instant controversy. More on that later.

You get instructional videocassettes and A Beka's very popular texts and teaching guides. Kindergarteners receive two and a half hours daily instruction from the videotape teacher and children in grades 1 to 5 spend slightly more than three hours watching their tapes. Students also have homework assignments. You return completed work and tests at designated intervals of six to nine weeks, depending on grade level.

A program is available for parents who want to host additional students in their home. Write A Beka for details.

I can't give this program an academic rating without seeing it. However, you can expect that the video teaching is of superior private school quality. A Beka's textbooks are widely used and generally well-regarded. See the A Beka listing for further details.

You will need a VCR for *each* student enrolled, unless one tunes in mornings and the other does his work in the afternoons. This is *not* the program for large families.

Now for the controversy I promised you! Some people have raised questions about whether a video approach is right for home schooling. (1) They worry about the eyestrain involved. (2) They also feel that in the one-on-one home school situation, a child does not need to spend that much time being "taught" by anyone. (3) Lastly, they fear that children will miss out on home school's greatest advantage: personal attention from their parents.

As the mother of a TV-free family, I sympathize with these concerns. However, I also recognize that most children watch a lot of TV, and they might as well be watching something edifying. As for A Beka, the first two problems can be minimized by simply not requiring the student to watch tapes or portions of tapes covering subjects he can handle on his own. Concerning objection three, my feeling is that A Beka is carving out a *new* market—home school for families who otherwise wouldn't consider it. Such parents might put the tapes to their best use by watching with their children and learning how to teach from the A Beka teachers—thus eventually moving on beyond video into "normal" home schooling.

Abilities Research Associates

With Anaheim Foundation School, you can buy course components separately. The complete ARA preschool program costs $200, as does the K-6 program. Grades 7 and 8 cost $250 each, and grades 9-12 are $300. AFS also offers an extremely wide array of electives, including such subjects as music, drama, swimming for beginners, and cooking for beginners.

Don't be confused by the two names above. Anaheim Foundation School was established as a private school according to California law in 1979. AFS offers families the choice of using any books and materials from any publisher or correspondence school across the country. However, most of their families use the wild and woolly Abilities Research Associates (ARA) curriculum designed by Sylvia Hare, described below.

ARA puts out the Individual Learner's Curriculum for Survival for Home Learning Centers (ILCS-HLC). This curriculum is, to put it mildly, unique. Its main academic focus is on helping the child become an independent learner, tackling problems and solving them on his own. To this end, the child studies *how* to study. He is shown how to detect when he or a friend is failing to understand: clues like yawning, blanking out, and irritation tip him off that perhaps he missed something on the way by. ARA's cure for misunderstanding is threefold: the Study Buddy system, where the learner has a buddy (who could be a parent or fellow child) check him out on what he just learned; doing "demos" of what he learned; and looking up words in the dictionary.

More about those "demos": ARA is the only program I've seen that uses object demos and clay demos as learning devices. In an object demo, the child takes a group of small objects— buttons, pencils, paper clips, or whatever—gives them names, and then uses them to act out what he is trying to convey. For example, a paper clip could be King Arthur, an eraser could be Guinevere, and a pencil could be Lancelot. Clay demos are similar, except that the child models the clay to (he hopes) resemble the people or things he is telling about. Each clay piece is labeled, and his buddy has to guess what the whole demo means. If it's a good demo and conveys the message, that section gets checked off on a checklist.

ARA uses the *World Book Encyclopedia* as its basic textbook. Anaheim Foundation School sells the encyclopedia at a reduced price. You also get a curriuculum guide and a Parent Folder that is added to throughout the year.

Although the booklet on teaching methods said ARA started with sight words, I actually saw a rather good little phonics program, consisting of the usual consonant and vowel booklets, plus a lot of writing, cutting, pasting, and general doing.

I haven't seen all the ARA material, but what I've seen looks very good. The curriculum has definite New Age patches, but Anaheim Foundation School does not itself hold a New Age position, and I was told that future editions of the curriculum will have a more Christian (or at least less New Age) emphasis.

AFS says it exists to "set the family free." Families fill out an extensive monthly report to meet state legal requirements, but are not told they must do this or that. The ARA curriculum is itself highly motivating, since the student gets to make many things that stand as a permanent record of his achievements, such as little books in the early reading/writing program, and those nifty (or silly, depending on how you feel about such things) clay demos. It is more organized than some other project-oriented programs I have seen, with a strong emphasis on mastering what is learned rather than filling out a lot of worksheets and then forgetting all about it.

However, this program may still be regarded as experimental, and you will want to be certain it meets your family's needs before signing on.

Advanced Training Institute of America

The advanced Training Institute of America (ATIA) curriculum is in a piloting phase and subject to change, so ATIA has requested that I just give you the barest facts. A project of Bill Gothard's Institute in Basic Youth Conflicts, the program reflects Gothard's message. ATIA materials use the Bible as the core of all learning and from that core are intended to lead students to master all areas of study. The program stresses the father's leadership role and the mother's homemaking role. Enrollment is limited to qualifying families: a preliminary qualification is that both parents have attended the Basic Youth Conflicts seminar and the Advanced Seminar. Write to ATIA if you want more information about the seminars or the ATIA curriculum.

American Christian Academy

Basic Reading $90. $300 1-8, $350 9-12 (includes five courses). Resource books, electives extra. Registration fee $50/student year 1, $25 thereafter. 10 percent off second student, 20 percent off third and rest. 10 percent prepay discount.

Zillions of tiny Christian schools are springing up all over America, like forget-me-nots after a spring rain. Many of these tiny schools use the Accelerated Christian Education (ACE) curriculum. In home school circles this curriculum goes under the name of Basic Education (see the review under that name), and it's produced by Reform Publications. American Christian Academy is one of the umbrella schools selling the ACE program to home schoolers.

Let's talk about American Christian Academy for a minute. American Christian Academy is on the list of schools that satisfy the State of Virginia's Home Instruction legislation. It is a member of the Texas Organization of Christian Schools, the New York Association of Christian Schools, and the American Association of Christian Schools. In addition, American Christian Academy is affiliated with the American Institute for Foreign Study. It offers the usual umbrella school services: standardized testing; individualized placement; all curriculum materials; periodic grade reports; a nicely-done Home Study Manual with helps for parents on setting up their program; phone counseling via a toll-free "800" number; and record-keeping. Legal assistance and support is promised "to the extent of our ability and financial resources." American Christian Academy has "retained an attorney who is available to answer legal questions."

Parents keep attendance, goal, and progress records and score daily work. Parents must communicate test scores to American Christian Academy monthly.

High school students get a student ID card and can buy a class ring. Diploma is granted on graduation.

American Christian Academy offers an easy-to-use program at moderate cost that should appeal to busy parents who aren't so much interested in turning out geniuses as in making sure their children know the basics.

American School

$379 one year, $479 two years, $579 three years, $679 four years. Everything included. Payment plan.

American School, widely known as The School of the Second Chance, is a *private* school offering an accredited high school diploma by mail. American School is accredited by the North Central Association of Colleges and Schools and by the Accrediting Commission of the National Home Study Council.

The school's ads are aimed mostly at adults. However, students of compulsory attendance age may enroll by attaching a note from their parents or guardians "explaining why this enrollment is necessary" and obtaining an exemption from local school authorities.

The first course American School will send you is Psychology Today (unless you've already taken it somewhere else). Most other correspondence programs do not require psychology.

American School lets you buy with confidence, allowing a ten-day free inspection of your courses and a generous refund policy for uncompleted courses. Also take note of this! *American School will either refund your money or provide you with free additional training if you are required to take a qualifying exam within six months of completing their course and fail to pass it.*

American School offers an immense array of job-related and enrichment courses.

Twenty small scholarships are granted each year to American School's top graduates.

I have not seen their courses, but with over 2,500,000 customers since 1897 and a reported 98 percent satisfaction rate, American School must be competent.

Associated Christian Schools

$450 Plan A, $300 Plan B, $150 Plan C. Books included. Shipping extra. $50 off students 2, 3, etc. No refunds.

The ACS Scope and Sequence tells you what is taught at various levels in the curriculum: $5. ACS Samplepac includes books from various grades and levels as well as a Scope and Sequence; this costs $29. Cassette tape entitled "Christian School Curricula: Good, Better and Best" compares ACS with other Christian school materials: $5. If you want any of these, don't forget to include 10 percent shipping (15 percent if you live outside the USA).

Associated Christian Schools was founded by Dr. Donald Boys in 1979 to provide an "educationally sound and biblically true" curriculum for Christian schools. Hundreds of Christian schools now use ACS's patriotic and fundamentalist materials. Almost all of the forty-two writers hold Master's and some hold Doctorates.

ACS provides three options for home schooling families. Under Plan A, ACS provides all books, answers, and tests; evaluates tests and assignments; keeps student records; sends report cards each semester; and awards diplomas when work is completed. This plan includes free testing. Plan B includes everything in Plan A except for placement testing and evaluation of the student's work. In Plan C ACS provides books, answers, and tests, and it's up to you to do the rest.

ACS has their own worktext series. Areas covered are Bible, English, math, science, history, geography (no "social studies"!), literature, and penmanship. Their Right Start Program for kindergarteners uses a strong phonics approach.

As a "back to basics" program, ACS employs a lot of drill, diagramming, and Scripture memory work. Every area is approached from an explicitly Christian perspective. Literature studied is classical and Christian. Composition skills are emphasized.

ACS curriculum is designed to be as easy as possible for the teacher to use. All the lessons for one week appear in one chapter of the large worktext. This eliminates the need for setting goals or drawing up lesson plans. Also, ACS is "the only publisher of school material that provides weekly quizzes."

The ACS material is "user friendly." Texts are addressed directly to the student and marked with good humor and wit. Lessons are straightforward and follow each other logically.

ACS claims that their material "is more of a challenge than ACE" (Accelerated Christian Education, listed in this guide under Basic Education) "or AOP" (Alpha Omega Publications: see their entry). As far as ACE is concerned, I believe this is correct, but I would question whether ACS is more challenging than AOP. Some areas, such as math and English, may be considered roughly comparable. AOP's reproduction and layout are superior to ACS.

Dr. Don Boys, President of ACS, says, "If you are not a Fundamentalist and a political conservative, you probably will not be satisfied with the ACS Curriculum." If you *are* the above and are looking for a fully-integrated, easy-to-use Christian curriculum that emphasizes straight-arrow morality and Baptist doctrine, check out ACS.

Calvert School
$165 K, $295 1-4, $315 5-8. Advisory Teaching Service, $150 1-6, $160 7-8. Five percent increase anticipated for '86-'87 season. Everything included. No discounts. No refunds once course begins.

Calvert School, founded in 1897, is the granddaddy of home education programs. Over three hundred thousand pupils have enrolled in Calvert over the years, many of whom have gone on to demonstrate considerable excellence in their chosen fields. Justice Sandra Day O'Connor, for example, is a graduate of Calvert's kindergarten program.

Calvert operates its own highly successful day school, and all home study materials are tested in Calvert's own classrooms. Calvert is an elementary grades program only, with courses for grades K (a readiness program) through 8.

Calvert is approved by the Maryland State Department of Education, and has the widest acceptance among state authorities of any elementary-grade home school curriculum in America. Calvert does not provide legal assistance.

Before we get into the program itself, you should know that Calvert definitely has "it," that special ambience that emanates only from the old, the rich, and the excellent. We hear that the Calvert Day Class of 1927 contained twelve descendants of the signers of the Declaration of Independence, and we aren't surprised. As Pooh Bear might say, "It's *that* sort of school."

The Calvert program is a structured, textbook-oriented, classical course of study. Academically it is very strong, with a commendable emphasis on developing creative thought and communication as well as basic skills. Calvert has a "Christian culture" flavor. Christianity is not taught, or presented as *the* truth, but it is not blatantly ignored or suppressed either. The historic accomplishments of Christians are recognized and morality is generally pro-Christian. Evolution is not stressed, but appears now and again in some science courses.

Textbooks in science and math are up-to-date. For language arts, Calvert often uses classics, some of which Calvert reprints itself. Lots of enrichment books and literature are included. *The Teacher's Manual is only leased from Calvert and must be destroyed or returned when the course is completed.*

Calvert's optional Advisory Teaching Service includes test grading, record-keeping, and correspondence by mail or phone with a certified teacher who will give suggestions and advice to the home-study student and to the home teacher.

Calvert requires more work from the home teacher in the early grades than most programs. To help you through this period, each lesson includes *everything* you need to teach it. Potential trouble spots are identified and solutions given. If you follow Calvert's excellent advice *exactly*, you can hardly go wrong.

Each grade becomes progressively more self-instructional, as the student learns to take control of his own education. Thus the parents work harder in the beginning than at the end. Also, required record-keeping is minimal.

For the student, Calvert is an excellent program. The format is straightforward, crisp, and logical and the lessons are interesting. Tests are bound into the Manual after every twenty lessons, so the student can see where he is heading and what progress he is making.

Calvert's emphasis on creativity includes serious attention to art in the early grades and a unique series on painting, sculpture, and architecture appreciation in the upper grades. Other special emphases: Social studies means history and geography, not "Sam's Visit to Niagara Falls." History studies include mythology. Handwriting begins in the first grade with Calvert's own simplified cursive script. Parents are given a wealth of classic stories to read to their young offspring. Another nice touch: *All* needed school supplies are included with each order—pencils, paper, crayons, art supplies, ruler, etc.

Calvert's lesson manuals are an education in themselves—for the parents! Any home school parent who uses Calvert for a young child will pick up some excellent teaching tips and techniques as a bonus. After using Calvert kindergarten, I felt competent to teach my children on my own.

Calvert is equally useful for the very bright student and the slower student, thanks to the excellent step-by-step approach. Many poor performers in school have gone on to do outstanding work after enrolling in Calvert.

Calvert deserves an A+ academic rating. A child can graduate from Calvert's eighth-grade course, take a few achievement tests, and go straight to the college of his choice. Think about it!

Christian Liberty Academy

$135 Jr., Sr. K; $210 grades 1-12. Everything included. Book credit when younger student reuses materials. No discounts. No refunds once books shipped. Supplementary enrollment, same price and terms. School Starter Kit, $70.

Could it be an omen? Christian Liberty Academy just bought a public school campus! With an active enrollment of fourteen thousand home study students, Christian Liberty Academy Satellite Schools (CLASS) is seeing its program grow faster than any other in the USA. Established in 1968, Christian Liberty operates its own day school where courses are originated and evaluated by its staff of well-educated professionals. Grades offered are K-12.

Low tuition includes all books and supplies and administration of the Iowa Basic Skills Test.

Here we have a strongly traditional, basics-oriented program with a heavy Bible emphasis. Though CLASS gets its materials from all over, most of them come from Christian publishers. The curriculum is Reconstructionist, patriotic, creationist, and profree enterprise.

CLASS curriculum covers more subject areas than many others: traditional math, phonics, reading, writing, Biblical studies, geography, history, the Constitution, science, and even languages (optional). Kindergarten programs include art, music, and character development.

CLASS places great stress on self-discipline and mastery of material. *All* of the workbooks provided for the many subject areas must be completed in their entirety. (However, parents may write requesting program alterations.)

Students receive individualized programs based on their test results (for grades 2-12) and on the information parents provide about their children's current level of skills (kindergarten and grade 1). Parents grade daily work; major tests and completed daily work are returned to CLASS. CLASS keeps records, issues quarterly report cards, and grants eighth grade and high school diplomas. CLASS also provides a large handbook for parents, with information on how to administer the program, and teacher's editions for some subjects. Parents are expected to produce their own lesson plans. Since study guides are *not* provided, parents must develop their own strategy for teaching subjects that come without teacher's editions.

Textbooks are up-to-date, with the exception of some Latin texts.

Phone counseling is available, as is legal advice and assistance. Rev. Paul Lindstrom, the Academy's principal, has a law degree and is very involved in home school activism. CLASS does expect families to exercise legal preparedness and not rely solely on them, and from the experiences of families in my area you would be wise to do so.

Expect to spend ten to twenty hours getting acquainted with the books and the handbook. You will also be designing lesson plans to meet your family's particular needs. CLASS provides a sample of a proper lesson plan, and you take it from there. This takes much more time at the beginning (especially since the handbook is not very well laid out), but gives the family more educational freedom.

CLASS is a *lot* of work for the student. You get a wealth of texts and workbooks to complete. Even four- and five-year-olds have a serious academic program, where they learn to read, write (in precursive), add, and subtract, as well as doing normal kindergarten art, music, and so on. Each CLASS grade covers work other schools don't assign this early. Thus CLASS grade 2 is more like public school grade 3 and their senior kindergarten is actually a serious first-grade program.

Latin and foreign languages are available starting at grade 7, for students who have already successfully completed a year of CLASS.

CLASS sends out special materials for home schooling parents from time to time. Examples: a *Home Education Journal* devoted to legal issues, a book on Biblical principles, a monthly newspaper.

The new "supplemental" enrollment feature includes curriculum only.

I like the freedom of making my own lesson plans, and in my view when it comes to questions of government, family, and the like, CLASS is among the most Biblical curricula on the market. CLASS operates as a ministry; therefore tuition is low and their concern for families is high. Doubling in size every year or so has caused CLASS chronic problems with staffing and inventory. They beg and plead with you *not* to enroll in August or September if you can *possibly* manage it, and you would be wise to take their advice if you want to get your materials swiftly.

A friend reports immense satisfaction with the first-grade program. The kindergarten and grade 2 programs (which we have used) are also excellent—many books for your money, all of them carefully chosen. Quality seems to continue through all grades. Quibbles: Some of the workbooks are voluminous and repetitive. You have to provide your own science equipment. The language arts approach in the upper grades could be more creative and fun (try supplementing with some Alpha Omega LIFEPACs).

The size of handwriting required of senior kindergarten pupils is more appropriate for older learners. For this reason I would suggest you stick with junior kindergarten if you want a kindergarten program at all.

Academically, I give CLASS an A. If you want a really solid, economical Christian curriculum with lots of "meat" both spiritually and academically; if you want the flexibility of designing your own schedule; if you have the confidence to teach without elaborate study guides; if you and your children enjoy hard work, CLASS could be the program for you.

Christian Light Education

Three enrollment options: (1) Info packet and order forms plus sampler kit, $20. *Basics for Beginners,* the teacher's manual for the Learning to Read program, $7.50 extra. Testing materials are extra. (2) $75 gets you a one-week parent training program, offered both by mail and at CLE's regular late spring and summer training sessions. CLE grants you a certificate upon completion of this program. You then can order materials on your own.
(3) $100 provides the full program: parent training, plus first year services that include CLE assistance and record-keeping. Option 3 required if student wants a CLE eighth-grade certificate or high school diploma. Successive years, $50 for full program. Workshops are available at no extra charge to Option 3 families. Also included is a free subscription to *LightLines,* the CLE school newsletter. Option 3 families may request the California Achievement Test and may call *collect* for assistance.

Curriculum materials are extra for all options. Cost is approximately $110/year/pupil.

Basics for Beginners is included free of charge with options 2 or 3.

Christian Light Education was established in 1979 as a part of the ministry of Christian Light Publications, a provider of school materials that emphasize a literal understanding and practical application of the Scriptures. While the materials are prepared from an Anabaptist-Mennonite perspective, they have received very positive acceptance by many others. Mennonites are followers of Menno Simons, a sixteenth-century religious leader who believed in adult baptism, pacifism, and unworldliness. The Pennsylvania "Dutch," or Amish, are one well-known Mennonite group.

Christian Light offers a worktext approach, based on their own revision of the very popular Alpha Omega worktexts. Christian Light's revised texts are more attractive than the original, with heavy kivarlike paper covers and colored ink used within. As revised, their curriculum is more down-to-earth; family-centered stories replace AOP's fantasy stories in the lower grades, for example. Pictures reflect Mennonite community values: women

have uncut, covered hair; dress is very modest; we see nice large families.

Christian Light incorporates several of its own hardcover textbooks and a few other resource books into the program.

You can sign up for a variety of high school electives, including consumer math, home economics, art, Greek, and Spanish, in the usual worktext format. Christian Light also carries courses in typing, carpentry, auto mechanics, small engines, survival car care, and bookkeeping. These courses are based on textbooks from other publishers and Christian Light provides brief guides explaining how to fit them into its program.

Religious orientation is gently Mennonite (they don't beat you over the head with it). Traditional family values and sexual roles are stressed. The curriculum is creationist, pacifist, and determinedly nonpolitical.

The curriculum emphasizes the basic skills as well as offering a strong program in science and social studies. First grade starts with the intensive phonics Learning to Read program, which is easy to teach and very inexpensive (less than $20 without Answer Key). As a whole, this largely self-contained curriculum stresses thinking skills. Christian Light believes in individuality (learn at your own pace) and personalized studies (matching content and teaching methods to the student's needs and abilities).

Teacher handbooks and answer keys are available for each subject. Some of these are Alpha Omega's original versions, which were designed with classroom use in mind. Still, they are easy to follow.

The worktexts are very easy to follow as well. Students can do most work without too much adult teaching.

Christian Light's record-keeping requirements are straightforward, but lots of scores are involved. Parents in Option 3 send in brief monthly reports of work done and final test scores. Record-keeping forms are available for those who want them.

The original Alpha Omega materials are very good in English and science, and Christian Light hasn't hurt these areas any. The social studies emphasis is different, reflecting Mennonite concerns. I consider Christian Light's changes to the early-grades materials to be an improvement.

Christian Light sells all needed materials for its science courses (with the exception of commonly available items like soda straws, toothpicks, etc.). This places their science program head and shoulders above most others. Send for their *free catalog* of science equipment and school supplies.

Children can progress rapidly with Christian Light's material, and they will truly learn how to learn. Academically, I give Christian Light an A.

For those favoring Mennonite religious and political beliefs, Christian Light is a "best buy."

Clonlara School

$300 per family for all services. Books and supplies extra, at school discount. CAT testing extra. Refunds: $25 fee for cancellation within five days after registration form received by Clonlara. No refund after five days.

If you're the mellow, free and easy type, you're going to like the Home Based Education Program operating out of Clonlara's independent alternative day school. Clonlara's staff is bristling with official credentials—the director, Pat Montgomery, holds a B.Ed., M.A., and earned Ph.D., for example—but this doesn't stop them from believing that parents, not institutions, are the primary educators of their own children. And Clonlara puts this belief into practice. As Dr. Pat Montgomery says, "Choice is our middle name!"

You get a curriculum to use as a starting-point for your own individually tailored program, a *Math Skills Guidebook,* a *Communication Skills Guidebook,* Clonlara's *The Learning Edge* newsletter, contact with other Clonlara families, a pen pal network for your children to plug into if desired, consultation with Clonlara staff on academic questions, and staunch legal assistance from the Clonlara staff. Pat will talk with your local school, if necessary, and her background and wide experience as an educator often soothe the troubled waters. It's hard to argue with a program that has been accepted and lauded by school officials across the U.S.A. and that has so impressed the Japanese that *three* books about Clonlara have been published in Japan!

You create your own individualized program with the help of Clonlara's curriculum listing. The listing tells you what subjects to study and what the objectives are in each area. Some families take it just as it stands, some don't bother with it at all, and some change it around to suit themselves. This latter is the option Clonlara recommends most: to use it as a working paper.

Clonlara's Skills Guidebooks are diagnostic tools that cover the basics. You can find out where your children stand by checking off their accomplishments on the chart in the *Math Skills Guidebook* and seeing if they are on track for their ages in the *Communications Skills Guidebook.*

The choice of textbooks and other materials is left entirely to the family. Clonlara suggests you go beyond texts by making wide use of the public library and building up your home library. I like this quote on their attitude toward textbooks:

"The *Time/Life* series, found in libraries, although not written specifically as texts, serve the purpose quite well. In some cases, they do a much better job of presenting the material since they don't offer a little bit in one text, a bit more in another, etc. Non-textbooks present all the information at once and students are left to absorb as much of it as they can. In this way, too, it is not necessary to change textbooks every year (thereby funding the textbook companies)."

Clonlara stresses manipulative learning tools and real-life experiences in place of endless workbookery. You choose the texts you do use based on the student's achieved grade level in each subject, not his age. You can order texts from any school publisher through Clonlara at a discount. This includes Christian texts: Clonlara provides a Christian Book and Materials Catalogue. They hope to expand to also provide Catholic, Jewish, Muslim, and other materials.

Each month you send in a Monthly Home Study Record to Clonlara, or if you prefer, a daily or monthly log. Clonlara provides report cards, transcripts, and a private school diploma on graduation. Graduation occurs when a student has completed his credits, whether he be fourteen or nineteen. A Clonlara diploma is widely accepted.

Action is a major part of the older students' program. A hundred and twenty hours of volunteer service in the community is one of the staples of Clonlara's secondary school curriculum.

Parents and students are not pressured into completing x amount of work and mailing it to Clonlara. Neither do you have to wait for Clonlara's judgment upon your work. Passage to another grade or subject does not hinge on Clonlara's approval. You decide what you are ready for and when you are ready for it. Who likes Clonlara?

- Families who follow John Holt's lead rank high on the list of those who find Clonlara compatible. This includes those who can "do it themselves," but want a friendly school's guidance and backup.

- Families who want to try freedom in education.

- Families who want to try the structure of a traditional program without the pressure of deadlines and punishments (such as withholding grades).

- Families who want Clonlara to handle all of the legal aspects, both administrative and dealing with school officials.

- Students who want to get away from the pen/paper/textbook treadmill and take an active role in making the world their classroom.

Hewitt-Moore Child Development Center
Full program, $250 for 1st student, $200 for 2nd and rest. Alternate program: $100 1st, $75 2nd and rest. Parent's Choice: $60 1st, $40 2nd and rest. Books and supplies extra ($50-$150). Optional testing extra ($35-$75). Readiness Program has been $150 full program, $100 alternate program, supplies included. 1986-87 school year will probably bring a new price structure. Secondary students pay by the course after tuition is paid. Course costs range from $15 to $95, depending on the course and what books and services are needed.
5 percent preregistration discount.
Since Hewitt programs are individualized, it is not possible to determine book costs in advance.

Hewitt-Moore is the brainchild of Dr. Raymond Moore and his wife, Dorothy, two pioneering experts in the home education movement. The Moores have written many books promoting their ideas of real-life learning and delayed formal education.

The program itself is new, begun in 1983. With four thousand students currently enrolled (including the children of one of my best friends), it is one of the fastest-growing home school programs.

Grades offered are pre-K-12, now that Hewitt has added a new program for secondary-age students. There is an informal Readiness program for applicants aged five to seven. Hewitt discourages applications for children younger than this.

Hewitt has no less than *four* separate plans:

(1) Full enrollment includes individualized curriculum design, twice-yearly thorough informal evaluation, record-keeping, and limited assistance with legal problems.

(2) If you need one of the Hewitt-Moore teachers to provide initial evaluation of your child, and their recommendations for books, you may enroll in the Alternate Program. Ongoing evaluations and counseling are not a part of this financial plan. Tuition is significantly less than for full enrollment.

(3) The Parents Choice Curriculum provides access to a select list of Hewitt-recommended educational texts and supplies to help you in planning your home school.

(4) An informal School Readiness program.

Hewitt's academic philosophy is to "place the child at his optimum learning level and then to proceed at his own rate." Some texts and workbooks are used, but these are meant for resource material, not as the primary source of instruction. Many Hewitt materials are exclusively theirs, and those I have tried have all been excellent. (See the Home-Grown Kids reviews.)

Secondary students are required to either establish a business (Hewitt provides a list of over two hundred possible businesses), become involved in civic or volunteer work, or become apprentices in a vocational program. This kind of practical work education is not required in the early grades, but is strongly commended as an excellent way of both building character and preparing the student for the realities of making a living.

The Moores' goal is "to provide a program that (1) contains carefully selected Christ-centered materials from a variety of publishing houses (as much as possible keeping the Scripturally based materials nondoctrinal and nonsectarian); (2) is not too structured or heavily workbook-oriented; (3) avoids myths and nonsense stories so that children may use their own imagination rather than simply be amused by adult-contrived fantasies; (4) plans for no formal schooling until age eight or later; (5) lists costs clearly and specifies what services are offered; (6) includes clear instructions for students and teacher; (7) encourages discussion, creativity, and independent thought; and (8) gives counsel in dealing with the law."

Legal information and guidance is available to Hewitt families enrolled in the full program. Dr. Moore continues to witness in court, as time permits and if his appointments can be adjusted to the court dates. Hewitt parents have seldom been called into court, partly because the Moores give "priority in counsel and intercession to help keep you out of court in the event of threats or harassment" to those enrolled in the full regular program. This is no idle promise, as Dr. Moore is nationally known and has established a reputation as a credible witness before judges, legislators, and even TV audiences. To date, only two established Hewitt families have been taken to court (both in the very tough state of North Dakota).

Hewitt's newsletter, *The Parent Educator and Family Report,*

is an extremely useful source of legal and other information.

Parents promise to consistently follow a daily program, keep a daily journal of activities, report twice a year, follow testing directions, and provide work experiences for their children. This requires more creativity and involvement than the traditional textbook approach.

For the student, Hewitt's approach definitely is less stressful. Hewitt wants to avoid meaningless rote work (e.g., filling out dozens of workbook pages on a subject the student has already mastered).

Slow learners, dyslexic, Down's syndrome, and handicapped children are welcome at Hewitt, as well as normal and "gifted" children. Hewitt staff is willing to provide advice on teaching these children; an additional $60 is added to the tuition fee for the first child, $50 for the second, to cover the additional counseling and evaluation time.

This curriculum looks like a lot of fun. I give it an A.

Read the Moores' book *Home-Style Teaching* if you want to find out more about this program's philosophy before enrolling.

Home Study International

$60.65 Pre-K, $205.30 K, $412.65 1, $376.95 2, $427.55 3, $420.60 4, $447.05 5, $413.95 6. Shipping extra, 1-6. Grades 7-8, $121/subject plus supplies and shipping. Grades 9-12, $92.50/subject plus supplies and shipping. $25 registration fee. 2 percent prepay discount grades 7-12 only.

Free legal packet answers questions about attendance laws. Request it in writing and tell HSI your present legal situation.

Excellent catalog lists all materials used in each grade. Parents only purchase items they lack.

Established in 1909 as a service to Seventh-Day Adventists, Home Study International has grown into a major supplier of home school programs. The Home School staff consists entirely of certified teachers, many of whom have Master's and Ph.Ds. HSI is accredited by the National Home Study Council and approved by the Maryland State Department of Education.

This is a standard, structured, school-at-home program. Young students are taught by their parents; older students are expected to work directly with the HSI staff, under their parents' guidance. HSI agrees to provide materials, Parents' Guides for each subject, test grading and record-keeping, advice, report cards, and certificates of promotion or diplomas.

Materials used include a number of Seventh-Day Adventist (S.D.A.) texts as well as some standard public school texts. Most books are up-to-date. Of special interest are the S.D.A.-revised version of the famous "Dick and Jane" readers used in the early grades. This program starts with sight words and then adds on phonics. All the S.D.A. texts I saw were professionally done and colorful.

HSI's own materials are conservative and profamily. Some of the public school texts HSI uses are less so.

Religiously, HSI is creationistic and evangelistic. Some Christian books are used and the Bible is taught. Seventh-Day Adventists believe that their founder, Ellen White, was a prophetess of God, and her writings are quoted in some Bible and Health sections of the curriculum, as well as occasionally in the Parents' Guides.

Parents are expected to comply with state laws and are urged to contact the Education Director of the local Seventh-Day Adventist council or their state Superintendent of Schools for details.

The HSI preschool readiness program is a superbargain. At only $60.65 it includes a very rich music program (with five cassettes thrown in), lots of arts and crafts activities, nature awareness, physical education, math readiness, and more! The heart of the preschool program is a super Parent's Guide, with *week-by-week* activities laid out—a very sensible approach! Like all HSI's programs, this includes optional Christian and Adventist teaching.

Elementary students are graded beginning in kindergarten. Subjects include art and music, Bible (optional), health/science, language, math, physical education (grades 3-6), reading, social studies, spelling, and handwriting. You can see there is a lot of work here!

HSI's upper grades cover few subjects and use fewer books, but still require a lot of work. Students of high school chemistry, for example, are expected to spend seven to ten hours a week on that one subject.

HSI's Parents' Guides are *great.* All lessons include stated objectives and list materials needed to do the assignment. Upper-grades lessons consist of a "commentary" section intended to substitute for the normal classroom lecture followed by assigned exercises. Guides directed to the student himself are written in a breezy style, while those addressed to parents are more serious in tone.

HSI has some terrific ideas that others would do well to emulate. Example: professionally-drawn Bible Activity Sheets printed on card stock enable young learners to make projects like an Ark (with animals!) that look great and will really hold together. Example: the Health curriculum teaches survival and first aid skills. Example: like the University of Nebraska, HSI provides a lab kit so upper-grades science students can do *real* experiments.

Math is the "new math" and reading is only partly phonetic. Judge if you feel up to using this approach.

HSI will appeal most to families who prefer modern educational methods and who appreciate HSI's professional materials and consistent Adventist flavor.

International Institute
   $45 K, $80 grades 1-8. Books $60 K, $195 grades 1-8.

Advisory Council $45 (n/a for K). 50 percent off tuition for 3rd student, 4th and rest FREE! (All applications must be received at same time to qualify for tuition discounts.) Also, 20 percent off on tuition and Advisory Council for full-time Christian workers. Book reuse option.

Founded in 1960 as a program for missionaries' children, over the years tens of thousands of students have used International Institute's courses. The staff consists of qualified Christian educators who look upon this as a ministry.

International Institute is unusual among Christian-founded programs in that at present it uses secular materials exclusively. With the exception of the Bible program, texts are chosen from among those approved by the public schools.

As far as International Institute knows, no student who has completed a course under the direction of its Advisory Service has ever been turned down or put back by any school anywhere.

Because International Institute uses up-to-date public school texts exclusively in grades 1-8, those courses amount to public school at home, *without* the extraneous public school classes on "values clarification" and sex ed and so on, and *with* an optional Bible course added. International Institute's philosophy is that the Christian teacher is competent to integrate Christian teaching in each subject herself. They have chosen secular texts because they feel those publishers have higher educational standards than the religious publishers they have investigated. However, International Institute intends to incorporate texts published by Christian publishing houses in the near future, since modern Christian texts are becoming more competitive academically by their standards.

The publishers International Institute chooses are among the more conservative philosophically (although there is still a lot of stress on "feelings" and self-disclosure, and subjects such as drug education are introduced). Format is textbook-workbook, with all teachers' editions supplied.

International Institute has an inexpensive Advisory Service. A professional elementary instructor grades tests, evaluates Achievement tests, makes suggestions, and assists you with problems. International Institute will also keep a file on each student, issue transcripts, and grant a certificate of promotion on completion of a grade to those using the Advisory service.

Kindergarten is a readiness program *and* a basic reading program. Kindergarten includes some Christian materials: a coloring book and several Bible story books. Public school math, readiness, basic reading, "listening and talking," and phonics materials are used, and all supplies are included (writing supplies, scissors—even gold stars!).

Handwriting starts with precursive and graduates to cursive

in grade 2. The method used stresses legibility over slavish conformity to a textbook norm.

International Institute provides an attractive teacher's manual for each grade. Their lesson plans are simple and straightforward. Because teaching hints are not incorporated in the lesson plans, but listed separately, it becomes much easier to tailor individual lessons to the student's working speed.

If you follow the instructions in the teacher's editions exactly, you will work yourself to death. You, of course, will not do this, because unlike the poor victims who teach in public schools you can stop "teaching" as soon as your student has learned the material. Armed with the teacher's editions, you can do as much or as little teaching as needed.

Students can expect to work hard in an International Institute course. Textbooks are drill-oriented, and there is a lot of review.

International Institute offers a novel "reuse" option for families who already have used their materials for one child, and now hope another child is ready for that grade. On receiving International Institute's approval and payment of a $25 reuse fee, International Institute will send workbooks only at their cost plus handling. International Institute also allows you to return any undesired book sent with the course for a full refund.

One of International Institute's most special features has to be its extremely low cost for large families, especially the families of Christian workers. Since the school is a nonprofit ministry, International Institute plans to lower rates even more as more families enroll (thus reducing their per-pupil overhead).

International Institute promises fast shipping—"within a few days of receiving your order (except in the rush months of July and August when it takes a few days longer)." Books lost or damaged in transit are replaced free.

Missionary mothers who want to start a kindergarten (or any grade level) program for native or missionary children can purchase additional student books for this ministry at cost. International Institute informed me that the same privilege is available for stateside mothers who wish to teach two or more students at the same grade level.

Students who are at or above normal grade level to begin with can progress well in public school-required skills in this curriculum.

Until International Institute switches over to Christian texts, families with strong feelings against public schools may find the present health, science, and reading materials not what they wish. This also applies to those who are looking for a course that overtly integrates Christianity into every subject area. If you do not fall into these categories, consider if you:

(1) have a large family and are looking for an economical curriculum;

(2) appreciate being supplied all teacher's editions;

(3) want a course that should be credible in the eyes of public educators.

Living Heritage Academy

$135 Basic Reading, $27.50 additional workbooks. $240 grades 1-8, $300 grades 9-12. $20 registration fee. $25 Diagnostic Test fee. Resource books, electives extra. 5 percent off on 2nd student and rest. 10 percent prepay discount.

Living Heritage Academy is Basic Education's own home school correspondence program. See the Basic Education review.

LHA provides a *Home Study Handbook* for parents, all needed materials, diagnostic testing, record-keeping, and *a choice of high school courses of study* (basic college prep, academic, and vocational prep). To enroll, you must send a copy of the student's birth certificate and a recent picture with the appropriate fees and a completed application form for each child.

The Basic Reading Program, though somewhat expensive for the first child, decreases in cost for each succeeding student since the family only needs to pay for the registration fee and an additional workbook.

If your main concern is that your children learn the basics, and you want a program that is extremely easy to administer, consider Living Heritage Academy.

North Dakota State Board of Education
Divison of Independent Study

$20/semester course, North Dakota residents. $40/semester course, nonresidents. Books and supplies extra (about $7-$30 for most courses). $5 handling fee on all course registrations.

Five thousand students are currently enrolled in this Independent Study program, making it one of the biggest in the country. So why has nobody ever heard of the North Dakota Independent Study program? It could be maidenly modesty, but I think it's likely that the educational house is divided against itself. Home education is just starting to get really big, and the people in state education have not yet begun to wake up to what a wonderful way this is of making a name for their program.

Getting down to brass tacks, what does North Dakota's Division of Independent Study have to offer? It's one of the few state-accredited high school programs, for one thing. That means that if your local school superintendent agrees to the plan, you can get a real live diploma through DIS. They have lots and lots of nifty electives, for another thing: stuff like creative writing, and journalism. North Dakota offers *six* languages: Latin, German, Spanish, French, Norwegian, and Russian (these courses include cassettes). They also have quite a variety of useful-looking art, business education, agriculture, home economics, and practical/mechanical courses. Not only that, but DIS's prices are extremely low. Book and supply charges are also slight (the program uses standard public school texts), and many textbooks can be returned afterwards for a one-half refund of the purchase price.

Students presently enrolled in high school or who are of compulsory school age must have their local school administrator sign the application and approve a supervisor for them, who must be a certified teacher.

Applicants for the diploma must have a transcript of their previous work sent to the Independent Study Program.

DIS courses are rather easy, as far as the assignments go. If you can understand the texts and syllabi, you can breeze right along. Science might be an exception to this rule, though the experiments are also easy to do.

DIS includes lesson wrappers in which you return the assignments (you pay the postage). You don't have to keep attendance records or grade anything.

Now, you're asking, what are the drawbacks? There are some, I am sorry to say. Some of the courses are not designed for success. You need a large vocabulary, for example, to understand the directions for the vocabulary-improvement exercises. The algebra course seemed to have new terms and concepts on every page. The science text I saw was dull, dull, dull and the experiments were rinky-dink. Science courses do not come with lab supplies. I'm not saying you can't learn from these courses, but they do not soar to sublime heights. Students with learning problems would be better off with University of Nebraska-Lincoln. Also, you need special permission to get your lessons returned to you.

On the brighter side, the student guides are livened up with copious appropriate cartoons. Some of the topics are quite interesting, such as a section on regional dialects in the language and composition course. The old-fashioned flavor of some of the courses is (to me, anyway) quite endearing. It's unusual to find a public school program that's not, shall we say, "supportive" of Russian totalitarianism.

Academically, at present DIS gets a good solid C.

If you want a secular high school diploma at a low, low cost and you can get permission from your local school superintendent, or if you are interested in some of DIS's unusual courses, check out this program.

Oak Meadow School

Tuition, $225/family. Curriculum alone, $49.95 each K-4. Grades 5-12, supplies are extra. Class Teacher Fee, $15/month K-4, $25/month 5-8, $12/month/subject 9-12. No registration fee. No discounts. Most supplies included. Some science supplies are available through Oak Meadow.

Since 1975 Oak Meadow has provided several thousand students with a curriculum based in the early grades on the educational teachings of Rudolf Steiner and continuing in the later grades with an extremely strong emphasis on self-awareness and closeness to the earth. Following Mr. Steiner's theories, Oak Meadow places more importance on art and "right brain" learning, including the use of fantasy, than any other program.

Oak Meadow curriculum has a "New Age" flavor. This is particularly apparent in the areas of the upper-grade curriculum that deal with ecology and our relationship with animals. In the early grades, the stress is on developing qualities of imagination and perception in the child. Thus math becomes the story of four little gnomes named Add, Subtract, Multiply, and Divide; the alphabet is taught through fairy tales that associate each letter with a real or fantasy object; science is first approached through nature experiences; and so on. Art, music, and crafts all have an important place in the elementary curriculum.

Students in grades K-4 "play" more than "work." Most assignments are informal and can be done anytime, and there is no pressure to meet deadlines. Once students reach grade 5, the parents are considered support and resource people and the Class Teacher takes over most teaching work.

Upper-grade students do have to work, although the amount of "nerdwork" is less than many traditional programs require. In grades 5-8 Oak Meadow curriculum strongly emphasizes "human values and ideals." Subjects are approached from the angle of how they affect people (subjectively) rather than as collections of objective facts alone. Grades 9-12 finally concentrate more on facts and the intellectual approach.

Oak Meadow provides materials, legal enrollment, transfer of records, Home Teacher training and a newsletter, and communication with school officials. In addition, every child has a Class Teacher. For grades K-4 the parents correspond with the Class Teacher; in grades 5 and up the student works directly with the Class Teacher, and the parents move into the background.

The record-keeping required is absolutely minimal. Parents of K-4 students communicate with the Class Teacher once a month. Upper-grade students send off completed material twice monthly.

Phone counseling is available, but legal assistance (above and beyond attempts to convince school officials of the validity of a child's enrollment) is not.

The curriculum for grades K-4 is self-contained. In the higher grades each student receives monthly assignments by mail.

Materials used are unique to Oak Meadow's program. Young children learn to play the recorder and sing a variety of uplifting songs, including a number of Christian hymns. Many books about nature and animals are included at the various levels. Some of these books are pantheistic.

As much as possible, "learning by doing" is built into the curriculum. Thus sixth-grade children study other countries by cooking their food, making their clothes, doing their crafts, learning conversational French, and so on. Science follows a "hands-on" discovery approach. Much attention is given to self-awareness, including many "personal" writing assignments with the student disclosing his feelings about a variety of situations.

Oak Meadow does use textbooks, but they are uncommon ones and generally not from major publishers. Exceptions are some excellent University of Nebraska courses and math materials.

Oak Meadow children learn to read and write and do their math. They also learn how to forecast their local weather, how to track animals, how to paint meaningful pictures, and a number of other things that do not find their way into the standard school texts. (See KONOS curriculum for the only Christian program that teaches all these things.) On the other hand, students get less practice and drill in some matters than those enrolled in more traditional programs. For creativity and imagination, give Oak Meadow an A. For traditional academics, give them a B+.

As a Christian, I could use Oak Meadow's kindergarten and grade 1 materials, but I would have to censor them lightly to omit the pantheism. In the upper grades my problem would become much more acute.

Parents who either are not Christians or who believe strongly enough in Oak Meadow's imaginative style that they are

willing to contend with the non-Christian elements will find Oak Meadow attractive.

Oak Meadow curriculum is for sale separately. They also have some "sampler" booklets that explain their philosophy. Write for a free brochure.

Our Lady of Victory School

$200 1A-6, $2.50 7-12. Books and supplies extra ($65-$132, depending on the grade). Optional Iowa Test extra. $25 registration fee. 10 percent off 2nd student and rest. Repurchase option: up to 50 percent of cost of reusable books.

Our Lady of Victory is an extremely traditional Catholic day school founded in 1978. The Home Study program has a staff of eight (plus, of course, all the parents who do the actual teaching!) and an enrollment of five hundred.

OLV's program is "the typically Catholic school format that was used successfully across the nation up until about 1960. We do not experiment with your child's mind. We give traditional grades, including F's if they are deserved. But, we don't abandon the 'F' student or place them in an 'educationally handicapped' group; we place them at the grade level they can handle and then we encourage them to advance from there."

Students with genuine learning problems (rather than those whose real problem is laziness) are welcome at OLV. They have had quite a few successes with this kind of student.

Lots of memorization and drill work is included in OLV's program, and lots and lots of Cathlic theology (so much so that when one priest saw an OLV second-grader's religion books he quipped, "Is he studying for a degree in theology?").

Parents are "required to duplicate our typical classroom as closely as possible." Special permission is needed for major deviations from the Home Study Program lesson plans, which must be followed for a regular nine-month school year. The lesson plan gives explicit instructions for each subject and is also an attendance record that must show work accomplished. You mail it in every two weeks. Students must follow dress code requirements, and parents are asked to send a photo of their uniformed child to the school. OLV reserves the right to dismiss students for unsatisfactory conduct.

A fair number of out-of-print Catholic texts are used, which must be returned to the school at the end of the year. Some Christian texts are also used. As much as possible, OLV attempts to avoid purely secular materials, relying exclusively on Catholic literature.

OLV believes students should work hard and develop self-discipline. Parents are also required to stick to a rigorous schedule. The amount of work in and of itself is not crushing, and many families have written to say they enjoy the program.

Record-keeping is straightforward, and can mostly be done on the lesson plan forms.

OLV's Kindergarten is a real learning experience, not a "play" time. Therefore cursive handwriting begins in Kindergarten (which they call "grade 1A" to show they are taking the Kindergarten student seriously). 1A students also learn reading, simple math, and so on.

OLV has a strong "basics" program, although they seem weaker in science than some others. Theology and Catholic devotion are the heart of the curriculum; in these areas students will be exceptionally well trained. Academically, give them a B+ to A−.

If you are not a Catholic you are unlikely to enjoy OLV, as so much of the curriculum *is* Catholicism. If your number one concern is that your children grow up Catholic, and you are leery of any exposure at all to secular thinking, OLV and you are a happy match.

Pensacola Christian Correspondence School
See listing for A Beka Correspondence School

Quest Academy

$200 plus annual $30 testing fee. Books and supplies: $160 grades 1-2, $120 grade 3, $109 grades 4-12. Bible courses: $32 grades 1-2, $24 grade 3, $18 grades 4-12. One-time family registration fee is $30. Shipping and handling are extra. 10 percent discount on second child, 19 percent on third.

Quest Academy was established in 1980 by Dr. and Mrs. Rudolph Moore. Both Moores (not to be confused with Dr. and Mrs. Raymond Moore of Hewitt-Moore) have extensive experience in teaching and curriculum development. Dr. Moore directed the development of the first two editions of the Accelerated Christian Education Curriculum and the Alpha Omega LIFEPAC curriculum. Mrs. Moore wrote the first six grades of math for both the A.C.E. second edition and the AOP curricula. Quest Academy uses what it considers to be the best of these materials, plus new material that the Moores produce.

Quest Academy's staff "is both qualified and experienced with M.A. and Ph.D. degrees from major universities. Our credentials include elementary, secondary, and college teaching certificates with guidance-counselor endorsement (K-12) and administrative certificates (K-12). Our combined classroom teaching experience amounts to more than 25 years at all levels."

Quest Academy offers grades 1-12, plus electives, adult education, and college courses. Placement is by diagnostic testing. The Wide Range Achievement Test (WRAT) is also used to measure progress.

Quest Academy provides Alpha Omega curriculum for each student, enrollment in their school, test grading, record-keeping, counseling, and a small Parent/Teacher Handbook. Legally, Quest is trying to keep a low profile. They are willing to "communicate the quality of our curriculum, the qualifications of our staff, and the effectiveness of our academic program" to school authorities, but prefer to avoid litigation if possible. Group legal insurance is available.

The work-text approach, which Quest uses, is about the easiest for both parents and students. Quest keeps all records, and grades all achievement and diagnostic tests and all major curriculum tests. You set weekly goals and check the daily work and self-tests.

You can purchase supplies for the curriculum's science experiments from the Academy.

Quest has an optional Bible course.

Canadian social studies is available, as are a number of high school and college electives.

See the Alpha Omega listing for an evaluation of Quest's curriculum. Administratively and academically, the quest staff certainly has worthwhile credentials.

Seton Home Study School
$150 K, $300 1-12. Books and supplies: free for K, $80 1-12. Registration fee: $25 first student, $15 second, $10 third, rest FREE! Discount on tuition: 10 percent off second student, 15 percent off third, 20 percent off fourth, 50 percent off rest. 10 percent prepayment discount.

Single high school courses: $80 plus materials.

Seton, a traditional Catholic school stressing academics, was established in 1981 as an outgrowth of Seton Junior/Senior High School, located in Manassas, Virginia. Four hundred students are currently enrolled in K-12 Home Study under the guidance of Seton's extremely well-qualified teaching staff. The director of Seton, Mary Kay Clark, is herself a home schooler, and the curriculum reflects her understanding of the special advantages of home schooling.

Seton's program is textbook-oriented, generally classical, flexibly structured, and very Catholic. "On all levels," Seton says, "it is important to remember that the primary purpose of home school is to teach proper Catholic attitudes about life, Catholic values, and the ability to see the integration of Catholic truth in all areas of knowledge and of daily living." Thus Seton emphasizes traditional Catholic distinctives: the Mass, the Rosary, prayers to Mary and the saints, and so on. The curriculum is also creationist and patriotic.

Seton also offers single courses in upper grade subjects.

Except for workbooks, *the books and lesson plans must be returned at the end of the course.* Kindergarten materials may be kept.

Kindergarten is a readiness *and* phonics program which includes handwriting. Each kindergarten lesson tells you what materials are needed and the objectives for the lesson (this is a good feature).

Seton's program is very thorough in all areas. Books come from a variety of publishers—some Catholic, some evangelical, some secular. From an academic standpoint, their choices are good.

Placement is by the S.R.A. test at no extra charge. Seton gives its students the Stanford Achievement Test at the end of their school year.

Educationally, Seton has a more relaxed attitude than other programs. The Seton staff believes in mastering a concept and then moving on, rather than continuing to fill out unnecessary workbook pages. They also believe strongly in individualized instruction and make special provisions for accelerated and slow students.

Seton's staff bends over backwards to help parents. Their teaching aids are excellent, in my opinion, although the dot-matrix printing leaves something to be desired. Curriculum is constantly revised and improved.

Seton is also very involved with its families. The director arranges a phone consultation with every family before sending out their books, in order to better understand the family's individual needs.

Although Seton tries to integrate Catholicism into its program as much as possible, to the point of using out-of-print Catholic texts in some subjects, the program is very strongly college-geared and therefore they introduce classical and modern secular literature as well.

Students in the full program are given placement and achievement tests, quarterly exams, periodic progress reports, permanent records on file, transcripts if necessary, and advice and counsel from the Seton staff. Graduates from this program are awarded a diploma. Parents are provided with course materials, lesson plans, teaching aids, and tests (which Seton grades).

Parents receive a suggested lesson plan and a blank lesson plan book. They then devise a schedule that meets their own needs. Each subject has its own teaching aids and enrichment suggestions. Parents fill out attendance forms and grade daily assignments. Quarterly tests and completed daily work are sent to Seton. Parents can expect to work hard, but to find their work interesting.

Students are given a great deal of material to cover, but unnecessary repetition of mastered exercises is not required, thus eliminating much school drudgery.

For Catholics, Seton appears to be in a strong legal position. They have a consultant lawyer and are in close touch with legislative realities. If problems arise, Seton deals directly with school officials, providing not only lesson plans, but their objectives and curriculum guidelines. Because an official Catholic encylical says parents are *not allowed* to send their children to a school they find morally objectionable, Catholics who aren't located near a parish school can apparently claim religious exemption for home schooling just as the Amish do with their upper-grade children.

Academically, Seton rates an A.

Families looking for a classical Catholic program which emphasizes individuality and flexibility will find Seton very attractive.

Summit Christian Academy

$125 K, $325 1-12. Materials included. $30 registration fee. $30 testing fee, grades 2 and up. $25 off second student, $50 off third and rest when paid in advance.

LIFEPACS only, order just the ones you wish. Complete curriculum for a year, including teacher guides and answer keys, $150. Individual subjects, $20; if you throw in answer keys and teacher handbooks, it comes to around $30/subject.

Information guide and ordering kit, $7.50.

Requests and letters answered within two days.

This Christian program was founded by Mel Hassell, an ex-Marine who wants to make Summit the "biggest and best" home school program in the country. I'm no prophet, so can't tell you whether he'll succeed, but I am impressed with what he and his staff have accomplished so far.

Summit is a complete home school program using Alpha Omega materials for grades 1-12. These are the very popular Christian worktext materials being used worldwide by more than sixty thousand students. For kindergarten, Summit has a program built around Romalda Spalding's excellent *Writing Road to Reading,* reviewed in this book's Reading section. And there's more! Summit is the only at-home correspondence school to offer a complete line of educational software for ages four to twelve for both the Apple and Commodore computers. (It's the Learning Technologies series, reviewed in the Computers section.) Plus, you can buy Summit's curriculum *without* enrolling, if you so desire, and it costs no more than if you ordered it directly from the publisher. See the listing under Alpha Omega Publications for a full description of the AOP materials that Summit uses in grades 1 to 12.

Summit's kindergarten course takes learning seriously. It includes the reading/writing/spelling program, a manual to teach it, *McGuffey Readers,* workbooks, and other teaching helps. Summit assumes the student *wants* to learn, and he is given solid teaching with much less emphasis on fun 'n games than other programs. He should be able to read good children's literature (*not* "vocabulary-controlled basal readers") and write hundreds of words by the time he completes the course. If your child responds well to this approach, you'll get a lot of progress for your money. Also, since the K course is not babyish, it can be used to instruct older nonreaders without embarrassment.

Students enrolled in Summit score in the top 10 percent on the Iowa Test of Basic Skills, and their graduates are scoring in the top 15 percent on A.C.T. college entrance exams. Summit says, "We know of no other school that has produced these results."

Summit provides all curriculum materials, diagnostic testing, parent teacher handbooks, grading of major tests, record-keeping materials for parents, quarterly progress reports, record-keeping, consultation and advice, and a high school diploma for those fulfilling their requirements. Also, teacher's manuals and answer keys come with each AOP subject.

Summit has an attorney on retainer in its effort to provide an effective legal umbrella for member families. Families are also urged to join the Home School Legal Defense Fund.

You get a two-fold testing program in grades 3 and above. Upon enrollment Summit sends you the WRAT. This achievement test tells what your child has learned to date. Next, individualized placement is achieved using AOP Diagnostic Tests. Also, during Spring and Fall optional Iowa Tests of Basic Skills are given if families request them.

Summit is patriotic, creationist, evangelical, and profree enterprise.

Parents can expect to do a lot of teaching in the earliest grades, but considerably less later on. Alpha Omega material, while not self-instructional, allows the student to take more responsibility for his own education as he matures.

Students will find the AOP materials challenging. Although AOP uses a worktext format, its material is comparable in quality to that of the better textbooks. There are a significant number of "thought" questions requiring essay answers or leading to projects.

Record-keeping required is fairly extensive: attendance reports and grading and averaging all the daily work. However, Summit makes your job easier by providing all the necessary forms.

Summit's booklet *Dare to Compare* contrasts their program with other major Christian programs on the market. Why not send for it?

Academically, give Summit an A.

The Sycamore Tree

$35/month (ten-month basis). Books and supplies extra (expect $150-$200 per child). $50/child registration fee. 10 percent discount on most catalog items for enrolled families.

Sycamore Tree is an alternative, individualized Christian program established in 1982 by Bill and Sandy Gogel, who between them hold about every teaching credential imaginable. Sycamore Tree also sells a wide variety of nifty Christian (and other) educational materials. Send for their catalog!

Sycamore Tree charges tuition on a per-family basis, payable monthly (on a ten-month basis, usually September-June). Thus they don't have or need a refund plan for tuition. Families get what they pay for and if they decide they don't like it, all they have to do is stop paying. (The Gogels, of course, hope you won't do this!) There is also a $50/child registration fee, which includes testing and curriculum setup.

Books and supplies are extra, but families are not required to get their materials from Sycamore Tree (although in most cases they would be wise to do so). All materials may be returned for a refund within fifteen days.

Sycamore Tree provides student evaluation and testing, assistance in developing an individualized program, assistance in selecting Bible-centered curricular materials, record-keeping, advice and counseling, support groups in each area where Sycamore Tree families are located, a student body card indicating your child is enrolled in a private school, group legal insurance, and a 10 percent discount on most items from their catalog. Sycamore Tree also publishes a monthly newsletter from September to June which they design as an educational aid to their families. You get fifty to seventy pages of enrichment material in each issue.

Sycamore Tree materials are creationist and nonpolitical and feature traditional family roles. The Sycamore Tree catalog includes a smattering of Seventh-Day Adventist material, none of which is required.

Parents keep attendance records, provide quarterly progress reports and student work samples, write lesson plans (with guidance from Sycamore Tree), and oversee the student's program. Sycamore Tree parents are strongly involved with their children's education.

The student's workload will reflect his and his parents' desires, since each program is totally individualized.

Sycamore Tree's catalog will make any true-blue home schooler drool with desire. The range of materials they have chosen to offer reflects sound taste and judgment. *You may order from their catalog without enrolling.*

Sycamore Tree materials are educationally sound and interesting. Here's just a sample of what they offer. The Alpha Omega curriculum. The Rod and Staff curriculum (see the review under Textbooks). Some Home-Grown Kids products, like Math-It and Winston Grammar, that are used in Hewitt's program. A wide variety of neat science and art equipment, including the best drawing text I have ever seen for young children. Foreign language materials. A whole host of Christian teaching aids that are hard to find elsewhere, including the fabulous Betty Lukens Through the Bible in Felt in a smaller, much more economical family size. I have not even begun to list the topics their catalog covers. You will just have to request one and see for yourself.

With all this variety of excellent materials to choose from, a family that *knows what it wants* should have no trouble setting up an A+ individualized program.

University of Nebraska-Lincoln
Division of Continuing Studies
$48/semester course, $38/half-semester course, Nebraska residents. $52/semester course, $38/half-semester, nonresidents. Books and supplies about $20-$30/course. Science supplies run $40-$100/course. Shipping extra.

Those who believe public schools need megabucks to produce quality education ought to take a look at Univerity of Nebraska-Lincoln's home-study program for high school students. Here, for an absolutely minimal financial investment, students can obtain the best *public* school education (in my opinion) in America today. No computers, no band practice or football team, no Olympic-size swimming pool, no "gifted and talented" kids playing Dungeons and Dragons—not only do U of N-L students survive without these things, somehow they surpass their schoolbound fellows!

U of Nebraska-Lincoln provides a state- and regionally-accredited high school diploma. Students under eighteen must secure the written permission of their local school administrator to enroll and obtain an "approved person" to supervise their program. This applies only to those seeking credit; courses are available to anyone who wants them.

All students get course syllabi, the texts and supplies they ordered, and the privilege of instruction and comments on their written work from an Independent Study High School teacher. Those enrolled for credit must also take tests under supervision. The texts used come from standard public school suppliers. U of N-L writes its own excellent syllabi.

Each course is so well laid out that students should experience no frustration. Although the workload corresponds to that in a public school classroom, there is no "busywork." Courses are self-instructional, and parents need not get involved. Since U of N-L is a state- and regionally-accredited program, if your school superintendent approves your enrollment attendance and other record-keeping should not be needed. Also, U of N-L grades all tests.

This is a fully legal, accredited program.

You can get *all* the supplies for every course from U of N-L, *including equipment and materials for all the science courses.* For this reason alone I would give U of N-L's science courses preference over those from any other program except Alpha Omega. Any science materials not provided should be locally available, and are clearly listed under the catalog entry for that course. Thus the student gets a real science course with real experiments, not just a book.

A limited number of scholarships are available. Write for applications to the K.O. Broady Scholarship Committee, Room 269C.

U of N-L provides some of the usual high school trappings, such as an honor roll, diploma cover, and high school pin.

U of N-L uses the best public school texts, and their syllabi are excellent. U of N-L writers make a real attempt to be objective, and while the result in some areas (I am thinking particularly of English and the social sciences) of necessity reflects secular thinking, it is still a whole lot better than you're likely to find in your local school.

As learning tools, the syllabi I saw were extremely well organized. Each step is clearly presented, each possible learning obstacle is illuminated and explained, goals and objectives are stated explicitly, and there are even self-check tests to help you decide whether you need to review any areas before you take a test.

Academically, the University of Nebraska-Lincoln program rates an A.

Those looking for a high-quality, traditional, secular high school course will be pleased with University of Nebraska-Lincoln's program.

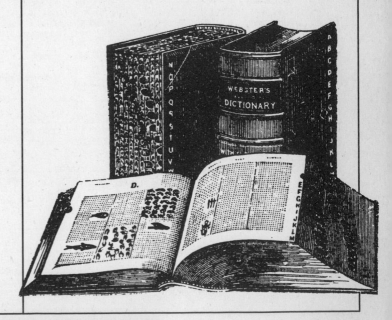

HOME SCHOOL COMPARISON CHART

NAME	YR EST	# NOW ENROLLED	GRADES OFFERED	PRICE RANGE	RELIGIOUS OUTLOOK	PROGRAM TYPE	INDIV/ PERSON	TEACHING HELPS
A Beka Correspondence School	1973	2,000	Nursery-12	MID-UPPER	Christian evangelical	A Beka textbooks	NO	Teaching curriculum used in A Beka classrooms.
A Beka Video School	1985	N/A	K-5	EXPENSIVE	Christian evangelical	Video teaching plus A Beka textbooks	NO	Handbook w/lesson manual
Advanced Training Institute	1984	1,000	Pre-12	UPPER	Christian evangelical	Bible/discovery	N/A	Seminar, aids
American Christian Academy	1980	2,000	K 1-12	BARGAIN MIDPRICED	Christian fundamentalist	Self-instructional. Basic Ed worktexts.	Indiv.	Handbook
American School	1897	2,000,000 since '97	9-12	BARGAIN-UPPER MID (# yrs)	Secular	Standard texts	Indiv.	Study guide for each subject
Associated Christian Schools	1979		K-12	MID-UPPER (option)	Baptist fundamentalist	Self-instructional. ACS's own worktexts.	Indiv.	Handbook
Calvert School	1897	5,000	K 1-8	BARGAIN MID-UPPER (option)	Secular, Christian flavor	Readiness Textbook, classical	NO	Study guide for each subject
Christian Liberty Academy	1968	14,000	Sr, Jr K 1-12	BARGAIN BARGAIN	Biblical Christian Reconstructionist	Textbook, lots of workbooks. Eclectic.	Indiv.	Handbook
Christian Light	1979	250	1-12	BARGAIN	Anabaptist Mennonite	Worktext. AOP revision.	Indiv.	Teacher handbook and answer keys
Clonlara	1967	2,000	Pre-12	BARG-EXP (# kids)	Neutral. You choose.	Wide open. Unschooling, traditional, in between.	Indiv.	Newsletter, Curric. guides for each subject
Hewitt-Moore Child Development Center	1983	2,000	K-12	MID-UPPER (# kids)	Christian Non-denominational	Discovery/project	Personal.	Curric. guides
Home Study International	1909	Thousands	PreK K 1-12	BARGAIN MIDPRICED UPPER-EXP (grade)	Seventh-Day Adventist	Textbook	NO	Parent's Guide/ each elem. subj. Study guide for each upper subj.
International Institute	1960	1,000	K 1-12	BARGAIN BARG-MID (# kids)	Secular plus Bible. Run by Christians.	Readiness/Reading Public school texts	NO	Handbook with lesson plans. Teacher's editions
Living Heritage Academy	N/A	N/A	K-12	MIDPRICED	Christian fundamentalist	Self-instructional. Basic Ed worktexts.	Indiv.	Handbook
North Dakota Ind Study	1935	6,000	9-12	BARGAIN	Secular	Public school texts	Indiv.	Study guide for each subject.
Oak Meadow School	1975	500	K-12	MID-EXP (# kids)	New Age	"Waldorf" K-4 Discovery/project 5-8 More texts 9-12.	NO	Curric guide K-4 Study guide 5-12
Our Lady of Victory	1978	500	K-12	MIDPRICED	Catholic	Textbook, devotional books	NO	Handbook with lesson plans
Quest Academy	1980	100's	1-12	MIDPRICED	Christian evangelical	AOP worktexts.	Indiv.	Teacher handbook and answer keys for each subject
Seton Home Study School	1981	250	K-12	MID-UPPER (# kids)	Catholic	Textbook. Flexible, classical.	Personal.	Study guide for each subject.
Summit Christian Academy	1982	800	K 1-12	BARGAIN MIDPRICED	Christian evangelical Christian	Reading thru writing AOP worktexts.	NO Indiv.	Manual Teacher handbook and answer keys for each subject
Sycamore Tree	1982	200	K-12	BARG-EXP (# kids)	Christian evangelical	Combination text/discovery	Personal.	Curric. guides
University of Nebraska-Lincoln	1929	5,000	9-12	MIDPRICED	Secular	Public school texts	Indiv.	Study guide for each subject.

Price Key		Preschool	Kindergarten	Grades 1-12
BARGAIN	=	<$100	<$180	<$280
MIDDLE	=	all other	all other	between $200 and $400
UPPER	=			between $400 and $500
EXPENSIVE	=			>$500

Some schools give a price break when you enroll more than one child, or when you select a particular enrollment option. These are indicated as (# kids) or (option) under the price code.

INDIV/PERSON KEY: "Indiv." means the program is individualized according to your child's ability levels in different subjects. "Person." means each child gets a program especially tailored to him alone. "NO" means each enrollee at a particular grade level gets the same program. Generally, the more personalized a program is, the more work the parents spend setting it up, so personalized programs are not automatically superior in all respects to standardized programs.

CHAPTER THIRTEEN

A SMATTERING OF SMALL AND ALTERNATIVE PROGRAMS

Yesterday's radical new idea is tomorrow's status quo. With this in mind, I have included a smattering of new programs and alternative programs. Even Calvert was new once upon a time, and who knows?—maybe ten years from now one of these programs will be the biggest in America.

Those who, like Thoreau, march to the beat of a different drummer here may find something to their taste.

WHAT IS AN ALTERNATIVE SCHOOL?

Alternative schools, otherwise known as "free" schools, believe in letting the child lead the way in his own education. In practice, this means large, messy rooms full of noise and lots of kids running around. I personally am skeptical of theories that credit children with an *unmixed* desire for self-improvement. Yet children are made in the image of God and can respond quite dramatically to the example of those who love learning and are good at doing interesting things. As John Holt so wisely observed, alternative schools stand or fall by the talents of the adults running them. Children aren't interested in learning from someone who has nothing interesting to teach, and this can become brutally clear in an alternative school where nobody is making them do anything.

John Holt, once a driving force behind the establishment of alternative schools, became a leader in the home school movement. Following his lead, you can expect more and more alternative schooling to be done at home. At the moment, existing alternative schools are acting as "umbrellas" to protect home schoolers from legal repercussions (as much as possible) while giving them a helping hand with developing a home program. Some, like the Open School Extended Program in

Corvallis, Oregon, go so far as to provide study materials on loan. These are helpful folk, usually not Bible-believing Christians, who love their kids and want to give them a chance to succeed without the trauma of grades, cliques, and sterile classroom teaching.

At home, the distinguishing feature of alternative schooling is its emphasis on learning by doing. (*All* normal families have messy playrooms and kids who like to run around!) Since no normal kid wants to sit still for hours of lectures (the conventional classroom fare), it follows that the way to get them involved in learning is to give them something to make or to take apart. Free kids are thus encouraged to write books or play with Cuisenaire rods or build a birdhouse or clip coupons from the newspaper or make a puppet theatre and put on a play . . . you get the idea.

Some alternative schoolers agonize over how much direction they can give their children and still have "free" children. "Does my child really *want* to use Cuisenaire rods for math, like *I* want him to, and not just for building neat little towers?" they wonder. These worries come from sentimental beliefs that children are holier than adults. Unsentimental (and successful) alternative schoolers know that "folly is bound up in the heart of a child," such folly including, among other things, laziness. We all need a figurative kick in the pants on our lazy days, and kids are no exception. In other words, anyone determined to raise an absolutely free child who also wants that child to have a decent education had better live in a fantastically rich environment and get rid of the TV set.

Alternative schools, then, provide a strong hands-on program sometimes combined with some rather permissive advice. If you want a hands-on math program, this is the place to get it. You'll also be on the cutting edge of what's new, like italic penmanship.

Sophisticated, liberal types, whether inner-city professionals or rural "dropouts," seem to like this approach the best.

A FEW ALTERNATIVE PROGRAMS AND ORGANIZATIONS

Corvallis Open School Extended Program

Fall and spring semesters, $75/semester/child. Optional summer semester, $50. Books and supplies extra. Buy-back option. Loan/rental program.

Corvallis Open School Extended Program (COSEP) operates on the same principles as open classroom programs in alternative schools. The staff believes in progress in learning, following the child's initiative. Each family's program is different, reflecting individual students' desires and abilities and the family's lifestyle.

The Open School staff consists of "experienced parents, homeschoolers, and alternative schoolers."

This is not a "graded" program. Children of all ages are accepted.

You design the program with the staff's help. COSEP provides "not a series of workbooks or lessons, but advice, suggestions, loans of material, evaluation procedures and unlimited consultations by mail or telephone (you pay long distance costs)."

COSEP follows the open classroom/alternative school educational philosophy. They prefer hands-on, principles-oriented materials rather than rote drill and fill-in-the-blanks. Reading and writing are integrated into all areas, rather than treated as separate subjects. Italic penmanship is preferred. Science, social studies, safety, health, art, and physical education are taught in a practical, active way.

The amount of work required is solely up to you. COSEP takes your family's lifestyle into account when planning the program.

COSEP does insist that you keep a daily learning diary and send it in every two to four weeks, so they can in good conscience claim your students are enrolled and are following a program. No testing or scorekeeping is required. Every three months the program is evaluated and updated if necessary.

Students are expected to get actively involved in their own education. They will do projects, complete math texts, and so on.

A "buy-back" option allows families to recover some of the cost for materials by returning them after the student has finished with them. COSEP also has a loan/rental program for course outlines, study programs, and equipment.

COSEP has a newsletter, and encourages parents to present discussion papers for distribution among COSEP families.

Academically, this program is what you make it. It certainly should not be boring.

Highly motivated families who are interested in a child-centered, innovative approach to learning will be attracted to this "alternative" program.

Santa Fe Community School

$100 per child per year covers the cost of SFCS correspondence services and record-keeping. Books and supplies extra.

Readers of John Holt's magazine *Growing Without Schooling* will recognize the name Santa Fe Community School. This small alternative school was one of the first to legally shelter home schoolers. In the early days, Santa Fe was quite busy galloping about on a white horse rescuing families from overzealous state officials. One father Santa Fe rescued had actually been served with a warrant for his arrest! (The happy ending: upon Santa Fe enrollment, all charges were dropped.)

Accredited by the Rio Grande Educational Association, Santa Fe Community School is a state-recognized alternative nonpublic school operating a regular educational program since 1968, now year-round. Ed Nagel, the director of Santa Fe, believes strongly in noncompulsory learning.

Santa Fe Community School is not a correspondence school. It assists parents in developing their own educational programs. The parents become "volunteer employees" of the school, and the home school is considered an extended part of Santa Fe's regular program.

Santa Fe has been operating home school extension programs since 1974. More than two thousand totally home schooled students have been enrolled over the years.

Santa Fe describes its program as "Multi-Lingual . . . Multi-Cultural . . . Ungraded . . . For Children Three to Eighteen."

Like most programs of this sort, Santa Fe requires that the parents keep journals of the children's projects and progress and report on their program from time to time. Work required varies with the family's interests and energy level.

To apply, send name, address, birth dates of children, phone number, and the name and address of the school(s) last attended, plus inclusive dates and grade levels.

National Association for the Legal Support of Alternative Schools

Yearly membership dues, $20. Directory, $5.

Ed Nagel is a man of many hats. Besides serving as the director of Santa Fe Community School, he is also the director of the National Association for the Legal Support of Alternative Schools, otherwise known as NALSAS.

NALSAS serves as a resource for those in the alternative school movement who find themselves embroiled in confrontations with state authorities. Its commodity is information, in the form of people to contact, legal briefs, legislative proposals, and a file of articles that support their position. If the information Ed Nagel sent me is current, NALSAS also operates a legal insurance fund. Premiums are quite low. Inquire for details.

Families interested in the alternative school philosophy and home schooling are advised to look into becoming a "satellite" of a nearby alternative/free/community school that already is legally in operation in their state. You can buy a current Directory of the National Coalition of Alternative Community Schools from NALSAS for $5, postage-paid.

NALSAS membership, for those interested, is $20 a year.

SMALL PROGRAMS

And now, as promised, here is a sampling of some smaller programs. Some of these are growing by leaps and bounds and might not deserve to be called "small" at all by the time you read this; still, they don't have the size or following of the largest ones and are more experimental in nature.

Most small programs are Christian. Some are not. The "umbrella" school concept is popular among smaller programs, and the Learning Center is a variation on this theme. Combining a home school program with the advantages of a support group, this option certainly will continue to grow in popularity. One of your local church schools may have a satellite program like this going. Ask; it can't hurt.

If you, after reading this section, feel like leaping up and shouting, "*I* could start a small program like these," why not do it? As Greg Harris, director of Christian Life Workshops, has said, there is a great need for home school coordinators, and you needn't feel ashamed to charge a reasonable price for planning field trips, ordering curriculum, and giving teacherly advice—*if* you're qualified! You don't necessarily need a teaching certificate, but you ought to have some successful experience in teaching someone somewhere and be an organized person. As Greg Harris also has said, this kind of job is made-to-order for single mothers who want to teach their children, but also kind of like to have bread on the table. Go to it! And if you're successful, I'd love to hear about it. Maybe you'll even get your school into the next edition!

Creative Christian Education Service

Family membership is $250 for the first child for one year, $100 for each additional child. Registration fee of 25 percent per student is not refundable. No refund is granted after "processing."

CCES believes it has been in existence longer than any other group home school program in California. 1985 was their ninth year of operation.

CCES is a member of the private schools of the State of California. CCES services include initial consultation and curriculum setup, testing, curriculum guides, record-keeping, a California affidavit legalizing your home program (California only), ongoing consultation, and a newsletter. In addition, CCES maintains a rental program. For a rental fee of $3 or less per book, you can obtain all the texts you need.

"All CCES representatives possess valid Teaching Credentials. . . . During the past 8 years not one student has been lost via public school pressures."

Parents keep a daily log in the record booklet provided, promise to follow a consistent educational program, and administer tests.

CCES offers various brochures describing their program for a nominal fee. Send SASE for an order form.

Discovery Christian Schools

DCS bills itself as "a network of independent and home schools." Its interest is in helping parents or parent groups to furnish basic Christian education to their children.

Both Patrick D. Clifford, the superintendent, and his wife, Ruth, have teaching credentials and experience. Mr. Clifford also has had sixteen years of administrative experience and possesses a State Life Credential in Administrative Services (preschool through junior college).

Services provided are clearly spelled out in the brochure.

These include training and curriculum seminars, given personally or on tape; curriculum recommendations; curriculum guides for each subject; attendance forms and advice on record-keeping; maintenance of student records in "safe, fireproof files"; testing; state report of private school (California only); consulting services; and newsletters and bulletins.

As with all such programs, you are in charge. Discovery Christian Schools gives advice and keeps you honest by requiring you to show you are doing something, but you choose the books and set the pace.

Family-Centered Learning Alternatives
You arrange fees with your local Center.

This state-approved home schooling program has Learning Centers in Indiana, Oregon, California, and scattered all over Washington. More than two hundred families, as of July 1984, were enrolled in more than forty FCLA Learning Centers.

Debra Stewart, FCLA's administrator, told me over the phone that she is willing to work with state boards of education in order to set up Learning Centers in other states beside those in which Centers are already operating.

FCLA parents are "instructional aides" working under the direct supervision of a certified teacher.

Each quarter begins with a conference between the student, parents, and teacher consultant. "The student selects his program and the educational objectives are then established accordingly." No one particular curriculum is used to the exclusion of all others. You develop a program that suits your family's religious and educational desires.

So far FCLA sounds like a lot of other programs. But wait! FCLA is actually a home school program and support group rolled up together. FCLA Learning Centers provide periodic group learning activities and field trips. You are part of a *group* of families that mostly study separately, but get together for special activities.

Parents keep a detailed daily log of activities. With the help of the teacher consultant, they select the methods and materials to be used each quarter. These must "incorporate all areas of state required curriculum."

In the states where FCLA is established, enrolling families are legally immune. FCLA families must, however, accept the principle of state regulation of their home school.

FCLA is a *group* learning setup. Your home school is affiliated, through the Learning Center, with other home schools and you get together for social events. As Debra Stewart says, "The question most often asked by outsiders, 'WHAT ABOUT SOCIALIZATION?' is easy to answer in a positive way with FCLA." (Although let's not forget that well-run support groups can provide the same group experiences.)

Gregarious types who prefer to cooperate with the public school establishment and who look upon the supervision of a certified teacher as an advantage will certainly be interested in FCLA.

The Learning Connection

$50 per family per year, plus a monthly fee of $25 for the first child and $15 for each additional children. Barter is acceptable when arranged in advance. Pay in advance and get one month free.

As of May 1985, fifty-nine students were enrolled in The Learning Connection, a private, nonaccredited Oregon school. Jane Joyce, a certified public school substitute teacher, helps families set up an individual learning program for each child. A typical program includes real-life learning situations, such as cooking a family meal or balancing a checkbook, field trips, or even an apprenticeship, as well as the familiar "academic" subjects.

Mrs. Joyce, evidently an energetic woman, arranges such things as potluck suppers, picnics, and educational toy demonstrations. The TLC newsletter also alerts members to opportunities like swim and gymnastics classes in the area.

Families consult with Mrs. Joyce, keep monthly logs, and follow their interests. Are they satisfied? Only one child so far has returned to public school. Is it legal? According to the *Freedom to Express* of May 1983, when someone called up the state to ask about The Learning Connection, the reply he got was that TLC "was the only one doing [home-based private school education] in the state, and they don't know why other people haven't thought of it."

School of Home Learning

Family membership, $35/year. Additional services extra.

Over eighty children are enrolled in the this state-attested private school that believes in "invited teaching." For the nominal yearly membership fee, a family gets: student ID cards, an attendance record sheet, a handbook and curriculum guide, record-keeping, six issues of *Growing Without Schooling*, a one-year membership in the California Coalition of People for Alternative Learning Situations (CC-PALS) and the National Coalition of Alternative Community Schools (NCACS), plus all other services offered at cost plus 5 percent.

Now, what *are* those "other services"? A Young People's Matching Network through which kids can meet, write to, or work together with other home schooled youngsters; a Contact Service to match learners up with possible apprenticeship/learning opportunities; a Skills Exchange Service; and a Reference Service to help members locate educational books and supplies that will meet their needs.

A credentialed teacher with a Master's in education directs the home-satellite program.

School of Home Learning is nonsectarian. The director is avidly involved in the "Beyond War" movement and a firm believer in the educational philosophy of John Holt, Ivan Illich, and Dr. William Glasser.

CHAPTER FOURTEEN

JUST CURRICULUM

Are you clever? Are you competent? Are you hard-nosed? Then you'll want to look over this list of "just curriculum." It's for people who don't want to enroll in a correspondence program, but who do want a prefabbed curriculum, and is as close to a roll-your-own program as any inexperienced home schooler probably ought to go at first.

The advantages of just getting a curriculum without enrolling in a program are cost and flexibility. In a program, you pay for all those telephone sessions and graded tests that are supplied with enrollment. You also in most cases have to do *all* the work the school sends you, even if it bores your young 'un to tears. On your own, you can pick and choose which exercises or activities you think are worth the effort, and you save some money.

On the other hand, you have no legal umbrella. You also might find a certain laziness seeping in, as many people find it harder to work without supervision, even if only a nagging memory that you haven't sent anything in to the school for two months and you really *must* get a package of work together soon.

Afterschoolers are definitely better off without formal enrollment, since a child can only stand to do so much schoolwork and you have no need to prove anything to anybody. The exception is when Summer School looms ahead and you'd *much* rather have your eighth-grader take the Calvert math course—for credit. Talk over such decisions with your school personnel, since they can get huffy about assigning credits for courses they haven't approved.

LIST OF CORRESPONDENCE PROGRAM CURRICULA AVAILABLE SEPARATELY

A Beka Books (not the video program, but the complete texts and teacher materials).

Alpha Omega (from them or Summit Christian Academy—same price both places).

Associated Christian Schools.

Basic Education (from Living Heritage Academy).

Calvert School.

Christian Liberty Academy (eclectic selection of books).

Christian Light Education.

Hewitt-Moore Child Development Center (use their Parents' Choice option or order much of the material from their Home-Grown Kids distributor near you).

International Institute (eclectic selection).

Oak Meadow School (K-6 curricula only).

Sycamore Tree (order directly from their catalog. Wide range of items).

University of Nebraska-Lincoln.

The following publishers *only* supply curriculum without enrollment services.

Alpha Omega Publications

LITTLE PATRIOTS Complete Kindergarten Program, $50 parent's kit, $100 student materials. $200/year for AOP grade 1-12 materials, each child (includes teacher guides, answer keys, and all other necessary materials).

Alpha Omega Publications (AOP) is not exactly the new kid on the block. Way back in the days of Jimmy Carter a team of over 250 Christian academic writers, most of whom held Master's or Doctorates, got together and produced an entire curriculum for grades 1-12. Why did they do this? Because, like so many others, they saw modern education slipping over the cliff and they wanted to provide a Christian alternative. At the moment AOP curriculum is being used by over 60,000 students in all fifty states and in twenty foreign countries. Most of these students are enrolled in small Christian schools; some are home schooled.

AOP doesn't publish textbooks. Instead, they have gone the workbook route, with consumable booklets containing both texts and assignments. These they call "LIFEPACS." Each subject for each grade has ten LIFEPACS, plus Teacher Handbooks and Answer Keys. You might scoff at Answer Keys, knowing you can always check out Junior's work without them, but when it's time to grade those hundreds and thousands of three-digit math problems, you will be *grateful* to AOP for providing them! Each grade has five subjects (including Bible), plus the usual and not-so-usual High School electives of Art, Consumer Math, Home Ec, Greek, and Spanish. It all is very professionally done, and AOP plans to upgrade its reproduction in the near future to include colored ink and other goodies.

AOP's English program, particularly in the upper grades, is excellent. Students not only read great literature but learn the arts of good writing, speaking, and listening. The Science curriculum is likewise excellent: lucid, logical, and thorough. AOP provides *real* lab experiments. If your children like to fool around with ice cubes and table salt, that's fine. But if your son is serious about Bunsen burners and ripple tanks and the like, AOP's got the stuff for him. You can buy all the equipment and supplies for the experiments from Christian Light Education (see their listing).

Social Studies is a bit more spotty, following the public school formula of "widening circles" from the student, to his family, his community, his nation, and the world. History and geography are also included, but the variety of authors works against a totally unified view of history and politics. Parts of the Social Studies curriculum could be considered overly "progressive" by some.

The Bible courses contain theology, book studies, and practical applications from a generally consistent evangelical viewpoint.

First grade materials are full of "I like me" and original (non-classical) fantasy stories. You decide whether you like this or not!

For kindergarten, A.O.P. is a distributor of the comprehensive, phonics-based kindergarten program THE LITTLE PATRIOTS produced by Mile-Hi Publishers. Its analytical approach to the American language is based upon Biblical principles. The program includes phonics, reading, writing, spelling, penmanship, numbers, history, and Bible. Teacher's guides organize the daily work with many worksheets and student workbooks to provide in-depth student practice. Researched and developed over more than ten years, AOP considers it a proven and effective kindergarten program.

AOP LIFEPACs are *not* self-instructional. Projects, compositions, essay questions and other "thinking" assignments fill the curriculum. This makes for a superior education, but more work for parents and students.

Overall, I give Alpha Omega an A. For English and science, you could stretch this to an A+. Although the curriculum has weak areas, generally speaking the more I see of what's available to schools (both public and private) the better I like Alpha Omega.

(If you want a correspondence program using AOP materials for grades 1-12, check out the Summit Christian Academy and Quest Academy listings. Christian Light Education also have a revised AOP program for the Mennonite community.)

Basic Education/Reform Publications. (Suggested retail price— $35 per course per year)

Lots of people are confused about what "Basic Education" is. No, it is not the Alpha Omega program. No, it is not Mennonite. Basic Education is published by Reform Publications, Inc. with headquarters in Lewisville, Texas. It contains four basic subjects— English, math, social studies, and science—taught through self-contained and self-instructional worktexts. Emphasis is heavily traditional and "back to basics." Courses feature lots of drill and fill-in-the-blanks.

Basic Education calls its courses "biblical" and "theistic." Materials are patriotic.

For the teacher, Basic Education is a very easy program to administer. Curriculum is mostly self-instructional, with the exception of the Basic Reading program, for which a complete teacher's manual is provided. No other teacher's guides are needed or provided.

Basic Education's program is equally easy for the student to follow. Layout is straightforward and logical, if unexciting, with a lot of repetition. Texts are printed in nice, clear type.

The Basic Reading program teaches thirty-five phonetic sounds through "visuals, coordination exercises, music, phonetic drills, writing of the letters, and stories" using an animal motif. Originally written for classroom teaching, Basic Reading is both a readiness and reading program designed to bring most children of five to six years to a solid reading ability in nine to twelve weeks.

Basic Education does provide a home school program. Families wishing to enroll in this program should contact Living Heritage Academy (see their listing). Satellite schools may qualify for a school account with Basic Education.

Some love Basic Education curriculum; some hate it. Critics complain that Basic Education does not teach real thinking skills, only rote facts. It is true that this program does not put the same stress on creativity as, say, Alpha Omega or Calvert. However, Basic Education still surpasses the public schools' results, since too often they teach *neither* thinking *nor* facts. Basic Education students have, in fact, been shown to significantly outperform public school children on standardized tests.

Basic Education says that after fourteen years of student use, two curriculum effects are visible:

1. Students completing the college preparatory course are consistent in attaining a 3.0 or better grade point average in a wide variety of colleges and universities.
2. Those who have completed formal education are being looked to for leadership in their work and community relationships.

It seemed to me that the curriculum would do the job of teaching basic skills and facts in a Christian context, which is what it set out to do.

Curriculum Development Centre
Joy in Learning, 602 pages, $35. *Teaching with "Joy,"* 170 pages, $8. *The Number and Shape of Things,* 267 pages, $18.
Membership in CDC is open to all who subscribe to its goals at an annual fee of $30.

CDC is an independent nonprofit organization. Its purpose is "to contribute to Christian day school education by developing and publishing curriculum materials, and by providing educational consulting services."

CDC publishes and sells curriculum for Christian schools under the name Joy in Learning based on their own "wholistic" and "integrated" view of education. This translates into "units" that attempt to contain many subjects. Thus children might study weather by doing a variety of activities using reading, writing, math, measurement, the effects of weather on people, and so on, instead of studying math, science, and language arts as separate school subjects.

Now available are *The Number and Shape of Things,* an integrated math curriculum with thematic activities, *Joy in Learning,* an integrated general curriculum, and *Teaching with Joy,* on how to implement integrated education in the classroom. All are for elementary-age children. Get a feel for these materials from the following quote:

> *The Number and Shape of Things* suggests many learning activities and directs attention to the mathematical aspects present in them. *These are not math activities designed to "get across" certain concepts.* They recommend ways in which experiences of the four realms of creation (the physical realm, plants, animals, and people living and working together) can be structured. And they can be used to lead children to the mathematical ideas and operations that will enrich their knowledge of the overall themes. (emphasis mine)

Used as supplemental activities to an existing program, the Joy in Learning approach might be valid, not so much for actual skills as for the learner's discovery of all the different ways there are to find out about things, and all the different questions one can ask about God's world.

The CDC Publications Catalogue provides info about their publications, consulting services, and current prices.

I cannot vouch for the Scripturalness of the program, not having seen it.

KONOS Character Curriculum
Volumes 1, 2, and 3, $32 each post-paid (Texas residents add tax). *Language Skills Checklist,* $2.50.

The KONOS brochure announces, "A WHOLE YEAR'S WORTH FOR K-6!" What is this, you ask? It's integrated units centering around Christian character traits that cover all subjects except phonics and math for one year of K-6. KONOS has a *Language Skills Checklist,* and by spending the few bucks necessary to acquire it you can also teach language along with the curriculum.

The KONOS curriculum consists of nine "theme" character traits. Each month's activities follow the theme for that month. The themes for Volume I include Attentiveness, Obedience, Orderliness, Honor, Trust, Stewardship, and Patience. Under the theme of Attentiveness, for example, children study how eyes and ears work (science), tell and retell the Bible story of Samuel (Bible, reading comprehension, creative expression), make a straw oboe and paper kazoo (music, art), read Davy Crockett's biography (history, reading), practice tracking (nature study), learn Indian sign language (language), and study Indian customs (social studies)—among many other things!

Since KONOS is not an umbrella school but a curriculum, you don't really have to do anything you don't feel up to (including role-playing ol' Dan'l).

KONOS relies on library books, which are free, for its supplementary literature and resource material. This makes it much cheaper than a standard curriculum.

Every activity has the corresponding subjects listed next to it in the margin. Examples: "Hammer a nail into wood. The next time rub the nail with soap and see if there is a difference." This activity has "Science" listed in the margin. "How old was Noah when he started building the ark?" = math. "Make your own sandpaper" (instructions follow) = art and science. "Learn Indian sign language and picture writing" (directs you to a book on the subject) = language.

Obviously attentiveness and obedience are wonderful things to learn, but can any sort of planned school experience really teach them? KONOS' answer is that by emphasizing a character trait for an entire month, parents will at least convey to their offspring that they are serious about that trait.

Applause goes to KONOS for *not* trying the "integrated" approach with the basic subjects. With social studies, science, and the artistic subjects it works much better. An advantage to this approach is that the whole family can learn together, on different levels. Little Sis can make her paper kazoo while Big Brother plays American folk tunes on his harmonica. The whole family can read Davy Crockett's story together, and go on a field trip to an Indian burial mound. The cost is also more than reasonable, since KONOS believes in using the public library. A wealth of resource books are listed after every section.

I did wonder if integrated units are sufficient to build up the necessary learning framework. KONOS now has a historical time line to pull together the history and literature. (See it reviewed under History.)

The KONOS writers believe in exposing Christian children to non-Christian ideas and values; thus the curriculum includes some activities (e.g., role-playing misbehavior) and books (e.g., *There's a Nightmare in My Closet* by Mercer Mayer, the prince of nasty kiddie lit) that I personally would skip.

The manual itself is professionally done and easy to use, and you get a lot of pages for your money (over 120).

The *Language Skills Checklist* is thirteen pages, listing all the language skills your child should master, and the grades in which children nowadays learn these things. It doesn't tell you how to teach these skills, but mentions a few choice books that will help you with this. For only $2.50 you'll be on top of your child's language arts program. Recommended.

Academically, KONOS deserves an A. (Remember, it does *not* teach basic math and phonics. You need to buy those materials separately.) Scripturally, at present I give it a B.

If you buy this curriculum, don't overdo it! The writers have included more suggested activities and field trips than you probably will be able to manage. Pick and choose, and have fun!

KONOS founders Carole Thaxton and Jessica Hulcy are also available for two- or four-hour seminars entitled "How Children Best Learn." Contact them through KONOS if you're interested.

Learning at Home

The Teaching Guides are sold both as grade level sets of language arts, math, social studies and science, or individually by subject area. Prices for the four subject Teaching Guide Sets are: grade 1—$32.00, grade 2—$36.00, and grade 3—$40.00. Prices for each single subject Teaching Guide are: grade 1—$9.50, grade 2—$10.50, and grade 3—$11.50.

So you say you don't need a lot of expensive services and fancy books? You say you just want a little help in figuring out what Johnny ought to be doing next and how to present it to him? Voila! Learning at Home has exactly what you need.

This small company offers professionally prepared Teaching Guides with Curriculum Outlines for grades 1-3 in language arts, math, social studies, and science. Hawaiian home schoolers have been successfully submitting Learning at Home Curriculum Outlines for four years to the Hawaii Department of Education.

The Curriculum Outlines, included with each Teaching Guide, are written in "teacher talk," and their main purpose is to reassure the authorities that you seriously intend to teach your kids. They also serve as a "Scope and Sequence" to give you an overview of the skills the schools supposedly teach in that grade, and the order in which you should teach them. The Teaching Guides, on the other hand, help you actually teach the stuff. Each new skill is covered step-by-step, so *you* know how it works and can explain it to your learners. This is all done in such a clean, taut style that you can't get lost along the way.

Let me tell you, these guides are *good!* I would recommend the Teaching Guides to any parents who are concerned about their children's education. By flipping through the "back issues"—i.e., the grades your little one has already finished—you can see very quickly if there are any weak spots, and what's more, you will have the information you need to correct the school's deficiencies right at your fingertips. By going through the Guide for your son or daughter's current grade, you can begin to take an active part in improving his or her education. All this for an absolutely rock-bottom price.

If you are using the KONOS curriculum, you might want to consider getting the *Math Teaching Guides* from Learning at Home, and perhaps the *Language Arts Guide* for the grade as well. If you are clever at teaching and don't need a special phonics program, in this way you can provide a complete grade-school education for any number of children at a minimal cost.

Learning at Home intends to produce Teaching Guide sets for grades 4-6 in 1986. They also have branched out into offering a test preparation series (see the Testing chapter) and a line of K-12 books and workbooks. Write and ask to be put on their mailing list if you're interested.

Learning at Home's staff also provides counseling and standardized testing services for local (Hawaiian) home schooling families, and tutoring for afterschoolers. If you live in their area, give them a call!

PRESCHOOL AND READING

CHAPTER FIFTEEN

PRESCHOOL AT HOME: THE SEEDBED OF GENIUS

See Dick run! Happy, happy Dick. Dick is at home. See Dick play. See Dick do things with Mom. Dick can do his ABC! Dick can count . . . one, two, three! See Dad bounce Dick on his knee! Glad Dad! Glad Mom! Glad Dick!

See Dick sit! Dick is at preschool. Work, Dick, work! No Mom. No Dad. Just Dick and Teacher and twenty other kids. No free time for Dick. No time to think and think. No tastes of cookie batter. No time for lots of questions. Keep it up for fourteen years, Dick!

I've read one or two articles about the lengths to which yuppie parents go in order to get their child into the "right" preschool, and it constantly amazes me that smart people don't realize that they can do a better job of turning out little geniuses at home! Parents fight and claw to get Junior into Ye Snobbe Childe Academy, and are devastated if Junior doesn't pass the stiff admission test (at age three, yet!). Actually, the only reason Ye Snobbe enjoys such a good reputation is that they are careful to take *only* children who would succeed no matter *where* they are taught. It takes no talent to teach Mozart music, or Rembrandt painting. The test of a good preschool program is its ability to succeed with kids who *aren't* in the 99th percentile already.

It just so happens that I know of a dynamite preschool with a one-to-one teacher/student ratio. The teachers truly love the students, and even spend their own money on classroom supplies. What is even more rare, the students truly love the teachers and were born wanting to please them! Better yet, this school accepts *any* child, even the most severely handicapped, and charges nothing whatsoever for its twenty-four-hour services. Naturally, I'm talking about your own home.

I'm not going to say that your home is as good a learning environment as the preschool: that would be a lie. Your home is a *better* teaching environment than any preschool! Learning to speak is harder than learning to read, and you've already taught your child to speak. Potty training is harder than learning to write, and I've never heard of a child whose parents didn't manage somehow to potty train him. Even without any help, you'd probably do a good job of teaching your children if you just put your native ingenuity to work. But with the access to tools and books and techniques that this book gives you, watch out! Another genius will be born!

It turns out, you see, that the greatest predictor of genius, the factor that shows up most often in case studies of geniuses, is the *large* amount of time they spent with adults and the *small* amount they spent with agemates. Of course, this refers to adults who *actively* spend time with their children. Plopping in front of the TV with your baby in your lap may be cozy, but it's not very instructive. But when children spend a lot of time helping adults, watching adults, talking to adults, going where they go and seeing what they see, those children grow intellectually by leaps and bounds. One would *expect* this to be so, since by an early immersion in the adult world, including the world of adult thoughts and language, these fortunate children are getting the raw data that will prepare them for *real* thinking about the things grownup people *really* think and talk about. Children isolated in a special little peer group of their own, on the other hand, are deprived of this exposure to adult thinking and ideas. They are being encouraged to *remain* childish and to function only in the artificial setting of the age-segregated group, a setting they will never again encounter outside of school.

It's easy to show that preschool at home is academically superior. So why don't more people do it? Actually, more and more people *are* doing it. But, academics aside, there is one big reason that out-of-home preschool is so fashionable at the moment, and that's the careerist movement. If it weren't bad enough that the men of America have been persuaded that their destiny lies in becoming corporation employees, rather than in striving to build up their own businesses, this same line has been handed to the women, too. If neither Dad nor Mom will stay home with Junior, then Junior gets zooped off to day-care or preschool.

What makes two-parent careerism even sillier is that Mom and Dad knock themselves out paying for the *best* preschool, at stiff rates, to be followed perhaps by years of expensive private school and years of outrageously expensive college, when they could be providing a far better education, without guilt, if only one or both of them would consider working at home.

When you teach your own, the more you have, the more you save! I've calculated that it takes $3 earned to save $1 spent, counting in taxes, donations, extra cars, office clothes, and other business expenses. So if you give one child the equivalent of $5,000/year education, it's like earning $15,000 a year. If you have two, you're making $30,000. Think about it!

Following is the information you need to assess the different methods of preschool instruction and to choose good products for your seedbed of genius.

PLAYERS, WATCHERS, AND TEACHERS

Early childhood education today is divided into three camps: the Players, the Watchers, and the Teachers. The Teachers believe that children need to be lectured and workbooked and activitied, in short *taught*, in order to learn anything significant. These are the people who had us wave our little arms in the breeze and pretend to be flowers when we were too young to defend ourselves. As Dorothy Canfield Fisher so perceptively remarked in her book on teaching Montessori at home, this "kindergarten" model has the teacher as the center of attention, with the children grouped around her.

Watchers, following Maria Montessori, believe in providing structured experiences for children, but also in letting the children discover on their own within that framework as much as possible. Thus a Montessori teacher will prepare a room filled with cleverly-designed material, such as lacing frames and graduated blocks, and hope that the children will use the material "properly"—e.g., for lacing and discovering number concepts, rather than for tying to a chair or building castles. This description is somewhat unfair to some Montessori teachers, who belong in the category of Players, but I believe is true to the approach of Montessori herself. Watchers do not intend to provide the child with total freedom—he must follow a predetermined path.

Players, the last category, let kids be kids. It's O.K. with them if their kids build sand castles, or throw sand in the air, or roll around in it, rather than industriously stamping out numerals with clever sand molds. When Junior builds a tower with his Cuisenaire rods, they compliment him on it. They let Sally scribble with her new crayons instead of anxiously showing her how to trace stencils. Their children only have to color inside the lines if they feel like it, and if they want to color Peter Rabbit green, that's great.

You will find precious few Players in the halls of academe, and only slightly more Watchers. All the hype is on for Teaching.

Miles of forest are being felled to produce propaganda asserting that children can only fulfill their potential if they are snatched from the very breast and plunked down behind a desk somewhere. This plan is very convenient for the hordes of eager young would-be Teachers who have been lured into selecting Early Childhood Education as their major, but in my view it is disastrous to children. Why? Because if the brain really does function in the way postulated in the opening chapters of this book, playing *is* learning, or at least the essential precursor of learning. Without raw data to chew over and digest—without a chance to become familiar with ideas and objects before being taught rules—learning difficulties multiply. The earlier the hopeful champions of early childhood education get their hands on our children, the better the chances that your son or daughter will be labeled "dyslexic" or "learning disabled" or, for heaven's sake, "hyperactive." *All* young children are dyslexic when first learning to read, and no normal three-year-old wants to sit for hours gazing at an adult's face. Force schooling down younger and younger children's throats, and soon they *all* will be labeled "learning disabled."

Childhood without any freedom is the pits.

Turning from this sorry scene, we discover that the home, in contrast to institutional settings, is an ideal environment for preschool learning. It's quite humorous to leaf through the catalogs of preschool and Montessori materials and see how many of them are copies of items found in any house. Play stoves, play pots and pans, little squares of different textures, trays for sorting little objects (remember Mama's button box?), dress-up clothes (what happened to raiding Mom and Dad's closet?) are just some of the products schools buy in an attempt to copy the home environment. Many more of the products you can easily make yourself, like beanbags and sandpaper letters. Some items nobody in her right mind would want, like parachutes for all those silly games where children have to follow shouted commands while they run to and fro holding on to an edge of the thing.

READINESS

Another major debate centers around "readiness." Do children just naturally become ready to learn certain skills, based on their own biological rhythms, or can the process be hurried along? Do children need particular training in perception in order to become ready to read and add, or not? Extreme views are held on this issue, with some contending that no child should receive any formal education whatever until the age of eight or ten, and others insisting equally vehemently that *every* skill would be improved by attacking it academically. Advocates of the latter theory are seriously suggesting that we start *teaching* children to speak, rather than our historical, haphazard (and effective) way of letting them learn by osmosis. The delayed formal education school is ably represented by Dr. Raymond Moore, and its opposite you probably know as the Superbaby movement.

I very rarely find myself in between two positions, but that's where I am in this case. If our children were all free to gambol about in flower-strewn meadows like Laura Ingalls, and if like her they had people handy who could bestow on them very rich oral teaching, then like her they would need no further preparation for formal study. If your children have ample opportunity to handle creation and you are able to enrich their minds orally, you can forget about reading readiness. Those of us, however, who live in more cramped quarters and who are not oral fountains of wisdom have good reason to teach our children to read as early as possible. Reading opens a window on the world which otherwise would be missing in my inner-city apartment. It never hurts to try a child on the ABC's or short vowel sounds. If he doesn't get it, drop it and come back to it in a month or so. Nothing could be simpler. Math is also fun for little kids, and science is a blast. If a child's natural environment is not very rich, I'm all for enriching it artificially . . . at home!

GOOD PRESCHOOL
MATERIALS FROM SCHOOL SUPPLIERS

The place to start with preschool supplies is the school supply people. These catalogs carry a huge variety of fun and clever learning tools. You can craft homemade versions of many of the products at home, and this is well to keep in mind when flipping through such a catalog. We have, for example, made our own jumbo-size flannelboard and our own beanbags. I collected the tops of gallon milk jugs to use for arithmetic counters and game markers, and the styrofoam trays meat comes packed in to serve as collage trays. Large disposable diaper boxes make excellent puppet theatres. Ingenious woodworkers can make jigsaw puzzles, beanbag targets, and building blocks (well sanded, of course!). Ingenious seamstresses can save fabric scraps to make their own doll clothes, stuffed puppets, and felt figures. Virtually any arithmetic manipulative can be made at home with the right tools. You can make a bug house out of an empty peanut butter jar with holes drilled in the lid. You can make your own play-dough (both *The Home School Manual* and *Home Grown Kids* have recipes). If fingerpaint you must, you can even make your own fingerpaint.

I am not suggesting that you should get a school supply catalog or two merely to give you ideas for homemade learning tools, though. These catalogs also contain an array of items you can't make at home, and that you probably won't want to do without. Let me tell you about some of them:

Write-on, wipe-off workbooks. These are colorful, lots of fun, and can be passed down through a dozen kids if properly cared for. The price is minimal, under $3 as of this writing, and they are great practice motivators. TREND makes the best ones. We have used all of theirs, but especially recommend the prehandwriting, manuscript, cursive, and numeral books. Of these, the prehandwriting book, which helps kids practice their loops, curves, and angles in a fun way, is for us practically indispensable.

TREND also makes a dazzling array of stickers, scented and unscented, for those of you who are into this form of approval.

Regular workbooks. The school supply workbooks cover the same subjects as ordinary school workbooks, with one important difference: they are fun. The more our public schools adopt the religion of humanism, the more sombre and preachy their required materials become. Supplemental workbooks seem so far to have escaped this curse. We like *Frank Schaeffer's* series. They are clear and uncluttered, and the activities appeal to little kids. Starting at grade 2, the workbooks begin to feature witches and other unseemly characters. This is my only quarrel with them. Frank Schaeffer (not to be confused with the Christian activist Franky Schaeffer) uses a phonics approach which is at least as good as the one the fancy textbook suppliers come up with, and his products are not nearly as boring or expensive.

Games and flashcards. These belong in the range of "I-could-make-it-myself-if-I-wanted-to-but-I-don't-have-the-time." *Milton Bradley* is king here. Their products are colorful and durable and not fussy. Flash cards go beyond $1+1=2$ nowadays; you can get geography flashcards, time-telling flashcards, traffic sign flashcards, alphabet flashcards, sight word flashcards, and on and on. And there is literally no skill that you can't practice with educational games: money games, biology games, geography games, and on and on. I have listed some of the most noteworthy independent game producers in the Toys and Games section, but you can also find shelves full of games at your local teacher supply store or in your handy school supply catalog.

Lauri's crepe rubber products. These are in a class by themselves. Quarter-inch thick textured crepe rubber is quiet and feels nifty; and *Lauri* uses it to make an abundance of colorful, inexpensive learning tools. I must confess that I have gone somewhat overboard here. We own the upper-case and lower-case alphabet puzzles, the numeral puzzle, the U.S. map puzzle, a multitextured fluffy bunny puzzle, the fraction discs, and a big just-for-fun train puzzle. We also bought the Beads 'n Baubles set, which is lots of differently colored shapes with holes in the middle that our little Sarah can string together. Lauri offers some very sensible items, like hexagonal crepe rubber counters that are quiet and don't roll about the room, and a crepe rubber version of Ring Toss, which likewise is quiet and won't wipe out your lamps if played indoors. For hands-on manipulation of letters and numerals, I don't think you can beat Lauri puzzles, and they cost far less than other store-bought products.

Special education materials. These books and tools, designed for use by older children with disabilities or who are academic late-bloomers, are fantastic for sharp little kids too! *Judy* makes a lot of hands-on stuff for special ed, engineered so even young and clumsy folk can handle it: stringing beads, color cubes, counters, abacus, peg boards, tangrams, parquetry, and last but not least, the famous Judy clock. This remarkably inexpensive piece of engineering has movable hands, working gears, and an "elapsed-time bezel." Of more concern to those who are immune to the charms of bezels, these clocks are *strong*. If you agree that little kids can learn to tell time better with a clock they can manipulate, you might want to invest in a Judy clock. Our young 'uns completely destroyed the Brand X clockface we brought home for them. Next time we'll know better!

More about special ed: the books designed for older readers who are having difficulties work just as well with little kids who are interested in adult things. These are called "hi-lo" readers, and with our national illiteracy they are proliferating. Ditto for workbooks. I see no reason why six-year-olds can't learn about world history or politics or marine biology, and the special ed materials can provide that kind of easy access.

Educational Insights has too many neat products to name. I have reviewed several outstanding ones in various places throughout this book. If it's fun, colorful, educational, and inexpensive, I'm not surprised if **Educational Insights** makes it.

This list is by no means exhaustive. Many other fine companies offer school supply products. Those above are my special favorites, whose products I have tried and tested.

For lists of school suppliers, see the chapter on School Supplies.

MONTESSORI SUPPLIES

Your next stop after the school supply catalogs should probably be the Montessori suppliers. If school supplies have more of an emphasis on play, Montessori supplies are decidedly structural. These supplies are excellent for children who have already had the chance to play with school concepts, and also good for very young children as long as the children are allowed to explore the materials freely before they settle down to working with them.

Montessori was an inventive and broad thinker, and her followers are alert to discover products that bring together concepts in a satisfying framework, as well as those that expose children to new ideas. The **Michael Olaf** catalog demonstrates this well. Under Music, for example, **Michael Olaf** sells a small harmonica for one-year-olds, an African slit drum for two-year-olds, a thumb piano and an assortment of children's music cassettes for three-year-olds, and at age four gets into a Great Composers series, a music history, a book about musical instruments, and books about ballet and theatre. Note the careful progression from hands-on music and listening to the "framework" books which begin to put it all together. This Montessori approach is excellent at home in every area, from foreign languages to geography to science to math to reading.

Michael Olaf has the most readable Montessori catalog. Items are listed under subject headings, like Music or Geography, and the catalog lists them in order of the suggested ages at which they might first be used. Each product is briefly described, but few are pictured.

Another Montessori supplier, **Montessori Services**, has an emphasis on the "practical life" Montessori materials. For the past nine years, **Montessori Services** has been providing these items and other supplementary materials to Montessori schools and teachers. As the business grew, these items began to be in demand for the home as well. **Montessori Services** specializes in child-sized tools for clean-up (brooms and mops, aprons, a carpet sweeper) and food preparation (apple slicers, vegetable peelers

and choppers, a juice squeezer, etc.), as well as items to help organize your child's environment (boxes and baskets). They also carry interesting selections in the areas of art, language and reading, and science and nature, plus books about the Montessori philosophy and a selection of Family Pastimes cooperative games. See also the review of several of the **Montessori Services** movement education products in the Physical Education chapter.

Lastly, the **Montessori World Educational Institute** has a catalog aimed at Montessori teachers. For instance, the catalog tells you how much it costs for a thousand Golden Beads, and assumes you know what Golden Beads are and for what they are used. This is the catalog for those who are mostly interested in the classical Montessori apparatus, since many of the materials Montessori invented are still handled by this company.

PRESCHOOL LEARNING
PACKETS AND CURRICULUM

If you want a total, structured, preschool program and don't mind spending over $60 to obtain it, you might want to turn to the Curriculum Buyers' Guide and investigate the schools that offer kindergartens and preschools. If not, you can construct your own program directly from school supply or homemade materials, or simply "wing it." For in-betweeners, I offer this listing of teacher's helps and one-book curricula.

Beacon Enterprises, Inc.
Pre-K Parent Kit (includes teacher training, teacher's manual, shape and puppet patterns, Animal Alphabet lace cards, pre-K tabletop flipchart, upper- and lower-case touch 'n feel cards, and Animals on Parade cassette), $106.10. Pre-K student materials, $16.90 each student.

A complete preschool for children from ages two to four that *includes all materials*—that's the Beacon Enterprises Animals on Parade program! It's fun and easy to follow. The Parent's Kit includes nifty things like touch-n-feel letter cards, patterns for puppets and other crafts, Beacon's Animal Alphabet pictures, a tabletop flipchart with teaching helps built in, the Animals on Parade cassette, a teacher's manual, animal stickers, and the Beacon Board (child-sized chalkboard with eraser). The student kit includes an activity book and Animal Alphabet book. The program was designed for four-year-olds, but is adaptable for threes and even twos with the easy adaptation chart. It covers one hundred and eighty days of instruction and is a full program, including prereading, math, discovery science, arts and crafts, and movement education.

Animals on Parade is very easy to use. Every day you follow the same master plan. First, arts 'n crafts 'n fun stuff. Next, alphabet training using the Self-Pronouncing Alphabet system (see Beacon's review in the Reading section). Following are blocks of time devoted to hands-on learning in all areas, social growth (for classroom programs), music, rhythm, movement education, and games. Doing similar activities at the same time each day builds up a rhythm that makes learning more fun and teaching less stressful.

Beacon has a reading/first grade program and an additional Bible program to follow Animals on Parade. Look for Beacon's listing in the Home Reading Programs and Bible chapters.

Carollie Company
Nutrition pack, $9.95 ppd. Alphabet patterns, $6.95 ppd. Monthly activitiy paks, $5.95 plus shipping or complete set of twelve for $63.50 ppd. *My Books,* all seven for $21.95 ppd. Mobiles $2.70 each.

Delightful activity packets geared to children ages two and a half and up include ministries, games, finger plays, arts and crafts, and other learning activities. They are sold as monthly packets or as a set. You can buy as many or as few as you wish. Consider these for summertime idea sparkers or an entire preschool program. Each packet includes twenty reproducible pages.

Carollie also sells *My Books,* which are books your own children create. Titles are: *Colors, Numbers, Shapes, Letters, Seasons, Rhymes,* and *Opposites.* They have a potpourri of other products, too many to mention here, including *Color Cut 'n Hang Mobiles* with seasonal themes, A-Z alphabet patterns, and a nutrition activity packet.

Carollie materials keep both parents and children busy. The parents are told how to make a wide variety of teaching aids, and the children are provided with lots of arts and crafts. Carollie's prices are not exorbitant, and the products are friendly and nonthreatening.

Creative Learning Services, Inc.
Preschool Workbook Program, $10 plus shipping.

All sorts of preschool materials: books, records and tapes, puzzles, and workbooks. Some materials are CLS's own, some are not.

CLS's Preschool Workbook Program has ten developmental workbooks, each 8½ x 11″ and 64 pages long. It includes a picture dictionary and a box of crayons.

CLS's books have a definite public school feel. Moms with careers, no-fault divorce, and behavior modification are among CLS's selection of topics.

Easy Education
Pre-School Mini Pack $49.95. Maxi-Pak $95.95. Shipping extra.

Easy Education is aptly named. Annemarie Zimmerman, its founder, has developed the easiest preschool program around. Covering prereading (including reading, writing, and sounding the alphabet), premath (the value and shape of numbers, writing numbers, and simple addition), telling time to the half hour, and geometric art projects that familiarize children with the concepts of shape and color, the entire program takes only fifteen minutes a day. That's the theory, anyway. In practice you'll likely find your children wanting to spend more time on the art projects.

You get an instruction book that lays out the program step by step, a preprimer, and a twenty-bead adder. The latter is a frame with twenty hardwood beads on a rod, and is used for early math concepts. Math is patterned and drilled; handwriting is ball and stick manuscript.

This is not a full program like some others, but it does cover the academic basics.

Easy Education also offers a reading program, a grade-school math booster kit, a grade-school reading booster kit, and a maxipak that includes all of these materials plus the preschool materials and a cassette of songs in other languages to help your child retain his natural ability to make non-English sounds.

Educational Book Distributors
Janan Curriculum, $15.95. Sing-along cassette to accompany it, $9.95 plus shipping.

EBD carries the materials of several smaller publishing firms. They have an assortment of preschool books. Prominent among these is the *Janan Curriculum.*

Billed as "A Pre-School/Kindergarten Teacher's Handbook," the *Jana Curriculum* is a big, beautiful book full of all the activities and ideas you need to put together a one- or two-year program for young children. The first fifty-seven pages are devoted to teaching tips and ideas on how to organize. It is all very well laid out and interspersed with charming graphics.

The *Jana Curriculum,* in spite of being written by a Southern Baptist, has a decided public school flavor. One-world government, feminism, divorce, and other similar themes are woven throughout the program. This makes *Janan* state-of-the-art as far as public educators are concerned, and is a hint of what we can expect from government-funded early childhood education.

Educational Insights
EI's Funthinker kits are a neat way to introduce little folks to shapes, color, the alphabet, numbers, and so on. Each kit comes in its own plastic carrying case and includes a write-on, wipe-off card or two, supplies like crayons and scissors, and activity suggestions. As the name suggests, these kits are a fun, unpressured way to approach new concepts.

Kimbo Educational
Kimbo has, as noted elsewhere, a huge assortment of music, filmstrips, and books for little people. From Raffi's *Singable Songs for the Very Young* to read-along cassette/book packs to all sorts of children's music and movement albums, Kimbo's got it. The catalog is attractive and easy to use. If you're looking for audiovisual materials to enrich your home, here's one place to start.

David S. Lake Publishers
Get Ready, Set, Grow! $8.95. *Learning Things* $10.95.

Lake's *Get Ready, Set, Grow!* is the least expensive one-year preschool curriculum I have seen. You have to supply all the materials, but many of them are items you already have around the house—pots and pans, catalogs, rice and measuring utensils, crayons, and so on. You get weekly (not daily) lesson plans, each with three Activity Units. These include such things as indoor play, art, music, homemade snack recipes that children can help make, Learning Times that get into science and drama, outdoor play, and storytime. The book is very attractive and easy to follow, and since the lesson plans are weekly you can easily flex them to fit your energy level, instead of getting the guilts for "not doing everything" on a given day.

Get Ready, Set, Grow! includes secular holiday activities (bunny for Easter, "Let's hide the matzoh" for Passover). At the end of the books you will find words (but not music) to the classic children's songs used in the program, as well as nursery rhymes, finger plays, circle dances, and a fine index to all activities, for those who want to look up the Playdough recipe or try the shopping mall trip on a week where it was not planned. The book is punched like a calendar so you can hang it on the wall. And it was designed for use not only by teachers, play groups, and day-care centers, but parents too! It makes a neat gift and can be used to supplement any other program you may be using.

In the same vein, Lake has another book titled *Learning Things: Games that Make Learning Fun for Children 3-8 Years Old.* The Lake catalog has all sorts of interesting arts and crafts for children of all ages. Look for these at your friendly neighborhood bookstore, or order them directly from the publisher.

Pecci Publications
Super Seatwork series. *Content Areas* and *Letter Recognition,* $7.95 each. *Color Words* and *Number Words,* $8.95 each. Shipping free on prepaid orders.

I was able to obtain review copies of all of Mary Pecci's *Super Seatwork* series, and glad I am of it. This series was designed in years of classroom teaching. Parts of it are correlated with Mary Pecci's reading method, which is reviewed in the Reading section. Other books in the series are for use in the classroom as seatwork to keep the children happy and occupied. But they aren't ordinary seatwork. They really *are* super!

Each book contains an immense variety of interesting activities, one per page. Some of the activities are standard classroom fare: drawing five balls, matching lower-case and upper-case letters. But most of the activities are really art projects, some of the most clever I've seen. For example: Using the *Color Words* book, so far my older son has constructed a log cabin, a covered wagon complete with horses and occupants, and a sled with two riders. His four-year-old brother has colored the *Mayflower* and colored and cut out a butterfly which even now reposes on his bedroom wall. You don't really need a 130-page book to teach color words, but you might, just possibly, be glad of a great rainy-day activity book or two with seasonal projects.

Content Areas has projects centering around associating words with pictures. The content areas are: parts of the body,

people, clothes, things in the home, things at school, animals, food, toys, occupations, tools, ways to travel, and holidays. *Number Words* and *Letter Recognition* are the most scholarly volumes, but even these have goodies like Alphabet Puzzles, Alphabet Tic-Tac-Toe, Number Word Puzzles, Color By Number, and more. The artwork is big, bold, and friendly. The activities are simple and fun. The books are real, bound, thick books, not chintzy workbooks. What more can we ask?

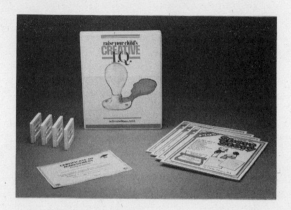

Perception Publications
IQ Booster Kit, $85, including four cassettes. Developing the Early Learner series alone, $19.80 for all four workbooks. Individual workbooks available separately.

Perception Publications' IQ Booster Kit is the one and only perception-training program that I have seen and liked. Drawing on her ten years as a classroom teacher, Simone Bibeau has produced a four-workbook series that exercises your child in these four areas: Motor (left-right tracking, mazes, eye movements, hand-eye coordination), Visual (similarities, memory, figure ground, space orientation), Auditory (similarities, memory, rhyming), and Comprehension (categories, sequence, language, awareness). This all sounds very complicated, but it's really not. The exercises are laid out in a carefully graduated sequence of fun activities. None of these require strain on your or your child's part. He practices drawing lines from here to there without running his lines into the "obstacles," he solves mazes, he colors the happy face if the birdies look alike and the sad face if they don't. For the auditory exercises, you might need to ding a spoon on a cup or thunk a book on the table while Junior listens with his eyes shut. Even this small effort can be removed by buying the accompanying cassette pak which has the auditory exercises on it.

We bought this series for our oldest son, who absolutely loved it. "When do I get to play 'Same and Different'?" he would ask. I could almost visibly see his mind sharpening up as he did the exercises. Let me mention that when the IQ Booster Kit has been tested, ninety-five percent of all children tested significantly increased their learning abilities by using the program.

The art is engaging, and since the books are all black and white your child can have the added fun of coloring them in. If your son or daughter is old enough to hold a crayon, you could start them on the first book of the series. By the time a child gets to book four, he is solving complicated mazes and figuring out the answers to questions like "House is to tent like glass is to—?"

Each book contains a diagnostic Progress Chart, and suggested exercises for testing and remedying perceptual handicaps.

Four cassettes come with the complete IQ Booster Kit. The first two share the program's educational philosophy and train you to use the Kit effectively. The last two contain the auditory exercises. We were able to use the books fine without them, but if you want the extra confidence (and the plastic carrying case), there they are.

Perception Publications

151 Fun Activities, $30. *Creative I.Q. Program,* $65.

Perception Publications must be having success with the I.Q. Booster Kit, because Simone Bibeau has just brought out two new products based on the same philosophy.

151 Fun Activities for Children is a two-tape set with accompanying manual and binder that gives parents an understanding of what it means to train in thinking and motor skills, plus 151 easy-to-do activities that develop those skills.

The *Creative IQ* program is a four-tape set with four accompanying "creative writing" workbooks, certificate of achievement, and binder. Simone explains on tape why creativity is vital to your child's success and the keys to developing a creative climate. She also discusses creative communications skills, creative writing and performing, creative problem-solving skills, and gives artistic activities for you to pursue.

I personally don't think it would be that much fun to fill out the workbook pages. Your student would end up doing an awful lot before he or she ever finished a story, since a lot of the work is prewriting exercises to generate ideas. What *would* work is to ask the workbook questions and either (a) tape your child's answers, (b) let Mom or Dad act as secretary and write down any answers you agree are important, or (c) just ask the questions and forget about writing the answers. You can describe the main character's appearance and character verbally before beginning to write, for example. It is not necessary to write down all these details in advance. It *is* good to learn to think like a writer, though, and going through these workbooks will definitely help your child do this.

Plough Publishing House

Songs books, $11.95 each. Hardbound. *Shepherd's Pipe* cassette, $4.95, choral book $2.50. All cassettes and records, a very reasonable $4.95 each, all choral books $2.50 each. Many other booklets and books. Add 10 percent for postage and handling.

Here's something different—poems and songs for young children from the Hutterian Brethren. Formed as a Christian commune generations ago in Germany, the Bruderhof share Mennonite values and practice pacifism.

Popular offerings: *Sing Through the Seasons* and *Sing Through the Day* are both gorgeous songbooks splashed freely with pictures that, as Lois Lenski remarked, reflect both "the beauty and guilelessness of childhood." These books are *large,* being 10¼ x 11"—just the size that little ones love—so big and important! Other books are available, as well as poems and Christmas celebrations, theology, and thoughts on education.

The Bruderhof also have records and cassettes to accompany their songbooks, as well as an original Christmas cantata called *The Shepherd's Pipe.* The singing is simple, direct, clear, and unforced. I realize that your preschooler is probably not into cantatas (though you never know!), but I did want to mention the Brethren's music somewhere in this book.

Sing, Spell, Read and Write

Workbooks for preschoolers, $7.50/set of two. Teacher Manual/Alpho Cards, $6.95. Level I workbooks, $7.50/set of two. Shipping 8 percent.

From the people who brought you the delightful *Sing, Spell, Read and Write* reading program come several sets of preschool and early school workbooks with a Raceway theme. *On Your Mark* and *Get Set* are readiness workbooks. *On Your Mark* has a pair of shoes pictured on its back cover, with punched-out holes and real shoelaces for practicing lacing. This workbook covers colors, shapes, visual discrimination, matching, opposites, classification, sequencing, and seasons. *Get Set* has a giant clock with turnable handles on the back cover, and includes letter shapes and sounds and recognizing beginning letters. *SSR & W* is in the process of redoing these workbooks with fancy new art. The accompanying Teacher's Guide is friendly and helpful, and includes readiness activities to go along with the workbook exercises.

You may want to skip readiness and go straight to the Level I workbooks. *Off We Go* starts right in with the letters. Each giant letter has a page to itself, and children also cut and paste, match letters, do dot to dot, and learn to write both capital and small letters in precursive. The book is simple, clean, and fun. The *Raceway Book,* also included in the Level I set, follows this up with words to write that correspond to each of the *SSR & W* storybooks, activities, and vocabulary and comprehension tests. The book is intended for first-graders, but once your preschool child finishes *Off We Go* I see no reason why he shouldn't tackle the *Raceway Book.*

Directions for doing the workbook exercises are printed on each page of the Level I workbooks. They're supereasy to use!

MAGAZINES FOR PRESCHOOLERS

You thought that magazines were only for people who could read? Not any more! The very babe in arms has his own magazine today, and we are not referring to the old issue of *National Geographic* his fond parents allow him to tear up.

Many entrepreneurial inventions aimed at young children are exploitative, and some kiddie magazines do fit into this category. For older children, we see this in the rock star-worshiping tabloids. Just because a magazine for young children claims to be "educational," we don't have to fall all over ourselves handing over our $10. Still, magazines are a good habit to get into. Unlike books, which I know from sad experience take months or even years to get together and put out, magazines can stay on top of new developments in a field. In practice, I have discovered that you can learn more about any new field by subscribing to a couple of trade magazines than by taking a college course.

Judge for yourself if it's worth the $10 or whatever, not only for the actual activities and knowledge contained in a kiddie magazine, but for the exposure to the world of printed ideas.

My Big Backyard
   $10/year (twelve issues).

National Wildlife Federation nature mag for the preschool set. Beautiful pictures, few words, large print, parent-initiated suggested activities. For more info, see the review under Nature Study.

Sesame Street
   $9.95/year (ten issues).

Establishment educational strategies sugarcoated with the Muppets. I am one of those who is less than enthusiastic about the behavior modification techniques and pressures that *Sesame Street* fosters. Lots of color, tons of activities.

Stork: The Magazine for Nursery Dwellers
   $9.97/year (eight issues), $17.97/two years.

A magazine, as the subtitle says, "for nursery dwellers." If there can be such a thing as a magazine for babies, *Stork* is it. Large, bright pictures, very few words, very simple activities. I like the magazine's unpressured style. *Stork* also unfortunately includes a "parenting" section for the grown-ups, with the usual infallible "expert" advice.

Stork is one of a series of magazines published by the Children's Better Health Institute, and reflects this concern with health. The others are *Turtle* for preschoolers, *Humpty Dumpty* for kindergarten, *Playmate* for first grade, *Jack & Jill* for second grade, *Child Life* for third grade, and *Children's Digest* for fourth grade. Subscriptions for each of these cost the same: $9.97/year.

CHAPTER SIXTEEN

THE NO-GIMMICKS, NEVER-FAILS, TEACH-YOUR-CHILD-TO-READ STRATEGY

Reading is like toilet training; until your little one does it, you're afraid he never will. Nothing brings out the paranoia in a modern father or mother like the fear that Johnny will grow up illiterate. And the corporate giants out there in the publishing field know it. Every year we get more and more offers in our mail for "reading programs" which are actually packages of regular kids' books that the publisher touts as supermotivators to get kids reading. The problem here is that, as willing as frightened parents are to clutch at straws and spend huge sums on cute little storybooks, children do not learn to read merely by having books thrown at them. Moreover, those who push these programs are careful not to encourage parents to teach their own children to read. The task is reserved to "real" teachers, and parents are shunted off to left field, there to act as coaches only. ("Hey, Jimmy, you can do it! Put some oomph into it! 'At's my boy!")

Why are modern parents scared silly about Jimmy's reading? The answer is simple. For several decades *the schools have been teaching reading all wrong!*[1] As a consequence, children who would have learned to read under a sensible reading program are now dubbed "learning disabled." The federal government goes along with the scam by giving all kinds of funds to school districts for "remedial" programs and "special education."

American literacy has declined from nearly 100 percent literacy in 1910 to its present sorry state directly *because* of bad teaching methods.[2] But those responsible for foisting bad methods on the public never take the blame. Instead, they blame the children. They invent dozens of "learning problems" that never existed in 1910, when we had almost 100 percent literacy, and don't exist now. They say our children are suffering from these nonexistent problems. They ruthlessly label children for life as stupid, and wash their hands and say, "That's why the schools

we control don't teach children to read." Then they turn around and demand we *reward* them! The more illiteracy the NEA bureaucrats produce, the louder they howl for more and more tax money for themselves, so they can pretend to "remediate" the problems they *caused!*

If I sound angry, it's only because I am. It is a national disgrace that we permit so-called experts to blame their failures on our children. If the reading program doesn't work in Soviet Russia, they demote the fellow who dreamed it up. If it doesn't work here in America, the man who invented it continues to be honored as a leader in the field, and the children whose academic future he blighted are told *they* are stupid.

In the Special Education section I discuss ways and means to uncrunch labeled children. For now, let's zero in on the nefarious reading method that caused our national epidemic of "learning disability."

Once upon a time there lived a man, a good man, a reformer, named Thomas Gallaudet. Mr. Gallaudet was concerned about deaf children. He wanted to help them learn to read. Deaf children could not sound out words like hearing children; so to get around that difficulty Mr. Gallaudet devised a method of picture-word association. The child would be shown a picture of a cat and the word *cat*. By memorizing the configuration of the word, the child could build up a very limited reading vocabulary. The reason his vocabulary would of necessity be limited is that so many words look like each other: bag and bay, ball and bell, play and ploy. As the child tried to memorize more and more words *by their appearance alone*, sooner or later his memory would give out. This method was, however, useful in its limited way and for its original audience.

As Kathryn Diehl, the author (with G. K. Hodenfield) of *Johnny STILL Can't Read—But You Can Teach Him at Home,* says, "Why it was ever decided that this would be an effective way to teach children who *can* hear and speak remains a mystery to this day." But that is exactly what happened! Since good readers read whole words, someone decided it was time to skip those silly phonics lessons and get right into "real" reading—sort of like skipping the swimming lessons and trying to swim the English Channel.

The nefarious "look-say" method whereby normal children are taught to read "whole words" by memorizing their configuration a la Gallaudet rather than by sounding out the component parts is the real reason why today's children are such poor readers. At this point, entire publishing empires have been built on supplying the hundreds of little vocabulary-controlled readers and millions of consumable workbooks that look-say requires. More than a few inflated reputations are at stake, not to mention big bucks in remedial education programs and years and years of employment for reading teachers, as reading instruction now continues beyond the elementary level, yea even unto college itself. These entrenched interests aren't about to let the look-say goose that is laying them such big fat golden eggs get killed without a struggle.[3] That is the real reason for our reading crisis. Until we dump look-say and get back to the old phonics method that required no more supplies than a blackboard, chalk, and a few library books, no amount of political thundering will help.

Discouraged? Don't be. In the privacy of your home you can short-circuit the system. I am delighted to announce that there are literally dozens of home reading programs that really work. If you have "teaching blood," there are some excellent books on the whys and hows of teaching reading. If you haven't a teaching bone in your body, several methods "have the teacher on the record" or tell you everything you have to say. Prices range from a few measly shekels to over $200 for a *complete* language arts program that includes all your child could ever hope to learn in this area from the best private school in the country.

First we'll look at the process of teaching reading, then at the programs, and finally at some organizations that purport to help would-be teachers of reading.

HOW TO TEACH READING

I was tempted to churn out a long dissertation on the subject of how to teach reading. But why reinvent the wheel? The following books will make you a reading expert. I strongly suggest that you buy or borrow them if you feel any compassion for the plight of the labeled and abandoned reading failures of our school system. Once you have learned to teach reading, you can make a tidy income as a tutor, or simply go into it as a service to the community. *Your* children, grandchildren, nieces, and nephews can be rescued from the Reading Trap!

A comment before you begin learning from those whose success proves them to be genuine experts: Kids need to be read to and to see lots of different sorts of print to build up a picture of reading in their minds, which the reading method can then tie together. You may think you have no skill whatsoever as a teacher. If you read to your children, though, you are giving them the foundation without which even skilled teachers have difficulty succeeding.

To paraphrase the old rock 'n roll song, "You gotta scribble, babble, and hear" before you can write, talk and read. Children need to be read to in order to build up an understanding of what reading is. When Suzy snuggles up to you and begs for *The Cat in the Hat* for the hundredth time, she is not being a nuisance; she is requesting prereading instruction. Children who are read to learn that the little black squiggles on the page always say the same words. They discover the different story forms—adventure, mystery, fairy tale, poetry—and become aware of rhythm and rhyme. Our little ones were inventing their own stories almost as soon as they could talk. What a head start this is when it's time for them to write!

The more print of all sorts a child gets to see, the better his chances of understanding what's happening when the grown-ups decide it's time to teach him to read. Or, in the case of those laid-back folks who insist that children should initiate their own education, the more likely it is that Johnny will someday ask you to teach him to read. He will have imbibed the necessary data. When you give him the framework, it will not strain his little brain, but will fill in the answers to his own unspoken questions.

It is also important for children, if at all possible, to learn to write at the same time they learn to read. Because of a muscle weakness, our oldest son was not able to write when he learned to read. Teddy, being a very visually-oriented little chap, learned nonetheless. Joseph, on the other hand, kept switching his *b*'s and *d*'s around until he learned to write them himself. By feeling and manipulating letters, and ultimately writing them, children with the dreaded "dyslexic" tendency can learn to read as well as anyone else.

The framework you will use, of course, is intensive phonics. "Since 1911, there have been 124 studies that have compared the look-say approach with phonics programs. *Not one study showed the look-say approach to be superior.*"[4] To turn this statement backwards, *every study ever done has shown phonics to be superior.* The reason is simple. Phonics is a logical approach that helps kids organize their way of attacking new words. Once children have learned a few rules, the exceptions won't knock them for a loop. (In fact, even the "exceptions" have some phonetic elements. In *do, the,* and *said,* for example, these three common "sight" words are at least 50 percent phonetic, and the irregular sounds can be easily figured out from the sense of the sentence.) The look-say approach, in contrast, is *all* exceptions. Each and every word has to be memorized on its own, and there is no end to this task. No wonder children give up in despair!

One of the most exciting things about teaching phonics is the way it brings back hope to children who have been taught by the schools to consider themselves stupid. You need no gimmicks or frills to accomplish this miracle—just time-tested phonics.

One last comment: The very best thing you can do to improve your children's reading costs nothing at all. Unplug the TV.

RECOMMENDED PUBLISHERS AND BOOKS

Johnny STILL Can't Read—But You Can Teach Him at Home. $4.50.

Armed only with this book, I taught our oldest son to read before he turned four. Kathryn Diehl explains why you need to teach phonics and how to do it. The book is inexpensive and reusable. Drawback: The author's layout is somewhat confusing, alternating as it does between reading instruction and comments on the philosophy of reading. Nonetheless, those who themselves were taught phonics can have success with this book.

William Morrow and Co. *Writing Road to Reading.* $9.95.

Romalda Spaulding's *Writing Road to Reading* is a fantastic book. Going further than *Johnny STILL Can't Read*, Mrs. Spaulding lays out her logical system of teaching reading through "phonograms"—that is, the consonants, vowels, and letter combinations such as *oi, sh,* and *str* that make up our different English sounds. Her emphasis on teaching reading through writing is much needed, and the discussion of how to teach handwriting is invaluable.

Summit Christian Academy has a complete kindergarten program centered around this book.

Pecci Educational Publishers
At Last! A Reading Method for EVERY Child, $19.95 postpaid.

The third book I would really urge you to buy, if you are interested in understanding how to teach reading, is Mary Pecci's *At Last! A Reading Method for EVERY Child!* This book's strong points are: (1) the discussion of *all* known methods of teaching reading, and (2) Mary Pecci's method itself. She has trimmed the teaching of reading down to seven steps only (compare this with the so-called "Mastery Learning" method of over one hundred steps!).

Mary Pecci begins by teaching the alphabet *in order*, so children by looking at an alphabet strip can help themselves find the letter they need. She then teaches the consonants, divided into "good guys" who make a sound like their name and "tough guys" who change their sounds or don't sound like their name. Next the blends (*bl, br, scr,* etc.) and diagraphs (*ch, sh, th, wh*). Now, vowels, both short and long, followed by some "sight" phonemes (*ay, oo, er, tion,* etc.). That's it! The rest of the book shows how to teach this information by getting children to ask

"What's the family?" (at, cat, sat) and "What's the clue?" (teaching them to approach weird words like *do* and *friend* by connecting with the regular sounds in the word).

Children using Mary Pecci's method can use *any* written material, not just phonics readers, from early on. It is just a wonderfully organized, teacher-pleasing approach with which every reading teacher should be familiar.

Going the extra mile, Mary Pecci has also developed a Super Seatwork series with some really fun supplemental exercises for young learners. I especially like the build-'em projects, like the log cabin with furniture (all labeled by name). These reproducible books have soul, and are easy to use at home or school. Activities are seasonal, which means I had to snip a few pages of Halloween witches. They are all clever, motivating, and correlated with her reading method.

Even more, Mary Pecci has a book entitled *How to Discipline Your Class for Joyful Teaching*. Without brutish authoritarianism or wimpy wobbliness, teachers at home or school can learn how to encourage good learning behavior and control foolishness. The psychology is sound, not faddish, and the author's sweet attitude towards the foibles of hapless young learners shines through.

Macmillan Publishing Company chose Mary Pecci's reading book as a Teacher's Book Selection of the Month. Good going, Macmillan. Now may all teachers everywhere get going and buy it!

Research Publications
NEA: Trojan Horse, $11.45 postpaid.

Sam Blumenfeld doesn't write with a pen; he uses a switchblade! *NEA: Trojan Horse in American Education,* Blumenfeld's expose of the NEA, documents how this organization and its consorts have been the driving force behind our academic failure. Part Three of this book, "The War Against the Independent Mind," contains the most clearly written and documented explanation of *why,* although we have the means to cure illiteracy in our hands, Johnny still isn't allowed to read. Plus Part One unveils how we got into public education in the beginning, although American children were almost perfectly literate *before* compulsory attendance laws!

Blumenfeld, the author of several books on the literacy problem and of a very successful phonics instruction method called *Alphaphonics,* is a widely recognized expert on this subject. *NEA: Trojan Horse* brings all the strands together in a fast-paced, riveting package.

CHAPTER SEVENTEEN

HOME READING PROGRAMS

Although we are normally stay-at-home types, occasionally our family goes out to eat. When we do, we go to a smorgasbord restaurant. The beauty of smorgasbord is that you can select your dinner from a wide choice of tempting dishes. It can be difficult to decide which foods to taste and which to leave until the next time, but that's a problem we enjoy!

In the same way, you are about to browse through a smorgasbord of reading programs. Every one of them has been successful to a much greater extent than any of the most popular public school programs. Your problem is not to find a good program, but to choose the one that's best for you.

I have my favorites, of course. The reason I can't just tell you their names and leave it at that is that you may have different needs than I do. Some of us prefer to save money and do a lot of teaching ourselves. Others wouldn't even consider teaching reading without the help of explicit instructions or a recorded teacher. Some need only a bare description of how to teach phonics; others are looking for devices to motivate a child who has already failed with other methods. Some demand workbooks; others hate them. Some love smiley-face stickers and gold stars; others think those kind of rewards are demeaning.

Not all methods are designed for the same age group, either. *Professor Phonics*, for example, does not work well with very young children because of the small print and lack of pictorial excitement—although it has been very successful with children of first-grade age and older. Two of my favorite programs, *Play 'N Talk* and *Sing, Spell, Read and Write*, are obviously designed for younger children and may seem childish to your failing sixth grader (although if he can swallow his pride they will do him wonders).

Add to these differences the wide variety in price among the better reading programs, and you'll see that it's up to you to carefully decide what you want to pay for. Do you want music and games to reinforce learning? Are you looking for a complete language arts program or just a little help over a tough spot? Whatever you are looking for, it's out there waiting for you.

Ashley's Home Tutor Kits
$24.95 plus 10 percent postage for the Reading Kit

Ashley's Kits feature a programmed approach. Every last thing you do and say is spelled out for you. The Reading Kit consists of a 282-page *Reading Textbook,* a cassette of all the letter sounds and examples of how to teach them, and a 118-page *Home Reader.* Both books are bound with two steel rings, which is very convenient when reading with a child on your lap. Print is a little larger than normal adult book size.

The only drawback is that there is no separate unit on beginning and ending blends.

The Kit is guaranteed to work and has in fact been successful with both adults and school-age children.

Beacon Enterprises. Beginning-to-Read Parent Kit, $176.95. Student materials, $69.80. Bible program, materials available separately.

Our English alphabet is a trifle mixed-up. Some letters have several sounds, and some sounds can be produced by several letter combinations. This is confusing to beginning readers, especially latebloomers.

Enter the *Self Pronouncing Alphabet* (S.P.A. for short). Using a system of dots on the ten letters with first and second sounds (a-e-i-o-u-y-w-c-g-x), the English alphabet is remade into a mostly one-on-one sound-symbol system using thirty-six basic sounds. Silent letters are also indicated. Children are taught to read with the modified letters, a relatively simple process, and are soon transitioned into the standard twenty-six letter alphabet through writing and spelling activities and reading standard English. The complete S.P.A. system not only features the "modified" reading alphabet, but includes a thirty-six letter "animal" alphabet (both upper and lower case) for introducing the sounds—e.g., Ape-A, Albatross-A; Bear-B, etc. with catchy jingles to reinforce the sounds.

The S.P.A. Reading System comes in three basic levels: Pre-K (2, 3, and 4 years, reviewed in the Preschool chapter), Beginning-To-Read (5, 6 and 7 years), and Remedial (8 years and up). All programs include training in basic language skills, manuscript writing, music, games, art, physical developmental activities, and stories, flash cards, preprimers and primers in the "notated" alphabet. A Bible program in the S.P.A. script is also available, whereby beginning readers get into the *King James Version* Gospel of John.

All of this is fun for the student and rewarding for the teacher. Note: some students may have trouble making the transition to the standard alphabet, especially if they are not given enough practice. S.P.A. has worked well with students for whom traditional phonics has proved too complicated.

Intended for classroom use, the program is also packaged for home teaching. Felice McGowan, editor of the *Stay-Homish Trading Post* (see the review in Chapter 7) recommends it highly.

Creation's Child

Teacher's Manual, $10.95—115 pages in the second edition. Alphabet picture cards: 3 x 5″, $3; 4½ x 7½″, $5.50. $2.50 shipping.

This program's beginning phonics are based on Bible words, and includes Bible verses, rhymes, sound jingles, definitions, Bible memory verses, hand motions, and art and science activity ideas for each letter. Children learn the letters A-Z and their sounds, and how to decode simple three-letter words. The program also includes alphabetical lists for Bible animals, foods, plants, alphabet songs, and an alphabetical Bible word list. The program is complete in itself, but some people use its Biblical content to supplement other phonics programs.

You cut out and color the flash cards yourself. Small ones are printed four to the page; large ones are two to the page.

Other course components are available: a cassette tape, notebook pages, and phonics games.

Eagle Forum Education Fund

Headstart Reading Course #1, $26 (includes *Phonics Workbook A,* teacher's edition of same, and *McGuffey's First Reader*). *Headstart Reading Course #2* includes *Phonics Workbooks B* and *C* plus teacher's editions and *McGuffey's Second Reader:* $46.

Phyllis Schlafly taught her children to read at home and thinks you can do it, too! Eagle Forum, the profamily volunteer group Phyllis founded, made this its first educational project.

Workbooks are the time-tested *Hay-Wingo-Hletko Lippincott Phonics Workbooks* and are the same intensive phonics system Phyllis used with her own children. Phyllis' method was to teach reading to five- or six-year-old Schlaflys at home, and then enroll them at age six directly in second grade. All have gone on to do outstanding academic work. Phyllis believes that any child who can't read anything he or she wants by midyear of the first grade has been cheated and should transfer to an intensive phonics-first system such as this one.

Eastern Mennonite Publications

$89.25, entire program. Components available separately.

As you may have guessed from the name, this is not your average secular phonics course. Consisting of pupil workbooks, worksheets, teacher guides, a word practice book, a Bible story reader, flash cards, and posters, the series is designed to lead into the Rod and Staff Bible Nurture and Reading series. Intended for classroom use, the total program is rather expensive. You can, however, economize by leaving out wall cards and some of the seatwork.

I haven't seen the program, which is billed as "A Phonics Reading Course for First Grade," but I have seen the Rod and Staff material which is to follow and can attest that children have to really have their reading down pat to tackle it.

You can order a sample packet, which is free if returned unharmed within thirty days. You pay the shipping.

Easy Reading Kit

Kit, $17.50. California residents add $1.05 tax.

This very simple method is designed for teaching young children of ages five to eight how to read. You get easy instructions on how to use the Kit, four packets of nicely-done flash cards, an Achievement Chart, and sheets of shiny stars. Children first learn the sounds of the consonants, including the "soft" sounds of *c* and *g,* then the vowels (both long and short), vowel and vowel-consonant blends such as *ar, ea,* and *oy,* and consonant blends (including diagraphs). There are flash cards for each grouping, printed on colored card stock with professional *large* type and drawings. Examples of words using the phoneme in question are included on the cards, as are irregular sounds of that phoneme. As the child learns a sound, he gets to place a star on the chart in the appropriate space.

The Kit also includes lists of irregular sounds such as *tion* and *ould* and *pn,* a list of silent letters (like the *b* in "lamb" and the *t* in "hasten"), plus a list of the more common prefixes *with* their meanings and sounds.

Intended as an introduction to reading and spelling, Leora Stanfield's Kit certainly gives you value for money. The flash cards are appealing, the instructions are clear and uncomplicated, and the Achievement Chart is motivating. The publisher herself supplies the only caveat: the Easy Reading Kit is not a *complete* phonetic program. However, with your explaining a few words such as "of," "was," "come," and so on, which can't be sounded out 100 percent phonetically, your kindergartner can be reading at a first grade level in six or seven months.

Educational Insights.

Course with records and one workbook, $17.95. With cassettes, $22.50. Extra workbooks, $2.95 each. Course with records and ten workbooks, $39.50. With cassettes and ten workbooks, $42.50. *Apprendiendo a Leer* for ESL Classes, cassettes and one workbook, $24.95.

I really like just about everything Educational Insights produces, and their *Hear-See-Say Phonics Course* is no exception. Designed for classroom or home use, the *Course* comes with three records or cassettes and a pupil workbook. Classroom teachers can buy the *Course* with a set of ten workbooks, or buy extra workbooks individually. The *Course* is also available in a version called *Aprendiendo a Leer* for ESL classes, with introduction in Spanish and the sounds in English.

Here is how it works: Instructions for the entire program are on the record (or cassette). A young female teacher gives the instructions, and your learner answers along with the recorded "alpha kids." Once you have gone through the record with him, the learner can follow the program in his workbook all by himself. Beginning with the sounds of the alphabet, the *Course* progresses to digraphs, the common endings *ck* and *ing*, short and long vowels, diphthongs, and blends. The alpha kids answer very rapidly, so Junior might be hard pressed to keep up with them at first. However, the alpha kids' obvious competence acts as a spur—if they can do it, so can he! Periodic quizzes are integrated into the easy-to-use thirty-three-page workbook.

Hear-See-Say is not a complete phonics course. It does have charm and is *very* easy to use, since the teacher is on the record. Literally millions of kids have used the *Course* in schools and homes. It is recommended to beginning readers ages five to seven, or as remedial practice for ages eight to eleven.

Kerr Publishing Company

Sound Links kit, $35 postpaid.

Sound Links is billed as the "You Can Teach Anyone to Read" program. It's a book and kit combination designed to teach *anyone* between two and a half through adult how to read. Using a different picture to represent each English sound, Sound Links is phonics with rebuses: visual phonics with look-say picture clues.

According to the brochure, when the author, Leo Kerr, tested Sound Links with five hundred children in 1978-80 under a Title IV-C federal grant, Sound Links students "achieved twice the growth when compared to students using other reading methods." Leo Kerr also informs me that *Sound Links* has been successfully used with students of all ability levels, including mentally and emotionally handicapped and ESL classes.

The Kit includes an easy to understand teaching and learning text, flash cards, fun pages for practicing skills, a 1200-word illustrated resource list for beginners, and two chalkboards with chalk; so you'll be getting your money's worth.

Life for Little Learners

LLL offers a *correspondence program* of four phonics workbooks. The complete package is a total language arts program, including such things as syllabication, contractions, suffixes, prefixes, and the uses of the apostrophe. It can be used to supplement another program or all by itself. According to the brochure, if your learner works six pages a day he will be reading independently in ten months. The only supervision required is that you read the instructions and give directions where necessary. LLL grades all the lessons and sends rewards periodically as a recognition of your learner's achievements.

LLL has other home schooling materials, reviewed elsewhere in this book.

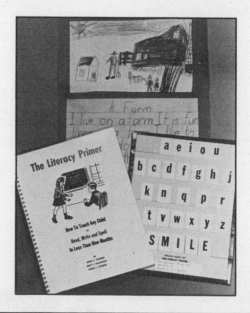

The Literacy Press, Inc.

Complete package, $35. $1.50 postage, forgiven on prepaid orders. Components available separately. Quantity discounts.

This small mail-order firm has an offer that's hard to beat: if, after trying their reading program with your most difficult pupil, you aren't satisfied that it's the best method you've seen, "return the USED BOOK with the shipping label for a full refund." The kit is designed, in the publisher's words, to "Teach Any Child to Read, Write, and Spell in Less Than Nine Months." Used as directed, children will read independently in eight to ten weeks, and be writing well-spelled compositions at the end of nine months.

How does it work? You get a *Literacy Primer,* which contains the lessons (in large type) and teacher's notes (in small type). The *Primer* is reusable, since children finger trace and say the letters in the book, writing them on separate paper (provided in the Spelling Kit) or a chalkboard. The trace-and-say method is supplemented with a Spelling Board Kit, consisting of a sturdy cardboard frame with accordion pockets into which single letters are placed to spell out words. The many kinesthetic drills using tracing and the Spelling Board reinforce reading concepts, and are a great help for those children who the schools like to label "learning disabled." Moreover, using the Spelling Board Kit, children can spell all the words they can read even *before* they learn to write. This is a feature not found elsewhere. (You can buy the Spelling Board separately.)

The Teacher's Supplement, also provided, is a minicourse in how to teach reading, spelling, and composition skills. Classroom teachers will find the teaching tips absolutely invaluable. These include time-tested motivational ideas and helps for getting problem pupils over the "humps."

And then there are the accompanying *Homestead Readers.* These delightful little books (*Jon and Jim on the Homestead, Homestead School,* and *Jon and Jim Discover Alternate Energy)* include drawing activities and questions for the children to show their comprehension of the story. Very thoughtfully, the writers have provided an appendix of simplified line drawings for this purpose. These drawings, like the rest of the art, are rather amateurish: not gorgeous, but acceptable.

In *Homestead School,* each story describes how to do some pioneer activity, like making soap. In *Alternate Energy,* you guessed it, the stories tell about alternate energy sources. Stories contain some Christian emphasis—hearken, Christian schoolteachers!

Quibbles: Writing taught is ball-and-stick manuscript rather than the more useful precursive, and the type in the *Readers,* although large, is not the easiest to read, being sans-serif with evenly spaced letters. You can overcome quibble #1 by simply using precursive strokes for the same letter shapes.

The people at Literacy Press have a lovely attitude, as this quote shows: "We do not feel that others who are promoting LITERACY are our competitors. The need is wide." Amen!

Play 'n Talk

Complete program, $210. Components no longer available separately. Budget plan; pay total sum with series of postdated checks. Please include credit card info.

Play 'n Talk is the Rolls Royce of reading programs. It has taken me hundreds of hours of research to reach this conclusion, and I'll stand by it. Yes, *Play 'n Talk* is a sizeable investment, but it's worth it if you can possibly scrape up the cash. Here's why:

- *Play 'n Talk* is a *total* language arts program, containing every phonics rule and exception in the English language, plus instruction in manuscript writing, spelling, and even diction (thanks to the fine quality of the recordings).

- The teacher is on the record. You need only start your little one off with the slightest of assistance, and thereafter he can teach himself with the help of the records.

- *Play 'n Talk* is a classy program. Harpo Marx's son did the very genteel mood music. A Disney artist did the illustrations. The program itself comes from that used by the Isabelle Buckley School in Southern California, one of the top private schools in the nation. In over fifty years of operation, they have *never* had a reading failure for any child who enrolled before third-grade level.

- You get value for your money. Not only does *Play 'n Talk* include 217 recorded lessons, but also a linguistic color-coded typing program, a spelling "slide rule," a spelling bingo game, a set of three "Riddle 'n Rhyme" records with read-along books, and more. Literally everything you need (except paper and pencil) is included. In fact, *more* than you need is included. What other phonics program gets into touch-typing—so useful in our computer age?

- *Play 'n Talk* is time-tested. The program has been around, and outstandingly successful, for over twenty years. Think on this, ye who bemoan our national illiteracy. The solution has been in our own backyard the entire time.

- You get workshop tapes describing how to use *Play 'n Talk.*

- *Play 'n Talk* takes only two ten-minute periods each day for a few weeks to obtain visible results.

- The entire program is nonconsumable. That means that if you are careful with the records, not only your children but your grandchildren can all learn to read without spending a dime more than the initial investment.

The *Play 'n Talk* story is fascinating. Marie LeDoux, the designer-inventor of the contour chair and once the youngest female tycoon in the country, became aware of the reading problem because of some difficulties she was having with her top executives. She would send them memos, and instead of acting on her directions they would make mistakes. Inquiring into this, Mrs. LeDoux discovered the problem was that these very bright, university-credentialed young people had *never learned to read well!* Around the same time, Mrs. LeDoux became a Bible-believing Christian and retired from her financial enterprises to raise a family. It sounds a little nutty, but Mrs. LeDoux says she had a literal vision that led to the idea of *Play 'n Talk.* Mrs. LeDoux is a solid citizen, though, and after hearing her account of the vision and what happened thereafter (available on tape, by the way) I find it entirely plausible. Her story is tremendously interesting and inspiring.

Mrs. LeDoux has been a guest on over twelve hundred radio and TV shows, including Mike Douglas, David Frost, and many other major national programs. Play 'n Talk also did a series for ABC-TV in 1967.

How does *Play 'n Talk* work? You put the record on and turn to the correct place in the accompanying book. (There are four record series, each with its own book—twelve LP records in all. All are included.) The teacher on the record takes it from there. All instructions are on the record. A group of children do all the exercises right on the record. For some reason, that kids' chorus proves irresistible, and your child will want to join in with them. A perfectly delightful young lady with just a slight upper-class English accent did the narration. Mood music sets the stage throughout each lesson, and each lesson comes to a definite musical close.

A story line moves the program along. Your children meet the alphabet family and different word families. All the phonics groups are portrayed as people. For example: "Here are Mr. and Mrs. Digraph, and their children. WH is a fat one. He puffs out his name!" "Long Vowels wear straight hats. Short Vowels wear laughing hats. They turn up like the corners of our mouths do when we laugh." Little kids love it.

To give you an idea of how effective *Play 'n Talk* is, my youngest daughter was trying to join in on the *Sing 'n Sound* record, which teaches the alphabet through songs and with large flash cards. The little nipper was getting the idea, too. Sarah is one year old.

Older children (ages ten and up) may be put off at first by the sweetness of the lessons in the first two series and the youth of the kids' chorus. Even they can learn from *Play 'n Talk*, though; it's just a matter of swallowing their pride. (The *Play 'n Talk* Instructor's Guide outlines several clever ways to motivate older children.) Adults who never had real phonics instruction in school report learning right along with their kids!

You can now also get a *Play 'n Talk* video of Mrs. LeDoux teaching part of the program to a demonstration class.

Recognizing that $210 is a stiff chunk of cash for most families, *Play 'n Talk* will take postdated checks, allowing you to pay the entire price up front, yet only deduct a monthly amount from your actual checking account. Personally, I wouldn't flinch at the price, even if it meant eating beans for two months! When you look at all you get, the program could hardly cost any less. And when you stop to think that reading is the foundation for *all* academic achievement, and that *Play 'n Talk* costs less than *one* college course, it's a bargain.

Children *can* learn to read without *Play 'n Talk*, and parents who are confident of their teaching ability can do the job with materials that cost less. Still, I know of no other program that does almost all the work for you *and* covers all the necessary skills.

Play 'n Talk has been used in tens of thousands of homes and thousands of schools. All *Play 'n Talk* items are approved under all Federal Fund Titles NESEA.

St. Ursula Academy
Professor Phonics program, $14.70. Components available separately.

A Sound Track to Reading, student's book $3.80, teacher's manual which includes student's book $4.80. $1.50 shipping; 10 percent shipping on orders over $23.

I ordered the *Professor Phonics* kit when our three-year-old seemed ready to read. To my dismay, the print was too small and the exercises too uninteresting to hold his attention. The program does work well for children six years of age or older, for whom it was designed.

You get a combined practice book/reader that contains a total intensive phonics program. The accompanying manual gives page-by-page instructions. Alphabet picture flash cards and a spelling and reading word list round out the package.

Marva Collins, a woman who has had phenomenal success in teaching inner-city minority children, recommends *Professor Phonics* highly as being "one of the simplest methods of teaching children to read." That it certainly is. What it lacks in tinsel and pizazz *Professor Phonics* provides in simplicity.

Reading begins on the very first lesson page, as children learn the sounds of *m, s, t,* and *a* and immediately blend them into words. This immediate reading, and the association of pictures with the sound, differentiates *Professor Phonics* from the other systems.

You will notice that *Professor Phonics* is the least-expensive total phonics program around.

Monica Foltzer, the program's author, has also produced something that every reading instructor should be aware of: an incredibly inexpensive advanced phonics program for the older student. It goes by the name *A Sound Track to Reading* and is deliberately adult in its approach. Quickly reviewing (or, in the case of foreign students, introducing) the basic sounds, *Sound Track* swiftly moves to words and sentences. By the simple device of adding a few common endings like *ing* and *ed* to root words, which older readers can easily learn to do, babyish vocabulary is eliminated from the start. Now where else can you get all this for under $7?

Sing, Spell, Read and Write
Complete Home Kit including one set of Level I workbooks, $89. Additional workbooks, $7.50 for a set of two.

Preschool workbooks, $7.50 for a set of two. Level II workbooks, $7.50/set of two. Level III, $7.50/set of two. Extra set of seventeen *Storybook Readers,* $29.10. Sing-along videotapes, $24.95. Shipping, 8 percent. Make checks payable to CBN University.

Here is another program I really enjoy. *Sing, Spell, Read and Write* is a total language arts program for grades K-3 including—what else?—singing, spelling, reading, and writing!

SSR & W comes in the most exciting package I have seen. Upon opening the outer box, your child finds a teacher's manual, two student workbooks, and a treasure-chest made of sturdy cardboard. Opening the chest he finds:

- Six color-coded song cassettes.

- Seventeen colorful phonics readers.

- Several reading and spelling games, including Bingo chips and colored cards.

- A bag of fifty little prizes.

- A tiny magnetic car.

- And, a large, colorful Raceway chart that you can stick on your refrigerator. The little car is placed on the step your child has just completed. After two laps he has learned it all!

The impact of unwrapping all that is immense. It's like Christmas in July! (Hint to grandparents: *SSR & W* makes an impressive and useful gift!) It made *me* wish I could learn to read all over again!

SSR & W teaches precursive script (one point in its favor) and acquaints children with *both* the printed and type alphabet symbols (another good point). I am not aware of any other program that does both these things. The workbooks are delightful—just enough exercises, not overdone, and a lot of fun reinforcement. The games are likewise delightful. And what kid could resist a chance to win *fifty* prizes?

The songs, which are intended to teach such things as the alphabet, short and long vowel sounds, and digraphs and dipthongs, have catchy lyrics and nice tunes. They are sung by children with professional orchestration. The little phonics

readers are cute stories about various children, pets, talking bears and bugs, and so on. I liked their strong family emphasis.

You have to do a lot of teaching with *SSR & W.* But the teaching is fun. And there are only thirty-six steps!

To make *SSR & W* more self-instructional, purchase the VHS or BETA videotapes. These include twelve songs and activities for your children to do along with the children on the tape.

If you can't get the videos, I'd suggest that you get *SSR & W* with records rather than cassette tapes. This way your child can replay individual songs without the hassle of rewinding and finding the right spot, and he can repeat the entire record again and again until it drives you crazy and he has learned it thoroughly.

You can get a preschool workbook for younger children. More advanced workbooks are also available. Level III workbooks cover English language and grammar up to grade 8. These workbooks are not included in the basic Home Kit; order separately.

As enticing as the brochure is, it doesn't do the program justice. In real life the contents are much more colorful and exciting than they appear on the brochure picture. (It's better this way than the other way around!)

SSR & W is the *ideal* supplementary reading program. The activities, games, and songs reinforce phonics lessons learned elsewhere. To my mind, the perfect phonics program would be *Play 'n Talk* for basic instruction, and *SSR & W* for reinforcement. By combining both programs, you get the benefit of *Play 'n Talk* self-instructional teaching and patterned drills, and *Sing, Spell, Read and Write* would supply the phonics readers, songs, activities, and extra games. I honestly don't see how you could miss with this combination. Both programs are almost totally nonconsumable, and together they would be a lifetime investment in your children's future.

SSR & W is also a good program on its own, although it is not self-instructional like *Play 'n Talk.* In its price class, you can't beat *Sing, Spell, Read and Write.*

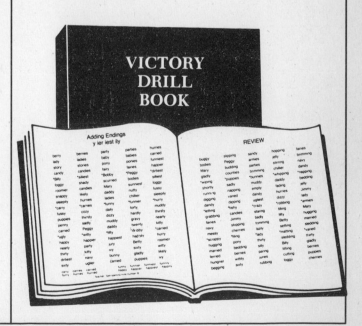

Victory Drill Book
   VDB, $8.25. Teacher's guide, $7. Cassette tape, $5.25. Worksheets and learning activities, $11.75. Predrill book, $3. Shipping, $5 on orders under $30. Total program, $35.25 postpaid. Quantity discounts.

   Every household should have a copy of the *Victory Drill Book*. I'll tell you why in a minute. First, let's look at the total Victory Drill program.

   You get the *VDB*, a teacher's guide, a cassette tape of the phonetic sounds along with teaching tips, worksheets, and a predrill book that teaches short vowels and consonants and how to write a ball-and-stick alphabet. The heart of the program is the *Victory Drill Book* itself. This very attractive hardbound book consists of word lists and sentences. There are no stories or pictures, except for the initial alphabet pictures at the beginning of the *VDB*. Students learn the phonetic sounds and then practice their skills with *timed drills* on the word pages. After achieving the speed considered necessary for his age level, the student goes on to the next phonetic combinations and the next page. After finishing the *VDB* the first time, he can freely read anything he wants. The publishers recommend that students go through the *VDB* a total of three times to ensure that total mastery has taken place.

   Why should every family have its own copy of the *VDB*? Because with the exception of Samuel Blumenfeld's *Alphaphonics*, which I can no longer find anywhere, this is the only book to drill and review all the reading skills with no distractions. No matter what phonics program you use, it will pay your youngsters to run through the *VDB* once or twice. You'll

catch any weaknesses in their reading before they develop into serious problems. The hardbound book is durable enough to hand on to your great-grandchildren, should God so bless you. For the price, this is an investment you shouldn't miss.

   The *VDB* was developed for Christian schools and includes prayers to God and references to preachers and church.

   What do I think of the total *VDB* program? It's definitely meant for serious students, lacking the frills of other systems. Well-disciplined children with a yen to read can certainly succeed with this method. Also, if you are looking for phonics worksheets, the *VDB* worksheets beat all others, in my opinion. The type is large enough for very young learners, there are just enough exercises to practice the concepts, and you do *not* get endless pages of pictures to "color if the object pictured begins with the letter *p*." The focus is on words, not illustrations, as it should be.

   The *VDB* emphasis on *timed* drill keeps you alert to where your learner actually is. At home, you can time drills just for the fun of it and avoid the invidious comparisons of the classroom.

   VDB also makes sure the *teacher* is able to teach phonics. Get the cassette tape if you are at all unsure of yourself in this area.

   To sum up: The *VDB* program is functional but not exciting. The worksheet packet, cassette tape, and *VDB* are valuable adjuncts to *any* phonics program. The approach is equally useful for older and younger students, not being the least bit cutesy. *VDB* does not include as much tactile input as some other programs, and this is a factor to consider if your child is a late-bloomer or shows signs of learning difficulties.

   VDB students have achieved outstanding scores on standardized tests. *VDB* is used all over the USA and in other countries.

CHAPTER EIGHTEEN

READING STUFF 'N NONSENSE

Stuff 'n nonsense! That's what this chapter is all about. I've put all my reading "leftovers" in this chapter—public and private school programs, reading accessories, and reading organizations. In every one of these categories you will find useful items ("stuff") and some that are frankly bogus ("nonsense"). The "stuff" is handy, and the "nonsense" is good for a few laughs.

SOME SCHOOL READING
PROGRAMS AND MATERIALS

Following is a selection of the best, worst, and weirdest public and private school reading programs. Neither you nor I have time to crank out and read reviews of every individual program, and it is in fact unnecessary, as all straight sight-word programs can be rejected out of hand, thus wiping out 90 percent of the contenders. Nor do we have the inclination to go into even the better programs in great depth, with a few exceptions, since most home programs beat the standard programs hands-down. The programs critiqued are either (1) used by a significant number of parents, (2) deserving of wider publicity in the school market, or (3) freaky enough to make interesting review copy. It's up to you to figure out which is which!

American Guidance Service

The Peabody Rebus Reading System is designed as an intro to sight-word systems, and you know what I think of those! You have to admire the cleverness of the people who thought this one up. Starting with rebuses—that is, pictures that symbolize whole words—the learner advances to reading stories told in rebuses. Eventually the real words are introduced in conjunction with the rebuses, and finally the real words take over. (Do not, by the way, confuse this with Kerr Publishing's Sound Links program, which uses *phonetic* rebuses.)

Students are given a little sponge in a colored plastic holder, with which they can test themselves. How do you test yourself with a sponge? AGS gives multiple-choice questions in the workbooks. To respond, the student wipes a wet eraser across the ribbed response area beneath the answer of his or her choice. If the answer is correct, the ink will turn green. If the wrong answer is selected, it will turn red. By using a cardboard answer mask, the same problems can be retested.

AGS says this program is especially helpful for handicapped students. It *will* accomplish the following:

• Students will learn to "read" left-to-right.

• They will learn to associate symbols with words.

• They will learn to associate concepts with whole words.

• They will learn to interpret information from printed symbols.

• They will learn the basic "readiness" skills, like following directions and distinguishing differences.

The rub comes, of course, when making the transition from rebuses to real words. No phonics is provided; thus a child who is a successful rebus reader can only learn the new words by sight. AGS gets around this difficulty by suggesting you use the Peabody Rebus program for *pre*reading instruction in place of whatever other program you were using to teach left/right, visual and auditory discrimination, and the other readiness topics.

Criticisms: The stories are colorful and interesting, and as an adult you can figure them out in ten minutes. However, one story has a flea father curing his air-sickness problems with "seven purple pills," and the continuing, repeated stress on how the pills make everything fine is insensitive, particularly in view of the huge drug abuse problem in the public schools. You absolutely must follow Peabody Rebus up with a strong phonics program if you hope to produce successful reading, and the children may have already learned the bad habit of guessing at words. As prereading instruction it certainly is a lot of fun, and as long as you stick to the rebuses only, "reading" success is certain. It is not *real* reading instruction, though, unless some smart cookies decide to translate a significant number of books into rebuses, for deaf people. And why don't they?

Distar

It always pleases us when we come across some folks in the public school market who are actually doing the very best job they can. SRA's *Reading Mastery: The Distar Reading Program,* and the schools that use it, are an example of this helpful spirit.

Based on a direct instruction model (hence the name *Distar*), the teacher's manual prompts the teacher to seek responses from the students while working with them in small groups. Everything the teacher must say is spelled out, which makes life easier for him. Example.

> [Point to m.] My turn. When I touch it, I'll say it. I'll keep on saying it as long as I touch it. mmmmmm [Pause. Point to m.] Your turn. When I touch it, you say it. Keep on saying it as long as I touch it. [Pause.] Get ready. [Touch m.] mmmmmmm. [Lift your finger.]

Instructions on how to correct mistakes are also spelled out. The *Teacher Presentation Book* also contains the graphics for the lessons: in this case, a large letter *m* to touch. This format *eliminates lesson planning!*

Distar also uses a modified English script. Letters that are frequently confused are printed with exaggerated differences rather than in standard type. This distinctive orthography is gradually faded out and standard English script introduced. One other feature I liked: the *Reading Mastery: Distar Reading*

Program contains *complete* stories and novels, not just excerpts. The Distar method has proved more successful than any other public school approach, but unhappily seems to be mainly used by poor and minority school districts and remedial reading departments. It will depress your soul to see the ugly, barren, concrete classrooms where Distar instruction takes place, as pictured in their catalog.

The course is not funsy and does require teacher initiation. However, it does have the merit of being approved by school districts, if any reader out there is a classroom teacher who would rather not save the good programs for "remediation" after all her students have failed with the standard ones.

Educators Publishing Service

Hurray for Educators Publishing Service! These helpful people have set up their catalog of language arts materials to do more than inform you what books are for what grade level. They have put a little "house" symbol beside items that are adaptable for home use. What a neat idea! It saves parents hours of struggling with catalog descriptions to figure out whether product X is usable in their home.

EPS carries more material about reading than I could ever hope to review in one listing. Of special interest: EPS has Orton-Gillingham-oriented materials specifically designed to help students diagnosed as having a language learning disability. Request their O-G materials list if you're interested. EPS also has a special Home Use Materials catalog for all their materials in the different subjects that are useful at home. This catalog includes the invaluable *Johnny STILL Can't Read. . . ,* reviewed above, plus Samuel Blumenfeld's well-liked book *How To Tutor.*

More goodies: EPS has a vocabulary-building Wordly Wise series. Unlike other alleged vocabulary-builders that I've seen, Wordly Wise is interesting, entertaining, and useful. Several major home school correspondence programs include it in their materials. EPS also has a number of reading games: Alphadeck, Rule-ette (for spelling rules), several bingo-style games, and Type-It, the linguistically-oriented touch-typing manual for beginners.

Regardless of which phonics program you choose (and EPS has several), you will probably want to get the EPS catalog for the sake of their hard-to-find-elsewhere games and other goodies.

J. B. Lippincott Co. (now a part of Scribner Educational)

Rudolph Flesch, the author of *Why Johnny Can't Read* and *Why Johnny Still Can't Read,* praises the Lippincott phonics readers highly. Phyllis Schlafly used their workbooks. Eagle Forum still sells those workbooks, and you know *they're* no bunch of fluffheads!

Open Court Publishing Company

Open Court offers phonics kits priced attractively for the classroom but expensively for the home. Some individual items, like flash cards and phonics records and cassettes, may be of interest. Their Real Phonics workbooks are inexpensive (under $4).

Science Research Associates (SRA)

Besides its *Reading Mastery: Distar Reading Program,* reviewed above, SRA also has a Corrective Reading program and a Fast Cycle program for accelerated students. All have demonstrated excellent results in the public schools where they were used. So why don't all school superintendents insist that their schools use SRA or Distar? Don't ask me—I don't even know why they don't use *Play 'n Talk!*

The Corrective Reading program begins by unconfusing the student. He is forced to decode lists of unrelated words (shades of *Victory Drill Book!*) in order to get across the idea that one does *not* read by guessing on the basis of story context. Once this idea is hammered home, an intensive phonics approach using "surprise" words (to prevent backsliding into guessing) and lots of stress on the commonly confused letters and words is wheeled into place. After students finish all three levels, they should be able to read one hundred and fifty words per minute with an accuracy rate of 99 percent—quite an improvement from total illiteracy!

SRA also has a Corrective Comprehension program to unconfuse fuzzy-minded or (more likely) ill-taught students about what on earth they are there to learn. Exercises in logic, categorizing, and following directions, as well as drill in classroom terminology, make up the meat of this program, which also has three units.

Fast Cycle is more of the same as *Reading Mastery: Distar,* only faster.

READING ACCESSORIES, THE GOOD AND THE WEIRD

This next section is the place to shop for accessories to your reading program. Some, like sandpaper letters and stencils, aren't strictly necessary with most children, although they are fun. And there are goodies such as fifty-cent workbooks as well.

Don't forget to also check out the Preschool section, as all the purveyors of Montessori equipment have reading and prereading accessories, as do most early childhood education suppliers.

Happy browsing!

DIDAX

DIDAX is the place for all sorts of nifty hands-on reading aids. Sandpaper letters, stencils, alphabet stamps, phonics activity cards, word-building puzzle cards, flip books, and reading games are all there in the pages of this fascinating color catalog. If your child learns by grabbing things and making lovely messes, he will profit from getting his mitts on some of this stuff.

Learning Systems Corporation

I am adamantly opposed to almost all phonics workbooks, as they are unhelpful, drawn-out exercises in tedium. Not so with Learning Systems Corporation's material. For one thing, the workbooks cost a measly fifty cents. Yes, you read that right! Five thin dimes will get you one of a wide selection of 20-page miniworkbooks. The workbooks are approximately 5 x 8" inches, in two colors, professional in appearance, and clever in execution.

Not only does LSC have workbooks for learning the alphabet and for practicing basic phonics skills, but also vocabulary-builders, books on syllabication, using the dictionary, punctuation, and a host of other necessary skills. Since the workbooks are so small, these skills are not overtaught.

LSC also has math materials, reviewed in the Math section.

"No-Name Press"

In keeping with my policy of not embarrassing companies by name whenever possible, I would now like to discuss a phonics workbook series that keeps turning up in home programs. Inaptly titled *Phonics Is Fun,* the series contains some of the most dreary exercises my children have ever suffered under. Page after page after weary page is loaded with thrillers like, "Color in the picture if the word ends with x." Older kids get to write the actual letter it ends or begins with, unscramble scrambled sentences, and churn out pages of similarly tedious exercises. Like Richard Mitchell, I abhor the exercise of unscrambling sentences. When in real life is this necessary? Sentences scrambled in never print almost appear. Why, talks like this nobody almost!

I believe it was the Carnegie Commission that recently reported American students spend too much time on reading workbooks and not enough time actually reading. Think about it.

READING ORGANIZATIONS

Finally, we turn to other people. Who out there can help you with reading problems or with access to materials that meet your needs? Who out there is trying to mess you up? Learn to distinguish the muggers from the friends . . .

International Reading Association

An establishment association of "classroom teachers, reading specialists, administrators, educators or reading teachers" and the like, the IRA discourages parents from trying to teach our own children to read. Concerned with such things as "strategies which have been effective in dealing with and eliminating sex stereotyping," the IRA is not exactly striking at the root of our national illiteracy. In fact, they continue to push look-say in spite of the hundreds of studies that show it *doesn't work*. Mere laymen can join, if they so desire, for an annual fee of between $30 and $100, depending on how many of the society's journals they want delivered to their mailbox.

The Orton Dyslexia Society

More promising for the parents of labeled children is the Orton Dyslexia Society. Samuel T. Orton, M.D., and his associates worked out an approach to teaching dyslexics that appears to have real sense. Using phonics, multisensory input, and an individualized teaching method, the Orton Dyslexic Society believes that "every undamaged person (and even many less fortunate) can learn:

- to understand and speak the language he/she hears;
- to read with skill and comprehension to the level of his/her inborn intelligence;
- to write legibly;
- to spell passably well;
- to put his/her thoughts into clear, understandable, spoken or written words."

Educators Publishing Service of Cambridge, Massachusetts carries materials based on this method.

Reading Reform Foundation

Ta da! Here come the folks in the white hats, galloping up to save the day! Formed in 1961 to combat illiteracy in America (not to study "sex stereotypes"), the Reading Reform Foundation exists to "encourage the correct teaching of systematic, multi-sensory phonics." No mush-mouthed fence-sitting here! The RRF is convinced that look-say is a disease, and phonics the cure. A donation of $10 or more will get you on their mailing list for a year.

RRF is interested in crusading for a cause, not in pumping up their leaders' and members' reputations. Consequently, they are a very busy group, offering workshops, speakers, courses, referral services, and consulting services. And let me tell you about their mail-order bookstore. Containing both documentation of reading research and the history of American reading instruction, and books and programs for actually teaching intensive phonics, the RRF order form is a great resource for any teacher of reading. Many books recommended in this book of mine are offered for sale: Romalda Spaulding's *Writing Road to Reading*, with phonogram flash cards and tutoring outline; *Johnny STILL Can't Read . . . But You Can Teach Him At Home*; *Professor Phonics* and *A Sound Track to Reading*; Richard Mitchell's books; Sam Blumenfeld's books; plus a number of programs and books that I have had no time to review, but look excellent.

All materials RRF offers are very reasonably priced, and RRF members get discounts on some items.

From what I have heard, the folks at RRF are truly helpful, and they certainly are in touch with the people who can solve your reading problems.

PART VI

LANGUAGE ARTS

CHAPTER NINETEEN

GRAMMAR

I don't know if you'll believe this, but grammar has been forced underground. At least that's what Richard Mitchell, the Underground Grammarian, says, and he should know, having written several devastatingly funny books on the subject.

Grammar never used to be a barrelful of belly-laughs, and it would not be now but for some egregious foolishness in the halls of academe. It seems that the same free 'n easy spirits who gave us "affective education" instead of the three R's have, quite naturally, determined that correct speech is not terribly important. Enter the Irate Grammarian to put them in their place:

> It had to happen. Last month we granted the world's first DEd . . . and now everybody wants one. Two new candidates present themselves, and they are not some silly educationists but *bona fide* associate professors of English out at what they call Eastern New Mexico University.
>
> Laid-back folk. Arlene Zekowsi, Stanley Berne. Hate apostrophes. Rules. Arbitrary. Down sentences! Up feelings expressing! Up Zekowski! Up Berne! Right on!
>
> Or, if you prefer, On right! "We're professors of English," says Berne. (Hm. Shouldn't that be "Were professors of English"?) "We are concerned with the idea of expressing feelings. Arbitrary rules of grammar prohibit that." (Cmon, be patient. Sure he talks that tired old grammar, but only because he has to get to we elitists.) Hes wright. No, thats not expressing feelings. He rite! Wordsworth feeling-expressing fouled-up by verb-subject agreement. Shakespeare shot down—Donne undone by nonrestrictive clauses. Whitman comatose from commas.
>
> Zekowski: "Grammar is elitism. I wish to destroy what is dead, lifeless and snobbish." . . .

> We support the idea of expressing feelings 1,000 percent. That's *exactly* what we should be teaching these kids. For one thing, it's a cinch, like playing tennis with the net down, as Frost put it. Another: if we let them in on the secrets of logical sentences and coherent discourse, the ignorant little b——s will go on to take away some of our cushiest jobs, perhaps even as associate professors of English, and that will be the end of lifeless elitism as we know it. . . .[1] (bowdlerization mine)

Mr. Mitchell, a professor of English at Glassboro State College, has much more to say on the subject of education, including some howlingly funny exposures of the way our professional educrats mangle the language they claim to teach. Do rush out and buy his books, *The Graves of Academe* and *The Leaning Tower of Babel*, both published by Little, Brown and Company of Boston and Toronto. You will laugh yourself sick. You will also have a box seat for the battle: Right and Wrong, Rules and Logic on one side, and on the other, in the gold boxing trunks, Muzzy Thinking, Soupy Feelings, Professional Ineptness, and Pompous Nothings. At the moment the Pompous Nothings have bribed the judge and are trying to persuade Rules and Logic to take a dive—hence the underground habitat of our grammarian hero—but if enough of the crowd will just get out their kazoos and give the villains the old Brooklyn raspberry maybe truth and righteousness will prevail. Who knows? Maybe Junior even will learn to unsplit his infinitives and stop dangling his participles all over town.

Why is the war, in Mr. Mitchell's view, being waged on the slender battlefield of Grammar? Because, as our Socialist friends who slid the knife into American education know, if you can't think straight you can't defend yourself. No kid whose vocabulary consists of "Huh?" and "Yeah" and "Like, y'know what I mean?"

will ever threaten to turn the world upside down. Even punk rockers have to know what they're mangling in order to mangle it effectively.

As Mr. Mitchell says,

Children *always* learn something in school, but what they learn is seldom what we had in mind to teach. Children who grow up under the influence of the humanistic education mongers, what do they learn? They learn that hosts of errors will be forgiven for even the pretense of good intentions. They learn that shabby workmanship brings no penalty, especially in the context of anything silly or self-indulgent enough to be put forth as "creative." They learn that the mastery of skills is of little importance, for even the supposed teachers of skills have found comfortable jobs in spite of their indifference to those skills and, not infrequently, in spite of an obvious lack of those skills. They learn to be shoddy workers in any endeavor, comforting themselves, as their teachers did, by fantasies of a holistic excellence unfettered by precision in small details. . . .[2]

Down, Zekowski! Down, Berne! Up, Mitchell!

Which brings us, at long last, to grammar itself. You do believe children and adults should know whether us goes to McDonalds, or us go, or we go, or nobody goes. You would rather know where to put the commas than remain in blissful ignorance of punctuation. It does not trouble you to write sentences that make sense (you elitist, you!). How, then, shall we go about handing on this knowledge to the next generation now that Miss Ritchie, your sixth-grade English teacher, has retired and been replaced by Berne-ists and Zekowski-niks?

As another enlightened grammarian has remarked,

The textbooks on grammar grow steadily thicker, but students arrive more often than not in their eleventh- and twelfth-grade classes barely conversant with phrases like "clause" and "phrase." Moreover, prevailing teaching philosophy has it that one must never ever study or teach grammar as grammar in an enlightened ("interdisciplinary"?) age. Grammar must only be looked at glancingly in connection always with the study of composition itself, it is said. And composition in turn must never be separated from what is "relevant" to the adolescent's own emotional slew, or some such folderol. The result, of course, is that nothing is looked at directly and no useful information imparted.[3]

As this same man, a Mr. Slade Schuster and author of the highly esteemed *Slade Short Course* in grammar and composition (reviewed below) goes on to say, "It *can* be done more simply. There *is* a time grammar should be studied in concentrated doses *as grammar,* and there *is* a useful handful of terms worth recognizing and learning to use."[4] You said it, brother Slade. It's almost heretical, but I'll say it anyway. To learn grammar, students have to *study!* Amazing! However, as physical exercise can be either the drudgery of calisthenics or the pleasure of a good tennis match, grammar study need not necessarily be mental drudgery. There are some good books, kits, and games for would-be grammarians. See below!

GOOD GRAMMAR MATERIALS

Any and every Christian textbook publisher will have a grammar book or two that follows the classical method and is free of objectionable sermonizing.

I'm not saying these books will be free of *legitimate* sermonizing, though. It's one thing to say "Thus saith the Bible," and quite another to sneak in little sermonettes pushing humanism in a supposedly neutral public school text. The first is straightforward, and if you don't like it you can at least argue with it. The second aims to indoctrinate subliminally, so that the victim doesn't even know what hit him, and is unable to fight back.

If a schoolbook is going to sermonize, I like to be warned. As C. S. Lewis said, it is an affront to get the fulminations of amateur theologians when you thought you were paying for the work of professional grammarians. Christian schoolbooks zap you with it right between the eyes. Public schoolbooks sneak up behind and stick you with it.

Alpha Omega Publications
Exploring Truths worktext $5.95, answer key $2.95. *Exploring Truths through Diagramming* student text with answer key, $3.95.

Did you know that Sunday school was invented to help poor children learn to read, and that their text was the Bible? For centuries the Bible was used as a text for reading, literature, grammar, and composition, and Sunday school was just one of the educational enterprises in this tradition.

Alpha Omega Publications has just come out with a new series based on this old concept. *Exploring Truths* is subtitled "A systematic approach to learning English through the Bible." Designed to be used by individuals or groups who possess at least sixth-grade skills, *Exploring Truths* is for anyone who wants to "learn grammar through studying God's Word." AOP suggests that the text can be used by individual students for review or enrichment, or by the whole family.

Exploring Truths Through Diagramming revives the honored custom of learning grammar and parts of speech through diagramming sentences. The sentences in question are based on the Bible book of Joshua.

Educators Publishing Service

For those who themselves have a reasonable command of grammar and wish to help others, whether children or adults, who are not so fortunately endowed, *Learning Grammar Through Writing,* published by Educators Publishing Service, is a wonderful tool. "The central idea of *Learning Grammar Through Writing* is to teach grammar to students by having them write compositions regularly and then correct their own work, at a level which they can reasonably be expected to achieve." The book is divided into thirteen categories—e.g., Verbs, The Sentence, Punctuation—and within each category you will find all the necessary rules and examples *in nice large print.* The book is inexpensive and reusable.

Harcourt Brace Jovanovich

Warriner's English Grammar and Composition has long been

regarded as a standard-bearer for genuine grammar instruction. The series consists of several books for the late junior high and early senior high grades, culminating in the one you should buy, *Warriner's Complete English Grammar and Composition,* which contains *every* rule.

Unhappily, the updaters have gotten their little hands on this series too. Will the "All New! Revised!" examples be grammatical illustrations or sneaky sermons on the joys of feminism? I can see no other reason for updating it: grammar is grammar is grammar and doesn't change all that often.

The old copy your library has will be good. So will the ancient version the high school is throwing out or that you can pick up at a yard sale or a used bookstore.

Hewitt Research Foundation
Winston Grammar, $30. *Advanced Winston Grammar,* $20.

The folks at Hewitt are not given to wild hyperbole; so I almost believe them when they claim to have latched on to a product that actually makes grammar *fun,* even for little kids who aren't neat and orderly types. It's called the Winston Grammar series, and as far as I can figure out without actually seeing it, the product teaches grammatical constructions by pattern-building with colored flash cards. Hewitt tells me the kit is good for three to four years of grammar instruction. Then the *Advanced* kit takes your child through high school. *Winston Grammar* comes in a box to which the *Advanced* set can be added. I've almost bought the kits any number of times, but hesitated because of the price. If you have a Home-Grown Kids demonstrator in your area, have him or her show you the kit.

Independent School Press
The Slade Short Course, a piddling $3.50.

It's a pleasure to find a book like *The Slade Short Course.* Mr. Slade Schuster, a teacher at Shattuck/St. Mary's, one of those exclusive private schools, has produced a slim volume that contains, in his own words,

> All ye know on Earth
> And all ye need to know
> About grammar
> In eight lessons.

The book would be embarrassingly thin if Mr. Schuster had put in nothing but those eight lessons. So he threw in another seven lessons that very judiciously lead the young author through the mazes of composition.

The book is not a beginning grammar text. You have to know about nouns and verbs in a rudimentary way before embarking on the *Slade Course.* Also, Mr. Schuster has wisely left out the rare exceptions which so litter comprehensive texts. Who cares about appositive phrases anyway? (Mr. Schuster assures us that the thingummies are just truncated adjective clauses.)

The Slade Course includes the Grammar Game. Students get points for identifying all the parts of speech, noun positions, and phrases, clauses, and sentence types. Sample sentences are provided.

In the Composition section, *The Slade Course* concentrates on the sentence by drilling students on the several rhetorical forms. This shows genius. We learn by patterns; why not use them?

The *Slade Short Course* is more for less, and it costs so little that I don't see why everyone shouldn't buy a copy.

Little, Brown and Company
The Graves of Academe and *The Leaning Tower of Babel,* $14.95 each.

These books aren't about grammar, strictly speaking, but they are about strictly speaking. Richard Mitchell disembowels the stupid notions of those who think that teachers should do everything *but* teach, and he does it with pizazz.

Sing, Spell, Read and Write
Trophy books 1 and 2, $7.50/set.

This two-workbook series for third-graders or bright second-graders isn't quite as inspired as the rest of the *Sing, Spell, Read and Write* program, but it still beats the standard public school texts. Book I covers alphabetical order, kinds of sentences, capital letters, and punctuation. Book II has Writing Letters, Writing Stories, Word Usage, Language Manners, the Parts of Speech Song, Articles, Nouns, Adjectives, Pronouncs, Verbs, Adverbs, Conjunctions, Prepositions, Interjections, and Practical Everyday Reading Skills. Both books have a spelling section in the back, with ten words for each of ninety-five days, and accompanying puzzles, crosswords, word searches, and other games.

What I like about this set is that it goes through in one year what regular schoolbooks drag out over ten. If a youngster really learned this stuff, he'd be better off than 80 percent of our high school graduates without ever taking another English course. I would, however, recommend that you also get him one of the other short grammar courses for older students listed in this section—why not have him do better than 99 percent instead of just 80 percent?

Wff 'n Proof
On-Words, $13. *LinguaSHTIK.*

Wff 'n Proof games are to Milton Bradley and Parker

Brothers as Shakespeare's plays are to my scribblings. Of course, it takes more mental oomph to understand Shakespeare than it does to understand the sentence you are now reading. True. In the same way, Wff 'n Proof games give your brain a much more thorough workout than ye average board game. But this sort of exertion is *good* for the brain, and some similar sort of exertion is *necessary* to understand grammar, which is the subject we're talking about (remember?)

Two of Wff 'n Proof's games might be helpful to grammarians young or old. First, there's *On-Words*, the game of word structure. You play it like *Equations*, which I have described at length in the Math section and have no intention of redescribing here. In *On-Words*, the resources are letters, and, for the Advanced game, dictionary symbols. By requiring, permitting, or forbidding the use of these resources, players try to force each other into making moves that make it impossible to reach a predetermined goal. If the goal is 6, for example, it must be possible to make a six-letter word from the permitted, required, and remaining resources, or perhaps to make two or more words whose letters add up to six, Scrabble-wise. It's like playing Scrabble without ever laying anything down until the end. Does that sound tough? It gets worse! In *Adventurous On-Words*, each player can change the game by adding new rules as he goes

along: for example, "The word must be a noun." *Adventurous On-Words* can range over the whole field of single-word grammatical constructs, with suffixes, prefixes, inflectional endings, and so on, as the authors are at pains to point out. The game is infinitely expandable and can be as easy or as hard as you like. It *will* increase spelling and dictionary skills.

Second, we have *LinguiSHTIK*. This creative, open-ended language game gets much more heavily into grammar. Played in a manner similar to *On-Words*, players may make demands like, "The word to be formed must be a noun (a verb, a preposition), an object of a preposition (a linking verb, a direct object), it must contain a prefix (a suffix) . . ." When *LinguiSHTIK* is played in the Academic Games League, you must not only challenge correctly or be incorrectly challenged in order to win, but also write a sentence using the word correctly. You may choose to dispense with this rule if you like.

Both *On-Words* and *LinguiSHTIK* are fun to play, and with a little practice you can become quite ingenious in your demands. ("The word must be used in apposition. Hah!") Both games come with an instruction guide and sets of colorful letter dice. *LinguiSHTIK* has letters only. *On-Words* has number dice (for setting the goal) and the above-mentioned dictionary symbols. Both are attractively packaged and a steal at the price.

CHAPTER TWENTY

HANDWRITING

In the wishful spirit of welcome mats that proclaim, "Dull women have spotless homes," it has been said, "Poor handwriting is a sign of genius." I would like to challenge the latter statement. Granted, doctors and top executives are often guilty of illegible scrawling. But they usually develop this annoying incommunicability only after they have acquired a secretary who is capable of deciphering what amounts to modern Sanskrit. You don't get to be a corporate president by, as a little boy, having all your school papers returned with points marked off for illegibility. No, the written hash produced by busy leaders is really the sad remains of what used to be decent handwriting.

It has also been said, in educational circles anyway, "Kids don't really need to learn to write any more. They can just learn to type on a computer keyboard. After all, everything's computerized nowadays." Sorry, but that won't wash either. Human beings sometimes need to write down ideas when they are more than six feet away from a wall outlet. Henry David Thoreau would have had a pretty poor time of it trying to write *Walden* at a computer console.

So let's just give up and admit it; children should learn to write legibly. Now comes the crunch: *how* shall we teach them?

Today four major methods are contending in the handwriting field. They are:

(1) *Ball and stick*. One group favors manuscript writing ("ball and stick") for young children because it is so easy to teach (all strokes begin on a line) and it resembles print, thus making the teaching of reading less confusing. Unhappily, ball and stick degenerates into a hash of bouncing balls and chopped-up sticks when students are trying to write fast, and once a child has started with ball and stick he has to make the dreaded transition to cursive from scratch.

(2) *Precursive*. Recognizing the flaws of ball-and-stick manuscript, a number of companies are now vending a type of manuscript handwriting that is closely allied to cursive. Letters are formed with a single stroke rather than with several as in ball-and-stick, and generally they follow the cursive form. What's left out are the connectors. Precursive moves smoothly to cursive, with only a few letters changing (such as *b* and *f*). The goal here is to end up with legible cursive writing.

(3) *Starting with cursive*. It is possible to begin with a simplified cursive script and stick with it, thus making no transitions at all.

(4) *Italic*. Here the ultimate goal is to develop a beautiful and functional calligraphic hand, rather than a ballpoint cursive. Students begin with precursive and move towards italic mastery. A big difference in this system is that the capitals are the manuscript forms, rather than the fancy and hard to read cursive capitals. Furthermore, since calligraphy is an art form, children are encouraged to develop their own style rather than to adhere to a uniform model.

Personally, I much prefer the italic approach. Why settle for merely legible handwriting when it could be gorgeous? Also, I find cursive capitals frustrating, and cursive hands very easily get out of control and end up being illegible. Properly done, italic is much more legible than cursive and just as fast to write. Furthermore, since most cursive methods stress connecting all the letters all the time, this places a burden on creative students, who, handwriting studies show, are more inclined to want to leave letters unconnected.

However, in the final analysis, handwriting style is a matter of personal choice. If your daughter is learning at home and she just loves old-fashioned copperplate writing, indulge her. Similarly, if she likes to print everything, let her. The only reason schools struggle with standardized handwriting systems is that they don't have the resources to deal with students as individuals. As a parent, you do have these resources. As long as the results are legible, you and your children are free to choose any system at all—even ball and stick!

HANDWRITING PROGRAMS AND RESOURCES

American Guidance Service
Complete program, $89.50. Components available separately.

"I'm an inchworm, my name is itl. I'm really quite a friendly fellow. But when I slither and I squirm, People yell out, 'ih, a worm!' "

Now why in the world would anyone name a worm, "itl"? It's because the letters i, t, and l are the easiest to write. AGS's *itl* Early Writing Program introduces all the letters of the alphabet through fifty-nine lessons. Children start with the lower-case precursive alphabet and go on to capitals. They also learn the signs for all the letters. The letters are introduced in families: those starting with a vertical stroke, namely i, t, and l; then left-curving letters like a, d, and g; next right-curving letters like b and p; and last of all the letters with diagonals, like x and v. Each lesson has a little story about itl and his friends, and the story ties into the letter's shape and sound.

The complete *itl* program includes a lesson guide, the *Writing Is Child's Play* handbook, a *my itl book*, eighty-five activity sheets, twenty-eight full-color Large Character Cards in their own folder, an *itl* puppet and poster and audiocassette, fifty-two black and white Tello cards boxed, a writing slate, a pencil, a handwriting crayon, a plastic gripper, and a carrying case to hold it all. Additional slates, pencils, crayons, and grippers may be purchased for group use.

Children listen to stories, say letters, draw and color, write letters in the air or with pencil or with crayon or on a slate—all over the place!

The program sounds like a lot of fun. It's a mite expensive for the home unless you think of it as a minikindergarten, which it is. Writing is one of the best ways to learn reading, and the *itl* phonics approach beats out the competition in exploiting this angle.

Collier Books/Macmillan Book Company
The Italic Way to Beautiful Handwriting, $6.95. Bookstores have it.

Fred Eager's book, *The Italic Way to Beautiful Handwriting,* was recommended to me by a home schooling college professor who was using it with his own children. This is the book to use if you want to learn italic yourself and then teach it to your children. The book is very reasonably priced, contains everything you need to know, and is full of inspirational "before and after" examples.

Cursive Italic News, the Barchowsky Report on Handwriting
Three issues/year. $12, U.S. subscribers. $15.50 on U.S. bank, Canadians.

If you are really excited about handwriting, you'll be glad to know of this new publication. "It brings you to a variety of perspectives on handwriting from the U.S. and abroad. It will help you to improve your own handwriting or that of your students, it will keep you abreast of the current role of handwriting in school curriculums, it will give you some of the history of letters and more. Subscribers have the opportunity of receiving whatever individual assistance we can provide, such as resources and references," say the publishers.

Ginn Company
My ABC Book, $4.20.

My ABC Book is a colorful, high-quality workbook designed to teach little kids how to read and write their ABC's in manuscript. A teacher's guide is in the back of the book, with many clever games to introduce and reinforce the letters. As a special bonus, the page ends are designed to be cut off and bound into a personal ABC book that the student helped make by tracing the letters. For ball and stick fans I recommend this book.

William Morrow
The Writing Road to Reading, $9.95. Phonogram cards also available.

Morrow publishes Romalda Spaulding's great book, *A Writing Road to Reading,* reviewed in the Reading section. The book is also superb as a handbook for handwriting instruction. Mrs. Spaulding's step by step instructions leave nothing to chance, and she is prepared to deal with every possible learning obstacle. Cursive method. Highly recommended.

Mott Media
Complete Spencerian set, including theory book and all five copy books, $13.95. Individual copy books $2.25, theory book $4.95.

Lovers of classic schooltexts, take note. Mott Media has resurrected ye olde Spencerian handwriting books from ye tombe of oblivion. These books were used for over one hundred years, and are based on the method of Platt Rogers Spencer.

If John Henry was born with a hammer in his hand, young Spencer was born with a pen. As a child he first drew letters on a birch bark, and soon he was scribbling everywhere. A born calligrapher, Spencer greatly admired John Hancock's elegant signature on the Declaration of Independence and desired to design a handwriting system that would produce that kind of grace, yet be easy to learn. The result, carried on by his disciples, was Spencerian writing, a complete system based on a few simple arm movements and seven basic strokes. Every letter is broken down into those strokes. The result is a gorgeous "copperplate" system of writing, quaint and elegant.

Spencer's theory book reads like a catechism, with its questions and answers. "Will you measure and analyze small r? . . . How should the small r be formed?" The five accompanying consumable copy books take the student from writing the "short" letters on graphed paper to penning such sentences as "Angels are guardian spirits" (this was before the ACLU, remember) and "Modesty always charms." Like all Mott's Classic Curriculum, the books can be used at all age levels and at any pace that fits the student.

A. N. Palmer Company

Palmer Method Handwriting is based on the so-true idea that handwriting practice should *be* handwriting practice, not poetry-composing time or puzzle-solving time. If the learner has to concentrate on language arts at the same time as practicing his handwriting, obviously his task will be complicated. As they say, "Handwriting class should be to teach 'how' to write so the rest of the day may be used to teach 'what' to write." The method is over a hundred years old, and is still the company's only product. The handwriting produced is a very lovely cursive hand. Students are encouraged to cleave to the norm rather than to invent their own style. Workbooks are less than $3 in all grades, and teacher's editions are under $10.

Aa Bb Cc Dd Ee Ff Gg Hh Ii Jj Kk Ll Mm Nn Oo Pp
Aa Bb Cc Dd Ee Ff Gg Hh Ii Jj Kk Ll Mi
nan nbn ncn ndn nen nfn ngn nhn nin njn nkn nln nm
CURSIVE ITALIC ALPHABET NUMERAL DESK STRIP (INCLUDING BASIC ITALIC)—NO 202
q Rr Ss Tt Uu Vv Ww Xx Yy Zz 0 1 2 3 4 5 6 7 8 9
Nn Oo Pp Qq Rr Ss Tt Uu Vv Ww Xx Yy Zz
nn non npn nqn nrn nsn ntn nun nvn nwn nxn nyn nzn

Portland State University

Books A through G and Instructor's Manual, $3.95 each. Specimen Set containing all the above, $28. Supplementary Packets A-G, $25 each, $20 to schools. Classroom Charts, $5.65/set, $4.50 to schools. Two sets: *Basic Italic Alphabet and Numerals, Cursive Italic Alphabet and Numerals.* Alphabet Desk Strips, $5.65 set of thirty, $4.50 to schools. Specify Basic Italic or Cursive Italic. Shipping and handling $1.50 on all orders.

Believe it or not, some public school systems are getting into teaching italic handwriting. The series they are using is published by the Portland State University. It begins with prewriting exercises and goes all the way to a very professional italic hand. The series is spread out over eight grades, like most public school courses; but you don't need to buy all the workbooks if you are using them at home.

My inclination would be to skip Book A, which is merely the italic alphabet with one letter per page. There are no review pages; so the student could easily forget all the early letters by the time he gets to the end of the book. Joins are first introduced in Book C, and thereafter the letter size gets smaller and smaller. Books B through E seem the most valuable of the series, if you don't want to buy the entire set. Or if you want only one book for

yourself or an older student, Book G has a self-teaching approach to the whole system.

You can also get an Instructor's Manual, which includes teaching techniques, a Scope and Sequence, and the theory behind the course. Schools may be interested in the Supplementary Materials packets, which contain reproducible master for follow-up practice.

Rinehart, Inc.

Home Study Program, $20 per student. Teacher Training Correspondence Course, $35.

Rinehart's main product is something very useful: a correspondence program for improving your handwriting. The Student Remedial or Home Study Program contains a manual, individual prescriptions, evaluation and diagnosis, remediation, and before-and-after testing. The course takes a minimum of six weeks, but it may span up to six months. Two courses are offered for school-age students, manuscript and cursive. State the student's grade level when enrolling.

Rinehart also has a Teacher Training Correspondence Course. This, too, is meant to train teachers in handwriting skills, so they can be an example to the class. Either manuscript or cursive can be learned.

Rinehart also sells handwriting accessories, such as desk tapes, duplicating master transparencies, manuscript/cursive cards (8½ x 7", choice of blue or yellow), and pencil grips by the bag. Rinehart teaches a slanted, precursive manuscript and a classic cursive.

Scott, Foresman and Company

D'Nealian Handwriting is a very popular precursive to cursive program used by at least one major home school correspondence program that I know of. As S-F's ad says, "From the start, D'Nealian establishes the letter formations, rhythm, size, slant, and spacing used in cursive writing. Children build on what they know." Unlike other programs, D'Nealian Handwriting does not require total conformity to the model. Children are allowed to slant their letters in the way that is comfortable for them, for example, so long as the slant is uniform. This method incorporates language arts instruction, and I mark it down for this. Why should students have to struggle with composition skills during handwriting period?

name _____   BOOK **C**

Pen + **Man** + **Ship**

E-Z as A-B-C
Through the year workbooks
FOR BOYS AND GIRLS

*FAIRFAX CHRISTIAN
CURRICULUM SERIES*

Thoburn Press
Set of three workbooks and teacher's guide, $20. Each workbook, $4.25. *Teacher's Guide* $7.25.

Perhaps the ultimate resource for Christian teachers of ball-and-stick manuscript is Thoburn Press's very lovely E-Z as A-B-C Penmanship series.

Book A begins with numbers, alphabet letters, and digraphs. Individual letters are then introduced according to their characteristics: "circle letters" like c and o, "candy cane" letters like h and r, "slant stick" letters, look alikes, tall stick letters, straight line letters, and so on. Both the upper- and lower-case manuscript alphabet are handled in this book.

Book B goes on to handwriting practice with short vowel words, long vowel words, sight words, and *s* sounds like *z* words.

Finally, Book C has students copying the names of Bible people, books of the Old and New Testaments, the twelve disciples, some kings and women of the Bible, and so on.

Instead of blah black lines to write on, each workbook uses "stop light" (green, yellow, and red) color-coded lines. It's all in a clean, easy-on-the-eyes format and reinforces any good phonics program.

TREND, Inc.
Buy through school suppliers. All wipe-off® books, $2.95 each.

I wouldn't want to be without TREND's colorful write 'n wipe handwriting books. The Pre-Handwriting book lets children trace the different shapes and strokes they will use in writing. The Numbers book gives practice in writing numerals and in counting. You can use the Manuscript book as a precursive intro by just having your student start some letters differently and using one continuous stroke. TREND even has a Cursive book, with a silly racecar theme. The books are great for practice, lively and colorful, and can be used again and again by every kid in a family of twelve.

TREND's wipe-off® crayons, for use with the books, are supercheap and come in assorted zippy colors.

Zaner-Bloser
Manuscript and Cursive Correspondence Courses, $18 each.

The king of handwriting suppliers! Zaner-Bloser sells absolutely everything to do with writing. Prewriting fun stuff like Kin-Tac Alphabet cards (plastic with large upper- and lower-case letters recessed into the card for kinesthetic and tactile learning), alphabet activity books, and more! Zaner-Bloser has a large selection of handwriting paper for all ages, finger-fitting pens and pencils, even *The Zanerian Manual of Alphabets and Engrossing* for those who are really into handwriting. I don't have space to list all their accessories. Do get the catalog and see for yourself.

Zaner-Bloser has recently introduced its latest handwriting correspondence course for teachers. Each course includes a 128-page workbook, paper tablet, pencil, six self-evaluation forms, and six preaddressed envelopes. You even get an official certificate of completion when you finish!

Zaner-Bloser also has an array of handwriting books and filmstrips.

Zaner-Bloser integrates language arts with handwriting practice in their classroom material, which as noted above is fun for the advanced students and murder on the slower ones. Also, cursive doesn't begin until third grade unless specifically requested. I must say that if you believe in the "integrated" approach, Zaner-Bloser's handwriting activities are about as motivational and interesting as I've seen anywhere.

Many home school programs use Zaner-Bloser materials.

CHAPTER TWENTY-ONE

LANGUAGES

Why learn a foreign language? Here are some intellectual reasons: a desire to broaden your mind through exposure to another culture, the need to communicate with non-English speakers in your business, or just for the fun of cracking a strange code. In years past, the man or woman who didn't know at least one language other than English was considered only half-educated. Now that so few American students are even learning to grapple with English successfully, the demand for fluency in another language has considerably abated. Yet it still is true that those who know several languages have an edge on those who do not.

Why learn a foreign language? Here's an economic reason: it can land you a job. I was amazed, during a visit to New York City, to see how many ads there were in the paper begging for executives who were fluent in German. It also doesn't take a genius to see that we could use a few good men in the computer field who speak Japanese, or that an importer of African artifacts might want to know Swahili. And knowing the languages in which English has its roots—namely, French, German, and to a lesser degree Latin—increases your command of your own native tongue. One of the most famous classic texts on preaching recommends that ministers study French and German for this very reason.

Learning another language sharpens not only your speech, but your thinking. The habits of analysis and organization are increased by the study of the multitudinous patterns that make up any language.

You've now heard most of the arguments that foreign language teachers marshal in order to convince someone (anyone!) to *please* enroll in their classes. They really are good arguments. The only reason more students don't act on them is that you can get just as many credits for Basket Weaving I as for Advanced French I, and learning a language is, frankly, harder than learning to weave a basket.

You, however, are made of sterner stuff than the average basket-weaver. For you, the question is not so much, "Ought I to learn another language?" or "Should my children learn another language?" as "How do I go about it?"

ESCAPING THE TYPICAL TEXTBOOK TRAP

I am well qualified to speak on the subject of foreign languages, having had ten years of French instruction, two years of German, and one year of intensive Russian. All these classroom courses, none of which resulted in actual fluency, have burned into my soul several basic truths about how *not* to learn a foreign language.

The first thing you must watch out for is the Typical Language Textbook. It comes in all sizes and colors but only one flavor: boring. You can recognize the Typical Language Textbook by the endless drills and listless dialogues that make up 99 percent of the book. The writers of these books have got it into their heads that you do not want to *speak* the language: rather, you want to *read* it. Furthermore, the stories you want to read all have sentences like "Jean rode his bicyclette to the store. Marie rode her bicyclette to the store. See Rex catch the ball. Run, Spot, run." This Dick-and-Jane approach to foreign languages not only leaves you gaping with boredom, it also leaves you fluency-free, as no normal Frenchman, or Italian, or Bulgarian talks like that.

Another trap to watch out for is the Cute Language Textbook. This is the Dick-and-Jane-go-to-the-disco version. We still get Dick and Jane, or maybe Jean and Marie, but now our young friends are doing "contemporary" things. Unless you really just want to read teenybopper magazines in the target language, this approach won't get you much of anywhere either. Furthermore, in their anxiety to be "with it," publishers tend to overstress the negative aspects of youth culture abroad. Life in France isn't an eternal no-adults-allowed camping trip, like some books make it out to be, any more than it is here in the good old U.S.A.

The last all-too-common trap is the language "course" that consists of phrases you're supposed to memorize. My first year of junior-high French was larded with dialogues sans grammatical explanation, and my classmates unanimously agreed that it was a waste of time. Some adult self-study courses for tourists do this also. Naked phrases go into short-term memory, which they quickly evacuate on the slightest excuse. Pattern drills, on the other hand, whether or not they incorporate overt grammar, lock the language into place.

THE BASIC TOOLS OF FLUENCY

Obviously the best way to learn another language is the way that already has worked for you once. You know English: how did you learn it?

First, people talked to you a lot. Your mother grabbed your chubby little foot and said, "Foot. Foot." Or perhaps she said, "My ittle baby has a cutesy itty-bitty footsie," in which case it took a while longer to catch on to what she was talking about. In any case, you heard the word "foot" a lot in many different contexts ("Yike! I hurt my foot!" "Stick your foot in the shoe.") until finally you made the connection. This was the intake, or data-gathering, stage.

Then one day you tried to say, "Foot." If you were really successful it came out sounding like "Foo." If you weren't so successful, it might have been "Doof" or "Voob." Why did you try to say "Foot"? It wasn't because you needed to pass a test. No, you needed someone to do something and do it *right then.* Perhaps your foot hurt or you wanted to put on your shoes. If your father or mother caught on to what you were trying to say, you all were happy. If not, you tried again. "Boof? Foob?" Sooner or later you made a noise that was close enough, and everyone was ecstatic. "Our baby is talking!" Take note of this: they did *not* try to make you feel like a fool for your mispronounciations. Instead, they encouraged you. If they didn't do this, it's a fairly sure thing that you were slow in learning to talk.

You also developed a pattern of asking for data in a certain way, and your parents responded predictably. "What dat?" "That's the saltshaker, Johnny. Saltshaker. Saltshaker. No, don't grab it, dear." You also became accustomed to the rhythms and patterns of English through hearing thousands of simple sentences. "Give Mommy the spoon." "Lift up your arms." "Swallow the nice medicine." You heard additional thousands of sentences not addressed to you, that you were under no pressure to translate, but were curious to understand. "Little Johnny spat out all his medicine all over his shirt this morning, and I had to feed it to him four times before I got any down him."

So kids learn to talk by seeing and feeling objects and asking other people to do things for them and doing the things that other people ask them to do and hearing sentences that nobody even wants them to understand. But how do we ask kids to learn foreign languages in school? Too often, it's by filling out workbook pages. They only get to hear the language spoken an

hour or so a week in language lab, and even if the classroom teacher is a native speaker of the language, he or she only has the students for another few hours.

If you or your children really want to learn to *speak,* not just read, another language, at minimum you will need:

Cassettes or records of the language as it is spoken.

Transcripts of the above, so you can make some sense out of it.

Translations of the above, so you don't get stuck forever wondering what *izquierda* or *wiederkommen* means.

Plus a reasonable framework for the language's patterns, which may or may not need to resemble a conventional grammar.

You will also desperately need some manageable memory devices to help you keep track of the thousands of slippery little words you will be learning.

If you only have a few hours a week to learn a language, it makes sense to spend as much of the time listening to it as possible. At home you can listen to a cassette again and again until you have it memorized from sheer repetition. More and more publishers are adding songs to their material, making use of the musical part of the brain to help you retain your lessons. One publisher that I know of uses pictures in all his courses to help you associate the spoken word with a visual image. With the advent of the VCR, expect to see courses developed featuring sound-sight association. These are all steps forward in foreign language instruction.

I don't know of one course that does it all—gives you extensive hearing practice, action practice, sight-sound association, and pattern drills. Still, you can learn quite a bit from some of the select programs following. For children, look especially for songs, action practice, and pictures, for if all these features are lacking in a program, few children will bother with it. For adults, look for a clean, logical framework coupled with lots of data. We adults can make up our own action practices and drill ourselves, being more accustomed to self-discipline.

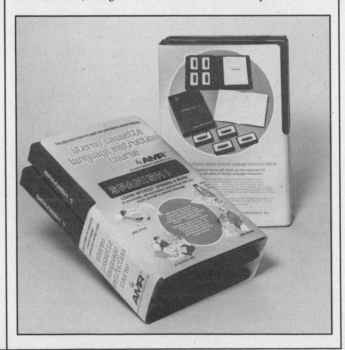

LANGUAGE COURSES FOR ADULTS

AMR Educational Systems
   French, German, Italian, Latin American Spanish: same format for all.
   Level I, $110. Level II, $130 (Italian not available).
   Strictly Vocabulary, Levels I and II, $49.50 each.
   Practical Spanish, $79.50.
   Japanese and Mandarin Chinese, $135.

What kind of foreign language courses would two Wheaton college professors design? Believe it or not, the profs don't want you to hit the books. In fact, AMR lets you learn the language right off the cassettes. Courses are recorded in stereo, with the foreign language and the English translation on separate tracks. Thus you can fade out one or the other, and test yourself. This method, unique to AMR, is protected by U. S. Patent.

AMR very graciously sent me their French I course for review. All Western languages follow the same format (your choice of French, German, Italian, and Latin American Spanish). You hear a short, useful dialog with very soft mood music in the background. On the cassette, each foreign sentence is followed by the English translation. Next, individual words and phrases are repeated with their translations. Finally, the dialog is repeated without translation, so you can try pronouncing the phrases and see if you understand it. Each dialog introduces new grammar; for example, the "I" form of the verb might be used for the first time.

After several dialogs, AMR has a short section on how to expand your speaking power by adding extra vocabulary words and phrases to what you have already learned. This section also includes very simple explanations of some essential grammatical features.

AMR uses native speakers, both male and female, carefully chosen from different regions of the target country so you get a cross-section of the different regional accents.

AMR's accompanying manual contains a complete transcript of every cassette, plus informative cultural notes.

AMR's approach would be suitable for anyone except young children, who, not seeing the need for learning the language, would be bored by the adult dialogs. For the traveler, AMR is excellent. Not only do you learn the essential vocabulary for coping with life overseas, but AMR includes cultural notes in its accompanying manual. These notes are obviously written by someone who has been there and who understands that Americans need to know if French hotel rooms have a bathroom (most do not; in fact, you're lucky to have a bathroom on your floor) and other vital facts.

Japanese and Mandarin Chinese are available in Level I only, and are different from the others in that they have been adapted to include significant features of Chinese and Japanese culture. Each course teaches a phonetic form of the language using the English alphabet. The Japanese and Chinese written characters are also provided as they correspond to each dialog.

Each course contains eight one-hour stereo cassettes, a manual with cultural notes and the transcript of the recordings, and a dictionary listing words used, all bound in two very impressive gold-stamped, vinyl-leather cases.

AMR also has Practical Spanish courses for medical workers, policemen, and firemen. These are less expensive than the foreign language courses, probably because nobody had to fly overseas and locate native speakers. You get six high quality C-60 cassettes, and all the other gear included in the regular language courses.

AMR also offers a Strictly Vocabulary series using its patented Bilingual Stereo Self-Test method. This series, available in all the languages mentioned above, is arranged in topics and supplements the Level 1 and Level 2 programs. The price is quite reasonable, for a memory and pronunciation tool covering about two thousand words. Those using a standard language text might want to consider getting AMR's Strictly Vocabulary program to help them with pronunciation. In this way, you could create a total language program for around $60. (It will, of course, be more work than if you got the total AMR language course.) Contents: four cassettes, dictionary of words used, and vinyl-leather case.

AMR's program is among the best for those who want to learn a foreign language with reasonable fluency, but do not plan on permanently moving to the country in question. It is not boring, the recordings are excellent, and you can test your progress as you go.

American Map Corporation
   $13.95, two-cassette courses: French, German, Greek, Italian, Spanish. *Lilliput Dictionary,* $1.75: English/Danish, Dutch, French, German, Italian, Latin, Portuguese, Spanish, or Turkish. Also Danish, Dutch, French, German, Italian, Modern Greek, Portuguese, Spanish, and Turkish/English. *Pocket Dictionary,* $6.95: French, German, Classical Greek, Classical Hebrew, Latin, Portuguese, Russian, and Spanish. Polish Pocket Dictionary, $8.95. Translator 8000, $69.95: French/English, German/English, Spanish/English. Other helps available.

Langenscheidt, "the world's foremost publisher of bilingual dictionaries and foreign language instruction for more than 125 years," is distributed by AMC.

Two LP cassettes plus a 96-page text with the foreign language and English side-by-side are what you get with Langenscheidt's Quick and Easy language series. Langenscheidt also puts out a series of dictionaries, from the matchbox-sized *Lilliput* with ten thousand entries to standard and college dictionaries. The most useful dictionary for most purposes is the pocket-size. It's a 3¾ x 6″ with between thirty-three thousand and fifty-eight thousand entries.

For high-tech types who eschew dictionaries, AMC has the Translator 8000 Pocket Electronic Translation Machine. Type in the word you want in either English or the target language and if it's in the eight thousand word memory, you'll see it on the little screen. It comes equipped with a calculator and, one presumes, batteries.

Audio-Forum
   Individual courses all have different prices. Price range from about $100 to over $200 for FSI courses. Languages: Many Spanish courses, including Business, Medical, Spanish for Policemen and Firemen, Spanish for Health Professionals, and Household Spanish for Home Managers, plus FSI Spanish (several levels). FSI French,

plus Basic Haitian Creole and several dialog series. German. Italian. Modern Hebrew. Arabic (several dialects). Chinese (several dialects). Portuguese. Japanese. Polish. Russian. Modern and Classical Greek. Classical Latin. Scandinavian languages. Eastern European languages. Turkish. Urdu. Thai. Vietnamese. Khmer (Cambodian). Trade languages of Africa. Survival English. In all, more than one hundred courses in more than forty languages. Less expensive courses available.

Audio-Forum does not develop their own courses. As they say, "We have drawn on the expertise of our academic advisory board to help us identify and locate the most effective courses in use anywhere in the United States or abroad. We then obtained the rights to offer these by mail throughout the English-speaking world."

Most Audio-Forum courses are duplicates of the Foreign Service Institute courses used to train U. S. diplomats and overseas personnel. These are the full-length, in-depth courses. Unlike others' language programs, Audio-Forum FSI courses do *not* all follow the same basic format. They do, however, offer a wider variety of languages than anyone else, including Arabic, Cantonese, Hungarian, Hebrew, and Vietnamese, to name just a few. If you want to dig down to your family's "roots" and learn the language of your non-English ancestors, Audio-Forum probably has it.

How does it work? Repetition, repetition, repetition, repetition . . . FSI students normally memorize the dialogs, and one can understand why, since you hear the same one over and over and over. I was surprised to hear the street French of the French I series: *Juizreux* or some such mangled remnant for *Je suis hereux*. That may be the way they talk in France, but it puts a stumbling-block before beginners to not hear extremely distinct pronunciation. We don't mumble at babies, after all!

FSI courses come with culture notes and big, fat textbooks. Make no mistake about it—FSI is the heavy artillery of language instruction.

Audio-Forum is starting to carry Living Language video courses. Vid languages are brand new, so I can't tell you much about them. Ideally, such a course should both have sight-sound association and a reasonable framework to help you remember the individual words and phrases.

Audio Forum also offers the lower-priced Language/30 and No-Time courses. The former was invented by Charles Berlitz and the latter by the sci-fi writer A. E. Van Vogt. No-Time courses are entirely on cassette. You learn the target language alphabet and sounds, then progress to spelled-out sentences. The Language/30 series includes cultural tips. They both sounded pretty good to me.

Berlitz Publications

One-hour course, $9.95: Arabic, Chinese, Dutch, Finnish, French, German, Greek, Hebrew, Italian, Danish, Japanese, Norwegian, Portuguese, Russian, Serbo-Croatian, Spanish (Castillian and Latin American), and Swedish. Basic Home Study Cassette Course, $59.95: French, German, Italian, Spanish. Comprehensive Cassette course, $140: same four languages. Berlitz also has travel guides and phrase books for almost everywhere—get these at bookstores.

Berlitz is now, according to itself, "the world's leading publisher of books for travelers . . . plus Cassettes and Self-teaching courses." Berlitz, as you may recall, started as a you-attend-the-classes language school. The company has wisely decided to put together inexpensive courses using the Berlitz method. These are aimed mostly at the tourist market.

The bottom of the line is Berlitz's one-hour cassette course. You get basic phrases spoken in four voices and a little booklet with the text of the recordings, plus translation. I don't think much of these phrasebooks as a serious learning tool. If all you want is a taste of the language, that's all you'll get.

The Berlitz Cassette Course looks more promising. You get a ninety-minute "zero" or beginner's cassette with ten basic lessons in four voices. These are not just random phrases, but follow a grammatical plan. This is followed by two more sixty-minute cassettes. You also get two illustrated books with the text of all lessons plus helpful notes, a rotating verb finder, a Berlitz phrase book, and a pocket dictionary.

The Berlitz Comprehensive Cassette Course includes all the above, plus two more C-60 cassettes and four more illustrated manuals.

I believe in "baby-talk"—slow, exaggerated pronunciation—for beginners, and Berlitz apparently does not. The Spanish cassette I heard didn't quite race along at Puerto Rican speed, but was pretty brisk nonetheless.

Conversa-phone

"Round-the-world" courses, $8.98: Indonesian, Serbo-Croatian, Chinese (Mandarin and Cantonese), Hindi, Arabic, Czech, Ukrainian, Eastern European and Scandinavian language courses, Turkish, Malay, Irish Gaelic, Korean, Yiddish, Thai, Afrikaans, and Tagalog, plus all the standard European and Asian languages. "Modern Method" courses, $17.98: French, German, Italian, Spanish, Portuguese, Swedish, Russian, Modern Greek, Mandarin Chinese, Advanced Spanish. Many courses available on cassette. Also English for Foreigners series, $17.98: twenty courses, including European, Asian, and Scandinavian languages, plus Arabic and Greek. $2 shipping for the first course, 50¢ additionals.

Let me skip quickly over Conversa-phone's "Round-the-world" courses. These are one record plus text. You can get the standard courses on cassette or 8-track as well, and the "exotic" languages on cassette. In the latter case, the price goes up to $11.98.

I'm skipping over these little courses because I am anxious to extol the Modern Method courses. These come boxed, with your choice of four LP records or two C-60 cassettes, plus a one hundred-lesson illustrated instruction manual. In my estimation, as one who has suffered under many language teachers, these courses are the cheapest, most effective means of brushing up a previously studied language around. You not only get the recorded text plus translation—all companies provide this—but a number of lists and simplified grammar lessons, plus pictures of hundreds of subjects. The text is even witty in spots, and since the text goes beyond the cassettes, you are not limited in your learning to what can be said in two hours of recording time. The whole course comes conveniently boxed.

Conversa-phone evidently hasn't upgraded its graphics since the 1960s, so their catalog and packaging look out-of-step. But don't let that put you off. Nowhere else can you get so much for so little.

ESP

ESP has the very cheapest language instruction around. For $8 you can get a cassette with sixty minutes of instruction, plus a student workbook and tests. For a low-risk taste of another language it sounds reasonable. Available in Beginning, Intermediate, and Tourist Spanish and Tourist French.

General Services Administration

The U.S. Government developed the FSI courses, and surprisingly enough the U.S. Government sells them. Most cassettes are monaural, and you get the slow, slow government delivery.

In my opinion, if you want good service on FSI courses you'd be smart to stick with Audio-Forum. If all you want is good prices, you might get both catalogs and compare.

LANGUAGE COURSES FOR CHILDREN

Courses for children are universally simpler, and often more appealing, than courses for adults. Therefore, any adult who is intimidated by another language and yet wants to learn it might find a children's course congenial. The pace is nonthreatening, and the content is learnable.

School kids range in age from five to eighteen; so keep that in mind when looking at the following selections. You'll find everything from language courses you can use with your baby to courses for senior-high students. Frankly, I'd pick any of these over a college course. The difference nowadays between high school and college is that college texts are more confusing and use more jargon. Since college, by lowering its standards, has become high school, why not stick with high school texts, which at least have to be understandable?

Addison-Wesley

Addison-Wesley has a brand new program for French instruction called "Accents." It's designed for grades seven through twelve. The catalog ad says, "Accents combines carefully paced, manageable lessons with motivating topics and cultural perspectives of interest to secondary students. Throughout this innovative, two-level program, the accent is on active communication, with a special emphasis on listening comprehension." The entire program contains students' texts, workbooks, cassettes, and all sorts of stuff for the teacher. It's so

new that most prices are unannounced as of this writing, and I couldn't wangle a copy to review it. Classroom teachers might want to check this one out.

Alpha Omega Publications
$19.50 for complete set of ten LIFEPACS, each course. Greek Manual, $3. *Textus Receptus* (Greek New Testament), $9.75. *Greek/English Lexicon,* $16. Spanish Instruction and Testing Tapes, $10 for each LIFEPAC unit ($100 in all). Shipping 10 percent.

AOP has LIFEPAC worktexts for both Spanish and New Testament Greek, one full year of each. The Spanish course comes with a set of two cassette tapes, one for practice and one for testing. Along with the dialogs and grammar, each LIFEPAC in the series of ten Spanish worktexts has sections on Cultural Activities, The World of Music, and a What Does the Bible Say? translation exercise.

New Testament Greek covers the essentials of grammar, with plentiful exercises for translating both Greek to English and English to Greek.

AMSCO

AMSCO has texts, workbooks, and dictionaries for French, German, Italian, Latin, and Spanish. Unlike other publishers, AMSCO has third-year texts for all its languages, and even a fourth-year text for Latin. Texts are inexpensive, and sample copies may be obtained by writing on school letterhead.

Audio-Forum
Pronunciation and Reading, Ancient Greek and Classical Latin, each language $19.95.

I'm assuming that Latin and Greek materials belong in this section, because most of the people studying these languages nowadays are preppy kids. Audio-Forum's *Pronunciation and Reading* guides to ancient Greek and classical Latin each come with a booklet and two cassettes. I hope some adults out there will, like me, repent of their youthful unwillingness to tackle these languages. There is no comparison between the prose of those taught by the classical method (which included studies of the language and literature of Greece and Rome) and those turned out by a school system that doesn't even expect its students to learn English. May the Lord hasten the day when men have enough mental oomph to write and understand periodic sentences, and when Newspeak is replaced by words of nobility and vigor.

Christian Character Concepts
Conversational Spanish I, $11.25 postpaid.

Sing, play a board game, make paper bag puppets, and flip flash cards with Christian Character Concepts' new Spanish I and II programs for young Christian children. The songs are really cute (if anything, *too* cute!) and the activities are fun. The lessons include forty to fifty vocabulary words and expressions. Some of the speakers have a Texas accent, but the music is professional and kids will like it. (Shucks, *I* wander around the house singing the songs!)

Hammond
Qu'est-ce Que C'est?, $34 for schools.

Hammond has come out with something that every French enthusiast will want: a visual dictionary. Thousands of pictures and photos show familiar objects, with all the parts labeled in both the target language and English. Now you won't have to stumble around wondering what the French word for *wheel* or *shin* is anymore. It's called *Qu'est-ce Que c'est*, which is French for "What's What?," which is the name of the original English visual dictionary. Although *Qu'est-ce Que C'est?* isn't really a language course, I put it in this section because it looks like a fine addition to a language course.

Independent School Press
Preparatory Latin, Book I and II, $7 each. Many more texts available.

Eager as I am to see classical studies revived, I rejoiced to hear of ISP's Latin text for junior-high students. Bright elementary pupils could use it too, in my estimation, which is a giant step towards providing Latin for suckling infants: my fond dream. *Preparatory Latin* was intended to help young preppies prepare for that inevitable moment when they are flung into a sea of Latin translation. As is so often true, in striving to make a text usable by younger students the authors have produced a book that makes their subject accessible to all, not just the young.

Prep Latin is not merely simplified explanations. It incorporates a variety of teaching methods: "the Traditional, the Aural-Oral, the Linguistic, to name a few." Technical terms are not introduced until absolutely necessary. Grammatical elements show up one at a time before being pinned into a framework. Drill consists of thirty brief sentences per lesson that include the elements being drilled. Also, you get the romance of Pauline the Ant called, you guessed it, *Pericula Paulinae* or *The Perils of Pauline*, complete with cliffhangers.

ISP has a dozen or more other Latin texts, including such gems as the ever-popular *A Latin Crossword Puzzle Book*. (Hey, be honest. It's probably the *only* Latin Crossword Puzzle Book.) Other gems: *Freddus Elephantus*, a Latin elephantasy about pachyderms and show biz. Plus old standbys like *Latin Word Lists* and *Lively Latin* and *Review Latin Grammar* for those made of sterner stuff.

International Linguistics Corp.
Courses in English, Spanish, French, German, Chinese, and Russian. Four books, each with accompanying set of five cassettes. Each book $6, each cassette set $32 except for the set for Book 2 which contains six cassettes and is $38. Intermediate series in English and German only, another four books plus cassettes, same prices. 10 percent discount and free postage on prepaid orders.

International Linguistics invented the first language program designed especially for very young children. Unlike other programs, which stress repeated sentences, grammar, and drill, International Linguistics teaches language through word-picture association. Cassettes accompany picture books; each sentence or phrase goes with a picture. This results in "natural" learning—the way a baby learns. No written words are in the text, either English or in the other language. International Linguistics is

insistent that you must learn through sounds only. It is possible to get a transcript of the tapes, but I.L. does not sell translations. This is an unnecessary hindrance, and the only feature to which I object.

Pictures are in amusing but understandable cartoon style. The stories are clever. Our sons love the sequence with the baby throwing eggs at the window and the harried mother rushing about looking for a paper towel to wipe up the mess, and request it over and over again. Every language uses the same picture book, so subsequent languages can build on the first one learned.

Book 1 has one thousand sentences, as does Book 2. Stories begin in Book 2, and you are introduced to prepositions and pronouns. Book 3 has more complex stories and gets into verb tenses. Book 4 has complex sentences. The Beginner Series of all four books contains a total of three thousand basic words and grammatical constructions. The Intermediate series, available only in English and German, teaches one thousand five hundred words and advanced grammatical structures. When you buy a whole series (Beginner or Intermediate), International Linguistics throws in a vinyl cassette case. You can buy a little at a time, and easily branch out into new languages.

I recommend that you buy a separate picture book for each learner (they are not expensive), as otherwise squabbles develop over who gets to hold the book. We found that mealtimes are a good time to turn on the cassette player and learn a little French, and you might try it too, if you don't mind getting the pages greasy!

R. S. Publications
Learning Spanish Through Spanish, $27.50 complete program. Extra student manuals, $4.75 each.

You don't have to know Spanish to introduce your children to it with this program. Designed for elementary school-aged children, it includes a teacher's manual with detailed lesson plans and lots of suggested activities, a student's manual, a tape of Spanish folk songs, and two tapes to accompany the book exercises. Children sing the folk songs (which are not just played, but *taught* on the tape), dance, do some Hispanic arts and crafts, and learn a little about Hispanic culture. The pronounciation is authentic, and the language is introduced in a natural way. You get a medium amount of vocabulary, sufficient to prepare youngsters for more advanced Spanish courses.

Learning Spanish Through Spanish is a really fun, comfortable program that younger children should respond well to.

Regents Publishing Company
Tune in to English and *O, Susanne*, $5.25 each text, $25 accompanying cassettes. *First Steps in French*, $3.25. *First Steps in Spanish*, $3.50. *Everyday Spanish Idioms*, $5.95. Hundreds more inexpensive ESL, Spanish, French, German, and Chinese materials.

I am not down on public school textbook providers as a group, only those who allow themselves to be bulldozed by special interest groups into using their texts for propaganda. It is with great pleasure, then, that I review the excellent and creative language programs put out by Regents Publishing Company.

Let me say right off that anyone who is seriously interested in teaching languages to young people, or in learning a number of languages, should get Regents' catalog. I don't have space to list all the fascinating methods Regents texts use, but here are some of the humdingers.

Uwe Kind (that's the author's name) thinks you can learn English through music. Take a song like "This Old Man." Change it to teach a specific language function. Put it in songbook form and on cassette, add nineteen more songs, throw in games, puzzles, and other activities to review the language, and presto! You've got *Tune in to English.* Not content with English, Uwe Kind got together with Ursula Meyer to produce the same sort of "Audio-Singual" method in German. It's called—are you ready?— *O Susanne, Ja Konjugier Fur Mich!*, which according to my faulty memory of German is something like *Oh, Susannah, Conjugate for Me!* The title song, roughly translated, goes,

> I work from one to two
> You work until three
> She works the whole day long
> And Sundays she has free.
> Oh, Susannah, you work too hard [all day]
> [Oh, yes] you work from dawn to dusk
> You have no time to play.

In this way, each verse conjugates a verb such as "work," and you couldn't forget the conjugation form even if you wanted to.

Regents also carries Margarita Madrigal's *First Steps* and *Open Door* materials. *First Steps* (in French and Spanish) introduces little kids to the target language through pictures and cognates. A cognate is a word that is very much alike in English and the target language, and Madrigal's genius lies in using these extensively to build much larger vocabularies than would be possible otherwise. It takes no effort at all to learn a cognate. I'll teach you some right now. English words ending in *or* are often the same in Spanish, with the difference that Spaniards put the accent on the last syllable. So color is colór, doctor is doctór, and so on. See how easy it is? *Open Door* is Madrigal's approach dressed up with classroom exercises and language cassettes.

One great stumbling-block when learning languages is mastering the idioms. For immigrants, Regents has several books of American idioms. I like the title of this one: *Colloquial English: How to Shoot the Breeze and Knock 'em for a Loop While Having a Ball.* And for Americans, Regents has books of idioms in other languages. *Everyday Spanish Idioms* is a rich treasure-house of idioms, proverbs, proverbial comparisons, and riddles. This kind of book is a peek into the soul of another nation, and worth reading even if you have no intention of learning the language.

I could go on and on. Regents' catalog is full of enticing titles like *Do's and Don'ts for the Japanese Businessman Abroad* and *Word Games in English.* There are dozens of different programs and hundreds of texts and thousands of cassettes. Don't miss this catalog.

GENERAL LANGUAGE STUDIES (LINGUISTICS)

Independent School Press
Phenomenon of Language, Latin or French, $7 each.

What do you get when you cross Latin with an introductory course in linguistics? It sounds awful, like pasta with barbecue sauce, but really it's great. It's *The Phenomenon of Language,* a sprightly text that uses Latin (or, in the second version, French) as a vehicle for giving students a method for learning all languages quickly and efficiently. Besides the charming Roman-style cartoons and clever activities, the student spends a lot of time discovering how languages work. The exercises are designed according to the Platonic method: students are gently led to draw the correct conclusions on their own.

I cannot overemphasize the usefulness of a text like this. Competence in handling language is really competence in thinking, and as Dorothy Sayers says, the student who masters these processes will reduce by at least 50 percent the amount of effort it takes him to learn future subjects. Latin is a particularly happy choice for this approach, as the structure of all the Roman languages (French, Spanish, Italian, and Portuguese) grew out of it, as did the Norman French portion of our own native English. By combining the study of Latin with the study of language, *The Phenomenon of Language* lays the intellectual foundation for a classical renaissance.

Summer Institute of Linguistics

S.I.L., an affiliate of Wycliffe Bible Translators, is where it's at in modern real-world linguistics. Christian missionaries sweat in the jungle and freeze in the tundra in order to learn, from scratch, the languages of their fellowmen and translate the Bible into them. Thus Christian missionaries have become the world's foremost linguistic experts, and S.I.L. publishes their scholarly works: dictionaries, grammars, linguistic treatises, and so on. If you're looking for uncommon works like an introduction to Cheyenne literature or a trilingual thesaurus in Sedang, Vietnamese, and English, S.I.L. is the place. The huge collection of beginning grammars in non-Western languages, such as *Saramaccan for Beginners,* will light up any linguaphile. If you'd like your son to grow up to be a missionary and to accomplish something really worthwhile in that capacity, try to interest him in S.I.L.'s catalog.

Wff 'n Proof Learning Games Associates
Queries 'n Theories, **$16.**

Delving now into the realm of the arcane and abstract, we come to what might be the ultimate game for eggheads. *Queries 'n Theories* pits a Native against one or more Querists. The Native invents basic sentence structures (represented by colored chips) and rules for legitimate constructions (also represented with chips). The Querist tries to figure out the "language" by asking questions with chips. From here it gets complicated, so don't expect me to explain it in a paragraph. It all has something to do with linguistic theory, and resembles the setup of the LISP computer language, which I know makes it all clear to a select few computer buffs and even foggier to the rest. Linguistics aside, the game stretches your thinking and is really fun to play. It comes nicely packaged, with small vinyl mats and lots of colored chips, plus an instruction booklet and carrying case.

LITERATURE IN OTHER LANGUAGES

Adler's Foreign Books, Inc.

Here is your source for French and German books, including kiddie books in both languages. You won't want to miss the great classics, like *Die Geschichte von Peter Hase,* better known as *Peter Rabbit,* not to mention Tom Sawyer and the Laura Ingalls Wilder Little House series in German. Somehow I just never thought of German kids playing cowboys and Indians! Adler's also has a good selection of genuine German literature, like the adventures of the irrepressible Till Eulenspiegel. Adler's also carries a select list of children's books in Greek, Hungarian, Serbo-Croatian, and Czechoslovakian.

For adults, Adler has German, French, Greek and Latin books. There is a whole catalog devoted merely to German teaching materials. Adler very kindly translates all its catalog items into English for you, so you are not left to flounder in a sea of *wiedersprechen* and *langewerdenalletogethergejammen.*

Adler's is the source for textbooks and materials from *all* German publishers.

American Bible Society

ABS has Bibles in many languages. I remember reading a novel whose main character learned new languages by studying a Bible in the target language. This method could work well if you (1) know the Bible very well and (2) only want to read the new language, or (3) also have cassettes to help you with pronounciation. If you're a Christian and want to talk about Jesus in a foreign country, it wouldn't hurt to have some Scripture memorized in that language. Avoid the "classical" translations that correspond to our King James Version; nobody overseas understands these any better than we understand Elizabethan English today.

ABS's "Scripture Resources in Many Languages" catalog lists Scripture publications in the forty most popular languages, about half of the languages they normally have available. Many Scriptures can be specially ordered even if they are in a language ABS does not normally offer for sale.

All ABS materials are inexpensive.

Caedmon Tapes

Caedmon has recordings of literature in several languages. The Caedmon catalog is immense and you're bound to find something you want in it, whether in English or not.

Jeffrey Norton Publishers

The company that owns Audio-Forum (see the Adult Language Course review) also has a wide line of spoken-word cassettes, including literature in other languages. You can get stories in Chinese, songs from Israel, an Italian interview with Federico Fellini, or Alexander Solzhenitsyn reading *One Day in the Life of Ivan Denisovich* in Russian. J-N also has the complete New Testament on cassette in Spanish, French, Arabic, Hindi, Mandarin, Italian, Portuguese, English, Urdu, German, and Korean. Plus *A Recital of Ancient Greek Poetry* and other classical Greek works, and *Selections from Cicero* in Latin.

Regents Publishing Company

Classics of Spanish and French literature, reasonably priced, some abridged. Don't miss Regents' wacky but effective language programs, reviewed above.

CHAPTER TWENTY-TWO

LITERATURE

It is true that children (and adults) can read for hours armed with nothing more than Spiderman comics and the backs of cereal boxes. If you want your children to fit right in with the current literary trend, this is indeed the best training they could get. For some time American comic books have been getting better—not in a moral sense, but in the quality of the stories and art—and novels have been getting worse in both morals and quality. However, instead of blowing the whistle on the gutter-loving writers who are so busily foisting off their deviant fantasies as literature, our Literary Moguls are actually celebrating the disaster! Indeed, the *New York Times Book Review* has gone so far as to inquire if we are living "in a Golden Age of the American Novel."

Now, it goes without saying that people who are living in a Golden Age of anything do not spend their afternoons asking one another if they are really living in a Golden Age, but the stragglers of 1980 didn't know this, and the response to the questionnaire was almost touching in its fevered loyalty to the dead faith. Yes, yes, they *were* living in a Golden Age, said everybody tearfully, and it was going to get better and better, and everything was going to be All Right.[1]

The point nowadays is to be shocking: film flies crawling around on your nude wife as per John Lennon, make giant soup cans, a project any fifth-grader could have mastered (Andy Warhol—the shock here is at the pettiness of the "art"), or flash your fanny at the screen a la Frank Ripploh. To be a modern literary great, go and do ye likewise. Scribble about child-molesting (Vladimir Nabokov was only the first), marital infidelity (Gay Talese), torture, especially of women and children (William Goldman), or ceaseless "creative" fornication (Henry Miller, followed by too many other "greats" to mention). If possible, wrap the sex and sadism in a melange of disconnected and absurd scenes. Even better, put it all in the first person and ramble on interminably about yourself. If you do this, the critics will fall all over themselves praising your boldness and creativity.

Perhaps the lowest of many low points came when a "blue-ribbon commission" charged with supplying the White House with "great recordings reflecting the wide range of American cultural interests" decided to fulfill their 1980 responsibilities by awarding the President of their nation a copy of a new recording called *Never Mind the Bullocks,* by those great reflectors of the wide range of American cultural interests, the Sex Pistols. But the laugh was on the beribboned authorities, because the Sex Pistols weren't really monuments to the American culture at all; they were monuments to the culture of the United Kingdom.[2]

BOOKS THAT HELP US KNOW WHICH LITERARY PRODUCTS TO DOUSE WITH ROTTEN EGGS AND WHICH TO READ

What to do? The very first step to take if you want to improve your own or your children's literary sensibilities is to read Bryan

Griffin's *Panic Among the Philistines*, quoted above ($5.95, under Regnery Gateway's Discipleship Books imprint). Mr. Griffin's book exposes the spiritual, literary, and literal nakedness of the present Cultural Establishment. It's the bracing tonic we all need, and is good for a few hearty laughs beside—for the real problem in many cases is that we have been taking the laughable seriously. Expanded from an article published in *Harper's* in the summer of 1981, this book is the literary "shot heard round the world." No serious reader should miss it.

While you're at it, you might also pick up a copy of C. S. Lewis's *The Abolition of Man*, published by Macmillan and now in its zillionth printing. Written in Lewis's delightful prose, *Abolition* uncovers the termites who even back in the Forties were gnawing steadily away at our cultural heritage. Further, Lewis explains why great art can't exist without classical values, and why an easy toleration of the obscene and ugly results inevitably in unfreedom. This might sound pretty heavy, but the book itself is short and will not overwhelm any reader who has courage enough to think through these matters.

And if your question is, "Can you please tell me some good books for my children to read?" have I got a book for you! Zondervan's *Honey for a Child's Heart*, subtitled *The Imaginative Use of Books in Family Life* ($5.95), is the most fantastic, inspiring book about books that I have ever read. Gladys Hunt, the author, expertly deals with the questions of what makes a good book a good book and explains how to make family reading a rich part of your life, as well as providing fifty-eight pages of suggested reading for different age levels. The book is illustrated with pictures from recommended books and is an absolute delight to read.

And for those who love America and want a family reading program that reflects this, the Foundation for American Christian Education's *Family Program for Reading Aloud* contains discussions of more than one hundred patriotic books. Three chapters introduce reading aloud and the listening-learning skills. Three more sugget books to read to the youngest (FACE is pro-Mother Goose). Six chapters introduce American themes, including immigrants and ethnic groups, pioneers and Indians, and even American horses! The last two chapters help you evaluate your family reading program.

Last of all, for those looking for Christian books for their children, Tyndale House has published a *Parent's Guide to Christian Books for Children* by Nancy L. Nehmer. It's an annotated list of one hundred and thirty books, "carefully selected and evaluated from more than 350 Christian books from 30 publishers." Each entry lists title, author, publisher, reading level, length, and publication date, plus a brief review of the book. *Honey for a Child's Heart* covers some of this ground, but

since the *Parent's Guide* is only $2.50 it won't hurt to pick it up too.

What more remains but to rediscover the genuine literary treasures of the past? Here those of us who are Christian immediately run smack dab into a problem. Those great old books weren't all evangelistic tracts. And certain folk in our own small version of the Cultural Establishment would have us totally ignore anything that doesn't arrive embossed with the Praying Hands.

If you're all tied up in knots over this problem, I suggest that you read Franky Schaeffer's *Addicted to Mediocrity*, published by Crossway Books. Its premise is essentially correct: reality *is* God's world, and you don't need to plaster Bible verses all over art to make it edifying or Christian.

In Philippians Christians are told to seek after what is true, noble, right, pure, lovely, and admirable. I believe that as this applies to art, we are to look for what is *true to life*. God does not condemn fiction, for Jesus Himself told parables. The point is that evil should not be glamorized, or even *explicitly* described. God tells us, for example, that the men of Sodom were sinners. The Bible does not glamorize their sin though, or give us "how-to" details about how to sodomize strangers. Thus stories of heroism, true or fictional, can be Christian even if the protagonists do not spend their entire time preaching, and scenes of evil that show its ugliness without dwelling on how it is perpetrated are also legitimate. Classical literature shows good and evil in their true lights; most modern literature, sadly, does not.

Following is a selection of sources for classical and modern literature, with a definite tilt to the classical. Some sources are extremely worthwhile, some less so. I have included sources for recorded books because a story is a story, and we can all learn how to improve our reading aloud by listening to professionals. Excuses aside, cassette stories are *fun!* There are books for beginning readers and books for adults (*not* "adult books!"). Some magazines and papers are included for their offbeat or literary qualities.

And of course, don't forget the library!

LITERATURE ON RECORDS AND TAPE

Caedmon Tapes
Most cassettes and records, $8.98 each. Sets cost less per recording.

Caedmon has a vast collection of spoken-word recordings of literature—modern, classical, ancient, British, American, European, and other, for people both young and old. Some recordings, like Carol Channing's performance of *Winnie-the-Pooh*, have music as well, and this is indicated by a little black musical note in the margin. Many are abridged, the better to fit on a C-60 cassette. The selection includes novels, fairy tales, poems, legends, science fiction, and fantasy. Many works are read by the authors. Some *poseurs* are included here also, but the good outweighs the bad.

Caedmon cassettes are not narrated, but "performed" by the likes of W. H. Auden, Dylan Thomas, Carol Channing, and Michael Bond (of Paddington Bear fame). The recordings are not all entertainment, though. You can get several Great Speeches sets featuring speeches that changed history, Studs Terkel's story of the Depression in the words of those who lived it, Camus reading his own novels (in French, naturally). Eggheads, in short, are in for a feast.

Caedmon's catalog is prosaic, and prices are not cheap (most cassettes are $8.98 and up). For diehard cassette fans, there is a way around the price boondoggle: sign up for the Library Subscription Plan. Of the four options, the one most likely to interest home schoolers is the Small Budget Children's Plan. You agree to buy each new Caedmon release in that category at a reduced rate, for a maximum investment of $55/year for ten cassettes. In return, you get 40 percent off on all Caedmon recordings and all Arabesque recordings (classical music and opera).

Mind's Eye

Most cassettes $5.95 each, including *Color Book Theater.* Sets are less per cassette.

This gorgeous, easy-to-use catalog contains mystery, intrigue, Ray Bradbury sci-fi, horror (those I skip), and set after set of classic tales that I drool over and hope to buy someday. For only $5.95 each you can get fairy tales (fully dramatized), classical children's stories, Mark Twain, Charles Dickens, Tolkien, dramatized biography, radio classics, Greek classics, American novels, and more!

Of interest to parents is *Color Book Theater,* for children ages three to eight. Each *Color Book Theater* pack contains a cassette, a coloring/story book, and a box of crayons. A special "act-with" feature allows a child to become the hero, as Side 2 contains the same story without the hero's lines. By reading the appropriate lines in the accompanying book (which are printed in boldface) your child can become the main character. Twelve children's classics are in this format. Someday we'll buy some; in the meantime, I've ordered gifts from this catalog.

Jeffrey Norton Publishers

Jeffrey Norton has a smallish selection of famous writers reading their own works.

Recorded Books

Thirty-day rental or sale. Prices start at $14.95, which includes a "durable bookshelf album with color cover art and contents information."

"Cover to cover studio recordings of the very best in current and classic fiction brought to life on standard-play cassettes by professional narrators." Rental available. Some "adult" cassettes. RB has lots of good stuff, too: P. G. Wodehouse, Tolkien, Jane Austen, James Hamilton narrating the New Testament, Gilbert and Sullivan operas with libretto, and Solzhenitsyn, among others.

SBI Publishers in Sound

Children's classics cassette library, $5.75 each, $65 for a set of twelve. Slow-playback cassette recorders start at $120 (with discount).

Parents magazine recommended SBI's Children's Classics Library. SBI offers adult classics as well. Some material is substandard from a Christian viewpoint; all is superbly read. All titles are unabridged.

SBI offers slow-playback titles also (eighty in all). The advantage of slow-playback is that much more material can be recorded per cassette, thus bringing the price down and sparing you unnecessary trips to flip the cassette. SBI also sells slow-playback cassette players.

SBI's forty-five-day rental plan is the longest in the industry.

I'm really tempted by the slow-play machine. Imagine taping an entire three-hour meeting on one C-90 cassette! SBI thinks the industry will move this way because it is so much more economical. If you're looking for economy and/or innovation, you might send for this catalog.

CHILDREN'S LITERATURE, REAL AND ABRIDGED, AND OTHER STUFF IN PRINT

AMSCO School Publications, Inc.

Paperback classics, $3-$4 range. Hardbacks, $5-$6.

These incredibly inexpensive, library-quality paperbacks and hardbacks run the gamut of old and new classics. Some come with a Reader's Guide that "focuses the reader's attention on the humanistic and aesthetic elements of a specific literary work." These teacher-written Guides look at such things as plot, character, and literary devices, as well as exploring unfamiliar vocabulary. If you would rather face literature without a teacher holding your hand, fifty-seven of the titles come without a Reader's Guide.

AMSCO offers discount prices to schools; so if you *are* a school, be sure to mention this. The selection includes classics like *Wuthering Heights, Vanity Fair, Huck Finn,* and *Tom Sawyer,* plus Dickens, Hawthorne, Shakespeare, and so on, as well as some modern works like *Flowers for Algernon,* a genuine science fiction classic. All books are complete and unabridged, and most are under $4 (for schools).

Capper's Books

Capper's has been around for a while; Laura Ingalls Wilder was reading *Capper's Weekly* before the turn of the century. The folks at Capper's, therefore, can tell the difference between a classic and a new-hatched dodo. They stock the former and avoid the latter.

According to Capper's, "our true specialty is in our strong selection of popular children's classics." These include such titles as *Mrs. Wiggs of the Cabbage Patch,* which thankfully has nothing to do with Cabbage Patch dolls, *A Girl of the Limberlost,* and nature-lover Thornton W. Burgess's 1909 classic, *Old Mother West Wind.* These gentle stories contrast sharply with the selfishness, nastiness, and flippishness of much of what now passes for children's literature.

Christian Light Publications

Christian Light offers literature they consider suitable for young children, chosen in conformity with Mennonite moral standards. Each work offered comes with a code that explains just how good they think the book is and if they recommend it with any reservations.

Crestwood House.

Horse, Tech, Movie Monster, and Crisis series, each book $8.95. Values clarification, $9.95 each book. Back to Nature, Survival series, $7.95 each book.

Crestwood House has published several series of books designed for the *interest* level of older students, with the *vocabulary* level of younger students. Jam-packed with photos and illustrations (the publisher tries to include something visual on every two-page spread in every book), Crestwood books are supposed to tempt reluctant readers. All come durably bound, and the hardbacks are library-bound. Crestwood books come highly recommended by the school establishment.

I like "hi-lo" books, but not for the usual reasons. Home schoolers do not usually have reluctant older readers who need books with limited vocabulary. We do, however, have younger children who could stand being exposed to something more profound than the books publishers consider appropriate to their "age level." Hi-lo books make the adult world more accessible.

The series on horses and the one on technology both look interesting. The Horse series is eight volumes dealing with different kinds of horses, with a special volume on Ruffian, the thoroughbred racer. The Technology series, also eight volumes, describes how various items are made. There's a book each about sport shoes, cassettes and records, video games, trucks, microcomputers, books, racing cars, and balls. You may want to consider this latter series for your home program, as it shows children how the various disciplines combine in the real world to produce a product.

Crestwood House's best seller is the Movie Monster series. Nobody thinks these are good literature, but schools and libraries buy them because kids will read them.

You probably won't want the Values Clarification series or the Crisis series. Life is tough enough already, and since these were prepared for the public school market they are not allowed to contain any real spiritual answers. The Wildlife series looks delightful except for the constant concern about how man is stealing the critters' habitat. Crestwood's various series on sports (including disco dancing!) concentrate on stars and unusual sports in an effort to gain children's interest. The Back to Nature series and Survival series sound most edifying of this group. The Survival books are *true* stories of people struggling for life in wilderness situations. Protagonists range from a fourteen-year-old boy to a seventy-seven-year-old man, providing this series with a depth of human interest often lacking in children's literature.

Since the books are relatively expensive, you might want to check your library before sending for Crestwood's catalog.

DIDAX

Ladybird books, $2.50 each.

If you're looking for classics recast in Dick-and-Jane vocabulary, DIDAX has the stuff. From England DIDAX imports the Ladybird books, brightly colored and lavishly illustrated redoings of classics and fables. This grew, as you can guess, out of the "sight word" approach. Ladybird also sells a sight-word reader series of thirty-six (count 'em) little books plus two picture dictionaries and workbooks, very aptly titled The Key Words Reading Scheme. (Not that they aren't cute and clever little books—it's just that any program which can persuade teachers and parents to buy thirty-six readers deserves to be called a "scheme.")

But we digress. The Ladybird books are inexpensive (singly) and supereasy to read, and will provide a diluted taste of the real thing for very young readers or those whose progress has been temporarily crippled by look-say.

Ladybird also has a clever little series for beginning readers featuring huge print and instruction about numbers, time, the alphabet, and so on.

Educational Insights

Each set of twelve cartoon books, twelve spirit masters, and teacher's guide, $19.95. Accompanying read-along cassettes for each set, $40. Thirty-six-booklet sets, $50. *Read-Along* cassettes, $110.

What do you get when you cross Spiderman with Edgar Allan Poe? Something I wouldn't want to meet in a dark alley—or the Educational Insights literature comics. Yes, you read that right! Educational Insights has compiled several boxes of four-page comics. Each comic tells, in compact form, one classic tale. And there's more! For the really hard-to-motivate literary dilettante, you can also purchase read-along cassettes to accompany the comics!

Each box also contains a number of spirit masters equal to the number of comics, and a teacher's guide. The spirit masters, one presumes, are for testing the carefree readers to see if they were really reading or just had a schoolbook propped open inside the comic.

Sets are: American Short Stories, which has thirty-six different comics by thirty-six different authors; Short Stories Around the World, which has twelve stories each at second, third,

and fourth-grade reading levels; three series of Adventure Stories (Ghosts and Monsters, Adventures in Mystery, and Adventures in Science Fiction), each featuring twelve tales; and three series of Classic Tales (Tales of Robin Hood, Tales of King Arthur, and Tales from Shakespeare—the latter "in modern dialog"), each likewise containing twelve tales. Oh, yes, I almost forgot the set of Great Sports Stories, perhaps because it doesn't really count as literature in the finest, truest sense of the word.

Your child will not discover great writing by reading comics, but he will at least become aware of the main plot of many masterpieces and perhaps become interested in the masterpieces themselves. I read several of these comics, or something like them, when I was in pigtails and it didn't cripple me for life. (What almost *did* turn me off to the classics was trying to read the agonizingly long *Lorna Doone* in an unabridged version at the age of eight.) We do not scoff, then, at Educational Insights' humble efforts to bring the classics to the people.

Foundation for American Christian Education (F.A.C.E.)

Webster's, $30 retail, $16 to Christian schools, churches, study groups, and home schoolers.

Not everyone reviews dictionaries. But then we're not looking at any ordinary dictionary. FACE sells a facsimile edition of Noah Webster's 1828 *American Dictionary of the English Language.* Not only is this volume a stunning addition to your library shelf (being hardcover, gold-embossed, and over two and a half inches thick), it also is a fascinating landscape of the American language as spoken when peope believed in God and grammar. FACE calls this edition of Webster's "the only American Christian dictionary," and although Bob Jones University may dispute that, this classic Webster's certainly breathes forth a refreshing air.

One very evident use of this volume would be to look up those obscure words with which old literature is dotted. Thus, if in perusing Chaucer one is puzzled by the word "swinker," flip to the spot in FACE's Webster's and discover that the term once meant "laborer" or "plowman." Webster gives a literary reference for many words, a la Dr. Johnson in his famous lexicography, as well as an etymology. The definitions clearly emanate from a sober and serene mind, and for that reason reading Webster's is very calming. The print is decently large and the definitions enticing.

Grolier Enterprises

One morning you unwittingly open your mailbox and there it is, lurking inside. It looks innocuous enough—an ad for a children's book club. The one I got most recently said, "Your child's lifelong love of reading begins with . . . 4 books for only $1.95, Plus A FREE Tote Bag."

So what's so dangerous, you ask? Just this: Grolier Enterprises' Beginning Readers' Program may do *exactly* what it says! Are you ready for a *lifelong* love of reading? Are you ready to have your arm jerked off every time you try to walk your children past a bookstore or a library? Reading can get to be a *habit,* you know!

The initial four books, at $1.95 for all four plus shipping and handling, are just to hook you on the program. Thereafter, every four weeks you will be sent two more books. If you want to keep them, you will pay $3.99 each plus shipping and handling. If you don't want to keep them, you will have to repack them, drive to the Post Office, and return them. This must be done within ten days. It is, in short, a *lot* of effort to return the books. Keep that in mind when considering enrollment.

The Beginning Readers' Program features the likes of Dr. Seuss and the Berenstain Bears. How do I know you can get hooked on Seuss? Because those are the books my father used to teach me to read, and I wore out three library cards before I turned fifteen!

Grolier has a similar program, entitled Disney's Wonderful World of Reading. The ad for this one offered two free books and a bookrack, plus a chance to win a sweepstakes. Terms are the same as for the Beginning Readers' Program. The books are, you guessed it, Walt Disney productions like *Pinocchio* and *Cinderella*. You know as much about Walt Disney as I do, so I leave this offer to your judgment.

Open Court Publishing Company
Lit Kit prices between $30 and $60. From eight to eighteen books per kit.

Open Court's Lit Kits are, according to the publisher, "The best in children's books grouped by grade and interest level." I really like most of their selections, but as a Christian I have trouble with the witch/dragon stories that make it into many of the kits. Sheerly from the viewpoint of literary quality, each kit's selections are well chosen.

An example of one kit (for second grade): *Make Way for Ducklings; Pickles and Jake; Madeline and the Bad Hat; Madeline and the Gypsies; Jack Jouett's Ride; Dandelion; Stone Cutter; Magic Michael; Hildilid's Night; The Shy Little Girl; Blaze and the Forest Fire; Frederick; Swimmy; Bearymore; Bedtime for Frances: Moon Mouse*. You can see you get your $51.75 worth. You can also see that not all kits contain occultic lit. When you consider how popular that genre is nowadays, Open Court is actually very conservative in the amount included.

The books are paperback, and per book the price is certainly right. The Lit Kit is certainly an easy way to build a home library.

Silver Burdett
Hardbound classics, $3.25 each.

I couldn't believe the price when I first saw it, and I still find it hard to believe. Where else can you get a complete, unabridged, hardbound classic for under $4? The selection is not very large, but all are genuine classics. Each includes a Study Guide with "short-answer questions, background information, composition skills practice, research topics, creative activities, a bibliography, and an audiovisual list of resources."

LITERARY CRITICISM ON CASSETTE

Everett/Edwards Cassette Curriculum
Each cassette, $12.50 postpaid.

> What you hear is what you get:
> Hundreds of critics on cassette.

Everett/Edwards says, "The true purpose of a 'critic' . . . is to aid and enlighten the student. . . ." Strong in this noble purpose, E/E has assembled a veritable army of critics and turned them loose on the literary giants. E/E believes that by listening to the critics criticize, the student will learn to analyze and ultimately to think for himself. It does help, of course, if the student reads the work in question, and E/E is the first to point this out.

E/E has an American Folklore series which includes lectures on all the principal genres as well as such ersatz themes as "The Military in Folklore" and "The Folklore of Social Elites." If I were a schoolteacher spending department money I might look into it; having only our own money to spend, I shall wait. E/E also has a Women's Studies series (intended for schools, mind you) which includes such objects as *Was Jesus a Feminist?*, *Women, Witches, and Worship*, *Open Marriage* (a euphemism for consenting adultery), and *The Prejudice of Parents*. Ironically, E/E suggests we should "Give Cassettes for Christmas." We might consider this if E/E would kindly get rid of the portions of its curriculum that knock Christ and Christianity.

Jeffrey Norton Publishers
Most cassettes are $12.45 postpaid.

This company, which also owns Audio-Forum and Video-Forum, has a catalog entitled Sound Seminars. Captured on cassette are a host of critics dissecting the works of other people. If this sounds like a good idea to you, Jeffrey Norton has, besides individual cassettes of individual critics, a series by Heywood Hale Broun and another by Gilbert Highet, both of which have been hailed as provocative, intelligent, and, in Mr. Highet's case, charming. You can also get Norman Mailer talking about existentialism, Stephen Spender talking about everybody, and Shakespeare talked about by everybody. Auden discusses poetry, and Frost reads his own poems.

MAGAZINES FOR YOUNG LITERATI

Classical Calliope
One year (four issues) for $13.95. Single issue $3.50. Quantity prices and back issues available.

Homer is looking for a few good men. Well, a few good boys and girls, anyway. The optimistic folks at Cobblestone Publishing actually believe there are American children who are interested in such things as the temple of Artemis at Ephesus, Greek and Roman coinage, and other trivia surrounding the vast amount of Greek and Roman writing known as "the classics." Myth and fable are cunningly resurrected, illustrated, and explained in hopes that American youth will show some slight interest in this part of our Western cultural heritage. Picture now the bespectacled hordes of Homer-lovers invading our libraries in search of an authentic rendering of *The Iliad!*

Besides myths retold and articles about classical society, *Classical Calliope* contains games, a section on English abbreviations that arise from classical language, a section on word origins, and another on the history of language. Even the page numbers are in Roman numerals! All is done with finesse, including the illustrations.

Cricket magazine

One year (twelve issues), $19.80 U.S.A., $23.80 Canadian and foreign. Single copy $1.95.

Cricket has been called "the New Yorker of kiddie lit." Each issue is a work of art: beautiful illustrations and stories written by top writers. *Cricket's* editor, Marianne Carus, is very, very picky about what goes into the magazine. She has been known to turn down stories offered by the likes of world-famous writer William Saroyan. Saroyan later tried again with a better story, which she accepted. What other magazine comes with a personal recommendation from Isaac Bashevis Singer? *Cricket* has won many awards for excellence, including finalist status in the National Magazine Awards competition—the only children's magazine so selected.

Of interest to home schoolers: Nancy Wallace's son Ishmael once "placed" in a *Cricket* writing competition. (See *Better than School*, reviewed in the Basic Books About School and Home School Chapter.)

The magazine's mascot is (surprise!) a cricket, who with his buggy friends, collectively known as Everybuggy, cavorts around the margins helping readers better understand the stories. Cricket also has his own adventures and his own comic strip in each issue.

Stories range from Sid Fleischmann's howling funny McBroom tall tales to true tales about volcanic eruptions (remember Krakatoa?) and "realistic" stories about kids and their relationships, with everything in between. Many stories have fantasy themes (friendly ghosts, brave mother dragons, and the like).

Cricket reflects the values of modern, sophisticated, fashionable culture.

THOSE FAMOUS *McGUFFEY* READERS

One last word: McGuffey. No discussion of literature would be complete without some mention of the famous *McGuffey Readers* used by millions of American children. McGuffeys are coming back "in" for sure. You can find them in the strangest places—like a catalog mostly devoted to Jack Daniel whisky paraphernalia.

The question is not, "Should we get a set of *McGuffeys?*" You either love McGuffey's Christian emphasis and moralizing or you don't. The question really is, "Which set of *McGuffeys* is the best?"

There are, you see, McGuffeys and McGuffeys. Mott Media prides itself on offering the *original McGuffeys*, a la the 1836-37 version compiled by Rev. McGuffey himself. (Seven volumes: hardback set $69.95, paperback $39.95.) Others are quick to point out that Mott's version is not an exact reproduction; words have been changed, the grammar has been amended, and the layout has been revised. The only completely authentic original McGuffey's around is the facsimile edition of the *Pictorial Eclectic Primer* sold by Buck Hill Associates. Buck Hill also has a version they call a "faithful reproduction" of the originals, seven illustrated hardbound volumes for $32.50. Is it a facsimile edition also? I don't know.

Now that we've settled (or confused) the issue of authenticity, several contenders still remain in the field. Thoburn Press has published a very successful Christian School Edition of the revised edition of 1880. The Primers in this version are much more useful for actual teaching reading than the originals, following a more phonetic plan. The price is right, too ($42.75 for seven hardback readers or $24.95 for all seven paperback volumes in an attractive slipcase).

Hewitt Research Foundation has gone all the field one better and put out the *Moore-McGuffey Readers* with new illustrations in color. Unafraid to tackle the venerated script, Dr. Raymond Moore has edited McGuffey with an eye to practicality in teaching reading. The grammar has been updated and some stories rewritten to remove spiritual teaching Hewitt considers misleading or offensive. Condensed into four volumes, Hewitt's entry is popular in spite of its expense ($55 for the set of four hardbound books: $14 apiece).

I am not much help in picking out *McGuffeys*. Although we have owned three different sets over the years, when friends ask my advice about *McGuffeys* I suggest that they forgo the use of "readers" entirely and patronize the library. For its moral character, McGuffey's is worthwhile, as are a host of other books written at the time. As an introduction to hearty American and English literature, McGuffey has its uses. But the point of studying literature is to study *literature*—the actual books themselves. It takes more than a passing handshake to get to know Shakespeare, or Longfellow, or Donne, or Dryden. Reverend McGuffey kindly offers to introduce us to the greats, but if we knew what we were doing we could introduce ourselves.

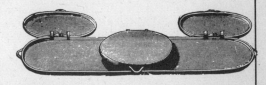

CHAPTER TWENTY-THREE

SPEECH

Have you listened to your teenager today? If you did, could you understand what he or she said? I don't have a teenager of my own, but I do get to talk to people of that age occasionally, and it's alarming how many of them are completely innocent of any kind of decent diction. What is this inarticulate mumbling, this rambling sprinkled with "uh" and "um," this helpless inability to communicate? Why do many of even the smartest teenagers sound like words are hot potatoes burning the insides of their mouths? Why *can't* the English teach their children how to speak?

John Holt has a fascinating explanation of the agony of the inarticulate. He points out that American schoolchildren very rarely get any practice in speaking. They must be silent in class, silent in the halls, and in some cases are not even allowed to speak in the lunch room! Once home, youngsters flop in front of the TV (more practice in silence) or struggle with homework (it's hard to work up a good conversation with a math worksheet). Mute all day, it's not surprising that their very speech is unclear and hesitant.

Not *all* American children suffer from this condition, and we are glad to meet the exceptions. Still, millions tiptoe into adulthood insecure about their communication abilities. This is tragic, because people judge you even more by your speech than by your dress or background. You can prove this to yourself by a simple mental test. Who would you suspect of being a member of the local country club: a young man in ragged jeans and T-shirt who spoke eloquent English with a slight Harvard accent, or another young fellow with identical features who, dressed in a fancy suit, fouled up his grammar and mumbled constantly? A gentleman may go slumming, yet be recognized by his accent, and uneducated social climbers are likewise instantly known by their speech.

Some of the following resources were designed to help overcome speech problems, from incorrect diction to actual physical difficulties. Others help to build a good foundation before problems arise. Still others are for those who want to increase their speaking power and persuasiveness. Why suffer from "fluff-in-mouth disease"? Let the pros show you how to harness pitch, speed, modulation, and pronunciation to your chariot, and how to give what you say "oomph" by increasing your vocabulary.

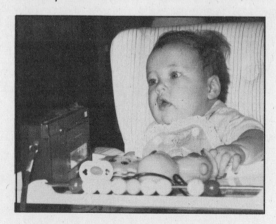

RESOURCES FOR INCREASING YOUR SPEAKING SKILLS

Achievement Basics
Communication Commercials, record or cassette, $11.25/set. *Bright Baby* tape, $5.95 including Parents' Booklet.

The *Communication Commercials* are a fun way for kids or adults to improve their speaking and dramatic skills. A professional announcer introduces or narrates the commercials, each of which is designed to illustrate a particular vocal skill. One commercial, for example, is a diction drill. Another helps you practice speaking with enthusiasm. By imitating the taped commercial, the listener can loosen up and try new skills without inhibitions. The commercials come with a transcript and instructions on how to use them.

The *Bright Baby* tape babbles to your baby in a sequence designed to stimulate the necessary developmental steps. You will be encouraged at how much "developmental babbling" sounds like the normal lovey-sounds you probably already make to your baby. If you are the strong, silent type, you could either (1) play the tape for your baby so you don't have to make all those gooey noises, or (2) play the tape for yourself until the gooey noises sound normal and you lose your fear of sounding silly.

The *Bright Baby* tape is pleasant to listen to—gentle voices, music, and simple sound effects. It can be used any time after two months of age.

We kid-tested this tape and found, to our surprise, that our baby was quite interested and willingly imitated the taped sounds.

Advanced Memory Research (A.M.R.)
English Vocabulary 1 and 2, $80 each. Sharpen Your Public Image, $59.50

Some wit has said that the 1980s are the era when *everyone* will be a star . . . for ten minutes. In the spirit of "The Gong Show," hundreds of TV and radio stations, not to mention thousands of newspapers, are desperately searching for new guests to interview. If you're not careful, you might get drafted! What will you do then? AMR has the answer. The *Sharpen Your Public Image* series shows you how to handle yourself in interview situations "from newspaper interviews to nationally televised talkshows." It includes tips on dress and body language as well as on how to communicate your message under pressure. You get four C-60 stereo cassettes, a manual with transcripts of all recorded materials, and one nifty bookshelf-sized binder to store your ticket to stardom.

AMR's *English Vocabulary* series is designed to increase your word power. Words are presented in groups of four related words and four contrasting words. This method helps you develop "word sense," the ability to find the exact word you want. Each word is presented with its definition, spelling, pronunciation, category (noun, verb, etc.), and an illustrative sentence. *Vocab 1* introduces over five hundred words that you can use in your writing or general conversation. *Vocab 2* presents "over 500 words in a number of specialized subject categories" such as "Business, Economics, Diplomacy, Debate, Politics, Fine Arts, Sociology . . . Medicine, Law, Psychology, Religion . . ." Each set comes with eight C-60 cassettes, a manual containing a transcript of all the recorded material, and a reference dictionary, all attractively bound in two bookshelf-size cases. The advantage of the cassette presentation, if it measures up to the quality of the other AMR recordings I have heard, is that you will be exposed to hours of correct pronunciation and diction, as well as getting a crack at increasing your vocabulary.

Audio-Forum
All Speechphone courses, $39.50 each.

Audio-Forum has latched on to the Speechphone series developed by speech specialist Hazel Brown. Billed as "not just a recorded speech course," but "an actual private study method," the Speechphone series has been used for almost thirty years "in leading colleges and universities in this country and abroad." You listen and repeat the words, sentences, and phrases, which according to the brochure "are paced so that . . . improvement will be apparent from the first lesson."

The Elementary Course is for foreign-born learners who can read simple English but have trouble communicating, and for Americans who suffer from limited vocabulary. The Intermediate Course is for those who want to eliminate a local accent (e.g., who no longer want to "pahk the cah in Hahvad Yahd"). Advanced foreign students are directed to this course as well. The Advanced Course finds Americans and the foreign-born now tackling "the finer nuances of the language." Each course consists of three cassettes and a sixty-four-page Study Guide, plus a word list.

And for those who are uncertain of their pronunciation, Audio-Forum has a Word List on three cassettes that offers "up-to-date pronunciation of more than 3,000 words." It comes with a 130-page book.

Caedmon Tapes
Most two-cassette series go for $19.95

The great Welsh preacher Dr. Martyn Lloyd-Jones used to say that the best way to learn public speaking was to attend the debates in Parliament. Since our abode is nowhere near those hallowed halls, are we then doomed to miss out entirely on the fine speaking of the ages? Nay, dear friends. Caedmon Tapes has preserved for us some echoes of the vocal extravaganzas of the past through its Great Speeches and Great Debates series. Each set contains two cassettes. Most are performances of the speeches rather than recordings of the speeches themselves. The exception: the Great American Speeches post-1931, which recording technology has preserved for us. Recreated bits of eloquence cannot perfectly duplicate the originals. Still, if you want to move others, you might inquire as to what has moved men and women in the past. All performances are professional (Patrick Magee helps out with the Great British Speeches, for example).

You can get Great: Indian Speeches, American Speeches (1775-1896, 1898-1918, 1931-1947, 1950-1963), Black Speeches (of the nineteenth century), and British Speeches (597-1625, 1628-1780, 1783-1812, 1867-1940). The Great Debate series are (1) Hamilton vs. Jefferson and (2) Lincoln vs. Douglas.

Conversa-phone
Speak-Well Course, $8.98. Advanced English course, $17.98. Shipping extra.

For quick and cheap speech improvement, you might want to look into Conversa-phone's Speak-Well Speech Improvement Course. You get one record with every English sound both in isolation and in words and phrases. Read from the accompanying manual, listen to the record, and then adjust any differences. Plus the manual contains breathing exercises, simple diagrams for mouth movements, a complete Speech System Chart, and a Sound-Age Chart that lets you know how soon you should expect Junior to thtop lithping all over the plathe.

Conversa-phone's *Advanced English* course has demonstrations of the correct use of colorful words, phrases, and idioms done in four voices on three LP records, plus an instruction manual. The idea is to help out your vocabulary and diction at the same time.

DIDAX
Form sound cards, $16.96/set.

Anyone ever told you your mouth was too big? Take comfort: the "Mr. Big Mouth" speech training program makes all mere human mouths seem dainty by comparison. It's a transparent reproduction of the oral cavity with (get this!) removable incisors, for demonstrating correct tongue and mouth position.

If you're not in the mood to twiddle incisors, Didax also sells cards with pictures of mouths making our English sounds. Each card has a mouth photo, the letter being pronounced, a word beginning with that letter, a picture of the word, and the deaf/dumb "sign" for the letter. The set includes a teacher's guide. Its usefulness for therapy is obvious.

Developmental Learning Materials (DLM)
Tok-Back, $13.75. *Land of S, Land of R,* $18.50 each. *Therapy Fun,* $23. *Remediation,* $30.

It would weary both of us for me to try to describe *all* DLM's speech therapy products, especially since they're all laid out so nicely in DLM's free color catalog. Let's just look at those that off the bat are most geared to families.

Tok-Back is a speech mask that reflects the sounds children make right back into their little ears. You get to hear what you *really* sound like wearing this blue plastic contraption, which attaches to both ears and then kind of curves around in front of your mouth.

Land of R and *Land of S* are board games meant to entice unwilling youngsters into practicing their *r*'s and *s*'s, respectively. The troublesome letters are practiced both in isolation and "in blends in conversational speech." Both games were "designed for four different levels of articulation ability."

DLM also has items like *Therapy Fun With /s/ and /z/* (what a name!) and the more prosaic *Remediation of Vocal Hoarseness,* which teaches chronic screamers to relax, already, and stop warping those vocal chords. DLM's prices are not abusive, so if you're in the market for this sort of thing you might give them a whirl.

Play 'n Talk
$210, complete program.

Play 'n Talk, reviewed and recommended in the Reading section, is a complete language arts program on records, plus many supplemental items. Youngsters who learn to read with this method will at least be exposed to some superb diction, in the persons of the female narrators. Moreover, *Play 'n Talk*'s phonics approach allows learners to become acutely aware of the different speech sounds. Although not mentioned as a benefit in the *Play 'n Talk* brochure, I found my diction improving from merely hearing the records.

Toastmasters International

The public speaking club, Toastmasters offers programs for older youths and adults. At club meetings, members practice different roles: toastmaster, timer (of speeches), introducer, evaluator, and of course the speechifier himself. Toastmasters believes in applauding all performances, no matter how insipid, so nobody is humiliated for even feeble efforts. If you do decide to join, unless you have scads of free time don't let them draft you into serving as a club officer! This happened to my husband, Bill, and though we survived, it was a struggle!

Youngsters don't have Toastmaster Clubs of their own, but Toastmasters occasionally take pity on them and conduct speaking courses for the younger set. I don't know what would happen if a younger person tried to join Toastmasters. My guess is that he or she would be welcomed with open arms.

CHAPTER TWENTY-FOUR

SPELLING

English is a lot of things,
But E-Z it is knot.
To lurn to spell, it wood be swell.
But then, there's words like "caught"—
And "through," and "new," and "blue," and
* "do,"*
That sound just like each other, too,
Their spelling out of Latin grew
Or French, or German, or Hindu
And you are left without a clue—
Or so your teachers taught.

But wait! When phonics comes to play
Upon this lingo ours,
The sense it makes will quash mistakes,
Increase your spelling powers,
And you will gladly come to see
That English is no mystery,
It can be spelled consistently
E'en by the likes of you and me
And all the rules that set you free
Just take a couple hours.

Now you've endured my doggerel
And shown your patient side,
Look down below, for it will show
How spelling gets untied
From all its knots and nots and naughts,
I've found you lots and lots and lots
Of ways to slip those words in slots
The finest money ever boughts!
(You see, a poet I am nots.)
The finest ever buyed!

As Ogden Nash says, "I think I'd better end this song." Don't let my poetic ineptitude stop you from getting the point, though, which is that *phonics cures spelling problems.* It does, that is, if the people who make up the program make sure to work on the translation of English-to-letters (spelling) as well as on letters-to-English (reading). A child may read *hill* and *well* and *doll* hundreds of times without ever stopping to think that short words ending in *l* following a short vowel generally have *two ls*. Phonics programs are admirably suited to pointing these things out, and most of those reviewed in the chapter on Home Reading Programs do get into spelling at least a little.

The look-say, or whole word, or sight-word method whereby children are forced to memorize words by their shape has been a disaster for spelling as it has for reading. Lacking systematic patterns, and loading short-term memory up with data fragments, look-say is the opposite of that logical order which English more or less follows.

In home school circles, the spelling debate is not between phonics and look-say, most home schoolers being firmly in favor of phonics. The new kid on the block is something called "invented spelling." "Let Johnny read and write and don't bother about his spelling," it is said. "In time, as Johnny becomes more acquainted with English in the course of his reading, his spelling will straighten out on its own." Does this idea have merit? Empirically it has been shown to work in a number of instances. I suspect that the key ingredients to success with invented spelling are lots of reading and basic phonics instruction to begin with. In the cases I've heard of, children started out writing phonetically, and then progressed without adult aid to become good spellers. A mind logically trained to *de*code Enlish—that is, any child taught to read phonetically—may very well in time discover the rules of *en*coding English.

Because most schoolchildren are *not* taught phonetically, and are *not* allowed unpressured time to develop correct spelling on their own, the following spelling programs might be of help.

I'd like to end this section with three thoughts. The first, after John Holt, is that the only word lists worth practicing are lists of the words *you* have missed in *your* own writing. Why practice words you already know how to spell or that you never use? The second is that a good learning-to-read program, followed by enough *corrected* writing practice, will produce good spellers. It is not a good idea to make children rewrite whole papers for the sake of a few misspelled words. That cramps their writing and develops fear of using unusual words. Practicing misspelled words separately, in order to gain mastery, is very different from having your entire composition condemned for a spelling error. The third thought is that spelling is not worth stressing at all until the learner has had enough reading practice to form a framework of phonics rules and known words. More than one "creative" speller has developed into a model of spelling accuracy without any adult intervention at all. Older children should be expected to produce more professional work, but younger children can be allowed a certain time to develop their writing skills. Don't squash writing for the sake of spelling!

SPELLING PROGRAMS

Christian Schools International

Student workbook, $6 each grade. Teacher edition, $12 grade 1, $14.40 grades 2-6.

CSI's *Spelling Spectrum* curriculum "helps students care about spelling as a way to love and serve God and others." Good thought. Now how do they propose to accomplish it? CSI begins at the beginning with an explanation of how our language developed, thus cluing students in to why our words look the way they do. Unique features include allowing the student to choose his favorite of three learning methods, spelling games, and a spelling progress chart. You get "varied, realistic, daily activities in 36 lessons."

Spelling Spectrum is a new series, published in 1984; so your chances of scarfing up used copies from your friendly local Christian school are poor. At the price, I'd want to see how it went with the student workbook alone before investing in a teacher's edition.

Distar

SRA offers two classroom-style programs for your spelling pleasure, both based on the Distar® method of teaching: *Corrective Spelling Through Morphographs,* and *Spelling Mastery.* If the first title doesn't really grab you, let me explain what a morphograph is. It is a hunk of a word that has meaning of its own: e.g., *re, pre, un, ed, ing, able.* You may recognize these particular hunks just listed as being prefixes and suffixes. Thus the word "disreputable" consists of four morphographs: dis, re, pute, and able. By learning how to spell the morphs and learning a few simple rules for combining morphs (e.g., "when adding

able to a root ending with *e,* drop the *e*"), students quickly discover how to spell anything they want.

Like the other Distar programs, both spelling programs feature fully scripted lessons (everything you do and say is spelled out) and student feedback. This Direct Instruction approach has been shown to be the most effective public school teaching method.

Distar comes highly recommended by schools that have used it.

Educators Publishing Service

EPS offers more than a dozen different workbooks for students with spelling problems. *Power Over Words,* for fifth- through seventh-grade students, is a "discovery" workbook series. Students "develop a visual-phonetic-thinking method" for spelling words. You can also get a workbook of spelling exercises, a multisensory spelling program for students with reading difficulties, and so on.

Leonardo Press

Spelling Mastery Kit, $59.95. *1,001 Affixes,* $8.95. *Spelling Book of Verbs,* $8.95. All orders add 10 percent shipping.

Raymond E. Laurita is a man with a mission. Disgusted by the practice of teaching schoolchildren spelling by means of "word lists," Professor Laurita set out to uncover the patterns of English spelling. English, Laurita believes, is essentially a regular language. While proving this thesis, Professor Laurita has assembled a number of extremely useful tools for those who care about spelling and language.

1,001 Affixes and their Meanings: A Dictionary of Prefixes, Suffixes and Inflections may not sound like it will ever hit the Top Forty. Nonetheless, the home teacher will find it invaluable. Laurita has divided those troublesome little morphs that make up English into their three categories: prefixes, suffixes, and inflections. He has then defined each and every one, with examples of its use. For example, "ptero- indicates feather, wing or winglike part: *pterodactyl* (ptero dact yl), *pterosaur* (ptero saur)." Reading through this book should improve both your spelling and your word power.

The Complete and Simplified Spelling Book of Verbs is another humdinger of a title that conceals a thoroughly useful work. Laurita shows that 98.5 percent of all English verbs are regular. He also (and this is the truly useful part) includes a complete list of *all* irregular verb roots in the language, organized into thirty categories, according to underlying vowel construction.

The Spelling Mastery Kit is a complete K-12 spelling program. You get a 5 x 8″ plastic box with two hundred color-coded cards containing over twelve thousand words, all placed in categorical order; ten student lesson pads; ten student folders; the manual *Five Steps to Spelling Mastery;* and the booklet *Spelling as a Categorical Act.* The Spelling Mastery Kit is Laurita's *vowel-centered* approach to spelling. There are five levels of difficulty, all related. In Level 1 the learner spells, for example, *ee* words: deed, feed, heed, need . . . In Level 2 he spells *ee* words that use blends: bleed, sleep, fleet, flee. Level 3 brings in digraphs: cheer, sheet, cheek. Level 4 adds inflectional endings: sleeting, cheekiest, cheered. Level 5, the last, adds affixes (prefixes and suffixes): uncheerful, sleety, cheekily. There is, of course, no reason why at home the entire program should take more than a few months. Once mastered, your learner can spell *anything!* And the kit comes with enough workbooks *et al* for all the children in your family, and perhaps some grandchildren as well!

Laurita has produced a number of items specifically designed for home use which also work well in the classroom. Contact Leonardo Press for details.

Phonetic Spelling Lab and Learning Network

Will some reader with marketing pizazz please take pity on Gene Lehman and help him work up his phonetic spelling materials into a jazzy package that will impress schools? Mr. Lehman has invented some very clever spelling helps, including pages and pages of limericks that you have to solve by filling in the blanks with the appropriate morphographs, a set of wooden Phonetic Spelling Blocks, and several levels of Phonetic Spelling Packs.

Mr. Lehman, an erstwhile schoolteacher and once a student for the Catholic priesthood, himself admits that his low energy level has prevented him from giving his Phonetic Spelling Lab the push it deserves.

If you like the offbeat approach to learning and don't mind living without flashy packaging, you're bound to like PSL's nutty, and educationally sound, exercises.

And now for a sample out of Mr. Lehman's grab bag, which includes Scramble Rhymes, Scramble Words, Hidden Rhymes, Hidden Words, Pattern Rhymes, Prank Blanks, Palindromes, Back-Words, Homophonics, Homics, Infernal Rhymes, and Group Games. The following Limer-Trick is taken from a page entitled "Higher Yearning":

> "M _ th - Taken"
> To secure a kingdom's rel _ _ _ _ ,
> Jason s _ _ zed a Golden Fl _ _ _ _ ,
> (Matched Medea's cap _ _ _ _ s
> For people in pie _ _ _)
> Packed it home in his val _ _ _ .

Or this, from another entitled "Political Punditry":

> Un _ _ sounding
> In order to set matters stra _ _ _ _ ,
> Carter agreed to deb _ _ _ .
> President F _ _ _
> Pr _ bably sc _ _ _ d,
> But only the silence was gr _ _ _ _ .

Who can resist?

Play 'n Talk

Entire program, $210. Includes four series of phonics records, one alphabet record, accompanying read-along books, games, typing program, riddle records, and more.

Seems I'm reviewing *Play 'n Talk* all over the place. As I keep mentioning, this program contains everything you need to teach the language arts, including spelling. *Play 'n Talk* includes several spelling games and manipulatives, as well as the basic phonics program which (unlike others I've seen) includes instructions in morphographs in the advanced series.

Slide 'n Sound is a plastic-coated picture of a bay, including dock and lighthouse. Using two plastic-coated slide rules that fit into slits in the picture, young learners are able to construct a large variety of words. The accompanying record spins a fanciful tale about little words gliding up to the dock and will appeal to little kids. Included are quite a few of the little slide rules and a pad for scoring how many words you were able to construct out of a given set of two slide rules. Example: using the beginning consonants and the family *at,* how many words can you construct? At, bat, cat, fat . . . The maximum totals for each combination are given in the accompanying book. You can build over eighteen hundred one-syllable words twiddling those little slides! Slide 'n Sound is good manipulative practice and helps cure reversals and other spelling problems.

Spell Lingo is a set of twenty-four Bingo spelling games. By using the game cards, you can pinpoint your learner's spelling problems as well as providing practice in overcoming them. The game cards are designed to diagnose whether skills are being learned as expected. Spell Lingo is an easy and fun way to help you stop spelling problems before they start.

Unhappily, these kits are not available separately.

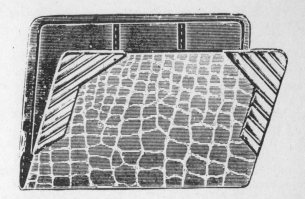

Zaner-Bloser

Spelling Computer Software, $34.95 each grade.

Zaner-Bloser has a standard spelling program, featuring lists of words that share some common feature—say, words with soft *c* and *g* or color words. This does not interest us nearly as much as Z-B's own Spelling Computer Software.

Each diskette contains "eight different learning-with-fun activities." Try your hand at Alphabetize, Speedspell, Anagrams, and Super Anagrams, plus games that deal with antonyms, homonyms, synonyms, and abbreviations. If the games are actually fun and not just dressed-up drill, this could be interesting. Diskettes come by grade level, with grades 1 through 8 available.

CHAPTER TWENTY-FIVE

WRITING AND COMPOSITION

Wordsmithery is what this section is about: finding the right words and hammering them together into shapely sentences. We're talking about *writing*—not handwriting, but the art of expressing your thoughts on paper.

Writing receives less attention in the public school curriculum than any other core subject. It takes time to teach children to write well, and teachers are overburdened. It takes attention to detail, and many teachers have been taught to believe that details are petty. It takes, most of all, an appreciation and understanding of good writing, and the present generation of teachers has itself been denied this instruction.

Happily, writing is easy to teach at home. All you have to do is (1) buy a copy of *Any Child Can Write* by Harvey Weiner, published by McGraw-Hill, and (2) put it into practice. *Any Child Can Write* is absolutely the best book ever written, and quite possibly the best that ever *will* be written, on teaching children to write. It's simple. It's inspiring. It's thorough. It's based on the author's own extensive experience teaching in schools, and on his experience teaching his own daughter at home. Melissa Weiner was writing and illustrating before she was four, and by the time she was five she was coming up with imagery like this:

> This is me. I like to dance and sing a song like a robin. I love to ice skate in red skates. I slip and slide and go *errrrr* on the freezing ice.

Do me a favor. Check out *Any Child Can Write* from the library. Then, if you're like me, once you see what a fantastic book it is, you'll gladly invest $12.95 in your very own copy.

I can't tell you anything about writing that Dr. Weiner hasn't already put in his book. Here are some of the high points for beginning writers. Writing begins with speaking. Encourage complete sentences, and draw your children on to describe what they see and feel as crisply as possible. Once a child learns to write, *let* him write! Letters to Grandma and shopping lists make things really happen. Mom or Dad can act as secretary and write out Johnny's stories if handwriting is still a struggle.

Dr. Weiner's great contribution is in showing parents how to nourish the creative process. The vitality and joy that children pour into their poetry and prose when they have discovered how to see the world with an artist's eye make this book a delight to read.

Following is a smattering of writing programs you may want to use along with *Any Child Can Write,* and a listing of magazines that publish children's work. I have included both the snobby mags that dispense rejection slips and the grateful zines that print everything you send them. Something for everyone—so get out those pencils!

WRITING PROGRAMS AND HELPS

A Beka Books

A Beka's *Handbook of Grammar and Composition* for eleventh and twelfth grades is now available in hardcover ($11.95) and softcover ($7.45). A Beka says, "This handbook provides a thorough treatment of all of those elements of grammar, mechanics, and usage that are necessary for correct, clear, and effective writing." Topics include The Writing Process, Specific Compositions, The Research Paper, Composing the Sentence, Choosing the Right Word.

A Beka's Language series, which I have used, does not turn me on. There is no need to write an entire sentence to practice capitalization, for instance. Also, the "story starters" fail to excite ("Write three interesting sentences about an unusual pet").

Alpha Omega Publications

Ten LIFEPACs/grade, $1.95 each. Teacher guides, answer keys extra.

Alpha Omega's "English" LIFEPACs are available separately. These feature an excellent worktext approach to composition. All forms of writing are covered, including some secular tales, and analyzed from a Christian perspective. The series emphasizes creative thinking and (unlike some others) actually gets the student writing a goodly number of compositions.

Students using Alpha Omega's English program have scored several grade levels above students using conventional texts.

AMSCO School Publications, Inc.

AMSCO's "Writing About" series covers Amusing Things, Fascinating Things, Curious Things, People, with separate workbooks on Writing Creatively, Writing Logically, and Writing Practically. You can request a sample copy of any of these workbooks by writing to AMSCO on school letterhead.

Christian Schools International

Teacher Guides, $25.97 each grade. Student Activity Sets (package of five folders and five sets of activity sheets), $24.99, grades 1-6. You can either combine orders with your friends or skip the student sets and work directly out of the Teacher Guide.

CSI's brand new K-6 *Writing Rainbow* series looks exciting. Unlike other programs, *Writing Rainbow* recognizes that children need to be filled with experience before they can write. Prewriting experience is, then, built into the exercises. Next, CSI emphasizes writing-to-be-read, rather than wastebasket "for the teacher only" writing. Practice in all the different forms of writing is afforded by the logical layout of this program, which includes instruction in grammar and ethics as well as composition skills.

See these two units from the grade 4 workbooks:

Unit Nine   WISE WRITERS PLAY WITH POETRY

Lesson 1 Words Sound Off!

Lesson 2 Cinquains Have Five Lines

Lesson 3 Poets Go Beyond the Senses

Lesson 4 Colors Are Alive With Feelings

Lesson 5 Poets Express Feelings

Lesson 6 We Can Express Feelings in Poems

Lesson 7 Know the Poets

Lesson 8 Rewrite the Classics

Lesson 9 Poetry is for Sharing

Unit Ten   WISE WRITERS ADVERTISE RESPONSIBLY

Lesson 1 Advertisers Want to Persuade You, Part I

Lesson 2 Advertisers Want to Persuade You, Part II

Lesson 3 How Should We Advertise?

Lesson 4 Writing Truthful Advertising Scripts

Lesson 5 Lights! Camera! Action!

See how the authors introduce poetry and ideas about poetry before requiring actual poetry from the students. Note also the emphasis on ethics.

Or how about this unit from the kindergarten book:

Unit Four   WRITING COMES FROM WITHIN

Lesson 1 Writing Requires Invented Spelling

Lesson 2 We Can Write Information on Charts

Lesson 3 We Can Write Conversation

Lesson 4 We Talk Together at Home

Lesson 5 Pictures Suggest Stories

Lesson 6 Stories Are Embedded in Wordless Books

Lesson 7 A Puppet Makes a Good Story Character

Lesson 8 Greeting Cards Give Messages

Lesson 9 A Newsletter Reports Our News

Do you see how the kindergarten student is exposed to the idea of writing to build a foundation for writing of his own?

Teacher Guides contain background information, daily lesson plans, evaluation ideas, and follow-up activities. You also get ten to twenty-five pages of tearout cards for supplemental writing activities. Students in grades 1 to 6 get two-pocket folders for storing their writing assignments and a complete set of activity pages.

Harper & Row

The first book I wrote took me twenty drafts. Seventeen of them I ground out before reading Sheridan Baker's two excellent books, *The Practical Stylist* and *The Complete Stylist and Handbook*. I gladly recommend the older editions of both these books. They will help any aspiring writer perform the needed surgery on his or her fulminations. *The Practical Stylist* is shorter and therefore a better book for beginners. *The Complete Stylist* is meant for use as a college text (which means Mr. Baker has to spin things out a bit more). Your public library probably has both books.

MAGAZINES FOR YOUNG WRITERS

The Jibber-Jabber

This is the one and only magazine I know of entirely written and produced by preteen kids. Laura Duncan does the honors as editor, and the contents reflect the actual achievements of kids, starting with those who are barely able to hold a pencil. To me, this is the most inspiring format of all, since "I can do *that!*" is a lot more likely to lead to results than an awestruck admiration of another's work. All submissions are welcomed. Send Laura a couple of bucks to pay for her expenses (she doesn't require this, but it's the friendly thing to do) and get your kid's work in print!

Loaves and Fishes: The Magazine for Kids by Kids
One issue yearly, $5.00.

Bruce and Jeanette Mosier felt Christian kids needed an outlet for their writing talents. "Let's start a kids' magazine," they said. And they did it! Daughters Andrea and Rachelle are the apprentice business manager and apprentice editor, respectively. Intended for kids aged five through twelve, *Loaves and Fishes* has Letters to the Editor, poems, a Computer Page, recipes, book reviews, puzzles 'n games, and "how to" articles, as well as various feature articles and sections entitled "Writing Tips" and "Light on the Word" (the latter referring to the Bible).

Unlike the *Jibber-Jabber, Loaves and Fishes* has submission guidelines. They like submitted articles to be neat, preferably typed double-spaced, otherwise written very neatly on one side of the paper only, with wide margins. Your name should be on each page, pages should be numbered, and skip the staples. Art work and photos should be very clear, with a lot of contrast, or they won't show up well when reproduced. If you want your work returned, enclose a stamped SASE.

These guidelines, by the way, are good for almost any magazine, including grown-up ones, if you feel inclined to spread your wings a bit.

The type and repro weren't stunning on the issue I saw, but the content was good. I tried the recipe for banana nog. Yum! All articles are wholesome (the editors demand this!). Also, the Mosiers do not believe in patronizing children—another good point in this magazine's favor.

The McGuffey Writer
$5 for three issues, spaced throughout the school year.

Rev. McGuffey had nothing to do with this literary magazine by and for kids, which emanates from McGuffey Hall at Miami University. Most contributions are by public school kids; so some stories include killing, monsters, disrespect for authority, and so on. Content includes poems, short stories, and essays. Black and white illustrations are considered for publication. Manuscripts are *not* returned.

Stone Soup: the magazine by children
$17.50 membership in Children's Art Foundation includes subscription.

Stone Soup is a product of the Children's Art Foundation. They are picky from a literary viewpoint about what they print, as they want this magazine to serve as an inspiration and example to other children. In the issue I saw, the selections seemed mainly drawn from the upper-class cultural milieu.

Stone Soup is printed on quality paper and stapled into a hefty booklet. An Activity Guide correlated with the magazine is bound into each issue, primarily for the benefit of schoolteachers who want to use *Stone Soup* in their classrooms.

Young Writers' Club
Magazine, $9.95 for ten issues. Young Writer's Kit, $17.95.

Deanna King and Charles Thiesen started the Club in 1982. It began as a regular club meeting in their home, and now has its own magazine, *Wordworks.* A large percentage of the children's submissions are published. There are some articles by the adults involved also, on suggestions for things to write, like "silly sentences" and acrostics. Again, the writing reflects most contributors' public school training: ghosts, monsters, and mixed values. The magazine itself is not large (the issue I saw did not top twelve pages) and has no color, but is professional in appearance.

PART VII

COMPUTERS

CHAPTER TWENTY-SIX

SO WHAT'S THE BIG DEAL ABOUT COMPUTERS, ALREADY (AND WHICH ONE SHOULD I GET)?

Computers—the biggest thing to hit education since ditto masters, right? That's what everyone is saying, but I'm not sure I totally agree. After all, kids can ruin their eyesight just as well in the traditional way, reading under the bedsheets with a flashlight, as by sitting for hours mesmerized by the tiny flickering lights on a computer screen. And as for the great educational benefits, most of the "educational" software on the market now is just glorified flash card drill, with a little animated song-and-dance to reward the student for getting the answer right.

For millennia the human race has learned its needed academic skills without the benefit of computers. The average eighth grader of the last century could read and write better than most of our modern college graduates, even though he never sat at a keyboard or twiddled a joystick.

So what's educational software's big selling point? *Motivation!* Any device that can get a normal kid to spend hours drilling himself on school subjects without an adult standing over him is bound to have audience appeal. Software can make drillwork more interesting. And a few rare programs actually top the computer's power by allowing students to create and discover instead of merely regurgitating facts.

When it comes to writing, computers are much friendlier than typewriters and much faster than the well-chewed #2 yellow pencils we struggled with in our youth. Today's kids can invent and print out endless letters, stories, reports, and so on with a tithe of the effort required in years past. Learning to type is easier and more interesting when the screen "talks back" to you, and editing is a snap.

Computers are also a fun way to get kids involved in the world of business: balancing the family checkbook, keeping inventory for the family business.

If you don't have a computer, relax. Your children don't need one, despite all the ballyhoo about "computer literacy." The hardware field is changing so rapidly that anything a child learns about computers in second grade will be out of date in sixth, let alone when he graduates high school. Furthermore, any child who has been given the "tools of learning" can learn what he needs to know about computers when and if he needs to know it.

ESSENTIAL BOOKS ABOUT COMPUTERS AND SOFTWARE

Having said all that, let's suppose the Smith family is in the market for a computer. Father Eric hopes to organize the family finances, mother Samantha wants to automate the mailing list for her women's organization, and kiddies Ignatz and Ermintrude are all agog to play some games on it. Where should the Smiths begin?

Far and away the best place to begin is with these two books: (1) *Computer Wimp* by John Bear, available from Ten Speed Press for $9.95. Dr. Bear warns you about every horrible mistake you can make in buying computers and their accessory "stuff" (peripherals, supplies, software, etc.) and explains how to do it right with such wit that the book is worth buying even if you're not in the market for an electronic beast of burden. (2) *The Whole Earth Software Catalog* is what its name implies, a catalog of software compiled by the folks who brought us *The Whole Earth Catalog.* Doubleday publishes it under their Quantum Press imprint. Any bookstore has it. I got my copy on sale from Quality Paperback Book Club, who were offering it as a premium to new enrollees. A lot of midnight oil went into producing this oversized quality paperback, and the editors aren't shy about sharing their opinion of the most popular and/or best products in every major software and hardware category. After checking out more than a few of the programs myself, I have to admit that the Whole Earth people's reviews are generally helpful and accurate. The two books between them cost less than $25, a puny investment compared to the agony you'll experience if you get stuck with an electronic lemon.

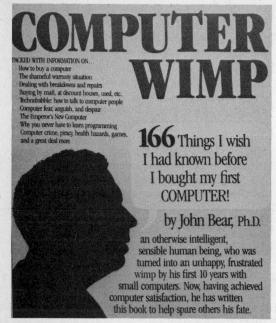

For keeping up with the Joneses, there's the *Whole Earth Software Review.* Eighteen dollars a year gets you four issues of what's happening now. Unlike other software magazines, *WESR* ignores the arcane and trivial. Is it usable? Is it useful? Does it beat the competition? These are the questions *WESR* reviewers ask. It's a consumer's guide to software.

If you want to go beyond store-bought software and learn to program, or if you have a son or daughter who's frantic to get into BASIC, your best bet is Mario Pagnoni's *The Complete Home Educator,* $10.95 postpaid from Larson Publications. The title is misleading, because although Mr. Pagnoni has a lot to say about education and home schooling (and I don't agree with all of it!), his strong suit is the extended discussion of home computing. Written specifically for the home schooler, Mr. Pagnoni's book will ease you into these troubled waters.

SOME SOURCES FOR COMPUTER BOOKS

Computer Literacy Bookshop

Are you anxious to load up on computer knowledge? A good place to start might be Computer Literacy Bookshop, the world's largest store devoted to computer and electronics books. Located in Silicon Valley, Computer Literacy carries every title recommended in the *Whole Earth Software Catalog* and nearly ten thousand others. They publish both a bi-monthly newsletter (free upon request) and also a catalog ($5, oriented toward computer pros). Computer Literacy says they will gladly answer any book questions you may have.

Learning Systems Corporation

People who like to pinch a penny until it bleeds will be happy with LSC's introduction to BASIC. At just fifty cents it's a friendly handshake to Apple, Atari, Pet, and TRS-80 programming. Miniworkbook, sixteen hand-sized pages.

Love Publishing Company

Books on computing for beginners, kids, and teachers. Love's selection seems good.

NASCO

Along with a new, expanded software section that includes reams of math programs, NASCO has a large section devoted to books about computers and programming.

AN APPLE TODAY GETS YOU SOFTWARE TO PLAY

It wouldn't really be fair to put in several chapters about educational software without giving you at least a hint about which computer system I think is your best investment.

My husband, Bill, is an M.I.T. grad and a professional computer programmer (his title at the moment is senior systems programmer/analyst). I myself have several degrees in the area of computer design and software engineering. So we have more than a passing interest in the subject of which PC (personal computer) is the fairest of them all.

Rather than just giving you the fruit of our research and leaving you to take it on faith, here are the steps that led to our endorsing the Apple as the computer to get.

The most essential thing for the average family to consider when buying a computer is, *what software runs on it?* Hackers who can write their own compilers and assemblers and read hex code dumps don't have to worry about software support, but the normal American who doesn't know what a compiler or assembler is and who thinks hex code is something Amish farmers put on their barns has to face facts and realize that any software he uses he will have to buy.

This being so, the field of sensible choices narrows down to the Big Five:

Apple

Commodore

IBM (and its compatibles)

Atari

TRS-80 (Radio Shack)

These are the computers for which most educational software is written, in order of how much runs on each.

You *can* pick up some small-time computer (say a Texas Instruments model) for a rock-bottom price. This computer will have maybe twenty to fifty programs that run on it. So far it looks good. But what if you want a different kind of program that is not offered, or if you don't like the ones that are? It's just too bad. Big software companies don't put out versions for small-time computers. All the really excellent programs reviewed in the following chapters are only offered for the computers listed above.

If you're serious about using your computer for educational purposes, you had better stick with the Big Five.

But how do you choose which of the Big Five to buy?

At this point many people start thinking price. This can be a serious mistake. A computer is more than a toy; it is an expandable piece of equipment. Used rightly, it can be one of your most powerful home tools or even launch you into an independent home business. If you are sure you will never want to write a book on your computer, or prepare tax returns, or hook into an electronic information service, or do any heavy statistical work, or use it for mass mailings, or any of a thousand other possible uses, then go ahead: buy cheap. But if you would like to keep your options open, there are other matters besides price to consider.

Atari and Commodore are the cheapest all-purpose computers for which a decent amount of educational software has been written. The reason we do not consider Atari and Commodore as good options for the home computer is that they are not very powerful or expandable. These computers are *slow,* compared to Apple or IBM or the TRS-80. If you try to use them for serious number-crunching or word processing, you will see what we mean. Both Atari and Commodore were originally developed for playing arcade-style games, and although these companies have struggled to adapt their equipment to wider use, they are still just not a professional's choice. Also in the case of Commodore we have heard complaints about the hardware's reliability. A computer that keeps breaking down is not worth buying.

Eliminating Commodore and Atari leaves Radio Shack, Apple, and IBM as the contenders. In our estimation, the Radio Shack computers are overpriced for their quality. They also have far less software support than either IBM or Apple.

So it's IBM or Apple. You can forget about the IBM PCjr. It was immediately labeled a dog upon its first entry into the market. We're talking about the IBM PC and its compatibles versus an Apple IIc, IIe, or Macintosh (or any expanded version of these that might have appeared by the time you read this).

The IBM PC is a good business machine, and if you're primarily looking for business hardware and only secondarily considering it as an educational machine, it's an OK investment. This also goes for the Apple Macintosh, a computer that really appeals to us for its ease of use and nice large screen.

But if you're looking for an educational computer *now,* and only thinking about expanding into other applications sometime in the future, the Apple IIc or IIe is your machine.

Almost *everything* educational runs on Apple. Apple has sold more personal computers to the school market than anyone else, and the software companies are aware of this.

The Apple IIe is also *expandable.* The reason this computer is still around after so many years is that its farsighted inventors designed it to accommodate endless hardware updates. Our little IIe, which came with 128K of RAM (128,000+ bytes of usable memory), can as of this writing be upgraded to hold more than three million bytes of RAM. We could add on cards to make it run ten times faster, to produce stereo-quality synthesized voice or music, or to turn our home appliances on and off. In addition, we could add on external memory devices that hold an extra ten million bytes, and there's talk of mass memory in the *trillions* of bytes being soon available. It seems there is no limit to the speed and size of a little Apple.

The Apple IIc is a nonexpandable version of the IIe with adequate power to meet all normal applications. Its virtue has been a lower price and that it comes already set up. You don't have to know anything about what hardware cards you want to start running your IIc. I wrote this book on a IIc.

It is possible to remove the IIc's cover with a screwdriver and plug in a new memory card, thus upgrading your supposedly nonexpandable IIc. We hope to do this with ours. Apple has frowned on this practice, but may change their mind since expandability is such a big selling feature for their computers.

So unless some totally unforeseen new computer bursts on the scene accompanied by thousands of fantastic programs, our advice to you is to

(1) Subscribe to *A+* magazine. *A+* will acquaint you with what's new in hardware and software for the entire Apple family (including the Mac). You will know what you want when you go shopping so the dealers can't put anything over on you. *A+* is also loaded with ads from hungry discount dealers, who sell both hardware and software at bargain prices. You can then play these dealers against your local Apple dealer. (You want to buy hardware locally if possible, since you can then expect better support, but you don't want to pay outrageously large sums for the privilege of buying locally.) Know the prices you can get at discount and haggle your local dealer down.

(2) Choose the system you want. For games a color monitor is very nice, although many games can be played without one. Two disk drives are almost essential if you do any writing or number-crunching. A printer is necessary if you want to write on your computer (and you will). Don't buy a clunky, noisy letter-quality printer if you can possibly get by with one like the Imagewriter II that delivers near-letter-quality print and speedy drafts and also prints graphics. Extra memory is a luxury needed only by those who use their computer as a business tool, and you can always pick it up later.

(3) Buy your Apple.

CHAPTER TWENTY-SEVEN

BABYWARE

When your baby is old enough to refrain from drooling on the keyboard, he's old enough to play with some easy educational programs. Parents of young children are the biggest buyers of educational software, and in consequence software writers have come up with a crop of helpful programs for the gooey-fingered.

Let me stress it one more time: you *can* teach your children anything they need to know without a computer, and don't let any industry hack tell you differently. But the computer can make teaching both more fun and less work. Once a child has mastered a program, he can play with it on his own. It's like having a perfectly patient private tutor. You, the adult, can kibitz if you like. The colors (if you have a color monitor) and song and dance also make practicing new concepts fun. You won't have chalk dust all over the rugs or piles of paper to throw away, either, if Junior does his scribbling and drill on a computer screen.

What do discriminating parents look for in a piece of babyware?

- Is it truly easy to use? Programs that require the user to select a specific keyboard character are too difficult for this age group. The better programs allow your child to do all his input with one large key, such as the spacebar. The best programs let your child input by hitting *any* key on the keyboard.

- Does it manipulate the user? In line with the behavior modification taught in teacher training courses, some programs "reward" correct answers with happy faces and songs and "punish" wrong answers with frowns and obnoxious noises. This type of program is using the child and teaching him to confuse right and wrong with correct and not correct. Is it a *sin* to think 1+2=4? No, a thousand times no!

Better programs gently indicate if an answer is incorrect. They might just ask the question again, or they might give the right answer after a number of incorrect tries. They might ignore the incorrect answer by dropping it off the screen (a very visual way of saying it is gone and forgotten and you can try again without penalty). This is not to say that computer programs should reward shoddy work. It is possible to design a program so a desired result only occurs after a certain number of correct answers, without rubbing children's noses in their mistakes.

- Is it fun? Appealing graphics are nice, but in the long run they don't matter as much as an intrinsically enjoyable program design.

There is a place for drill-and-practice programs. But the most enjoyable program design is one that puts the user in control. This is probably why the *Stickybear* programs, which really don't teach all that much, are such a hit. The child tells the program what to do instead of vice versa.

- What does it cost per hour of expected use? A cheap program that loses your child's interest after five minutes is less of a bargain than one which costs twice as much but is loved and used for months.

BABYWARE

American Guidance Service
Apple family. Each Soc program, $44.95. Set of 6, $250. Storybook, $12.50. Doll, $10.50.

AGS has an interesting concept in its MicroSoc series. Soc is a little character who travels around the world. Each disk has Soc visiting a different place: Washington, D.C., Tokyo, Paris, Australia, and outer space. Three arcade-style games are on each disk. SocSort is for classifying: four levels of difficulty, from first grade through seventh and up. SocLink is for word association: two levels, primary and intermediate. SocMatch has four levels like SocSort and centers on identifying common attributes. SocMate is a game of analogies played among the koalas and kangaroos of Australia; three levels. SocOrder is sequencing games with three levels, K to 2, 3 to 5, 6 and up. SocPix is for prereading classification skills. You can get Soc stickers, a Soc storybook, and a cute little Soc doll. This series sounds useful, especially since all the games can be played on different levels.

Learning Technologies
All programs $19.95. All programs for Apple II family and Commodore.

Pay attention to this company. Learning Technologies has leaped into the educational software market with a real splash. Each program in their software library

- sells for only $19.95,
- includes a certificate that entitles the buyer to a free accompanying learning kit (value $4.95),
- comes with clear, simple on-line and printed documentation,
- and has random challenges for repeat use.

More about those free learning kits. You send in one dollar to cover postage and handling and get three reproducible worksheets, a lesson plan, a colorful poster, and reproducible award certificates. The worksheets contain ideas and activities on the concepts taught in the programs. And don't expect "worksheet" to mean "boring." The exercises are challenging and engrossing.

Learning Technologies programs presently cover preschool through grade six, and the company hopes to expand its line to the upper grades as well.

For babyware, LT has programs that teach pattern and shape recognition, memory, and matching.

Lion's Workshop features a grouchy old lion who has hired an assistant (you) to help him with packing and repairs. You move objects up and down on a conveyor belt and select the proper one. The conveyor belt is a neat idea and works well graphically, and if your child can put up with getting frowned at for wrong answers it's a good program.

The Flying Carpet has a stardust-scattering genie who is interested in finding out what shapes make up the objects he constructs. Counting is necessary for this program, but keyboarding numerals is not, since LT cleverly has the child "count" by repeatedly clicking the spacebar.

Shutterbug's Patterns and *Shutterbug's Pictures* cover the areas of visual discrimination, pattern recognition, and part-whole relationships, with the additional interest of a time challenge to your visual memory in *Shutterbug's Pictures*.

Same or Different is what its name suggests. You know all about this from Sesame Street.

Although I can see some ways these programs could be improved (it should be possible to correct a counting error on *Flying Carpet,* for example) they are so inexpensive you could consider them disposable. When you consider the value of the free learning kit, your actual cost for the software is just $15. And if you don't like it, you can get a full refund. The programs take no time to learn, and as you will see, those for older children get really challenging. How can you go wrong?

Springboard
Apple II family, Commodore 64, IBM PC, PCjr.

Springboard's *Early Games for Young Children* looks like a value for the money. You get nine simple games that can be played without adult supervision, including shapes and letters and addition and subtraction (with colored blocks).

Easy as ABC, which I have used, is one of the very best choices for young children. You get options not found on other early learner programs, such as Dot to Dot. Children do *not* need to type letters or numbers: everything can be done with cursors (or, on the Commodore, the IJKM keys) and the spacebar. Move to the right answer with the cursor and select it with the spacebar. The games include letter recognition and matching (Match Letters), alphabet sequencing (Dot to Dot, Lunar Letters, and Leapfrog), and upper and lower case recognition (Honey Hunt). Delightful graphics and sound effects make *Easy as ABC* kid-appealing.

Sunburst Communications

Getting Ready to Read and Add, $59: Apple II family with 48K; Atari 400, 800, XL series with 16K; Commodore 64 (Disk); IBM PC (64K), PCjr (128K). Color graphic card and monitor required for IBM. *Teddy's Playground,* $59: Apple II family with color monitor and 48K. *Muppet Learning Keys,* $79.95: Apple IIe, IIc with 64K; Commodore 64 (Disk), IBM PC (64K), PCjr (128K).

Getting Ready to Read and Add has six programs. Kids match letters, numerals, and shapes. They associate upper- and lower-case letters, and numerals with amounts. The graphics are cute, and every effort is rewarded. Especially helpful is the design that allows kids to participate by touching *any* key on the keyboard, instead of having to find a particular letter or number. Our one-year-old daughter enjoys this disk, as does her five-year-old brother, who already knows all that stuff!

Teddy's Playground has little Ted waiting to zoom down his slide. Dangling from nearby trees are shapes with different textures and colors. You bring matching items to the steps of the slide. Once three matching objects have arrived, Ted climbs a step. After three steps up, he gets to slide down. Ted also wants you to do some SeeSaw Sorting and Swing Games. Simple and cute.

Muppet Learning Keys is a special kid's keyboard. It is really cute, with letters in alphabetical order on a simulated blackboard, numbers lined up on a ruler, colors as paints in a paintbox, a four-way compass (for moving up/down/right/left) with Kermit the Frog grinning from its middle, and an open "comic book" with "Oops!" and "Help!" and "Stop" and "Go" on its four "pages." Plus the essential "eraser." By touching the appropriate spots, kids can input everything adults type in on a standard keyboard, plus some. *MLK* comes with special software to teach letter, number, picture, and color recognition. Hit "Help!" and Miss Piggy answers. "Go" animates the screen and "Stop" ends animation. Three programs to teach letter, number, picture, and color recognition come packaged with *MLK. MLK* is also compatible with *Teddy's Playground* and *Getting Ready to Read and Add.*

Weekly Reader Software

Stickybear programs, $39.95 each. Apple II family with 48K; Atari with 48K. Much better with color monitor, but color not strictly necessary

The Stickybear family love to play, shop, and eat junk food. (Maybe that's why they're sticky!) These programs for little learners have great graphics and are very entertaining. For all practical purposes they are animated storybooks. *Stickybear ABC* flashes screen after screen of beautiful pictures, each associated with a capital letter and a word beginning with that letter. Aside from associating the input key with the screen level, there is not much opportunity for interaction, and that is true of *Stickybear Numbers* as well. With the latter, you get a huge numeral and that number of objects dancing about the screen. *Numbers* counts forward and backward and shows assembled objects, and that is all. *Opposites* and *Shapes,* which I have not seen, look to be more of the same from their printed descriptions.

You get some great packaging, including a colorful hardbound Stickybear storybook, a poster, hints for using the program more effectively, and of course some Stickybear stickers. If you think the programs are worth it for the fun, go ahead. But don't expect them to do more for your kids than you could do with an ABC or numbers book from the library.

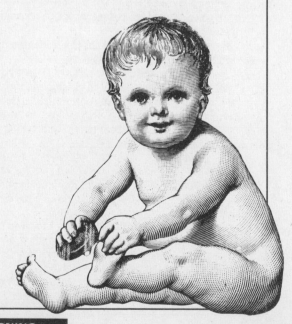

CHAPTER TWENTY-EIGHT

THINKWARE

*"Like all other arts, the Science of
Deduction and Analysis is one which
can only be acquired by long and
patient study . . . Let the inquirer begin
by mastering more elementary problems.*
Sherlock Holmes

Did you know there really once was a live, breathing Sherlock Holmes? Sir Arthur Conan Doyle, the man who gave us the keen-minded Holmes, was himself the prototype of his own creation. His son, Adrian Conan Doyle, in a fascinating introduction to the International Collectors Library edition of *A Treasury of Sherlock Holmes,* lays the matter before us:

> Holmes was to a large extent Conan Doyle himself. Incidentally, and it stands to their credit in view of my father's reticence, this fact was recognized almost from the very first by the police chiefs of the world who, speaking or writing from America, France, Germany, China, India, or Egypt, paid him tribute. The exception was, of course, Scotland Yard, whose silence put to shame even that of the immortal Colonel Bramble. Scotland Yard owed too much to Conan Doyle and it is always painful to acknowledge large debts.
>
> The use of plaster of Paris for preserving marks; the examination of dust in a man's clothing to establish his occupation or locality; the differentiation between tobacco ashes; all these were introduced into the science of criminal detection by my father through the mask of Sherlock Holmes. Far above all else, his own work in the famous Edalji case resulted in the introduction of the Court of Criminal Appeal into the British legal system. And to change the British legal system is almost equivalent to bailing out the English Channel with a teaspoon. The facts are there for all to read, including some noteworthy instances of my father rescuing the innocent from the clutches of the police by using the very methods which he had invented for his man in Baker Street.

It appears, then, that Sir Arthur Conan Doyle knew something about how to think and observe, and that the advice of Holmes at the beginning of this chapter can be taken seriously.

Once again, let the reader remember that Sir Arthur did not possess a personal computer; it is possible to have the sharpness of Holmes without the help of RAM. However—and it's a big "however"—in some ways educational software is ideal for developing thinking skills.

I'm talking about *good* educational software of course— software that is worthy to be called "Thinkware." A question, an answer, and a "Very Good!" flashed on the screen do not a piece of Thinkware make.

Computers can take in new information and make changes based on it, unlike flash cards. You should be able to build, draw, move, or explore with a good Thinkware program. Or, alternatively, you should be able to improve your memory or your spatial skills with the problems provided. Some Thinkware programs are puzzles that require careful thought to solve. Others allow you to invent a puzzle. But, unlike Schoolware which is designed to teach specific subject skills, Thinkware massages your brain directly. It makes you smarter.

The beauty of the computer is that it can constantly propose new problems. It can match wits with you on command. It can provide you with simulated tools for doing projects you would never get the chance to do in real life, and to rapidly run through many of these projects. You can build your own city, run your own business, or invent your own world, all without leaving your chair.

What makes this all possible is the genius of the man or woman who wrote the software. The computer is merely a tool for letting you sharpen your wits with the help of some of the sharpest people now living on earth.

The point of this all, of course, is to use your sharpened wits in the real world. Kids who are glued to the monitor all day turn into glassy-eyed, limp noodniks. Wise computer-users take their brains outdoors and into company now and then, and wise parents of the computer-bound children insist on the same for their offspring.

BEST OF THINKWARE

The Learning Company

All programs reviewed run on Apple II family, IBM PC family and PCjr, and Commodore 64/128, except *Robot Odyssey I,* which does not have a Commodore or IBM version. *Rocky's Boots* and the *Gertrude* series come for Compaq. For Tandy 1000 you can get *Rocky's Boots. Rocky's Boots* and *Robot Odyssey I* are available for Tandy Color Computer. Color monitor recommended; required for *Rocky's Boots, Gertrude,* and *Moptown.*

Prices: Moptown series $39.95 each. *Gertrude* series $44.95 each ($29.95 for C-64 version). *Rocky's Boots* $49.94 ($34.95 C-64). *Robot Odyssey I* $44.95. Add $3 shipping if ordering directly.

One of my husband Bill's colleagues is an avid computer hacker named Dave. Dave had been bugging Bill for a long time about Learning Company software. "You really should get some," Dave urged. "I know your kids would love it," Dave pleaded. We hate to see a grown man cry, so with a certain amount of skepticism I obtained some Learning Company programs.

And lo and behold, the man knew whereof he spake. (As usual: Dave was also a guiding light behind our purchase of not one, but two Apple computers, which turned out to be the best hardware decision we could have made.) I say it as a mother, and I say it as an engineer: These programs are *good!!!*

Let me start with the simplest Learning Company thinkware. *Moptown Parade* is a matching and sequencing game. The user needs to know how to find a specific key on the keyboard and match it with a code, placing *Moptown Parade* beyond the range of babyware, but the tasks themselves are simple. The graphics characters are Bibbits and Gribbits, who may be fat or thin, tall or short, red or blue. The seven games included on this disk include making a twin to the displayed character, recognizing differences, making opposites (for the game's purpose, a Gribbit is the opposite of a Bibbit), creating the character who should come next in a sequence, creating a character who differs by a chosen number of traits from the previous character in the parade, and discovering the rule that selects which characters may enter a clubhouse. A child who can master the first game may take quite a while to learn to play the last, making *Moptown Parade* worth its price. *Moptown Hotel* carries these skills (analogies, sequences, pattern recognition, and hypotheses) further, being aimed at the eight- to twelve-year-old.

Gertrude's Secrets has to be the most "enabling" educational software for the just-barely-school-age child. The game consists of a series of rooms. You zap about from room to room by means of cursors or a joystick. When you enter the game, a friendly tutorial shows you how to move around, how to pick up and drop objects, and explains the game options. There are three official logic games—loop puzzles, train puzzles, and array puzzles, each with multiple levels of difficulty. But the geniuses who designed this game also included a room where you can edit the shapes of the pieces used in the games, and it is to the Shape-Edit Room that my two sons fly like homing pigeons the minute the game is turned on.

If you play *Gertrude's Secrets* in the orthodox way, you carry Gertrude the goose to the puzzle room of your choice and drop her there. She then will fly back with puzzle pieces for you, and

once you solve the puzzle she will return bearing a treasure for you, which is kept in the Treasure Room. If you play it like my sons, you edit the shape of not only the game pieces kept in the storeroom, but the treasures and even Gertrude herself. "What's that funny little house sitting in Gertrude's room?" I asked Ted yesterday. "Oh, that's Gertrude," he explained. "Ha, ha."

Children really are in control with *Gertrude's Secrets* and with its sequel, *Gertrude's Puzzles* (which is on my wish list). They can leave puzzle pieces scattered everywhere, change them at will, or even solve a puzzle if the fit takes them. It's a rewarding way to learn about learning without making any real-world messes, and you will not regret buying it.

The last two Learning Company programs that belong in this section are two software classics that are possibly *the* greatest learning software ever invented. These are *Rocky's Boots* (for grades 4 and up) and *Robot Odyssey I* (for grades 7 to adult).

Both programs have the same universe-of-rooms format as the Gertrude series. Both also let you pick up and carry around items on your screen. But with these programs, you are not only solving problems, but building machines.

Rocky's Boots, after guiding you through an excellent tutorial, has you building machines with AND, NOT, and OR gates, plus assorted flipflops, clackers, clocks, and delays. These are elements of computer circuit design that allow you to turn electricity on and off depending on what kind of input you give them. For example, a NOT gate connected in the program to a blue sensor will be off if a blue object touches the sensor and on if no blue object is touching it. This may sound like *Rocky's Boots* gets into electrical engineering, which it does. But these logical design strategies are useful in all kinds of reasoning. You can practically feel your brain growing as you think through these problems.

Such arcane concepts aside, *Rocky's Boots* is fun to play. You get to drag components around, hook them up, and disconnect them. You turn on machines and turn them off. The intellectual challenge is stimulating, and the process itself is enjoyable. "Let's see. I need to select blue diamonds and crosses. Let's get a blue sensor and some AND gates . . ."

Robot Odyssey I takes *Rocky's Boots* one step further. You are not only designing little circuits, but programming robots to help you escape from the devious maze of Robotropolis. You can test robots out in the Innovation Lab and save your spot in the game.

Each level requires more complex programming, and eventually you'll be burning chips that contain chips that contain chips full of your original circuits. Figure on several months of steady play to get out of Robotropolis. You won't outgrow this program in a hurry.

I hope I didn't make *Rocky's Boots* and *Robot Odyssey I* sound too formidable. The genius of these games is that you don't have to be a genius to play them. The games teach you every step of the way, and you gain genuine thinking skills and not a little computer knowledge. And they are FUN!

Learning Technologies

All programs $19.95; includes certificate for free Learning Kit. Apple II family and Commodore 64/128.

Is it worth twenty dollars for a piece of thinkware and a learning kit? Learning Technologies has cracked the price barrier with this outrageous offer, which we hope other companies will emulate.

I have a shelf full of LT programs. Although LT's schoolware is decent for the price, their thinkware is better than a bargain.

First, memory programs. *Animal Hotel* shows you which animal is staying in which hotel. You pick how long you get to look. Can you remember who was where? The game has two levels and great graphics. *Bike Hike* goes one step farther, with animation. Two children are pedaling down the road while various creatures hop, crawl, run, or fly by. At the end of the hike you indicate which creatures you saw, and how many times you saw them. These games were both designed for ages four to eight.

Slightly more tricky is *Clowning Around*. You pick a category, for instance fruit, and objects from that category are displayed on a grid. Then they vanish and you have to match the object now displayed with the places where it appeared on the grid. This you do by moving a marionette clown up and down a two-sided number line. The program's concept is fine, but I couldn't live with the clown's obnoxious treatment of wrong answers.

Learning Technologies has several fine programs that develop spatial skills. *Sliding Block* is based on those puzzles our Aunt Rosie gave us when we were young. They came with one empty spot and little interlocking pieces that you slid around until the correct picture or pattern emerged. The computer version includes much tougher levels (I don't think I will ever solve the twenty-five-piece puzzles) and several different puzzles. Our childhood hand-held versions didn't have color graphics or rocket ships that blasted off when put together either, both of which features enhance the computer game.

Pipeline is another spatial skills game. You hook together different types of pipe to feed water to objects that need it. The game has three levels of play and you can set yourself a time deadline, making it challenging enough for any age. This game is a favorite at our house.

Speedy Delivery requires you to help the postman deliver his packages to all the houses in the randomly generated maze without ever visiting the same house twice. This is also a challenging game that requires planning ahead.

For classic problem-solving skills, Learning Technologies has a computerized version of the game known as King Tut's Pyramid or the Hindu Pyramid. Called *Monkey Business*, it asks the user to move a stack of monkeys from one location to two others. He can only put a smaller monkey on a larger. I spent more hours than I'd care to admit in eighth grade figuring out how the puzzle worked, and I still remember the rush of satisfaction when I understood the trick of how to do the puzzle in the least amount of moves. *Monkey Business* has three levels, with a stack of three, four, and five monkeys respectively, so if you don't already know how this puzzle works you can spend some time finding out.

And now for Learning Technologies' two best thinking programs.

Scrambled Eggs presents you with an expectant hen and four eggs. You deduce which number is in which egg by making guesses and analyzing the computer's response. It tells you (1) how many of your guessed numbers were in the eggs but not in the position you guessed and (2) how many numbers were in the right position. You'll be doing some heavy-duty thinking by the time you get these chicks hatched.

Alpine Tram Ride is the same sort of puzzle as *Scrambled Eggs*, featuring a menagerie of animals rather than a brood of chicks. Of the two, *Alpine Tram Ride* is more colorful and also somewhat harder to use, since instead of displaying the numbers you selected, as in *Scrambled Eggs*, the screen shows you the animals corresponding to each number code. The accompanying learning kits for these two games were really fun to work through.

I'm not afraid to recommend Learning Technologies programs, because of their excellent refund policy. If you usee and no likee, you getee money back.

Open Court

Open Court has put together a list of the best learning software, with reviews that explain what is which and why and how to use it. For one-stop shopping that reflects Open Court's emphasis on high-order thinking skills, send for their Quick Finder.

Scholastic Inc.
Apple II family, all programs. *Agent USA* also available for Atari series, Commodore 64, IBM PC, PCjr. $39.95.

Colorful, yes. Interesting, yes. Educational? Sometimes. That's my opinion of Scholastic's software. It's O.K. to just have fun, and you should keep this in mind while browsing through Scholastic's free color brochure, which tries to label *every* one of its over sixty programs as "educational."

I sent away for those that looked most promising and was not disappointed. *Agent USA* has a mission: find the FuzzBomb that is turning normal Americans into goofy FuzzBodies. You travel about the U.S. on trains, evading FuzzBodies and collecting crystals that turn the F.B.'s back into solid citizens. It's a pretty sneaky way to develop survival geography and thinking skills. Our kids love it.

You can also get a program for making posters (with musical accompaniment!), for dissecting a frog (yuk!), for making up crazy stories, for pattern recognition (build your own spiderweb), and on and on.

I found the brochure descriptions to be honest. These are not programs you will quickly outgrow.

Spinnaker Software
Almost every Spinnaker program is available for Apple, Atari, IBM PC, and Commodore 64. *Trains*, $39.95. *Delta Drawing*, $50.

Spinnaker has simple stuff, freaky stuff, clever stuff, and heavy stuff. As their motto says, "We're Not Just Playing Games."

Not everything Spinnaker sells appeals to me. Their nursery rhyme programs look to be entertaining but easily outgrown. And *Prime Ducks* seems a roundabout way to teach the math concepts of primes, factors, and exponents. Aside from those few examples, though, everything else looks attractive.

Trains teaches the management of a small shipping business. The train company has suppliers who pay the company to take goods off their hands and customers who pay for the goods when delivered. The job of the train is to get the goods from the suppliers to the customers in the most efficient way. As the train moves, it uses up coal which has to be replenished when the supply gets low. There are eight levels, ranging from one product with two suppliers and two customers to four products with one supplier and one customer for each. The game is very absorbing, but not extremely educational.

Other alluring Spinnaker products: Type "The boy sat on a cat" and see it happen with *Story Machine.* Construct faces and animate them, or match prebuilt faces, with *Facemaker. Kidwriter* is another picture-story maker (see *Story Maker* from Scholastic). *Fraction Fever* present fractions both visually and numerically in an arcade-style game. And the widely-regarded *Snooper Troops* series requires intensive deduction and note-taking to solve the mysteries.

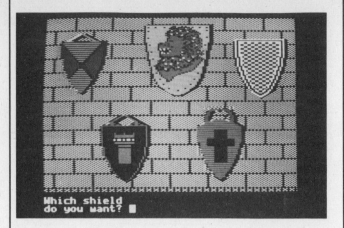

Sunburst Communications
Most programs in the $45-$59 range. Everything runs on Apple. Most programs also run on Atari, Commodore, TRS-80, and IBM PC or PCjr. Something for everyone. Send for Sunburst's catalog.

Mirror, mirror, on the wall—who has the some of the finest software of all? Sunburst, that's who. I have used scads of Sunburst products and loved them all, with only one exception *(Teasers by Tobbs).* Sunburst's eight Home Programs have won 121 well-deserved awards. And then there's Sunburst's School software, most of which fits neatly into the home library as well.

What makes Sunburst so good? The answer is that Sunburst is one of the few companies I've seen whose products *only* make sense on a computer. Sunburst's programs are not glorified flash cards or dancing TV cartoons. Most are open-ended, allowing the user to continually discover new delights. Sunburst also stresses thinking rather than rote drill. The packaging is super, the programs are clean and tight, and the price is not out of sight.

First, the Home Programs. (You can order a color brochure describing them, by the way.) *Memory Castle* has you scurrying through a castle trying to remember where you should go and what you should do. It gets pretty tricky, and you can forget whether you are going to the Shield Room to pick up the yellow shield or trying to open the Talking Door. Neat graphics and a real memory-sharpening workout.

The Factory is one of my favorites. You are in charge of a factory with three types of machines. They can rotate, drill, or draw a stripe down a piece of stock. Each of these operations has variations (round or square holes to drill, rotations of different angles, different numbers of stripes of different widths). You can create an assembly line of up to eight machines. Put in the stock and see what you made. Then let a friend try to duplicate it! You can ask the computer for a finished piece of stock, and try to duplicate it yourself. This is a great workout for spatial skills which would be impossible to practice on paper.

Sunburst also has a new *Super Factory* program that processes a cube instead of a flat disk.

The Pond is a game of logic, pattern-recognition, and experimentation. Your frog wants to gaily leap from lily pad to lily pad until he reaches "home." Only one pattern will get him there. Can you recognize it? It *sounds* easy, but since you only see part of the pond at a time, you have to carefully hoard your test jumps. *Pond* isn't quite as much fun as some others, but if you like this kind of mental challenge, its six levels of difficulty will keep you hopping.

I had doubts about *The Incredible Laboratory* before I saw it, mainly because I try to shun products that stress monsters and horror. The monsters that you invent just stand there, though, since the program's emphasis is on deducing how they are made. Briefly, you have to figure out which chemicals produce what results. In the Novice level, the same chemical always does the same thing. In higher levels, you're looking for combinations that react together to produce the monsters' characteristic (high heels or cowboy boots, three eyes or two eyes or cat eyes, etc.). You'll be grabbing for pencil and paper before you're through. As an introduction to scientific deduction, *Incredible Lab* is cheerfully motivating.

M-ss-ng L-nks sounds silly at first. Who needs to practice filling in missing letters? The hidden power of this program is how it develops a feeling for language. As you work your way through excerpts from classics like *The Secret Garden* and *The Wind in the Willows*, guessing what letter or word is missing, you develop a sense of sentence structure and grammar (not to mention the spelling practice!). I didn't expect to find this program absorbing, but was pulled right into it. The computer never rebukes you—it simply fills in the missing part for you after you've flubbed it enough times. The only incentives are a desire for a good score (few mistakes) and the pleasure of reading some excellent literature. By the way, you can also get *M-ss-ng L-nks* with classics from heavyweights like Hemmingway, Thurber, Freud, and Solzhenitsyn, or with excerpts from a MicroEncyclopedia that's a potpourri of factual trivia, or in the Foreign Language Editors version that shows you how to input passages of your choice in French, Spanish, and German.

Now, on to the School programs. Why these are not yet on the home market is a mystery to me. The only observable difference is their somewhat klunkier packaging. Send for Sunburst's Educational Courseware Catalog and find out about goodies like *The King's Rule, Whatsit Corporation,* and *Muppet Learning Keys,* plus dozens more.

Unlike other math games, *The King's Rule* was designed to help learners develop *un*obvious hypotheses. In order to progress to the throne, you must recognize the pattern which defines three numbers. But watch out! The simplest answer is not always right! For the numbers "1, 2, 3" for example, the rule may be "All numbers under 10" instead of "Whole numbers in counting sequence." You test your hypotheses on new number sets until you think you have it down. Then you challenge the computer and see if you're right. With six levels of play, it can get plenty tricky.

Whatsit Corporation lets you run a simplified small business. You make business decisions: to take out a loan or not, to hire a consultant or not, to hire employees or not. You price your product, advertise, keep records, cope with problems, and try to make a profit. So few programs (or textbooks) consider entrepreneurship that *Whatsit Corp* really stands out.

"BE"-WARE: COMPUTER FANTASY GAMES

There is something unhealthy about continual immersion in fantasy, and this is even more so when the fantasy is witchy or violent. This is why I do not include the shoals of role-play games in this book. Many of these do not sharpen thinking as much as mold character; your decisions are ethical as well as intellectual. But what kind of character are they molding? Ruthless adventurers with convenient morality who enjoy thrusting themselves into the society of villains? Not one of these game "heroes" ever *works* for a living. Some worship demonic gods. Others simply hack and maim for the thrill of it. And don't think that fantasizing murder and witchcraft helps release harmful tensions, as some ineffective psychiatrists tell us. What you train for is what you become. As a man thinketh, so is he.

This doesn't mean that I think we should rush out and demand Pollyanna fantasy games. There is something to be said for training in courage and resourcefulness. Some of the realistic military strategy software looks good, for example. So do other realistic simulations that let you try on the responsibilities of command, whether it's a program for practicing your corporate management skills in a simulated business or a computer drill for driver ed. I do, however, question how far twiddling a joystick can prepare anyone for real-life challenges.

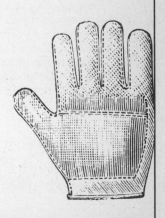

CHAPTER TWENTY-NINE

SCHOOLWARE: THE THREE R'S

We've come a long way . . . maybe. Today our children can get back to the basics in BASIC. They can also spend endless hours doing mindless computer drills, locked to the computer like a slave to the galley oar.

Computerization alone can't rescue school subjects from mediocrity, because mediocrity begins in the hearts and minds of the people. Much flotsam continues to clog the halls of academe. Some education professionals actually believe that if a program is simple and fun, it can't be worth much academically (at least unless the user offers up a sacrifice of accompanying blackline masters).

This attitude is by no means totally dominant in the schools, for which we give thanks. But the institutional structure of modern compulsory education, which has transferred the teacher's academic freedom to bureaucrats in state capitals, still works to stifle intelligence and joy in the classroom. For that reason—beware! Some of the popular programs for school subjects are very, very good, but some of them are horrid.

Beware of:

- Programs that rely on superficial rewards (and even worse, punishments) to motivate the learner. Endless flattery or nagging breeds contempt, not excellence. Successfully completing a worthwhile task should be the user's main reward.

- Automated flash cards. Some software just demands answers. This is not using the computer properly. Good software uses the computer's visual abilities. Better software gives the user choices he couldn't have with flash cards, like rotating a geometric object on-screen. The best software lets the user run the program and change his on-screen environment.

- Score-obsessed software. Some programs spend more time testing the user than teaching him anything.

- Programs where you're paying more for the workbooks than the software. In most cases, you won't want desk activities at all. (Learning Technologies, with its simple, fun learning kits, is a notable exception.)

- Labels that proclaim a product is "educator-approved." Some of the worst software is NEA-approved. So is some of the best. You just can't tell a program by its cover.

There is so very much schoolware out there that I had to break it up into two categories: the three R's (reading, writing, and arithmetic), and the rest. This chapter focuses on software for the three R's.

Surprisingly enough, the computer can help with these very basic subjects.

Until voice synthesis really catches on, you won't really be able to use a computer to teach the basics of word attack. And nobody I know of has any serious hardware/software developed for teaching handwriting via computer (though it wouldn't be hard to invent). But the youngster who knows the letters and their sounds can choose from a bevy of programs that help him build words and improve his spelling. Your young scholar can learn to type with computer software, thus gaining an adult skill that propels him beyond his physical handwriting abilities. He can write stories and illustrate them on-line. And he could even learn all his arithmetic at a keyboard, math being a subject ideally suited for computer instruction.

Nobody needs a computer to learn the three R's. But if you have a computer and a child, why not put the two together?

READERWARE

Reading is itself the best reading practice. I only know of one reading game that's really worth the money:

Reader Rabbit by The Learning Company (Apple II family, Commodore 64/128, Atari, IBM PC/PCjr family, Compaq, and Tandy 1000: $39.95).

Reader Rabbit is for beginning readers (better readers don't *need* computer reading practice). Children play with words, looking for words that begin or end with the same letters, or have the same letter in the middle. They look for words that differ by only one letter and play a rather neat memory/matching game that involves pairing words, or parts of words, with pictures. They even build words, using letters from a preselected list. All this without having to type a single keyboard letter! It's all done with cursor keys and a spacebar.

In the Word Factory, children "sort" words into shelves or into the garbage can, selecting their sorting speed. They label shipping cartons with words from the Beginning, Middle, and Ending Letter Boxes. Each new car connected to the Word Train must have only one letter different from the car before it. And Matchup has nine categories of objects to match plus six levels of difficulty.

Reader Rabbit is great fun, and actually exercises reading skills.

SPELLING AND GRAMMARWARE

Although, as I did, you can find dozens of spelling and grammar programs out there, current consensus has narrowed the contenders down to:

- DLM's *Spelling Wiz, Verb Viper, Word Invasion,* and *Word Master*—straight drill 'n practice.

- The Learning Company's *Magic Spells.* You play against a demon, *not* my choice of a computer opponent, unscrambling and spelling flashed words.

- Sunburst's *M-ss-ng L-nks* and *Wally's Word Works.* In *M-ss-ng L-nks* you fill in letters within words in order to read a fine piece of literature. *Wally's Word Works* has Wally the Wallaby plopping words in parts-of-speech pockets. You control Wally and he helps you control your grammar.

I am unenthusiastic about spelling and grammar programs, believing that he who reads and writes a lot and whose spelling and grammar get corrected will become good at the same. These programs are fun, though, and in the case of Sunburst the software is designed to be thinkware as well as spellware. See the review of *M-ss-ng L-nks* in the Thinkware chapter.

WRITERWARE

It is possible to write with ballpoint pen and paper. It is possible to type clean drafts over and over again on a typewriter. You can cut and paste by hand, and redo everything countless times from scratch. But is it *fun?*

When little children flock to the keyboard, they are showing good sense. Writing is hard. Typing is easy. And computers have made even *re*typing easy, a boon which is only fully appreciated by those whose previous books went through ten retyped drafts.

Children, and adults, can do excellent work without a computer. But if you have a computer, why live without a word processing program?

Broderbund Software
    Bank Street Writer. Apple II series $69.95. Commodore 64, Atari, $49.95. IBM PC $79.95.

Bank Street Writer paved the way for all those little kids who were longing to get their hands on a keyboard. Back when most word processing programs came wrapped in technospeak so dense that grown men could disappear into the fog and never be seen again, the people at the Bank Street College of Education had a better idea. And this is it: a very easy to use word processor, with a very easy to follow tutorial, that can be used even by the youngest writers.

Naturally, others rushed into the market with their own kiddie word processors, so Broderbund Software has been upgrading the original *Bank Street Writer.* It now comes with both the original easy-to-read forty-column format, and a new professional eighty-column option. You switch between the two modes via a utility program that comes with the disk. This utility program also is used to tell *Bank Street Writer* what kind of printer you have, and to set up special printing options, like boldface or underlining, so they will run on your printer. You may think, "Yuk. Utility programs." But *Bank Street Writer's* utility program also makes it possible to use everyday blank disks, instead of special preformatted ones like some other programs require. You can buy a pack of disks from your friendly local software store and set them up for writing on the spot. And though *Bank Street Writer* saves its files in a binary format which cannot be read by other programs, the utility program can convert these files into readable text files.

Bank Street Writer has all the essential word-processing functions, including block copy and find/replace. The program also provides UNERASE and MOVEBACK commands for the fumble-fingered.

Unique features:

- Unerase and Moveback—to reverse mistakes.

- You can view the end of pages and move the page boundaries until the document looks right.

- Files can be converted from internal format to text and back again.

- *Bank Street Writer* has one-character special printer function commands.

Shortcomings:

- I find it clumsy to use the tab key to select an option on the edit menu. If you go past your selection, you can't back up, but have to skip over the other eight options to get back to the one you want.

Milliken Publishing Company

The Writing Workshop, Apple II family: $69.95 includes Program diskette and file cabinet diskette plus a backup program diskette, documentation, student activities, and teacher activities, all in a binder. Ten extra file cabinet diskettes, $30.00.

As I said, Broderbund now has competition in the kiddie word processor market. Milliken's *Writing Workshop* is a *very* simple word processing program, possibly the best for youngest writers. The center of the program is the "desk," a selection menu with a picture of a desk. You see a filing cabinet, a manual, a typewriter, and a piece of paper with pen and pencil. These pictures represent the four different sections of the program. The Help Manual option displays a picture of a looseleaf binder containing a concise tutorial; Writing Tools is the editing and writing option; File Cabinet displays the filing and retrieving menu; and Typewriter prints the paper.

The graphics are simple, attractive, and easy to understand. My five-year-old followed the instructions on the screens easily.

Unique features:

- Easy to follow graphics.

- Help manual readily available.

- Print to screen option—displays the shape of the final draft on the screen as it will appear on the printer.

Shortcomings:

- The buffer will only hold about eight thousand characters—about three pages.

- Although *Writing Workshop* has block move and block delete commands, there is no block copy, and though there is a find command, there is no replace option.

This, like *Bank Street Writer,* is an excellent first word processor.

Sunburst Communications

Magic Slate, Apple II family: $89.95 includes two Program diskettes with backup diskettes, documentation, Student activities, and Teacher activities, all in a binder.

If you have a lot of young people in your family, or are looking for a word processor that both Junior and you can use, you may want to consider *Magic Slate*.

Magic Slate comes in all three character sizes: twenty column, forty column, and eighty column. The letters in the twenty-character version are large enough for even the youngest eyes to see, though the editing window is small, only eight lines of twenty characters each. The eighty-character version has a full-size editing screen, twenty lines of eighty characters.

Magic Slate is not quite as easy or as fast for a beginner to use as *The Writing Workshop* or *Bank Street Writer.* But *Magic Slate* has advanced functions which allow it to be used for the most complicated word processing tasks.

Unique features:

- Twenty, forty, and eighty-character versions of the program.

- Help panels appear right on the screen.

- Icons on the main menu of the twenty/forty character version make it easy for a beginner to understand.

- Prints in seven different type fonts, including italics and outline for printers which support graphics.

Shortcomings:

- The procedure for using block commands is more complicated than in other word processors.

- Because there are so many commands in *Magic Slate,* it is hard to learn them all.

- *Magic Slate* only keeps 2560 characters of your document in memory at any given time and uses the diskette for temporary storage for the rest. This allows the program to edit documents longer than 2560, but slows down editing considerably.

• When you format a data disk, there are a lot of programs that need to be copied onto it before *Magic Slate* can work with it. Making a data disk requires multiple swaps of the *Magic Slate* disk and the data disk if you only have one disk drive.

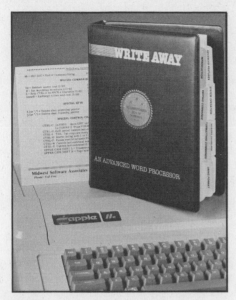

Peregrine Software
Write Away, Apple II family, Franklin Ace, BASIS-108. $119.95. Written in machine language, works with any printer. Not copy protected. Compatible, inexpensive sorting and programming software available.

And in case you are wondering, in my opinion the best word processing program for the *serious* writer with an Apple is *Write Away*. Because the program can't be learned in twenty minutes, some major reviewers, like the Whole Earthers, have passed it over. But *Write Away* has more power, speed, versatility, and extra features than any other Apple programs I have seen, all at an unbeatably low price.

You can do literally *anything* you want to with *Write Away*: center text, move or delete huge blocks of text, create automatic page titles, set tabs, indent any way you like it, automatically number pages, find any text you want and change all occurrences of that text, word wrap, right and left justify, and on and on and on. Eight easy-to-use function keys let you stick in a string of up to thirty-two characters with one keystroke (like the name of your novel's hero, Fauntleroy Wilbersham). You can write *large* documents, like the book you are now reading. A normal book chapter can fit in *Write Away's* text buffer, and you can merge an unlimited number of files to form a document of any length.

Using *Write Away*, you switch back and forth between "enter text" mode and "edit" mode with a single keystroke, and you don't even have to change modes to erase a mistake you just made. Printer features such as boldface, underline, subscript, and superscript are handled by inserting control characters at the beginning and end of that piece of text, again with just a few keystrokes. *Write Away* handles virtually all printers, maybe *all* printers by the time you read this. And no other program matches *Write Away's* blinding speed of editing. To move a hunk of text of any size, from a word or letter to entire paragraphs, all you have to do is find the beginning of the text, hit the double quote, then jump to the end and hit single quote. The text now disappears. Thereafter, whenever you hit the single quote in "edit" mode, that text will reappear where your cursor is. That means you can use this feature for copying; just reinsert the text in its old location before (or after) putting it wherever else you want it. It's child's play to duplicate or move sections of text. Compare this to such supposed superstars as *WordPerfect* where you must hit open-apple-0, Open-apple-9, 1, move the cursor to where you want the text, 4, and open-apple-0. And you have to consult menus at several of these steps!

Write Away is loaded with powerful features. You can set up each page to accommodate footnotes (although *Write Away* does not automatically number and insert footnotes for you—the only feature it lacks). You can switch text between cases (uppercase to lowercase or vice versa) with a single keystroke. *Write Away* has "soft hyphens" that allow you to suggest ways the program can hyphenate long words which otherwise would just go on the next line in one big chunk. You can scroll up and down by a line, a screen, a specified number of lines, or a specified number of characters, or to the beginning or end of your document. You can delete forwards or backwards, and by lines or characters. You can define top and bottom titles, and change them as often as you like. *Write Away* will automatically number pages for you, and start the numbering at a number of your choice. You *never* have to mess with submenus and subsubmenus with *Write Away*; all your options are right there.

Like *WordPerfect*, *Write Away's* editing screen shows only the line and column position of the cursor. The bottom of the screen shows whether you are in "enter text" or "edit" mode. You don't have to stop working on your document to look at what's on a disk, read or write from disk, delete files from disk, and if you have a printer buffer you can continue working while your document is being printed.

Powerful? *Write Away* lets you chain macros to instantly execute any series of commands you choose, as many times as you choose. You hit the t key to execute the macro once; /t executes it repeatedly until the document's end is reached. And *Write Away's* built-in mail merge capability includes conditional commands in your text that can, for example, create letters for specific zip code areas or select different titles for the addressee based on his or her sex. I have used it to create labels and personalized form letters to suppliers—thousands of them by now.

Because *Write Away* is written in machine language, most commands are executed *instantly*. Even with a full twenty-eight thousand characters in memory, *Write Away* can locate any section of text in less than one second. Files load fast and are written fast. It takes less than twenty seconds to load a ten-page paper.

Versatile? *Write Away* has electronic communications built right in. You won't have to buy a separate program to use with your modem. *Write Away* has a complete Mail Merge system and interfaces with VisiCalc, DB Master, Sensible Speller, and other popular programs.

Write Away comes with a fine tutorial program and well-organized manual. Because of all the powerful options, you're going to spend some time learning how to use the program, but it's time well spent. I've been using *Write Away* almost daily for more than a year, and it has met all my needs as I wrote this book, sent out numerous mass mailings, accessed data bases through a modem, and wrote letters.

Yes, *Write Away* can't access those miles of extra RAM that users who get *WordPerfect* and a memory expansion card can. But even so, I have chosen *Write Away* on an unupgraded Apple IIc over all the joys of memory expansion and hard disk. It's faster. It's easier to use. It handles whole chapters at a time even *without* expensive memory expansion. I just couldn't bear to clunk along with screens and subscreens with one of the highly-advertised "super word processors" when *Write Away* soars like an eagle and lets me write and edit as fast as I think.

Write Away was awarded the recommended seal of approval by the Professional Software Programmers Association.

Scarborough Systems
Mastertype, $39.95: Apple II family, 48K; Atari, 32K; Commodore 64; $50 for IBM PC.

Mastertype is for learning to type, and for improving your speed and accuracy. You select the keyboard row you want to drill, or ask for a free-for-all. Select the rate, and zap the letters or words zipping at you from all sides of the screen by typing them correctly before they hit your world and destroy it. Everyone agrees this program is more fun than the very professional *Typing Tutor III,* which calculates your speed to the tenth of a word per minute and which I have never had the heart to try. My only complaint is that the practice words are not randomly generated. You have to input your own practice words if you want a change of pace.

MATHWARE

All-Purpose Catalogs

Creative Publications

If you're into math, you're probably going to send for Creative's catalog anyway. It also includes a nice twenty-three-page section of software, books, and accessories, with such goodies as computer art posters. The program selection is good (Creative carries both *Bank Street Writer* and *Milliken Word Processor,* for example) and each product is thoroughly described, most with color pictures of sample screen graphics.

NASCO

NASCO is getting into computers in a big way. Their latest catalog has pages and pages of math software and computer books. If you want special-purpose math software, like for instance a trigonometry program, you can get it from NASCO.

Arithmetic Games

Daybreak Software
Salina Math Games, $29.95 each. Apple II family, TRS-80 only.

Daybreak's math games vary from straight teacher-style drill to *Math Baseball* (still drill, but student gets rewarded by moving players around a baseball field) to drill based on board and arcade games *(Salina Math). Simple Algebraic Equations* spits out randomly generated equations on three levels, and gently helps the student correct his mistakes. These products are mostly acceptable, but unexciting.

Developmental Learning Materials (DLM)

Computerized flash cards. That's DLM's popular math software series. We tried it and did not like it. Especially bothersome was the way the problems on *Alligator Mix* came jiggling across the screen, ruining your eyes while you were trying to think of the answer. The games have arcade-style timed action and various hungry critters who want to eat your answers.

Learning Technologies
All programs $19.95, include certificate for free Learning Kit. Apple II family, Commodore.

Learning to Add and Subtract is what its name implies. You get three games on your disk: an addition game, a subtraction game, and "Addition in a Different Way." For each problem in the basic games, that number of creatures or objects appears on the screen. E.g., for "5+2" first five buses might appear, then two more. The user gets several tries at the answer, and then can ask to see it. The game that makes this software memorable is "Addition in a Different Way." The screen displays a tower matrix (a 10 by 10 grid slashed in half) and a hovering helicopter. When a question is asked, a space on the grid flashes. Correct answers put a check mark on the grid, incorrect ones an x. Each correct answer causes the helicopter to drop another piece of a rocket, and questions answered incorrectly are asked again later on. When the entire matrix is full of check marks, the completed rocket takes off. This game, then, drills *every* addition fact for sums less than ten.

Let's Go Fishing is both simpler and harder. Simpler, because all you have to do in its two games is catch the correct number of fish or string the correct number of beads. Harder, because you must hook just the right fish and because your necklace of beads keeps zipping about the screen. These are basically counting games, with hand-eye coordination drill and visual discrimination thrown in.

Spinnaker
Apple, Atari, Commodore 64, IBM PC, PCjr, Coleco Vision/Adam.

Fraction Fever is an arcade game that has you matching fractions. Some are visual fractions: four circles of which three are filled in for 3/4, for example. Some are multiples: 8/12 is the same as 2/3, for example. You hop along on your pogo stick trying to beat the clock and not fall through the floor. Sounds interesting.

Springboard Software
Piece of Cake Math, $34.95. *Fraction Factory,* $29.95.

The best math drill I've seen is Springboard's *Piece of Cake Math* and *Fraction Factory.* In *Piece of Cake,* you add, subtract, multiply, and divide cakes. Everything is explained with visuals, and there is a multiple-level drill section as well, called "Catch-a-Cake." Nowhere else do you get *all* these arithmetic processes in one lean, clean program. The only problem is that our sons find it funnier when the cake splats on the floor than when they answer correctly and "catch" it. *Fraction Factory* follows a similar style, with color visuals, explanations, and hints for slow learners.

Mathematical Thinking Games

EduSoft

Simulated Computer, $39.95: Apple, Atari.

Grub around in your micro's guts with *Simulated Computer.* You run sample programs and the screen shows what happens to your input, output, registers, and memory locations as each step is executed. If innards turn you on, this award-winning program is for you. Personally, I think you get as good an understanding by working it through on paper.

Learning Technologies

$19.95 price includes certificate for free Learning Kit. Apple II family, Commodore.

Math in a Nutshell takes whole numbers and arithmetic about as far as they can go, and would be an excellent preparation for Wff 'n Proof's *Equations.* You are given three, four, or five numbers with no operators in between. Your task is to find the operators that make the equation on the left match the number on the right. You do this by hopping an almost idiotically happy squirrel from one apple to another, selecting the operator on the correct apple. If this sounds too easy, try finding the answer for 6 3 5 3 2 = 19. For children who know their math facts, *Math in a Nutshell* can really crank up mathematical thinking.

Scholastic

Quations is an electronic version of the board game, a sort of Scrabble with equations. It's one of the simpler thinking games, since you get to lay down your pieces occasionally and you get to see part of what the opposition is up to.

"Why," I asked the lady at Scholastic, "would anyone want to spend money for software when they can just get the original game?" "Because," she replied, "the computer can play with you." "Ah!" I said, and wandered off to ask my math-degreed husband what *be* thought of it. "Yes, you can play against the computer or against another person," Bill explained. "This little bird called 'Quato' comes on the screen and challenges you. I didn't think that much of the bird," he continued, "until it started beating me."

Sunburst Communications

The King's Rule stretches your ability to invent theories to explain mathematical facts. Given the series 1,3,4, the answer *might* be "series where the last number equals the sum of the first two" or "numbers under 5" or "series where the last number equals the product of the first two numbers plus one," etc. Form your hypothesis and test it on several new series. Then make your challenge. If you're correct enough times, you pass all the obstacles and are crowned King! Colorful graphics and lots of new puzzles make this an attractive game.

Wff 'N Proof Learning Games Associates

DIG math preview disk, $10. Three-program Home Learning Package (includes DIG preview, *Intro to Equations,* and *Equations Challenge Matches,* plus user manual), $49.95. Four separate *Challenge Matches* disks available as above, or all four for $119.95. Apple II family, DOS 3.3 or PASCAL, min. 64K; IBM PC, PCjr, 128K.

Equations, that peerless math game, is now computerized. Schools may want to look into outfitting their math classrooms with the DIG (Diagnostic Instructional Gaming) *Equations*-based program. Useful for classes from fourth grade through high school, DIG math dramatically increases students' ability to apply math concepts taught in the program.

Not every school will be enlightened enough to get DIG, so Wff 'n Proof has produced a home miniversion with an *Introduction to Equations* and some *Equations Challenge Matches.* It is *much* easier to learn to play *Equations* this way, and the computer will match wits with you even if nobody else feels bright enough to do so.

Equations, as we have intimated in the Math chapter, is the Porsche of math games. Schoolkids who play it industriously do far, far better at math than they have ever done before. Get it for Junior and see his brains bulge.

Wff 'n Proof is in the process of computerizing their entire line of brainbusters. Write if you want to find out what they're up to.

Geometry, and Developing Your Spatial Sense

Daybreak

All geometry games, Apple II family. $49.95 each.

Daybreak's geometry tutoring programs are interactive and visual. *Fundamental of Geometry* gets into basic terminology and points, rays, lines, segments, parallels, angles, triangles, and quadrilaterals. *Areas of Triangles and Quadrilaterals* squirts out random problems covering areas of triangles, rectangles, squares, parallelograms, and trapezoids. Daybreak is proud of their *Circles* program: they say it "covers virtually all aspects of angles, lines, and segments connected with circles." *Circles* messes around with radius, diameter, circumference, central and inscribed angles, secants, tangents, and our old friend pi.

Also of interest is Daybreak's *New Angle on Geometry.* Three programs on one disk cover geometry fundamentals, areas of triangles and quadrilaterals (with detailed graphics and an infinite problem set), and circles. "Programs are highly tutorial and progressive," says the brochure. "Wrong answers bring immediate branching into detailed explanations." Geometry being such a visual subject, this software might be useful to some.

EduSoft
Superplot, $49.95: Apple II family, 64K. Other programs from $29.95 to $39.95

Superplot is a jazzed-up version of *Plot* with zoom and scrolling features. The program graphs any function in standard algebraic notation. Superimpose other functions, zoom in and out on either axis or both axes, scroll in all four directions, change the limits. If this sounds like fun, you'd better apply to M.I.T. at once.

The Learning Company
Bumble Games: Apple II family, Commodore 64/128, Atari, IBM PC/PCjr, Tandy Color Computer. *Bumble Plot:* Apple, Commodore, IBM, Tandy Color Computer. Each program $39.95.

Learn the basics of plotting and graphing with the Bumble series. Both feature Bumble, a beelike character from the planet Furrin. Being a Furriner, Bumble keeps losing things, like his butterfly and his cousin. In the first games on the *Bumble Games* disk, you guess where the butterfly or cousin are hiding by naming a point on a grid. Arrows tell you if you need to go left or right, up or down. In the next level of difficulty, your directions are spelled out (e.g., "Go right and down"). The last two games have you plotting lines on a graph, first to duplicate Bumble's own pictures (only a few are included) or to make your own.

I wish the program allowed you to draw more than ten lines on a graph, and also that there was a way to pick up your cursor and put it down elsewhere without drawing a line. But even so, *Bumble Games* is about as engaging an introduction to geometry and graphing as you can find.

Bumble Plot carries the concept one step further, with negative numbers.

Learning Technologies
All programs $19.95, which includes a certificate for a free Learning Kit. Apple II family, Commodore.

For an enjoyable, user-friendly introduction to spatial visualization, check out the *Pipeline* review in the Thinkware chapter. For a maddeningly difficult workout of the same skills, try *Sliding Block,* reviewed in the same place.

Sunburst Communications
The Factory, $55: Apple II family, Atari, Commodore 64, IBM PC, PCjr with color graphics card, TRS-80 Color Computer. *Super Factory,* $55. Apple II family, 64K.

The Factory and the new *Super Factory* are the best programs I've seen for developing spatial sense. In *The Factory,* you have machines that can rotate, drill, or paint your stock. Set up the machines and see what they do. (The graphics that show the stock being fed through the assembly line are great!) Or ask the computer for a problem and see if you can figure out what setup produced the result! *The Factory* operates on a square piece of raw material: *Super Factory* processes cubes.

Algebra Tools

NASCO

NASCO has a full range of math software, from the simple and fun to the hairy and tedious. Personally, I'd stay away from anything labeled *Factoring Binomial Equations* or similar dispiriting titles.

CHAPTER THIRTY

SCHOOLWARE: MORE SUBJECTS

Art! Music! Geography! Social studies! Bible! Languages! Journalism! Science! No subject is safe from being computerized these days. The word in academe is that you'd better talk software and carry a joystick.

At the risk of being called repetitive, let me implore you for the last time to always, always remember that nobody *needs* a computer to learn these subjects. Rembrandt lived before *Delta Drawing* was invented. Mozart did not learn his trade with *Magic Piano.* Dr. Livingstone, we presume, did not cart about an Apple IIe on his rambles through Africa. George Washington Carver figured out three hundred new ways to use peanuts without the help of computer simulations.

Anyone who implies that home schooling, or home learning in general, is substandard because "children need computer exposure" or "today's subjects can only be grasped through computerized education" is simply puffing hot air.

Learning is not the exclusive property of the wealthy. Who learns more: the devoted reader of *Organic Gardening* magazine who raises earthworms, composts her kitchen scraps, and puts into practice the lore of companion planting and raised beds, or the purchaser of a garden simulation program? Who knows more about the history of the American Revolution: a child who has read *Johnny Tremain,* the Declaration of Independence, Jean Fritz's books, and the *Federalist Papers,* or one who fiddles with a computerized time line? Who is the better scientist: the boy messing around in the basement with his Sears chemistry set, or his brother who sits upstairs with his nose glued to a science simulation? Would you learn French better by going to France or by using a French language program?

Computers are remarkably efficient substitutes for real-life learning. But they will never replace it.

Schoolware is at its best when it simulates experiences we are not likely to have. Few of us are international jet-setters. Therefore a program where the user travels around the world can be a helpful (although second-rate) substitute for the experience of actual traveling. Most little kids don't get to mess with soldering irons and powered machines. Therefore a program like *Rocky's Boots* that allows the user to build and test digital circuits is a happy introduction to this art.

Also useful are the "challenge games" where the computer takes the place of an infinitely patient friend. Few of us have a piano teacher who will spend hours coaching us on rhythm, as *Magic Piano* does.

And, since most of us make mistakes when learning a new skill, software that lets us try out new ideas and play with them *without* penalizing honest mistakes can remove some of the tedium from subjects that must be grasped through trial and error.

The real world is not Plastic City, and human beings are not just fingertips connected to a keyboard. But as a supplement to lots of hands-on learning, good schoolware can be a very friendly tool.

ABOUT THE FOLLOWING REVIEWS

I couldn't possibly review every piece of schoolware on the market. So I didn't try. Think of the following as an introduction to the scholastic smorgasbord rather than as a "Best Of" list.

The reviews are in alphabetical order by subject: All-Purpose Catalogs, Art, Bible, Geography, Journalism, Languages and Culture, Music, and Science. In those categories you will find some of the most popular programs reviewed, plus ideas of what to expect in the future as educational software heads from its tentative infancy towards a more mature adolescence.

ALL-PURPOSE SCHOOLWARE CATALOGS

Life for Little Learners

Huge array of Commodore 64 programs for home education on both disk and cassette, including *Basic Self-Taught*. Programs are available for other computers as well. Write for details.

Open Court

Open Court has put together a list of the best learning software, with reviews that explain what is which and why and how to use it. For one-stop shopping that reflects Open Court's emphasis on high-order thinking skills, send for their Quick Finder.

ART AND DRAWING PROGRAMS

If you want a computer primarily to do art, you want an Apple Macintosh. You also want several expensive grahics programs and perhaps several expensive programs for fancy text as well. Its graphics capabilities are why I periodically have to fight off the temptation to go get a Mac.

But these professional programs, interesting as they are, are not the ones most people start their children with. Children's art programs are much less expensive. They come in two categories:

- Drawing programs (with on-screen brushes and colors).

- Design programs (these graph designs on the screen that produce results similar to those achieved by a Spirograph toy).

Below is one example from each category.

Spinnaker Software

Delta Drawing, $39.95. Disks for Apple, IBM PC. Cartridges for Atari, Commodore 64/128.

Delta Drawing is a command-driven program. By entering commands such as D to draw or R to turn to the right, you can draw just about any picture you want. The program allows you to save a sequence of commands as a function which can then be used repeatedly in the drawing. You can make the drawings as finely detailed as you want.

Is it kid-appealing? My sons were fighting with my husband to try *Delta Drawing*. Is it useful? Many of the techniques used in

Delta Drawing are very similar to techniques used for programming. Master this program, and you will be well on your way to computer mastery.

Springboard Software

Rainbow Painter, for those solely interested in drawing, has ten categories of line drawings (such as Dinosaurs, Flowers, Fairy Tales, and Space), plus fifty different brushes and thousands of color patterns. This is not a Logo-style preprogramming item like Spinnaker's *Delta Drawing*, and you can't write any stories on the screen. You can, however, sit in front of the screen for hours and produce some nifty pictures.

BIBLEWARE

Look for programs that help with Bible research and games that lead into real Bible discovery. Who needs PacMan with Bible verses? Also, do avoid those programs whose advertising implies that kids will find the Bible boring unless it's dressed up with arcade antics.

Ascension Designs

Right Again!, $32.99. Commodore 64/128.

Right Again! is an arcade-style game with three clue levels and two skill levels. Solutions to the first clue level are found in the accompanying colorful Bible storybook. Second-level clues come from the story, but may be not mentioned specifically in the text. Third-level clues can come from anywhere in the Bible. Angel Dominic escorts you through time and space to find the answer.

Right Again! is a Bible Games, Inc. product and runs on Apple or Commodore. Reviewers praise it highly.

Baker Book House

Early Bible Heroes (Genesis), *Searching for a King* (1 Samuel), *Boy Jesus* (Gospels), *Early Church* (Acts), each $29.95. Apple II family, Commodore 64.

Also: *Bits, Bytes, and Biblical Studies*, $6.95.

The authors of Baker's Bible software series have cleverly invented the gimmick of having the Baker Street Kids dress up and act out the Bible stories, thus avoiding the problems associated with trying to authentically reproduce events nobody now living has seen. You get fifteen stories on every disk. Pick a story and you get a full-screen picture featuring one or more Baker Street Kids. By repeatedly pressing the space bar, you cause the Bible story to appear in a page by page fashion. At the end of the story, you pick your difficulty level: Tough, Very Tough, or Super Tough. The questions are multiple choice, and answers are selected by using only the Return key and spacebar. If you miss a question, the program can take you back to the part of the story where the answer resides and highlight the appropriate text. Get five out of six correct answers, and the picture is animated for your reward.

The Bible stories are written by the editor of *Christianity Today* and his son. They are decent little stories, but why settle for stories when you could have the real thing? More quibbles: The Super Tough questions weren't hard enough. Also, questions are the same every time you read a story. This is probably because the graphics take up so much room on the disk.

A kid who can read, but who has never read the Bible, could learn something from these programs. Better-instructed users would find the series too simple.

The Bibleware product you won't want to miss is *Bits, Bytes, and Biblical Studies* by John Hughes. Thomas Nelson publishes it, but Baker will be distributing it also, as will local Christian bookstores. It discusses and explains "nearly all currently available Bible oriented programs—including ancient language texts, bibliographic data bases, concordances, and games." As a special bonus, all info is categorized for novice and advanced operators. Let Hughes tell you all about it and make up for my deficiencies.

Christian Computer Users Association.
Christian Computer News, $15/yr.

If you want to keep in touch with what's out there in Biblical software (e.g., the NIV on disk) and church-related software, you'll want to subscribe to *Christian Computer News,* a CCUA publication.

GEOGRAPHY, OR WHERE-O-WARE

Daybreak Software
Regions of the U.S., $39.95. Apple II family, Commodore 64, TRS-80 Models III and IV.

Daybreak's *Regions of the U.S.* computer game is a quick, interactive way to practice your state recognition, as well as to pick up a few facts about our country's geographical regions. You recognize the states in the context of their regions. The Beginner's Quiz tells you the names of the states in that region and you pick the correct one. Super Quiz just shows you the region and you have to type in the state name. After you've flubbed a few, you can always turn to the Review section, which identifies the states. The Regions Quiz contains twenty clues about each region. Examples range from the obvious to those requiring some geographical knowledge. Examples: "The Pilgrims landed in this region" and "Farming has always been limited in this region because it is so rocky." Did you guess New England? Right!

Regions of the U.S. was designed for schools, so the computer is very stern about mistakes. It is not open-ended; after you've been through it a few times, you should know it all. But since that's what you're trying to accomplish, *Regions* is a decent, if unexciting, little tool.

Developmental Learning Materials (DLM)
Atlas Action games, $44 each, Apple family.

U.S. Atlas Action and *World Atlas Action* are two computer map games that might unveil new horizons in geography drill. I was hoping they would be out in time for me to review them personally. Next edition, maybe! In the meantime, here's the catalog description.

U.S. Atlas Action features: * colorful maps of the 50 states * a map of the entire U.S. (including Hawaii and Alaska) * an exciting arcade-action game designed to help players learn locations and important facts about each state.

Players can also create, play, and save more than 20 individualized map games and more than 20 individualized arcade games.

Players have the option of assigning symbols on each map, with each symbol depicting such categories as mountain ranges, rivers, cities, birthplaces of famous persons, etc. This makes *U.S. Atlas Action* a source of unlimited learning about the United States.

Other features of the *U.S. Atlas Action* include game instruction screens, an "items missed" screen to provide players with a visual listing of their errors, and options including speed, length of play, one or two player games, keyboard or paddle control, and game sound effects.

Game content is directly linked to geography curriculum typical for grades 3 through 12.

Well! Doesn't that sound interesting? Open-ended geography drill is sure a step up from flash cards.

World Atlas Action does not promise quite so much. You get thirteen maps of major regions. "Players will be able to learn locations and important facts about each country or region, plus learn the names of continents, island chains, oceans, and major seas."

JOURNALISM

Here are two products for budding journalists: one for the very young and one for the rest.

Scholastic Software

Story Maker lets kids write their own stories: *illustrated* stories. Kids can pick up to eight different type styles and dozens of different pictures to illustrate the text, or they can draw their own. Erasing is easy, as is editing, all being done with icons at the bottom of the page. (Naturally, you need a joystick for this program.) Pictures can be made large or small, and when you make your own you can choose from sixteen colors and textures and two line widths. It all can be printed out, too. We found the drawing process to move very slowly at first, but the children never lost interest.

Springboard Software
The Newsroom: Apple II family, IBM PC 256K and color graphics, $59.95; Commodore 64/128, $49.95. Needs dot matrix printer, supports modem, joystick, and Apple mouse.
Clip Art Collection: Apple II family, IBM PC, PCjr, $29.95.

The ultimate accessory for a computer-age writer would be a newspaper-creating program that lets you prepare texts in different fonts, create banners, position and reposition photos while the computer automatically rearranges your text, sends and receives text and pictures between all computers that can run the program (including different companies' models), and finally zaps your creations out on your trusty dot matrix printer.

The Newsroom by Springboard Software is one of the best-selling programs around because it does all the above. You can select from a library of six hundred pieces of clip art, or twelve hundred pieces if you add on Springboard's *Clip Art Collection*. These pictures can be used in text or to make banners, and you can alter and customize them if you wish. Now it is easy for anyone with two disk drives to make professional-looking newspapers and booklets. (Contary to what the manual says, for most applications you will do fine storing pix and text on the same disk.)

Springboard has also promised to add another volume to its clip art collection, a complete section of business clip art. It probably has arrived by the time you're reading this.

The clip art on *The Newsroom* disk is mostly cartoons in a sophomoric style. *Clip Art Collection* clip art contains art more suitable for serious applications, plus a number of cartoons. For some unknown reason, there is not one pleasant-looking baby and most of the men are fat or stupid or both. On the other hand, virtually every female character is good looking and posed energetically, and many of them are portrayed doing things like running jackhammers and fixing plumbing.

I have run machinery and swung a wrench in my day, but most women have not. I therefore question how useful it is to have clip art which substitutes women for men in the occupations actually dominated by men in the real world. And it surely is unfair that the female workers are glamorized while the males are pictured as duds. Will you do something about this, Springboard?

LANGUAGES AND CULTUREWARE

Voice synthesis is finally becoming a reality. My latest issue of *A+* magazine has several ads for programs that will help you learn foreign languages at your Apple—with the computer giving the proper spoken intonation, yet. I'm not sure that I'm ready for a computer that speaks English better than I do, let alone French! But if some clever linguists match up with the voice synthesizing scientists, we could have programs with the visual advantages of video training *and* the user control of good software.

Keep your eye on this field for what could become a breakthrough in classroom language training.

American Map Corporation
Languageware, $39.95, Travelware, $49.95. (Each available for Apple II family, DOS 3.3, 48K, one disk drive.)

For visual drill alone, you might consider American Map Corp's Languageware. Arcade-style computerized vocab and comprehension development programs are available for Spanish, French, German, Latin, and English.

And to go along with this, you can get Travelware from Baedeker's. "Unique programs with amusing situations, graphics, sound effects, and folk music present cultural differences and help travelers avoid social blunders." Hm. *Correct Behavior* Travelware comes in either English or the language of the country for France, Germany, and Mexico. The Japanese version is only available in English.

Daybreak Software
Annam, $49.95.

Just as a sample of the cultural simulations being vended to schools, consider Daybreak Software's *Annam*.

In *Annam*, you are the leader of a small Asian country threatened by a Communist superpower. Your job is to keep your country free. Your people are very touchy, and you can be overthrown from within as well. Based loosely on the experience of Vietnam, *Annam* allows the user to face an ever-changing set of problems. If you keep Annam free for twelve years, you get a city named after you and win the game. *Annam* is fascinating to play and offers some insight into intenational affairs. The conditions are somewhat biased against the U.S.A., as American intervention hardly ever seems to help in this game.

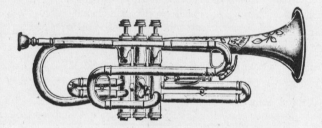

MUSICWARE

Once upon a time the Commodore was *the* computer for music-makers. It had music keyboards and programs that would do everything your little musical heart desired. But the Apple is striking back!

Not only are programs coming out that let you *hum* your compositions into the Apple, but with a MIDI interface and a synthesizer, some clever software can actually teach you to play the piano. There's much more to come, all of it expensive so far.

Some affordable software does exist for those who want to play with music, not make it a career. Kids, for instance. See the reviews below.

Springboard Software
Music Maestro: Apple II family, Commodore 64, IBM PC, PCjr, Atari. Disk only. $34.95.

Music Maestro is a very basic introduction to some musical ideas. You can select any one of several programs from a changing picture menu. "Treble Clef" displays the notes of the treble clef and then tests you on which note goes on which line of the clef, and "Bass Clef" does the same for the bass. It would have been helpful if the program provided mnemonics, such as *EG*ad, *B*ill, *D*on't *F*all for the treble clef lines. You can "Perform" a song (with uniform staccato rhythm only), "Record" it, and "Playback." Pick the "Kaleidoscore" option and the screen will put on a color show to your music. All so far is usable, if unexciting. But *Music Maestro* falls down in its "Melody Tutor" program. The idea is that the computer is going to teach you a song. But instead of leading you through the song by phrases, and letting you echo back as large a chunk as you can master at one time, here is how "Melody Tutor" does it. The computer plays one note. You play one note. If you get it right, the computer plays two notes. You play two notes. If you get it right, the computer plays *three* notes. Your beard will be long and gray by the time you ever get to the end of any song with this method of instruction.

EduSoft

Magic Piano, Apple II family, $49.95.

Forgive my fiendish howls of glee. I *know* it's not nice to gloat because *Magic Piano* is only available for Apples (like mine), but it's about time some decent, inexpensive, educational music software came out for something besides Commodore!

With *Magic Piano,* you can play, record, and playback songs in any rhythm you choose. Not only that, you can print your masterpieces, and they will come out in beautiful standard music notation. More: *Magic Piano's* "Simon Says" game helps you develop your musical ear. The computer plays a tune (you pick how many notes long), and you try to reproduce it. If you miss any notes, the computer tells you if you were too high or too low, and replays the song. If you absolutely can't figure it out, you can beg to see the tune displayed. Anyone from kids to symphony orchestra players can enjoy this game, as the two-note selections are very easy and the long pieces are very hard.

And to top it all off is a little number called the "Rhythm Game." This is Simon Says with rhythm: the computer belts out a rhythm and you try to duplicate it by hitting the spacebar in *exactly* the same rhythm. Again, you can choose your difficulty level. Not only can you pick easier or tougher rhythms, but you can decide whether the computer will be lenient and let a close try through, or persnickety and demand rhythmical perfection.

You "play" the computer by tapping the number keys. Easy as do-re-mi!

SCIENCEWARE

If you're looking for science simulations or flash card style drill, NASCO is a good place to start. NASCO's science catalog lists hundreds of science programs for students in junior and senior high. Watch blood pump through a heart and identify heart parts. Pretend you are a fish trying to survive in a Minnesota lake (it shouldn't be *that* hard!). Fiddle around with the periodic table. Practice dissecting the standard critters (earthworm, crayfish, and so on). Learn to identify major constellations. Most NASCO software is in the $27 to $50 range.

If, on the other hand, you want to develop your scientific thinking and engineering skills, you want to rush out and buy *Rocky's Boots* and *Robot Odyssey I* from The Learning Company. These two $44.95 programs are the greatest introduction to scientific reasoning and experimentation that I have yet seen. See their reviews in the Thinkware chapter.

PENNY-PINCHING

I do hope you don't plan to buy too much major software at retail prices. It's so unnecessary. Just subscribe to any major computing magazine, and you'll find half a dozen full-page ads from discount dealers who knock 20 to 50 percent off their stock. You might prefer to rent a program for a month (the going rate is 15-20 percent of the retail price) and there are companies that will accommodate you. The reviews in the magazine will more than pay for themselves, cluing you in to what's new, what's great, and what's not.

If you can't wait long enough to get a computer magazine, one source for discount software is The Computer Software Store. This company has a wide selection of the best software for Commodore, Apple, and IBM machines in the categories of business, education, recreation, and home use. The software is listed by company name, with no reviews. (This is, by the way, standard operating procedure for discount firms.) If you know what you want, you can get it here for 20-40 percent off (larger discounts on the more expensive programs).

Computers. Are they "changing the way we live and learn," a phrase beloved by hack writers? No. *We* change the way we live and learn. And one of the changes is that now we have the opportunity to use a fine little tool called a computer.

Enjoy!

PART VIII

MATH AND SCIENCE

CHAPTER THIRTY-ONE

HEALTH

Fifteen men on a dead man's chest,
Yo ho ho and a bottle of rum.
Drink and the devil had done for the rest,
Yo ho ho and a bottle of rum.
(Old English sailors' song)

Health is now a required course in the public schools. It is therefore easy to get health textbooks, and any who are content with standard school fare can find a variety of sources in the Textbooks section.

Why do I object to standard health texts? Because they spend so much time talking about drugs and drunkenness and venereal disease and so on, and refuse to say that any of these things are *wrong.* All is reduced to "risk-taking." While the general public thinks that Junior is getting a sermon against (for example) drugs, he is actually being taught to play the odds. The text, not being allowed to say hedonistic chemical-pumping is wrong, weakly stutters that Junior is taking a chance with his health by so indulging. Junior, of course, gets the message that he won't *necessarily* harm himself—there's only a *chance* he will.

He's also subtly being conditioned to consider drug abuse a respectable option. So yo, ho, ho, and a bottle of rum.

Most of the "health" subjects really don't belong in a health course at all. Drug use, or abstention; premarital sex, or chastity; suicide, or life—these are all *ethical,* not strictly medical, choices, and should be taught by the family and church, not the school. Children who know right from wrong don't need to suffer through gruesome units on the physical effects of cocaine or syphilis. Even children who *don't* know right from wrong fail to profit by what amounts to hours of how-to instruction in breaking the laws of God and man.

Anyone who *wants* his sons and daughters taught how to commit suicide, or how to masturbate, or how to take drugs, is certainly free to purchase that sort of materials. But if you think public school health materials mainly teach good nutrition and exercise, you're in for a shock.

NUTRITION AND EXERCISE

Jack Sprat could eat no fat.
His wife could eat no lean.
And so, between them both, you see,
They licked the platter clean.
(Mother Goose rhyme)

And speaking of nutrition, don't expect standard school texts to be too much help in this area either. While growing numbers of Americans are baking with whole wheat and sprinkling sesame seeds on their salads, school texts still babble on about the "Four Basic Food Groups." You remember these from your own school days—Meat, Dairy, Breads 'n Grains, Fruits 'n Veggies. You were exhorted to eat one item from each group at every meal, if possible. So let's have chicken with apple stuffing and vanilla ice cream for breakfast! You can *kill* yourself with the Four Basic Food Groups, or at least grow exceedingly fat: steak 'n potatoes 'n broccoli with hollandaise sauce 'n chocolate pudding, to name just one meal with all four "essential groups." O.K., it sounds yummy, but is it *healthy?* Is the perfect meal *really* a Big Mac with shake and baked apple pie?

While up-to-date nutritionists debate about the virtues of Natural Hygiene's dairy-free and largely frugivorous (fruit-eating) diet or the virtues of complementary protein (combined grains with dairy or legumes to enhance one's protein intake), school texts plod along twenty years behind, informing kids of such earth-shaking concepts as "get plenty of fresh air and exercise." Now you tell me—does it make sense to sit *inside* filling out workbook pages about the virtues of being *outside?* If kids really learn by doing, they'd be better off playing volleyball in the school yard.

The best nutrition texts to read, in my opinion, are the popular books on this subject written for adults. Since most publishers won't print anything with more than an eighth-grade vocabulary, literate kids can get their nutritional ideas straight from the horse's mouth. And since most books of this ilk include recipes, your kids can learn to press their own cheese and grind their own wheat flour and bake their own all-natural corn chips and do whatever it is that people do with tofu.

I don't claim to agree with all the theories the following books teach. That would be impossible, since they disagree with each other: protein-combining versus skip-the-dairy; megavitamins versus no capsulized vitamins of any dosage. But since nutrition *is* such a hotly debated field, it makes sense to at least become acquainted with the major *practical* theories.

Herald Press
 $9.95. Available from Puritan-Reformed for $7.96.

The *More-With-Less Cookbook* is the simplest, most useful introduction to the doctrine of "protein-combining"—i.e., eating combinations of foods for your protein instead of noshing on steak at every meal. The religious group that put this out has a notion that if Americans eat less meat, somehow hungry folk on the other sides of the world will find more rice in their dinner bowls. You may remember this as the, "How can you leave all that food on your plate when there are children starving in India?" school of thought. Anyone who can't read the book through without feeling guilty should read David Chilton's *Productive Christians in an Age of Guilt Manipulators,* reviewed in the Economics chapter. Apart from the guilt, it has a lot of useful nutritional data (tables of protein amounts in various foods, etc.) and some very decent recipes.

Rodale Press

Rodale Press publishes *Prevention,* the world's largest circulation health magazine, and another biggie, *Rodale's Organic Gardening.* While they're at it, the folks at Rodale Press also publish fifty or so new books each year. Cookbooks, gardening books, and health books are their specialty, with the emphasis on fresh food, minimal use of fertilizers and pesticides, and natural management of the soil and one's self.

Warner Books
 Fit for Life, **$16.50.**

Fit for Life, by Harvey and Marilyn Diamond, is your introduction to Natural Hygiene. The grabber is that this is a weight-loss diet as well as a permanent lifestyle. Natural Hygienists are interested in how the body absorbs and eliminates food, and figure that by making the process more efficient, excess weight will also be eliminated. Their basic tenet is that the body *wants* to be healthy, and is always working towards a healthy weight and trying to get rid of toxins. Some New Age thinking is sprinkled throughout, along with the sesame seeds. You also get a section of reasonably easy recipes.

ANATOMY

There was a young lady from Lynn
Who was so excessively thin
   that when she essayed
   to drink lemonade
She slipped through the straw and fell in.
(Anonymous)

Now that we've debated what Jack Sprat and his wife should eat, we can study what their peculiar lifestyle actually does to them. Anatomy uncovers the digestive, endocrine, muscular, skeletal, and reproductive systems, among others. Part of the required health subject is the study of all these layers of anatomy.

American Map Corporation
 Anatomy Wall Charts, $29.85/set. *Anatomy Atlas,* $2.25. Notebook Anatomy Charts with transparent identifying overlays and index, $17.95.

AMC's *Anatomy Atlas* is ridiculously cheap, with sixteen pages of full-color labeled drawings and short text for each. Like the publisher says, it's "virtually a complete course in basic anatomy." The same drawings are available in a set of fourteen Wall Charts, 29 x 37".

Ideal for self-testing is the new Colorprint-Schick Anatomy Charts notebook. Spiral-bound, it has thirty full-color drawings with transparent nomenclature overlays. This means the part labels are on a separate see-through sheet, so you can first try to identify the parts you are studying and then flip the accompanying transparent page over the drawing to check out your answers.

Carolina Biological Supply Company
    Large price range. Plastic is cheaper. Catalog, $10.95.

You can get *real* animal skeletons, too, as well as plastic human skeletons, from Carolina Biological. Ever want a nice set of shark jaws? The small size is under $20, and you can get a single large shark's tooth for less than $6. Fishermen, think twice before throwing away the next catch's bones: a nice fish skeleton, fully articulated and mounted on a Plexiglass plate in a display cabinet, goes for about $60. Unmounted bullfrog skeletons can be had for under $25, whereas a snake skeleton is between $50 and $150. I should mention that you can generally get just a skull, too: a chicken's skull is under $25. More exotically, there are rattlesnakes, moles, opossums, armadillos, wallabies, fruit bats, and muskrats. Cats and dogs, rabbits and rats, sheep and pigs are for sale in their bony state. You can get feet and limbs of some of the larger mammals. These come in natural bone.

Now, on to Man. Most human skeletal preparations come in very realistic plastic, this being one case where art is preferable to nature. You can get all different bones, individually or in you-assemble sets or all together and hanging from a rod.

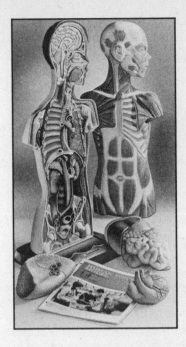

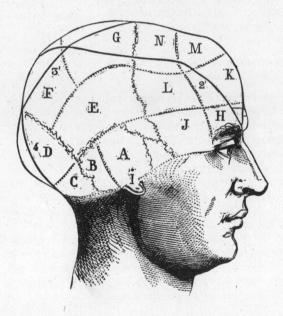

Educational Insights
    Human Body Kit $21.95, Heart Kit $19.95, Brain Kit $19.95, Skull Kit $21.25.

These are the lowest-cost anatomical models I've seen. Each kit contains twenty-five activity cards, reproducible worksheets, games, student and teacher record sheets, and quizzes. The Human Body Kit includes not only a transparent human form with muscles molded inside, but also a small plastic skeleton with some abdominal organs exposed. The Heart model can be taken apart. The Brain model has four sections. The Skull model can also be taken apart. All models look very nice, at least as nice as this sort of thing can. Where color is appropriate, color is used.

Hubbard

Kits for investigating your own body, including respiratory system, muscles, vision and hearing, personal health, and visual coordination and control. These are a miniversion of the classroom-sized kits Hubbard sells and are rather expensive; prices start at $45. Apparatus for the investigation is available separately, and if you just want to do a few of these experiments, the price is affordable.

Hubbard's plastic models for anatomy are excellent quality, but might be expensive for a home program. However, you can learn a lot by just looking at the color pictures in Hubbard's free catalog.

Ideal School Supply
    Most models under $15.

Calling Dr. Frankenstein! Ever want to build your own . . . thing? Ideal School Supply has unassembled anatomical models. You supply the glue and paint, and Ideal supplies a model of the eye, ear, heart, brain/skull, body, skeleton, nose/mouth, and even a pumping heart! Inexpensive, and it makes a change from Sopwith Camel and dragster models.

Milliken
    Diagrammatic Prints, $8.95 per package.

For low-cost anatomy studies you might also want to consider Milliken's full-color Diagrammatic Study Prints. *Systems of the Human Body* and *Organs of the Human Body* are each a set of eight poster-size prints with anatomical items clearly labeled. Each comes with four review sheets and a teacher's guide.

Sycamore Tree

Sycamore Tree has a great selection of health and anatomy materials for home study. *Anatomy* coloring book is meant for high school students. Descriptive text accompanies each drawing. Sycamore Tree has several other books on the body and health. Some are Adventist. Skipping over all these, let me tell you about the Betty Lukens felt Human Body Set. When I saw the picture in the brochure, I knew this was the teaching tool to get! It is an incredibly beautiful set of felts, containing all the innards and muscle layers, etc. that you'd ever hope to see—even a womb with a little baby inside! Ten talks accompany this set, plus the I Am Joe's Body series from *Reader's Digest,* which was the most popular series ever printed in their history. The Human Body Set costs $25.95, and with care it will last almost forever. Where else can you get a life-sized *overlayable* model?

HEALTH AND SAFETY RESOURCES

Jack and Jill went up the hill
To fetch a pail of water,
Jack fell down, and broke his crown,
And Jill came tumbling after.
(Mother Goose)

I'm only going to recommend one series on health and safety. Here it is.

A Beka Books

Bright, cheery, colorful *Health, Safety, and Manners* series for grades 1 to 3.

Books cost around $6 and follow the typical A Beka "programmed" format, where the text talks to the child in the first person (e.g., "I will take care of my body"). I was impressed by the thoroughness of this series, and enjoyed the emphasis on manners.

FIRST AID AND MEDICINE

Up Jack got, and home did trot
As fast as he could caper.
Went to bed, and wrapped his head,
In vinegar and brown paper.

I find it somewhat ironic that school texts advise children to use alcohol and illegal drugs "responsibly," yet take it for granted that only doctors are wise enough to dispense medicine and medical aid. Kids can get marijuana and cocaine and heroin in the friendly neighborhood school yard, but their parents aren't allowed to get their hands on a bottle of penicillin without a doctor's prescription. Strange.

Let me hereby cast my vote for teaching kids *real* medical skills. Unlike such esoteric subjects as the ecology of freshwater marshes and the nomenclature of plants' reproductive systems, both commonly taught in schools and both hardly ever used in the students' real lives, first aid and practical medicine will be needed by almost everybody at some time.

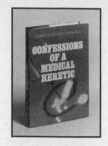 

Contemporary Books.
Confessions, $9.95. *Healthy Child,* $13.95.

Confessions of a Medical Heretic and *How to Raise a Healthy Child . . . In Spite of Your Doctor* should be required reading for those who believe in required reading. Let me just *suggest* that these two books, written by the eminent Dr. Robert Mendelsohn, will help you see the need for achieving some practical medical skills. If absolute power corrupts, absolute faith in a man doth cause that man to sometimes behave like a ninny. Doctors do *much* better when we don't encourage them to play God, as Dr. Mendelsohn points out. Both books give strong reasons for becoming more medically self-sufficient, and provide resources for those interested in putting Dr. Mendelsohn's message into practice.

Merck & Company, Inc.
Merck Manual, $19.75

Increase your word power and get a handle on medical procedures with *The Merck Manual of Diagnosis and Therapy.* This is the very same book your doctor uses to help him diagnose and prescribe. *The Merck Manual* is fascinating browsing for those with a large medical vocabulary; extremely helpful in medical emergencies (it's comforting to be able to check out the diagnosis for yourself); and the definitive test of whether Junior really wants to go to med school (can he hardly tear himself away from the *Manual,* or does he nod out after reading a paragraph?). Dr. Mendelsohn recommends it.

The Merck Manual won't tell you about nonconventional treatments. Nor will you be able, in many cases, to act on its recommendations without a doctor's prescription. But it will educate and inform you about what is going on in the medical world for every disease known to man.

Medical Self Care

The publishers of *Medical Self Care* magazine have assembled a catalog of medical tools 'n stuff for folks who want to keep things medical at home. Buy your own stainless steel stethoscope and other widgets. But the magazine itself is sometimes too far out to take seriously. Is herpes really "no more serious than the common cold"? Come on, now.

Your Library

The library is sure to have a number of good books under the headings "First Aid" and "Self Help." Also try "Doctors," "Physicians," "Disease," and "Medicine."

SEX EDUCATION

Suzy and Johnny, sitting in a tree
K-I-S-S-I-N-G.
First comes love,
Then comes marriage,
Then comes baby in the baby carriage!
(Children's rhyme)

First comes love. *Then* comes marriage. *Then* comes baby in the baby carriage.

DEATH EDUCATION

Now I lay me down to sleep,
I pray the Lord my soul to keep.
And if I die before I wake
I pray the Lord my soul to take.
(Old American rhyme)

CHAPTER THIRTY-TWO

MATH

In some cultures kids have it easy. They only have to learn to count, "One . . . two . . . many." That's it! In our computerized, money-minding society, though, life is not quite so simple. Every day we have to make change, or fill out order forms, or balance the checkbook. All this record-keeping and money handling requires math skill. True, we now have electronic calculators, but the only people who seriously preach that calculators have made personal math skills obsolete are (1) calculator manufacturers and (2) the writers of bad arithmetic texts. Without a grasp of arithmetic, who can tell if the result the calculator spits out is reasonable or if an error was made in the input? Without arithmetic, where will we get our scientists and engineers and bookkeepers and sales clerks?

Because of America's present math illiteracy, McDonald's has been reduced to importing cash registers that have little pictures of hamburgers and shakes on the keys instead of numbers—but McDonald's is not happy about it. Ignorance is not progress. Like the rest of us, McDonald's management would like teenagers to be able to count and cipher.

Our national confusion about arithmetic arose, you'll remember, with the introduction of the New Math. Hailed as a breakthrough in math instruction, the New Math concentrated on teaching kids mathematical principles in place of rote instruction. In this way, the math profs reasoned, children would be prepared for real math when they had mastered arithmetic. Unhappily, the New Math generation didn't even learn their arithmetic, let alone emerge as math geniuses.

Now that "math anxiety" and "math failure" are so widespread, what should we do about it? Debate rages. Some resort to flash cards and rote drill. Others believe children need to discover math for themselves with the use of colorful manipulatives. My personal belief is that the truth lies somewhere in between.

If it is true, as we suggested at the beginning of this book, that we learn by first assembling raw data and then fitting it into a framework, then arithmetic should first appear as a real-world process. We count things with our children. We add pennies. We subtract forks. The children don't have to be able to count or add themselves in order to benefit from simply seeing it done. This initial number play is essential to producing the raw arithmetic data that children's minds need to work on.

When a child learns to count (which he does by rote repetition), he is well on his way to learning arithmetic. Counting is adding by one. Subtraction is counting backwards. Multiplication is adding by groups (2×3 is the same as adding two three times—e.g., $2+2+2$). Division is subtracting by groups. All of these concepts grow directly out of counting. If counting is an abstract series of noises, so is arithmetic. If counting is what you do to find out how many buttons are on your jacket, then arithmetic is much more likely to seem real to a child.

I personally believe in showing children the patterns ("principles") of arithmetic and, after they are comfortable with them, then drilling on the actual "facts." The "9's" pattern is that adding nine to a number is the same as adding ten and then counting backwards one time. Whether a child discovers these patterns or you reveal them to him does not seem to me as important as making sure that he does become aware that arithmetic is full of patterns.

Drill alone does not build a framework. We need it, though, to become quick in performing arithmetic operations. But drill need not be boring. Try drilling with games!

ARITHMETIC PROGRAMS AND GAMES

Addison-Wesley Publishing Co.

A-W's Workjobs texts are activity-centered math learning. Also, be aware of *Mathematics Their Way,* "the most popular activity-centered math curriculum in use today," $22.84.

Addison-Wesley is very proud of their math curriculum. I haven't seen any home school programs use it, but it's popular with public schools.

American Guidance Service

Complete set including all three Teacher and Pupil editions plus the *Complete Book of Fingermath,* $59.75. Beginner's set, containing *CBF* plus first Teacher and Pupil books, $31.75. *CBF* alone, $16.95. Teacher editions of workbooks, $9.50 each. Pupil editions, $4.75 each.

AGS's Fingermath series turns your kid's hands into a calculator. It only takes ten to fifteen minutes a day to help your learners develop facility with a math method that is literally at their fingertips!

How does it work? The right hand is used for units, the left for tens. Each finger has a value of 1, except for the thumbs: the right thumb has a value of 5, and the left thumb a value of 50. By pressing down the appropriate fingers on a tabletop or desk, you can "feel" any number from 1 to 99. Twenty-seven, for example, is your left little finger and ring finger plus the right thumb, index finger, and middle finger. Children learn to add, subtract, and even multiply and divide using finger manipulations. To do this quickly, they practice "short cuts" that give them a real feel for math. To add five, for example, you can either add a free right thumb or substitute a left finger (value 10) for a pressed right thumb (value 5), since 10-5=5. To add 8, you can either add a right thumb and three fingers (5+3) or add a left finger and subtract two right fingers (10-2).

Little kids using Fingermath have beaten adults with calculators in a TV showdown. The method can be extended to numbers over 100, as the book's final chapter shows.

You wouldn't want this to be your children's only exposure to math, because it sidesteps the storage of math facts in the brain. Still, as supplemental math practice, or as a brand-new successful experience for a student in the grip of math anxiety, Fingermath appeals. Children who learn best through their hands ("kinesthetic learners") and those labeled dyslexic or learning-disabled should especially benefit.

I wouldn't bother with the teacher's editions and workbooks, which mostly dwell on coloring in fingers on printed hands and matching fingers with dots—the usual seatwork fare. All you need for a home program is in *The Complete Book of Fingermath* itself.

Ashley's Home Tutor Kits
Home Measurements, $7.95. Add 10 percent shipping.

All Ashley's Kits feature a programmed approach similar, on a home level, to Distar's Direct Instruction. Everything the teacher says is spelled out for him or her.

Along with the programmed instructions, the *Home Measurements* book includes practice problems for each new skill and an answer key. The book is ring-bound, making it easy to use while sitting comfortably on your couch with your little one nearby. Topics covered include capacity, weights, units, length, time, and metrics.

While not as fancy or professional as some other offerings, Ashley's Kits are ridiculously easy to use. The *Measurements Book* includes exposure to the actual quantities along with the teaching and drill, thus accomplishing as much as one can expect in this area.

Bob Jones University Press
Student worktexts: K $5.25, 1 and 2 $7.95 each, 3-6 $13.25 each, 7-8 $15.95 each, Algebra I (grade 9) $19.95, Geometry (grade 10), $19.95. Teacher's Editions, $27.50 each grade K-6, $29.50 each grade 7-10. Wide variety of supplementary materials available.

If you're looking for an excellent basic math program, here it is. We've seen and/or used them all—A Beka, Rod and Staff, Holt, Laidlaw . . . In my opinion, the BJUP math program towers over the competition.

Unlike other series, BJUP math combines a variety of drills with "thinking" exercises. Concepts are introduced first, and then cemented with practice and applications. New kinds of exercises on every page of the colorful texts give fresh insights into the particular area being studied. These include math tricks, games, and riddles; geometry play; charts, graphs, and so on.

Everything about this series is first-class, including the art and even the bindings. Starting with third grade, BJUP's math books are quality hardbound textbooks. You will be able to use these books for years. The earlier grades' books come with quality kivar bindings.

While not as devotional as a series like Rod and Staff, BJUP does incorporate Biblical principles into their math program. This is done in a very natural, unforced manner.

Because BJUP is so thorough, you might want to get the text from your child's last grade level instead of his present one. Although our Ted had finished grade three of another publisher's series, I found that the BJUP grade 3 text was just right for him. The same went for Joseph, who had finished grade 1 of another series and started over with grade 1 of BJUP.

Creative Publications

Creative Publications is your source for offbeat and imaginative math drill and practice materials. A small sampling: Solve problems and fill in number patterns to connect-the-dots in *Dots Math.* Try your hand at *Math Practice with Ridiculous Recipes.* Get a "Mickey Math Rule" to find answers to all sorts of problems. With colored plastic strips you can tackle a surprising number of math topics, says a kit called *Those Amazing Tables.*

There are mystery problems and code problems and file folder games. Creative's best seller, *Aftermath*, is an enrichment program for grades 5 to 9. Each book contains "over 100 pages of puzzles, games, and cartoons to make math fascinating." These activities are designed for self-study.

Honestly, there is just no way to list all the dozens of different clever books and games that Creative has. Weird and crazy people (all math fans, that is!) will love this catalog.

Distar

Math from the folks who invented Direct Instruction. This public school program is designed for small groups. Everything you do and say is in the book you flip today. Programmed instruction includes kid responses. The emphasis is on math strategies instead of memorization. "Students use their strategies to handle a wide range of basic problems and to derive unfamiliar arithmetic facts based on an understanding of about 35 facts."

Arithmetic I series covers from Rote Counting to Problems in Columns and Written Story Problems. Arithmetic II gets into multiplication, fraction operations, telling time, and negative numbers, among other topics.

If your school uses this program, or if you choose to use it at home, be sure your child also gets practice in arithmetic drill. It's nice to be able to derive things, but it's even nicer to *know* them.

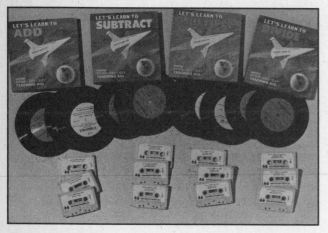

Educational Insights

Let's Learn to: ADD, SUBTRACT, MULTIPLY, DIVIDE, $14.95 each, records or cassettes. *Mixed Math Drill,* $14.95, records or cassettes. Complete Math Facts course, $72.50 (records) or $82.50 (cassettes). *Thinkfast!, Capture the Flags!,* and *Gotcha!,* $4.95 each.

Using the same "Hear-See-Say" formula used in their basic phonics course, Educational Insights created a series of math drill records. Directions are recorded: this is a self-teaching program. The teacher on the record gives the problems; then your student tries to answer along with the Math Kids. Each set comes with three LP records or cassettes and a test pad.

EI also has a new line of Math Card Games. Each competitive game uses all four basic arithmetic processes: addition, subtraction, multiplication, and division. *Thinkfast!* is for two players only, and can be played using addition only, or subtraction only, etc. In *Capture the Flags!* players roll dice and try to capture the cards laid down by finding one that equals any combination of the dice. If the numbers 2 and 3 are rolled, for instance, you can take a 5 (2+3), a 1 (3–2), or a 6 (2x3). But you have to be the first! *Gotcha!* players win by capturing the opponent's cards. If my 4 and 2 equal your 5 and 1, I can take them—if you don't figure it out first!

Home Grown Kids

Pre-Math It and *Math It,* $30 each. *Advanced Math It,* $15. Math concepts book, $8, covers math learning for all three sets.

As usual, Hewitt Research Center has come up with some great products. Professor Elmer Brooks' Math-It series leads kids through the basic math principles *and* drills them on arithmetic facts. Math-It is not only painless but fun! Instead of memorizing dull tables, kids learn how to derive the answers (e.g., adding nine is the same as adding ten and subtracting one). *Pre-Math It* involves exercises with dominoes (included). *Math It* tells you "How Stevie Learned His Math" and includes the Addit, Dubblit, and Timzit games. *Advanced Math It* has Percentit and Dividit. Each kit is nonconsumable and covers several years of math.

Key Curriculum Project

Key to Fractions, $6.40/set of four books. *Decimals,* $6.80/set of four. *Algebra,* $5.60/set of four. *Geometry,* complete set of eight books $22.10. *Geometry Starter Set,* three books, $5.55. Answer Books $1.85 each subject, except geometry where there are separate answer books for books 1-3, 4-6, 7, and 8.

You won't beat this guarantee. Peter Rasmussen, the publisher, says, "I unconditionally guarantee that *Key to . . .* worktexts will substantially improve your students' math skills and enjoyment. If, for any reason, you are not satisfied, return your books—even if they're used—and I'll give you a 100% refund. No questions asked."

Why is Mr. Rasmussen so confident? Because these worktexts assume nothing. Each page contains only one concept. Sample problems are handwritten to reduce student intimidation. Visual models are used wherever possible, such as shaded-in area when studying fractions. Examples are worked out step-by-step. New terms are explained and underlined. Students get plenty of workspace and lots of exercises which gradually increase in difficulty. *Everything* you need is in the inexpensive worktext.

Key to Algebra is an algebra introduction, and *Key to Geometry* includes no proofs.

You'd probably want more review than this series offers to be sure your children remember the concepts forever. As an introductory framework to these often difficult areas, though, the *Key to . . .* series looks good.

Learning Systems Corporation

Fifty-cent workbooks. Shipping 10 percent; $1 on orders under $10.

These professional two-color miniworkbooks are excellent for the home schooling family that needs to pinch pennies. Each skill is clearly presented in just a few pages along with exercises for practice. Because the workbooks are so small, there is no danger of boredom. Also, your learner gets an instant sense of accomplishment when he masters a new skill. Instead of just finishing a chapter, or section of a chapter, in a massive textbook, he finishes a whole workbook! This sense of having completed a task is vital to keep a youngster's motivation strong.

Math miniworkbooks include Time, Money, Place Value, Addition with Regrouping, Subtraction with Regrouping, Fractions, Word Problems, English Measurements, Metric Measurements, and a number of workbooks on multiplication and division of whole numbers and fractions, materials on decimals, percent, graphing, and geometry. You can't beat the price, and they cover the field.

Leonardo Press
Arithmetic Mastery Kit, complete program, $99.95. Masters for students worksheets, $7.95 per category. Manual, $5.95 per category. Criterion-referenced tests, $2.95 per category. *Math Anxiety* manual, $5. Individual category, all materials, $19.95. Other components also available separately.

I am really enthusiastic about this basic math program developed by Raymond Laurita, Phillip Trembley, and two others. It covers six categories: addition, subtraction, multiplication, division, fractions, and decimals. In each category a series of "prescriptions" laid out for the student to master. So far it sounds pretty standard—but wait! Unlike other programs, the student learns through *copying a model.* Instead of a brief teaching time followed by reams of student exercises, which are actually tests in disguise, the method Professor Laurita and friends uses has the student either orally copying the teacher's example or physically copying models that are provided on his worksheet. Models are provided in a pattern, another excellent idea, so the learner can get the "feel" for math that is so essential for developing a mental framework. The next fine touch is that the worksheet problems are *written out,* rather than typeset. This has also been shown to reduce student anxiety, as it makes the exercises more human and doable. Everything the teacher does and says is also spelled out, another excellent feature, eliminating teacher anxiety.

And my very favorite feature of all: the program is perfectly designed to let you follow it at your own pace. The entire program is laid out on a single sheet of paper. Since each subject area is taught independently, you can teach addition along with subtraction if you wish, and get into multiplication and division and the rest at the earliest opportunity. In this way, you can get your child cooking on all the arithmetic burners at once, as much as he is ready for, instead of building an artificial fear of the "tougher" areas by putting them off for years. Thanks to the program's excellent design, you can see at a glance how you are progressing in each area and how much remains to do. Children get a real feeling that they have accomplished something when they can see their progress in relation to the total amount to be learned before they have mastered an area.

Brief tests are included to ensure that the student is actually learning. However, most of the stress is on providing input for the student rather than forcing him to come across with output. This feature alone makes the Arithmetic Mastery Kit unique, as most basic math programs demand far more output from far less actual teaching. Your student literally *cannot* fail, unless he

refuses to even try or has an organic disorder that interferes with learning.

This program has been classroom-tested with over one thousand Title I students, with excellent results.

You get folders for each area (addition, subtraction, multiplication, division, fractions, and decimals) that include reproducible student worksheets, a teacher's manual, individual progress charts, and criterion-referenced tests. In addition you get a manual, *Dealing with Math Anxiety,* and a Scope and Sequence outline of the entire program. The Kit comes in a sturdy cardboard box. All folders are color-coded, as are the tests, progress charts, and manuals within, for easy access.

The price may seem steep, but remember that you are buying *six years of arithmetic curriculum,* plus all necessary materials. You can save some money by buying the teacher's manuals only and making your own worksheets. This will be easier if you have bought one complete folder so you can get a feel for the program. If you decide to buy the Kit, you need only purchase replacement sets of worksheets for subsequent students, or xerox the reproducible sheets you have (all the children in your family count as your "class"!). This amounts to $16 per year for the first student and $8 for each following (less if you xerox). For kids with math anxiety, this may be the answer.

Margwen Products
Match-a-Fact card games. *Addition, Subtraction, Multiplication, Division,* $8.95 each. Set of all four, $33. $2.50 shipping for first game, 60 cents each additional game.

Instead of dull, dreary flash cards, why don't you try *Match-A-Fact* for your math drill? Each set of cards comes with six games: *Concentration, War, Solitaire, Match-A-Fact, Beat the Clock,* and *Flash Card Frustration.* You get a problem deck (cards with math problems like "2+5" on them), an answer deck (whole number cards—1,2,3 . . .), a self-checking answer key, instruction booklet, and progress chart. *Match-A-Fact* is no kitchen-produced job, either. The cards are real playing card quality, and the packaging would look quite at home in any school supply store.

How does it work? Some games use both decks, some just one. For *War,* children deal out the cards in the "problem" deck. The child whose answer is a higher number takes both cards. You remember the game from your youth. Thus 8-1 beats 5-4, for example. Children can resort to the answer key if they forget the answer. You can see how much drill they will get in math facts from just this one game! *Concentration* involves spreading all the cards in both decks face-down, and turning over two at a time. If you match a problem with its answer, you get to keep the cards. This is an excellent memory drill as well as a math drill. Don't forget, each box has four more games, plus you can make up games of your own.

Match-A-Fact has gone over big wherever it has been used. Children request it for birthday presents and parents who see it used at school buy their own copies for home. It really is fun to use, and not much more expensive than a batch of commercial flash cards.

Math by Mail
All materials are free.

Michael K. Jones presides over a pile of math worksheets, explanations, riddles, and so on, some in Esperanto and some in English. All are in the public domain. You can't build a math program with this stuff, but you might enjoy playing around with some of it.

Math Mouse Games
$18.95 postpaid for eight basic games plus variations.

Christian math games? Who ever heard of such a thing! Well, you have now. This appealing set of games did start out as a kitchen table job, developed by a Christian home schooling family, but that just increases its charm. (The games are now professionally printed.) The only distinctively Christian game is the *Gardening* game, where Scripture references to sowing, weeding, watering, and reaping are included on the gameboard. The other games are math drill with a lot of soul. In *Grocery Store,* for example, you visit the four food groups and try to spend a total of $40 on your trip. But be careful: you can't spend more than $10 in each category! Grocery Store is played with a gameboard, pawns, dice, and Math Mouse Money. The set as a whole contains five folding cardboard gameboards, a fraction/decimal card deck, six special dice (including one with fractions), a number line, pawns, spinner, play money, round markers to cover up spaces in some games, and an instruction book. Games are *Gardening, Grocery Store, Space Race, Roll a Problem, Multiplication Board, Add Off, Fractions and Decimal War,* and *Gobbling Fractions.* All basic math concepts are practiced. The learner also gets an introduction to economics in the grocery store and the garden.

Math Mouse Games are really cute and kid-appealing, and you get a lot for your money.

Mott Media

If you're into classics, you'll be glad to hear that Mott Media has resurrected a whole series of the texts America used in the days of Reverend McGuffey and Laura Ingalls. One of these selections is *Ray's Arithmetic.*

NASCO

In case you don't already know this, NASCO is a one-stop shopping company for art, science, and . . . math! NASCO carries many of the best math products reviewed in this and other chapters, including Lauri crepe rubber counters and fraction circles, Unifix cubes, geoboards, math games, problem and puzzle books, Judy clocks, and so on. NASCO has also recently expanded its computers section to include pages of software for all grades and ages of computer books, all of which look quite decent. NASCO also has some exclusives, like their Algebra Model kit which, for $10.50, is supposed to help your student see algebra concepts. (It can't hurt, right?)

Open Court

Open Court's Real Math series looks interesting. Unlike other textbook-based programs, Real Math includes games, manipulations, and drill as well as workbook exercises. Open Court prides itself on developing thinking skills, and the word problems and teacher-led Thinking Stories reflect this concern. I was boggled by the number of games the curriculum includes: forty-two in all for grades 1 to 6.

Christians and those favoring traditional family roles will not find much comfort in the story problems, which stress careerist values along with the typical public school push for metric measurements (when *are* we going to start buying potatoes by the kilogram?).

SRA

SRA, the folks who brought us Distar (see above), have a Corrective Mathematics program for math flunkees in grades 3 and up. The program is based on the Distar model.

I have been entertaining a growing suspicion that Corrective courses might be the best ones to start with. If you can bring a kid up to grade level with your Corrective method, why are you teaching another one that caused him to fall behind in the first place?

Thoburn Press
Animal Number Families, $5. Other prices to be announced.

A cute and cuddly math curriculum for little kids is Thoburn Press's new *Creative Oral and Written Drill Math Series.* This program has been used successfully in the prestigious Fairfax Christian School of Fairfax, Virginia. You get a daily teaching guide with 180 days of instructions that teaches beginning arithmetic to four, five, and six-year-old children, including addition to twenty using single digits, tens concept, and counting to one hundred. Each number is introduced with a little tale about an animal: Mrs. Two and her two little mouse children, for example. The children's names are 2+0 and 1+1, so you can see that this is just a comfortable way of introducing the math facts.

The activities that go along with the program are really fun. Children color and cut out the Animal Number Families, and put the "children" inside manila envelopes with the "mothers" on the outside. The number families will now serve as flash cards. In the student book, children write numbers, do dot-to-dot, color by number, make number lines, count, match numbers to sets of objects, recognize symbols and shapes, and much more! The art is as good as you'd see in a standard secular text, and warmer and more engaging. Biblical characters are included, as you might expect.

This curriculum has some clever teaching tricks that I haven't seen anywhere else.

You'll have to write for prices, as they weren't firmed up yet when I was writing this.

Wff 'n Proof Learning Games Associates
  Equations game, $13. *Real Numbers,* $2.75. *Wff 'n Proof,* $16. Imp Kit #1, $1.25; #1-5, $4.25; #1-10, $8; #1-21, $15.50.

Equations is the ultimate math game. You win by never winning, by never making it impossible to win, and by never letting your opponent win. Does this sound just a trifle confusing? *Equations can* be hard to figure out at first, but let's persevere in the knowledge that inner-city fourth-graders have figured it out.

Briefly: The game comes with number dice, symbol dice, a game mat, an indispensable instruction manual, and an efficient and elegant carrying case. You roll the dice. One player sets the "Goal" using the dice. This will be a number, such as 2. On each following move, one die must be put in the "Forbidden" or "Permitted" or "Required" area of the game mat. The remaining dice are the "Resources." The idea is to make only moves that don't allow a solution to be built with the addition of only one more die, and that don't prevent a solution from ever being built. You can challenge another player's previous move as violating these rules, or you can try to trap him by deliberately violating a rule yourself. It's actually not hard to follow, once you've worked through a couple of the sample matches in the manual.

The beauty of *Equations* is that it forces the players to continually make creative arithmetic calculations. You have to consider *all* the possible arithmetic combinations that can be built with the allowed dice. In the classroom, students quickly develop math strategies in order to help their teams win *Equations* tournaments. At home, you can discover these strategies with Wff 'n Proof Imp Kits, instructional math play solitaire kits that each teach a specific mathematical lesson from the *Equations* game.

Real Numbers is a handy and very inexpensive introduction to *Equations.* You get colored number and symbol dice cleverly clipped to a ballpoint pen, plus an instruction booklet that shows you how to play the game with real, rational, irrational, integer, and natural numbers. Kids six years old can play the easiest of the five games that comes with it.

And don't let's forget *Wff 'n Proof.* It sounds like the name of a Saturday morning cartoon show, but actually Wff stands for Well Formed Formula and Proof means logical proof. It's a beautiful game for your family or to give as a gift—actually, twenty-one beautiful games, since the kit comes with an instruction manual listing twenty-one games of increasing complexity. Six-year-olds can play the first game (Wff), and from then on it gets steadily hairier. *Wff 'n Proof* is a game of logic: if this, then that. Physically, it is thirty-six colored cubes with letters and funny symbols on them and an hourglass with pink sand in it, both reposing in a blue foam cutout in a hard blue vinyl carrying case. Mentally, it's a real workout and brain organizer that has been shown to *raise IQ by up to 20 points* in dedicated players. Financially, it is a steal, at less than $1 per brain-stretching game. Potentially, it is your child's introduction to higher math thinking that could perhaps even lead to him going on to make it his vocation.

PREMATH AND MATH MANIPULATIVES

What about "math manipulatives," those colorful little sticks and blocks and cubes and so on? Manipulatives are supposed to facilitate "discovery" learning. By manipulating the objects, children theoretically figure out arithmetic patterns for themselves. Some manipulatives are sold with the idea that they provide a "concrete representation" of abstract principles like decimal place and fractions. The question here is whether children need this kind of symbol, or whether they can learn just as rapidly working with numerals or real-world objects. In my own experience, children who have been exposed to counting, adding, etc. as real-world processes have no trouble understanding the more abstract ideas when the time comes.

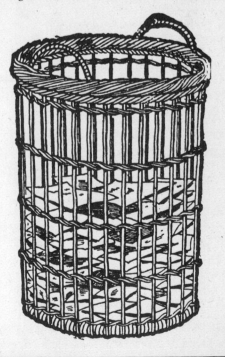

Families who learn at home can present fractions more effectively with an actual blueberry pie that needs to be cut into quarters (or sixths, or eighths) than with felt "pie segments." Decimals, being a specialized form of fraction, can be understood by anyone who understands fractions.

I am not happy to find that manipulative producers are lobbying state legislatures to *require* the use of manipulative products in math classrooms. Texas House Bill 72 (1985) *forbids* teachers to do drill and practice work until their students have fooled around with manipulatives. Is this academic freedom?

Manipulatives are a lot of fun to play with, and if kids are allowed to mess about with them as pure play objects before settling down to use them as math symbols they can actually learn something from them. But they are not essential.

Activity Resources

Good selection of manipulatives, measurement tools, and supplementary workbooks. Activity Resources sells a selection of materials from Key Curriculum Project, Creative Publications, Cuisenaire, and other sources. If you want Miquon Math Lab books, widely used by alternative schools, this is the place. Forty-six-page black and white catalog.

Christian Curriculum Project
Kindergarten manual, $30. First grade, $35. Second grade available spring '86; third grade, fall '86. Manipulatives for K and 1, $15. Shipping $3.50.

CCP's *Making Math Meaningful* is a delight. Designed specifically for home use, it leads children gently from observation to interpretation to application. Example: Your child observes you sorting forks into a set of long forks and a set of short forks. When he understands what you are doing, you sort some other objects into "long" and "short" piles. The words "sort"

and "long" and "short" arise naturally out of this activity. Finally the child does some sorting into "long" and "short" piles himself.

I just shared the first activity in the first module, "Equal and Unequal." As you go through the curriculum, activities move from real objects to manipulatives to pictorial representations to, finally, the math symbols themselves: the numerals and operands. The child gets to "mess about" with real objects and manipulatives before he does serious work with them. Instead of moving from the familiar to the strange, this curriculum makes the strange familiar.

Topics in the first-grade book include: Comparison Sentences, Order Sentences, Equalizing Sentences, and Joining and Separating. Children learn to write, solve, and validate mathematical sentences (0-20) with unknowns about a variety of situations, using objects or pictures.

Topics in the kindergarten book include: Equal and Unequal, Equalizing, Serial Ordering, Comparing and Ordering, and Representing. The latter includes graphing. Children also learn to write the numerals. Basically, you get all the normal kindergarten math readiness, plus a firm foundation in math thinking.

Making Math Meaningful is not the easiest-to-use primary math material I have seen (because you spend so much time gathering and playing with actual objects), but it is very well organized. Each separate activity lists materials needed and tells what concepts the activity will develop. The Lesson Plan tells parents exactly what to do and say. All necessary student activity sheets are included, and the whole thing is packaged in a three-ring binder for easy accessibility. The Manipulatives Kit includes fifty Unifix cubes, one hundred colorful plastic links, and one hundred checker-style variously colored counting chips in a Zip-Loc bag. I applaud the authors for not overwhelming us with manipulatives. This lean collection is all you really need.

Creative Publications

As well as having zippy drill materials, Creative also has a nineteen-page color section devoted entirely to manipulatives. Manipulatives for sorting and counting, for operations and place value, for geometry and problem solving, for fractions and decimals, are all among Creative's wares. All the biggies are there: Cuisenaire, Unifix, Multi-Links, tangrams, math balances, attribute blocks, and more. Prices are standard—the bonanza here is completeness, not price.

Cuisenaire Company of America
Cuisenaire Rods start at $6.75 for an introductory set.

Math manipulatives, games, puzzles, books, and computer software. I remember using the famous Cuisenaire rods when I was a little girl. They are very pretty little rectangular wooden rods in varying length, each with its own color. Lots of books are available with clever ideas on how to use the rods, both from Cuisenaire and from other publishers. Cuisenaire carries several other lines of its own manipulatives and is not above selling other companies' products either. Cuisenaire's catalog compares with Creative Publications' in the manipulatives area, with perhaps a touch more geometry and measurement equipment.

DIDAX

The DIDAX catalog has thirty-one color pages of math games and manipulatives, including some you won't find elsewhere. Giant number dice! Geo-fix solid geometry construction kit (make 3-D shapes!). Fraction flip books! Multiplication dominoes! Sandpaper numerals (at a good price!). Plastic shapes counters (dogs, ducks, horses, butterflies . . .)! Plus more Unifix materials than I have seen anywhere else. And don't forget that DIDAX has hands-on stuff for language arts and art also.

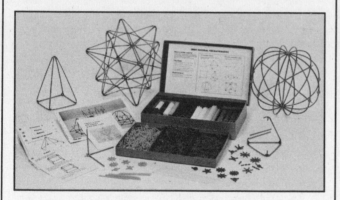

Burt Harrison and Company

Low, low prices on popular manipulatives and unusual items are Burt Harrison's specialty. Burt has Unifix cubes for the lowest price in the USA: 100 for $10, 500 for $42, 1000 for $74. Prices are similar on Burt's other manipulative stock.

Now for the weird stuff. Burt has a kit called *Orbit* that contains thick plastic straws and little connectors, plus twenty-eight activity cards and a teacher's guide. The whole thing comes from England in a sturdy storage box with a sectioned tray for two-tiered storage. Every little bit and straw has its very own home. You get over nine hundred pieces—enough to build the craziest 3-D structures—for guess how much? Fifteen dollars. I'm not kidding! The same kit is selling in Canada for over $45, and I've seen it here in America for almost $30.

Another weird item: the Calendar-Clock. It's over a yard in diameter, hangs on the wall, sells for $12, and tells the day, month, and season. It's coated with vinyl, so you can color in

important dates like birthdays and holidays with a wipe-off crayon. Now what is it *good* for? You can't keep appointments by a clock that doesn't give the hour or the minute . . . but you can "mark time" with the big hand and develop your kids' sense of how long a month, a season, and a year take.

Burt is also into geoboards (he swears his has the lowest price in the U.S.A. and is the best), tangrams, measurement, chip trading kits (shades of wampum!), and something called Sportsmath. Plus the standards: Cuisenaire, base ten blocks, loads of measurement devices, and math balances and games.

Home Grown Kids

Pre-Math It is a gentle first introduction to math for the very young. See more about Math-It materials in the Math Programs section.

NASCO

NASCO has lots and lots of math manipulatives, plus math stuff for all grade levels. If you want manipulatives for the youngsters and also are looking for something to liven up math for the older children, you might want to consider this catalog.

ALGEBRA AND OTHER HAIRY MONSTERS

Algebra is where math fear really begins to grip. Happily, it is not a required subject for graduation. You *can* skip it.

Skip algebra? As a former math major, I know that sounds heretical. Life has not convinced me that algebra is necessary, though. Or that we need geometry, either. These subjects were among my favorites in school, so it's not sour grapes that lead me to this conclusion. It's just that I very seldom need to calculate the height of a tree by the distance to the tree and the angle of the treetop to a predetermined position on the ground. Even less often do I need to determine how long it will take Smith and Jones, working together, to do a job if it takes Smith three days working alone and Jones five days working alone. The latter problem cannot be solved by algebra, although it is a standard, because as everyone knows, Smith's work performance will be affected by Jones. If both like to chat, they may take *longer* together than they did alone! Algebra is useless in predicting human behavior.

Actual math, of which algebra and geometry are the merest beginnings, is only really useful in a technological career in one of the disciplines which have their finest hour in dealing with machines. Try as the statisticians will to make math apply to humans, plants, and animals, the *living* world exists quite nicely without them. If your interest, or your children's, is to be found among the living, then "survival math" or "consumer math" is your best bet. Algebra and geometry you can study just for fun.

And you *can* study algebra and geometry just for fun, thanks to the prodigious efforts of one John Saxon. Mr. Saxon, whose career includes both military service and teaching, has developed a math series that has tripled the algebra enrollment at schools where it is used, as well as sending achievement scores through the roof. How does he do it? By introducing only one new concept at a time, providing witty problems to work that include a lot of real-life examples, and (this is the key) *reviewing* all previous concepts all the way through the course. Children learn to expect success, since they are given as long as they need to catch on, and are allowed to reap the rewards for understanding throughout the entire course. More about Saxon's algebra is in the review under Grassdale Publishers.

Creative Publications

Pizzazz! series, $8.25 each book, $29.50/set of four prealgebra books or four algebra books. $31.75 for set of four in three-ring binder. *Algebra in the Real World,* $15.95.

Pre-Algebra with Pizzazz! and *Algebra with Pizzazz!* are each a four-workbook series of self-checking math activities. The pizzazz comes from the jokes and riddles incorporated into each activity. To get the joke, you must solve the problem. This would be fun supplemental material for any prealgebra or algebra program.

Key Curriculum Project

See review under Math Programs. *Key to Algebra* and *Key to Geometry* look like decent introductions to these subjects.

Grassdale Publishers

Math 76 (for seventh-graders or smart sixth-graders), $18. *Algebra 1/2* (introduction), $18.20. *Algebra I,* $19.40. *Algebra II,* $20.75. *Geometry-Trig-Algebra,* $23.40. $2.25 shipping for one or two books, $3 for three to five books. *Math 65, 54, 43,* price to be announced.

What modern crusader has infuriated NOW, upset the math establishment, and raised children's math scores by incredible amounts? John Saxon, that's who! When this ex-Air Force officer took to teaching, he wondered why only 10 percent of his algebra students passed the final exam. Unlike so many modern teachers, who have been trained to blame the students, Saxon blamed the text. Moreover, he decided to try an experiment. He invented lesson plans that not only simplified math concepts, but reviewed the same types of problems again and again, once introduced, rather than moving on immediately to new ideas.

This "incremental" approach to math teaching produced unbelievable results. Students, for the first time, had a chance to let math settle into their bones. Instead of desperately treading water, trying to cope with new idea after new idea, Saxon's students had time to become familiar with math. They also had a chance to experience success, because once they had learned a skill that same skill continued to be included in their problem sets. Math became, as Saxon says, a time for "showing off" instead of for failure. Another Saxon saying: "Time is the elixir that turns things difficult into things familiar."

In a recent *Reader's Digest* article (March 1985—reprints available) these amazing results were reported.

In Del City, Oklahoma, junior-high students who usually earned C's and D's were introduced to the Saxon book and—by as much as 147 percent—soon outscored A and B students relying on a conventional text. In Hillsboro, Ohio, less than 60 percent of high-school students had elected to take second-year algebra; after teacher Diana Harvey introduced the Saxon book, nearly 90 percent of her students signed up for the course.

Dramatic increases in algebra enrollment occurs wherever the Saxon texts are used. One high school increased its algebra enrollment by 500 percent!

After all the publicity, I expected to see a very colorful, almost gaudy book. But Saxon's books look quite sombre: black and white, no pictures. The excitement comes from the learning itself. Saxon's texts support and encourage the student, not by babyish Behavior Modification ("you're doing great! Keep it up!"), but by allowing him to go step by step and rewarding him for learning. The problems themselves sparkle with wit and display Mr. Saxon's wide reading and awesome vocabulary. Example:

The goliards sang songs before the banquet. If the ratio of ribald songs to scandalous songs in their repertoire of 3102 songs was 7 to 4, how many ribald songs did they know?

Again:

Miltiades and his army marched to Marathon, the site of the battle, at 2 miles per hour. After the battle Pheidippides ran back to Athens with the news at 13 miles per hour. If the total traveling time was 15 hours, how far was it from Marathon to Athens?

Saxon also includes lots of problems using chemical terms and measurements in order to try to remove fear of science from his students. One problem starts, "Since knowledge of chemistry is useful even in non-scientific fields, three-eighths of the students elected to take chemistry." This kind of preaching I don't mind! Saxon's texts talk about "boys" and "girls" and occasionally have the boys beating girls in foot races. Perhaps this is what incensed the NOW folk—or perhaps they saw the words "hoyden" and "virago" in some of the problem sets and jumped to conclusions. It's all just good clean fun, and that's the most probable reason why some Establishment folk want to suppress it. No sermons about female astronauts? No Values Clarification, or discussions of contraceptive effectiveness? Horrors!

I wouldn't dream of trying to teach algebra without Saxon. You have got to admire this man, who in spite of all the opposition and even after having a quadruple heart bypass is still working on bringing his incremental method to students in the early grades. Mr. Saxon hopes to soon have texts available for even third-grade students, presenting arithmetic in the same easy-to-learn style. And if he does, I will buy them.

Order Saxon's texts from Thompson's Book Depository.

NASCO

Don't forget NASCO for supplementary algebra and prealgebra stuff. NASCO has games, puzzle books, scads of upper-level math computer programs (including some of the goodies reviewed in the Computers chapter), an Algebra Model Kit, and lots of other stuff designed to tame the algebra tiger.

CHAPTER THIRTY-THREE

NATURE STUDY

Many great trees grew there, planted long ago, falling into untended age amid a riot of careless descendants; and groves and thickets there were of tamarisk and pungent terebinth, of olive and of bay; and there were junipers and myrtle; and thymes that grew in bushes, or with their woody creeping stems mantled in deep tapestries the hidden stones; sages of many kinds putting forth blue flowers, or red, or pale green; and marjorams and new-sprouting parsleys. . . . The grots and rocky walls were already starred with saxifrages and stonecrops. Primeroles and anemones were awake in the filbert-brakes; and asphodel and many lily-flowers nodded their half-opened heads in the grass; deep green grass beside the pools. . . . (From The Two Towers by J. R. R. Tolkien, part of the Lord of the Rings trilogy, published by Ballantine Books)

Nature! Tolkien does not arouse our imaginations only with his superb word-painting, but with his profound knowledge of the created world. For Tolkien, flowers and herbs and trees had names. He could tell sprouting parsley from marjoram, and a tamarisk from a terebinth. This intimate acquaintance with things natural is unhappily not true of us, the products of modern schooling. Most of us wouldn't know saxifrage if it flung itself in our path, not to mention wild parsley. Many of us can't even tell an oak from a maple!

One branch of nature study is especially well-fitted to our ignorance; we can call it "Nature Lore." Here is the habitat of such as Euell Gibbons, the wary asparagus-stalker. Nature Loremasters can walk down an old city street and tell tales about every tree and squirrel. They know which wild plants are good to eat and which are deadly poison. They know how the Indians made birch-bark canoes and how Robin Hood constructed his bow of yew. Loremasters are conversant with squirrels and wise in the ways of deer, foxes, mice, skunks, and great horned owls.

The very best way to become a Loremaster is (1) to live in the country and (2) to follow around another Loremaster. You should certainly try to draft grandparents, especially those who live on farms, to serve as your Professors of Lore. The second-best way is to prowl around your own neighborhood, filling up on questions. What is that tree with the thorns and berries? What is that purple flower? Why do squirrels run around to the far side of the tree when they see you coming (and is it possible to sneak up on one and catch him unawares? Try it!)? When your cup of ignorance is full and running over, then turn, if you must, to a book. Books there are on tree identification, and wild foods, and suburban animals; some of them are listed below. Any good library will have enough in your areas of interest to answer your questions and spark some more.

SOURCES OF NATURE LORE

One caveat before you plunge into these reviews: primitive pagans have always worshiped the earth, the sun, the rat, the cow—in short, any and all created objects, including themselves. Some moderns, having rejected God, are again resorting to this ancient foolishness. Thus modern nature lore is divided between those who worship the creation and those who admire it *as* the creation. More on this later.

American Museum of Natural History

Museum annual membership fee of $20 includes one year of *Natural History* magazine, free admission, travel opportunities, discounts on mail order items, etc.

The "hope you will join us" letter makes it clear that Museum membership is for worshipers of Sacred Nature:

> From all indications available to us, you're a rather uncommon sort of person.
> One who has a special *reverence* for our natural surroundings . . . an endless and *respectful* curiosity about the quirks of animal and human nature . . . an unabashed *sense of wonder* and fascination in the presence of our legacy from the past. . . . [emphasis mine]

Unlike other nature mags, *Natural History* spends a lot of time looking at people. We are examined just like other animals, in terms of our interesting behaviors and characteristics. Can superb art and scintillating text make up for a fundamental lack of "soul"?

Carolina Biological Supply
Huge color catalog, $8.

From Carolina's Biology/Science Teaching Materials Catalog you can get rabbits, frogs, protozoa, and all sorts of other creepies and crawlies. Plus, of course, food, bedding, and "habitats" for same. Anyone for leeches? No? Tarantulas (not sexed)? Fiddler crabs? How about unusual corn ears, for studying genetics?

Also of interest is Carolina's wide selection of biology and general science books, records, filmstrips, and games. These are geared to public schools and reflect those values. Among the huge selection I found some items I liked: the bird-song records and hard science books and some of the science games.

Educational Insights
Critter Condo, $14.95.

Ed Insight's Critter Condo is the top-of-the-line home for whatever animal, insect, or whatever your little one brings home. It can be used as a terrarium when the hunting is bad, an ant theater, a butterfly hatchery, and even an aquarium. Educational Insights has so many other neat "hands-on" items in all fields, including science, that you won't want to pass them up.

Hubbard Company

Much more pleasant than Carolina's offerings, but not as complete, are the Hubbard Science catalogs. Hubbard's Biology Equipment catalog includes terraria, tanks, and other aids for studying real live beasties. Take note of the MicroEd System, a full semester general bio program with lab manual, earthworms, and everything you need to study the same (plus the "bacteria, protozoa, algae, fungi, nematodes, mites, and flies" that "develop regularly in the bedding material"). Making the best of things, Hubbard cleverly incorporates all the little critters developing in your earthworms' bedding into the study. Total cost, $36.25. Lots of other interesting things, some low-priced enough to be within reach.

Mother's Bookshelf

Wide selection of lore books for nature-lovers. Stalk the wild asparagus, risk your life picking wild mushrooms, identify birds and bushes, learn how the pioneers struggled along without Tide and Cheer. The selection is tempting and the books useful.

National Audubon Expedition Institute

"Wild America Is Our Campus," reads the ad. Don't know why this program keeps turning up on home school lists—home schooling it is not. High school, college, and grad students can enroll in the Institute, which consists largely of treks about America. Communal values and eco-doctrine are instilled through hands-on exposure to Amish farms, backpacking, spelunking, etc.

National Geographic World
$9.95 U.S., $16.25 Canadian funds ($12.75 U.S. funds) per annum.

National Geographic World is a bright and beautiful kids' picture mag. Inside are stunning photos and interesting stories, some about nature and others about science, history, young achievers, and other subjects of interest to children. *World* is careful to present up-to-date scientific theories *as* theories, striving to avoid partisan causes and stick to the facts.

World's adult counterpart, the *National Geographic* magazine itself, has some nature lore tucked in along with the sociology, politics, geography, and what not.

National Wildlife Federation
Ranger Rick (for kids six to twelve); twelve issues $12. *Your Big Backyard* (for ages three to five); twelve issues $10.

Nature lore reigns supreme in these two magazines for kids. National Wildlife Federation does have a conservation agenda. *Ranger Rick* is more like a "grown-up" magazine with feature articles, letters to the editor, and the like. *Your Big Backyard* comes wrapped in a "Parents' Letter" that has teaching suggestions for using the magazine. The photos are gorgeous, and the activities are interesting. Both magazines have kid-appeal and are a value for the money.

Nature Friend Magazine
$9.25/twelve issues.

Aimed at readers from four to fourteen, this Christian magazine includes read-aloud stories, a readers' forum, child-submitted pictures and poems, a "You Can Draw" page that guides children to produce their own nature drawing, and activities, projects, and puzzles. With a creationist emphasis, and a smorgasbord of nature books and products offered for sale through the magazine, it sounds like everything a Christian family could wish for in a nature magazine. The price is right; so it won't hurt to see an issue or two.

Nature Friend's Nature's Workshop 1986 Catalog features tested nature-study products and books. Books are either evolution-free or have "guideline sheets" included. Bird feeders, binoculars, ant farms, telescopes, pocket knives, pocket compasses, nature study guides, and nature coloring books are all offered at very reasonable prices. Send $1.00 for catalog (refundable with first order).

Zoobooks

Each colorful Zoobook is about one animal. Uncritically evolutionary, the series traces each animal's fancied family tree.

Consider such amusing but ridiculous "evolutionary facts" as a series of supposed elephant ancestors pictured complete with their trunks and proto-trunks. This is particularly fascinating because trunks, being cartilaginous, are never preserved as fossils.

The photos and pictures are chosen from thousands and are visually superb. Where the facts *are* facts, they are fascinating. You subscribe to the series and pay for each booklet as it comes. The price is low.

STUDYING THE SKY

Orion Telescope Center

For one-stop astronomical shopping, Orion Telescope Center is hard to beat. Established in 1975, Orion is "the nation's largest independent telescope dealer." Just reading the Orion catalog is an education in itself. Total ignoramuses like myself can benefit from the catalog articles describing the difference between reflecting and refracting telescopes; devoted hackers can pick up the latest astronomical info. But then, devoted hackers probably already have this catalog! You can get one, too, by calling Orion's toll-free number.

Sky and Telescope
$20 a year (domestic), $2 single copy.

Latch on to an issue of this magazine and you'll have *no* trouble locating astonomy books and supplies. The ads are often worth more than the articles in a publication of this sort, leading you on to dazzling vistas and brilliant ideas that you would never have discovered on your own. Amateur astronomers do occasionally make serious discoveries, it turns out, and S & T is certainly the magazine for the serious amateur.

ECOLOGY

Nature Lore is, as I have said, one area of nature study. The other area, much studied in schools, is ecology. Ostensibly the study of how animals and plants live together, ecology has become a cover for some pretty heavy social activism. It is hardly possible to find a section on ecology in a school text which does not preach the following errors:

(1) Man is the destroyer of the planet. According to this dogma, all was fine in nature until Man came along. Man, that greedy ape, rampages about heedlessly destroying precious ecosystems. We are robbing the lions and lemmings and rats and roaches of their just domain. In this way of thinking, every time some poor African builds a grass hut, he is usurping the territory of the sacrosanct animals.

I call this the "It's Okay If An Elephant Does It" doctrine. Elephants, as everyone ought to know, stomp about ripping up trees, mangling the bark, and generally wiping out whatever range they are in just like untended cattle would. But it's O.K., you see, for elephants to act that way. They are only animals. It's our *duty,* or rather the duty of the African blacks, to leave huge gobs of land for free-ranging elephants. Only Man, you see, ever destroys.

The crassest expression of this philosophy that I ever saw was in an article in the *Mother Earth News.* The article's authors, pious ecologists all, had spent lots of money and lots of fuel flying to Africa to observe some apes in their natural state. These apes live in a protected national park in Rwanda. Nearby are African farmers, so poor that

> The wooden stakes marking [the park's] boundaries are often surreptitiously moved back by local residents hoping to gain even a few more feet of farmland or a tree or two to cut for scarce cooking fuel.

Pity the poor Africans, right? Wrong. The authors lament that

> In spite of this, the money necessary to install more permanent cement boundary markers has been slow to materialize.

Continuing into the article, we get some insight into the plight of the Africans:

> An even greater concern arises when local people, wishing to supplement their protein-poor diet, attempt to snare some of the parks' antelope.

The ecologists' solution:

An internationally sponsored project now pays for guards to patrol the 30,000-acre refuge, and the officials do bring in a number of poachers each week, dealing with them fairly harshly. [Goody! Punish those wicked Africans trying to provide food for their hungry families!] But there simply aren't *enough* guards, and there's very little money to provide those already on duty with such basic necessities as guns, ammunition, and uniforms.[1]

The article continued with rhapsodies over the fifteen gorilla groups that are allowed to roam over the thirty thousand acres (two thousand acres per gorilla family). No attention whatever was paid to the people of Rwanda (529 per square mile[2]). In closing, the authors made a fervent plea for money, to help— who? The dirt-poor blacks of Rwanda? No such luck. Remember, the guards who are dealing harshly with Rwanda's families need guns and ammo! The plea, directed in cooperation with Paul and Anne Ehrlich, the parents of the We-Are-Overpopulated movement, was for money to help protect the *gorillas.*

But it's O.K., folks. It's not insensitive to burn up supposedly irreplaceable jet fuel toddling over the globe to gape at gorillas. White people can *help* gorillas by flying to Rwanda, since the tourism brings money to Rwanda's bureaucracy. Maybe then Rwanda can really get to work on its problems by pledging allegiance to doctrine number two:

(2) We need less people on the earth. I have *never* seen a section on ecology, even in Christian texts, that does not drag out this doctrine. In my first book, *The Way Home,* I showed how the myth of overpopulation is both inconsistent with real Christian doctrine, and inconsistent with the known facts about population, land area, food population, and the like. If the entire human population of the planet moved to Texas, we would be less crowded than certain parts of New Jersey and New York are right now.[3] Look up the facts and work it out for yourself.

This "hate humans" philosophy makes a very convenient excuse for certain antichild lifestyles. As the self-righteous ecologists don backpacks and traipse off for a delightful weekend disturbing the wilderness, they can content themselves with the thought that only they, the Anointed, will disturb those hallowed hills. They will not share the pristine wild with anyone, even their own children.

The Overpopulation Myth also provides a convenient rationale for totalitarianism, since totalitarians always know how to dispose of "extra" people. We are seeing the fruit of it already, as it is selfishly suggested (and selfishly acted upon) that we simply don't have *enough* food, medical help, land, or whatever, and that therefore this handicapped baby or this unwanted child or that old person would be, ahem, "better off" dead.

All this dogma belongs to the area of ethics, where it cannot hold up its head. That is why it is hiding out under the innocuous label of ecology. Ecology, properly understood, is the study of the marvelous way in which all the living things on the earth help each other. Man, as one of the living organisms, *belongs* here. We are not foreigners or intruders on our own planet! Further, it is not our duty to lie down and die so the Sacred Animals can romp about our empty cities. Man was told to make the earth a garden, and insofar as man obeys God, he does so.

People will tell you that Christianity is responsible for pollution and the destruction of wildlife. This is not true. The most ardent nature lovers, including J. R. R. Tolkien, have been and are Christians. Only those who know the Painter can truly enjoy the painting.

Simply stated, the issue is this: Should nature be left "undisturbed" or are we humans allowed to garden in it? Viewpoint #1, the Hindu viewpoint, leaves no room for people. We might, with great difficulty, tiptoe through life without stepping on the ant, but try as we might, we can't pass through this world without leaving any traces. We must harvest the Sacred Vegetables to eat (muttering a charm as we do so). Even if we let our babies die of hunger in the streets while the cows and rats eat up the crops, unless we are willing to commit mass suicide ourselves we cannot help changing nature somewhat. At what point is survival allowed? May we take the bracken to make our homes? (No, there are guards with guns to protect the gorillas who roam through that bracken.) May we farm the land? (No, it is needed for the gorilla's habitat.) Be glad that African eco-freaks aren't visiting America to help *us* with our problems.

Viewpoint #2, the progarden viewpoint, says that Man *is* the lord of creation, but that he is not autonomous. God is the Lord of man, and He will require an accounting. Man is to regulate the physical world, to order it, and to make it fruitful. In this viewpoint, the solution to the "Elephant Problem" would be to let the Africans herd the elephants. If you want to "protect" an animal, you do so by giving it an owner, instead of by fencing people out. If the Ehrlichs want to see animals running free on thousands and thousands of acres while people scrabble for a mere existence nearby, let them buy Rwanda. If, however, they would like to see both humans and animals thriving, let the humans own the antelopes and gorillas instead of poaching them. Those whose ownership interests incline them towards nonuseful animals can set up zoos and preserves (purchased with *their own* money). Nobody forces us to grow flowers; yet most of my neighbors have a garden. If nobody forced us to keep out of the wild, many would be inclined to tame the wild and bring it home. As long as it's illegal to own hawks, hawks will be endangered. Make hawking legal, bring it back as a sport, and hawks will be everywhere.

I understand how Christopher Robin felt when he lay on his back on an island, looked up at the sky, and said, "There's nobody else in the world, and the world was made for me." It's fun to think of being barefoot, running through the wild grass with the antelope and zebra, unfettered and free. But this is the real world, other people are in it, and we have to decide whether the animals shall rule or the humans. I vote for the Africans—let the gorillas go to those who love them best.

Books about the Environment and Pollution

Puritan-Reformed Discount Book Service

J. A. Walter's *The Human Home: The Myth of the Sacred Environment* is a Lion paperback, published in England. Thankfully, P-R sells it here, and a gem it is. Walter, a sociologist by training, became interested in the question of how people see and experience their environments. The book goes deeply into matters of art, architecture, and city planning, along with its expected look at the politics of ecology. All is done with that fine British sense of the lovely and the absurd. Let me share one of the author's insights:

> So there is a problem, deriving from the juxtaposition of three geographical facts:
>
> First, contrary to popular belief, there are masses of wilderness in the world. [Proof follows.] . . .
>
> Second, there are lots of pretty places in the world, and lots of safe places.
>
> Third, there are rather few places that are both wild and pretty, dominated by nature yet safe for humans; and still fewer that are readily accessible for the urban masses. . . .
>
> Together, these three facts cause a problem because, though the overt definition of wilderness is that it is wild, natural and unpopulated, the covert definition insists that it also be pretty, safe and accessible. So there has grown up a myth that *wilderness is scarce,* and fast disappearing. Virtually any valued wild place is believed to be 'the last wilderness.' . . .
>
> This belief in the scarcity of wilderness greatly enhances its sacredness. Something common could hardly be a viable replacement for God; the substitute must surely be rare, yet accessible; of a different order, yet approachable if one goes through the correct preparatory ritual. Without the myth of scarcity, the religion of nature could hardly continue.

All in all, this book will lead to some heavy thinking in the whole area of environment.

Regnery Gateway

Coercive Utopians, $7.95, paperback. Introduction by Franky Schaeffer.

The Coercive Utopians, by Rael Jean Isaac and Eric Isaac, is a readable, in-depth investigation of modern utopianism, including environmental utopianism. Particularly useful is the way the book debunks the spiritual aura surrounding those claiming to act "in the public interest."

Simon and Schuster

Edith Efron's *The Apocalyptics: How Environmental Politics Controls What We Know About Cancer* is a massive tome, not for the fainthearted. Why do I recommend it? Because here are assembled the unemotional facts which prove that the apocalyptic screams emanating from the eco-freak community are not based on any scientific proof. The book's real value is the way in which Edith Efron shows how the scientific community has become trammeled by politics, to the point where serious scientists are afraid to say anything contrary to the religion of Sacred Nature and Unholy Man.

Books about "Overpopulation"

Paul Ehrlich, *The Population Bomb,* **Ballantine Books, 1968.**

See Ehrlich predict worldwide famine and death on an unprecedented scale, to occur in the 1970s, or the early 1980s at the latest. Discover how, in order to save us from this terrible doom, we need government to step in with some "apparently brutal" solutions such as loading up the food supply with antireproductive agents and cutting off food aid to India. How *did* we make it through the Seventies, anyway?

Germaine Greer, *Sex and Destiny: The Politics of Human Fertility,* **Harper and Row, 1985. 492 pages. $19.95, cloth.**

Greer, one of feminism's original guiding lights, has traveled around the world with her eyes open and seen much that Dr. Ehrlich missed. Her massive, spirited book wipes out many of the common prejudices against fertility, particularly those which are commonly used to force infertility on poor women in underdeveloped countries. Greer knows how to write with a scalpel, and her section on Ehrlich is particularly instructive.

Jacqueline Kasun, *The War Against Population: The Economics and Ideology of Population Control,* **Green Hill and Jameson Books, 1986. 350 pages. $16.95, cloth.**

This book should be titled *The War Against People.* Jacqueline Kasun, professor of economics at Humboldt State University in Arcata, California, reveals in chilling detail how the war on population increase is a convenient ideological smoke screen for a war on our freedom and right to privacy. What do the population bombers want? Could it be totalitarian control? See how overpop dogma is being used to usher in a dictatorship of the bureaucrat. Some chapters, such as the one on sex education, will curl your hair.

Kasun is no lightweight or deep-end right-winger. She has been published in *The Wall Street Journal, American Spectator,* and *Commentary.*

Mary Pride, *The Way Home: Beyond Feminism, Back to Reality,* **Crossway Books, 1985.**

The chapter "Who's Afraid of the Big Bad Baby?" contains a brief synopsis of the more compelling arguments against overpopulation mythology. The book also gets into some of the social and political consequences of this belief, and documents how overpop myth is a precursor to totalitarianism.

Julian Simon and Herman Kahn, *The Resourceful Earth: A Response to 'Global 2000,'* **published by Basil Blackwell, 1984.**

Readable but heavy, this volume is top-heavy with heavyweight scientific contributions. In every area of apocalyptic environmentalism, real experts present the facts.

Julian Simon, *The Ultimate Resource,* **Princeton University Press, 1977.**

In-between the chattiness of *Grow or Die!* and the learned weightiness of *The Resourceful Earth,* this book shows how humans are not a detriment to the environment, but the earth's greatest resource.

James Weber, *Grow or Die!,* **Arlington House, 1977.**

Easy-to-read refutation of "overpopulation" doomsday thinking.

Ecology Resources and Games

Ampersand Press
Predator Game, **$6.25.** Available in English, Spanish, and French. *Krill Game,* **$6.75** (English only). *Pollination Game,* **$6.95** (English only). Shipping extra.

If you want to understand how food webs work (that is, who eats who and how it agrees with them), try playing some of Ampersand Press's inexpensive and classy games. *Predator* is a deck of forty nice-looking playing cards based on a forest food web. Each card shows a plant or animal, tells who eats it and what it eats, and assigns it Energy Points. *Krill* is similar, but it uses an Antarctic Ocean food chain card deck. Both decks have the usual levels in their food webs: producers, three or four consumer levels, and decomposers. Many games can be played with the cards: classification games, *Concentration, Solitaire, Rummy,* and of course the *Predator* and *Krill* food web games.

   Pollination is about the birds and the bees, following a similar format.

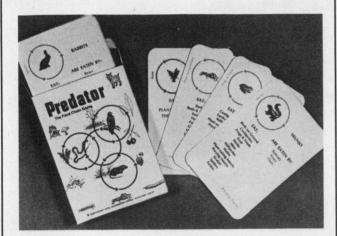

These games furnish a great introduction to *real* ecology at a very manageable price.

Rodale Press

   To my mind, the best ecological activism is gardening. Instead of "Fence Man Out!" let's help make the earth both beautiful and productive. Rodale Press has hundreds of practical books on this theme: homesteading books, gardening books, books on composting, books on herbs, books on natural landscaping, books on the care of farm animals, and on and on. Most books have very little, if any, antihuman philosophy, being mostly concerned with helping you and me become *practical* ecologists.

CHAPTER THIRTY-FOUR

SCIENCE

O LORD, our Lord, how majestic is your name
    in all the earth!
      When I consider your heavens, the work of
      your fingers, the moon
and the stars, which you have set in place,
      what is man that you are mindful of him,
      the son of man that you
care for him?
      You made him ruler over the work of your
      hands; you put
everything under his feet;
      all flocks and herds, and the beasts of the
      field, the birds of the air, and the fish of the
      sea, all that swim the paths of the seas.
      (Psalm 8:1, 3, 4, 7, 8)

Science has traditionally been understood in these two ways: thinking God's thoughts after Him, or becoming god oneself. In the first view, expressed by the Psalm above, man searches out the whys and wherefores of things primarily as an act of worship. Through understanding the world around him, he can better know and serve God. Scientific investigation is not presumption, but veneration. As the proverb says, "It is the glory of God to conceal a matter; to search out a matter is the glory of kings" (Proverbs 25:2).

The second view, man-becoming-god, is sometimes known as Religious Humanism. In this view, man studies his environment only in order to control it. Power is the goal, and knowledge the means. If man can learn to manipulate himself and the world successfully, he will have become as god and the world will supposedly be a Utopia.

Both forms of science may study the same objects, but their methods and responses are very different. The theistic (or Biblical, or Judeo-Christian) approach regards the very objects being studied as important, the artifacts of a worshiped God. There is then a case for treating animals, plants, and the earth itself ethically. As the Bible says, "A righteous man cares for the needs of his animal, but the kindest acts of the wicked are cruel" (Proverbs 12:10). Curiosity alone is not sufficient reason for maiming God's creation. Since the end of scientific investigation is to better serve and worship God, the means must match the end. Also, discoveries are weighed in the balance of their usefulness to the service of God. The drive is not to show that it *can* be done unless it is first determined that it *should* be done.

Humanistic science, on the other hand, is concerned with increasing man's power, and thus is constantly embroiled in ethical dilemmas. It is not considered "nice" in modern America to trample one's fellows underfoot, and yet much of modern science is devoted to giving one group of men the tools to do that to others. If power is the goal, is it *my* power or *your* power? Increasingly the rules of science are being broken by those who see some immediate gain (power) to be grasped through falsified data and fake experiments. Even more devastating is the defection from true science by those who, without God, can find no reason for believing that absolute, immutable truth exists. As Edith Efron, herself a humanist, observes,

> In all branches of the humanities and the social sciences, there has been a rejection of the criteria and disciplines of the field and a slide into a subjectivity which serves as a vehicle, overt or covert, for ideological values. These trends are now institutionalized, and are well known to a generation of scholars in the humanist world, whether they have capitulated to the irrationalists or are fighting them. Most humanists, however, have not realized that *the same trends have infiltrated science.*
>
> I gradually discovered that scientific intellectuals were aware of the problem. I learned from Ernest Nagel, a philosopher of science, that many biologists in the 1960s had rejected the analytical and abstractive disciplines of science. I learned from a discussion of a book entitled *Science, Technology and Society,* edited by Ina Spiegel-Rosing and Derek DeSolla Price, that many biologists in the 1970s were rejecting the most crucial "norms" of science: "universalism, communality, disinterestedness, organized skepticism, and more lately originality and humility." I discovered a paper by Bernard David of Harvard, a prominent geneticist, observing that "some scientists appear to be losing confidence in the objectivity of scientific knowledge. . . ."[1] [emphasis mine]

All of us, believers and humanists alike, need to watch out for the kind of thinking that makes reality fluid. Pantheism and feelings-fondling may be in vogue, but they are essentially antiscience and reality contradicts them daily. I don't make reality; I can only work with the reality that exists. All the little kids who really believed they could fly like Superman went splat when they tried it, as did George Reeves himself.

SCIENCE RESOURCES

When purchasing science equipment or courses, it's not necessary to copy the schools. A Sears & Roebuck microscope or chemistry kit may do your child (or you) just as much good as a fancy course with workbooks—perhaps more. In science, learning is supremely by doing, and those who *do* will beat out those who memorize and fill out workbook pages every time. I had a sad experience of this in engineering school, where the fellows who had spent their high school years putting together Radio Shack kits breezed about enjoying their electrical courses, while I, who had never even seen a transistor before, had to struggle out my grades through sheer rote memory, and afterward promptly forgot most of what I had "learned."

Hacking about in the basement is a great way to get into science. If every school kid were allowed to read novels during science period, but given a chemistry kit and a microscope with prepared slides to play with at home, would we see those paranoid articles in the paper about how superior Russian children are to Americans scientifically? As Gollum said, "We wonders, aye, we wonders."

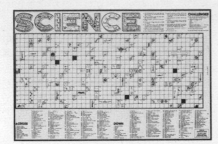

Ampersand Press
AC/DC game, **$6.75**. *Science Participoster,* **$3.95**. Shipping extra.

The neatest introduction to the study of electricity that I've seen, Ampersand's *AC/DC Electric Circuit Game,* is played with a deck of special cards. Cards depict energy sources, wires, switches, energy users, and fuses. The object of the game is to construct workable circuits. Players may get "shocked" or "shorted," so watch out! You can't help but learn the rudiments of electricity playing the game. I wish someone had given me this game before I went to engineering school (but then, it probably hadn't been invented way back then!).

The *Participoster* is a huge crossword puzzle loaded with science questions.

Ampersand Press also has some nifty ecology games, reviewed under Nature Study.

Backyard Scientists
Book **$5.45** ppd. California residents add 32¢ tax.

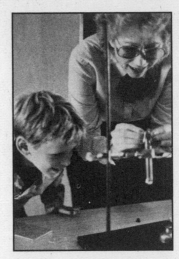

Backyard Scientists is a book that gives children a "fun hands-on introduction to science," with thirty step-by-step science experiments that four- to twelve-year-olds can perform using things found around the house. The author, Jane Hoffman, has received national attention for her "backyard science" program, now in its sixth year. Mrs. Hoffman now works as a consultant to school systems. Her book is highly recommended by the National Science Foundation.

Bob Jones University Press

Bob Jones has a textbook science series for Christian schools that has met with a great deal of approval in home schooling circles. They also carry all the lab apparatus you are ever likely to need, and chemicals in classroom-sized portions.

Christian Light Publications

It's not cheap, but if you want science equipment to perform all your high school experiments, CLP has it. Geared to the Alpha Omega Publications curriculum, CLP's lab materials are available in complete sets or as individual components. If your children are serious about science, I'd look upon this as an investment. All the lab materials to set up all your kids with real experiments costs less than a good stereo system or a fancy racing bike.

Creation-Science Research Center
Science and Creation series, all books under $3 each. Eight volumes, some with accompanying student handbook.

The name speaks for itself. Here is your source for creation science resources. Books, filmstrips, cassettes, and more.

Crestwood House
$8.95 per book, **$71.60** the series. Library bindings. 48 pages.

Another series on how things are made, Crestwood House's Technology series is high-interest, low-vocabulary. Topics: balls, trucks, books, records and cassettes, racing cars, micros, sport shoes, and video games.

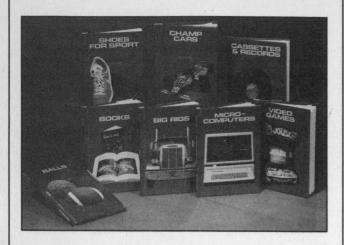

DIDAX

Ladybird series, $2.50 each, set $27.75. Junior Science Series, $2.50 each, all eight for $18.50.

From England, the Ladybird How It Works series covers cars, rockets, airplanes, more, for ages nine to eleven. The Junior Science Series has simple, safe experiments with magnetism and electricity, light, air, botany, zoology, weather, and more. A great "hands-on" catalog.

Edmund Scientific Company

Every neat scientific widget under the sun. Microscopes, telescopes, stethoscopes, orotoscopes, binoculars, and the ever-popular sextant (don't leave home without one!). Crazy gifts for the man who has everything, from quarters that "blast off" when you tip the waiter, to your personal robot. For serious tinkerers and investigators. Plus a pile of science kits with kid-appeal.

Now tell me honestly, where else can you get a kit to build a working model of the Gutenberg press (only $42.95!) or a giant gyroscope ($6.95) or a fossil collection ($14.95) or a paper clock kit ($7.95)? Sea monkeys! Butterfly collecting! Make your own perfume! Garden hydroponically! Stargaze! Much, much more! Plus survival gear, tools, photography supplies, and everything else far out and technological.

Educational Designs, Inc.

Mini-Labs, set of thirteen, $75. Individual prices, $4.50 to $6.89, most around $6. Comprehensive Labs, $11.95-$29.95. These are school prices.

For all-in-one colorful, inexpensive hands-on science, Ed Design's Mini-Labs look hard to beat. Electronics, solar energy, chemistry, physics, even paper airplanes—it's all here. If you're a school, you're entitled to the special school price and can order directly from the manufacturer. If not, you can send in a prepaid order or find a store that stocks them.

Ed Designs also has Comprehensive Science Labs—Power-Tech Electricity, Physics, and Chemistry labs, Electronics 60, World of Radio and Electronics, Solar Energy, Sky Full of Plane Aeronautics lab, and a 45x telescope.

Educational Insights

Sticky Things, Beautiful Things, $4.95 each. *Solar Encounters,* $3.95

Quite a selection of experiments with simple things: some on cards, some in books, some with accompanying materials. The Fun with Art and Science series has two books, *Sticky Things* and *Beautiful Things.* The *Solar Encounters* print-making kit is very popular—make prints with light. Science centers, experiment books, selection of inexpensive microscopes (up to 900x), and more.

Heathkit

For the novice hobbyist or serious student of electronics, Heathkit has both home-study courses and of course its famous kits. Build your own oscilloscope, or TV, or IBM PC-compatible computer (which Heath says is faster than the original). You won't save all that much money, but it's great experience.

Burt Harrison & Company

Batteries and Bulbs Mini Kit, $19.95. Book alone, $6.50 $2.50 shipping and handling.

Science books, games, equipment for hands-on experiments, and "things." Kid's photography equipment, plus all the necessary glop to develop pictures. "Kitchen physics." Equipment for measuring and looking. Fantastic prices (example: 100X microscope for $7).

Burt's niftiest science kit is the *Batteries and Bulbs Mini Kit* (a larger size is available for schools). Suggested for children aged eight to twelve, but also usable for impatient four- to seven-year-olds, the kit is a whole pile of materials for investigating magnetism and electricity, including (believe it or not) four batteries! Now when's the last time you ever saw a supplier include batteries with *anything?* Kids not only "perform experiments," but come to understand the basic principles of electricity and magnetism while making a flashlight, galvanometer, electromagnet, telegraph key, and buzzer. The activity book reveals all, and if our children's reaction means anything, your red-blooded American tyke would love it, too. Small fry need adult help, of course.

If you love widgets and whatzits, don't miss this catalog.

Home Grown Kids

Science with Simple Things, four volumes: Balancing, Electricity, Magnetism, Pendulums and Metric Measures. $14 each.

Hewitt does it again with some very nifty hands-on science experiments. Science with Simple Things series uses sugar cubes for measuring volume, paper clips and rubber bands for experiments in balance, minimagnets for studying magnetism, and the like.

Hubbard Company

Combined Earth Science/Life Science catalog, Biology catalog, Jewel Terrarium catalog. Just ask for the Science catalogs. They make great browsing, and you'll get lots of ideas for your home curriculum. Much of the material is classroom-priced (Hubbard's prices are reasonable compared to the competition's), but some kits and equipment would be within the reach of the home lab.

Institute for Creation Research

Another source of creation science materials. Especially liked books are those by Duane T. Gish (*Evolution: The Challenge of the Fossil Record, Scientific Creationism,* and, for little kids, *Dinosaurs: Those Terrible Lizards*). You'd better send for the brochure, which also includes videos, filmstrips, 16mm films, and slides, plus a large number of other good books, if you're trying to build a strong home science library. Find out what the ACLU is afraid to let into the public school classroom!

Jerryco

Wonderful widgets from the world of surplus. Only the Jerryco catalog can make a petri dish sound enticing. The man who writes the catalog description has a wry sense of humor and a *lot* of imagination. Catch this description of a humble security cable:

SHORT TETHER
Which is just the way you ought to feel about your computer keyboard, the demo item on your showcase top, the wire stripper everyone borrows, and the other items with a tendency toward wanderlust. Brand new 36″ cable assemblies made up from plastic coated 1/32″ dia. aircraft cable. Very flexible, reasonably tough. That is not to say that a serious and well equipped crook couldn't chew thru one, but the casual

acquaintance who intended to bring it back right away will be suitably discouraged. . . . Make an honest statement about your faith in mankind.

Jerryco not only sells motors and sprockets and gears and everything else, but generously shares ideas about what to do with all these gizmos, as witness this ad:

REAL MEN DRINK BEER OUT OF BULLETS!
Real 76 mm (3″) shell casings from WWII's Sherman Anti-Tank guns. A touch over 21″ long with the classic bullet-like overhanging rim at the bottom. The overpaint gives them a greenish color, but you may be assured they are steel. We should have said, "Real Men Dribble Beer out of Bullets," as these shells were demilitarized by punching out the primer and detonator with an out of round ½″ punch. Real men plug such holes with day old quiche. . . .

I absolutely can't resist one more:

SWEDISH BAYONET
Vintage: 1940. Condition: Excellent. Length: 13″, 8″ of which is blade. Markings: Odd crown with "C" under it. Appearance: Menacing. Purpose: Nasty. Great barbeque knife for the macho cook. Fine letter opener for the macho executive. Fingernail cleaner or toothpick for the macho macho. We're packing the thing in one of our World War I sheaths, which is described separately below. As with so many of our friends' marriages, the two look a little funny together, but they work.

Many items are military surplus, as you may have guessed, but a lot are components of mass-produced items that bombed in the market. Clever folks can make something with them. Unclever folk can just get their belly laughs reading the catalog.

Master Books

Formerly Creation-Life Books, this is yet another source for creation science.

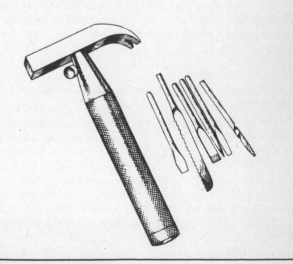

NASCO

I just found out about NASCO's Science catalog as this book was in the final editing stages. Even though it was late to add anything, I just had to give a plug to what must be one of the best single sources for science equipment and supplies for private schools and home schoolers.

The NASCO Science catalog is *complete*. You can get everything from animal housing to T-shirts, including lab benches, lab equipment, dissection specimens, skeletons (yuk!), slides, aquaria, computer programs, chemicals, activity kits, safety equipment—in short, everything your little scientific heart could desire. Other companies carry a lot of this stuff, but they don't have NASCO's reader-friendly layout or excellent choice of materials. Many of the items recommended in this book are sold by NASCO: Milliken's *Diagrammatic Study Prints* and activity books, Ampersand Press's nature games, and Hubbard kits and models, to name just a few. Many NASCO items are priced affordably enough for the home, and some are just plain fun, like the Model Rocketry kits.

National Teaching Aids
$6 per viewer, $3.50 per title. Five-year guarantee.

Here is a nifty idea! Since most schools can't afford high-powered microscopes for every student, why not take pictures of slides as they would appear under ideal viewing conditions and then let children look at those in lieu of expensive specimens? National has a wide range of labeled "photomicrographs" (spell *that* and go to the head of the class!) plus explanatory text folders. You need a viewer, of course, and National also sells those. The viewers are rugged, coming with a five-year guarantee against breakage. These materials have been used by over one hundred and forty *million* students.

Resources for the Gifted
Glop Shop, $19.95. Science Scopes, $39. Go Power, $14.95. Shipping extra.

This company features materials for "gifted" children. Glop Shop is a bunch of just plain stuff (wire, a small motor, assorted widgets) that a smart kid can turn into . . . well . . . a working model of something-or-other. Science Scopes is a kit of sixteen optical projects, including materials. Make your own kaleido-scope, periscope, microscope, chromatrope . . . *Go Power* is propulsion exploration: balloon rockets, rubber-band crafts . . . RFG is continually coming out with new products that feature heavy-duty thinking.

Silver Burdett Company

Silver Burdett's Science Lab Demo Packages for grades K-6 let you set up a complete public school science program in your home. Designed to accompany the Silver Burdett Science series, the labs cost between $85 and $150, depending on the grade. A 30x microscope is the only extra item to buy, at the nominal cost of $5.95.

Sycamore Tree

Sycamore Tree distributes some of the neatest science books and equipment you will ever see. More and more I value Bill and Sandy Gogel's shopping expertise. Example: *Bet You Can't!* features science gags—trap a friend into trying to lift a book with his head on the wall and knees locked! Mom can do it, but Dad can't! All Sycamore Tree's line is a value for the money and either beautiful or clever or both.

Things of Science
$20 per year. Canada and Mexico, $26.50. Other countries, $29, U.S. dollars. Back units, $2 each, three for $5.25.

The gift that keeps giving all year long. Every month the subscriber gets a science kit in the mail. Designed for children ages ten to sixteen, the kits have explored such topics as optical illusions, seed growth, aerodynamics, fossils, and herbs. Each month the topic changes.

What you get is a sample of the material being studied or some small piece of equipment and a booklet of information and ideas for study. The Seashells kit was a big hit in our house because the kids love seashells. The text they conveniently ignored.

Things of Science is aggressively evolutionary, a fact which is only obvious to those who read the entire booklet straight through. Many units do not touch on origins, to be fair. The booklets are erudite, but not stellar in their lucidity (rather like this sentence).

Those inclined to taste before buying might try ordering a back unit. These are available at a nominal price, as per above.

University of Nebraska-Lincoln

U of N-L's accredited high school science courses have the additional benefit of including all necessary equipment at an outrageously low price. Avid young scientists might enjoy one of these courses as a gift. For more details, see the U of N-L review in the Correspondence Programs section (it's one of The Biggies).

Wff 'n Proof Learning Games Associates
Queries 'n Theories, $16.

Queries 'N Theories is a simulation of the scientific method that allows you to create and test hypotheses in the course of trying to break the code your opponent just invented. It's my very favorite Wff 'n Proof game, partly because it develops scientific thinking and partly because I get to play with all those neat little colored chips.

Creation Science

For materials on creationism, you may want to obtain some of those on the following list, compiled by Creation-Science Research Center.

Books

J. Kerby Anderson and Harold G. Coffin, *Fossils in Focus* (Grand Rapids, Mich.: Zondervan, 1977), 95 pp., $2.95.

James F. Coppedge, *Evolution: Possible or Impossible?* (Grand Rapids, Mich.: Zondervan, 1973), 350 pp., $3.95.

G. Richard Culp, *Remember Thy Creator* (Grand Rapids, Mich.: Baker, 1975), 207 pp. $3.95.

Bolton Davidheiser, *Evolution and Christian Faith* (Nutley, N.J.: Presbyterian and Reformed, 1969), 372 pp., $4.95.

Duane Gish, *Evolution, the Fossils Say NO!* (San Diego: Creation-Life Publishers, 1973), 129 pp., $1.95.

——, *Speculations and Experiments Related to Theories on the Origin of Life* (San Diego: Creation-Life Publishers, 1972), 41 pp., $3.50.

Gertrude Himmelfarb, *Darwin and the Darwinian Revolution* (New York: W. W. Norton, 1968), 510 pp., $2.95.

John W. Klotz, *Genes, Genesis, and Evolution* (St. Louis: Concordia, 1970), 540 pp. $5.95.

Walter E. Lammerts, editor, *Scientific Studies in Special Creation* (Nutley, N.J.: Presbyterian and Reformed, 1970), 343 pp., $6.95.

Norman Macbeth, *Darwin Retried* (Boston: Gambit, 1971), 178 pp., $6.95 hardcover, $2.95 paper.

Frank L. Marsh, *Variation and Fixity in Nature* (Mountain View, Calif.: Pacific Press, 1976).

John N. Moore, *Questions and Answers on Creation/Evolution* (Grand Rapids, Mich.: Baker, 1976), 110 pp., $2.95.

Henry M. Morris, *Scientific Creationism* (San Diego: Creation-Life Publishers, 1974), 217 pp., $3.95.

John G. Read with Dr. C. L. Burdick, *Fossils, Strata, and Evolution* (Culver City, Calif.: Scientific-Technical Presentations), 63 pp., $1.95.

Evan Shute, *Flaws in the Theory of Evolution* (Nutley, N.J.: Presbyterian and Reformed, 1969), 286 pp., $3.50.

Harold S. Slusher, *Age of the Cosmos* (San Diego: Institute for Creation Research, 1980), 76 pp.

Paul M. Stedl, *The Earth, the Stars, and the Bible* (Grand Rapids, Mich.: Baker, 1979), 250 pp., $5.95.

John Whitcomb and Henry Morris, *The Genesis Flood* (Nutley, N.J.: Presbyterian and Reformed, 1961), 518 pp., $7.95.

A. W. Wilder-Smith, *The Natural Sciences Know Nothing of Evolution* (San Diego: Master Books, CLP, 1981), $5.95.

R. L. Wysong, *The Creation-Evolution Controversy* (East Lansing, Mich.: Inquiry Press, 1975), 450 pp., $15.00 hardcover, $7.95 kivar.

Repossess the Land, collected convention papers, 15th anniversary convention (Minneapolis: Bible-Science Association, 1979), 224 pp., $7.50.

Periodicals

Acts and Facts, Institute for Creation Research, 2100 Greenfield Drive, El Cajon, CA 92021.

Bible-Science Newsletter, Bible-Science Association, 2911 E. 42nd Street, Minneapolis, MN 55406.

Creation Research Society Quarterly, 2717 Cranbrook Road, Ann Arbor, MI 48104.

Creation-Science Report, Creation-Science Research Center, P.O. Box 23195, San Diego, CA 92123.

Creation Social Science—Humanities Quarterly, 1429 N. Holyoke, Wichita, KS 67208.

Origins, Geoscience Research Institute, Loma Linda, CA.

Students for Origins Research, P.O. Box 203, Santa Barbara, CA 93116-0203.

Cassettes, Slides, Filmstrips, and Films

The Creation Concern, Inc., 9445 SW 62nd Drive, Portland, OR 97219.

Creation Filmstrip Center, Inc., R. 1, Haviland, KS 67509.

Creation Life Publishers, P.O. Box 15666, San Diego, CA 92115.

Films for Christ Association, North Eden Road, Elmwood, IL 61529.

Scientific-Technical Presentations, John Read, P.O. Box 2384, Culver City, CA 90230.

T-Q Productions, Box 5115, Eugene, OR 97405.

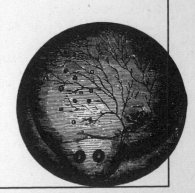

PART IX

SOCIAL STUDIES

CHAPTER THIRTY-FIVE

BIBLE

Why include a Bible chapter in the Social Studies section? Because social studies covers the range of social relationships, and there's nothing more sociable than getting in touch with God, and no relationship more highly to be prized. Those who don't agree need not bother with this chapter, although even nonbelievers stand to gain by a study of the book that, more than any other, has influenced Western arts and sciences.

Believers, too, need help with their Bible studies. Just as the public schools are producing illiterates, because they spend too much time preaching humanism and too little teaching facts and skills, our Sunday schools are producing religious illiterates. Christian children today do not know the Bible as they should. Even after years of Bible college and seminary, too many believers are abysmally ignorant of Bible facts and doctrine.

When my husband Bill and I entered seminary, we both had to take a Bible Knowledge test. I was apprehensive about how well I would do, since I had just recently become a Christian and before that had scarcely ever opened the Bible until I began studying it a year earlier. Most of the other seminary freshmen were Bible college graduates or had been brought up with years of Sunday school training. Picture my astonishment when I was told that I had done better than 80 percent of my fellow test-takers! They should have left me in the dust after all that training. But the sad fact is that they had really had *no* training. Their teachers had spent years *preaching* to them instead of *teaching* them. Consequently, the seminary found it necessary to introduce remedial Bible courses for students who had spent literally thousands of hours in Bible classes already!

I fervently hope and pray that this situation will change, and that the current rage for sermonizing instead of instructing will fade. In the meantime, if you want your children to be exceptions to the mediocre norm, or if you can see that you yourself have suffered from lack of instruction, you will have to take matters into your own hands.

THE BASICS OF BIBLE STUDY

I shouldn't really have to mention this. But since so much stress is put nowadays on "Bible memory" and "daily devotionals," many of us have fallen into the habit of going over the same chapters and verses over and over again and neglecting the rest of Scripture. For anyone, child or adult, to become thoroughly familiar with the Bible, he or she must consistently *hear it read*.

First of all, just hearing the words sets up your brain with the raw data. Secondly, and this is an important point that has been ignored for years, *the Bible itself stresses the act of hearing God's Word*. See, for example, 1 Timothy 4:13, Deuteronomy 5:1, Psalm 95:7, and all the hundreds of other passages that command people to *hear* the word of the Lord. With all our modern emphasis on "daily Bible reading" we have completely overlooked the fact that *hearing*, not *seeing*, is the Bible's recommended way for storing up God's Word in our hearts. I haven't studied this in depth, but I will hazard a guess that we memorize words better through our ears than through our eyes. Consider how hard it is *not* to memorize TV ads, even though the text of the ads is not printed on the screen.

Father can easily reestablish the honored custom of reading the Bible at meals or other convenient times. And it is even easier to pop one of the numerous Bible cassettes now available into the cassette player. By hearing God's Word over and over, you'll store up a lot of stories and phrases without really trying.

Once family worship is established, with the Bible being read aloud, it takes the pressure off to spend a prescribed number of minutes a day casting your eyes over the pages. We can *listen* while we work or eat dinner; this is not true of reading.

After you and your children have become familiar with the Scriptures in this way, it becomes appropriate to start studying them more academically. Time lines, Bible book studies, character studies, and theme studies all have their place, as does the study of archaeology, ancient culture, and the original languages. This is the time to memorize the Catechism, if you belong to a confessional church, and to memorize the Ten Commandments and the Lord's Prayer.

These more intensive studies can be livened up through the use of visuals and other props. For little kids, acting out Bible stories with puppets is fun. Older children may want to put on a minidrama of their own, tramping solemnly seven times around "Jericho" (a block city, perhaps) which obligingly falls down after they sound their trumpets. A good set of felts or other visuals enhances the Bible lesson for everybody. And novel ideals like chalk talks and object lessons liven up the family study.

Individual Bible reading, as time permits, is very helpful, particularly for those who are not yet well acquainted with the Bible. As soon as our sons learned to read, we bought each of them their very own *large-print* Bible. Children don't mind using such a large book. It makes them feel important! And unlike the so-called children's versions with their tiny print, a large-print version will not make reading an effort or ruin their eyes.

Those interested in making the Lord's Day a delight will be happy to find the many kid-pleasing Sunday toys and books listed in this section. For Sunday to be holy it must be *special,* and that means special things for your children to do that they will enjoy and that focus their thinking on God. It's made a great difference to our family to find these things, and it will to yours.

A WORD TO THE WISE

The Romans had a saying: *Caveat emptor,* or "let the buyer beware." Today we need to be doubly cautious when using Bible study aids, because some folk, in a desire to "prettify" the gospel, have painted over the Cross. The great Christian and Missionary Alliance preacher A. W. Tozer aptly called this adulterated message the "need-meeter gospel." God is pictured as a helpless grandfather, wringing his hands over His wayward grandkids and bribing us to come back to Him. Jesus is not portrayed as Lord but as our slave. He exists, in this view, for only one reason: to

meet our needs. No room here for talk of hell or judgment, or even of repentance. The only reason to get "saved" is to get something in the here-and-now: more money, better health, a happy life, or some other carnal goal. The Christian life becomes the pursuit of happiness rather than the pursuit of holiness. Sin (if it is even mentioned at all) becomes an impediment to total self-actualization rather than an objective offense against a justly angered God.

The world rightly disdains this wimpy message, and Christians should disdain it too. Unhappily, almost every major provider of Christian products has succumbed to it to some degree. My solution to this problem has been to ignore the iffy parts of the teaching dialogs and so forth that accompany these products, and to just use the visuals and strictly factual portions.

For an excellent discussion of this whole issue, see Walter Chantry's little book *Today's Gospel: Authentic or Synthetic?* Puritan-Reformed has it for under $3. A. W. Tozer's writings are also very lucid on this point. P-R has those too.

BIBLE TEACHING AND LEARNING HELPS

Alpha Omega Publications
Bible LIFEPAC's, $1.95 each, ten per grade. Bible teacher handbooks, $3.95 per grade. *Bible-Based Math,* $2.95 each, two per grade. *B-B M Teacher Handbooks,* $3.95.

AOP's Bible course for grades 1 to 12 contains seven major strands: Christian Growth, Theology Themes, Attributes of God, Christian Evidence, Bible Literature, Bible Geography and Archaeology, and Special Themes. In grade 6 AOP has a preliminary Bible Survey, which is followed up in grade 9 by a New Testament Survey and in grade 10 by an Old Testament Survey.

The book studies are quite good. As a whole, I do not think the "seven-strand" approach is the best, since it doesn't stick with a subject long enough to build a really good framework.

In the early grades, the Bible course is integrated with language arts instruction, which means you get word exercises, phonics drills, and so forth.

On the positive side, you can hardly find a more inexpensive set of Bible worktexts. The upper-grades material is of a calibre worthy of adults, and new Christians might want to consider using it as some of their first study material. All AOP's products encourage thought—there is little rote fill-in-the-blanks.

AOP also has a brand-new math enrichment program, *Bible-Based Mathematics.* This series not only provides valuable practice for the math concepts at each level for grades 2 to 7, but directs the student to worship God as the Creator of our regular, mathematical universe and to use math to obey Him. This is not as strained as it sounds—honesty in business revolves around honest weights, measures, and prices, for example. The *Bible-Based Math* series costs more than other *LIFEPAC's* because it is two-color and the worktexts are thicker. AOP suggests that it could be used at home devotionally, as well as for math enrichment.

Baker Book House

Baker, a major Christian publisher, now has a nice large newsprint catalog brimful of helpful stuff for Christians of all ages. The back page of the fall '85 catalog consisted entirely of Christian Activity Products, meaning neat Sunday stuff for little kids. Coloring books! Stick-a-Story books! Color 'n Rub Bible verses! Sticker fun! Prestofun! And more! Plus the catalog itself has Bibles (all versions, including large-print), Bible story books, Bible study aids, children's books, and lots more.

Baker distributes books from other publishers, as well as their own line. Let me give you an example of just one of Baker's own books for kids. *101 Bible Activity Sheets* is a good way to reinforce Scripture learning. Reproducible pages feature dot-to-dot, cut and paste, mazes, crosswords, puzzles, etc. Every kid in the family can find something to do, unlike other activity books designed for a narrow range of ages. Walter Kerr's illustrations are charmingly innocent.

BCM Publications (a ministry of BCM International, formerly Bible Club Movement)

Relevant, Bible-centered lesson materials for all ages (including visuals); special songs, fact books, missionary stories and songs. Supplementary catalog of flannel backgrounds, Bible club supplies, cassette tapes, booklets, and other helps. Visuals are mostly acceptable quality colored pictures on flocked paper—you cut them out. Stick-on Storiboard is used for littlest kids.

Several programs are available. *Footsteps to God* and *Footsteps of Faith* combine to make a complete three-year sequential Bible curriculum for Sunday school, usable for family worship or Sunday study. *Tiny Steps of Faith* for preschoolers has four volumes. For $12.95 you get teaching visuals (plastic figures, teaching pictures, and paper bag puppets) and a teacher's guidebook, a color and action book kit sample, and a Bible Word Card sample. From twelve to sixteen lessons a volume. One dollar a week is not too much to spend, now is it? *Steps of Faith for Special Children, Steps to Higher Ground* (for teens and adults), and *Steps to Maturity* (for teens and college) are also available at similar prices.

Spanish and French Bible lessons are also available.

BCM has the cheapest flannelboard: $10.95 for a 27 x 36″. Compare this to commercial prices of $32.99 and up!

Plus Five-Day Bible Club programs, missionary lessons, etc.

Search magazine for kids is $3 a school year (ten issues) and includes a Bible contest with prizes, action stories, a puzzle page, fun food recipes, and subscriber feedback. The few pages are nicely done, and considering the price it's worth it.

BCM has been around for years and years.

Beacon Enterprises Inc.

Bible program alone: Parent's Materials $51.15, Student's Materials $9.50. Virtually all materials reusable for next child.

If you're looking for a beginning-to-read program that gets new readers into the *King James Version* Gospel of John, Beacon Enterprises has the stuff. Beacon's Self-Pronouncing Alphabet notation is coupled with a nondenominational, complete year's daily Bible program. I kind of like the looks of it—it's easy to use and thorough. Doctrine is taught concept by concept instead of chronologically or randomly, straight out of the Bible instead of from storybooks or other teaching aids. You don't have to use the S.P.A. reading program to get the Bible program, but the regular reading program includes both.

For more info, see Beacon's review in the Home Reading Programs chapter.

Bible Games, Inc.

Family Edition, $19.99 in stores, $24.99 postpaid from the publishers. Youth Edition is less.

Bible Challenge is the best Bible board game I've seen. The concept is simple and effective; the game is elegant. Each player tries to collect seven different-colored rings, each representing a different question category, while moving around a board whose squares represent books of the Bible. The game includes twenty-one hundred well-chosen questions on three hundred cards and is expandable with the purchase of additional packets.

All members of the family can play the Family Edition. Our small fry can answer some of the questions, but even Bill gets stumped occasionally—so adults won't necessarily always win.

You can register your game and thus replace any lost or broken pieces. It comes in a beautiful, durable box that can be stored like a book on a shelf. Everything about this game is professional and high quality. It's the nicest way I've seen of testing our children on their Bible knowledge, and giving them the incentive to gain more.

Bible Lovers Correspondence School

Diploma Courses, $10 each.

Alan Heffren's father, a prolific preacher and writer, founded Bible Lovers Correspondence School, and his son carries on the work. BLCS has a wide variety of books, booklets, and tracts, very reasonably priced, mainly dealing with basic doctrines from an evangelical Baptist perspective and prophecy from a amillennial viewpoint. BLCS also offers three diploma courses: *The Sign of His Coming, Things Which Become Sound Doctrine,* and *The Mission of the Messiah.* The nominal price for these correspondence courses includes course text, question booklet, correcting the quizzes, and the diploma which signifies you have completed the course.

Bible Visuals, Inc.
Visualized Bible volumes, $4.95 each. Available for less in sets. Twenty-three volumes for Old Testament so far, forty-six for New Testament. *Mini-Visualized Bible* volumes, 50¢ each. Twenty-nine Old Testament titles, twelve New Testament.

Bible Visuals celebrated its twenty-fifth anniversary in 1985. BV is yet another supplier of children's church and child evangelism materials. For the home, BV's *Visualized Bible* series is one of the simplest to use. Each volume is a large 14 x 10" book with teaching hints on the inside covers and lesson plans in the middle. Each book contains four lessons. The rest of the book is given over to sixteen large illustrations of the lessons. No flocked paper to cut out, no gimmicks. I have not seen the whole series, but the art in the one sample volume I did see was just right—not too much detail, but not oversimplified either. And what a relief to see drawings of Jesus that makes him look *Jewish* and *strong* instead of Aryan and weak!

Bible Visuals also carries visualized missionary stories, visualized songs, mini-Bible stories, five- and ten-day packets, and Spanish materials, plus other supporting items. The minibooks are exceedingly inexpensive and contain the same illustrations as the large volumes, but without lesson text.

Bible Visuals takes care to assure us that they teach "*Bible* doctrine (not *church* doctrine)." I can't vouch 100 percent for their Biblicalness, not having seen every volume, but the one volume I saw was remarkably free of flights of fancy and irrelevant sermonizing.

Bob Jones University Press
Student worktexts: K4 children's packet, $9.25; K5 and grades 1, 5, and 6, $5.25 each; grades 2-4 $4.35 each. Teacher's Edition, $27.50 each grade. Cassettes, storybooks, and so on are extra.

We are absolutely delighted with the Bob Jones University Press Bible Truths series. The first two grades provide a chronological overview of the entire Bible. These books impart some solid knowledge along with the salvation emphasis, covering the Children's Cathechism along with the Bible and emphasizing simple "Bible Action Truths." Both K and 1 include enjoyable memory and handwork activities. Grades 2 through 4 systematically study the fundamental doctrines of the Christian faith. Grade 5 is a New Testament survey, while grade 6 surveys the Old Testament.

Like all other Bob Jones products, the art, layout, and general quality of these books is impeccable. The content is clean, clear, educationally excellent, and contains nothing "iffy." Eschatology is handled separately from other subjects, making it possible for families with diverse eschatological views to use these books.

The expensive Teacher's Editions are not essential for a home program. Without the teacher's edition, the program price is quite reasonable.

The series was designed for use in daily Christian schools, making it deeper than Sunday school-style materials.

Century Gospel Film Library
Free catalog of Christian films.

Child Evangelism Fellowship
Teach Me Now, four volumes, $19.95 each.

Good things come in twos! We can be glad that both BCM (see above) and Child Evangelism Fellowship exist, since between them they offer a tremendous array of Bible lessons and Christian teaching helps both for your own family and for child evangelism.

CEF's visuals are mostly colored, flocked pictures that you cut out, and large flash cards (usually spirally bound into a book with the teaching text). All art is of acceptable, professional quality. Their selection is larger than BCM's, and more individual units are included (BCM materials are mostly in course form).

Of special interest: *Teach Me Now* preschool lessons come with musical cassette, songbook, games, finger plays, visuals—both flocked and unflocked—and complete instructions. Personally, I would only use the instructions as suggestions. The series comes in four volumes. If you can only get one, make it Volume 1, as this presents God as Creator, tells about the Fall, introduces Jesus, and presents the gospel.

Biblegrams and *Missiongrams* each contain five or six lessons on their respective subjects. Prices are in the $4 to $9 range. *Growgrams* are single lessons with activities on Christian growth. *A Look At God's Book* introduces kids to the Bible; $9.29 including flocked visuals. *Salvation Songs* is four volumes of the best; $1.79 each. Plus filmstrips ($13.99 each), visualized Bible verses, and more!

For all these flannelboard materials you're going to need an easel, and CEF has the cheapest easel around: $12.00 for a good quality folding wooden easel (three folding legs and tray, 64" high, hardwood). We use it all the time and are well satisfied. Like BCM, CEF's flannelboard is 27 x 36", of masonite construction, and folds; however, CEF's has handles as well, for $18.79. For home you may prefer CEF's tabletop easel—only $6.75.

CEF's visuals and true stories are excellent, but the fictional characters in their "application" stories are shallow and the dialog is often unrealistic. The CEF stories I've seen avoided all mention of hell.

CEF missionaries give seminars and workshops on how to evangelize and disciple children. We attended one of those in our area and found it to be an excellent presentation. Some of these are available on video. Each five-part video course is $95.

Christian Book Distributors

Personally, I prefer Puritan-Reformed. However, if you're looking for Arminian or neoorthodox or liberal works, CBD carries them whereas P-R won't. Discounts of 20 to 90 pecent on over three thousand titles, from fifty publishers, including major sets necessary for the library of every serious Bible student. Also Christian records and cassettes. Inventory tends to be "heavy stuff"—few children's books. Membership is $3 a year.

Cornerstone Ministries

Vast selection of Christian films and filmstrips, on subjects ranging from cults and the occult to family living to Bible study to personal and church growth. Cornerstone has lots of films and videos on teen problems, some more edifying than others—also Bible study films and children's material. Most major producers are carried. Cornerstone rents or sells. Make your own movie and see if they'll distribute it!

Derek Prince Ministries

Home Bible courses from a charismatic, premill perspective.

Family Life Institute

Single orders $7.95 per record or cassette. Club price $5.95 per recording, $1 shipping and handling. Sample cassette $1.

The Bible in Living Sound is the name of a series of four hundred and fifty fully dramatized and orchestrated Bible stories on record or cassette. The early Genesis accounts had a Seventh-Day Adventist flavor. When I inquired I was told that the series was a collaboration of writers from many denominations. I didn't notice any sectarian emphasis in the later recordings. All recordings are very well done, with professional actors and appropriate sound effects and music. When possible, the actors quote the *King James Version.*

The series is entertaining and indulges somewhat in creative imagination. Example: Izhar and his family are crossing the Red Sea during the Exodus. Izhar scolds his son for almost driving their donkey into the wall of water, and asks him why he did that. Reply: "I saw a fish in the water, and I was trying to catch it." Parental response: "You'll catch it from me if you don't do as you're told!"

Unlike other series, *The Bible in Living Sound* can be purchased through a monthly club. Membership in the monthly story club is free and may be canceled at any time. Club members each month get a $3.50 record (or two) or a $7 cassette (equivalent to two records). The total set is $262.50. Accompanying workbooks, cassette binders, and a record carry case are also available.

Global Visuals

Visualized Christian materials, $2.75-$7.75 each.

Cute little visualized stories and visualized songs. Some are illustrations of Bible verses, others are doctrinal lessons in fictional story form. Get a feel for Global's offerings from these catalog descriptions, chosen at random from among hundreds:

> SG107-PRIZE CAKE
> Forgiving was hard for Ruby, especially since Warren had cut the cake she had ready to enter in the baking contest!

> SG108-WHICH ONE ARE YOU?
> The proud peacock, strutting giraffe, and lowly camel help us learn a lesson in humbling ourselves.

Global's artwork is professional and the storyline sounds like it has kid appeal in a corny, innocent sort of way.

Good Things Company

Cassette tapes with booklet, $12.50. Paper chart, $14.50. Laminated chart, $19.50.

What do you do if you're a Sunday school teacher who has carefully put together the genealogy of every major character in the Bible, plus quite a few minor ones? With fear and trembling and a lot of prayer you work it up into a beautiful four-color wall chart, which to your surprise becomes a hit and sells thousands of copies!

The *Adam and Eve Family Tree* is a veritable hobbit's delight, showing who was related to whom and what they were up to for all of the Bible history until Christ, plus giving selected Scripture references for further study. Talk about genealogical research! The chart is accurate and easy to use, and will provide hours of educational browsing for any Bible lover. (We all hope our kids will be Bible-lovers, don't we?) And it's so handy to have a *laminated* chart which the little folks can't shred before they're old enough to appreciate it!

The chart comes in both laminated and plain paper styles, both colorful and very beautiful. You can also get a tape and booklet that explains how to use it.

Home Life

Tired of "Christian" fluff? Want books that apply the Bible to today and show you how to make a difference? Home Life has 'em! Responding to the frustrations of those who would have liked, for instance, to buy the books Franky Schaeffer put on the *Christian Activist's* "MUST" list, Home Life decided to bring all these books, and others like them, together in one place. These include titles like Samuel Blumenfeld's books, *NEA: Trojan Horse* and *Is Public Education Necessary?*, Richard Mitchell's *The Graves of Academe,* and Jacqueline Kasun's *The War Against Population,* reviewed elsewhere in this book. The list also includes all the Schaeffers' activist books, an abridged version of the *Gulag Archipelago,* Bryan Griffin's devastatingly funny *Panic Among the Philistines,* and other titles recommended in the *Activist.* Some of the titles are by professing Christians, some are not, but all open up areas for Christian thought. Home Life also carries a Christian Discovery line, books like *The Danger of Self Love* by Robert Brownback, *Today's Gospel: Authentic or Synthetic?* by Walter Chantry, *Productive Christians in an Age of Guilt Manipulators* by David Chilton, *Bringing in the Sheaves* by George Grant (the best book ever written on how your church can start a mercy ministry—it could replace Welfare!), and even *The Book of Psalms for Singing.* All books are from major publishers and competitively priced.

Implanted Word

Have you ever heard of "rebuses"? A rebus is a picture symbol that represents a word. Implanted Word has a program of Scripture memory for very young children, using rebuses and songs. Printed on heavy card stock, each verse has a page to itself. The verse is visualized with rebuses, and also printed with a few helpful comments. Flip the page on the wire spiral binding to go on to the next verse. The oversized book is designed to stand by itself and is suitable for teaching small groups as well as for use in the home.

The accompanying cassette has each verse in song form. Usually the words are repeated in several musical lines. Verses come from a variety of Bible translations: NIV, KJV, NASB.

"For ages birth to 8," the brochure says. Really, any child old enough to focus his eyes could begin to use this program.

Janzen Specialties

Unlike BCM, Child Evangelism Fellowship doesn't produce their own flannel backgrounds for Bible stories. The Janzens sell Smith Backgrounds, which are uncolored, functional backgrounds mainly used by CEF people. Colored backgrounds are available, if requested in advance. Art is usable but not scintillating; similar in quality to BCM backgrounds. Inexpensive.

Janzen also now carries "Edith Mackay" Tabernacle Backgrounds.

LIFEWAY

Bible curriculum K-8, and junior high literature electives. Teacher supplements, teaching aids, flannelgraphs, story cassettes, children's books, reference materials. LIFEWAY has a new preschool course. Write for details.

Life for Little Learners

Instant Bible, $12.95. *Bible Memory Cards,* $5.95. *Prophecy Chart,* $2. *Books of Bible Visual,* $2. Shipping extra.

Life for Little Learners carries supplementary teaching aids for home education. In the Bible category, LLL has a collection of creative memory aids. The *Instant Bible* is a combination map/puzzle with accompanying book. It covers the history of redemption in a graphic way, with Bible verses included. LLL's *Bible Memory Cards* are 8½ x 11″ and bound with a plastic spiral. Designed for use with nonreading young children, the cards have KJV verses interspersed with rebuses and come forty-eight to a set, coded in six categories. LLL's *Prophecy Chart* also looks like a value for the money. It's colorful. It's a Bible overview. It's 12 x 36″. It's printed on a durable Tyvek paper. And, not last of all LLL's wares, but the last I have space to mention, the *Books of the Bible Visual* is a poster-size memory device for teaching the names of all sixty-six Bible books.

Living Scriptures

Dramatized New Testament, $286.20. *Dramatized Old Testament,* $286.20.

Living Scriptures has produced a dramatized Bible using a large professional cast and expert sound effects. The stories on the sample tape were Scriptural and quite well done. In fact, they were better done than other dramatized presentations I have heard.

The series as a whole employs imagination to make the stories more like playlets. This venture into the realm of what-might-have-been introduces extra-Scriptural elements, but is done with restraint.

It seems that you must buy the entire set, not separate tapes, and according to the buyers' agreement, you have to pay the entire price even if you decide you don't want the rest of your tapes after all. Tapes are sent at the rate of two per month, and you get a binder for every twelve tapes.

Betty Lukens

Let me rave for a bit about the most gorgeous set of Bible-teaching visuals I have ever seen. Not flocked pictures, but actual air-brushed felt! *Through the Bible in Felt* comes in two sizes: the expensive large size (12″ figures) and the affordable regular size (6½″ figures). Background scenes of the same superb quality are also available. A teacher's manual to help you present the Bible in a three-year sequence (once a week) is also included. The manual could be more helpful; it merely shows two felt scenes, lists the items needed, gives the Scripture, and leaves you to figure out how to tell it.

Although some of the later history of Israel and Judah is not covered in the manual, there are more than enough figures to tell any story you choose.

The regular set is about $55, and if you order all the backgrounds and the indispensable storage case (which organizes the whole kit and caboodle onto outlined velour sheets) you'll spend just under $100. That sounds like a lot, but what you're getting is a lifetime investment in Bible teaching that you can use even with the smallest children in your family, and perhaps pass on to your grandchildren. The price is really low for all you are getting—because *you* are going to cut the figures out! I look upon this as a fun family project, and it has been for us, with even our five-year-old cutting out some "easy" pieces.

Sycamore Tree sells all the Betty Lukens sets. You can get a free color brochure describing the flannels from them. Then if you can resist them, I'll be surprised!

Message of Life Publications

"Krata-Kraft" Bible lessons are printed in bright colors on durable stock, either in book form or on ovals and circles for use on flannelgraph boards. Some have pictures that pop off for an element of surprise. Pictures are prepunched, but you have to peel off and adhere felt circles to the backs (these come with the package). Simple and straightforward, not tedious or "talky." Gospel emphasis throughout.

Thirty English Bible lessons, twenty-eight Spanish lessons. Also in Spanish only: twelve five-day DVBS courses (songs, maps, workbooks, etc.). Plus seven fifteen-week illustrated Bible studies with workbooks and take-home papers.

These are the most economical visual lessons around, costing around $2 or less each.

The good folks at Message of Life offers a 25 percent discount for Christian schools (including home schools) when you prepay and tell them you're a school.

Moody Correspondence School

Adult credit courses are also suitable for intelligent Christian kids: $10.45 each. Many subjects covered pertaining to the Bible and the Christian life. Dispensational emphasis.

You can earn a certificate for completing each series and with perseverance even earn an Adult Bible Certificate. An A. A. in Bible studies is also available to those who take Moody's college correspondence courses ($45/semester hour plus $45 for materials/course). V.A. will pay for some college credit courses. Final exam must be proctored.

NavPress

"Discipleship!" is the war cry of this follow-up organization. Founded by a man who saw the need for instructing new converts, the Navigators' main stress has been on teaching neophytes how to study the Bible, how to pray, and how to witness. They also carry quite a large line of inductive Bible study materials, which lead the student to answer the question, "What does it mean to me?" This material is open-ended and discovery-oriented.

I am not thoroughly impressed with the Navigators' Bible memory programs, which consist of memorizing verses relating to a theme. This method bypasses the verses' context completely, and also very quickly loads up your short-term memory, forcing you to continually review, review, review. Much more worthwhile, in my estimation, is the practice of constantly rereading and rehearing the same books until whole sections become almost involuntarily embedded in your memory.

NavPress items are available in any Christian bookstore.

Puritan-Reformed Discount Book Service

Puritan-Reformed changed my life. Bill and I were new Christians, unsteady on our feet, and unable to find a bookstore that had anything but frothy testimonies and Christian cookbooks. (There are many fine Christian bookstores, but we were living in a spiritually deprived neighborhood.) Enter P-R. All of a sudden we had a selection of thousands of the finest Christian books, both classic and modern, at greatly discounted prices. We joined, we read, we learned.

P-R also has a wide selection of Christian music on LP's and cassettes. More, they also have hundreds of children's books. This is the book service to join if you buy any of the above on a regular basis. Membership is $5 a year, and if you're canny and wait until the special offers for membership extension roll around, you can upgrade to a life membership for less than $50.

Superfast delivery, toll-free ordering, and prices that can't be beat.

Reformed Presbyterian Board of Publications
Book of Psalms for Singing: Looseleaf edition $12.95. Hardbound $10.95. Bulk prices, cassettes available. Order from Home Life.

You've just got to get this hymnal if you care at all about reviving godly worship in your home. The Bible says we should sing "psalms, hymns, and spiritual songs" (Col. 3:16). Unhappily, so much time has been spent justifying the use of hymns *in addition to* psalms that nowadays most churches sing hymns *instead of* psalms! The few psalms in the modern hymnbook by no means reflect the Psalms' actual richness. What are we missing? Psalms for times of despair. Psalms for the repentant sinner. Psalms that promise victory in the battle with God's enemies. Psalms about the Messiah. Psalms on every topic of the *real* spiritual life, not the trimmed-down, always-grinning version.

Although the Reformed Presbyterian Church, which publishes this book, believes in singing unaccompanied by instruments, they have besides the lovely gold-stamped original Psalter a looseleaf edition which can be propped on the piano while you puzzle out the tunes. Many of the tunes are familiar to hymn-singers, and most of those that aren't are easy to learn. For the convenience of those who don't know how to read music, the RP Board of Publications also offers cassettes of some of the most popular psalms.

What difference does singing psalms make? They give you courage. They prepare you for real life. No heresy here; no questionable verses; no mindless choruses. Just God's word to man.

Roper Press

If you're looking for a book-by-book Bible study with courses for all ages, Roper Press's *Through the Bible* looks like one of your best bets. Unlike other courses that start over in Genesis again and again and never get you out of the wilderness, Roper Press goes through the whole Bible several times. For home school families this format is ideal, since all ages from eight years old and up can study the same books on different ability levels.

You get student workbooks and a teacher's manual for each course. The Bible is your textbook. Ue the manual with discretion, as although the stories and teaching hints are generally sound you may want to adapt some of them.

Little children get pictures to color, cut, and paste and other kiddie activities. Older ones move into inductive Bible study.

As a plus, this series can be very easily coordinated with the fabulous Betty Lukens Through the Bible felts, which Roper Press also sells.

If you want to taste before buying, Roper Press has an Administrative Kit with samples of the materials at different grade levels and a cassette that explains the program. A home school group or church could easily obtain one and pass it around to those interested. It's $15.95 and returnable for a full refund.

Sentinel Teachers Supply

"Christian Books and Supplies" catalog features teacher training, Bibles, gifts and awards, visuals, creative activities, etc. The Bibles, Books, Literature Supplies catalog has an overwhelming mass of different Bible studies for children and adults. Plus fun stuff for children, songbooks, tapes, filmstrips, records, Bible correspondence courses, and novelties. Nondenominational.

The Sycamore Tree

Some of the best products listed in this category, plus many more, are carried in the Sycamore Tree catalog. Bill and Sandy Gogel's reviews make armchair shopping easy. Get Betty Lukens's felts, Standard's paper models, Bible readers, activity books, and more here. Some Adventist materials.

Standard Publishing

This catalog is a "must" for anyone interested in low-cost, high-interest Bible visuals and activities for children.

Standard's Bible visuals come in large and regular sizes and economy packs. Large size *Pict-O-Graphs* have eight to eleven stories, and forty or more precut figures (just punch out to use) up to 11″ tall. Artwork is superior and colorful. More than fifty Bible stories are covered in these packs. The only drawback is that there aren't more of them! Also available are patterns for making large-size background objects, supplementary objects (altars, wineskins, etc.). Standard also has many how-to books for teachers.

Standard's Visual Talks series includes many object talks centering around such items as a football, salt, a telephone, and other common household items. They're ridiculously inexpensive.

Standard also has puppet packs; quiz books; game books; Bible study charts (fantastic for kid's room); maps and charts; craft ideas; seals and stickers (some with a Christian message); complete Bible activity programs; classroom Bible activity books; teacher training resources; songbooks; and much more!

We have used a number of Standard products, and are well-pleased with the quality. You get more for your money here than anywhere else.

CHAPTER THIRTY-SIX

CHARACTER EDUCATION

He knew which was the right tree at once, partly because it stood in the very centre and partly because the great silver apples with which it was loaded shone so and cast a light of their own down on the shadowy places where the sunlight did not reach. He walked straight across to it, picked an apple, and put it in the breast pocket of his Norfolk Jacket. But he couldn't help looking at it and smelling it before he put it away.

It would have been better if he had not. A terrible thirst and hunger came over him and a longing to taste that fruit. He put it hastily into his pocket; but there were plenty of others. Could it be wrong to taste one? . . .

While he was thinking of all this he happened to look up through the branches towards the top of the tree. There, on a branch above his head, a wonderful bird was roosting. I say "roosting" because it seemed almost asleep: perhaps not quite. The tiniest slit of one eye was open. . . .

"And it just shows," said Digory afterwards when he was telling the story to the others, "that you can't be too careful in these magical places. You never know what may be watching you." But I think Digory would not have taken an apple for himself in any case. Things like Do Not Steal were, I think, hammered into boys' heads a good deal harder in those days than they are now. (From *The Magician's Nephew* by C. S. Lewis, one of the *Chronicles of Narnia*, published by Collier/ Macmillan)

I think most of us agree that C. S. Lewis was right. Do not steal and the rest of the Ten Commandments *were* "hammered into boys' heads a good deal harder" a few generations ago. Assuming that we still cherish these values, which most of us do, the question is, "How can we pass on these values today?"

The Bible's answer is that we should tell our children the Ten Commandments as we "sit at home" and as we "walk along the road," when we lie down and when we get up (Deuteronomy 6:7). Our environment should be permeated with written reminders of the Commandments as well (Deuteronomy 6:8, 9).

There was a time in American history when virtually everyone paid at least lip service to the Ten Commandments. It wasn't all that long ago, either. Strangely enough, in those bygone days hardly any children ever committed crimes. As short a time ago as 1950, "in all of America, only 170 persons under the age of 15 were arrested for what the FBI calls serious crimes (such as murders, forcible rapes, robbery, and aggravated assault)."[1] That was .0004 percent of the under-fifteens in the country, or 1 in every 250,000.[2] Since that time, now that the Ten Commandments never appear in classrooms and kids have been trained to do "their own thing," the ugly fruits have emerged. "Between 1950 and 1979 the rate of serious crime committed by children increased 11,000 percent!"[3]

The media roam about saying the Ten Commandments are passé and ought to be ignored, and I roam about saying that in this case the media are passé and ought to be ignored. If we're going to get rid of these rules for living and character standards, which at least *claim* to be divine and I believe *are* so, then what are we going to replace them with? Dr. Spock? The Care Bears? The latest craze along these lines is "character-building books." These are peddled not only as supplements to home character training, but as the character training itself. Supposedly, reading these little sermons will make Junior kind, unselfish, courteous, and get him to pick up his room. One kiss from the Care Bears and the frog turns into a prince! Love cures all ills, and the love doesn't even have to come from a family member—cartoon characters can do it all!

It really is hard to build a sturdy foundation for strong character without any absolutes. Without a "Thus saith the Lord," anything adults want kids to do pretty soon looks like tyranny. So secular "character-builders" concentrate on that great character-builder, self-interest. "If you're generous, Johnny, people will like you. If you study hard, Johnny, you will get good grades. If you work hard, Johnny, you'll make lots of money." The problem with this method is that Johnny is never learning to do what is right *in spite of* adverse circumstances. Johnny is also learning to judge every action by its benefits to *him*. What if he prefers short-term benefits (like a drug high) to long-term benefits (becoming corporate vice-president)? America is covered with young people who live for *now* and *self*. We need more of this?

Since most Americans profess some kind of belief in God, why be embarrassed at passing down His laws *as* laws? Johnny should not steal because God says, "Thou shalt not steal." He should learn to share because Jesus said, "Do unto others as you would have them do unto you." As long as the child understands that his parents are also under God's laws, and are not merely using the Bible to tyrannize him, he will readily accept these rules.

There is, of course, more to character-building than laying down rules. We lack space here to go into the whole question of discipline and how to raise happy, self-disciplined children. I commend to your attention the products in the Parent/Leadership Training chapter, as a number of them provide good answers to these questions.

PRODUCTS TO HELP PARENTS DO THEIR JOB OF CHARACTER-BUILDING

The following list, then, contains materials for values education from a number of religions and denominations, including some materials that are purely secular. I have not bothered to include the Care Bears 'n Rainbow Brite 'n Cabbage Patch school of character education, partly because it is in my estimation academically worthless and partly because you can hardly escape it even if you want to. Nobody needs special instructions on how to order products that line every shop counter and whose main characters star on major cartoon shows. It's hard for me to understand why the preaching of the Care Bears or the Hugga Bunch is more culturally respectable among sophisticated people than that of Jesus Christ—but if that's what anyone out there wants, he knows where to get it.

Advanced Training Institute of America

Bill Gothhard's Advanced Training Institute curriculum, reviewed in the Curriculum Buyers' Guide in the Biggies section, has a character development emphasis.

American Reformation Movement

On Teaching is a sprightly newsletter series written by Dr. David Gamble that develops a Christian philosophy of education. Recommended for thinking parents who want their children to have a truly Christian education, not a baptized secular one.

Bible Games, Inc.

Besides the *Bible Challenge* game, recommended in the Bible section, Bible Games is also coming out with a line of peel-n-stick Bible stories and Bible action figures. You might want to consider these as substitutes to the gruesome or banal fantasy play items that have become so popular.

C. M. G. Productions, Inc.

The Christian Mother Goose, now in three volumes, has ignited quite a controversy in Christian circles. Majorie Decker, the author, thought the original Mother Goose rhymes were substandard in terms of Christian values and contained needless violence. So she paraphrased dozens of them (example: "A dillar, a dollar/ a ten o'clock scholar,/ He's on time for his church school!") and added some longish poems of her own about little animal characters who inhabit a place called Dandelion Sea. No publisher would touch it, so Mrs. Decker published it herself, with illustrations from her own pen and that of a friend. Naturally, she made a mint. Enter the critics, claiming Mother Goose needed no improvement, castigating the illustrations, and knocking the new verses.

Well, CMG still selleth quantities, and now Fleming Revell distributeth it. If you want it, get it from Puritan-Reformed, where they offereth discounts.

"Children's Bible Hour"

For decades CBH has been on the air with Christian stories aimed at the young. Some stories have an evangelistic emphasis; some concern Christian growth; all are interesting, and available on cassettes as well. Some CBH tapes are available for $3 each. Others are $5. These include song albums by the Children's Bible Hour music staff. CBH also has cartooned filmstrip stories ($15 each). The program is aired on over seven hundred stations—check yours.

Cheery Chats, CBH's bimonthly magazine, features poems, a story, a song, and letters from listeners. *Search the Scriptures* is CBH's correspondence course of ten lessons from the New Testament. *Keys For Kids,* their family devotional booklet, is free, but you'll send $1 to pay for it if you're nice folks! *Keys* contains stories and activities for kids, and noncynical types are bound to like it.

CBH, unlike some other Christian groups, isn't afraid to share the *whole* truth—including the reality of hell. All material is of professional quality. Stories are sweet but not sugary. I'd avoid the occasional tale that features Christian kids' misbehavior, because although they always repent, it can be a poor example. Otherwise recommended.

Christian Character Concepts

Fluffy Tail Home Package, $38 postpaid. Sample Packet (one tape and handwork), $8 postpaid.

Dr. Karen Evans and her energetic associates are busy these days! They have produced an introductory Spanish program for young learners and are working on a sequel (see the Languages section) and have also come out with the Fluffy Tail character training series.

Fluffy Tail is a little bunny rabbit. He and his friends eat ice cream, go to preschool, keep fish and cats for pets, and engage in other unbunnylike behavior. Through a series of adventures and misadventures, these thoroughly middle-class bunnies learn various character lessons.

The Fluffy Tail stories are sentimental and appeal to young children. Each story is repeated five times on one side of the tape. On the other side is a Bible story, also repeated five times. Each story has its own catchy song, also quintupally repeated, and a Bible verse, ditto.

The Bible stories are not always the most traditional choices for teaching a particular character trait. For example, the story of Daniel is used to demonstrate responsibility and faithfulness instead of courage. The stories are written so that young children can identify with Bible characters and understand the meaning of different character qualities. The important role of parents in teaching character qualities to their children is seen in both the Fluffy Tail and Bible stories.

An Activity Packet accompanies the series, which contains clever exercises for reinforcing the concepts. Color filmstrips of all the stories are also available.

Constructive Playthings

Holiday puzzles, $16.95 each. Crepe rubber alphabet puzzles, $7.95 for set of two.

Constructive's free catalog of Jewish educational materials is designed to familiarize children with Jewish traditions, holidays, and beginning Hebrew. It includes such things as Hebrew holiday puzzles (Shabbat, Passover, Purim, and Chanukah), magnetic Hebrew letters, two crepe rubber Hebrew alphabet puzzles, Jewish songs, and Israeli games. Chanukah decorations, a free ninety-six-page carnival catalog for your Purim carnival, and more!

Evangelizing Today's Child

Child Evangelism Fellowship puts out this very useful, colorful magazine full of teaching tips for Christian education, including hints just for parents. Included are techniques for

teaching visuals, parents' tips, info on child development, lots of special departments; and one free visual lesson is bound into every issue! Now how can you go wrong when all this is only $12 a year?

Fellowship of Christian Puppeteers

The Puppeteers hold an annual convention, featuring puppetmaking, scripting, drama techniques, and other technical aspects of puppetry.

God's World Publications

Q: What's black and white and read all over?
A: *God's World* weekly newspapers for Christian children.

What an intriguing idea—the news for kids from a Christian viewpoint! GWP has papers for all different reading levels, carefully matched to the interests and abilities of children of that age. Following a newspaper format, you get feature stories, reports on hot news items, editorials, cartoons, and letters-to-the-editor. Each issue also includes an activity for kids. No fuzzy-wuzzy copouts here, either; the editors know what the Bible says and aren't ashamed of it.

Happy Times Magazine

One year (ten issues), $18.95. Two years, $35.00. Free sample issue with trial subscription.

This kid's mag is entirely devoted to character-building. *Happy Times* is colorful and kid-appealing. Each issue has a different theme, such as developing talents, positive self-image, work, integrity, etc. There are games, crafts, activities, stories, and articles on famous people like George Washington Carver and Thomas Edison.

Harvest House Publishers

Christian Charm Course and *Man in Demand:* teacher's manual for each course is $7.95, and the student manual is $4.95. *Bible-Time Nursery Rhyme Book,* $11.95.

Harvest House carries the best-selling *Christian Charm Course* and *Man in Demand Course,* for teenage girls and boys respectively. These provide methods for improving the outer appearance along with spiritual instructions for developing beautiful inner character, and were written by Wayne and Emily Hunter. Harvest House now also distributes Emily's *Bible-Time Nursery Rhyme Book.* The book includes doctrinal and practical rhymes and Bible stories in verse. The illustrations, also by Emily, are pleasant and innocent, and some are in color.

Compared to *The Christian Mother Goose,* the *Bible-Time Nursery Rhyme Book* has superior artwork and far more Scripture content. It's only fair to remember, though, that *CMG* blazed the way.

Jewish Museum Shop

Individual Member, $35. Associate Member, $30—available only to those living outside a hundred-mile radius from New York City. Family Member, $45. Student Member, $20 with copy of ID. Senior Citizen, $25. Lots of expensive memberships for big spenders. Free Museum admission, all members. Mail-order shop.

All sorts of materials "for preserving and perpetuating the Jewish Experience." Sabbath, holiday, and festival supplies. Posters, graphics, and Ketuhabs exhibition catalogs. Jewelry. Mezuzahs. Notecards. Children's gifts. Books, Bible and holiday books for children. Art books. Books on Jewish holidays, philosophy, religion, archaeology—children's sections. Hebrew calligraphy. Dictionaries. Fiction. Holocaust books. All available to the general public—15 percent discount to members.

Konos Character Curriculum

See the Smattering section of the Curriculum Buyers' Guide for a review of this complete one-year academic curriculum that covers all subjects for K to 6 except phonics and math and that stresses Christian character development.

Living Stories
All titles $2.50 or $2.75

Twenty-two colorful, visualized stories designed to present the gospel message. These are not Bible stories, but stories like "Little Red Hen," "Miss Bump," and "Barney's Barrel." Full instructions for teacher. Large, durable books.

Betty Lukens

Betty Lukens, besides her fantastic Through the Bible felts, also has a small series of Christian character-building felts. Order the Betty Lukens felts brochure from Sycamore Tree.

Gospel Mission

This nonprofit ministry of a small Reformed congregation has blossomed into a large wholesale Christian book outlet. Gospel Mission singlehandedly reprinted a number of Christian classics, and has since coprinted a number of others. Their Children's Heritage series of classic Christian tales from the nineteenth century is widely acclaimed, not only for its large print and nice pix, but for the enduring values it contains. Puritan-Reformed carries a lot of the same books; be sure to compare prices.

Maher

It's enthusiasm time again! Anyone who is the slightest bit interested in visual teaching will love Maher's free catalog of ventriloquist dolls, puppets, and visual instruction (balloon, chalk talk, clowning, etc.). For the novice Maher has a home-study ventriloquist course (thirty lessons for $79.95) that is unconditionally guaranteed. Maher's selection also includes dialogues, scripts, cassette tapes, books, and novelties. But best of all is the Christian emphasis in Maher's inventory. It seems that a goodly chunk of the world's practicing "vents" are Christians engaged in it as a ministry, and they've written all sorts of books of gospel dialogues and how-to's for Christian ventriloquism.

Maher also offers deluxe vent figures that they rebuild from commercially produced dolls. These have a lot of features for a base price of less than $190. Add-on features, such as winkers, raising eyebrows, and spitting (some people want that!), cost extra. For young folks, Maher has some animal characters (Eagle, Buzzard, Sheep Dog, . . . and Grumlett!) for $39.95 each, or rebuilt commercial figures for $59.95. Catalog of Knee Pal professional dolls costs $2 (refunded with order); prices of these dolls start at $260.

Maher Workshop

Once you have decided to learn ventriloquism and amaze your friends, it's time to think about investing in a deluxe ventriloquist figure of your very own. Maher Workshop has "the most complete selection anywhere of characters with Personality and Audience Appeal." Chuck Jackson hand-carves his basswood figures and adds a lot of quality touches, which is why the Junior Series starts at $469 and the Standard Professional Series starts at $599. Molded figures for the beginner are available for under $200. Special effects can be added to the "Pro" figures, such as raising eyebrows, winking, and shaking hands. Fifteen-year warranty, 100 percent satisfaction or money back within first two weeks. Recommended by missionaries and pastors. Figures available in all colors, both sexes, and all ages. Catalog, $2.

Fleming Revell Company

Some home school resource lists have mentioned Revell's Christian Character series. The Kit itself is suitable for groups of preschool children and priced accordingly at $125. Of more interest to parents are the two accompanying books (*Bible Adventures* and *Everyday Adventures*) at $8.95 each. Revell also offers a two-volume set for grades K to 3, *A Child's Book of Character-Building,* by Ron and Rebekah Coriell, at $10.95 each.

Sparrow Distributors

Speaking of character-building, Sparrow has a Look, Listen, and Learn book/cassette series featuring the Agapeland characters. Stories and songs are intended to teach topics under each fruit of the Spirit (love, joy, peace . . .). Only $4.98 each, so you might hop down to your Christian bookstore and check them out.

Son Shine Puppet Company

Puppets from $8 to $99. Teaching materials and dialogs, many under $5.

Everything you can imagine having to do with puppets, all designed for use in puppet ministries. Patterns for creating your own muppet-style puppet with a changeable face! Stage plans! Dialogs! How-to books! Prerecorded puppet music and soundtracks! Larger than life-sized costumes! Children's church lesson units! And, of course, lots and lots of puppets.

What does all this have to do with character education? I dunno, but seems to me that making your own puppet would develop *perseverance* and bombing out on your first three performances would build *humility* and not getting mad when your little brother ate the puppet's nose would teach *forgiveness. . . .* And there's always the possibility that some of those puppet stories might teach something useful.

Son Shine conducts puppet training seminars for beginning and advanced puppeteers, as well as teachers interested in learning new techniques and teaching ideas. Contact Randy and Glenda Hoyle at Son Shine for more info.

Word Books

Survival Series, $8.80 for each two books. Twenty-four volumes in all. Books sent on approval.

Since the Survival Series for Kids by Joy Wilt Berry has already sold five million copies, I may not be telling you anything you don't already know. Still, here goes. It's a pile of books that tell kids how to do such things as be kind to guests, get good grades, take care of their clothes, clean their rooms, answer the phone, and so on. The name of each book begins

with "What to Do When Your Mom or Dad Says" and that's what they are all about: what to do, how to do it, and why to do it.

The illustrations are a character education in themselves. Kids doing bad or useless things look bummed out; kids behaving properly look cheerful or downright smug.

The books won't do everything the enormous full-color direct mail ad says they will. No book turns a lazybones into a model of industry all by itself, except the Bible! But they at least provide the how-to to go along with your what-to.

Word is offering the Survival Series with one of those send-for-the-first-two-books-and-get-one-free offers. If you are prompt in getting to the Post Office with books you don't like, it's a good way to look over the series.

Young Companion

$4/year, monthly issues.

Our home school group took a field trip to Amish country not long ago. While we were there visiting the harness shop, buying cheese, and so on, I ran across a copy of this magazine for Mennonite young people. The publishers are anxious to preserve virtue in their community, and concerned about such things as young Mennonites marrying "outside" or picking up worldly habits like playing pool. Ah, lost innocence! It looked like quite a charming little zine and certainly represents a different point of view than "Dallas."

Young Pilot

$9/year U.S. $11 Canada.

I had to laugh when I saw the white envelope labeled "North America's Best Kept Secret Inside." *Everyone* is getting into advertising hype these days—even the solid folks at Prairie Bible Institute! *Young Pilot* is their magazine for Christian children. It's loaded with tear-jerking stories, cartoons, stories about courageous Christians, activity pages, some of those silly riddles kids love, letters to the editor, and even a centerfold (the issue I have displays a kid leading a horse along a wild riverbank).

Young Pilot is a blend of professionalism and old-fashioned sentimentality. The stories might have been written one hundred years ago. The literary quality does not reach the heights of such secular creations as *Cricket* and *Cobblestones,* but is still commendable.

The magazine is organized around a monthly theme, such as stewardship. There also are drive-you-crazy serial stories (remember Flash Gordon?), complete with cliffhangers. Will Sarah's father ever give those worthless Darnley boys their comeuppance? Will Sarah's mother ever get well? I don't know about how well *Young Pilot* will instill other character traits, but readers of their serials are bound to develop great gobs of patience.

CHAPTER THIRTY-SEVEN

ECONOMICS

Economics is the art of predicting how people will make and spend their money. That's all there is to it! Many of us have been dazzled by charts and graphs and statistics into believing economics is a "science." Not so! People in the mass are just like people as individuals—human, not robots. We obey certain laws of our inner nature, and thus our behavior is sometimes predictable, but no scientist will ever be able to predict a new social trend like the Cabbage Patch fad or the computer boom.

Economists nowadays are divided into two main schools. The Keynsian school, as represented by President Carter's advisors and the New York *Times,* believes that the more you spend the richer you get. Thus they support deficit financing of everything from washing machines to Great Society programs and believe that the piper will never show up demanding to be paid. They also firmly believe that "the economy," meaning your and my decisions about how we spend our money, needs a wise and powerful elite, meaning them, to regulate and control and strangle us into submission.

The other school of economics believes that there ain't no such thing as a free lunch and that "the economy," which you'll recall means you and me, will work out things better for its individual members if said individual members are allowed to make their own decisions. This school, known as Free-Market Economics, is less than grateful to those who want to "help the people" by plundering those very same people and filtering their money through a bureaucracy. Its members are quick to point out that there can be no such thing as Irresponsible Capitalists Exploiting the People without (a) the Irresponsible Capitalists commiting actual crimes, for which they can be punished, or (b) the active cooperation of bureaucrats emitting regulations that stifle small business and entrepreneurial competition.

The two schools, then, divide on the issue of bureaucratic control. The Keynsian side says, "Bureaucracy is great! We need more of it!" The Free Market side replies, "Horsefeathers! Bureaucrats *cause* all those scarcities, monopolies, and price fixings that you claim we need bureaucrats to solve!" Bureaucracy, for or against, is the main battle line. There are other areas of conflict: Keynsians love it when the government hemorrhages billions of dollars of unbacked paper money into the economy, and Free Marketeers hate it. But since the only reason the government is so anxious to spend money it doesn't have is to pay for more bureaucracies, this too is a symptom of the basic conflict.

So economics is not a dull, dry, dreary struggle with dusty statistics, but a full-fledged war. One side believes in itself, and wants all power for itself; the other side believes in the people. One side has its hand in your wallet; the other is trying to get you your wallet back. One side gushes fog and irrelevant statistics to conceal its actions, and hypocritically deplores the sad state of Inflation or The Deficit, both of which it zealously creates every time it gets a chance. The other side writes muscular, readable books and strives to dispel confusion.

BOOKS ON ECONOMICS FOR BEGINNERS

Where to start? The very best book for the beginning economics student is John Pugsley's *Alpha Strategy* ($13.95; order from Home Life). Ostensibly a book about the best way to invest your money, *Alpha Strategy* begins by explaining (through the medium of clever little stories) what the free market is, why it works, and how government intervention in business affairs is actually nothing more or less than one group's attempt to get rich by breaking the rules. As a bonus, Pugsley explains why investing in tangible, useful objects (rather than stocks or gold) is the most effective way to increase your net worth. The best of us, of course, also believe in investing in heaven's bank, where riches never are stolen or decay. But Pugsley's reasoning will help you be a productive steward of whatever capital remains after you have done your good deeds. It will also help you increase your opportunities to do good.

A close second, and perhaps the grand prize winner for Christians, is *Productive Christians in an Age of Guilt Manipulators* by David Chilton ($9.95 from the Institute for Christian Economics, less from Puritan-Reformed). Written as a response to Ron Sider's *Rich Christians in an Age of Hunger,* Chilton's book devastates economic and political myths left and right. Chilton's style is both witty and argumentative. He will have you avidly flipping pages to see what he'll say next. Once you've read Sider's book and Chilton's book, you'll have a good understanding of where the economic battle is and which side is wearing the white hats.

Two more excellent books, verging on the inspirational, are George Gilder's *Wealth and Poverty* and *The Spirit of Enterprise.* Gilder's strength is his eloquent ode to the virtues of capitalism, and the noble entrepreneur in particular. If the words "noble entrepreneur" sounds foreign to you, it's because you've never read these books. Gilder not only shows how entrepreneurs are the most valuable economic asset of a country, but inspires you to become one yourself!

Now that you've read these books, you're able to make sensible decisions about economics programs for your children.

ECONOMICS PRODUCTS AND RESOURCES

"Establishment" economics (that is, texts that reflect a Keynsian and statist approach) is available from almost any major public school textbook provider. Creeping capitalism is making some inroads; still, the vast majority of this country's elite are still happily devoted to a philosophy that allows them to *remain* the elite and keep us masses in our place. Since establishment economics is so easy to come by, from the New York *Times* to your public library, I haven't bothered to list any sources. The writings of Keynes himself are an exercise in tedium (Keynsian economics is rightly called the "dismal science"), as are most books that reflect his views. Still, you can find them if you want them at any college bookstore.

What is truly hard to find are writings and products that reflect an exuberant entrepreneurial spirit. This, if I am not mistaken, is what most parents are interested in providing for their children. Hence the selection below.

Addison-Wesley Publishing Co.
   Lifegames, $12. *Our Economy: How It Works,* $11.22.

Addison-Wesley has a variety of activity-centered learning programs in economics. *Lifegames* is a set of eighty games, simulations, and activities meant for very young children. The text covers goods and services, specialization and jobs, resources, and money and the bank. No reading is required for most lessons; everything needed is included. *Our Economy: How It Works,* written for junior- and senior-high students, traces the production of jeans, bread, and paper from raw materials to finished product. A supplementary activity book is available for less than $5.

Conservative Book Club
   Membership book club. Take one introductory book free or at a bargain price, promise to buy four more in the next two years. All books discounted. Some superbargains—hardback books for $1 or $2! Occasional closeouts with many superbargains.

An unparalleled source for great books on economics at discount prices. Many books are hardbound. I bought *Wealth and Poverty, The Spirit of Enterprise,* and *The Alpha Strategy* from CBC.

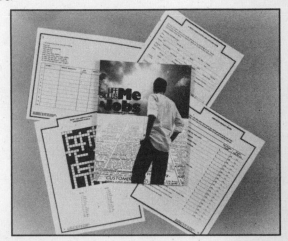

Educational Design
   This company offers workbooks that prepare students for obtaining jobs and help them come to grips with the proper attitudes so necessary for success in the working world. If you must start out as a wage slave, as most of us must, at least learn the ropes.

Foundation for Economic Education
   Books and tapes about economics from a free-enterprise position. Classics no educated person should miss: *The Law* by Frederic Bastiat ($3.50 cloth, $2 paper), *The Wealth of Nations* by Adam Smith ($12.50 paper). Includes many modern writers as well. The Austrian School is well represented. If you never understood economics before, it's probably because of that Keynsian fog that glommed up your school texts. FEE has the antidote.

FEE also publishes a journal called the *Freeman,* which is only for heavy readers and hard-core economics enthusiasts, being thick and loaded with small print to boot.

Harper & Row
   Publisher of *The Alpha Strategy: The Ultimate Plan of Financial Self-Defense* by John A. Pugsley, reviewed above.

Institute for Christian Economics

What you see is what you get—economics from a Biblical Christian viewpoint. ICE is "reconstructionist"—that is, they not only believe they have found some answers, but they think that it's time to do something about it. Luminaries such as Gary North (the nationally known economic advisor who founded ICE) are pushing for an economic revolution featuring such heretical ideas as a flat tax rate of no more than 10 percent, no more government financing of education, and abolishing the whole system of price supports that affects fields from farming to automobile manufacturing.

ICE published David Chilton's *Productive Christians,* reviewed above.

Laissez-Faire Books

Another fruitful source for good books on economics, this time from a libertarian standpoint. The libertarian viewpoint is that people are basically selfish (which is true), and what the hey, we should all have an equal crack at doing whatever turns us on (which is sometimes true and sometimes false). They are less inclined to cast an evil eye on your pocketbook than most groups, understanding that this opens them up to being plundered also. If you are well acquainted with the heavy line between liberty and license, Laissez-Faire offers many volumes of merit for your discriminating taste.

Jeffrey Norton Publishers

Why Socialism Always Fails, A Conversation With Milton Friedman, $11.95 each. *How Government Destroys Our Money,* $10.95.

With enterprising evenhandedness, Jeffrey Norton Publishers carries cassettes both by free-market economists and by the like of John Galbraith who want to "redirect the system towards the public interest," which naturally means more meddling by public bureaucrats in their own interest.

Ludwig von Mises, rightly titled the dean of Austrian economists, has an innocuous little number called *Why Socialism Always Fails.* Nobel Prize winner Milton Friedman tells us why there ain't no such thing as a free lunch in *A Conversation with Milton Friedman.* Murray Rothbard chimes in, explaining *How Government Destroys Our Money* (by hemorrhages at the printing press and our lend-money-you-haven't-got banking system). Dr. Rothbard also traces the dismal history of government abuse of money. (Q: Why do bureaucrats always want more money? A: Because it's *there!*)

Penny Power

$11.95/year (six school-year issues); $14.95, Canadian and foreign. *Teaching Guide,* $3 (six issues), $4 Canadian and foreign.

Penny Power is "A Consumer Reports Publication for Young People" and thus puts more stress on spending and saving than on earning. This full-sized, colorful zine is fun to read. Since most of the issue is devoted to *Consumer Reports* style products tests, there are more articles than activities, although *Penny Power* does have a regular Puzzlers department and throws in such things as recipes from time to time. I'd like to see more

articles on kids with businesses. The issue I saw had a two-page spread on "Kids in Business," but they were all extremely small-time operations. It's true that kids can get inspired by seeing something they could easily do, but I'd also like to see some stories on under-fifteens who hit the big time.

Penny Power has great graphics, and the consumer articles on such things as musical instruments, trivia games, fruit snacks, and markers will be of interest to those who have enough money to consider buying these items: i.e., everyone whose parents are willing to pay the price of the subscription.

Simon and Schuster

Publishers of George Gilder's *Wealth and Poverty* and *The Spirit of Enterprise,* reviewed above.

Visual Education Corporation

Exploring the Working World, eighteen cassettes, $180. *Entering Without Specialized Training,* twelve cassettes, $120. *Expanding World of Tech Careers,* six cassettes, $60. All the above for $330.

I may not be playing with all my marbles on this one, especially since I haven't heard the product myself. All the same, Vis Ed's Careertapes series sounds intriguing. It's on-the-spot interviews with young workers in a variety of occupations—*not* including homeworking or small business.

Exploring the Working World is eighteen forty-minute cassettes ranging over every wage-slave category defined by the U.S. Office of Employment. "Each cassette includes four interviews, beginning with entry level positions and ending with jobs requiring advanced degrees." For example, in the Environment category you get a sanitation worker, air quality technician, wildlife specialists, and urban planner. The series stresses feminist careerism.

Entering the Job Market Without Specialized Training explores "career areas that permit direct entry after high school without further specialized training or education."

The Expanding World of Technical Careers has to do with jobs that do require technical education, such as aircraft maintenance technician, dental assistant, computer systems technologist, and video technician—twenty-four jobs in all.

Obviously, most individuals won't have the shekels to spring for this series. Just as obviously, it is foolish to rush about picking

a specialty without gingerly feeling the ropes that are about to bind you. See if you can sweet-talk your high school or library into buying this series. And if you want to put in your apprenticeship at something technical, you might want to go ahead and make the $60 investment in that series.

ENTREPRENEURSHIP— STARTING YOUR OWN BUSINESS

Achievement Basics
Do Your Best, Where's the Wall, and *You Can Lead,* $6.95 each plus $1 shipping or $17.95 for all three. *Up and On,* $7.50. Parent/Teacher Guide included free. *Communication Commercials,* $11.25 postpaid.

Achievement Basics offers something unique: A Junior Business Basics series designed to teach entrepreneurial skills to kids from fourth grade on up. The series is correlated with an optional Junior Business newsletter for inspiration. It comes with a Parent/Teacher Guide with cartoon pages.

The cassettes for younger children are dramatized stories of lovable Uncle Hersh and his nephew Dow and niece Joan. *Do Your Best* teaches kids about productivity and setting standards. In *Where's the Wall on Wall Street?,* Dow and Joan go to the stock exchange. You also get a wall poster and sample stock certificate. *You Can Lead a Horse to Water, But . . .* is about incentive, profit, and loss and includes the Junior Business File Folder that teaches bookkeeping and budgeting.

Up and On with Productivity is a motivational cassette for teens, stressing the free-enterprise message. It includes tips on how to be productive and successful with obsessive hype.

Communication Commercials are a cassette or record set for training communication skills through an "ad" format. Clever!

All cassettes are done by professional actors or announcers and designed for home use.

Mother's Bookshelf

The *Mother Earth News,* to which I will once again subscribe as soon as it ceases publishing Anne and Paul Ehrlich's tiresome antibaby tirades, regularly has how-to articles on home business. Mother's Bookshelf, an operation of the magazine, also carries lots of titles on this theme. Some are just gee-whiz hype, but others are solidly useful. It's a good place to start.

Jeffrey Norton Publishers
Successful Entrepreneurship, $89.95. *How to Start a Home Business, Great Home Businesses, Teenage Business Opportunities,* $10.95 each. Shipping extra.

Home business and entrepreneurship on cassette! I haven't heard any of these courses, mind you, but I'd like to. *Successful Entrepreneurship,* by A. David Silver, includes a two hundred-page book and six cassettes on the following subjects: Characteristics of Successful Entrepreneurs, The Entrepreneurial Process, Survival Plans for Entrepreneurs, Financing Strategies for the New Business, What Kind of New Business to Start, and Entrepreneurial Growth Techniques. If you're not playing in this league, *How to Start a Home Business* by Gary Null is only one cassette. *Great Home Businesses,* by the same author, includes case histories. Richard Berman also has several tapes. The title *Teenage Business Opportunities* might interest you, and according to the blurb, "this cassette is packed with solid, practical information about how teenagers can make as much as $200 a week after school and during vacations." Plus many more cassettes on the theme of small business.

CHAPTER THIRTY-EIGHT

GEOGRAPHY

If it's true that finding all the wrong answers is one of the best ways to discover a solution, I should be a geography expert. Geography was my very worst, absolutely lousiest, subject in school. This may be partly due to my very low level of navigational ability. I can get lost crossing the street! Still, looking back on my school experience, I see that I was taught by some pretty lousy methods.

We had units on Tundra and Plains and Mountains. We memorized (and promptly forgot) Famous Rivers and Famous Forests. We studied Large Bodies of Water. We memorized State Capitals and State Flowers. After years of this sort of training, I still thought Missouri was in the far west somewhere! The only geographical fact I retained from those days was the shape of Italy, because of a homework assignment that required us to make an outline map of that country.

Out of all this emerge two grave errors so commonly employed when teaching geography, and one sound method of instruction. The Grave Errors are (1) to present facts in a meaningless way and (2) to make learning passive. Who cares about tundra and plains and mountains, anyway? These geographical features are extremely important in understanding the people who live on or near them, and for the history of wars and commerce; but none of my teachers emphasized this. Eskimos are interesting; tundra is not. Geography is one of those subjects that needs a peg to hang on. Otherwise it is stored in short-term memory and quickly lost. You can memorize the map and its geographical features, but unless this is related to the needs and history of the people (and to a lesser extent, animals) who live there, geography is not only forgettable but valueless.

Passive learning means that kids are supposed to sit there and soak up geography. But if there ever was a subject meant for discovery learning, geography is it. Everything that any person has ever done was done somewhere. Look up that "somewhere" on a map or globe, and the map and globe come to life. It's boring to watch a hockey game if you don't know anything about the players. It's just as boring to look at places and not know what happened there. Also, when studying shapes (the outlines of nations, states, and continents and the course of rivers, etc.) the best way to get these into the brain is to copy the shapes. I am not a particularly kinesthic learner, but I will forever remember that Italy looks like a boot because I had to copy its coastline.

Drill has its place, in my opinion, and as far as geography is concerned, that place is supplying simple facts and shapes again and again until we are comfortable with them. It then is easier to fill that data with content. When the Sudan comes up in dinner conversation, you'll at least have a vague idea that it's on the other side of the world. You won't think it's one of the fifty states or a province of Mexico!

We are now blessed with a superabundance of colorful and fun geography products. There are books to introduce geographic concepts, hands-on projects, drill products, and maps and atlases and globes. All of these (1) help you get from point A to point B in your personal travels or (2) provide the "where" of "Who did what where?" If these points are kept firmly in mind, geography study can be a thrilling discovery—as it is now for me!

GEOGRAPHY CURRICULUM AND MAPS

American Map Corporation

Here's everything in maps, including some surprises! Colorprint maps, an AMC product, are the least expensive around. The Colorprint Student Pack, consisting of maps of the world, the U.S.A., and the solar system, costs only $6. Colorprint also has maps for all major land areas, plus a Star Chart, a Bible World map, and a Fantasy Land map with nursery rhyme and storybook characters.

AMC also has a full line of map accessories like wipe-off crayons for laminated maps and pointers. Outline maps and transparencies, and a huge line of business maps, are also AMC standards.

AMC sells Hallwag European travel maps, holiday maps, and even astronomy maps. The travel maps are quite inexpensive, and it can be fun to plan an imaginary journey to another country on one.

Unrelated to the above, AMC also carries a large line of anatomy charts and study aids.

Hammond
Wonderful World of Maps, $6.95. *Atlases,* $3 and up.

Maps and atlases are Hammond's strong suit. They have great prices for some really fine geography material. *Wonderful World of Maps* is an introductory atlas for young readers. The first part of the book teaches map skills (symbols, direction, distance, scale, different types of maps, latitude and longitude, time zones, etc.), while the second part presents world and regional maps. The book has been named "outstanding" by the National Council for the Social Studies. The NCSS is right on, in my opinion. *Wonderful World of Maps* covers everything geographical with finesse, looks great, and even smells good (because of the high-quality ink and paper).

Hammond's World Atlases (which come in models from economy to deluxe) feature an index right next to each map (where you need it the most) as well as a separate master index in the back (in some versions).

An unusual offering is *Hammond's Antique Map Reproductions.* These are full-color repros of the original old-time (mostly before 1700) maps.

Hammond has a separate Education catalog, which I recommend. Hammond's Map Skills program will interest some home schoolers, particularly since it is so inexpensive and well laid-out. Student atlases start as low as $3.45. Plus reference maps for less than $2 and a wide selection of other maps and globes.

Hubbard
Relief maps start at $14.95. Map Reading Model, $31.

Hubbard is the place for raised relief maps. You can get regional maps (West of the Rockies and some eastern areas), National Park maps, U.S.A., and world maps, all framed or unframed.

For geography study, Hubbard has a map reading model packet that includes a plastic terrain model with five stacking contour sheets, five unprinted stacking contour sheets, a wall map, fifty student project sheets, and even a grease pencil.

Hubbard's catalogs are free, and the map catalog is well worth sending for.

National Geographic Society
Membership, $15; includes the magazine. Most maps: $3/paper, $4/plastic.

You know all about *National Geographic* magazine, and if you don't you can find out in the Social Studies chapter. As befits an originally geographical society, NGS has maps, maps, and more maps. Lands of the Bible today. Bird migration in the Americas. Mural maps to cover your wall. Ocean floor relief maps. Space maps. U.S. regional maps. Canadian provinces. Antarctica (plan in advance for your trip!).

NGS also has a couple of fancy atlases and a quint of fancy globes.

Rand McNally
Family World Atlas, $12.95.

No listing of geography materials would be complete without Rand McNally, the people whose maps help America navigate on her summer vacations. Rand McNally has bunches of atlases for the incurably curious, including a number of astronomical atlases. Does anyone you know need a map of Jupiter? Of more interest to the average family is Rand McNally's *Family World Atlas,* so called because it has information of interest to any age bracket. This atlas has sixty pages of tables, charts, intriguing facts, and comparisons. It's always fun to get down the *Family Atlas* and browse with the kids, and it makes a great resource for discovery projects. What is the largest island in the world? How much of Australia gets by on less than ten inches of rain a year? Kids will like the Today's World in Maps section consisting of colorful regional maps devoted to different attributes, such as landforms, natural hazards, minerals, etc.

Rand McNally's catalog also features some very decent kids' books, including some Christian books. The dedicated armchair shopper may want to send for it.

GEOGRAPHY GAMES, KITS, AND PUZZLES

Developmental Learning Materials (DLM)
World Map Games, $11.50, U.S. Map Games, $17.

DLM also has two nice, simple map games. You get a set of large laminated maps. Each map (six to a set) has important places and geographical features marked with a numbered red dot. Players put tokens over all the dots, and then throw dice to determine which place or feature they must find. Pick up a token, and find out if you're right! The *World* game has maps for: Land Masses, Mountains, and Deserts; Oceans, Seas, and Rivers; Large Cities; North America—Mountains and Important Bodies of Water; North America—Large Cities; and South America (Countries and Geographical Features). The accompanying booklet has facts and figures about all these areas. You could also write on the laminated surface with plastic crayons, making the maps suitable for all kinds of projects (tracing Columbus's sea voyage, for instance.) These make nice family games.

Educational Insights
Geography Know-It-All, $7.95. *Name That State*, $9.95. Globe Kit, $12.95.

Essential for geography drill is that old favorite, *Geography Know-It-All.* You probably remember twirling a disk inside of a plastic holder to learn the capitals of states. Educational Insights has taken that one step further by adding eleven more disks. Now your kids can quiz themselves on two hundred and forty questions covering oceans, seas, rivers, states, etc. As an upgrade, *Geography Know-It-All* even has a teacher's guide and a plastic case.

Name That State is a red-white-and-blue board game correlated with a U.S. map. Name the state whose number you land on. It's painless geography drill, slightly overpriced.

Educational Insight's last winner is something dear to the heart of all who love hands-on learning: a map globe kit. Yes, you blow up the balloon, cover it with papier-mache, and by carefully following the patterns make either an awesome mess or a world globe. The kit comes with a base, reproducible project pages, and a teacher's guide, plus the indispensable balloon and patterns.

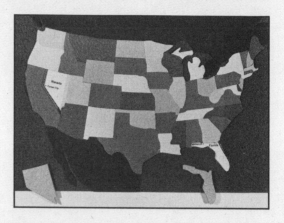

Lauri
Fit-A-State, $16.50. *Fit-A-World*, $17.95.

I went out and paid money for Lauri's crepe rubber maps. If you know how stuffed my storage cabinet already is with things geographical, you'd realize how great I think these Lauri maps are! First, they are beautiful. Nations, in the world map, and states, in the U.S. map, are different colors of crepe rubber. Second, they have texture and heft. The pieces are ¼" thick and feel great. Third, they are puzzles. You *have* to learn something about geography just by putting the puzzles back together! Novices quickly learn to look for clues: the funny-shaped, tiny states come from New England, and the big blocks from Out West. State names are shown on the underlay, so you can see what you are looking for. And if you lose Rhode Island, Lauri will replace it for 50¢.

Milton Bradley Company

Global Flash Cards and *United States Flash Cards* are just what the names imply. Drill your kids on the outstanding features of each region you are studying—not just its shape, but a whole pile of interesting characteristics. U. S. cards list state abbreviations, capitals, nicknames, date of Union entry, state flower, largest city, natural resources, and major products. Several cards of fascinating facts are included, such as a card of important dates (from the Stamp Act to the first moon landing), a card describing the origins of the various state names, a card listing important lakes, rivers, and mountains, and more. The *Global* cards are 8½ x 11" regional cards plus smaller country cards. Major cities and geographical features, date of independence, and exports and imports are listed on the front of these colorful cards, while the back is a black outline map for use in identification games. When we bought them, the *Global* flashcards were $6.95 and the U.S. cards were $4.50—truly a reasonable price for this information-packed discovery tool.

CHAPTER THIRTY-NINE

GOVERNMENT

Ever since the days of Dewey, American schools have required students to take courses in politics. These come labeled as "Civics" or "Government" or "Citizenship." The idea is to teach kids how American government operates . . . and to get them to accept a certain political agenda. Less independence. More government. Above all, more bureaucracy.

Of the pile of American government texts I have seen, each and every one encouraged dependence on government bureaucrats. The examples given of how "reformers" have "used the American process" always concentrated on how certain people got laws passed that created *more* bureaucracies. I can't recall a single textbook example of a citizen or group of citizens getting together and *eliminating* a bureaucracy. The "citizenship" taught in these volumes consists of exhorting our children to elect officials who will, in the words of the Declaration of Independence, "erect a Multitude of new Offices, and send hither Swarm of Officers to harass our People, and eat out their Substance." The moral? "You can't fight City Hall."

I happen to believe you *can* fight City Hall, and that the time has come when we'd *better* fight City Hall. Power corrupts; absolute power corrupts absolutely; and modern bureaucracies are seeking absolute power. And the NEA bureaucrats are careful to make sure that public school texts never discuss the case against bureaucracy.

Even if you don't agree that modern bureaucracies pose a grave threat to our personal liberties, you owe it to yourself to become aware of tools for influencing the system. "Citizenship" courses that exhort students to "Vote for the candidate of your choice!" hardly get to the roots of our political process. Picketing, lobbying, writing letters to the editor, getting on the media; local party meetings, district canvassing, direct mail; citizens' groups, forums, political conferences—all these and more should be in the political syllabus. It's one thing to choose not to get heavily involved politically. It's another to be unable to do so even if you want to.

You also owe it to yourself to become aware of the real political issues. When Republicans and Democrats debate, it's often Tweedledum versus Tweedledee. Either side can and often does compromise a consistent position for perceived political advantages, thus robbing the debate of clear-cut arguments. Reason is swallowed up in a dense fog, from which yet another bureaucracy predictably emerges.

You already know one side of the issues. "Life is so complex. There are no simple answers. We must look to the experts." And so on. Editorial pages are full of this sort of stuff. So are school texts. I need not list sources for this point of view: it is inescapable. (If you really want textbooks that push this view, select any of the civics texts published by any of the standard public school publishers. The addresses are in the back.) The other side of the issue is that there *is* right and wrong, government exists to punish the wrong and let the citizens get on with doing the right, and if you want a job done right you'd better do it yourself. The schools do their best to suppress these ideas; all the more reason to take them seriously.

The following list will give you and your children the tools to be informed about the "other side" of our political issues, and to be active citizens in the land of the free and the home of the brave.

TOOLS FOR UNDERSTANDING POLITICS

American Vision

Books and tapes promoting a Biblical world view. American Vision is in the process of developing a Biblical World View Library. The three-volume *God and Government* series is the first topic covered in the Library. These volumes together comprise the most comprehensive treatment available on the Biblical principles of government. The series is used by hundreds of home schoolers and makes up part of the curriculum of Christian Liberty Academy. It sells for $12.95 plus 12% shipping and handling, with 20 percent discount (minimum of three) to schools ordering on letterhead stationary.

Conservative Book Club

Very inaptly named. There's nothing "conservative" about wanting to do away with nine tenths of our government bureaucracy, or in advocating sudden death for murderers and rapists. CBC sells books from what could be called the New Right position (as opposed to the Old Wrong). These run the spectrum from Biblical Christian to atheist libertarian, and covers all issues of interest to thinking people (not just politics).

You join by accepting one of CBC's terrific book offers, which for a while now have been heavily advertised in national conservative magazines. We got a complete hardback set of *McGuffeys* for $10 for joining the Club. Another excellent offer I saw was the Sam Blumenfeld's *Alphaphonics.* Whatever the bait book may be, it's one that's interesting and valuable reading. Once you're in, you need only buy four more books at the discounted club price. Every so often CBC sends you a mailing about their current specials, along with Neil McCaffrey's terrific reviews.

Recent offerings have included: Jeane Kirkpatrick's *Dictatorships and Double Standards,* George Gilder's *Wealth and Poverty,* a book entitled *The Pentagon and the Art of War* whose thesis is that the former could stand to learn more about the latter, Michael Novak's response to the Catholic bishops' increasing socialism called *Freedom With Justice,* and a book suggesting corporal punishment for criminals called *Just and Painful.* I have chosen these titles almost at random. CBC also carries books that would appeal to almost anyone, such as

Classics to Read Aloud to Your Children and a guide to doubling your living standard called *Move South Now!*

Please note that the particular titles I mentioned may not still be available by the time you read this. CBC continually adds new titles and sells out the old. These were mentioned to give you an idea of what to expect.

We have been CBC members for several years now and are well pleased with their service and selection.

Foundation for American Christian Education (FACE)

Russians raise little comrades on a steady diet of Marx and Lenin; so little U. S. Citizens cut their eyeteeth on the Constitution and the Declaration of Independence, right? Wrong! Ignorance of our basic political documents, and of the thinking on which America was founded, is widespread.

F.A.C.E. is trying to revive the "Principle Approach" to government, an approach based on Biblical law, on which they say the U.S.A. was founded. Their material, which is directed to adults and mature teenagers, traces America's Christian roots through source documents. F.A.C.E. does not seek merely to acquaint students with history; they want to bring back the same spirit that animated our Founding Fathers. Political freedom begins with self-government, F.A.C.E. says, and self-government begins in the home.

Everything F.A.C.E. makes is beautifully bound, gold-stamped, carefully written, and incredibly cheap. You can line a short library shelf with F.A.C.E. books that look like a million and cost less than $50.

See the History section for a detailed review of F.A.C.E. products.

Green Hill Publishers
What Makes You Think We Read the Bills?, $7.95.

Ever wonder what exactly your elected representatives *do?* State Senator Bill Richardson (California) has managed to write a book that is both hysterically funny and strictly factual at the same time. It's called *What Makes You Think We Read the Bills?* and is an invaluable addition to anyone's political education. Discover why your elected rep can't read the bills he's voting on, even if he wants to. Find out why State Senator Richardson says, "A full-time legislature—yuk!" You'll learn about the insidious peer-group shift and the ancient origins of lobbying. Here's the inside poop on legislatures—their good side and their bad—written in a clean enough style so you don't have to lock up the book.

If you'd like to know a little more about how American government works than they taught you in civics class, grab this book. In fact, grab the whole Green Hill Catalog while you're at it.

Heritage Education and Research Organization (HERO)

With a name like HERO for their organization, you'd expect Bill and Penny Bowen to at least have bulging biceps and a big red letter S stenciled on their shirts (where *is* Superman when we need him?). Sorry, friends, the Bowens are a normal middle-aged couple whose power lies only in their message.

HERO is out to expose our silent counterrevolutionaries, those government bureaucrats and their hangers-on who want to crush all individual initiative and family ties in order to implement Super-Bureaucracy or one-world government. Their books are certainly a different point of view from the fare on TV, and offer a clear, documented look at how the bad guys operate. This serves as an instructive lesson in How to Grab Unreasonable Power in a Democracy, and may perhaps prod some of us into getting rid of the grabbers.

Heritage Foundation

Journals, bulletins, policy studies, and books on topics of current interest. Unless your kid is a genius, he won't go for this stuff. Although Heritage Foundation writers spew less fog than most who handle these issues, it takes a certain acuity of mind and familiarity with close reasoning to follow them.

Those who like to at least try to find answers to problems will find some solace in Heritage's catalog.

Ideal School Supply
Our Government, $4.95. *Presidential Posters,* $12.95.

Our Government is a set of four posters with a simplified explanation of the branches of government. *Presidential Posters* are 8½ x 11″ full-color portraits with accompanying bios of each man and important events during his Presidency. Discussion topics; teacher's guide. Make 'em into a book, or let your kid paper his room with them. Hey, it's better than having to stare at Prince or Madonna!

Laissez Faire Books

Libertarians believe in "Lib and Let Lib," or as it is sometimes put, "Get Your Laws Off My Body." For years those subscribing to this view have been a small, but literarily acute, minority. And for years before that, those subscribing to this view were running this country. Laissez Faire has their books: some serious, some wicked, some funny, some sad. These are the classics of yesterday that modern school kids aren't allowed to read, mixed in with a certain amount of atheistic and anarchistic works. Serious political thinkers will want to at least consult this catalog.

Mayflower Institute
Journal, $15/year suggested donation.

Mayflower's bimonthly journal "contains provocative articles on the application of America's Christian history to the problems of our day and updates on the growing movements toward restoration of America." Also cassettes and study guides that deal with topics such as, "Is there any reason why pastors today should not be able to preach the Word of God as it relates to government?"

Plymouth Rock Foundation
Biblical Principles, $4.95. *Fundamentals,* $6 Study Manual, $6.75 Guide Book.

Plymouth Rock's study course in Biblical principles of government, *Fundamentals for American Christians,* is currently used in several thousand Christian day and home schools in the USA (including Christian Liberty Academy) and in some fourteen foreign countries. Designed for upper high school students and adults, it is four hundred pages loaded with charts, tables, and study projects, and comes three-hole punched to fit your standard ring binder. Are you *really* a fundamentalist? Get *Fundamentals* and find out!

Another Plymouth Rock entry that has met with great acceptance is the formidably titled *Biblical Principles Concerning Issues of Importance to Godly Christians.* This is a compendium of Plymouth Rock's scrappy little fact sheets, filled with terse comments on current issues such as abortion, Dungeons 'n Dragons, you name it. First the issue is stated. Next you get facts and statistics. Finally, Plymouth Rock states the Biblical position. The Fac-Sheets are written in telegraph style to pack as much info as possible in four pages, rather like this book you are now reading; so they sometimes lack normal grammar and other niceties, ditto.

Plymouth Rock has more books and booklets, periodicals and cassettes dealing with Biblical principles of government, Christian education, and America's Christian heritage.

Resources for the Gifted
Political Strategies, $8.95

RFG's *Political Strategies* book was intended to teach young smart alecks the nitty-gritties of campaign politics. It's actually a nifty little how-to manual for neophyte politicians and their supporters. If you want obedient kids, you'd better not show them the section on lobbying. It includes hints on how to lobby *you.* The author reveals dirty tricks along with clean campaign tactics. Those same dirty tricks are what you're going to run into in real life, so I regard this as a plus. The book switches back and forth between adult politics and exercises in student government. Something for everyone.

School of Statesmanship
How to Elect Statesmen, five-hour video, free if you send a blank video cassette and a little postage; $20 otherwise. Audio cassettes, $15. Free Literature.

Here are videos, audio cassettes, and piles of stories and clippings for anyone who's interested in restoring our Federal Republic. The free literature made quite interesting reading. I had no idea Davy Crockett once got into trouble for voting relief to a burnt-out area, or that Abe Lincoln refused to give the bankers a cut of the action with his "Lincoln Greenbacks." It's a different point of view: Power to the People, and Bureaucrats Go Home!

Visual Education Corporation
Each Speaking For . . . series, $76/six cassettes.

If you're curious about who has the nerve to consider they speak for all America, Vis Ed has the answer! Vis Ed's *Speaking For America* set consists of three separate series. First is the Six Presidents series. You get selections from significant speeches and remarks by Herbert Hoover, Franklin Roosevelt, Harry Truman, Dwight Eisenhower, John Kennedy, and Lyndon Johnson. O.K. so far. After all, we elected these men to speak for us. Next comes the Twelve National Leaders series: John Gardner, Hubert Humphrey, Henry Jackson, Martin Luther King, Jr., John L. Lewis,

Walter Lippman, Douglas MacArthur, George McGovern, George Meany, Daniel P. Moynihan, Clinton Rossiter, and Adlai Stevenson. "Hm," I said. "McGovern might speak for Massachusetts and D.C.—after all, they voted for him—but is this exactly speaking for America? And I wonder how many people even know who Clinton Rossiter is, let alone want him to speak for them?" Well, sliding rapidly leftward we end up at the last group of people anxious to speak for you and me, the series of Twelve Activists. The club includes Julian Bond, William Sloane Coffin, Karen DeCrow, Ralph Nader, and a whole slew of lesser-known feminists and assorted leftist agitators. Nary a Phyllis Schlafly nor a Jerry Falwell in the bunch. Those who are comfortable with the world according to Doonesbury will undoubtedly find this group inspiring. Others will find their "visions of a better America" sinister or amusing.

Each series comes with a Listener's Guide: the usual background info and discussion questions.

Wff 'n Proof
Propaganda, $13 postpaid.

One of the most acute problems when dealing with political issues is recognizing propaganda. The *Propaganda* game, coauthored by Lorne Greene of "Bonanza" fame, consists of definitions of propaganda devices and a series of sample statements, each of which contains one such device. Students play by either challenging the group consensus (in which case the authors' solutions are consulted) or by going along with it. You get points for challenging correctly and lose points for incorrect challenges. You can also play *Solitaire,* checking yourself against the solutions.

Once the basic games have been played several times, students are encouraged to invent their own problems, using the *Congressional Record* or an old newspaper.

Propaganda is an attractive, fun, inexpensive way to bring a little reason to a field that notoriously lacks it.

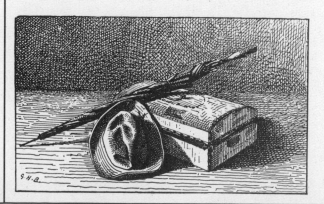

CHAPTER FORTY

HISTORY

History is a tricky subject. Unlike mathematics, which follows logical rules no matter who the mathematician is or what his political party, history changes depending on who is telling the story. We can all sit down to memorize (and subsequently forget) the dates and places: Columbus sailing the ocean blue in fourteen hundred ninety-two, or the Declaration of Independence being signed on July 4, 1776. But even something as innocuous as memorization is not without its perils. Do we memorize Susan B. Anthony's birthday or Phyllis Schlafly's? Is Mrs. Rosa Parks' refusal to move to the back of the bus more important to the history of America than John Paul Jones bellowing, "I have not yet begun to fight"? Beyond the few major dates on which all agree, there is room for strife aplenty in choosing which events and people are worth our attention and which are not.

Not only are skirmishes fought in the halls of academe over the relative importance of Date A and Person B, but war also rages over the *interpretation* of events. Even if all sides finally would agree that the Pilgrims landed at Plymouth Rock, that would not be the end of it. Was the Pilgrims' landing a great step for mankind, or a disaster for virgin, Indian-populated America? Historians agree that Custer and his men died at the Little Big Horn. But was Custer a hero or a cad? Name your event and you'll find at least two, and more likely ten, different interpretations of its significance and results.

Let's list off as many major theories of history as we can remember, and we'll see the vast difference each theory makes in how history is interpreted.

(1) *Cyclical.* Everything repeats itself, and history goes around in circles. This is one ancient view of history, and it is all tied up with bonds of reincarnation and karma. Nothing you or I do will make the slightest difference. The wheel keeps turning around.

(2) *Random chance.* Everything happens by accident. No historical events have meaning or purpose. Existentialists and nihilists like this view.

(3) *Marxist.* History is the result of a class struggle between the masses and the wealthy. When class distinctions and religion finally are annihilated, Utopia will rise from the ashes. In the meantime we need censorship and an army of bureaucrats and an army of KGB men and an army of conscripts and an arsenal of nuclear weapons and a first-rate Olympic team. On with the struggle, comrades! Workers of the world, unite!

(4) *Feminist.* History is the result of a struggle between men and women. When sexual distinctions and religion finally are annihilated, Utopia will rise from the ashes. In the meantime we need sexually unbiased textbooks and an army of bureaucrats and an army of social workers and an army of day-care centers and a third chance at the ERA. On with the struggle, sisters! Women of the world, unite!

(5) *Conspiracy.* A group of clever, evil men have plotted for (take your pick) years/decades/centuries to centralize world power in their hands. They are so clever that every war, recession, bank failure, and crop failure is their doing. Their nefarious plots almost always succeed. Therefore we are heading into another Dark Age.

(6) *Modernist* or *Evolutionary.* Things are getting better and better, and pretty soon we will end up living in the best of all possible worlds. Why? Cause it just happens that way! Since we are the smartest generation that ever has lived, we don't need to learn from the past. Chuck out those history books! Or if you insist on studying history, make sure it's all stated in terms of

today's political program. You know—"The Puritans and Feminism" or "John Adams and Nuclear Disarmament."

(7) *Great Man.* Individuals with exceptional ability determine the course of history. Some nihilists like this view, too. Most conservative history books sold in America tend to take this position.

(8) *Providential.* God controls history and is working out His plans on earth. History in this view is cause and effect. If a nation or an individual sins, it or he can expect troubles. If a nation or individual is obedient to God, then in due course God bestows blessing. Some trouble is part of the normal human condition, and necessary to keep us from getting soft, but by and large history's grand purposes can be discerned.

So, you see, there is *no neutral theory of history!* Every one of those theories offends people who believe some other theory. If you try to mix any of these theories, with the exception of #3 and #4 which go very well together, they will blow up in your face. And every history text you read, whether intentionally or not, will be coming from one of these directions.

There is no harm in reading a history text written from a viewpoint you dislike *as long as you are equipped to recognize points of interpretation and errors of fact.* For this reason, I strongly recommend beginning the official study of history with what are called "source documents." By looking at the books, newspapers, posters, and artwork that people produced in the past, we can get inside their heads. We can see what was really important to them, and what moved them to action. This view of history is more exciting and earthy than sterile textbook tours guided by a committee of dusty scholars.

For very young children, you are in their source documents. Begin by telling them your family history: how you met and married, how they were born. Oral storytelling is a root of history, and every child needs his own personal roots besides.

Texts have their place, in providing a framework for us to fill in ourselves. In many cases a simple time line would suffice for the framework, but as the history student begins to possess his facts, to really know them, he is ready to venture out into the world of ideas, good and bad, and search for writers of kindred spirit, who he is by now trained to recognize.

ORAL HISTORY AND SOURCE DOCUMENTS

Let's start with history as our fellowmen saw it. What did they say? What artifacts did they leave behind?

Buck Hill Associates

What a find! Buck Hill's catalog lists over six hundred posters, handbills, broadsides, prints, and advertisements from America's past. These authentic reproductions trace the political and social history of America from its beginnings to the recent past. As on-the-spot records of America's heritage, they bring history alive.

Most of the reproductions are printed in black ink on white paper, as the originals were. Some posters are in color or on colored paper, and are so described in the catalog.

Now get ready for some excitement! How would you like a copy of George Washington's recruiting poster . . . early American tavern rules ("no more than five to sleep in one bed, no dogs allowed in the kitchen") . . . Lincoln's campaign poster . . . and more! On the darker side of our country's history, there are posters offering "Negroes for sale" or rewards for the capture of runaway slaves. Balance this against the 1883 cartoon that predicts an all-black class except for a white pupil in a dunce cap, and the 1904 cartoon picturing an all-black Harvard football team. Showbills, ads for patent medicines, "Wanted" posters for desperate criminals like Butch Cassidy and Jesse James. Posters of all sorts. Most posters are under $1.

Dime novels that once cost just one thin dime are at Buck Hill for $1.25 each, which is not bad for an authentic reproduction. Plus facsimile reprints of all the *McGuffey Readers,* including the *Eclectic Primer.* The price is affordable for a complete hardbound, boxed, seven-volume set.

If you are at all interested in history as it really was, you've just got to get this catalog.

Caedmon Tapes

Caedmon carries *Great Speeches* and *Great Debates,* which are sometimes the original recordings and sometimes reenactments. The reenactments are recorded with no audience, so lack pizzazz. See the Speech chapter for more details.

Capper's Books

My Folks books, $4.95 each. *Too Good to Keep,* $5.95.

My Folks Came in a Covered Wagon and *My Folks Claimed the Plains* are two collections of true pioneer and homesteading stories, including chapters of original recipes and homestead homemaking secrets. Find out how dog power churned the butter and what Grandma prescribed for fever and ague.

For more "you were there" history, Capper also has *Too Good To Keep,* a fascinating collection of articles and illustrations that appeared in *Capper's Weekly* from 1879 to 1979. Did you know that in 1894 Kansans knew it was love when a young fellow helped a girl to pen the pigs, whereas in Texas a young fellow was thought to be in love if he absentmindedly forgot his revolver when he went to a dance?

Foundation for American Christian Education (FACE)

FACE's very lovely hardbound books are mostly quotations from original American and other source documents. See the Parent/Leadership Training chapter for detailed reviews.

Jeffrey Norton Publishers
Directory, $25.50 postpaid. Single cassettes, $10.95. *Voices,* $59.95 (five cassettes and discussion guide).

JNP's *Directory of Spoken-Word Audio Cassettes* has several pages of reviews of historical recordings and reenactments. JNP also carries more than a few oral history recordings: *Looking Back at Hiroshima, The True Story of Pearl Harbor,* and *Voices of the American West,* to name a few. Plus historical biographies on cassette, historical criticism, and more. Wide, interesting selection.

Visual Education Corporation

Decades series, $39/each decade (three cassettes and program notes). *Black Diamonds,* $39. *Eyewitness 1* and *2,* $76 each (six cassettes and guide). *Grass Roots,* $76. *They Chose America,* Volumes I and II, $76 each. *Voices of World War II,* $119/twelve cassettes.

I am delighted to be able to praise Vis Ed's oral history series. The *Decades* series is an overview of the thirties, forties, fifties, and sixties, straight from the horse's mouth. It's what was happening in Presidential speeches, on radio and TV entertainment and news shows, and in science, from actual recordings made at the time. The three cassettes for each decade cover politics, society, and technology. The production quality is excellent, and each decade comes in a nice binder. I got the 1930s tapes and found them absolutely absorbing. Herbert Hoover was right in so many ways, but he *sounded* weak. FDR, on the other hand, was a charging dynamo! Hear it happen yourself.

Black Diamonds is an oral history of blacks in baseball. Stephen Banker waylaid some of the best players in the old Negro leagues and got them to tell him what it was really like.

Eyewitness is a collection of eyewitness reports from people who lived through some of the major sensational events of the twentieth century. Two victims describe the San Francisco Fire and Earthquake. A man who joined in the Alaska Gold Rush tells what it was like. Custer's last stand, described by the last Indian who was there; the on-the-air report of the Hindenberg disaster; JFK's assassination; several views of the Woodstock Festival; a Confederate soldier's reminiscinces; plus more are all on *Eyewitness 1.* Volume 2 has a sea captain telling about the old sailing vessels; the stories of a woman homesteader and a suffragette; more women describing the Great Depression; the

London blitz, described by an ambulance attendant and a woman who survived a direct hit on the Cafe de Paris; the Hungarian uprising; the sinking of the Titanic; and more.

Voices of World War II covers the entire war, from Chamberlain's foolish pacifism to the Nuremberg trials. You also get to hear such media stars as Axis Sally and Tokyo Rose.

Grass Roots and *They Chose America* are reviewed in the next chapter. And a good thing, too—this writeup is long enough already!

TIME LINES

You can make your own time line by gluing or stapling strips of paper together, or by recycling the backside of a long strip of computer paper. Mark off the years, write down some names and dates, and you're in business.

Time lines can be as simple or complicated as you want. The simplest time line consists of a single line with only a few major events. More elaborate time lines incorporate color, pictures, or stickers to highlight particular types of data, and may include fairly complete histories of several nations. You can make parallel time lines for the history of politics, music, art, and inventions; fashion time lines; or family time lines. It's a great way to organize and get a grip on data that otherwise would overwhelm you, as well as graphically demonstrating the relationships between events that otherwise would have been missed. See how art influences philosophy, or theology politics.

Since making your own time line from scratch can be such a massive chore, I've included reviews of two different time line products. Both look nice on your wall. The first contains information you very likely would never find yourself, and the second employs your children in putting together the already printed pieces.

Creation's Child
Historical Time Line Chart, $17.35 postpaid.

S. C. Adams was a man of many talents: pastor, educator, state senator, Oregon pioneer, and farmer. In 1871 he published a time line, and *what* a time line! Over fifty feet long and five feet high, lavished with color engravings, Adams' time line covered the history of the world from creation to his day, including the vicissitudes of nations (with a separate stream for each), discoveries, inventions, alphabets, political events, and much more. Besides Western nations, Mr. Adams' time line also covered China, Persia, Assyria, and a host of other countries normally forgotten in our historical studies. Adams was a bit of a modernist, although still committed to Biblical chronology, and his effusions on the marvels of 1871 technology are amusing.

The original chart is on display in a museum in Oregon. But you can get a copy of this beautiful extravanganza that's a usable fifteen feet long, composed of five poster panels, from Creation's Child. As a data-organizing tool, this time line is not as helpful as it could be, since dates are incorporated into the "streams" instead of being firmly separate and viewable on the top of the paper. However, it contains a wealth of information and is an invitation to historical browsing.

Creation's Child has many other materials of interest for learning at home. See their listing in the Catalogs and Parphernalia chapter.

Thomas A. Edison

KONOS

Time Line Packet, $45. More volumes to come.

It cost me a pang to send back the copy of this time line that KONOS loaned me. What you get are sturdy, laminated, colored sheets with time lines printed on some pages and little cutout figures on others. The time line covers 2099 B.C. to 1999 A.D., with three lines each for the 1400s on (so much was happening!). You get sixty-eight people, with dates of birth and death if known, some carrying insignia of their profession, others with little colorful stickers to identify them. Prophets carry staffs, mountain men wear coonskin caps, humanitarians have a red heart, preachers and missionaries carry a Bible, and so on. The people in Volume 1 are those studied in Volume 1 of the KONOS Character Curriculum, reviewed in the Curriculum Buyers' Guide. This time line contains a preponderance of Biblical figures, along with major cultural leaders like Michelangelo and Martin Luther King, Jr.

The price reflects the extra cost of providing laminated time strips and figures, which render the product much more attractive and durable. KONOS suggests you mount the time line in ascending and descending steps around a doorway, with B.C. on one side and A.D. on the other. Their time line looks nice enough so your children's room will look decorated rather than defaced.

I should also mention that the kit contains a number of "free" figures, so you can add the people of your choice: family members, for example.

KONOS plans to come out with future volumes of both their curriculum and the time line, plus special-purpose time line packets such as Scientists and Inventors or Presidents.

HISTORY TEXTS AND RESOURCES

A Beka Books

I like the entire A Beka history series, from the colorful workbooks for little kids to the equally colorful textbooks for junior- and senior-high students. Our sons have no trouble at all understanding the early A Beka texts, which besides history include American customs, songs, and other vital parts of our cultural heritage. The entire curriculum includes an emphasis on geography mastery (you get twenty-two pages of map skills and a mini-atlas in the *Old World History and Geography in Christian Perspective* book for fifth graders, for instance). A Beka's series includes both American and world history, and like all real Christian history it starts in the Garden of Eden, not mucking about among scattered bones in Africa.

Addison Wesley

Pursuing the Past, Volumes 1 and 2, $12.72 each for student book and teacher guide.

A-W is an energetic and enterprising company. *Pursuing the Past* has a good idea: let kids investigate history on their own. Kids learn techniques of historical investigation by programmed assignments. In Volume 1, students dig into oral history, photos, family history, and grub about in cemeteries. Volume 2 pushes on to maps, architecture, city and neighborhood history, and the "working world" (I hope that last isn't just a cover for pitching more careerist nonsense).

I haven't seen it, but the underlying idea is great.

Cobblestone: the history magazine for young people

$18.50/year (twelve issues). Back issues, $2.95 each. Discounts for bulk orders (three subscriptions or more).

Would you believe a history magazine for kids with a growing circulation of more than forty thousand? (Encouraging, isn't it?) This very professionally done magazine has lots of kid appeal, being loaded with pictures, puzzles, cartoons, and lots of short, zippy stories. Whoever locates the pictures does a terrific job, as they include a lot of rare and apt photos, woodcuts, engravings, and whatnot that truly add to the depth of the stories.

Each issue of *Cobblestone* is organized around one theme. Over the past five years, themes have included America's Cowboys, the Boston Massacre, Harriet Tubman, Old-Time Schools, and the Pony Express. A recent issue on the theme of Newspapers had a two-page time line beginning with Roman slaves sweating out newsletters by hand and ending with the Columbus, Ohio *Dispatch* whipping off the first totally electronic newspaper. Articles took off on tangents. Newspaper illustration, war correspondence, rural papers, and specialty presses were some of the unusual subjects covered. The whole issue was held together by several major articles on the history of printing and the freedom of the press. I've described half of that one issue; if it whets your interest, why not send away for a back issue, perhaps choosing one of the themes above? Back issues are available in bound annual sets as well as individual copies.

You can also get a teacher's manual that provides over sixty activities that can be used with back issues of the magazine, and a cumulative index.

Cobblestone is secular, but what I've seen of it is historically accurate and not polemical.

Living Scriptures

Living Principles, thirty-six cassettes, $286.20. Individual cassettes, $11.95.

A history of America on cassette. Professional dramatizations and sound effects.

Mountain Craft Shop

Toys from $1 to $23. *American Historical Cards:* large, $7; small, $5. Shipping extra.

The Mountain Craft Shop is your source for authentic reproductions of antique American folk toys. The Shop also carries reprints of old books with a toy or game theme, like the one hundred-year old Pop Up Book series, or the 1859 Hand Shadows books. Plus books on how to make your own toys, books of folk games and songs, and more!

Local artisans make the toys, and famous museums carry them. Owner Dick Schnacke's *American Folk Toys: How to Make Them* is a standard in this field. (It's $8.95 from the Shop.) The Shop deals with both wholesalers and the general public.

What does this all have to do with history? Well, history is about people, and children are people, and children spend a lot of time playing, and here are the toys, hundreds of them, that our great-granddaddies played with!

The Mountain Craft Shop also carries a line of large and small *American Historical Cards,* which are fifty-two portraits of famous folks, plus info about them.

Our Christian Heritage

Workbooks for grades 1 to 6 with a Scriptural approach to the studies of geography, history, and government. History is the biggest component of the three. These workbooks are well-liked by Reconstructionists. Christian Liberty Academy uses some of the volumes. Each is $4 or just slightly more, and you may obtain an evaluation copy by sending a check for the price. If you don't like it, send it back unused for a full refund.

RESOURCES FOR USING THE "PRINCIPLE APPROACH"

Of the eight historical theories listed in the introduction to this chapter, those receiving the least attention in the schools are #1—the Cyclical Approach, and #8—the Providential Approach. I can't help you much with materials for #1, as this view of history is inextricably intermingled with primitive mysticism and mythology, and is scarcely history at all, as we understand it in the modern West. The Providential Approach, although equally neglected by modern scholars, has an entirely different background. It was once the dominant view of most Western historians, and the view of many of the famous men and women whose lives formed our history.

Several organizations have recently sprung up to revive the Providential theory. They have banded together to contend for a Principle Approach to the history we study and the history we make. Devoutly Christian, these groups believe in the spread and triumph of Christianity the way Marxists believe in the spread of their religious antireligion. According to the Principle Approach, the behavior of nations is governed by God's immutable laws, and nations advance or decline proportionally as they obey or offend. America's success is then explained in terms of the colonies' early convenants with God, and because our laws were patterned on Biblical models. Our current bouncing from crisis to crisis occurs, according to the Principle Approach, because we are breaking God's laws for national and personal conduct. This sounds

remarkably like what the Russian writer Aleksandr Solzhenitsyn has been saying about both America and the U.S.S.R., showing that the Principle Approach transcends national and political boundaries.

Principle Approach materials are in their first generation, and therefore mainly addressed to adults, who then have to present the ideas directly to their children. But busy hands make light work, and perhaps by the time you read this, some of the groups listed below will have materials for young children as well.

Christian Heritage Studies

Seminars for the home, church, or school. Subjects: Introduction to America's Christian History: The Principle Approach; Intro to America's Christian History and Government; A Reading Program: McGuffey and His Readers; the Principle Approach.

Rev. Christopher R. Hoops is available as a consultant on the Principle Approach and as a seminar leader.

Foundation for American Christian Education (FACE)

In the Mayflower Compact, this nation was dedicated "for ye glorie of God, and advancement of ye Christian faith." FACE would like to reconstruct America according to the Christian principles of the Founding Fathers, beginning in the home and with the teaching of America's Christian history.

FACE has published a number of very attractive volumes on this subject, and offers substantial discounts to schools and home schoolers. All volumes quote heavily from source documents, and all are quite a bargain for the price.

FACE's Rosalie Slater originated the Principle Approach, so named because one starts with Biblical principles and then builds one's education plan from there. (Actually, the Apostle Paul originated it, but you know what I mean!) You'll find more info on FACE in the Government and Help! chapters. Do send for their free brochure if you are interested.

Mayflower Institute

Role of Patriot Pastor, four tapes, $24.95. *Pilgrim Seminar,* eight tapes, $29.95. *American Covenant,* $9.95. Study Leader's guide, $4. Bimonthly journal, suggested donation of $15. Bulk prices available on books. Shipping 10 percent.

Mayflower sells FACE materials, and also has tapes on matters such as The Role of the Patriot Pastor in Colonial America: A Challenge for Today and the tape of the first annual Pilgrim seminar. Marshall Foster, the Institute's president, and Mary-Elaine Swanson, its resident scholar, have written a book called *The American Covenant: The Untold Story.* You can get an accompanying study guide for *The American Covenant,* or even order a fifty-two-minute documentary based on the book that was aired on the "700 Club" in ten episodes. (Order the movie from Gospel Films.)

Mayflower also issues a bimonthly journal geared toward contemporary applications of the Biblical principles it sees in America's Christian history.

CHAPTER FORTY-ONE

SOCIETY AND CULTURE

Back in the days of William Holmes McGuffey, no American student had ever heard of "social studies." This portion of the public school curriculum, a hybrid of history, geography, sociology, anthropology, and psychology, emerged as the so-called social sciences began to come into favor.

The first thing to understand in order to see social studies steadily and see it whole is that *there is no such thing as a social science.* Science is based on objective, reproducible facts about observable reality. Measurement must be totally objective. A real scientist might drop a stone from the top of the Tower of Pisa, for example, and measure how long it takes to hit the ground. He might repeat this experiment with stones of different weights. In the end he has enough measurements to formulate a hypothesis, which is his best guess at why stones drop at the rate they do. After hundreds of stone-droppings he is sure—*all* stones dropped from the Tower of Pisa fall at the same rate. Figuring out why the stone-dropping rate is constant takes many more experiments, dropping different objects from different heights and, since gravity ends up being involved, observing the movements of the planetary bodies. When the scientist finally has his theory ready, anyone in the world who can obtain different results can disprove it.

The "social sciences," however, deal with people, not stones, and that is where the trouble begins. You can, of course, drop people off the Tower of Pisa and observe their flight patterns, but social "scientists" aren't concerned with these mere physical observations. They are interested in human *behavior. Why* do we do the things we do? What sort of things *should* we do? To answer the first question, you have to get inside the human spirit. To answer the second, you must become acquainted with the Spirit of God. This is entirely outside the realm of true science.

Every observation a social "scientist" makes comes through a grid of human interpretation: his or the subject's or possibly both. Unlike the time it takes a stone to fall, which can be measured by machines, human behavior can't be scientifically quantified. Another problem is that people behave differently when they are being observed. Still another problem is that the types of people who willingly allow themselves to be observed, or who spill their guts to researchers, are not quite typical of the rest of us.

In the schools, social studies has been the chosen vehicle for carrying propaganda. Kids are indoctrinated with socialism and antireligious ethics, presented as "scientific." Now, come on. Just because a dying tribe of Eskimos eat each other and drive their old folks out to freeze on the ice floes, does that really mean *we* have to do it?

There certainly is a place for research about human behavior. Human curiosity demands it. We can get a better understanding of the human condition by seeing how different men, women, and children behave in different times and circumstances. But these observations or the theories that spring from them are not "science." Misused, the study of humans and society leads to intellectual tyranny. But when well done, it is an *art.*

SOCIAL STUDIES MATERIALS

Again, I have not included any standard school sources on this list. Those textbook suppliers are listed in the Textbook sections. The list that follows is of materials both innovative and inventive. They involve the student in making his own observations and discoveries. Not all share my ethical outlook, but all have a high information content.

Who are our fellowmen? How do they behave? Look below and find out!

Cobblestone Publishing

FACES, $16.50/year (ten issues), $20.50 Canadian and foreign. Single current copy, $1.95. Back issues, $2.95 each. Bulk rates available for single issues and subscriptions.

The *People* magazine of other cultures—that's *FACES,* a children's mag put out by Cobblestone. Each good-looking issue of *FACES* has photos, features, and stories from societies around the world and focuses on a single theme. The contents are kid-appealing. Most are selected from tribal cultures. The perspective is a la public school—e.g., what is, is right.

Educational Book Distributors

European Cultures, $12.95.

EBD has quite a few books about other cultures, including a wide selection on the subcultures of California (Hispanic, Indian, Japanese, and so forth).

The EBD series I like the best is their one on cultural activities. *European Cultures,* a book in this series, has sixteen cultural activities for K-6 children. Children make their own Mother Goose book (rhymes and pictures supplied) which they correlate with a map of the British Isles to see where each rhyme takes place. They make Scottish scones (yum!). They make flags of many nations, and store them in an envelope. They play matching games—which animal is found in which country? Paper dolls! Gypsy tambourines! Foreign money! Every activity is easy to do and really fun. The rest of the series follows this format.

God's World Publications

God's Big World (K), *Sharing God's World* (grade 1), *Exploring God's World* (grade 2): $6.50; includes teacher guide. *It's God's World* (4-6), *God's World Today* (junior high), $8.00; includes teacher guide. Class-sized orders receive substantial discounts. Class orders received after September are billed only for the issues remaining through the end of the school year.

A different slant on social issues. *GWP* has weekly newspapers for elementary children of all ages at a really reasonable price. Lots of activities and discussion questions, with Biblical ethics applied throughout. Know what the issues are and see how different people respond. *GWP* papers also carry items about the trivial and sensational: which town made a two hundred-foot strudel for its annual festival, what German carved a stone Mercedes (every home should have one, right?), what Floridian now gives underwater haircuts? Keep on top of the zany as well as the serious!

Museum of the American Indian

The Museum publishes exhibit catalogs, scholarly studies, a book on recommended films by and about Indians, photographs, postcards, and note cards. The Museum Shop also offers a selection of books from other publishers. For information on what is currently available, send a stamped, self-addressed, #10 envelope.

National Geographic Society

National Geographic magazine comes with Society membership of $15/year. *World,* $9.95/year (twelve issues).

My dad bought us a station-wagon-load of old *National Geographics* when I was eight years old. I was supposed to fall on them with yelps of joy and read them cover to cover. In sober fact I found them boring, and only read the insurance ads on page 2. Not to put down *National Geographic;* still, without someone to explain why stories about strange people and animals on the other side of the world are relevant, even the most colorful, well-written, well-researched information available will fall by the wayside.

National Geographic is gorgeous and loaded with information about other cultures. Its pictures are a great source for collages, scrapbooks, and other discovery projects.

National Geographic World, the picture mag for kids, is very beautiful and easy to read. Very little of the content has to do with other cultures, except incidentally. It really is a nature magazine.

The National Geographic Society also publishes books and records about things historical and geographical and all creatures great and small.

Our Christian Heritage

Complete set of 5 books, $19.50. Books A-C, $4 each. Books D and E, $4.25 each. Add 8 percent shipping.

If you're looking for a series that fuses history, geography, and government without a morass of "social science" thrown in— in other words, an old-fashioned social studies program—OCH has it. Very strongly Christian, the five-book series depicts the Western movement of Christianity from Europe to America up through the 1800s. The books are worktexts and quite reasonably priced.

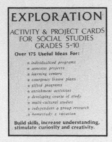

EXPLORATION

ACTIVITY & PROJECT CARDS
FOR SOCIAL STUDIES
GRADES 5-10

Over 175 Useful Ideas For:

■ *individualized programs*
■ *semester projects*
■ *learning centers*
■ *emergency lesson plans*
■ *gifted programs*
■ *enrichment activities*
■ *developing course of study*
■ *multi-cultural studies*
■ *independent & group research*
■ *homestudy & vacation*

**Build skills, increase understanding,
stimulate curiosity and creativity.**

R. S. Publications

Exploration: card stock $7.50, paper $3.75. *Explore U.S.A.,* cards $9.95, paper $4.25. *Explore Literature,* cards $7.50, paper $3.75. *Explore Natural Science,* cards $7.50, paper $3.75. Entire set, paper, $12.50. All prices postage-paid.

R. S.'s *Exploration* packets are the niftiest social studies activities I've seen for elementary and middle-grades students. All are available on 8½ x 11″ heavy card stock or on bond paper bound into folders. Buff-colored cards are "foundation" activities, and ivory-colored cards are for enrichment.

The *Exploration* series begins by introducing the student to the different categories of social scientists (that unfortunate term again!). After looking up the definitions of these professions in the dictionary, he is given a number of social problems and asked to decide which profession goes with which problem. After this very sensible introduction, the foundation cards go on to maps and their use, different cultures, symbols and graphs, and other necessary tools. Enrichment cards suggest activities in such areas as flags, families, folk dances, coin and stamp collecting, and world travel. Here's one of the several dozen possible activities on the coin collecting enrichment page:

Make a display or poster of the money of one country as it has changed from the past to modern times. Show how we can learn something about a country's history from the changes in its money. Make a timeline of historical events showing the money used at various important times in the country's history.

For those who prefer less work and more thinking, there is the question: "If you were to replace money as a means of exchange, what would you use?" The questions in this category alone could easily lead students into the discovery of economics, geography, history, and politics. This kind of open-ended learning is fantastic for developing anyone's mental powers.

R. S. has also developed packets called *Explore U.S.A., Explore Literature,* and *Explore Natural Science,* for grades 1 to 6.

R. S. is very friendly to home schoolers, and has prepared special paper packets to make their series easier to afford.

Visual Education Corporation

Grass Roots, $76. *They Chose America,* Volumes I and II, $76 each. All three plus free American Heritage Learning Kit, $209.

And when you've finished studying the strange customs of people on the other side of the globe, it might be refreshing to rediscover a few of *our* strange customs, past and present. America has a little of every nation right here. Why not study America?

Vis Ed has several cassette series to make this study lively. *Grassroots* is an oral history of the American people, told by themselves.

Field recordings, selected from 17 private collections and from state, regional, and national archives are interwoven to depict the customs, ideas, viewpoints, and daily life of Americans. Mountain folk, miners, former slaves, seafarers, sodbusters, roughnecks, cowpunchers, homesteaders, and loggers sing and tell their stories in dialects as rich and varied as their origins.

Grassroots comes with a listening guide that includes an introduction by folklorist Alan Lomax, plus background info and sources for each selection.

These six cassettes, all over an hour in length, are grouped by regions: Northeast, South, Midwest, Southwest, Far West, and Northwest. "Sayings" of the Pennsylvania Dutch; accounts of seafaring life; rural Southern courtship and marriage; feuds between farmers and ranchers; homesteading; rodeos; whaling; Indian attacks and massacres on both sides and on and on are recalled in the words and dialects of those who lived through it.

They Chose America is a set of original interviews with forty-seven men, women, and children who came to America between 1902 and 1968. It comes in two volumes, each with thirty- to sixty-minute cassettes. Volume I has the stories of Chinese, Irish, Italian, Jewish, Mexican, and Polish immigrants. Volume II carries on with Cubans, Germans, Hungarians, Japanese, and Scandinavians.

The American Heritage Learning Kit, which comes free if you splurge and get both *Grassroots* and *They Chose America,* has a colorful wall chart showing where the immigrants came from and where they settled, plus a teacher's guide.

PART X

FINE ARTS

CHAPTER FORTY-TWO

ART

Scribble, scribble, scribble. Grab a chunk of crayon and splotch on some color. Snip, snip with the scissors. Glop on some glue. Oh, boy! Junior just created another masterpiece!

Little kids all love art—making it, that is—and that is just as well, because what would sustain them through fifth-period English if they couldn't scribble cartoons on the margins of their workbooks? Dr. Seuss got his start this way! But somewhere along the line, most of us learn that we are "not talented" and that we should leave art to those other chaps over there, those sporting the berets and the Paris fellowships.

I'm not going to deny that there is such a thing as artistic talent. But most of us have a lot more talent than we suspect. Why, then, can so few Americans turn out a workmanlike piece of art? Our training is to blame. Somehow the idea has taken hold in art instruction circles that the way for people to learn art is for them to make "five thousand mistakes" on their own. *Then,* after making all these mistakes, the talented will emerge and the rest will sink into the dregs. This is the way the schools teach reading as well, and it of course produces the same sorry results.

Contrast this with the ancient and honorable "apprenticeship" system, where the eager would-be artist worked under the direction of a master in his craft. At first the apprentice spent most of his time doing menial things: rehairing brushes, mixing paints, and so on. This phase gave him great intimacy with the physical tools of his art. Then the master would let him try some small exercises, and if he was successful he would perhaps get to contribute a minor part to one of the master's own projects. In time, he would learn most of the master's techniques (canny masters kept some back!) and would be ready to try something new on his own.

At each step the apprentice was *taught* the skills he needed.

He saw all the stages artwork goes through; he saw the finished result; he heard the master criticize his efforts, and make suggestions for improvement. He did *not* hack about making five thousand mistakes—the master wanted a productive apprentice, not a nitwit.

Children need to see good art if they are to produce good art. It's true that when freshly introduced to a new form of art they need to be free to mess about and familiarize themselves with the art media. But this play phase should be followed by real instruction, or frustration results. *Any* serious artist, whether five or fifty, appreciates teaching that helps him produce better work.

Below are resources that will help you avoid some of those five thousand mistakes.

INTRODUCTION TO ART VIA DRAWING

It is being overly generous to say that 5 per cent of our college graduates know how to draw. There is no successful drawing program in our public schools and educators know it. . . .

If you will evaluate our public-school art program, do not ask the art supervisor. The reply would probably sound much like the weaver's description of their goods in the tale, *The Emperor's New Clothes.* Instead, ask yourselves and your neighbors because you are the products of the public-school art program and NO EDUCATIONAL PROGRAM IS BETTER THAN THE PRODUCT IT TURNS OUT. . . .

Many art supervisors and teachers maintain that there is no "right" and "wrong" in drawing. . . . In a drawing program where there is no right and wrong and no rules, the children have nothing tangible to grasp and nothing to take home. They do not learn the right way; they do not learn the wrong way; they do not learn. . . .

One of the main objectives of today's public-school art program is "Free Expression (creative self expression)." We know that people who do not know how to draw cannot express themselves freely. . .[1]

Thus speaks a veteran public school art instructor who also put in a decade as a Walt Disney artist in the era when Disney's art was really something. As so often happens, Bruce McIntyre beat me to the punch. His book, aptly named *Drawing Textbook,* explains in crystalline detail *why* public school (and most private school) art programs fail to produce students who can draw. His analysis of what went wrong is combined with a stirring call to achieve drawing literacy in our day, and takes up the first thirteen pages of the book. Find out why the ability to communicate visually makes such a difference, and the *one* approach to art instruction that provides it. Then you and your children can tackle the 222 graduated exercises that make up the rest of the book! These start with simple stuff—a birthday cake, a TV set— and progress along merrily, introducing the Seven Laws of Perspective and other goodies until by Lesson 58 you're drawing realistic skyscrapers, by Lesson 94 you're getting down on paper a twisted candle that would make the Hildebrandt brothers proud, and by the last lesson you can draw ANYTHING! From here on in, it's merely a matter of adding to your visual vocabulary.

Sycamore Tree carries *Drawing Textbook* and sells it for the piddling price of $4.50 or so.

And while we're concentrating on drawing as the foundation of all art, don't miss *The Big Yellow Drawing Book,* a product of the O'Neill clan. Dan O'Neill is a cartoonist of some repute in flower-child circles. His *Odd Bodkins* cartoons gained quite a following in the Sixties and Seventies. Family members Hugh (a genuine EdD) and Marian also helped out, in ways not clearly defined in the introduction. The end result of their labors is a charming, simple introduction to drawing (in general) and cartooning (in particular) that has been proved 99 percent successful in teaching people of *all ages* to draw. You start by adding expressions, as per the directions, to cartoon faces, and go on to practice six principles of perspective. A mere $3.75 (postpaid!) to Hugh O'Neill & Associates gets you the book, which includes room for your practice exercises. Anyone four or five years old can tackle the beginning exercises. We got one for each member of our family. *The Big Yellow Drawing Book* makes a great stocking-stuffer (as long as you wear tights—the book is 8½ x 11").

And, for a complete drawing course intermixed with New Age philosophy and neurological speculation, I'd better not skip over *Drawing on the Right Side of the Brain* by Betty Edwards. Houghton Mifflin distributes this $9.95 book, and at the time of this writing you could get it discounted from Quality Paperback Book Club. After a lengthy introduction about right and left brains and artistic states of consciousness, the authors gets down to cases with a number of exercises to help you become aware of shapes, perspective, and proportion, with particular attention to drawing the human face. The book is full of before-and-after examples done by the author's students, and these are a powerful commentary on the effectiveness of her teaching methods.

ART SUPPLIES

ABC School Supply
Chasselle, Inc.
Hoover Brothers
Lakeshore Curriculum Material Center

These school supply houses all have a wide selection of arts and crafts materials at very attractive prices. I like the Lakeshore catalog best for art, although they all are good, because Lakeshore offers some crazy items the others don't: wiggly eyes for freaky collages, and a device that makes innocent clay into stringy "spaghetti" suitable for providing a clay model with hair, for instance. All the catalogs sell glitter, paints, pens, markers, clay, glue, and dozens of varieties of art paper: everything a young artist needs.

Curriculum Resources, Inc.
Price sampling: 12" bookshelf for $1.75; birdhouse for $1.30.

This company offers a large variety of craft kits for children and adults. Excellent prices, simple projects. Some unusual crafts: wheat weaving, quilling, smocking—plus basketry, latch hook, and dozens of other "standards." Some crafts come in bulk packs for group projects, and these are often used in schools.

Dick Blick
Five mail order addresses. Send order to the one closest to you.

Blick has a complete selection of art, craft, and related materials for all ages and skill levels. Blick's special emphasis is on fine and graphic arts; many supplies are geared to the working artist. You name the art medium or craft, from spinning to sign-making, from oil painting to light tables—they've got it. No serious artist, young or old, should miss this catalog. Worth the $2.

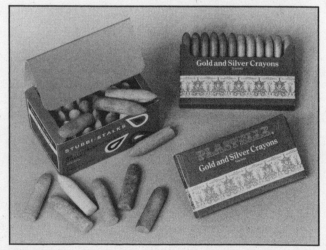

DIDAX, Inc.
Rubber stamps, crayons, and other fun stuff for kids. Small art selection, but nice. DIDAX also sells all sorts of manipulative

learning devices for other subjects. (See the listings under Math and Reading). If you like the "hands-on" approach to learning, you'll drool over this colorful catalog.

Dover Publications

Publishers of over three thousand paperbacks in all fields of interest, including many specially suited for home study and instruction. Most priced between $2 and $5.

Tons of economical art and craft books. Dover has a large clip art section, consisting of copyright-free designs and illustrations you can paste on to your own productions before duplicating for that professional look. Just for fun, Dover has paper models—you can cut and assemble the Emerald City or a Western Frontier Town, among others. I bet you'll get excited over their unique coloring book series (human anatomy; favorite birds; American Revolution uniforms; Bible stories; make your own calendar . . .). Also books on origami, books about art, books on "how to" almost anything.

The prices are great because the books are reprinted. Dover has books in all categories. Look for the reviews throughout this book.

Hearth Song

Superb quality art and craft supplies, small but well-chosen selection, some extravagant, some affordable. Over one-third of the items are under $6. Hearth Song emphasizes natural fabrics and materials—e.g., their wool-stuffed dolls. New Age flavor.

NASCO

Along with Dick Blick, this is the other major art catalog you will want to get. NASCO offers a lot of the same material Blick does, but looks more to the school-age market. Many items are discounted. Huge color catalog. Compare prices and save!

Optasia Fine Art Designs

Ten coloring postalettes for $5. Includes ten of one design on a variety of paper stocks and colors, plus gold stickers.

The SCHOOL • MASTER • PIECES Guideline Series of cards takes coloring practice to its artistic limits. These very lovely cards come on a variety of colored, high-quality papers to encourage experimentation with various artistic tools and techniques, and can be either sprayed with a fixative and framed or given as gifts. The publishers suggest that children can use fine line felt tip pens, pastels, wax pencils, and thick water colors (too much water wrinkles the paper).

It can be a great disappointment to a child to create a "masterpiece" on shoddy coloring book paper, which promptly tears or is otherwise destroyed. By using SCHOOL • MASTER • PIECES coloring cards, your youngster's best work can both really look good and be preserved. The cards make lovely gifts too, thus solving the problem of what your child can do with his excess artwork. I am also amazed at the price, which is less than you'd pay for many cheap mass-produced occasion cards.

SCHOOL • MASTER • PIECES crisp card stock is a treat for the fingertips, and the designs are a delight for the eyes. It's a way to both introduce your child to quality art and enable him to participate in creating art at the same time.

Sculpture Associates Ltd., Inc.

Everything for the sculptor. SA is growing; it recently bought out Sculpture Services. The catalog offers "fine tools, accessories and materials for the sculptor and artist," including books.

If you like to squish clay between your fingers or to chip away at large stones, SA will lend you a helping hand.

ART INSTRUCTION AND EXERCISES

Alpha Omega Publications

Art I, one-year course, ten LIFEPACs plus two (optional) answer keys and one (optional) test pac; $1.95 each LIFEPAC. Two resource items, Art-A-Color Plates ($5) and Construction Paper Packet ($1.25), are also required.

It is my policy never to endorse a product I haven't personally seen, and that is the only reason I am hesitant about piling on the superlatives for AOP's introductory art course. First of all, the price is right. Secondly, the course hits *all* the bases: fine art, applied art, commercial art, and art appreciation. The course layout, which I *have* seen, maintains Alpha Omega's usual standards of logic and thoroughness, so that each of these areas gets a real workout rather than a passing nod. Thirdly, and this is the part I like the best, the course is designed to provide *practical* art skills, giving the student the tools to use the artistic media (graphics, lettering, layout, cartooning, photography, and printmaking) as well as tools to analyze and improve his personal environment.

AOP says that the fine arts portion of the course can be personalized to fit the student's interests and opportunities.

Dover Publications

Dover, as I mentioned above, has lots and lots of art instruction books, as well as their make-it-yourself projects.

Growing Without Schooling

This very fine home school magazine consistently has articles on art. Readers write in to share their ideas and experiences, and Donna Richoux and the staff contribute their own. As a forum for creativity, *GWS* is unsurpassed. You'll get more ideas per column inch about teaching and learning art here than anywhere else.

David S. Lake Publishers

Papercraft series and Craft Workshop series are inexpensive books designed for home art and craft projects. Grades preschool through 8.

THE CHRISTIAN ART MANUAL

AN ART CENTER FOR THE HOME

ENHANCING THE IMAGE OF GOD BY TEACHING CREATIVITY & SKILLS

SHAPING, TANGRAMS, BUILDING, SEWING, PAINTING, FORMING, DESIGNING, COMPASS USING, CUTTING, PLEATING, WITNESSING, LATCH HOOKING, EXPANDING, BRAIDING, TRACING, MAZES,

STRUCTURING, MOLDING, DRAWING, PERCEIVING, PATTERNS, TAPING, TOY MAKING, GLUING, PRINTING, SLOTTING, WEAVING, MACRAME, COLORING, STRINGING, PUZZLES, FOLDING, QUILLING

OVER 200 IDEAS

☐ Enclosed is my check for $30.00 which includes shipping and handling.

NAME (Please Print)
ADDRESS
CITY _____ STATE _____ ZIP

All orders are filled on a 30-day approval basis. This means that if you are dissatisfied you may return your box at any time within 30 days of receipt for an immediate and unquestioned refund.

Motivational Art Training
Christian Art Manual, $25 plus $5 shipping and handling.

Here's a complete art curriculum for Christian kids. The *Manual* is truly Christian, as the exercises are designed to teach Christian truth by allowing the student to develop visual demonstrations of each concept. Example: Make a 3-D model to represent "me" as body, soul, and spirit. The art instruction itself is also excellent and covers most major areas of creativity: lettering, painting, modeling, etc. Each project has ideas for expansion, so the skill taught can be applied to other projects. List of easy-to-obtain materials are included.

The *Manual* is usable for all ages, including Mom and Dad, who are encouraged to have some artistic fun along with the young 'uns. Projects can be self-instructional for older children, but younger ones will need some guidance.

Originally sold to Christian schools as a motivational tool to reward good behavior, the *Manual* now comes in a home version at the lower price listed above.

Pecci Publications
Color Words, $8.95 postpaid.

What do you do when it's been raining for two solid weeks and the kids are about to eat the living room drapes from sheer frustration? I smile sweetly and say, "Go get Mary Pecci's *Color Words* book." Now you know that you don't need one hundred pages of assignments to teach those little color words—red, orange, yellow, and so on—so what are all those pages about? Aha! Good question! What we have here is the niftiest bunch of primary art assignments that I have ever seen. All you need are scissors, crayons, glue, and a brad or two and you can: Build a (paper) log cabin! Make an Easter egg which opens up to "hatch" a chick! Make Thanksgiving napkin rings featuring a Pilgrim girl and boy! Put together a 3-D circus parade! The activities are seasonal, which is great for emphasizing holidays, and the results are so charming that I have our boys glue them onto cardboard to make them last longer.

Sycamore Tree

Sycamore Tree carries hordes of home schooling resources, including some of the finest art instructional books I've seen. *Drawing Textbook,* reviewed above, features an approach to art instruction so obviously right that you'll wonder why you didn't think of it yourself—guaranteed to teach *all* children to draw! If you don't want to waste your time shopping around, just get this catalog for all your beginning art instruction needs.

ART APPRECIATION

Art Extension Press
Large (7 x 9″ or 8 x 10″) prints, $1.50 each. Small (3 x 4″) prints, $1.50 for packet of ten. Accompanying text, $17.50. Two hundred miniprints (twenty packs), $25.

Learn art history and appreciation through a graded series of fine art prints. The text, *Learning More About Pictures,* includes background on each artistic school represented as well as a small version of each print for cross-reference with the actual print. All major schools of Western art are covered, from Primitive to Renaissance to Modern, including each country's distinctive contribution. This is an excellent concept, marred somewhat by poor lithography, especially apparent on the smaller prints.

Dover Publications

And while you're thinking of art appreciation, try Dover first for those gaudy coffee-table books full of paintings. If they have it, it will cost next to nothing compared to the price from other publishers.

Publishers' Central Bureau

PCB is another source for low-cost coffee-table art books. They sell closeouts, and you can get lavish art books at decent prices. PCB also carries books in many other categories, unfortunately including what they are pleased to call "erotica."

PUBLICATIONS FOR ARTISTS

Periodicals published specifically for sculptors and artists include the following:

ARC
Rural Arts Services
P.O. Box 1547
Mendocino, CA 95460

Artspeak
305 West 28th Street
New York, NY 10001

American Artist
Dept. DA 139
1 Color Court
Marion, OH 43305

Art Journal
College Art Association of America
149 Madison Avenue
New York, NY 10016

Arts Magazine
23 East 26th Street
New York, NY 10010

High Performance Magazine
Karen McCarthy, Circulation Manager
240 South Broadway, fifth floor
Los Angeles, CA 90012

American Art Journal
40 W. 57th St. 5th floor
New York, NY 10019

Art Marketing Letter
R. Lubow Presentations
3608 Douglas Ave., Suite 404
Racine, WI 53402

ArtsCanada
3 Church St.
Toronto, Ontario M5E 1M2
Canada

Horizon
P.O. Drawer 30
Tuscaloosa, AL 35402

Art and Antique
Dept. DA 939
One Worth Ave.
Marion, OH 43305

Art Monthly
37 Museum Street
London, England, WC1A 1LP

Artspace
P.O. Box 4547
Albuquerque, NM 87106

Images and *Issues*
1651 B 18th St.
Santa Monica, CA 90404

Arts & Artists
Foundation for the Community of Artist
280 Broadway Suite 412
New York, NY 10007

Artforum
P.O. Box 980
Farmingdale, NY 11737

Artweek
1305 Franklin Street
Oakland, CA 94612

Leonardo
Pergamon Press, Inc.
Journals Department
Maxwell House, Fairview Park
Elmsford, NY 10523

The Art Economist
Box 600, Canal Street Station
New York, NY 10013

Artmagazine
Suite 306
234 Eglinton Ave. E
Toronto M4P 1K5
Canada

The Crafts Report
P.O. Box 1992
Wilmington, DE 19899

Portfolio
Circulation Department
271 Madison Avenue
New York, NY 10016

Art in America
Subscription Office
542 Pacific Ave.
Marion, OH 43302

Artnews
Subscription Service
P.O. Box 969
Farmingdale, NY 11737

Government and the Arts
1054 Potomac Street, N.W.
Washington, DC 20007

Vie Des Arts Magazine
373 ouest, rue St. Paul
Montreal H2Y 2A7
Canada

Reprinted from *Sculptword News,*
a publication of Sculpture Associates.
Used by permission.

CHAPTER FORTY-THREE

MUSIC

Some of us have suffered at the hands of music teachers, and consequently cast a jaded eye on the prospect of teaching or learning music at home, or anywhere else. Fear not. This section is pretty much free from the sort of musical exercises Miss Grump used to try to force your sweaty fingers through. Yes, some music teachers still make scale exercises and theory the meat of their diet, but they happily are few and far between.

Let me explain that I'm not down on playing scales or learning music theory. Scales and finger exercises are good for developing agility, and music theory provides one sort of framework for the art. It's just that people take music lessons to learn to play an instrument, not to learn *about* playing an instrument. I myself quit taking piano lessons when my teacher refused to let me attempt Tchaikovsky's *Nutcracker Suite,* condemning me instead to more weary months of Bartok piano exercises. I liked Tchaikovsky; I was familiar with the music (unlike Bartok, which always sounded to my youthful ears like a mistake). So why didn't my teacher let me try it?

That question propels us into a burning debate among music teachers. Do people learn music best by proceeding step by cautious step and not being allowed to even *try* advanced pieces until they have been "taught" how to play them? Another issue: Is it a good idea to concentrate on learning pieces you have never heard? One more question: Is it best to learn theory before, during, or after having mastered the elementary playing techniques?

According to the theory developed in the beginning of this book, it would be a good idea to become familiar with how a particular piece sounds before trying to play it yourself. Listening to music builds up your "data" on which your musical knowledge will be based. It would also be a good idea to mess about on the instrument before settling down to serious learning. "Playing" provides tactile data—you discover what movement makes what sound. Sight reading, a highly refined skill, would follow playing by ear in this view. You'd want to get a "feel" for the instrument and for music in general before superimposing a highly developed framework on it.

It just so happens that the musical approach outlined above is part of the famous Suzuki method. Shinichi Suzuki, a Japanese man, developed a method of music instruction that begins by exposing the student to lots of good music—in fact, the very pieces he will learn to play. Once he has become thoroughly familiar with these pieces, he is allowed to begin lessons. At first he plays around with the instrument a lot; then he moves on to making specific sounds. It is very important that the student feel comfortable with his instrument and that he attack the music freely. Music theory is only introduced after the student has already been playing for some time.

Mr. Suzuki has added some other touches as well. Children's parents are at least present for all lessons, and are encouraged to learn along with the children. Students also spend some time in group lessons and recitals, where they get to hear musicians of various ages and skill levels play. This gives them a taste of what they can look forward to accomplishing, as well as getting them used to playing before a friendly audience. All is done in a spirit of helping and comradeship (at least ideally). Using this method, very young children have demonstrated amazing musicianship.

Suzuki has not confined his thinking to music instruction alone. He is the founder of the Talented Education school of thought, which shares some of the spirit of the Human Potential Movement.

Controversy swirls about the questions of how much and if and when parents should make children practice, an issue over which Suzuki teachers have split. But access to an instrument of the right size; encouragement to handle it; a wide mental library of good music; the support of other musicians and the encouragement of one's family; putting off academic studies until the student can see the need for them—these ideas, to my knowledge, are no longer seriously questioned. The Miss Grumps of this world haven't risen up in a body to condemn Suzuki.

Another big name in music instruction is Zoltan Kodaly, a Hungarian man. Kodaly was vitally interested in singing as the best introduction to music of all kinds.

"That the teaching of music is best begun with singing," he writes, "that it is through singing, and before ever touching an instrument, that the child should learn to read music, are recognized as truths by a good many people. . . . Mechanical training in instrumental playing, without corresponding theoretical education; music-making with the fingers instead of the soul; the omission of any thorough musical grounding; and neglect of solfeggio—these are the direct causes of the present decadence of singing and of the increasing number of second-rate professional musicians. . . ."[1]

Kodaly's great crusade was to revive solfeggio, the ear training of being able to recognize notes and intervals in any key and sing them. We are familiar with this as the do-re-mi-fa-sol-la-ti-do style of singing. In this way, the student would be able to pick up a score of music, once trained in sight reading, and *hear* it in his head. He would also be able to translate music into staff notation, and duplicate it by ear in his instrument.

Kodaly was also a champion of Early Childhood Music Education. He deplored the use of the piano in teaching songs and choral music as a (possibly untuned) crutch that prevented children from appreciating "pure, virginal melody."[2] Kodaly also was active in encouraging music societies and choral singing, writing a number of volumes of choral exercises for young people. He then turned to popularizing the pentatonic scale, in an attempt to revive a national Hungarian musical consciousness. This was followed by the publication of *24 Little Canons of the Black Keys.*

They spring from the idea that, as in the case of singing, instrumental studies should start with the pentatonic melodies. . . The first sixteen pieces are transcribed in solmization signs [e.g., do-re-mi style], and only the last eight are scored conventionally. . . . Two other points of interest here are, firstly, that the two parts are recorded on the same line; and, secondly, that the eight conventionally scored canons are intended to be played a semitone higher than the score indicates. The purpose of this is to develop musical thinking and a facility for transposition.[3]

At the time the book I am quoting from was written, its Hungarian author said, "The principles embodied in this, and in the previously discussed works, have to-day become the basis both for musical training and for the teaching of singing in schools. . . ."[4] That was back in 1962. However, Kodaly's methods are by no means dead. Silver Burdett Company, a major textbook publisher, has a line of classroom music instruction based on Kodaly's methods, and Kodaly's name is familiar to students of music.

Suzuki and Kodaly are not, of course, the only names in music instruction today. But they are two you will keep running across, most likely. Between the two of them—Kodaly with his interest in solfeggio and in making the black keys and pentatonic tones accessible, and Suzuki with his stress on exposing the student to lots of good music and allowing him to uninhibitedly attack the music in a supportive atmosphere—you will find plenty of good ideas to start with.

MUSIC INSTRUCTION AND INSTRUMENTS

Ability Development

"The Suzuki Place." Violins, accessories, books, music, flutes, strings, cassettes, metronomes, novelties. Ability Development stocks an outstanding array of books about music, including of course all of Suzuki's books and many books about the Suzuki method. I found about $100 worth of books I wanted just by glancing through their catalog.

To make your shopping easier, Ability Development has prepared several Panda Packs for Suzuki beginners. These include essential books for understanding Suzuki, cassettes of the music your children will be learning, and the music sheets to go along with them.

A.D. has Suzuki series for violin, viola, cello, and flute, plus the instruments themselves and all necessary accessories.

A.D. also sells hundreds of classical recordings (both record and cassette and compact disc).

If you're serious about music, this is a catalog not to miss.

Birch Tree Group Ltd.

While you're looking up Suzuki suppliers, don't forget that *Suzuki Method International,* a division of Birch Tree Group Ltd., has some of the best material available for the Suzuki Method. They are the sole publishers for the world outside Japan and distribute the core music books and recordings for each of the schools: The Suzuki Piano School, Violin School, Viola School, Cello School, Flute School, and Harp School. In addition they carry supplementary material (both music and texts) for the Method. Shar, Kentuckiana, and Southwestern Stringed Instruments carry most of their line or your local music dealer can order direct from Birch Tree Group Ltd.

Summy-Birchard Music, another division of Birch Tree Group Ltd., carries other educational music methods/texts (i.e., Frances Clark ® Piano Method).

Holt Associates

John Holt was not only a major voice in the home school movement, but also an amateur musician of some dedication. Unlike many others, he believed that it's *Never Too Late* to begin learning music, and he published his musical biography under that title. Holt Associates sells the book, which contains valuable insights on the subject of music instruction from the viewpoint of an empirical thinker. Holt Associates also carries a select line of what can only be described as music counterculture: books like *How To Learn the Piano Despite Years of Lessons* and *Mrs. Stewart's Piano Method,* which encourages beginners to roam over the entire keyboard by applying solfeggio principles to instrument playing. Holt Associates also sells instruments, some standard and some outre. None of these items are inferior or frivolous. The choices simply reflect a different view of music: music for the people instead of music for the snobs.

Homespun Tapes

Each one-hour audio cassette comes with printed matter. Single tape, $12.95. Three-tape series, $32.50. Six-tape series, $65. Sixty-minute video cassettes, $49.95 each. Ninety-minute video cassettes, $59.95 each. These also come with printed matter. Shipping extra.

If I told you how much I like Homespun Tapes, you'd think I was exaggerating. So let's stick to bare facts. Here is a company run by professional musicians that sells music instruction tapes produced by themselves and other professional musicians. Styles covered are folk, blues, rock, bluegrass, country, and jazz. The instruction is mellow and familiar, and you can rerun the tape any time you want. Along with the tapes come printed matter giving the music scores and perhaps some explanatory notes. It's like having a private lesson with one of the best musicians in the country, and you can repeat the lesson as many times as you like!

Who teaches the courses? Well, for example: Livingston Taylor on "Hit Guitar Styles," Amos Garrett (several series, including "Electric Guitar"), John Sebastian and Paul Butterfield on "Blues Harmonica," and Lorraine Lee on "Appalachian Dulcimer." These are top musicians, folks, and you couldn't get a one-hour private lesson of this quality if you signed up and waited for a year, let alone one that cost less than $7.

Before I start listing some of the "fun" courses, please note this: Homespun Tapes sells an excellent series on ear training that teaches the principles of solfeggio. Matt Glaser does the honors, and I can't think of a better introduction to real musicianship for anyone mature enough to do the exercises. In other words, most five-year-olds won't dig it, but Mozart would have.

Homespun Tapes, besides its essential series on guitar,

harmonica, bass, banjo, fiddle, autoharp, and piano, has a potpourri of courses on unusual instruments and techniques. If we didn't live in a two-family building with very near neighbors, I'd get the Learn to Yodel two-cassette series. It's a great way to call the kids (or the hogs!) home. You can get a pennywhistle (not for a penny, unhappily) to go with the Irish Pennywhistle three-tape set. Folksy types can latch on to a selection of dulcimer courses, and weird ones can tackle something called "Dawg Mandolin." Some of the best courses are now on video, such as "Contest Fiddling" with Mark O'Connor, "Learning to Fingerpick" with Happy Traum, and "Basic Guitar Set-Up and Repair," a course that is *only* offered by video, for obvious reasons.

In all, there are sixty-six different series as of this writing, most consisting of more than one tape. Any musician can learn something with tapes from Homespun, and aspiring musicians will find Homespun a feast.

International Montessori Society

The Making of Music, Child's Book $10.50, Teacher's Manual $16. Shipping extra.

IMS isn't really in the music business, strictly speaking. However, I noticed that some of the Montessori materials they sell feature an innovative approach to music instruction. One in particular caught my eye: *The Making of Music* by Hestia Abeyesekera. Modestly subtitled, "Breakthrough in Music Education," this book can be used with or without a piano in the home. It "covers the entire keyboard through a series of thirty songs, specially designed for transposing on all the major keys and their minors, including their inversions." I don't exactly know how it works, but it's supposed to integrate "the educational philosophies of Montessori, Orff, Kodaly and Laban." The testimonials say *The Making of Music* is very good in its rhythmic training and that it helps children explore the keyboard freely.

Mandolin Brothers, Ltd.

If you're a music-lover, don't you dare send for this catalog unless you have at least several hundred dollars in hand. Mandolin Brothers specializes in new and vintage guitars, mandolins, and banjos, and the selection will knock your eyeballs out. The owner, Stan Jay, is a recognized authority on vintage fretted instruments, and offers goodies in his catalog such as a 1946 Martin D-28 Herringbone. "We don't know one player who wouldn't like to own this guitar," Brother Jay says. Too true. The lovely creation goes for $4975. Another Martin D-28 made in 1960 was advertised as "You be the judge—we can ship this guitar to you, on approval. $1800."

If, like me, you can't play in this league, Mandolin Brothers carries an outstanding assortment of fretted instruments for small-timers. Plus every fretted instrument accessory known to man, songbooks for dulcimer, fiddle, cello, acoustic bass, violin, mandolin, autoharp, and banjo. Plus instruction books in all the above plus guitar and bass guitar.

Rhythm Band

If you've got kids, and the kids like music, and you're willing that they should, you'll really like this catalog. Rhythm Band is one of those entrepreneurial success stories that public school economics courses keep forgetting to mention. Started with two employees and a borrowed $6,000, Rhythm Band has grown to be one of the largest conglomerates in the music industry, employing over three thousand people. The reason for this outstanding success will become obvious the minute you open RB's catalog. It has something for everybody, at prices anyone can afford, and covering 99 percent of the field of kids' music.

Rhythm Band has pages and pages of instruments for sale. Rhythm Band sells rhythm band sets (but of course!), in sizes for small families and for large institutions. Low-priced folk instruments from many countries. Beginning instruments for young players. Fun instruments even a baby can fool around with. High-tech instruments. Chromaharps. Pianicas. Metronomes. Orff instruments. Bells.

Rhythm Band also has instructional materials: pitchpipes, staff liners, musical notation flash cards, and books on music instruction. More, they sell educational games for teaching music concepts. The catalog has several pages of these, enough to make any music teacher lose control of her pocketbook. There's a page of Hap Palmer records and a page about Andre Previn's *Guide to Music*. Plus supplementary items like full-color prints of orchestra instruments and composers.

R.B.'s prices are outstanding. You can get an Aulos Soprano Recorder for only $2.50. We have one of these, and it's no Cracker Jacks job. No wonder schools, with their strapped music budgets, patronize Rhythm Band so freely.

The catalog is full-color and easy to use. Many school suppliers sell Rhythm Band instruments, but if you have a music-lovin' kid, why not go to the source?

Shar Products

Shar is really two companies in one. On one level, they're a heavy-duty supplier of violins, cellos, basses and all the paraphernalia that professional players of the same require. On the other level, they're a big-time Suzuki supplier, with a comprehensive listing of books about Suzuki, Suzuki recordings, and instrument outfits for little players.

Shar sells the Children's Music Series by Evelyn Bedient Avsharian. This contains workbooks and games for teaching music

reading by several innovative methods, plus fun and easy songs. Example: the *Mississippi Hot Dog Lonely Hambarger Band* is said to include "exciting pieces on the A string alone (!!!), E string alone, and both strings. Duets and rounds in two basic Twinkle rhythms." I'd be interested in seeing anything that made playing one note exciting.

Shar's listing of sheet music for string players and records and cassettes of string music is as complete as you can reasonably expect. You will probably want to send for this no-frills catalog.

Silver Burdett

Silver Burdett, a public school textbook company, has *Listen, Look, and Sing* a complete elementary Kodaly curriculum. They also sell Silver Burdett Music, "the most popular music program in America," for public schools.

MUSIC APPRECIATION

Animal Town Game Company
Music Maestro, $21 plus $3.50 shipping.

As a game, I personally haven't found *Music Maestro* to be all that thrilling, but it *is* a good overview of musical instruments and their functions and sounds. You get an audio cassette with the sounds of over twenty instruments, a gameboard, several decks of cards, and rules to play five games of increasing difficulty. Instruments included are classical 'n medieval, bluegrass, rock, and jazz. We have decided the medieval is our favorite period, and our favorite instrument is the one that sounds like a giant kazoo (now is that the rebec?).

Players not only identify individual instruments, but learn to place them in the correct ensembles and the correct period. Even little kids can play the simplest games—which, as I said, are not that exciting. Part of the problem is that the same instrument always plays the same song on the cassette, thus making it possible to identify instruments by the tunes on the tapes without really knowing which instrument makes which sound.

As a teaching tool, *Music Maestro* is worth the money. But a barrel of laughs it ain't.

Christian Curriculum Project
    $50/year plus $2.50 shipping.

Here's something perfectly delightful for music fans. Christian Curriculum Project's Music & Moments with the Masters series is a four-year music curriculum. Year 1 features J. S. Bach, Handel, Haydn, and Mozart. Year 2 has Beethoven, Schubert, Berlioz, and Mendelssohn. Year 3 it's Schumann, Chopin, Verdi, and Grieg. Year 4 you get Wagner, Brahms, Tchaikovsky, and Dvorak. For each musician you get one professionally narrated cassette tape that tells the story of the man's life interspersed with excerpts from pieces he composed during the period being narrated. You also get a second tape of the master's "Greatest Hits." Each year, then, has eight tapes in all, plus a small booklet giving background information and a valuable resource list for further reading and study.

CCP is using cassettes published by Allegro and CBS Records. The quality is superb and they have great kid-appeal.

ESP
    Worksheets, $5/set. *The Orchestra, $80. What's Music All About?, $80.* Each of the latter is twenty-four fifteen-minute lessons on twelve cassettes plus twenty-four spirit masters.

ESP, a public school supplier, has a line of spirit master worksheet exercises that cover such things as Introducing the Treble Clef, Music Signs, Music Notation, and so on. More ambitious are their two twelve-cassette sets, *The Orchestra* and *What's Music All About?* These also include a spirit master workbook.

The Orchestra covers: What Is an Orchestra?; The Symphony Orchestra; History of the Symphony Orchestra; Players in a Symphony Orchestra; The Conductor; Music Played by a Symphony Orchestra; Who Supports the Symphony Orchestra?; Instrumental Families of the Symphony Orchestra; The String Family; The Woodwind Family; The Brass Family; The Percussion Family; The Concert Hall; Enjoying a Concert; Other Kinds of Orchestras; Dance Orchestras and Jazz Bands; Bands; Small Orchestral Groups; Pop & Rock Groups; Accompanying Orchestras; Unusual Orchestras; Unusual Instruments in the Orchestra; How You Can Join an Orchestra; Future of the Orchestra in America.

What's Music All About? covers: Origin of Music; Early Musical Instruments; Basic Music Notation; Musical Notation Drill; Major and Minor Scales; The Chromatic Scale and Others; What Is a Melody?; Characteristics of Melody; What Is Rhythm?; Characteristics of Rhythm; What Is Harmony?; Characteristics of Harmony; Forms Used in Music; Common Terms; Identify Instruments—Visually; Identify Instruments—Audibly; Vocal Skills; Famous Composers; Classical Music; Music of the Opera; The World of Marches; Jazz; Music from Other Lands; Modern or Popular Music.

The Instrument Workshop

If you'd like to make your own old-fashioned keyboard instrument, this company is the source. You have to buy their catalogs of tools, parts and plans, replacement parts and accessories, kits, and plan sources. They also have a *List of Recordings of Historical Keyboard Instruments* of about one hundred and fifty listings of pre-1850 instruments with artist, record title and content, record company, and record number.

As for why this company is listed under Music Appreciation—after you've sweated over blueprints and hunks of wood for about two years, going blind from turning tiny screws with tiny screwdrivers, you *know* you're gonna appreciate *whatever* music the thing turns out!

Kimbo Educational

Kimbo has one of the largest collections of children's music. Nursery favorites, folk songs, sing-alongs, and so on.

LEARNING TO READ MUSIC

Christian Education Music Publishers
    K workbook $3.75, grades 1-4 $4.75, teacher's guide $3. Shipping 4 percent extra for workbooks only. Sample set includes all above for $19.50 ppd. (*All* workbooks are needed for the complete program.)

The *Your Musical Friends* workbook series is a music reading program for K to 4. Each musical symbol is carried by a cartoon animal. Quacker Treble Clef, for example, has a body made of the treble clef, a tail like a bass clef, and quarter notes for feet! There's Crescendo Whale and Forte Lion and Sixteenth Note Bird and Ritard Turtle—twenty-nine animals in all.

The kindergarten book introduces the characters in the form of a coloring book. The first-grade book, *Fun with Your Musical Friends,* gets into the two staffs and notes and rests. The second-grade book, *Enjoying Music with Your Musical Friends,* gets into line and space note values and the loud and soft signs. The third-grade book, *Learning More with Your Musical Friends,* gets into sharps, flats, tempo, repeats, and accents. Finally, the fourth-grade book, *Reading Music with Your Musical Friends,* covers the last details of dotted notes and so on, and launches into actual sight reading.

The series is *very* Christian. Each book begins with a review of the previous book. The exercises and stories are fun and colorful. An example: a fill-in-the-blanks-with-the-note-name exercise in the fourth-grade book about how Isaac Watts' mother had to spank him for continuing to drive her crazy by always speaking in rhyme gives Isaac's reply: "Mother, do some pity take. I will no more verses make!" Because the publisher is striving to keep prices low and therefore uses medium-grade paper, the art is muddy, but that is my only quibble. If your children want to know what all those funny little squiggles in the hymnbook mean, this is the series for you.

PART XI

SPECIAL TOPICS

CHAPTER FORTY-FOUR

PHYSICAL EDUCATION

Awright, ya guys! Up-down, up-down, one, two, three, four! Hey, Jergens, yer tryin' ta touch yer toes or just wavin' good-bye to yer girlfriend? Up-down, up-down, and put some muscle into it!" Such is the melodious song of a football coach in the fall. It is indeed difficult to duplicate this performance at home. For one thing, you need enough players to make at least one complete team. With a little stretching, my brothers and sisters and I made up a baseball team, but most modern families are not blessed with enough members to carry this off. Also, although dads do love to play coach, at home there is not enough incentive to run one's offspring ragged for months on end, like real coaches do for their teams. We must conclude that serious, all-out, gut-grinding, competitive team sports are not for the home. Shucks.

What *did* kids do for exercise before grown-ups invented Little League, anyway? Girls played hopscotch and jumped rope. Boys shinned up trees and played pick-up games of football, baseball, stickball, and street hockey. Everyone played catch and "It" and "Blind Man's Bluff" and dodgeball. Everyone tried to do somersaults and handstands and drove their parents crazy on rainy days running around the house.

Modern kids are fat and soft compared to their old-time counterparts, thanks to TV and adult-sponsored game leagues which force most children to spend hours waiting for a turn to play. The schools try to remedy this by providing "physical education" classes a few hours a week. These classes often provide very little exercise for the one's who need it most: just more standing around in line watching the athletes perform. We are almost at the point upper-class Americans had arrived at in 1920, not believing children will exercise unless some adult stands around and *makes* them.

There are, then, two kinds of exercise products on the home market. One is exercise furniture. There it sits, the jungle gym or climbing rope, trusting that children will hop on it and use it. The other is programmed "movement learning." Children are put through a series of movements and exercises in time to music. I have nothing against the second approach, as long as the movements result in a useful physical skill, such as folk dancing or ballet. But if movement education is used as an *exercise* program, it is a waste of time and insulting to children besides. Just because we adults are obsessed with the shapes of our bodies is no reason to dump this trip on a five-year-old! Baby aerobics is a monster that should never have seen the light of day.

PLAY AND EXERCISE EQUIPMENT

If you're thinking of making a major investment in play equipment, you might first want to send for Community Plaything's free illustrated booklet, *Criteria for Selecting Play*

Equipment for Early Childhood Education. The booklet is more interesting than it sounds, containing numerous candid pix of children playing with (naturally) Community Playthings' equipment. The booklet is both philosophical (stressing cooperative play) and a handy guide to what equipment is best for what age and what features make for superior equipment. There is also a section on the special play needs of handicapped children. You don't have to take all the suggestions as gospel (if you do, you will end up spending your year's wages!).

Childcraft Educational Corporation
Constructive Playthings

These companies both offer standard playground equipment, plus exercise equipment for indoors such as balance beams and mats.

Child Life Play Specialties
Sample prices: Jungle End Swing Set, $485. Complete Fireman's Gym, $385. Kinder climber, with platform, knotted rope, and climbing pole, $166. Knotted rope alone, $15 (it's manila, with large knots). Doorway Gym, $40. Prices slated to rise in '86. Kits are about 20 percent less. Shipping is extra. Ten-year warranty.

Play equipment is this Massachusetts company's *only* product. It's durable and distinctive too, being painted with lead-free forest green enamel. Products are all made from Northern hardwoods, except for chains and ropes and suchlike. The prices are quite acceptable considering the quality, and you can start with a basic frame and add on accessories such as swings and ladders. Some products are also available in kit form.

Child Life has quite a few small items, such as their Doorway Gym, their Knotted Rope, a Tree Hanger that attaches a

swing to any tree of at least sixteen inches in diameter, etc. Many items are clever and innovative. The Doorway Gym, for example, includes a flexible belt swing, a trapeze bar, steel trapeze rings with comfort-grips, and a blocked climbing rope. You just hitch the contraption to your door frame and let 'er rip. Kids can adjust the height of the paraphernalia themselves.

Do we have a Child Life swing set in our backyard? No, we do not. We bought a Sears set before I ever heard of Child Life, and you don't just toss out something made of steel that took several days of hole-digging and concrete-pouring to install. Do I kick myself every time I look at my Sears set, wishing it *were* a Child Life? Well . . .

Community Playthings
Sample prices: Variplay Triangle Set, $125. Kiddie Car, $39.75. Scooter, $65.50. Mini Scooter, $45.50. Shipping extra.

Good solid play equipment, originally designed for schools and day-care centers. The Hutterite community makes its living assembling and selling these items. Many are made of solid wood, and most have exceptional play value. Example: the five-piece Variplay Triangle Set can be a seesaw, a balance beam, a ride-a-plane, a go-cart, a wheelbarrow, a slide with steps, a steering wagon . . .

I should mention that Community Playthings' equipment is quite attractive, in a sensible, solid sort of way. The maple is clear-finished, wheel hubs are painted red, and some wood is stenciled. The catalog is adorned with pictures of Hutterite children enjoying play on the equipment.

All this equipment is designed to *last*. Community Playthings has testimonials from schools that have been using the same piece of equipment for twenty years. This explains why their products cost more—over $90 for a tricycle, for example. The machine in question has a *solid* wheel (no spokes), and a frame that Superman would get a workout trying to bend. Prices are significantly less than the other institutional suppliers, like Childcraft. It's a real alternative to the tinny, mass-produced items available in standard mail-order catalogs and department stores.

Rifton Equipment for the Handicapped

The Hutterites also manufacture very sturdy and useful exercise items for children and adults who need extra help in these areas. It all is quite attractive, as much as this type of equipment can be, and the prices are not any more outrageous than anyone else's.

MOVEMENT EDUCATION

Kimbo Educational

Kimbo's colorful catalog has more exercise and movement albums for children than any other I've seen. Kids can mess around with folk dancing, beanbags, parachutes, Hawaiian rhythm sticks, and so on. Page after page after page of gymnastic routines (with ribbons or without), preballet and ballet, tap dancing, stunts and tumbling, plus the usual leap-and-stretch stuff we all have seen for years on Romper Room. Many of the recordings feature simple, folk-style music. Some thump about with disco.

Kimbo has movement and exercise albums for adults, too: square dancing, slimnastics, jumpnastics, ethnic dancing, and of course the ever-present Jane Fonda. Kimbo has not forgotten senior citizens, either; they have exercises you can do sitting down and other gentle pulse-persuaders.

Send if you wish for Kimbo's free sample record, which also includes snippets of their children's music.

Montessori Services
Perceptual-Motor Lesson plans, Levels 1 and 2, $7.95 each. *Step By Step,* $14.95. Shipping extra.

Montessori Services devote the entire next-to-last page of their catalog to Movement Education of a "non-competitive, non-threatening" sort. Besides parachute activities, parachutes ($79 and up!), kits with rhythm sticks and beanbags, and a rope ladder, MS offers several sets of movement education lesson plans.

Perceptual-Motor Lesson Plans is twenty-five weeks of activities for gross motor skills, plus equipment construction diagrams for such things as a balance beam and a jump box. Level 1 is for ages two and a half to six; Level 2 is for ages seven to nine.

Step By Step is the output of one Sheila Kogan, a Montessori teacher, dancer, and movement consultant. It has eighty flexible lesson plans and a comprehensive index. The lessons use movement to teach physical concepts and reinforce academic concepts. Most activities require little or no equipment. The rest describe "innovative uses for balls, balloons, scarves, ropes and other inexpensive props." Example: "Throw the scarf in the air and catch it. Catch it with your elbow, head, shoulder, tummy, seat, hip, knee, foot, anything but your hands." Just like the rules for that ol' competitive soccer!

Moving and Learning
First five sessions (forty lesson plans, five cassettes, imprinted binder), $125. All ten sessions, $235. Sample lesson and demo tape, $2.

If you really want to get into movement education, Moving and Learning has the stuff. It's programmed. It's complete. It's developmental. It has lesson plans, a teacher's guide, and original music and lyrics. It stresses feelings. It culminates in actual dance steps and improvisation. It requires no special training—but you can get a video tape, or sign up for a workshop, if you wish.

Each of the ten sessions includes eight lesson plans you can tailor to your personality and needs. In the early sessions your child begins by imitating simple actions like jack-in-the-boxes and popcorn popping and working with easy locomotor and nonlocomotor skills. From here the lessons become progressively more challenging until, in the final units, he or she is learning dance steps and performing complicated imagery—the beginning of miming.

Each of the ten sessions takes approximately eight weeks to complete in the classroom, and probably less at home. The entire curriculum is nonconsumable and can be used for any number of children.

The curriculum is clever and complete.

Send for the sample lesson plans and demo tape if you're interested.

Pacific Cascade Records
Cassettes $8.98 plus shipping.

Children's songs on record or cassette are this company's stock in trade. Their material has a folksy feel, and includes several activity albums.

Some popular offerings: Nancy Raven's *Singing in a Circle and Activity Songs* and *Hop, Skip, and Sing.* Children participate along with these live-recorded albums. Another: Mark Weiss's *The Moving, Counting, Rhyming, Feeling, Up-Down, Left-Right, Look What I've Got Album.* Nancy Raven's albums consist of authentic folk songs, while Mr. Weiss's songs are originals.

A number of Pacific Cascade records have won awards.

Pacific Cascade's activity albums are not "movement education" in the strict sense. They foster movement, but do not *demand* it. The activities are fun and invigorating, but not "programmed" with "skill levels." Mellow folks will like it.

Silver Burdett Company
$76 total program. Volumes 1-4, $19.25 each.

This textbook company has "a movement program that teaches music concepts." Entitled *Move into Music,* it features professional performers, recorded directions, and specially-composed music. The series consists of four volumes, each covering two grades, and including a 12″ LP record and teacher's guide.

Sycamore Tree

Perceptual Motor Development Series, books 1-5, $4.95 each. *Good-Time Fitness,* $5.95. Shipping 10 percent.

Ya gotta shake, rattle, and roll! That's the message of the movement ed series Sycamore Tree carries. Each activity helps you "assess your child's motor strength and weaknesses and provide practice to develop his/her skills." The books can be used for grades K to 6. Titles in the series: *Basic Movement Activities; Ball, Rope, Hoop Activities; Balance Activities; Bean Bag, Rhythm Stick Activities;* and *Tire, Parachute Activities.* Sandy Gogel, co-owner of Sycamore Tree, says the tests and tasks require minimal instruction time, and reports much success with them with her own children.

Sycamore Tree is also the exclusive distributor of *Good-Time Fitness for Kids—A Guide for Parents, Coaches and Counselors.* The book is about proper exercise habits and sports conditioning, from birth on up.

PHYSICAL EDUCATION

If you want a school-style physical phitness program (everyone should be physically phit, eh what?) I only know of one that sounds like it could work in a home setting, and be phun besides.

Alpha Omega Publications

Dynamic P.E. for Elementary School Students, $32. *Lesson Plans,* $12. *Dynamic P.E. for Secondary Students,* $26.70 complete.

Alpha Omega has been serving home schoolers for a while now, and AOP's new *Dynamic P.E.* programs are being advertised to home schoolers as well as to traditional Christian schools.

Dynamic P.E. for Elementary School Students is a resource textbook with hundreds of simple activities for both fitness and recreation. Its how-to directions include rules, diagrams, and instructions. The accompanying resource book, *Lesson Plans for Dynamic P.E.,* details thirty-six weeks of activities for K-2 and 3-6 levels.

Dynamic P.E. for Secondary Students is the whole ball of wax in one book: lesson plans, instruction units, game rules, and everything else you need (except the balls and mats, of course!).

CHAPTER FORTY-FIVE

SPECIAL EDUCATION

As just about everyone knows, "Special Education" is a euphemism for classes for students labeled slow or learning disabled. In most cases, there is nothing "special" about it.

At home, Special Education becomes truly special. For the first time, the labeled child gets a chance to show himself or herself an individual capable of achieving. Unlike schoolteachers, who have been trained to always "blame the child" when his learning does not progress, parents have a stake in discovering a better teaching method. This is *your* child, and if he doesn't learn you can't chalk it up to fate and hope for a better group of students next year.

HELPING YOUR LABELED CHILD

Step one in helping your labeled child is to reject the label. Unless the school, or whoever labeled your child, can demonstrate that an *organic* problem exists, they're just saying, "We don't know why Johnny doesn't learn and we aren't interested in finding out." If Johnny has crossed eyes and can't see the blackboard, or his ear wax is the consistency of concrete, then obviously he will have learning problems until his eyes get uncrossed or his ears get cleaned. But if Johnny is labeled "learning disabled" or "developmentally delayed," these so-called diagnoses have no *medical* significance at all.

Albert Einstein's teachers thought he was stupid, and would have called him learning disabled if the term had been around back then. But Mr. Einstein was merely disinterested in their teaching; there was nothing wrong with *his* brain.

So if your child is doing poorly in school, consider some of the following possibilities:

(1) He is bored.

(2) He has a poor teacher.

(3) He is being taught by a poor method.

(4) He is not being taught in the way that suits his learning style.

(5) He is very bright and has contempt for his classes.

(6) He is very bright and is trying to "fit in" with the gang by acting stupid.

(7) He is a thorough chap who doesn't like to race on to new items until he has digested the old. (But school leaves no time to digest the old.)

(8) The class is graded subjectively, and the teacher doesn't like him.

(9) He is not well disciplined, and rather than dealing with his bad behavior, the school prefers to label him "hyperactive."

These nine possiblities are just the tip of the iceberg. The bottom line, when dealing with physically normal children, is this: shall we give up and blame them, or consider their failures *our* failures, and keep searching for the solution?

The following two organizations exist to help the parents of physically normal, labeled children.

Good News for Handicapped Children

Many communities today have toy libraries that deal mainly in materials for the handicapped and developmentally delayed child. For more information and the location of the toy library nearest you write:

- USA Toy Library Association
  Judith Laccuzzi,
  Executive Director
  1800 Pickwick Avenue
  Glenview, IL 60025

There is also a free newsletter for the grandparents of the handicapped and developmentally delayed.

- Especially Grandparents
  Kings County ARC
  2230 Eighth Avenue
  Seattle, WA 98121

Lekotek is another source. It is a toy library, a training program for professionals and it provides a number of family services.

- Lekotek
  613 Dempster
  Evanston, IL 60201
  (312) 328-0001

Reprinted from Constructive Playthings catalog.
Used by permission

Latebloomers Educational Consulting Service

Let me quote from the brochure:

LATEBLOOMERS offers a new model for viewing learning disabled children. Just as the buds on the freesia of LATEBLOOMERS' logo are
in different stages of growth and bloom in their own time, so too,
will children who are not flowering academically have their time to
bloom. . . .

LATEBLOOMERS believes many children who are experiencing difficulties in learning, overcome these problems and "latebloom" when they are in a trusting, warm, supportive atmosphere which allows them to move at their own pace and according to their own natural patterns of growth. . . .

Latebloomers provides individual academic therapy, educational evaluations which focus on *strengths* and potentials for achievement, educational materials for both parents and children, workshops, lectures, and consultations, and above all its "growth model" for lateblooming children rather than a "deficiency model."

Thomas Armstrong, the founder of Latebloomers, has lots of experience in these areas. You may be interested in hunting up the article he wrote for *Mothering* magazine in the summer of '83, entitled "Learning Disabilities: An Unhealthy Concept." Or better yet, send for his brochure.

Orton Dyslexia Society

If your son does cute little things like write *Z* backwards and read *saw* for *was,* and if you are teaching him at home, just ignore it. If, however, he is enrolled in school and the pressure is on to *do* something because for heaven's sake this child is *dyslexic,* don't panic. Get in touch with these folks.

True dyslexia is just a different way of processing information and doesn't need to be "cured." Dyslexics are often geniuses who only need the right teaching method to turn them loose on the world. Dr. Samuel Torrey Orton did pioneering work in developing these methods, and the society carries on his work.

It's very likely that your little one is not dyslexic at all, but just learning and making normal mistakes. Most so-called dyslexia

is actually the fallout from teaching the "look-say" method of reading in which children are required to memorize the shapes of every word in the language. This type of "dyslexia" can be instantly cured by a good phonics program, of which there are two dozen in the section on Reading.

In 1975 the Michigan Reading Clinic examined over thirty thousand allegedly dyslexic children. These had all been neatly labeled so that their reading failures could be blamed on them, instead of on bad teaching methods. Of all the thirty thousand only *two* children were found to be unable to learn to read.[1]

Since the Orton Dyslexia society uses multisensory, intensive phonics, which works equally well with dyslexics and nondyslexics, it can't hurt to send for a list of their materials.

Educators Publishing Service

Parents' Packet, $3. *Language Tool Kit,* $28. *Teaching Box,* $122.65; accompanying storybooks $19.30. *A Guide to Teaching Phonics, Orton Phonics Cards,* $10.65 each. *Reading, Writing and Speech Problems,* $3.50. Lots more.

Educators Publishing Service has a nice little brochure offering "Home Use Materials for Students with Learning Difficulties." EPS carries a number of Orton books and packets, plus Orton Phonics Cards and Orton-Gillingham Language Kits. You can also get reference books on learning problems, including Dr. Orton's classic *Reading, Writing and Speech Problems in Children.*

The *Parent's Packet* of articles from the Orton Dyslexia Society Reprint Series tell what dyslexia is, how to diagnose it, and how to remedy it using the Orton-Gillingham method. The booklet ends on an uplifting note, profiling eminent achievers who have had dyslexia.

Language Tool Kit of 119 cards and a teacher's manual can be used by a parent for teaching reading and spelling to a student with a "specific language disability." The *Teaching Box* is a very highly structured, step by step program for children with severe learning difficulties. You get sixty-nine groups of 3 x 5″ cards, separated by dividers. Two accompanying books explain how to use and supplement the cards, and explain dyslexia. One pack of phonogram cards is enclosed, and you can buy a set of fourteen storybooks to accompany the program.

There's lots, lots more that I have no room to describe. Hey, why don't you send for the brochure?

DEALING WITH PHYSICAL PROBLEMS

Let's assume that your child has not been labeled, but diagnosed. There is solid medical evidence that something is wrong with his brain and/or body. What then?

Popular prejudice to the contrary, these are the very children who need most to be taught at home. Very few professional therapy programs provide hours of individualized therapy every day, and those that do are prohibitively expensive. In the family, on the other hand, a special child can receive hours of instruction and help, *without* being made to feel abnormal.

The materials you will want to use depend on your child's special problems. Look in the School Supplies and Preschool sections and you will find loads of colorful, noisy, hands-on, grabbable learning devices. Many materials designed for early childhood education work well with special children. Make it as much fun as you can for yourself—pick stuff you would enjoy playing with, too! If you are able to take your time and let your child learn at his own pace, this takes off a lot of pressure.

Our first son was born premature and had to spend five weeks in intensive care. Ted was very slow in his physical and muscular development as well. On first diagnosis, one nationally known neurologist predicted that Ted most likely had the fatal disease of spinal muscular atrophy, and if not that, he at least would be handicapped for life. We called in the elders of our church and had them anoint Ted with oil in the name of the Lord. Ted did *not* have spinal muscular atrophy, as it turned out, and neither is he a cripple. Nor is he mentally retarded, another pleasant prospect that was held out to us. When the experts were busy trying to discourage us, my reaction was, "Even if they are right, I bet he *still* can succeed!" Today's "normal" kids are busy retarding themselves, lolling around in front of the TV set and wasting their lives trying to impress their peers. A "retarded" child who works hard at his studies should be able to beat a "normal" kid who never puts forth any effort. Ditto a "handicapped" child who exercises vs. a "normal" kid who lounges around all day. In fact, when a "handicapped" child really works hard, sometimes he or she even beats the "normal" kids who are trying! They said little Wilma Rudolph would never walk again, but Wilma's mother was determined enough to spend her one weekly day off sitting for hours on the bus, taking Wilma to get therapy. Wilma walked. Then Wilma ran. Then Wilma won the Olympics.

Rifton Equipment for the Handicapped

As I said, school supply houses and firms that cater to preschoolers are good places to start, especially those that carry Montessori materials. For physical therapy, Rifton Equipment for the Handicapped has the stuff. Exercise chairs, bolsters, wedges, play equipment, and so on—it's all here. Prices are acceptable for the quality, and it's possible that insurance may pay for some of it if you get a doctor's prescription. We've used similar equipment of our own manufacture, and it did Ted a lot of good.

National Academy of Child Development

Somewhat more controversial is the National Academy for Child Development. Founded by Robert Doman, a nephew of the Glenn Doman who runs the Institute for Achievement of Human Potential and who wrote those books on teaching look-say reading to your baby, NACD specializes in home therapy programs for the really hard cases. Children who have suffered severe brain damage, or who have neurological problems, or fits, or physical handicaps, are thoroughly diagnosed by NACD's staff and then presented with a home program tailor-made for them. NACD is expensive (hundreds of dollars a year per child), and many of their methods are severely criticized by the medical establishment. They do have some spectacular success stories, however, and their philosophy of optimism at least keeps them trying to achieve results, whereas medical experts seem to be getting more and more pessimistic these days. We were members of NACD for a while, and Ted just loved his program (all except the knee bends).

NACD programs are a lot of work for the parents and are highly patterned. You do exercise A for two minutes three times a day, and listen to tape B for three minutes twice a week, etc. NACD is also into the "dominance" theory of brain organization, whereby the goal is to be right-handed, right-footed, right-eyed, and right-eared, or conversely *left*-handed, footed, eyed, and eared. Thus your child may end up wearing an eye patch or earplug to assist him in "switching over" from right to left, or vice versa. NACD also believes strongly in the stages of development, and enrolled teenagers and even adults sometimes wind up crawling around like babies until they improve their coordination in that stage.

You can order NACD's introductory tape set, *The Miracles of Child Development,* for $75. The tapes are fascinating and inspirational; but take them with a grain of salt. B-mod is not the answer for all childhood discipline problems as Mr. Doman believes, though his suggestions for motivating children, and especially his stress on praise and encouragement, are worth hearing.

Home School Headquarters
Resource Guide, **$10 postpaid.**

America is a wonderful country. We have so many volunteer organizations devoted to helping people! The *Resource Guide for Home Education* lists dozens of organizations that serve the handicapped and their families, plus listing magazines, recreation opportunities, and educational resources especially designed for those with physical impairments. Plus the *Guide* lists hundreds of resources for researchers, home schoolers, and community leaders, many of which are not included in my book because of their specialized audience. If your child has been labeled, or has an actual handicap, the *Guide* can help you start networking with people who can help you.

Love Publishing Company

Lastly, if you are looking for standard public school materials for special children, Love Publishing Company has them. See what the schools practice and what they preach, if you're interested.

CHAPTER FORTY-SIX

TESTING

The world of testing is an unearthly landscape where queer creatures loom up out of the gloom. Unnatural sounds stray into your ears: "Raw Scores on Skills Battery," "Diagnostic Subtest Equivalency Norms." Now, if you like your scores raw and your best friend Norm's last name is Diagnostic, this doesn't sound so strange. But to normal earthbound creatures, the language of testing is mystifying. And so it will stay, because without the jargon that consecrates modern testing, it wouldn't sound scientific. And if testing didn't sound scientific, nobody would make children stake their entire future on it. And if kids' futures didn't depend on how they did on the tests, the testing companies would be out of business.

In some ways, parents who educate at home are in better shape because of the sanctity of modern testing. It's not that hard to teach a child to do well on a standardized test, and since the tests are sacred, good results command respect. Tests that check out objective skills, such as the ability to add and subtract or the ability to tell nouns from verbs, can be helpful in assessing a child's area of strength and weakness. But unhappily the testing story doesn't end there. The prestige that objective standardized tests have achieved is being used to huckster a whole range of *subjective, manipulative* tests. These are mislabeled "scientific instruments," when they are actually being used to promote a political agenda.

Early Childhood screening, for example, is being peddled as the cure for all our national academic ills (as if the same people who can't teach five-year-olds would do better if they got their hands on them two years earlier!). Legislators are being pressured to make Early Childhood screening *compulsory.* The kicker is that some of these screening tests are *designed* to find normal children deficient, so large numbers of little children can get forced into state schooling to "remediate" their supposed problems.[1] It's just another device for dragging children out of the home at an earlier age, and saves the bureaucrats the trouble of passing compulsory attendance laws for babies.

Tests of "Social Development" and the like are also excellent for suppressing nonconformists. Once you get out of the realm of $2+2=4$ and start testing *subjective* responses, the test-maker can impose his prejudices on the rest of us. Any response that he doesn't like can be labeled "immature" or "deviant" or "antisocial," and the unfortunate test-taker dragged off to receive compulsory behavior modification.

Since testing is so pervasive and uncontrolled, and can be so damaging, and since legislators are already under fire to make testing even *more* widespread, I would also like to propose a law. Instead of making testing ever more compulsory, how about making it less so? Nobody should be forced to take a test against his will, or the will of his parents in the case of a minor child. This is the only way we can effectively preserve our civil right to privacy, and it won't hurt legitimate tests one whit, because *people gladly take tests whose benefits they can see.* Even if colleges didn't require the SAT, most prospective college students would take it. Another example: few parents or children object to the Iowa Test of Basic Skills, and those few should be allowed to act on their valid objections. But to make testing a political football and impose it on the people from above, or withhold it from students who want it,[2] is plain and simple tyranny.

Even in states where home schooling families are not required to subject their children to standardized tests, one of the first questions prospective home schoolers raise is, "Where can we get our children tested?" Most parents are more than willing to personally pay to have their children's progress evaluated, without any coercion at all. Those who shun tests, in my experience, have serious reasons for so doing. Even though my own children are grade levels above the norm on standardized tests, I fully support the right of *any* family to choose or reject testing. The power to test is the power to destroy.

Following are listings of test options available to home schoolers, and testing companies that sell only to established schools. The latter list may be helpful to those founding private schools.

TESTING FOR HOME SCHOOLERS

The easiest way to have your children tested is to have them tested at a nearby private school. Your children just come to school on the day everyone is tested, do their thing, and then you take them home. The fee for this service is usually nominal. Be sure the private school is friendly to home schoolers before you ask to do this.

Bob Jones University recently announced it would sell the Iowa Test of Basic Skills to home schoolers. You need to locate a certified teacher to administer the test. The test is mailed to her, she administers it, and mails it back to Bob Jones.

Virtually every home school program includes testing. Some, like Alpha Omega, include both diagnostic and standardized achievement tests. Look in the Curriculum Buyers' Guide for more info.

You can just about forget any idea of buying tests directly from the publishers. Not only will you get lost in all the obscure names of obscure tests (DMI-MS and CMI Occ-U-Sort are just two examples), but since you are not an approved and accredited school, you will have to fill out a Purchaser's Qualification Statement. This statement asserts that you meet the standards for test-users established by the American Psychological Association. According to the APA,

> A test user, for the purposes of these standards, is one who chooses tests, interprets scores, or makes decisions based on test scores. He is not necessarily the person who administers the test following standard instructions or who does routine scoring. Within this definition, the basic user qualifications (an elementary knowledge of the literature relating to a particular test or test use) apply particularly when tests are used for decisions, and such uses require additional technical qualifications as well. A recurring phrase in discussions about testing is "the legitimate uses of a test." One cannot competently judge whether his intended use is among those that are "legitimate" (however defined) without the technical skill and knowledge necessary to evaluate the validity of various types of inferences.

> G1. A test user should have a general knowledge of measurement principles and of the limitations of test interpretations. Essential

> G1.1. A test user should know his own qualifications and how well they match the qualifications required for the uses of specific tests. Essential

> G2. A test user should know and understand the literature relevant to the tests he uses and the testing problems with which he deals. Very Desirable

> G3. One who has the responsibility for *decisions about individuals* or *policies that are based on test results* should have an understanding of *psychological* or educational measurement

and of validation and other test research. Essential [emphasis mine. What school official has any business making "decisions about individuals" or "policies that are based on test results" with the results of a necessarily *subjective* psychological test?]

> G3.1. The principal test users within an organization should make every effort to be sure that all those in the organization who are charged with responsibilities related to test use and interpretation (e.g., test administrators) have received training appropriate to those responsibilities. Essential

> G3.1.1. A test user should have sufficient technical knowledge to be prepared to evaluate claims made in a test manual. Very Desirable

> G3.2. Anyone administering a test for decision-making purposes should be competent to administer that test or class of tests. If not qualified, he should seek the necessary training regardless of his educational attainments. Essential[3]

In the CTB/McGraw-Hill catalog, purchasers are required to sign a form certifying that "I and/or other persons who may use the test materials being purchased by me 'have a general knowledge of measurement or principles and of the limitations of test interpretations,' as called for by the APA *Standards for Educational and Psychological Tests,* and that I/we are qualified to use and interpret the results of the tests being purchased as recommended in the APA Standards." Other publishers have similar forms and make you sign similar statements.

All this rigamarole might be necessary for large institutions, especially when those institutions start meddling with psychological tests; but surely something simpler can be devised for home-based instruction. As long as the states don't make the mistake of requiring a certain percentile level of achievement for home schoolers (a standard which is *not* required of public school kids, since even those in the bottom percentiles stay in public school), home schoolers will have no incentive to cheat on the tests. Any company coming up with a clean, inexpensive, home school achievement test should have no problem with test security. In the meantime, it's sign up for a home school program, write away to Bob Jones University, or go take the test at your local Christian school.

TEST SCORE BOOSTERS

More and more public school providers are coming out with test preparation series. Students using these workbooks learn how to increase their test scores. It's really a pity that teachers are forced to spend the little classroom time they have that should be devoted to actual learning just prepping kids for tests. My neighbor Mildred, a public school teacher, wishes she could spend classroom time on instruction, not test-taking skills, and there are many more like her.

However, since the public school kids are being groomed for test-taking, it behooves those of us in home-based private education to pull up our socks and make sure our students aren't lacking in this area. You could make out a good case for the contention that the only skill public school kids get consistent practice with is test-taking. If your home schooled child must take a test for some reason, he might need special training if tests are not a big part of your home curriculum.

Elementary Test Prep

Learning at Home

Set of teacher and student books, $10.25. Separate student books, $3.50 each. Shipping $2.50, orders under $20; $3 for orders over $20.

Although, as I said, many public school providers offer test-taking series, I'm only going to mention one elementary grades test prep series here. *Scoring High* is a "full program of instruction in test taking skills and strategies. SCORING HIGH is a proven practical series that has already helped millions of first through eighth grade students improve their test taking ability."

You can get *Scoring High* for the California Achievement Tests, the Comprehensive Tests of Basic Skills, or the Metropolitan Achievement Tests. These are the three biggies. Learning at Home is a company for home schoolers, and is glad to take your small order, which is why I suggest you buy your test prep materials there.

SAT and GED Prep

The College Board

10 SATs, $8.95. *College Board Achievement Tests*, $9.95.

If you want to see what the College Board's Achievement Tests or an actual SAT look like, the people who publish the tests have put together two books that contain actual, recently administered tests. *10 SATs* has, as the title suggests, ten actual SAT tests in its 304 pages, plus the College Board's official advice to students planning to take the test. You also get prep suggestions, instructions on how the tests are scored, and other useful info. *The College Board Achievement Tests* follows the same format, with 375 pages including fourteen actual tests in thirteen subjects. These are: English composition, literature, American history and social studies, European history and world cultures, math level I, math level II, French, German, Hebrew, Latin, Spanish, biology, chemistry, and physics.

Contemporary Books

GED: How to Prepare, $8.95. *GED Satellite Program* books—*Writing, Social Studies, Science, Reading, Math*—$6.85 each.

Contemporary's GED prep series has review, instruction, exercises, explanations, practice tests, and strategies. Contemporary's *New GED: How to Prepare for the High School Equivalency Examination* has, according to the blurb, been "used by hundreds of thousands of GED candidates to earn their high school diploma." Or, instead of this comprehensive one-volume prep program, you can get individual books on the five GED test areas. Sold by the publisher and through bookstores.

Educational Design

Inside Strategies for the SAT, $6.50. *GED Math, Reading Skills, Writing Skills, Science Test, Social Studies*, $5.75 each.

The cover of Gary R. Gruber's *Inside Strategies for the S.A.T.* announces, "Scores on the actual SAT have been raised an average of *133 points* and up to *300 points* by using the strategies in this book!" Dr. Gruber analyzed over twenty-five hundred actual SAT questions, and came up with thinking strategies for decoding the questions and answering them quickly and correctly.

Educational Design's GED series doesn't come with so much advertising hype. I hope that this is because it is so great it needs no introduction. The *GED General Review* is not tremendously expensive, and it might be a good idea to see how well your home schooled ten-year-old does on it. Just think how silly the state would look prosecuting you if your ten-year-old had already passed the GED!

TEST SUPPLIERS

American College Testing Program (ACT)

The ACT tests need no introduction. What you may not know is that ACT sells inexpensive materials to help prospective college students locate the college of their choice and find financial aid to get them there.

American Guidance Service

Absolutely dozens of tests, mostly aimed at early childhood screening and learning difficulties. Most tests can only be ordered if the examiner proves he has had special training or experience in testing theory.

CTB/McGraw-Hill

Source for the California Achievement Test and Comprehensive Tests of Basic Skills, plus tests in the following categories: Achievement, Early Childhood, Academic Aptitude, Criterion-Referenced and Diagnostic, Competency-Based, Special Education, Adult Basic Education and Guidance, and Customized Services. Only trained individuals may order tests.

The College Board

Books on college majors, careers, financial aid, picking a college, and everything else that might pertain to high schoolers' academic ambitions. And, of course, The College Board publishes the PSAT, the National Merit Scholarship Qualifying Test (NMSQT), the Test of English as a Foreign Language (TOEFL), and last but not least, the Scholastic Aptitude Test (SAT).

Developmental Learning Materials (DLM)

More Psycho-Educational Batteries, Early Childhood screening, tests of language development, and so on. DLM's catalog is easier to follow than the others I've seen.

Jastak

Ready for some alphabet soup? Jastak has the: WRAT-revised, DARE, WRIOT, WRIPT, ABS, WREST, TONI, SIT and SORT, EOWPVT, ROWPVT, LET, DSPT, QNST, LRS, MVPT, DTLA-Z, WBSS, ABC Inventory (a readiness screen), TOWL, WISC-R Compilation, and Stanford-Binet Form L-M Compilation. Jastak's prices are quite decent, the catalog is very easy to follow, the descriptions tell you what you need to know, and Jastak will take orders on institutional letterhead without asking you to sign your life away.

Scholastic Testing Service, Inc.

Scholastic is another company with a vast assortment of tests, from preschool to personality inventories for adults.

Science Research Associates (SRA)

These are the people who brought us Distar® and SRA Reading Laboratories, and numerous language and math kits. They sell the Iowa Tests of Educational Ability and their own SRA Survey of Basic Skills, plus a dozen or so other testing products.

PART XII

FUN
AND
ENRICHMENT

CHAPTER FORTY-SEVEN

SCHOOL SUPPLIES

Ah, what a treat! I am about to introduce you to my very favorite catalogs. These companies have a selection of toys that makes Child World look sick. They sell fairy tales and Dr. Seuss. They carry chemistry sets and ant castles. They have music and filmstrips and art supplies and playground equipment. They sell games, and flannelboard figures, and puzzles. And just to prove they are really education-minded, some of them even sell workbooks!

Parents and grandparents, you have been missing out if you have been doing your birthday shopping without a school supply catalog handy. Unlike the textbook market, which is dry and boring and loaded with ideology, the school supply market is bursting with creativity. You can teach your children the shapes of letters over thirty-five different ways with just the products Constructive Playthings carries (I counted). For just this one skill area, you can get: crepe rubber puzzles with alphabet pieces; textured, grooved alphabet blocks; alphabet letter molds; an alphabet stamp set; alphabet blocks; an alphabet flip book; alphabet stencils; an alphabet worm puzzle. And these are some of the *less* innovative products! Whether you are studying handwriting, or math, or science, or history, or you name it, the school supply people carry a constellation of exciting materials in your subject area. You can hardly keep from getting ideas for fun ways to learn just by reading one of these catalogs.

Why are textbooks so dull and school supplies, which sound at least as dull, so exciting? Because textbooks are "approved," a doctrinal routine which demands adherence to whatever dogmas are currently in vogue among the elite, and school supplies are not. Teachers have *much* better sense than the bureaucrats who actually run the schools, and when they get a chance to pick which materials they use, they demand good products. School suppliers are also heavily used by private schools, and this helps keep the school supply market more geared to materials parents would approve.

Since textbooks are supposed to carry the teaching load, school supplies can afford to be fun. Virtually everything in a good school supply catalog has kid-appeal. Kids *want* to use this stuff! Which leads us to a semiserious suggestion for the schools. How about throwing out the textbooks and using only school supplies? I know that it's un-American to teach kids without testing them every two minutes, but still it would be an interesting experiment.

SUGGESTED SUPPLIES FOR YOUR HOME CLASSROOM

Almost every book on home learning that I have seen includes a list of supplies for the home classroom. Almost every list that I have seen is a mile long. In time, you probably will accumulate all of those items, but at first glance it looks like home learning would break the bank and clutter up your home! I would like to offer the following thoughts in an attempt to simplify and economize.

First, desks. The kind with a storage space under the lid are great. But actually you don't *need* desks. Children can study at the kitchen table, or on the living room floor. Some of our family's best lessons have been given sitting on the living room couch. Just be consistent about whatever spot you pick, and in time it will develop that special "study area" feel during lesson hours.

Second, blackboards. The best kind is the white mark 'n clean style that you write on with special colored markers. These are much easier to read and work with, and don't get chalk dust all over your rugs. Again, you don't *need* a blackboard. We haven't used ours for a year, although at first the children went wild drawing pictures and writing all over it.

Third, paper and pencils. These you must have. Almost every office has reams of used computer paper whose backsides you can use for scribble paper. Tracing paper is helpful for drawing exercises and tracing letters. Colored construction paper can be used for almost everything. But watch out! Art paper also now comes in foil, tissue, fadeless, and corrugated. It's possible to go overboard when you see the selection!

Actually, you don't even *need* paper and pencils for most activities. Our great-grandparents used slates and chalk, thus eliminating paper litter and saving money. Although slates are hard to find today, every school supplier has kid-sized chalkboards, some especially designed to be held on the lap, and kid-sized mark 'n clean boards. When first learning to write, these boards are a boon. Kids can erase their mistakes and try again, and make letters as large as they like without wasting paper.

Fourth, art media. After trying markers, watercolors, yarn, Cray-Pas, charcoal, colored pencils, clay, toothpick art, and too many other materials to mention, we have settled down to scissors, glue, crayons, and Play-Doh as the "bare essentials." Older children who are responsible enough to work with expensive and messy materials on their own can accumulate whatever they can afford to buy; but when you don't have much time to hover over kids' art projects, ye olde cut 'n paste is great. Get rid of those scuzzy old bottles of wheat paste and get some glue sticks, and pasting becomes a neat activity. Anything a youngster wants to do with line and color, he can do with crayons. Anything he wants to do in 3-D he can do with Play-Doh or plasticlay. Until he learns the basics of drawing and modeling, all the glitzy stuff in the art catalog is not needed.

Once you have your basic art media, your basic writing stuff, and a place to sit, you have enough to get started. The beauty of learning at home is that home is *not* a classroom. All the other classroom paraphernalia—globes, an American flag, bulletin boards, chalkholders that draw musical staffs, and so on—can be added when and if you feel the need. It's better to get too little and have to make a second shopping trip than to buy too much and have it cluttering up your house.

SCHOOL SUPPLY CATALOGS

Besides being sources for all sorts of creative teaching tools, these catalogs are also the place to get your teaching supplies, such as chalk, crayons, blackboards, protractors, paper, and the like. If you're into stickers and happy faces, these people will be glad to oblige you. If your pressing need is for a BIG bottle of glue, or a small American flag, you can find it here. The only school supply I wouldn't get from a school supply firm is a student desk. Modern desks have just a flat writing surface and no place to store the books. This is realistic, considering the rate of theft in schools, but not functional at home. We got our desks (which the boys hardly ever use) second-hand through an ad in the local paper. My best friend got hers *free* when a school district threw out their old ones. See what kind of deal you can work out, or save your money and stick with the kitchen table. But for every other item, let your fingers do the walking!

ABC School Supply

Gorgeous color catalog of materials of early childhood education, elementary, and special education. Most materials are for preschool through third grade. ABC carries a few Christian products and seems geared to the private school market. Don't hold your breath waiting for your order to arrive—normally it takes four to six weeks.

Chaselle

Chaselle has more of an emphasis on teacher supplies and art supplies than most others.

Chaselle has separate catalogs for arts and crafts, basic "lifeskills" materials, preschool and elementary school materials, general school materials, and microcomputer materials. A smattering of the best of everything is in the general catalog, which is the one you'll probably want.

Christian Light Publications

Besides offering their own Mennonite version of the Alpha Omega Publications curriculum, Christian Light also vends science lab equipment, a smattering of literature and textbooks, and record-keeping forms for private schools. All prices are very reasonable, as CLP obeys the Christian injunction not to gouge one's brethren.

Constructive Playthings

Curriculum materials, supplies and equipment for everyone from newborns to preteens; also special education materials. Constructive Playthings' mostly black and white catalog honestly describes each product in a straight-forward way.

Educational Insights

Superselection of fun, motivational materials, all usable for home study. Over eleven hundred items. Educational Insights sells through school supply stores and catalogs, but will also sell directly to individuals.

Hoover's

Hoover's motto is, "Everything Educational" and they're not kidding. Their catalog is *huge*. We've shopped at their Teacher's Store here in St. Louis and admire the vast selection. If you ever think of starting a private school, Hoover's can even get you all the furniture you need for the library, gym, auditorium, etc. Much of this heavy-duty furniture is not listed in the catalog—contact them directly.

Since Hoover's carries so many products, you may find the catalog overwhelming. The selling point here is completeness, not glamour or layout.

Ideal School Supply

Full-service elementary supplier. Ideal is a producer of materials sold in other catalogs and teachers' stores—sixty-four-plus full-color pages full! Ideal's inexpensive science supplies would be especially helpful to the home classroom. Plus lots and lots of games and manipulatives for early childhood, special ed, math, language, and social studies. A complete listing of Ideal

dealers and distributors in your area can be found on the inside back cover of the catalog. This listing is a good way to locate handy school supply stores, since almost every good teachers' store carries Ideal supplies.

Lakeshore Curriculum Materials Company

Colorful catalog, slimmer than most, well-rounded selection, faster shipping (Lakeshore guarantees three-day shipment). Categories: infants, preschool, elementary, and special education. Whoever does Lakeshore's layout is a genius. It is impossible to thumb through it without being tempted.

Milton Bradley

Games, games, games, and flash cards, flash cards, flash cards. MB has gone into educational accessories in a big way. All Milton Bradley products are top-notch. Sold through stores and school supply catalogs.

Sentinel Teacher Supply

Decent medium-sized catalog with a good selection of educational supplies, plus the usual kiddie goodies. Less toys than Lakeshore, more curriculum-style materials than most. Usable for both home and school.

CHAPTER FORTY-EIGHT

SUPPLEMENTAL AND ENRICHMENT

A treasure chest of all that's neat and nifty, but is not intended to be the primary teaching tool for a subject—that's this chapter. Here you can find the fun and the freaky, your kits and accessories for practicing concepts taught elsewhere. After-schoolers should find this section especially useful, as should home schoolers who are looking for ways to pep up math drill or enrich their teaching of history. This is also the place for "gifted and talented" materials, which insofar as they are any good are good for *all* children.

ENRICHMENT MATERIALS

First, be sure to check the Catalogs and Paraphernalia chapter. These catalogs for home schoolers carry a wide variety of books, workbooks, and kits. You also can find supplemental materials for individual subjects under their subject listings. Math Manipulatives, for instance, are found in the Arithmetic and Mathematics chapter.

The following companies specialize in enrichment materials covering several subject areas. Jazz up your home program with their clever ideas!

Creative Publications

Math, language arts, computer, logic, and strategy activity books and games.

Dover Publications

Over three thousand paperbacks in all fields of interest, most priced between $2 and $5, many specially suited for home study and instruction. For those who want to enrich their own and their children's education, but who aren't rich themselves.

ESP Inc.

My Yearbook series, $15 each. Grades K-6. Many workbooks for 98¢ each.

School-style enrichment workbooks in every subject area. The *My Yearbook* jumbo workbooks have learning activities covering all basic subjects in the same order usually taught in schools. We have used these books and are well pleased. An inventive mother can teach the subjects from them, but in most cases they serve better as supplemental material. The books are *big*—beginning at 544 pages (grades K and 1) and increasing in size until grade 6 has a massive 832 pages. My only gripe is that they use manuscript handwriting right up through third grade. The books' tone is conservative and factual rather than preachy. Kindergarteners work with nursery rhymes, for example, rather than the moralistic little stories about feelings which are becoming such standard fare elsewhere.

This was the only "school" material our son Ted used for first grade, and he tested well into second grade upon completion of his *Yearbook*.

Economy Company

Public school supplemental materials.

Educational Book Distributors

EBD carries a good-sized line of "alternative" public school materials. Most of these don't have the heavy pomposity that so mars typical school texts. Categories are: Early Childhood Education, Social Studies, Life Skills, Language Arts, Special Education, Creative Learning Activities, and Math and Science. For Californians there are almost two dozen special interest titles, including *Gumshan: The Chinese-American Saga,* and books about Mexican folk art (you *do* it rather than *study* it), the Gold Rush, railroads, California Indians, and so on. If you want a California history coloring book, this is the place.

EBD's generally good taste is shown by their selling Mary Pecci's excellent reading method and Super Seatwork series (reviewed elsewhere). You can find unusual stuff here—teaching units on volcanoes, a noncoloring book (you finish the drawings), and Creative Quickies to add arts and crafts to every subject area. All items are reasonably priced, well within the reach of the average home budget. I cannot endorse the values taught by every one of their offerings, but *educationally* the material mostly ranges from interesting to sublime.

Educational Insights

Funthinkers, prices average $12-$15. *Charlie* battery model, $45. A.C. model, $70. *Rainbow,* $169.95. Drill packs of twenty cards, $10.95 each.

Huge assortment of some of the niftiest enrichment materials around. Every Educational Insights product has dash and flair. Prices are better than reasonable, in my opinion. A few examples from the enormous number of possibilities:

The *Funthinker* activity kits enrich your teaching of basic skills. Each comes in a plastic carrying case, and contains all sorts of goodies such as sing-along cassettes, stencils for tracing, storybooks, games, and even supplies such as scissors and crayons. The series presently includes *First Steps to Reading* (prereading exercises), *Learning My Alphabet, Understanding Numbers, Learning Values* (with Aesop's fables), *Beginning to Add and Subtract, Mysteries of Light* (an intriguing kit that contains a prism, a magnifier, and four color filters among many other things), and *Learning to Draw.*

For drill, EI has several different electronic tutors. Stick in a card and press the probe into the hole next to the answer you hope is right. Flashing lights and space-age sounds come from Charlie to let you know if you got it right or if you blew it. Rainbow, the more expensive model, has a touch-sensitive keyboard. If you'd like to add some zip to your drill, but can't afford a computer, one of these might be an acceptable compromise.

I have not begun to even skim the surface of the varied and imaginative product line. See any school supply catalog, or send for EI's own, and be overwhelmed!

Holt Associates

Donna Richoux and her associates are carrying on John Holt's work, including not only *Growing Without Schooling* but the Holt Associates mail order catalog. Donna and company write great reviews of home school products, and the products they particularly like end up in the catalog. Holt Associates merchandise is chosen with an eye for beauty, imagination, and simplicity. The resulting assortment is unique.

Holt Associates' literature selections are quite good, ranging from *The Bat Poet* to old favorites like the Grimm's fairy tales. For math, there is *Anno's Counting Book* and the indispensable *How to Lie with Statistics.* For science, there is *Powers of Ten,* a mind-boggling book that exponentiates sizes in jumps of ten (how many jumps do you think it takes to go from "people size" to the Solar System?). For music, there is *How to Play the Piano Despite Years of Lessons.* The catalog, of course, contains hundreds more books than these, but I wanted to give you a taste of the sassiness and originality of the selections. It's worth sending away for this brochure just to read the names of the books!

Holt Associates also sells some art and music equipment, again with an eye to the gorgeous and/or unusual. We bought our Aulos recorders here, and several boxes of Cray-Pas. Holt Associates sells some expensive equipment too—violins and cellos and (on the more mundane side) pianicas and metronomes.

The emphasis on beauty makes this catalog a joy to read.

Learning Systems Corporation

You can't beat the price: 50¢ miniworkbooks that do a decent job of exercising your youngster in his language arts and math. See the reviews in the Math and Reading sections.

Life for Little Learners

Wide assortment of supplemental materials especially chosen for home schoolers. The catalog includes: Bible memory visual aids, charts, a phonics course, all sorts of early-grades enrichment material, and educational software. Quite a diverse selection!

Michael Olaf

More than Montessori, Michael Olaf offers a good selection of supplemental materials for young children in all subject areas. Many of their items are imported. The catalog is easy to use and simple in an elegant way. Find out more about their selections in the Preschool chapter. I wouldn't pass this company up.

Milliken Publishing Company

Science Activities books, series of fifteen, $4.95 each. Children's classics on cassette, $5.95 each. Transparencies, each set of twenty $9.95.

Milliken has a huge assortment of workbooks in all subject areas for prekindergarten through twelfth grade. Decent as supplemental material, these workbooks are clean in layout and inexpensive.

Milliken also sells wipe-clean cards, duplicating masters, transparencies, filmstrip packages, and a nice little series of children's classics on cassette for only $5.95 each.

A really helpful resource is Milliken's Diagrammatic Study

Prints series. Each package contains eight poster-size, full-color prints with concise background information, four duplicating masters, and a teacher's guide. The prints are clearly labeled, and cover such subjects as The Solar System, Animals, Electricity, Plants, and Organs of the Human Body. Useful when you want to study what something is called or what it looks like.

Milliken also has science miniunits, science activity books, and a great series of full-color transparencies for studying the tougher biological areas like endoplasmic reticulum ribosomes and angiosperms phylogeny. Areas covered are Nature of Science and Origin of Life (non-useful for Christians), Cell Machinery, Monera and Protista, Plants-Angiosperms, Invertebrate Phylogeny—The Metazoa, and Vertebrate Phylogeny. Maybe it's just because I'm a science nut, but I freak out over full-color pinups of leaf cell structures.

Pecci Publications

Phonics Grab Bag, 138 pages, $9.95. *Linguistic Exercises,* 106 pages, $7.95. *Word Skills,* 238 pages, $10.95.

Mary Pecci's Super Seatwork series contains several volumes of supplemental phonics exercises that I really like. Correlated with her reading method (reviewed in the Reading section), the *Phonics Grab Bag* has twelve different fun types of exercises. Some are cut-and-paste, some involve drawing, some require writing. There are Phonics Picture Puzzles, Phonics Crossword Puzzles, Word Wheels, Let's Play Categories, and lots more! As with all Mary Pecci's seatwork, the book is big and the pictures are simple and entertaining.

Linguistic Exercises consists mainly of valuable word-family exercises. A page, for example, may feature repetitions of *ore, ote, ove,* and *oze.* Some the student just reads. Towards the end of the book he does some writing and drawing. This pattern-building is the way our brains construct frameworks for storing the data we feed them, unlike short-term rote memory which quickly fades away unless refreshed.

Word Skills is a handy compendium of all the ways we build onto words. Standard textbooks usually drag this out over years. Included are roots and endings, plus all the rules for irregular endings (change *y* to *i* before adding *es,* etc.), compound words, possessives, contractions, prefixes, suffixes, syllabication, and dictionary skills, including practice in unraveling those weird little dictionary pronunciation symbols. The exercises are simple and nonthreatening, gradually progressing without beating the student to death with overdone repetition. After going through this book, children who have had a basic phonics course should have no spelling or reading problems.

The Pecci preschool and basic skills enrichment workbooks are reviewed in the Preschool section.

Mary Pecci's books have a special friendly and human quality that I find irresistible.

Playing for Knowledge

PFK distributes enrichment materials from more than thirty publishers. The newsprint catalog is not the easiest to find things in, but it contains some gems. Examples: *Eight Ate: A Feast of Homonym Riddles,* or *It's Easy to Have a Snail Visit You,* one in a series that tells you how to catch and house and care for the

critters. The *Recyclopedia* has all kinds of projects you can make from trash. *Can* your daughter make a silk purse out of a sow's ear? Lots of books for "gifted" children. How-to-draw books, books on dinosaurs, David Macaulay's marvelous series on how great buildings are made, and more. Includes some of the standard messing about with students' feelings and values, but these selections are swallowed up in the large number of truly valuable ones.

Playthinks

Bill and I had an idea once upon a time. We'd put together some of the best materials from different manufacturers into kits to teach individual skills, such as handwriting or beginning art. Well, Playthinks beat us to it. Their colorful, yuppy-oriented catalog has kit after learning kit for all ages and stages, plus books for the parents. Kits are divided into three categories: Concept Kits, Specialty Kits, and Library Kits. Each Concept Kit is for a different developmental level (from birth to age five) and includes a number of colorful, multisensory learning tools, which you might recognize as games and toys. Specialty Kits include such topics as The Creative Cook, Abracadabra, a kit for handmaking Christmas presents, and a Hanukkah kit. Library Kits are collections of books like *Biographies of the Great* (Einstein, Mozart, and Da Vinci), *Science Information and Experiments, Timeless Classics, Early Reader's Shelf, The Present of Christmas, The Joy of the Jewish Experience, Shaping Values and Manners,* and so on.

Don't expect to find bargains in this catalog, with kit prices ranging from $20 to $42. You will find a lot of tempting sets— like *Tick, Tock, My Friend the Clock; A Child's Flight With Nature; How Do Things Grow?; Choo-Choose This For Your Train Lover; Around the World . . .*

School Zone Publishing Company

School Zone has enrichment and supplemental stuff for grades prekindergarten through six. School Zone's workbooks are specifically designed for at-home use. Each workbook covers a particular skill or subject area. These include perceptual skills, grammar, reading, math, spelling, and phonics. School Zone also has videotapes, audio cassettes, flash cards, puzzles, "Start-to-Read" books, and software.

In the industry, School Zone has established a reputation for excellent, swift customer service. School Zone books are mostly sold in stores, but their catalog is available to all.

Shakean Stations

Twelve-game sets, $14.95 each. Twenty-four-game set, $21.95. Seven-game sets, $13.95 each. Puzzle games, $5.95. Twelve manila file folders, $1.50. Twelve string tie envelopes, $1.50.

Delightful, inexpensive "file folder" games. You cut out the colorful game board portion and mount it on a legal-size file folder, then laminate or cover it with clear contact paper. (This last step is not essential, but it does help the game last longer.) Play pieces are stored in a string tie manila envelope that you mount on the back of the file folder. The whole process takes next to no time, and you end up with a long-lasting game for under $2, and in some cases less than a dollar.

Shakean games are sold in sets of five, seven, twelve, or twenty-four. *Reading Unlimited,* the only set of twenty-four games, covers phonics from alphabet recognition through syllabication. Games sold in sets of twelve include:

Smart Start, a set of reading readiness games.

Sports of Sorts, vocabulary and word-building skill games with a sports theme.

Number the Big Top, arithmetic practice and drill with circus-theme games.

Play the Numbers, intermediate arithmetic (including division, decimals, and other tougher operations).

The Space Place, math concept games.

Classroom games (which can be played with as few as two or as many as thirty-six players) come in sets of seven, for grades 1 to 4. These are *Everybody Plays* and *Play It Again.* Both these sets concentrate on phonics and language arts.

The *Puzzle Games* set comes with five gameboards and twenty-two word lists for practicing specialized skills, such as matching states and their capitals or working on antonyms and homonyms or drilling math facts. You pick the list you want to work on, and write each word twice, once on the puzzle square and once on the corresponding gameboard. Players put the puzzle together by matching the problem (like the capital of Alaska) to the solution (Juneau). Each puzzle is self-correcting, and if you cover it with contact paper (available in any school supply catalog) it should last and last.

Look at the prices Shakean Stations charges for their teacher-made games, and you will (1) agree that we still are blessed with some kindhearted teachers and (2) send for their free catalog.

Western Publishing Company, Inc.

Golden Step Ahead book/tape series, $5 to $7 each set. Color and activity books, 99¢-$1.49.

A variety of supplemental and enrichment materials, from the makers of the Little Golden Books series. Lots of cheap color

and activity books, starting at 99¢ and generally featuring licensed characters (e.g., Barbie, Donald Duck, Rainbow Brite). Western has lots of activity books, lots of games, lots of children's books, lots of puzzles, and even some workbooks, staying in tune with the new wave of demand for home educational products. Western is a *big* producer, and their products do have that very professional, mass-produced flavor.

Of special interest to home teachers is the new Golden Step Ahead book/tape series. It's instantly obvious how a "teacher on cassette" can spare Mom and Dad the effort of constantly repeating the alphabet or addition facts. So far the series includes *Beginning to Count, A to Z, Understand It* (a listening comprehension tape), and *Let's Add!* I would encourage any commercial producer reading this to think seriously about adding cassette teaching to his workbook series. Meanwhile, Western has shown they are wide awake and in touch with what's going on.

Western does have a big, expensive catalog, but they much prefer to sell through stores.

World Book/Childcraft International

Send for WB/C's Teaching Materials Catalog, which is actually a small brochure, to get your hands on some of the least expensive enrichment materials around. World Book/Childcraft is an enormous corporation that doesn't mind filling 25¢ orders. Their encyclopedias can only be ordered through local sales reps (try your Yellow Pages), but the Teaching Materials designed to publicize the encyclopedias and the uses thereof you can buy by mail.

Take note: reprints of selected articles from *World Book,* many of which include color pictures, are available *free* in quantities of one to teachers and librarians. If you are home schooling and have a school name and stationery, you are a school and need not feel embarrassed about sending for some of these. But don't abuse the privilege—give them a shot at selling you their product!

Another fantastic offer: WB/C has a Look-It-Up Club program, intended to teach the use of reference tools. Each book costs one thin dime. Titles are: *The Alphabet and Alphabetical Order, Parts of a Book and How to Use Them, How to Use the Dictionary, Using an Encyclopedia (Parts One and Two)*, and *Choosing a Subject for a Report.*

If you decide to buy one of these encyclopedias, you will want to invest one more dollar in their *Through the Year with Childcraft* or *Through the Year with World Book.* These forty-eight-page booklets have a whole year's worth of activities, games, and puzzles centered around the encyclopedia.

And if you want to know what the public schools are supposedly teaching, 15¢ will get you *Typical Course of Study.* I say, what they are *supposedly* teaching, because although the list of topics is impressive, and might be overwhelming to parents contemplating home schooling, in real life the coverage of same is shallow in the extreme. What does it mean for a third-grader to "study" ocean life along with sixty-eight other subjects? (Our five-year-old, incidentally, has already mastered all the public school third-grade subjects. For real. At home.)

WB/C has a set of classroom posters for $1 each, any four for $2. Some of these are quite helpful, such as the *Physical Map of the World* and *The Metric System at a Glance.*

Xerox Educational Publishers

Xerox bills you $7.32/month for the three summer months, or you can pay $21.96 in advance.

You know an idea is taking root when Xerox hops into the market with it. Parents really do care about their children's education, and they are starting to see that children *can* learn at home.

Xerox's Weekly Reader Summer Skills Library consists of a selection of the same Weekly Reader practice books used in the schools. The idea is that by working with these books over the summer, Junior can keep from falling behind, and maybe even move ahead!

Each Skills Library contains a Parent Guide, a selected set of Practice Books matched to your child's grade level, six paperback books for free-time reading, a colorful storage case, a free set of marker pens, and the indispensable Award Certificate which you can flash in front of his new teacher to show that Junior actually agitated his brains this summer instead of just roasting them in the sun. Skills Libraries are available for children entering grades 1 through 7. If you want to use this program for *teaching* this material, instead of for reviewing it, order the next-lower set. For instance, a child entering first grade orders Set A, but you could also use Set A for teaching kindergarten.

Naturally, Weekly Reader is a secular supplier, and those teaching at home for religious reasons will want to keep this in mind. You do get an awful lot for your money, covering *all* subject areas. This set might be a good idea for helping a child at home who needs extra practice in his schoolwork, too.

GIFTED AND TALENTED MATERIALS

About those school Gifted and Talented programs: It has been said, and I believe truly, that they constitute a device for

providing private schooling for the children of the elite at public expense. Like the Christian doctrine of election, G & T selection is purely by grace. Some anointed person declares a child gifted, and there he is. The anointed differ sharply among themselves as to who these gifted ones are, but the basic premise is that one is either born gifted or not. Children cannot earn, or learn, their way into these classes. No amount of sprucing up one's study habits or striving to do better will get your child labeled "gifted," but only the anointing from on high. Once in, "gifted" children are drilled rigorously in "open-ended"—e.g., humanist—thinking. They are trained to consider *all* possibilities: shall we feed Marvin his dinner, or kill Marvin and eat him for dinner? They are encouraged to consider themselves future leaders and led to believe in a future one-world Socialist government. They are trained to worship their own intelligence and to mock traditional answers. Now, individual families may hold the above values, and that is their business. But there is something disgusting about the State holding catechism classes in humanism at the same time that Christian teachers aren't even allowed to hand out Christmas cards.

You can enrich your enthusiastic child's education just as much at home, using the same materials the best G & T programs use, or substituting others of your choice. In this way you can ensure that creative thinking doesn't become an exercise in lack of compassion (if Marvin is hungry, killing him is *not* a viable option), and that training in political strategies does not evolve into training in challenging one's parents. You can also avoid the heady arrogance of having your child labeled "gifted," which is just the counterpoint to the pain felt by the child labeled "slow." One can't be lord of the roost unless one has lesser beings to lord it over; one can, however, be as excited about learning as one pleases without putting anyone else down. There is enough room in the world for *all* of us, and enough worthy tasks for us all to work on, even if we all were trained as geniuses.

I have never met a stupid child yet. I hear they are out there, but I have yet to see a dull-eyed baby or a vapid two-year-old. God gives different gifts to us all, but enthusiasm for learning was never meant to be the province of an elite. Though your child may not be considered "gifted and talented" by the school district, he *is* gifted and he *is* talented. His natural enthusiasm may have been blunted by passive entertainment and peer dependency, but if you can throw a tablecloth over the TV and liberate him at least temporarily from the clutches of his peers, his creativity and intelligence will amaze you.

Chart Your Course!

New reader subscription price, $15 (eight issues, October through May). Sample copy, $2.50. Canadians and foreign subscribers, add $4/year for postage; pay through U.S. banks or by international money order.

Magazine by and for "creative students." They are safe in this standard, as dullards by definition do not send in articles for publication. Loaded with all sorts of activities, art, poetry, puzzles, mazes, reviews, and so on, *Chart Your Course!* is edited by adults, but entirely written by kids. Activities may be reproduced for classroom use.

GCT Publications

New reader subscription price, $18. Sample issue, $4. Canadians and foreign subscribers, add $5 per year for postage and pay through U.S. banks or by international money order.

G/C/T, which stands for "Gifted, Creative, and Talented," is "The World's Most Popular Magazine for Parents and Teachers of Gifted, Creative, and Talented Children." It contains practical advice, home and school activities, special columns about computers and so on, reviews of books and resources for "gifted" kids, a calendar of meetings about same, an annual directory of summer camps and programs for same, interviews with "experts," and on and on, all in full color and adorned with pictures.

The company also has its own mail-order bookstore of games 'n stuff for "gifted" kids and their parents.

Kathy Kolbe Concept

Kathy Kolbe Concept, Inc. is a division of Resources for the Gifted. KKC operates through a nationwide network of educational consultants who demonstrate and sell the Think-ercises directly. If you would like to see such a demonstration, call Resources for the Gifted at 602/840-9770 and they'll be glad to give you the name of their nearest consultant.

Midwest Publications

Public school materials directed at improving thinking skills. They have workbooks on Syllogisms, Word Benders, pattern 'n puzzle Brain Stretchers, and so on. Midwest endeared itself to me by Question 15 in its *Inductive Thinking Skills* workbook, which begins, "Larry lives in Iowa. He doesn't like school." The problem proceeds with Larry trying to talk his folks into moving to south Texas so that he won't ever have to go to school again (we don't go to school when it's warm, and it's *always* warm in south Texas). If you can't figure out what's wrong with Larry's reasoning, you'd better buy this book.

From the examples given in the catalog, Midwest's

publications seem to really do the job of improving the accuracy of a student's thinking and exposing him to new possibilities within the confines of logic.

Resources for the Gifted, Inc.

Special offer evaluation and kit, $120.

Kathy Kolbe began Resources for the Gifted as a frustrated mother. When regular programs didn't respond to the needs of her two children, Kathy Kolbe decided to create brain-stretching alternatives to standard school fare. After the major publishers told her there was no market for materials specifically designed to teach thinking skills, she started publishing them herself. Mrs. Kolbe soon built her business into the world's largest producer of learning aids for gifted children.

RFG carries a full line of gifted/talented materials in every category. They are all stimulating, entertaining, and expensive. Suitable for kids from prereaders to high-school seniors, they encourage creativity and emphasize the teaching of problem-solving skills. Mrs. Kolbe also believes that the best way to motivate kids to learn is through a lighthearted approach. RFG encourages parents to use the materials with kids of all ability levels.

How do you choose the best RFG materials for your child? One way is by accepting RFG's Special Offer. They send you two Kathy Kolbe Intellectual Fitness (IF) profiles. You and another adult who knows the child will fill them out. Then RFG analyzes the results and sends you a collection of Think-ercises suited to your child's thinking style. The ad says, "You receive a $150 value for $120," which probably means they throw in the profiles free.

Treehouse Publishing Company

Resources for the gifted, much cheaper than Kathy Kolbe's materials. This public school-oriented series has quite a strong emphasis on the future and on options, which means I'd be careful and see if any values-molding is going on here. The catalog to get, if you want to look them over, is called World of the Gifted.

CHAPTER FORTY-NINE

TOYS AND GAMES

Headings are slippery things in a book like this. So many toys and games are educational, and so many educational products have gamelike qualities. I originally intended this section to be a listing of all the just-for-fun and crazy-weird catalogs that didn't fit in anywhere else. However, when I tried to force this neat little box over an appropriate assortment of companies, it split at the seams.

In the end I decided to include the educational-games people along with the kiddie-toys people, and let them fight it out as to who was educational and who was not.

WHO'S EDUCATIONAL?

Now that educational toys and games are in such hot demand, everyone wants to be educational. In one sense, it is true that all experience is educational. On the other hand, this can be carried too far. Consider this ad for an Interactive Posterior Stimulus Module: "Your children will have hours of fun learning from our IPSM. They can manipulate the circular shape and learn about density. (Don't forget, the IPSM can be used as a very large stencil!) Aural development is enhanced by rapping the IPSM smartly against its base and observing the variations in sound. Gross motor skills are fostered by lowering and raising the IPSM. The IPSM can also be used for values education. Remembering to always lower the IPSM at the end of an educational session is not only good exercise but also demonstrates kindness to others." I could go on and on. But why waste more space describing a toilet seat?

Beware, beware, beware! Get to know what the ad jargon really means. "The product develops gross motor skills," could refer to a Ring Toss game or eating. "Your children's perceptual ability will be enhanced" could be said of a nature walk or a comic book. "Children will have hours of fun playing with it" is a cheap shot aimed at your supposed desire to be rid of your kids' company.

In real life, virtually *anything* can be touched, tasted, smelled, and looked at, and most things can be shaken and listened to as well. Just because my baby daughter tries to teethe on my shoe as she plays on the floor does not mean shoes should be sold as a "tactile stimulus experience." Every house, except those of the desperately poor, has things to look at and listen to and taste and smell and feel. Good toys and games aren't "experiences": they are something to *do*.

TOYS, PRO AND CON

At the same time as the educational toy market is swelling to eight times its previous size, a movement is afoot to talk parents out of buying any toys at all. "Toys are childish!" voices cry. (True, of course.) "Children should use *real* tools and do *real* work instead of all this fooling around with expensive gewgaws."

It's bad enough that toys cost so much, and even worse if you have to feel guilty about buying them. *Should* we feel guilty about buying toys, or (more consistently) stop buying them altogether? Are Junior's Lego bricks a harmful influence?

After giving the matter deep thought, and riffling through more toy catalogs than I care to mention, I think I've found some helpful guidelines.

Passive toys, toys that do things without having anything much done to them, are educationally worthless. In this category put talking dolls, battery-operated miniature cars, and the TV set, as long as these items are used as designed. If the talking doll is used as a regular doll and not limited by the extent of her built-in vocabulary, if the minicar's battery falls out and it can be propelled about the floor on pretend journeys to Alaska, if the TV is turned into an aquarium, then they become useful.

Toys that duplicate adult tools are only useful if it will be years and years before your children are ready for the real thing. What is the sense of buying Junior a toy typewriter when, for the same price, you could get a real used typewriter that he could really learn to type on? Why get Suzy her own tiny set of breadpans and mixing bowls when she can help you with your real baking? Our five-year-old son, Teddy, frequently volunteers to do the real dishes in our real kitchen sink, and does a good job of it too. Sarah, our just barely two-year-old, mixes batter for me. Joseph, our four-year-old, gets upset when I don't let him stir the eggs for the omelet. Both boys help Dad screw together bookcases and do other carpentry work. It would be too much for a five-year-old to wield an adult-sized hammer, though, so a good set of children's tools is on our "Wish List."

Open-ended construction toys and art materials are good for fantasy play. Under this heading come all sorts of building blocks and construction kits: Legos, Duplos, Tinker Toys, Erector sets, Lincoln Logs, and so on. These are the products that really *will* give Junior "hours of fun," since they are limited only by his imagination. I do not include kits that only build one particular item, like a castle or a frontier town, in this category. These are fun only while the project lasts, and then you have to either store them for years or throw away hours of Junior's work.

Board games and other family games are great relaxers. This does not apply to the "wipe out your opponent" sort. Competitive games have their place, but I have never seen any happy results from families playing them. You can change a competitive game into a cooperative game by making the goal to have *everyone* win, which is how we do it. We don't stop playing until everyone is "home."

For children, play is learning. For adults, play is relaxation. If you relax too much, you get limp and sloppy. If you never relax, you get ulcers. The proper balance of play and work produces healthy bodies and minds. "A cheerful heart doeth good like a medicine" (Proverbs 17:22).

ABOUT THESE REVIEWS

Many of these products have been reviewed in other sections, since the toys or games proved particularly helpful in teaching some skill or another. These companies are distinguished by listing their names and the sections in which their products were reviewed.

ALL-PURPOSE TOY AND GAME COMPANIES

These are the stuff-it-all-into-one-big-catalog folks. Lovers of one-stop shopping will be pleased by these companies.

Animal Town Game Company

Cooperative board games, classic games from around the world, books about games, books for children, rubber stamps, "old-time radio" shows on cassette, lullabies, songs, and stories. When we want to retreat far from the madding crowd, instead of hopping into the car and burning oil for hours we play their *Back to the Farm* game ($19 plus shipping).

Animal Town's philosophy is profamily and Mother Earthish, somewhat sentimental for the olden days and with a California flavor. *Save the Whales* has been their best-seller for years, giving you an idea of where Animal Town and its customers are coming from. The board games are beautiful and Animal Town encourages you to change the rules to fit your family's needs, which we have done. Their own family-designed games are not cheap, but are very well made. Catalog items are fairly priced.

Childcraft (Phys Ed)

Childcraft's motto is "Toys That Teach." Their catalog is big, bright, and filled with an assortment of educational toys, equipment, and books in all subjects. Childcraft has lots and lots of play equipment and giant building materials: Big Waffle Blocks, giant cardboard blocks, a Combi Kit that can make toys big enough to ride on, the Quadro construction kit that makes a gym, and lots more. There's something in every price range, but yuppies will feel more comfortable with the prices than bargain-hunters. The selections have good educational and play value.

Constructive Playthings (Phys Ed, Char, School Supplies)

CP has two catalogs: a school catalog, loaded with institutional playground equipment and heavy-duty playthings, and a Home Edition. The latter has hands-on stuff only (no books or workbooks). I've seen a lot of catalogs, but this one has several unique crafts that tempted me: a shellcraft kit for my son who loves seashells by the seashore, and a early knitting kit that I'll try to give to my daughter if the boys don't get their hands on it first! The no-spill tempera markers also look like a good idea. We struggled with a set from another company that had paintbrush tops attached to bottles, out of which the paint stubbornly refused to flow. Constructive Playthings tests all its products in order to avoid lemons like that. You may also be interested in the large selection of family games, the free toy guide, or Constructive Plaything's new Jewish Education catalog. Lots of reasonably priced items for ages birth to eight, many under $5.

Developmental Learning Materials (DLM) (Computers, Geography, Speech)

DLM, a public school supplier, carries a large selection of their own educational games. These colorful games are reasonably priced and easy to play. DLM has games in many subject areas, including those listed above.

Discovery Toys, Inc.
Eighty percent of toys cost less than $8.

Discovery toys sells *only* through home demonstrations! Their product line is constantly changing to reflect the best available in the toy market. Discovery Toys are imported from all over the world, and the country of origin is mentioned in each of the catalog entries which your local home saleslady shows you. In case you're not quite sure about what a particular toy is good for, each item is described in terms of its "Educational Play Value." Every item is beautiful, every item is educational, and many are not to be found anywhere else.

Discovery toys does *not* send their catalog to the general public, preferring to deal only through local representatives. You may buy toys at a toy demonstration, or order through your rep's catalog.

By hosting a Discovery Toys demonstration, you can get a discount on the toys sold and perhaps even half off one of the most-wanted items (Babycycle Trike, Microscope, Children's Encyclopedia, several neat and expensive construction sets . . .). Discovery toys is also looking for people to do the selling at their home demos.

Dr. Drew's Toys, Inc.
Set of seventy-two blocks and bag, $34.95 plus $4 shipping. Thirty-two block set, $17.95 plus $2.50 shipping. Eighteen block set, $12.95 plus $1.50 shipping.

I never thought I'd find myself writing an entire review on a set of wooden blocks. Blocks are blocks are blocks, right? Wrong!

For one thing, Dr. Drew's blocks are made out of hardwood, not your typical soft pine. This means they clack together in a satisfying fashion and that they don't immediately develop a leprosy of dings and dents like common blocks. Dr. Drew's blocks are also slim and rectangular (3 x 2 x ½″), so even babies can grasp them easily and adults can build terrific constructions (see the accompanying photo). The blocks come in a natural, splinter-free finish, so they will go with your decor, unless it's Recent Plastic. They are truly a "discovery" toy, as only your imagination and the size of the set you purchase limits what can be made with them. The whole kit and caboodle comes with a durable and attractive canvas bag, so you will have someplace to put them (most other sets come with a cardboard box that almost immediately degenerates into a ragged eyesore if you try to use it for a storage container). Now you know why Dr. Drew's Blocks received the 1982 "toy of the year" award from the Parents Choice Foundation.

Oh, yes: the inventor, Walter F. Drew, is a for-real Ph.D. and early childhood educator. He would say that the simplicity and uniformity of his blocks make it easy for children to discover number relationships and basic geometric patterns and to develop their creativity through construction and free play. He would also point out that all ages can play with the blocks together. I will just say that these blocks are *fun* (I've personally tested them!) and that you will kick yourself if you don't buy the large set.

Families That Play Together

Large selection of clever and stimulating books and learning materials, plus some kits. Examples: *Make-My-Own-Book* kits (animals, shapes, alphabet, numbers), $4 each; paper soldiers from the Middle Ages that can be colored, cut out, folded, and used to reenact the Crusades, the Battle of Hastings, and so on, $3; diorama books with dinosaurs, cavemen, plains Indians, and African animals, $4.50 each.

FPT's special emphasis is on items that adults will enjoy sharing with their children, or vice versa. Nothing is boring, nothing is babyish. As the brochure says,

> We found that doing these projects together was as much fun for the adults as for the children; and that the experience brought us closer together, which is the whole point of Families That Play Together.

Growing Child

Would you like to bridge the generation gap? Growing Child offers a large selection of classy playthings, with an emphasis on classic toys that you might have played with and that can be handed down to your grandchildren. This is not another yuppy catalog: the prices are reasonable. All catalog items are age-graded (so you know which ones to get) and developmental.

Growing Child is not a bunch of aging nostalgia buffs, either. You can find many of today's best new classics along with the old-time favorites like wooden nesting blocks and counting frames. Goodies like Dr. Drew's blocks, a Noah's Ark puzzle with interchangeable pieces, and Lauri puzzles are scattered throughout the catalog. And Growing Child has a large selection of children's literature, including several pages of award-winning classics.

Hearth Song

"A Catalog for Families." Natural fabric kidstuff, books on parenthood, wool-stuffed dolls, art supplies, cookbooks, knitting 'n sewing stuff, Weleda plant-derived toiletries, books, seasonal gifts. Everything beautiful, no schlock.

Just for Kids

Definitely yuppy catalog of toys and clothing. Colorful, many pages, rather more frivolous and decorative items than other catalogs. No bargains here: some expensive toys like the Rocking Kitten ($139.95) or the Emigrant Doll Family ($149.95). Good service.

The Toy Factory

A family-owned business established in 1972, The Toy Factory carries toys from around the world, folk toys, make-your-own-toy kits and parts, and a large selection of children's books. The newsprint catalog appears geared to the better-off *Mother Earth News* subscriber. Lots of nature study and environmental stuff; lots of expensive toys made out of natural hardwoods. The children's books include series of Caldecott and Newberry Award winners, plus Mrs. Piggle-Wiggle, Curious George in all his misadventures, and other children's standards. Interspersed throughout the catalog are "parenting" tips from a secular standpoint.

Toys to Grow On

This one is a doozie. Toys To Grow On has a big, beautiful color catalog. So do lots of other companies. Ah, but who else sells kits designed to provide ninety-nine hours of fun for . . . babies, toddlers, preschoolers, and school-age kids? Each kit is $44.95, thus putting it out of *my* reach, but perhaps not out of yours. And there are such items as a Hermit Crab Lab (including two crabs and extra shells), a build-it-yourself roller coaster for marbles, minigolf with marbles, *Tot Trivia*, etc., etc.

But that is not what makes Toys To Grow On so amazing. Their *hustle* is what amazes me. Who else has a Never Forget Birthday Club? Who else gives away a No-Choke Testing Tube (it lets you know whether any given object is small enough to be swallowed by a young child) *free* with any order? Who else has a chatty company newsletter bound into their catalog, with enticing article titles like "Why Is This Man Skating Away with Your Toys?" Who else gives away $50 gift certificates to customers who send in interesting tidbits that get published in the catalog? Who else tells you how to gather a variety of insects in next to no time (hold an open umbrella underneath a low branch of a bush and *shake!*)? Hustle isn't everything, but in a country where people dress for success it's bound to help.

ACTION GAMES

Here's stuff for the sweat set. Climb! Run! Jump! Shoot little disks back and forth!

Child Life Play Specialties (Phys Ed)

Green outdoor play sets: modular, wooden, and rugged. Clever add-ons like climbing ropes. Indoor play equipment, too.

Family Pastimes

Cooperative games and books. Educational puzzles, game plan kits. Also wholesales to home businesses (take note!). Some action games (a la table hockey) and plans to construct same. Example: Huff 'n Puff game is won by puffing ball across table w/o dropping it into trap. Nonmacho types use the little squeezers provided. New Age flavor.

Into the Wind Kites

Kites, I daresay, are one of the few fun things left that haven't been packaged as "educational." However, kiteflying is no longer sheer frivolity, either. Men with muscles of steel now spend their free time hauling stunt kites about, or being hauled about by same, as a sport. New two-string stunt kites have been clocked at speeds in excess of 90 mph while still going through precise maneuvers.

Gentler sorts can still laze about in the grass watching their kites float about in the bonny blue. New kite materials make the devices both compact and lightweight, so you can stuff them in a bag and take them along for your family picnic.

Into the Wind has a selection of kites that range from elegant simplicity to downright weird. Some kites are shaped like stars, some like manta rays, some like shoeboxes. You can get a Sky Shark (it looks like Jaws aloft), an eagle, or butterflies, dragonflies, peacocks, goldfish, and other extravagant, colorful creatures. Dragon kites have long, long tails, Fringed Dancers have fringe, and Precision Star Cruisers have each other (you can stack six on a line). Airfoils! Amazing Flying Bird that winds up and flaps his wings! Windsocks! Airplane Kites! Wind Fish! Fighter Kites! Kitemaking materials and accessories! A little further afield in the field of flight, Into the Wind also has a pile of boomerangs.

Don't think this all means lots of money, either. A silk Oriental Dragonfly kite costs only $18, and a Rainbow Octopus kite is just $5. Well-heeled types can manage to spend $100 or more on a single kite, but most offerings in this free catalog are in range of the average kite fanatic.

Into the Wind's *Pocket Guide to Kiteflying* is sent free with kite orders. Otherwise it sells for a mere 25¢ and can help you pick the kite you want to buy . . . or make. Into the Wind has materials for kitemaking, too.

Where we live in the inner city, I have no more hope of finding a wide open space for kiteflying than I do of finding a nice dark sky to examine with a telescope. So we have neither. You, however, need not deprive yourself of a classy family exercise like this. A kite of beauty is a toy forever.

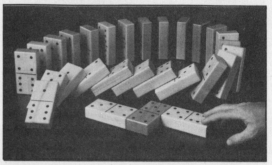

World Wide Games

Marble roller, $41.95. Table cricket and box hockey, $99.95 each. British ring toss, $23.95. Shoot-the-moon, $20.95. Maori Sticks, $4.95. Pommawonga, $8.95. Pic-E-U-Nee, $9.95. Backgammon, $49.95. Blocks, $75. Large Dominoes, $49. Hindu Pyramid, $9.95. Sponge Polo, $79.95. Wykersham, $42.95. *New Fun Encyclopedia,* $10.50 each volume.

If you like wood, you'll love WWG's games. They have marble mazes and table cricket and box hockey and British Ring Toss (toss rubber rings at hooks on a board). They have Shoot-the-Moon and Maori Sticks and Pommawonga and Pic-E-U-Nee (Ping-pong in one hand). Backgammon. Building blocks. Solid cherry wooden toys. Large Dominoes. Hindu Pyramid. Sponge Polo. Wykersham. Etc.

WWG also has books about games, such as the *New Fun Encyclopedia.* And for people who like to play in huge swarms, there are six-foot Earthballs and the ever-silly Parachutes.

WWG's Warren and Mary Lea Bailey stand ready to lead workshops on games and gameplaying. Warren can teach you how to make and fly a kite, and Mary Lea can unravel the intricacies of folk dancing.

BOARD GAMES/FILE FOLDER GAMES

Take it easy! Flop on the floor and push a little token around the board. No commercials, no raucous hucksterism, just a fun family time.

Animal Town Game Company

Animal Town has the largest selection of cooperative and noncompetitive games ever assembled. Animal Town has games from around the world, including some that have been classics for centuries. A family-owned and operated business, Animal Town also develops and manufactures their own extremely beautiful and slightly preachy board games, with values based on conservation, well-being, and social cooperation. Lots of other browsing stuff in this catalog!

Shakean Stations (Supplementary)

Fabulous collection of "file-folder" games; outrageously reasonable prices.

CHRISTIAN TOYS

In a reaction against the increasing brutality and amorality of children's toys, several Christian companies are now coming out with their own line of toys.

Bible Games, Inc. (Bible)

Bible Games, Inc. is the maker of *Bible Challenge,* my favorite Bible board game. By the time this book is out, Bible Games will have out a line of posable Christian action figures, a line of dramatized cassettes, Bible Peel 'n Play plastic stick-ons, and Bible software.

Praise Unlimited, Inc.

Praise Unlimited is a company on crusade. Listen to their brochure:

In the last few years changes have been occurring in the toy industry. These changes have shown movement away from traditional toys into a new era of violence-related, humanistic-type toys.

The innocence of tea sets, baby dolls, train sets and simple board games has been replaced with violent video games, voluptuously endowed fashion dolls, figurines encouraging destruction and fantasy role-playing that many times leads to an inability and lack of desire to cope with a real world.

The answer? "God-inspired" Christian toys. First there are the Praise Dolls: Joy, Hope, Faith, and Love. Just like the typical trademarked dolls, the Praise Dolls come in several sizes, and have all sorts of trademarked accessories. Unlike the Rainbow Brites and Strawberry Shortcakes, Praise Dolls make Christian comments when you squeeze them. Example: "Did you know that Jesus loves you and He is Lord!" Also, purchasers of the large twenty-one-inch model receive a Friendship Toy certificate which, if sent in and forwarded to Praise Unlimited, gets placed in a sixteen-inch Friendship Praise Doll box, and the whole kit and caboodle gets sent to an underprivileged child free of charge.

In the same line, Praise Unlimited has come out with a "Judah the Christian Soldier" action figure for boys. Judah wears the Full Armor of God, which is completely removable except for the shin-guards. Price includes the gift of a second Judah to a needy child, when a Friendship Card is returned by the purchasing child.

The Full Armor of God is also available separately in kid-size.

Praise Unlimited also sells a Noah's Ark kit, complete with Noah and his family and even some scenery pieces. Again, a small Noah's Ark goes to a needy child when a purchaser of the large set returns a card.

Judging from the pictures, all products seem carefully and professionally made. The brochure informs us that Praise Unlimited products meet all consumer safety regulations.

Praise Unlimited toys are sold through local distributors.

MAGIC

Magic tricks *as* tricks are just lighthearted fun, a spoof on how credible people can be. Some of the best magicians are Christians who use magic to introduce their street evangelism or illustrate a gospel message. I am not crazy, however, about the occult themes that some performers encourage gullible audiences to take seriously. You won't, I hope, want to get involved in pumping the Tarot cards or holding seances. These are especially silly since you can pay $20 and buy a trick that will show you how to produce these phenomena. But who needs them at any price? Disappearing coins and color-changing scarves are fine party fare, and none the worse for being innocent.

Fellowship of Christian Magicians

Organization with conventions and a newsletter full of gospel magic tips and ads from suppliers. Members must sign a statement of faith.

Hank Lee's Magic Factory
Catalog, 270-plus 8½ x 11″ pages, $5: or $8.95 with binder. Magic Club, $12/year.

What workshop is full of magical things and populated by elves? You're thinking of Santa's, right? Well, the mythical Mr. Claus has real-life competition. Hank Lee's Magic Factory in good old Boston (love that dirty water!) is staffed by such imps as Elmo, Joe-O, Bob-O, Phono ("Still answers the phone at night and on weekends"), and Byte-O ("The computer elf"). Hank Lee's catalog has an immense selection of magic tricks, equipment, props, and books. I find it easier to follow than Tannen's (see below). Let me warn you, though, once you pick it up you will have trouble putting it down! The descriptions of the magic tricks make fascinating reading, and the layout makes browsing a delight. Now who wants a pair of soft dice that change colors and produce baby dice . . .

To make it even easier for you to blow all your hard-earned shekels on magic, Hank Lee has invented a Magic of the Month club. Members get a membership card, "Noosletter" subscription, and discounts of 10 to 40 percent off selected books and magic, plus previews of the hottest new stuff.

And for the really dedicated magic fan who also has a computer, Hank Lee has set up a magic bulletin board. Call (617) 482-8750 between 5 PM and 8 AM Eastern time. The password is HANKLEE. You can leave orders using your credit cards, leave questions and messages (questions will be answered and left as EMAIL for the next day), check out the latest magical goodies, and so on.

Louis Tannen, Inc.
850-plus-page hardbound catalog, $8 postpaid USA, $10 foreign.
Summer Magic Camp, $300. *Magic Manuscript* magazine, $15/year (six issues). $3 for sample copy. Foreign and Canada, add $7/year for surface mail, $34/year airmail.

Another fabulous magic catalog: typeset, indexed, and illustrated. Tannen's catalog includes close-up magic, magic for kids, stage magic, silk magic, card magic, coin magic, and some heavy-duty illusions for professional magicians. The book section is huge. This is Tannen's fifteenth catalog (the 1985-87 edition), so you know they've been around for a while.

Tannen also runs a summer Magic Camp for boys and girls ages nine to eighteen. Held on the grounds of LaSalle Academy (which I *think* is in New York state), the camp fee includes a Magic Supply Kit (retail value $50) as well as the magic instruction. Campers get "a rigorous schedule of evening shows, celebrity performers, and finale appearances by the campers." Well-known magicians serve as guest teachers and lecturers. Some of Tannen's grads have gone on to perform professionally. I don't believe in sending kids to camp, but you've got to admit that this sounds like one of the more interesting camps around.

And if you should be looking for a full-color magic magazine, Tannen publishes the world's only. *Magic Manuscript* has news, reviews, interviews with the pros, and pictures of people making rings of fire or chopping lovely ladies asunder (temporarily, of course).

TOOLS FOR CHILDREN

I have only one listing in this category, because I only know of one company that specializes in quality tools for children. Schlock tools you can get from any major department store catalog.

Toad's Tools

I'm sorry, but I had to do it. I had no choice. There is no section in this catalog for "serious tools for children," so I had to put Toad's Tools in the Toys and Games chapter. What you get, folks, are kid-sized but serious tools. Prices are "reasonable"— e.g., $15 for a ten-ounce hammer and $4.40 for a set of three screwdrivers. This is not your typical made-in-Taiwan tinware.

The Toad's Tools basic set, which includes anything a young carpenter could ever need except power tools, presently goes for $135 plus shipping. All items are available separately. All items, except normal replacement parts like saw blades, carry an unconditional lifetime replacement guarantee.

UNUSUAL GIFTS

Many of the products mentioned in this chapter are unusual, but the following companies are *really* unusual. I very much doubt if your nephew Sidney will get two ecological card games or two logic games this birthday. Niece Brunnhilde is also unlikely to receive two corncob dolls or two sets of teddy bear stamps. These products are authentic, inexpensive, fun, and unique. What more could Sidney or Brunnhilde want?

Ampersand Press (Nature Study and Ecology, Science)

Card games which teach ecological and electrical principles.

Mountain Craft Shop (History)

One-stop shopping for hundreds of American folk toys. Mountain craftsmen make these authentic reproductions. It's a little bite of history at a very reasonable price.

Rubberstampede

Beautiful rubber stamps. The selection is eclectic, with offerings ranging from a mother bunny trundling her baby rabbits in a carriage to a piece of pizza to aid in teaching fractions. Cartoons and animals are intermixed with serious art. The catalog is large and contains every stamping accessory your little heart could desire. You can get personalized stamps and custom stamps and Rainbow Pads and uninked pads and metallic inks and stamp holders and stamp sets (Betty Boop or Teddy Bears, to name just two).

Rubberstampede's Alpha Bears™ set sells for $12.95 and has been a big hit with teachers.

Wff 'n Proof Learning Games Associates (Computers, Language, Math, Science)

Quick quiz: What company has managed to integrate Chicago schoolchildren where the federal, state, and local governments failed? Answer: Wff 'n Proof Learning Games Associates. It seems that some of our university profs are actually producing something useful—a series of educational games that really gets kids involved.

The game that got dozens of Chicago schoolkids, black and white, to voluntarily board buses and spend their Saturday mornings nerding math is *Equations*. This deceptively simple prealgebra game consists of a set of numerals and operations. One player sets a goal. Then everyone in turn tries to pick a resource from the remaining pool that will (1) not allow the goal to be reached in one or less steps and (2) not make reaching the goal impossible with the remaining resources. From here the description gets more complicated. Suffice it to say that it takes only fifteen minutes to learn to play *Equations,* but a math major like me or my M.I.T.-graduate husband Bill could spends weeks playing it without getting bored. In Chicago, kids play *Equations* in the Academic Games League. At home, they can play it with you, or (thanks to the folks at Wff 'n Proof) with the family Apple.

Nobody can play *Equations* without sharpening their thinking and their arithmetic skills. Boys tend to love it more than girls, but everywhere it's been tried the math skills have gone up and the absentee rate down.

Wff 'n Proof has a pile of other games for science, language, grammar, logic, and set theory. All stress abstract thinking. The *Wff 'n Proof Game of Modern Logic* has been shown to increase I.Q. scores by more than twenty points in avid users.

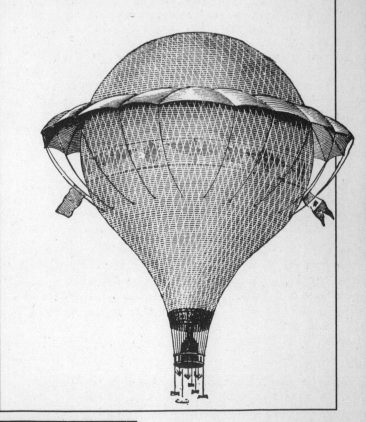

PART XIII

OF MAKING MANY BOOKS

THE TEXTBOOK BOONDOGGLE, OR: READING, SCHMEADING, WE'RE TOO BUSY CLARIFYING JUNIOR'S VALUES

"To read, or not to read, that is the question:
Whether 'tis nobler to suffer the slings and
arrows of outrageous textbooks
Or to take up arms against a sea of rubbish
And by so doing, end it. . . . (with apologies to
William Shakespeare)

If you want one word that sums up why millions of parents have taken their children out of the public schools, and why millions more are even now considering it, the word is: *Values!* And if you want one word that explains why textbooks have become such a political football, it's still the same: *Values!* Academics have been conquered by ideology. The people who run our schools are now more interested in *preaching* their peculiar values to our children than they are in *teaching* them anything. These values include:

Sexual Anarchy—School courses teach kids how to masturbate, fornicate, adulterize, sodomize, even commit incest, but omit the options of chastity and marital faithfulness.[1]

Amorality—Texts preach that there is no right and no wrong. Students are presented with both sides of the issue: shall we take drugs, or not? Shall we commit suicide, or not? Students are made moral eunuchs by being forced to choose an option from a list containing nothing but bad alternatives. This brainwashing is mislabeled "developing thinking skills" or even "teaching values."[2]

One-world government—American schoolchildren are taught that the world is inexorably moving towards centralized, monolithic government. And I don't mean *democratic* government, either. Children are being prepared to become little comrades under a totalitarian bureaucracy a la Stalinist Russia.[3]

Radical feminism—In school texts, housewives are to be neither seen nor heard. *All* women pictured must be engaged in outside occupations. *No* women can be shown pregnant, mothering children, or engaged in housework. Children are told this is an accurate picture of our present world.[4]

Dependence—From kindergarten on, textbooks indoctrinate children in the idea that they must end up working for someone else. All the "careers" emphasis boils down to brainwashing kids

into never considering the possibility of self-employment. Where are the small businessmen, the housewives with their home businesses, the owners of companies? Along with this, the individual, the family, the church, and voluntary organizations are presented as incompetent to solve any of society's problems. Only bureaucrats can redeem us, or so the dogma goes.[5]

Despondence—Texts rub the kids' noses in death and dying, and then tell them that suicide is O.K. After teachers have taught kids to write suicide notes, some children have gone out and killed themselves.[6]

Rejection of religious values—Supreme Court rulings aside, it *is* O.K. to mention the names *God* or *Christ* in public school textbooks. All you have to do is follow these guidelines: (1) Get across the idea that man created God. (2) Refer to religion in the past tense, as an outmoded, dying concept. (3) Use the name of Deity in swearing and profanity.[7]

Rejection of family—Learn to hate your parents. Learn to suspect them of incestuous intentions if they hug you, or to turn them in as abusers if they spank you or scold you or tell you to go to your room or refuse to let you eat all the Twinkies you want.[8]

If you think I'm kidding, read the footnotes. And these are just the tip of the iceberg. I've not only read books about the textbook problem; I've read the textbooks. The dogma isn't always crassly obvious when you first flip through, especially when texts are dealing with teaching a genuine skill, such as phonics or math. (Generally, the most conservative publishers academically also are the most conservative philosophically.) But after a while, you begin to see a pattern emerge. Why do the writers of history texts keep forgetting Patrick Henry's famous, "Give me liberty or give me death!" while giving full space to Susan B. Anthony's comments? Why do *math* texts need units on "careers"? Why do drug education courses forget to say using illegal drugs like heroin and cocaine is *wrong?* Why do sex ed materials preach the joys of irresponsible copulation while sweeping the heartbreaking realities of syphilis, herpes, gonorrhea, and AIDS under the rug? Again, why do sex ed texts assume *all* teenagers are "sexually active" (in itself a propaganda term that labels noncopulators as sexually *in*active duds). What do courses on nuclear war (which the NEA is currently trying to force on kindergarteners in every state) have to do with getting ready to read and write, which is why most parents send their children to kindergarten?

But why go on? The NEA has openly declared that it sees its function more as evangelizing students for its radical leftist agenda than as educating them. As Mary Futrell, the NEA's president, said in the *Los Angeles Times* of July 4, 1982, "Instruction and professional development have been on the back burner for us, compared to political action."[9]

Even if you agree wholeheartedly with the NEA's philosophy, the question remains: "Am I sending my children to school, or to Sunday school?" And if you don't agree with all the values above, the question is even stronger: "Why should I pay taxes to send my children to The First Church of What the NEA Hopes Is Happening Now?"

The only way to get back to basics is to eradicate this one-sided preaching from our textbooks. The only two ways to get one-sided religious values *out* and skills and facts back *in* are:

(1) Begin a parents' group. Go to school board meetings. Write your state education office for information on how textbooks are adopted, and then get the books and review them and go to *those* meetings. Get on the media and air your complaints. In general make this your free-time crusade.

I do not disparage this approach. However, most parents have a better chance of helping their families with the next option.

(2) Trash the bad texts *your children* are using. Get some good texts and use them. This may mean enrolling in a private school that uses academically superior texts, or a Christian or other religious school whose texts and teachers support, rather than offend, your values. It may mean home schooling. It may mean afterschooling, or summer schooling, at home, struggling with good texts to overcome the one-sidedness and academic inferiority of the bad.

The next two chapters are a listing covering 90 percent of what' out there in the textbook market, good, bad, and indifferent.

BOOKS DOCUMENTING THE TEXTBOOK DISASTER

If you're the sort of person who loves to read Edgar Allen Poe stories or H. P. Lovecraft novels on black nights when the wind is shrieking in the rafters, you'll love the following collection of books. Each one is stuffed with actual quotes from school texts and the actual stories of children whose lives have been ruined by them. Together, they form a new genre of horror literature. Hear little children crying that they would rather die than go to school, and see older ones hang themselves. One boy, assured by his chemistry teacher that drowning was rather pleasant, was found on the bottom of a swimming pool with a weight tied to his ankle. His face showed that he had discovered, too late, that

his teacher was wrong. Hear the screams of little girls, some as young as five years old, gang-raped by older students after a particularly instructive sex ed lesson. It all really happened, and it's all documented here.

The real horror is that we have been trained to accept crime and mediocrity as *normal.* When bright-eyed, cheerful kindergarteners turn into sullen, defiant, drug-using alley cats, we've been trained to respond, "Oh, it's just a phase they are going through," or "The world is different nowadays." If nothing else, the following collection of books is a reminder that not all our fellow citizens have agreed to accept depression as the normal state of childhood, and illiteracy as the inevitable fruit of schooling. These writings, by refusing to accept the darkness, constitute the only real vision of a brighter future for America's children.

Child Abuse in the Classroom, Phyllis Schlafly, editor. Crossway Books. 1984. $4.95.

From cover to cover, this book is red-hot. With the exception of a short Foreword and two small appendices, it contains nothing but testimonies given by parents, teachers, community leaders, and students as to what is really happening in their schools. The testimonies were given at official Department of Education hearings conducted throughout the nation in 1984. This is what's happening now, folks—from teaching kids to masturbate and commit suicide and use drugs to the tactics the bureaucrats use to harass any who disagree with them—told in the words of the people to whom it happened.

Change Agents in the Schools, Barbara Morris. Published by the Barbara M. Morris Report. 1979. $9.95.

Change Agents details the movement to change America from a basically religious, democratic country to a hedonistic zoo ruled by the one-world-government crowd. Barbara Morris quotes the very individuals who are anxious to use the classroom as a pulpit for their new antireligion, and shows how Uncle Sam has his hands deep in their dish. The book is irrefutable, and explains much about why things are the way they are in the public school textbooks and the schools themselves. Out of their own mouths they have said it.

What Are They Teaching Our Children?, Mel and Norma Gabler, with James C. Hefley. Victor Books. Available from Conservative Book Club.

An exposé of public school textbooks, pure and simple. The Gablers have won an international reputation as experts on textbooks, and specifically on weeding out the bureaucratic preachifying from the genuine academic content. Naturally this makes the unanointed preachers hopping mad. The Gablers get called a lot of names, like "ignorant, fear-mongering, right-wing fruitloops" (page 14; this gem of objective reporting comes from the *Dallas Times Herald* of July 21, 1983). And what dangerous questions do these right-wing fruitloops ask? "Are the students asked questions about family, neighbors, and religion which invade their privacy? Does factual learning take a backseat to behavior modification and attitude formation? . . ." (page 127). Naughty, naughty, Gablers! It's un-American to let school kids think their private thoughts and to teach them factual material! At least we gather that is the position of People for the American Way, which has opened an office in Austin just to try to thwart the Gablers in their nefarious drive to restore education to the schools.

When the light comes on, the roaches run for cover. If the schools were dishing out nothing but wholesome instruction in needed skills, they wouldn't wail so loudly when a couple like the Gablers turns the spotlight on their curriculum. This book is the spotlight.

Why Are They Lying to Our Children?, Herbert I. London. Stein and Day, 1984. $15.95. Available from Conservative Book Club.

This book's main focus is on the actual errors of fact taught to American schoolchildren—errors which lead them to despair about their future. Dr. London points out the problem, quotes the textbooks, and calmly refutes them. Eye-opening.

Book Burning. Cal Thomas. Crossway Books. 1983. $5.95.

Just why is it that *one* set of values (anti-Christian, antifamily, antihousewife, antibabies, etc.) is allowed to proliferate in school texts while the other side is relentlessly censored out? Why is it O.K. to use Christ's name in vain, but not to use it seriously? Why is it O.K. to show Daddy changing the baby, but not O.K. to show Mommy doing it? The Far Left likes to scream about "censorship," but as this book shows, they are the most ardent censors of all. Provocative reading.

Globalism: America's Demise, William M. Bowen, Jr. Huntington House, Inc. 1984. $9.95. Available from Heritage Education and Resource Organization (HERO).

The focus of *Globalism: America's Demise* is on the "why" of all the seemingly contradictory strands in public school curriculum. What does any educator get out of alienating children from their parents, or breaking down their sexual morals, or keeping them from learning to read? The answer is, "Nothing." It therefore seems strange that the educational establishment so stiffly resists every program that is shown to have good educational results, while embracing hundreds of no educational worth whatsoever. Strange, that is, until you read this book. Impeccably documented, it proves that certain people in high positions would like to have total control over all the rest of us,

and that in order to accomplish this goal they are trying to brainwash our children and isolate us citizens from all our nonbureaucratic attachments (such as family and church).

I am not the paranoid type who sees conspirators lurking under every bed. However, it is easy to see that modern government bureaucrats enhance their power by engineering crises. If we had no problems, bureaucrats would have no excuse for expanding their territory. Hence, the more illiteracy, drug use, and teenage pregnancies the schools produce, the more funding our educrats will get to "combat" these things. That being so, they need no motive stronger than self-interest to continue bungling our children's education.

Bureaucratic self-interest climaxes in the "one-world government" movement, which naturally means one-world bureaucracy, which means huge, centralized, uncontrollable power structures, which for bureaucrats and their hangers-on means fun, fun, fun! Naturally, the schools are full of courses pushing one-world government.

Mr. Bowen explains not only why we have crises in education (and everywhere else), but why we will never stop having them until we toss the rascals out. Their power *depends* on crisis, and this is how it works. Announce a crisis (which may or may not exist.) Demand power to deal with it. Fail to solve it. Use the continuing crisis (which is becoming genuine) to demand more power. And so on. If diagnosis is 90 percent of the solution, then all free people should read this book. The only missing ingredient is the conviction that God, who sits in heaven, will yet laugh these schemers to scorn (see Psalm 2).

ORGANIZATIONS THAT KNOW ABOUT TEXTBOOKS

You don't want to read every textbook in the country. *Really,* you don't! It's wearisome and sometimes gruesome work. But you do, perhaps, want to obtain a critical analysis of the merits and flaws of some current offerings. What do you do?

Two organizations can help you.

America's Future

Almost fifteen years ago, a nonprofit foundation called "America's Future," located in New Rochelle, New York, set up a Textbook Evaluation Committee which has since performed more than 800 in-depth studies in the fields of history, civics, sociology, and economics at the high school level. Out of all this effort has come a list of two hundred titles which the foundation recommends as being good instruments for teaching as well as giving a fair, balanced treatment of our form of government and economic system.

"Who does the evaluating? Eighteen of America's top teachers and college professors, chosen for their eminence and for their objectivity. Men like Anthony Bouscaren, Russell Kirk, George C. Roche III, A. H. Hobbs and Anthony Kubek.

"How are the individual book reports made available? Through concise printed pamphlets, each summarizing the book under study and giving the reasons for recommending it.

"What does it cost a school principal, superintendent, or board of education member to get a copy of each new evaluation as it rolls off the press? Nothing. I mean it; nothing at all. . . .

"So the next time you get so sickened by one of Junior's social science books that you feel absolutely compelled to raise cain with your school superintendent, you know now what to tell him when he purrs, 'We realize the book in question isn't perfect, but can you name a better one?' "

That's what Dr. Max Rafferty, the former California state superintendent of education, has to say about America's Future. Let me add to this that you can get a free list of the books that the Textbook Evaluation Project has reviewed so far, sample textbook evaluations, *and* the brochure "200 Recommended Social Studies Texts" by just writing to America's Future and asking for them.

It's a terrific accomplishment to have sorted through more than eight hundred social studies texts and actually located a number that, from a secular standpoint, are acceptable. America's Future would like very much to perform the same positive service for the schools' *reading* programs, which at present are badly in need of it. Their emphasis is to praise the good rather than to go about beating on the bad. Optimists that they are, they expect to find some good, and if enough people send in their shekels perhaps they will be able to do so.

America's Future also has free recommended reading lists for various age levels, to help you find good literature for your children.

The Mel Gablers, Educational Research Analysis

And Mel and Norma Gabler, down in Texas, are still working away with their small staff, evaluating textbooks and collating reviews that other people have provided. If you would like information on any particular book, send a small donation to cover expenses and ask for info on that book by name. (Large donations are also O.K.!)

The Gablers have over six hundred printed forms relating to textbook content, over thirty handbooks on subjects concerning textbooks and curricula, and thousands of individual book reviews prepared by fellow citizens from coast-to-coast, and even as far away as Australia. Send $10 for the Gabler's list of *Acceptable Texts for Private Schools and Home Schoolers,* if you're interested. Other handbooks, also available for a $5 donation, include: *Values Clarification, Sex Education, Acceptable Sex Education, Court Rulings Favoring Parental Rights, Drug Education, Death Education, Phonics, Scientific Creationism, "Dungeons and Dragons," MACOS: Man, A Course of Study* (the worst social studies curriculum ever developed, parts of which are continually recycled through other textbooks), *Sensitivity Training, Recommended Reading and Literature,* and *Background Information on Textbooks' Problems,* plus more. *Humanism in Textbooks* is the Gabler's most popular brochure. It includes "as many publishers, subjects, and grades as could be put on six pages" and proves how prevalent this state-supported religion is in our public school texts. You can get two copies for $1 or five for $2. Minimum order is $2 to help the Gablers and their staff keep on top of their enormous correspondence.

SUMMING UP: THE GETTUSBOOKS ADDRESS

Ten score and ten years ago our forefathers brought forth on this continent a new nation, conceived in liberty and dedicated to the proposition that all men are created equal.

We are now the victims of bureaucrats who do not believe that our nation, or any nation so conceived and so dedicated, can long endure.

We cannot consecrate, we cannot dedicate, we cannot hallow the educational blunders of the past.

So let's get rid of them!

CHAPTER FIFTY-ONE

TEXTS FOR PRIVATE SCHOOLS AND HOME SCHOOLS

Public schools are declining, and private schools are growing. The latest figures I heard announced that one out of every four American schoolchildren now is privately educated.

Private education, once the domain of the rich, has been taken over by the working class. The average income of a family whose children are enrolled in private schools is less than $15,000 a year.

Naturally, working people want the most for their money. Solid, practical texts are what we want, and solid, practical texts are what we get. Most of these are Christian, since the Christian school movement is by far the fastest growing sector of private schooling, with the possible exception of home schooling, which is also mostly Christian. The old-line private prep schools are still there, but because of their commitment to exclusiveness they *can't* grow as fast as Christian schools. Alternative schools, another corner of the market, tend to use hands-on materials for most of their curriculum, and when they use texts they use public school texts.

The following list, then, contains nine Christian publishers, one preppy publisher, and no "alternative" publishers.

CHRISTIAN TEXTBOOK PUBLISHERS

A Beka Books
For more information, see the A Beka Video School and Pensacola Christian Correspondence School reviews in the Buyers' Guide.

A Beka is a big-time supplier, no doubt about it. One of the major Christian school text publishers, A Beka is evangelical, creationist, and patriotic. Their products cover grades nursery through 12 and all subjects.

I have seen, and used, many A Beka texts. The elementary math workbooks which are colorful and provide needed practice in a sensible order. A Beka's upper-grades history, geography, and economics texts are likewise a straightforward, traditional look at these subjects.

In the lower grades, A Beka's science texts progress from rinky-dink to really interesting. For readability and kid-appeal they are fine; but in my view the earliest books in the series are more superficial than is necessary for children of those ages. A Beka's history series is interesting right from the start, introducing children to holidays, geography, and patriotic songs along with a brief look at history. In the A Beka scheme, history and science are taught "spirally"—that is, by going into the same subjects more deeply each year while introducing a few new ones.

We did not care for the elementary grammar materials, which were unimaginative and overdone. The Readers, on the other hand, are all very attractive and hugely interesting to children.

In the upper grades, A Beka follows the laudable course of including several entire literary works within each of its anthologies, along with excerpts from others. The Themes in Literature series for ninth graders, however, did not appeal to me at all, being an eclectic blend of popular writing laden with unimaginative "thought" questions that mostly centered around the actions of the characters (the realm of ethics) rather than the literary devices which make us willing to read about the characters (the art of composition).

Of more importance than my comments above is the fact that the catalog really does describe the books accurately; so you can make intelligent choices. You can now buy anything in the entire A Beka catalog. I would stay away from the classroom manuals even so, because they *are* classroom manuals and it is so much easier to teach one child straight out of the book.

Alpha Omega Publications

For more information, see the Alpha Omega review in the Buyers' Guide.

Alpha Omega produces a series of worktexts that come ten per subject per year. In some areas, notably upper-grades English and science, they are excellent. In others, they are still mostly quite good. All emphasize higher-order thinking and "spiral" teaching.

Alpha Omega curriculum encourages parental involvement. It is widely used and widely liked. If you forget about the goal-setting and just use the booklets on their own, they add quite an interesting fill-up to any program.

Associated Christian Schools

For more information, see the Associated Christian Schools review in the Buyers' Guide.

ACS material is as simple to use as Basic Education (see below) and laced with stimulating exercises and witty text. ACS is not fancy, but it's up-and-coming. The morality is fundamentalist and Baptist. I really hated to send the first-grade books I was reviewing back to the publisher (but you can't buy EVERYTHING!).

If this curriuclum were packaged with fancy art, glossy paper, and color, it would make a real hit with the solid citizens among us. It's not doing too badly even without them.

Basic Education

For more information, see the Basic Education review in the Buyers' Guide.

Families can buy the Basic Education worktexts used by thousands of children. All follow the same format: Instruction, questions based on the text, and a text test which requires a score of 80 percent or higher. All are self-instructional and exceptionally easy to use.

Basic Education materials have been criticized because of their "fill-in-the-blanks" approach, which makes it tempting for some students just to find the answers. If you supervise your

children's work and use the publisher's recommended controls, this should not be a problem. The question for potential Basic Education users is, "Do you want heavy-duty texts or do you want to provide the basics as simply as possible?" Many families report satisfaction with these materials, and test scores show users to surpass public school children quite substantially.

You would be wise, in my estimation, to count on supplementing Baic Ed texts with lots of free reading and some "hands-on" resources from the other sections of this book.

Bob Jones University Press

Now here's a big-time company that's *really* friendly to home schoolers! Bob Jones has a toll-free number for questions about their curriculum and a gorgeous glossy catalog loaded with everything you need from preschool through high school.

The BJU catalog contains a number of innovative ideas. For example, BJU's Multi-Grade Manual is a management scheme for classrooms containing four or more different grades. Designed for one-room schools, it can be used equally well when home schooling large families, if you are willing to use the Bob Jones curriculum, on which it is based.

BJU has been around for a while, and their material is really solid intellectually. The math and science programs, especially, have many fans. BJU sells books, workbooks, classroom equipment, and even science lab apparatus. BJU also offers a number of books for teachers and parents.

The enormous, ring-bound Teacher's Editions are great for Christian school teachers. At home, I personally would skip them unless you feel you need the extra help of lesson plans, teaching tips, and all sorts of supplemental activities. They are much more expensive than the texts.

BJUP is very friendly to parents, and will send you a free catalog on request. Their traveling sales reps are also willing to demonstrate their wares to parents' groups—you might give them a call.

A "must" catalog.

Christian Schools International

Another full-service schoolbook supplier, this time from a Reformed Christian perspective. CSI's products appear to be more functional, less glossy, and more intellectual than most publishers'.

One extremely interesting CSI offering is their Writing Rainbow series, reviewed in the Writing and Composition section. This opens up the art of composition both logically and creatively.

The catalog is very serious and sober.

Mile-Hi Publishers

Mile-Hi's *Little Patriots* curriculum covers phonics, reading, penmanship, spelling, and vocabulary. In later grades, grammar, composition, and speech are also covered. Mile-Hi does not believe in the Language Arts approach, whereby all these subjects are jumbled together. Their curriculum presents each separately.

Mile-Hi is also a company that believes in presenting the classics to little kids. Their curriculum contains three classics per year. Their notebook approach involves the student in making what amounts to his own text of the subject.

Mott Media

If you long for the days of Laura Ingalls Wilder, you might find a friend in Mott Media's Classic Curriculum. Mott has republished a whole line of classic textbooks from the golden age of American public education. The line includes an edited version of the original *McGuffey's Readers, Havey's Grammars, Spencerian Penmanship,* and *Ray's Arithmetics.* Mott also has a contemporary line of phonics and spelling helps, plus supplemental helps and parent-teacher resources (including Sam Blumenfeld's invaluable *How to Tutor,* which Mott publishes). Mott's Sower Series of Christian biographies is also widely used in Christian schools and home schools.

All of Mott's Classic Curriculum contains Christian values and is nongraded. Children learn at their ability level. Many Mott products also are nonconsumable and can be passed down from child to child.

Rod and Staff

We were saddened to hear that Rod and Staff had suffered a calamitous fire at their headquarters, but it seems that, in spite of having no insurance, they have been able to recover. Rod and Staff is a large, serious publisher of Mennonite schoolbooks. As one might expect, their books are very traditional and are filled with pictures of people in Mennonite dress. Home schoolers of all faiths enjoy them, and Rod and Staff is one of the most popular home school sources.

Being unworldly and serious does not deprive the Rod and Staffers of wit. My son and I had a happy five minutes giggling over this exercise from one of their books:

(In a section of the Bible Nurture and Reader series on giving thanks:)

Q: You have to work after school and do not have much time to play.

(pick one)
a. Be thankful you can work and help at home.
b. Be thankful you do not like to work.
c. Be thankful you know how to grumble a lot and show your mother how much you hate to work. (!!!!)

In keeping with an unworldly Christian outlook, all Rod and Staff materials are very reasonably priced.

School Supply Room

A supplier of Amish-Mennonite texts, grades 1 through 8, that is even cheaper and simpler than Rod and Staff. Dick and Jane in the first grades, German-English materials. Lots of Christian materials. School supplies. Some secular textbooks. All you get is a mimeo sheet with the prices on it in green ink. Surprisingly, it is not hard to figure out what you want from the extremely laconic descriptions. Example: "Color Book-Workbook; 50 States; Maps; State Flowers; State Birds; Cap.; Popu.; 1.50." And where else can you get the *McGuffey Primer* in German?

Thoburn Press/Fairfax Christian Bookstore

Not only does Thoburn Press publish its own facsimile version of the revised *McGuffey Readers,* it also carries a tremendous line of Christian books and texts. From a small but dynamic selection of books about education, including Robert Thoburn's *How to Establish and Operate a Successful Christian School* (he should know, having done it) to a fine section of creationist books, Thoburn Press has all you need to get started thinking in important educational areas.

As for school texts, besides the creationist books, already mentioned, Thoburn has the famous Lippincott New Reading With Phonics series, history books, phonics and math records, the original *Webster's Elementary Spelling Book,* and its own Fairfax Christian Curriculum Series. The first books in this series are the *E-Z as A-B-C* penmanship set, reviewed in the Handwriting chapter. Thoburn also has its own charming early math curriculum (see the Math chapter) and several other products.

PREP SCHOOL PUBLISHERS

Independent School Press

This small and not very splashy catalog contains books written by teachers and headmasters of private schools in all school subjects. Offerings display prep school values: modernist theology and values, classical literature and languages. ISP is an excellent source for classical language instruction, and carries foreign language materials as well. Find out what the other half's children are up to by sending for this catalog.

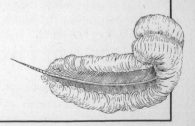

CHAPTER FIFTY-TWO

PUBLIC SCHOOL TEXTBOOK PUBLISHERS

"Instruction and professional development have been on the back burner for us, compared to political action."

(Mary Futrell, president of the National Education Association, *Los Angeles Times*, July 4, 1982)

SOME THOUGHTS ON THE NEA'S PRIORITIES

Mary Futrell
She said it well—
*   "The public school system can go to*

*   ____.*

"Forget education!
Political action
*   Gives us* much *more satisfaction.*
"Give us more money,
Give us more power,
*   And we'll be back asking for more in*
*   an hour."*

I really feel for the plight of public school textbook manufacturers, caught between a rock and a hard place. If they don't put in all sorts of NEA dogma, textbook selection committees won't approve their products. If they do put the horrible stuff in, parents will object. Although some companies are wholehearted believers in the New Doctrines of unisexism, careerism, bureaucratism and so forth, others would be equally glad to dump the whole boring liturgy and get on with the business of teaching. It's our job to make sure the people's voice is heard. No indoctrination without approbation!

FULL-SERVICE TEXTBOOK SUPPLIERS

Many companies supply the public schools with textbooks. Only a relatively few, however, are "full-service" suppliers, with texts for every subject area. Companies that sell texts in one area only are reviewed under that heading, if I've seen their materials and found them useful. The list following is of full-service, or almost full-service, companies.

Addison-Wesley Publishing Company

Two catalogs, K-8 and 7-12. This strange arrangement is necessary because some communities stuff the junior highs in with the high school students and others don't. The K-8 catalog has math, science, reading, computers (including a pile of Learning Company software packaged with A-W teachers' guides), social studies, English as a second language (henceforth referred to as ESL), bilingual materials, art, general resources, and earlier publications. The 7-12 catalog has all the above subjects with the exception of art, which shows that the people who make up our high school budgets esteem creativity less than football.

A-W is definitely out there on the cutting edge of new public school ideas. More than others, their books feature "hands-on" learning. Two of their books, *Workjobs for Parents* and *Mathematics Their Way,* have become minor home school classics. A-W's books for teachers look at least readable, which is more than I can say for most other publishers. If you know what you're doing, you can discover some interesting things in these catalogs.

AMSCO School Publications

AMSCO has texts on foreign languages, literature, mathematics, and composition. Their no-nonsense catalogs seem addressed to the high school market. See the Literature and Language chapters for more info.

The Continental Press

A potpourri of materials for various grades. Subject areas are: reading, language arts, math, social studies, science, special ed, bilingual, computers, and assorted teachers' stuff. These people publish the *Growing Up* take-home newsletter and *Growing Child* "parenting" newsletter, both of which reflect pop secular thinking.

Developmental Learning Materials (DLM)

Another big glossy catalog from a big company. DLM has: reading, language arts, speech, mathematics, educational software, "assessment" (a polite way to say testing), early childhood, practical life skills, social studies, filmstrips, professional resources, and an index to help you find them all.

DLM's somewhat stodgy catalog has bright spots in the geography section, as noted in reviews elsewhere. Mostly it consists of big programs written by Very Important Experts, and large, expensive kits. Frankly, I'd skip all these. DLM's games and accessories, which are generally free of both dogma and experts' initials, are what you're after. *Traffic Sign Bingo* ($18.75) and *Pronoun Pinchhitter* ($18.50) are just two of the sturdy games you'd never think to invent for yourself, but that DLM did.

Economy Company

K-8 materials in English and Spanish reading, language arts, social studies, and early childhood. The reading series is anything but economical, containing dozens of student books, teacher's books, "Skillmasters," practice masters, word phrase cards, etc., etc. One suspects from the catalog that this is not a pure phonics program.

Bowmar/Noble, a division of the Economy Company, has shown some imagination in its social studies support materials. These include *Sing a Song of People,* a program with "music, literature, drama, dance, and art." The program *is* "creative" as the catalog entry says, featuring recordings, miniworkbooks, and filmstrips with songs about different countries. It's a sad fact, though, that with all the push for "one-world government" we have to be careful of even innocent-looking, fun little things like this.

Bowmar/Noble also has a history program with audio cassettes and accompanying books. This too is clever and a good way of approaching the subject, but again be careful of the history presented.

Economy sells "Parent/Paraprofessional Kits" for use at home or school. These are for preschoolers or kindergarteners and cover the standard "readiness" areas with an activity card format. It's nice to see textbook companies becoming aware that

parents want to take a hand in their children's education. These kits cost $49.95 each.

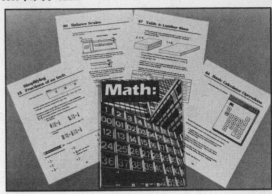

Educational Design, Inc.

E.D.I. carries two different lines. First, its no-nonsense Skillbooks. These inexpensive worktexts cover nitty-gritty stuff like developing a business vocabulary, the rudiments of composition, how to raise your test scores, kids and the law, and so on. These come under the headings: basic skills/language arts; remedial reading/writing/vocabulary; remedial math; adult living skills/consumer education; SAT/GED/gifted/computer literacy. Somewhat more ersatz are the booklets on employability skills and attitude development. These have to do with tracking the high school student into the employ of some company somewhere. Over all hangs an aroma of the dull-eyed almost-dropouts who this material is supposed to reach.

E.D.I.'s other line is its large filmstrip library. Some of the above subjects are covered, but most are in the area of social studies. The filmstrips are "interactive"—that is, students respond to worksheet questions as they watch the filmstrip. Filmstrips deal with "the natural and human-made environments * with heredity, race, ethnic groups, and culture * with individualistic and collectivist societies * with human needs *and values* * with facts and *attitudes,* with tradition and *change*" [emphasis mine]. The award-winning series features "photographs from every inhabited continent and major island area in the world." A lot of work went into this series. Now, what does it teach? The segment on Russia speaks favorably of communism (a "bold ideology" and a "strong central government"). It also goes to some pains to explain "why Russians support their system," giving us a hint of what to expect from the series as a whole.

Ginn Company

Ginn is another huge company with separate K-8 and 7-12 catalogs. In the earlier grades, some Ginn material is usable at home. Ginn's *My ABC Book* is a nifty little intro to ball and stick writing.

Ginn has very intelligently decided to create a set of "Parent/Home Newspapers" to be sent home with schoolchildren. They then somewhat blunted the edge of this fine idea by persistently referring to the one doing the activities with the child as the "Helper" instead of the "Mother" or "Father" or "Parent." The one sheet I saw was nicely done, with interesting and stimulating activities, albeit laced with the usual deplorable emphasis on "careers."

Ginn materials seem to be a mixed bag. Some texts (for little kids) use classic stories and noncontroversial teaching methods. Then we have the grades 11-12 *Parenting and Children* text which, right in the catalog, says, "The importance of preschool and day care programs is stressed." Is this proselytizing or what? It aggrieves me to see the schools use their compulsory requirements to push for their own programs (in this case, preschool). The same text gets deeply into "community agency services for both normal and special needs children," thus preparing young adults for a lifetime of dependence on outside "experts" when raising even *normal* children. Touches of these NEA dogmas reverberate throughout the upper-grades catalog (the "interdependency of all human beings"—a pitch for one-world government—in a home ec text, for example). Aside from the dogma, Ginn books are beautifully done.

Harcourt Brace Jovanovich

Yet another K-8 and 7-12'er. HBJ isn't just big—it's *huge*. Subjects covered in the K-8 catalog are: reading, language arts, grammar and composition, spelling, literature, humanities/art, math, science, health, social studies, foreign languages, earlier publications, and several indices so you have a sporting chance of finding what you're looking for. The grades 7-12 catalog has: literature, art/humanities, reading, English, math, science, environment, health, social sciences (a misnomer), ESL, and foreign languages.

I have seen HBJ's math and social studies material, and am unimpressed. HBJ's literature and reading offerings do include some interesting items. *Reading With a Purpose* is a workbook with over ninety documents and forms that students might encounter in real life. *How to Read Your Newspaper* sounds like a joke—this is what our schools have come to, folks! The literature series contains some classic anthologies (those with the old copyright dates). HBJ has an *Artists at Work* filmstrip series that would be worthwhile seeing if it didn't cost $60 a throw. Ditto for the *Writing of Poetry* filmstrip series at $54 a shot.

HBJ are the people who sell Warriner's *Grammar and Composition,* which has unfortunately been revised several times. Perhaps the Heritage edition would be still acceptable. You might try your library and used bookstores for an old copy.

Holt, Rinehart, and Winston

Holt is the only textbook company who did not send me a catalog. But no matter. We've used the early grades Holt math, and liked it except for the ever-present careerist preaching. Holt science, ditto: good material mixed with dogma. The Holt Reading series is kicking up quite a storm. One mother got arrested trying to remove her daughter from a classroom where Holt Readers were being used. (She is now suing for false arrest, by the way.) And on the schools go, showing how responsive they are to parents' feelings by arresting them.

McDougal, Littell & Company

Full-service textbook supplier for K-8, and English and social studies for 7-12. McDougal, Littell & Co. is particularly proud of its *Writing Better Sentences* and *Writing Better Paragraphs*

software for the Apple, which is however priced out of reach of most families. McD. L. & Co.'s literature series goes genre by genre (a logical approach) and also stresses discernment of literary techniques (most series tend to ignore this and beat "comprehension" to death). I can't say much about the selections, since I haven't seen them, but at least the methodology is sound.

World Geography strongly emphasizes issues related to our "increasingly interdependent world."

Charles E. Merrill Publishing Company

One-two-three-four-five separate catalogs here. Count 'em! The Readiness-Grade Eight catalog covers language arts, math, science, and social studies. There also are separate catalogs for science (pre-K-12), social studies (grades 7-12), math (pre-K-8), and language arts (pre-K-12).

Merrill has a phonics program. The accompanying readers are blighted by the emphasis, once again, on "careers" (now tell me, honestly, how many female airline pilots do you know?).

Merrill is very, very proud of their math program. It seems to be decent academically from the catalog description and sample pages.

Merrill's pure science texts look decent. They have considerably produced a biology text for noncollege-bound students and a simplified physics text, among other items. Merrill also sells Advanced Placement science texts.

Modern Curriculum Press

MCP has met with great favor among home schoolers because they stress basic skills and they contain less NEA preaching than most. In spite of all this, I am really forced to say that I do not like MCP's phonics workbooks. You *can* teach from them, if you have no other phonics materials, but the exercises are redundant and boring. Parents who have the time to ask Johnny, "What letter does 'bug' begin with?" don't need forty workbook pages with pictures of bugs and birds and baseballs to help Johnny practice recognizing beginning sounds.

MCP's Work-A-Texts are workbooks with built-in activities. Not all are supportive of Christian beliefs.

MCP's *See How It Grows* and *See How It's Made* are two multiple-book series that introduce kids to science and engineering for a very low price (about $1/book).

Much of the rest of this large catalog is given over to books for beginning readers. Some people really like the little phonics readers, and they don't cost too much.

Scott, Foresman

Very attractive, carefully prepared texts shot through and through with humanism. Scott, Foresman is a full-service provider, with even French and Spanish programs. Their health program is the most depressing I've seen. The lessons in this series center around remolding children's values to be "non-judgmental" about all physical sins. I was also not impressed with the math and science materials, which lacked depth in my opinion.

S, F's *D'Nealian Handwriting* program, on the other hand, is used by a number of parents. It allows children to develop their own writing style, within the limits of legibility.

The catalog closes with a selection of "Good Year Books," some of which are activity tips. One interesting entry from this public school publisher was *Loving and Beyond: Science Teaching for the Humanistic Classroom.*

Scribner Educational Publishers (formerly Harper & Row/J. B. Lippincott)

History time! Several years ago Harper & Row, one of the nation's largest publishers, acquired the J. B. Lippincott Company. Lippincott has been well-known for many years, especially for its phonics program, which is still used today. Then in 1984 Macmillan Inc. bought Harper & Row/J. B. Lippincott School Division and renamed it Scribner Educational Publishers. Both Harper & Row and J. B. Lippincott remain active publishers, but not of elementary and high school products.

Scribner's is a name with good vibes in the educational field. Its new catalog covers all grades, from readiness to advanced study texts, including such things as foreign languages, plus Latin and basic technical drawing. The selection isn't very deep, but there's something for every subject and every grade. Some of the selections looked good from a secular standpoint, like the biology text with a built-in lab exercise in each chapter. In all, the selection ranges from quite conservative to aggressively change-oriented.

Steck-Vaughn Company

This company sells state histories! Since most states require that all students take a course in the state's history, home schoolers might want to order Steck-Vaughn history through a nearby private school, textbook depository, or Textbooks for Parents! That is, if you live in AL, AK, FL, GA, KY, LA, MI, MO, NY, TN, TX, or VA. Some states have more than one history text to choose from.

Steck-Vaughn is a full-service K-12 supplier, more imaginative and less glitzy than most others. Subjects include: language arts, social studies, health, special ed (simplified texts), math, science, and adult education, including ESL materials.

Some notable S-V products: *Imaginary Line Handwriting,* a very cheap handwriting series that includes a workbook for adults who want to improve same. *Working with Numbers* is a no-nonsense math program used by several home school correspondence schools. GED prep booklets. Story Starter series. *Five Steps to U.S. Citizenship.*

Inexpensive, no-frills approach throughout.

Silver Burdett

K-12 textbooks and educational material. SB has the normal core subjects—language arts, science, social studies, and math—plus music and computer books and courseware. SB sells science lab equipment. You will probably be most interested in SB's accessories and supplemental materials.

SB has texts and/or workpackets on state history and geography for CA, NY, PA, VA, IN, WI, NC, and TN.

All offerings are pretty standard.

Zaner-Bloser

Elementary spelling, handwriting, and reading texts and supplies. Z-B is interested in preserving the past, not erasing it.

Z-B is without a doubt the king when it comes to handwriting instruction. I have reviewed their handwriting products at length in the Handwriting section.

Z-B's spelling programs are reviewed in the Spelling section. Now for the other tidbits in this catalog, which I should mention is heavily used by private schools and home schools as well as by public schools. Z-B's *Day-by-Day* kindergarten program is absolutely the best value and simplest around. The 128-page full-color pupil book includes prereading, prewriting, and premath for under $5. The accompanying 144-page full-color Teacher's Guide is just under $6. Z-B also has a Modality Kit (just over $100) for determining which way any given child learns best: through eyes, ears, or touch. The book, *Teaching Through Modality Strengths,* for $10 explains and documents how to teach each kid in the way most natural for him.

If you're serious about home schooling, go ahead and get this catalog.

A PUBLIC SCHOOL TEXTBOOKS SOURCE FOR FAMILIES

Textbooks for Parents!
Suggested packages $100 to $135, depending on grade.

There you are, one little family, and there are the enormous textbook companies. Will they enjoy doing business with you? Do they *want* to do business with you? Do you dare try to do business with them (after all, they're used to *big* orders)? Textbooks for Parents! is there to bridge the gap.

Carla Emery has put together packages of public school texts for each grade level. She can also get you the texts you prefer, plus teacher's editions. (The latter are not always available to individuals who order directly from the publishers.)

As an example of the Textbooks for Parents! approach, the standard second-grade package includes

Riverside's *Discovering Phonics We Use,* Book C

Economy Company readers and activity books

Holt School math worktext

Laidlaw Brothers English worktext and a hardcover health text

Zaner-Bloser *Creative Growth Handwriting*

Ginn Science Program, level 2

Macmillan Company (now Scribner) social studies

Houghton Mifflin spelling worktext

for a total cost of slightly over $100. If you like, you can substitute texts of your preference, leave out texts you don't want, add in extra texts for enrichment, or add a foreign language or two.

PART XIV

ESPECIALLY FOR ADULTS

CHAPTER FIFTY-THREE

ADULT AND VOCATIONAL EDUCATION

Money, money, money. It's not the only reason adults sign up for educational programs! Knowledge is power, but it is also satisfaction, confidence, and even entertainment.

Adult education has come a long, long way from the rows of high-school dropouts bent over dog-eared textbooks under the fluorescent lights of an after-hours high school classroom. For many people, adult education still means pursuing a diploma, but in their home, not a classroom. Nor are high school diplomas the only credentials available to after-hours scholars. You can get a college degree, a Master's, or even a legitimate Ph.D. at home!

Academic degrees are not the whole story, either. You can learn hundreds of marketable skills at home, from accident investigation to zookeeping. Upgrade your present job, or change jobs, *without* wearing yourself to a frazzle with late-night classes!

And then there's the sheer joy of learning. Dazzle your friends with your wok cookery! Learn how to make new slipcovers and design your own clothes! Immerse yourself in military history! Develop a gorgeous calligraphic handwriting style! Study French and read Blaise Pascal in the original, or Russian and grapple with Dostoyevski and Solzhenitsyn.

I'm not saying you should try to "reach your potential." You can *never* reach your potential! If you lived a thousand years, you could still be learning new things in your tenth century. And wouldn't it be *fun!*

FIRST, ABOUT THOSE ACADEMIC DEGREES

American College Testing Program (ACT)
College Planning/Search Book, $6 postpaid. Updated yearly.

If your heart is set on a traditional college experience, ACT's *College Planning/Search Book* is an excellent place to start. The Planning Section helps you decide what you're looking for in a college, and guides you through the application process. The Search Section displays up-to-date information about more than three thousand colleges in several helpful ways. You can, for example, look up schools that offer forestry, or colleges in Wisconsin, or the student profile of St. Louis U. Vital facts such as cost, religious affiliation, and composition of student body are laid out straightforwardly.

Moody Monthly

This Christian family magazine each spring puts out an issue highlighting Christian colleges and universities. If this is where you want to go, you need *Moody Monthly.*

Ten Speed Press
Bear's Guide to Non-Traditional College Degrees (Ninth edition), $9.95. Oversized qpb. Updated yearly.

BUY THIS BOOK!!! Dr. John Bear has put together the ultimate handbook of nontraditional education. "Nontraditional" means you don't spend four years in a stuffy classroom. Included are correspondence programs, short-term residency programs, after-hours and weekend programs, and even a section listing every known degree mill in the U.S.A. (just in case you want to buy Fido a Degree of Canine Knowledge for his birthday). This completely legitimate, incredibly well-researched book tells you how to get the degree you want, the way you want.

Unlike so many resource books, Bear's guide is delightful to read. Bear's lively descriptions of the colleges and universitites are accompanied by a little cartoon head wearing a graduation cap. If the little face is smiling, you're going to like this school. If it looks bored, the school is so-so. When the face assumes a Mr. Yuk expression, watch out—it's a real dog!

Bear gets his information both from extensive questionnaires and phone calls, and from the letters readers write telling him about their educational experiences. You can't find a better guide. Someone you know could save thousands of dollars by reading *Bear's Guide.*

NOW, YOUR ULTIMATE
SOURCE OF ADULT HOME LEARNING

But home education is much more than college degrees. It's vocational training, and hobbies, and religious instruction. It's courses on writing and art and fashion design. Where can you go to not only find academic degree programs, but also vocational programs and self-improvement courses? And if you spend a hundred to a thousand bucks by mail, how do you know you are getting a good product?

I firmly support the entrepreneurial spirit which moves people to set up new mail-order courses. And it's true that not every reputable home-study course is accredited by the National Home Study Council. Calvert School, for example, although it is accredited by the Maryland Department of Education, has not sought NHSC accreditation. But the National Home Study Council's *voluntary* accreditation program can increase a shopper's confidence, especially when you are unacquainted with the companies that offer the program you need.

The National Home Study Council has very kindly given me permission to reprint their listing of accredited home-study courses, and information about accreditation, for your information. The rest of this chapter is reprinted from their brochure, *NHSC 1985-86 Directory of Accredited Home Study Schools.* To receive a free brochure of your own, just write to the National Home Study Council office.

Comments from the National Home Study Council

WHAT IS HOME STUDY?
Home study is enrollment and study with an educational institution which provides lesson materials prepared in a sequential and logical order for study by students on their own. When each lesson is completed the student mails, or otherwise makes available to the school, the assigned work for correction, grading, comment, and subject matter guidance by qualified instructors. Corrected assignments are returned immediately to the student. This exchange provides a personalized student-teacher relationship.

Home study courses vary greatly in scope, level, and length. Some have a few lessons and require only weeks to complete, while others have a hundred or more assignments requiring three or four years of conscientious study.

ADVANTAGES OF HOME STUDY
Many courses provide complete vocational training. Others prepare you for upgrading in your present job, without losing experience or seniority. Avocational and hobby courses are also available.

Emphasis is on learning what you need to know. Instructional materials from accredited schools are up-to-date, clearly written and easy to understand.

Home study is especially suited for busy people who wish to increase their knowledge and skills.

With home study, you do not have to give up your job, leave home or lose income. You learn as you earn. The school comes to you. You receive individual attention, and you work at your own pace.

WHAT HOME STUDY ACCREDITATION MEANS
For 59 years the National Home Study Council has been the standard-setting agency for home study schools. The council has progressively raised its standards. Its accrediting program employs procedures similar to those of other recognized educational accrediting associations.

Each accredited school meets the following standards:

It has a competent faculty.

It offers educationally sound and up-to-date courses.

It carefully screens students for admission.

It provides satisfactory educational services.

It has demonstrated ample student success and satisfaction.

It advertises its courses truthfully.

It is financially able to deliver high quality educational service.

To become accredited each school has made an intensive study of its own operations, opened its doors to a thorough investigation by an outside examining committee, supplied all information required by the Accrediting Commission, and submitted its instructional materials for a thorough review by competent subject-matter specialists. The process is repeated every five years.

(Following is a complete listing of National Home Study Council Accredited Home Study Courses, with addresses, course information, and a cross-index of subjects taught. Have fun!—M. P.)

DIRECTORY OF
ACCREDITED HOME STUDY COURSES

1. **American Career Training Travel School**, 4699 North Federal Highway, Suite 106, Pompano Beach, Florida 33064. Founded 1982. Combination home study-resident course in airline/travel career training.

2. **American Medical Record Association**, 875 North Michigan Avenue, Suite 1850, Chicago, Illinois 60611. Founded 1928. Course in medical record technology.

3. **American School**, 850 East 58th Street, Chicago, Illinois 60637. Founded 1897. Complete high school diploma course.

4. **AMS College**, 10025 Shoemaker Avenue, Santa Fe Springs, California 90670. Founded 1976. Courses in computer programming and motorcycle mechanics.

5. **Andover Tractor Trailer School, Inc.**, 55 Hampshire Road, Methuen, Massachusetts 01844. Founded 1971. Combination home study-resident course in tractor trailer driving.

6. **Army Institute for Professional Development (IPD)**, U.S. Army Training Support Center, Fort Eustis, Virginia 23604. Founded 1976. U.S. Army specialist and professional development courses. Enrollment is restricted to Active and Reserve Component military personnel, Federal civil service personnel, ROTC cadets, and allied military students.

7. **Art Instruction Schools**, 500 South Fourth Street, Minneapolis, Minnesota 55415. Founded 1914. Courses in art, poetry, fiction and nonfiction writing.

8. **Aubrey Willis School**, P.O. Drawer 15190, 5840 West Concord Avenue, Orlando, Florida 32858. Founded 1970. Course in piano tuning, regulating and repairing.

9. **The Barton School**, Scranton Pennsylvania 18515. A division of North American Correspondence Schools—National Education Corporation. Founded 1977. Courses in medical and dental office assisting.

10. **Berean College**, 1445 Boonville Avenue, Springfield, Missouri 65802. Founded 1948. A division of the Assemblies of God. Degree and non-degree courses in Bible studies, evangelism, and theological areas.

11. **Biosystems Institute, Inc.**, 1430 West Broadway, Tempe, Arizona 85282. Founded 1972. Courses in respiratory therapy: entry level (technician) and advanced practitioner (therapist); health-related fields.

12. **California College for Health Sciences**, 1810 State Street, San Diego, California 92101. Founded 1978. Degree program and non-degree courses in respiratory therapy and health-related fields.

13. **Cambridge Academy**, Petti Building, Suite B, P.O. Box 1289, Banner Elk, North Carolina 28604. Founded in 1978. Complete high school diploma course.

14. **Citizens' High School**, 5582 Peachtree Road, Suite 107, Atlanta, Georgia 30341. Founded 1981. Complete high school diploma course.

15. **Cleveland Institute of Electronics, Inc.**, 1776 East 17th Street, Cleveland, Ohio 44114. Founded 1934. Degree and non-degree courses in electronics technology, broadcasting engineering, color TV troubleshooting, communications, engineering, and FCC license preparation.

16. **Color Me A Season, Inc.**, 1070-A Shary Circle, Concord, California 94518. Founded in 1977. Courses in color analysis and color cosmetic application.

17. **Columbia School of Broadcasting**, 5858 Hollywood Boulevard, 4th Floor, P.O. Box 1970, Hollywood, California 90028. Founded 1964. Courses in announcing (English and Spanish), FCC general broadcasting engineering, radio-TV commercial writing, and advertising time sales.

18. **County Schools, Inc.**, 3787 Main Street, Bridgeport, Connecticut 06606. Founded 1960. Courses in accounting, bookkeeping, drafting, hotel-motel management, food and beverage controller, interior design and decoration, tractor trailer driving, and travel agent training.

19. **Diamond Council of America**, 9140 Ward Parkway, Kansas City, Missouri 64114. Founded in 1944. Courses in Diamontology and Gemology leading to certificates of Certified Diamontologist and Guild Gemologist offered to members of the Diamond Council of America and their employees.

20. **Dorothea B. Lane Schools**, 955 S. Chapel Street, P.O. Box 9439, Newark, Delaware 19715. A division of USA Training Academy, Inc. Founded 1984. Courses in business secretarial topics.

21. **Early Learning Center for Montessori Education**, 8980 Brook Road, McLean, Virginia 22102. Founded 1978. Combination home study-resident course in Montessori teacher training.

22. **Educational Institute of the American Hotel & Motel Association**, Stephen S. Nisbet Building, Suite 310, 1407 South Harrison Road, East Lansing, Michigan 48823. Founded 1953. Courses and certification programs in hotel-motel, restaurant and food service operations.

23. **The English Language Institute of America**, 332 South Michigan Avenue, Suite 864, Chicago, Illinois 60604. Founded 1942. Course in practical English and command of words.

24. **Extension Course Institute**, United States Air Force, Gunter Air Force Station, Alabama 36118. Founded 1950. U.S. Air Force career development, specialized and professional military education courses. Enrollment is restricted to active duty military personnel, civil service, reserve, National Guard, and other specified personnel.

25. **Farmland Industries, Inc.**, Training Center, P.O. Box 7305, Dept. 23, 5401 N. Oak, Kansas City, Missouri 64116. Founded 1929. Courses in agriculture: accounting, cooperative development, management development, sales training, grain training, and commodities (feed, crop, and petroleum).

26. **Gemological Institute of America**, 1660 Stewart Street, Santa Monica, California 90404. Founded 1931. Courses in diamond grading and appraisal, gem identification, colored stones, colored stones grading, pearls, jewelry design, jewelry display, and jewelry retailing.

27. **General Education and Training, Inc.,** 12100 Grandview Road, Grandview, Missouri 64030. Founded 1971. Combination home study-resident course in tractor trailer driving.

28. **Grantham College of Engineering,** 10570 Humbolt Street, Los Alamitos, California 90720. A division of Grantham Schools, Inc. Founded 1951. Associate and Bachelor degrees in electronics engineering technology.

29. **Granton Institute of Technology,** 263 Adelaide Street West, Toronto, Canada M5H 1Y3. Founded 1934. Over 400 courses in business and management, engineering and technology, electronics and mechanics, repair and installation, hospitality and tourism, social and community services, and health and nutrition.

30. **The Hadley School for the Blind,** 700 Elm Street, Winnetka, Illinois 60093. Founded 1920. Over 100 courses offered. Courses for the blind in learning braille; high school, vocational, avocational, and college level subjects taught by braille or audio cassettes.

31. **Halix Institute,** 1543 W. Olympic Boulevard, Suite 226, Los Angeles, California 90015. A division of Hemphill Schools. Founded 1984. Course in computer programming (English and Spanish).

32. **Heathkit/Zenith Educational Systems,** Hilltop Road, St. Joseph, Michigan 49085. A division of Heath Company, subsidiary of Zenith Radio Corporation. Founded 1975. Courses in electricity and electronic fundamentals, advanced electronics, digital electronics, microprocessors and microcomputers, robotics, computer programming, mathematics and automotive electrical systems and tune-up.

33. **Hemphill Schools,** 1543 W. Olympic Boulevard, Suite 226, Los Angeles, California 90015. Founded 1920. Spanish language courses in art, automotive, diesel, radio-TV repair, electricity, air conditioning, refrigeration, accounting and English. Computer programming courses available in English language.

34. **Hollywood Scriptwriting Institute,** 1300 N. Cahuenga Boulevard, Hollywood, California 90028. Founded 1976. Course in professional scriptwriting.

35. **Home Study International,** 6940 Carroll Avenue, Takoma Park, Maryland 20912. Founded 1909. Correspondence courses for kindergarten, elementary (grades 1-6), junior high, secondary (with diploma), college and adult education.

36. **Insurance Achievement, Inc.,** 7330 Highland Road, Baton Rouge, Louisiana 70808. Founded 1969. Courses to prepare for the Chartered Life Underwriter (CLU), Chartered Financial Consultant (ChFC), Chartered Property/Casualty Underwriter (CPCU), Certified Financial Planner (CFP) national insurance designations and NASD Series 6, Mutual Funds and Variable Annuities, Series 7, General Securities Representative and Series 63, Blue Sky licensing examinations.

37. **International Correspondence Institute,** Chaussee de Waterloo 45, 1640 Rhode-St. Genese, (Brussels) Belgium. A division of the Foreign Missions of the Assemblies of God, Springfield, Missouri. Founded 1967. Degree and non-degree courses in Bible studies, evangelism, and theological areas.

38. **ICS—International Correspondence Schools,** Scranton, Pennsylvania 18515. Founded 1891. A division of National Education Corporation. Courses at the secondary and postsecondary level in technology, engineering, business, vocational trades, liberal arts, practical arts, and specialized industrial subjects.

39. **ICS Center for Degree Studies,** Scranton, Pennsylvania 18515. Founded 1974. A division of International Correspondence Schools—National Education Corporation. Associate degree programs in business, engineering, and electronics.

40. **ICS—Newport/Pacific High School,** Scranton, Pennsylvania 18515. Founded 1972. A division of International Correspondence Schools—National Education Corporation. High School diploma course.

41. **John Tracy Clinic,** 806 West Adams Boulevard, Los Angeles, California 90007. Founded 1942. Courses for parents of deaf children and deaf-blind children.

42. **The Laural School,** 2538 North 8th Street, Phoenix, Arizona 85006. Founded 1978. Courses in medical and dental office assisting, medical and dental receptionist, general business secretary, legal secretary and medical secretary.

43. **Learning and Evaluation Center,** 479 Drinker Street, P.O. Box 616, Bloomsburg, Pennsylvania 17815. Founded 1972. A home study "summer school" of subject extensions in areas offered to junior and senior high school students who fail during their regular school year. Student's school approval required.

44. **Lifetime Career Schools,** 2251 Barry Avenue, Los Angeles, California 90064. Founded 1944. Courses in landscaping, floristry, dressmaking, and doll technology.

45. **Marine Corps Institute,** Marine Barracks, Box 1775, Arlington, Virginia 22222. Founded 1920. Courses to improve the general military and technical proficiency of Marines. Enrollment is restricted to active duty military personnel, retired Marines, reserve Marines, civilian employees of the armed forces, NROTC midshipmen and allied military students.

46. **McGraw-Hill Continuing Education Center,** 3939 Wisconsin Avenue, N.W., Washington, D.C. 20016. Founded 1971. Courses in computers, electronics, automotive technology, air conditioning, appliance servicing, construction, and small engine repair.

47. **Modern Schools of America, Inc.,** 2538 North 8th Street, Phoenix, Arizona 85006. Founded 1946. Courses in gun repair, advanced gun repair, outdoor sporting goods repair, and small engine repair.

48. **MTA School,** 1801 Oberlin Road, Middletown, Pennsylvania 17057. A division of MTA, Inc. Founded 1968. Combination home study-resident courses in truck driving and diesel mechanics.

49. **MTA School—Connecticut Training Site,** 64 Oakland Avenue, East Hartford, Connecticut 06108. A division of MTA, Inc.

50. MTA School—North Carolina Training Site, 1061 Boulder Road, Greensboro, North Carolina 27410-9990.

51. MTA School—New Jersey Training Site, 1231 Route 22 West, Bridgewater, New Jersey 08807. A divison of MTA, Inc.

52. MTA School—Ohio Training Site, 3440 East Main Street, Columbus, Ohio 43213. A division of MTA, Inc.

53. MTA School—Ohio Training Site, 445 Glade Run Road, S.E., West Jefferson, Ohio 43162. A division of MTA, Inc.

54. MTA School—Pennsylvania Training Site, RD #4, Zeager Road, Elizabethtown, Pennsylvania 17022. A division of MTA, Inc.

55. National Center for Child Care Professionals, 5322 West Bellfort, Suite 103, Houston, Texas 77035. Founded 1980. Combination home study-resident course in Montessori teacher training and day care center faculty training.

56. NRI Schools, 3939 Wisconsin Avenue, N.W., Washington, D.C. 20016. A division of McGraw-Hill Continuing Education Center. Founded 1914. Courses in air conditioning, appliance servicing. TV-audio repair, microcomputers, electronic communications, automotive, building construction, locksmithing, robotics, telephone servicing and small engine repair topics.

57. National Safety Council, Safety Training Institute, 444 North Michigan Avenue, Chicago, Illinois 60611. Founded 1913. Courses in safety supervision and human relations for first line supervisors.

58. National Tax Training School, 8 Albert Drive, Monsey, New York 10952. Founded 1952. Basic and advanced federal income tax preparation courses.

59. National Technical Schools, 4000 South Figueroa Street, Los Angeles, California 90037. Founded 1905. Courses in robotics, microcomputers, digital logic electronics, TV and radio servicing, communications, automotive, air conditioning, refrigeration and home appliance servicing.

60. National Training, Inc., 1543 Kingsley Avenue, P.O. Box 1389, Orange Park, Florida 32073. Founded 1978. Combination home study-resident courses in tractor trailer driving and heavy equipment operation.

61. National Training Systems, Inc., 7140 Virginia Manor Court, P.O. Box 2719, Laurel, Maryland 20708. Founded 1976. Combination home study-resident courses in tractor trailer driving and diesel mechanics.

62. NHAW Home Study Institute, 1661 West Henderson Road, Columbus, Ohio 43220. A division of Northamerican Heating & Airconditioning Wholesalers Association. Founded 1962. Courses in heating, air conditioning, mathematics, and business management for contractors.

63. North American Correspondence Schools, Scranton, Pennsylvania 18515. A division of National Education Corporation. Founded 1959. Courses in animal science, accounting, conservation, drafting, firearms, motorcycle repair, secretarial, and travel.

64. Northwest Schools, 1221 Northwest 21st Avenue, Portland, Oregon 97209. Founded 1946. Home study-resident courses in travel agent/reservation sales agent and heavy equipment operator training.

65. Northwest Schools—Arizona Training Site, 1700 E. Thomas Road, Phoenix, Arizona 85016. A division of Northwest Schools.

66. The Paralegal Institute, 1315 West Indian School Road, Drawer 33903, Phoenix, Arizona 85067. Founded 1974. Course in paralegal assistant training.

67. Police Sciences Institute, Scranton, Pennsylvania 18515. A division of North American Correspondence Schools—National Education Corporation. Founded 1977. Course in police sciences and investigation.

68. Sallwright Academy, Route 1, Columbia City, Indiana 46725. Founded 1978. Course in sailmaking.

69. Seminary Extension Independent Study Institute, 901 Commerce Street, Suite 500, Nashville, Tennessee 37203-3697. Founded 1951. Courses in Bible, Christian doctrine, Christian history, religious education, and pastoral work.

70. Southeastern Academy, Inc., 2333 E. Spacecoast Parkway, Drawer 1768, Kissimmee, Florida 32741. Founded 1974. Combination home study-resident courses in airline/travel career training and hotel/motel front desk training.

71. Southern Career Institute, 1692 N.W. Madrid Way, Boca Raton, Florida 33432. Founded 1976. Course in legal assistant/paralegal assistant training.

72. Stenotype Institute of Jacksonville Beach, Inc., 500 Ninth Avenue North, Jacksonville Beach, Florida 32250. Founded 1940. Courses in court reporting, convention reporting, notereading, and steneotype machine shorthand.

73. Superior Training Services, 3334 Founders Road, P.O. Box 68115, Indianapolis, Indiana 46268. Founded 1974. Combination home study-resident courses in tractor trailer driving and heavy equipment operation. Send inquiries to number 75.

74. Superior Training Services—Heavy Equipment and Truck Driving Site, Camp Atterbury, Edinburgh, Indiana 46124. Send inquiries to number 75.

75. Superior Training Services—Administrative Offices, 1817 North 7th Street, Suite 150, P.O. Box 33157, Phoenix, Arizona 85067. Send inquiries to this address.

76. Superior Training Services—Heavy Equipment Training Site, 600 East Baseline Road, Apache Junction, Arizona 85220. Send inquiries to number 75.

77. Superior Training Services—Truck Driving Training Site, 27th Avenue and Thomas Road, Phoenix, Arizona 85008. Send inquiries to number 75.

78. Superior Training Services—Heavy Equipment and Truck Driving Site, 140 West Agua Mansa Road, P.O. Box 606, Rialto, California 92376. Send inquiries to number 75.

SUBJECTS TAUGHT BY ACCREDITED SCHOOLS

This is a PARTIAL list of subjects offered by accredited home study schools.

In many cases, courses on a given topic are available from more than one school. However, each school presents its courses in its own way. Therefore the content may vary in intent, range, and volume.

Because of this it is important that prospective students write to each of the schools which offer courses in the desired subject field. Each student should obtain from each of the schools complete descriptions of course offerings including course objectives, the quantity of materials to be furnished by the school, and obligations of both the student and the school.

NUMBERS refer to schools listed above in the Directory of Accredited Home Study Courses.

A
Academic Degrees . . . 10, 12, 15, 28, 37, 39, 70, 91
Accident Investigation . . . 29
Accident Prevention . . . 57
Accounting . . . 18, 20, 22, 25, 29, 33, 39, 63
Advertising . . . 17, 29
Advertising Art . . . 7, 29
Agribusiness . . . 25, 29
Agriculture . . . 25, 29
Air Conditioning . . . 29, 33, 38, 46, 56, 59, 62
Aircraft Technology . . . 29
Air Force Career Specialties . . . 24
Airline Ground Personnel Training . . . 1, 63, 64, 65, 70, 81, 89
Animal Hospital Assistant . . . 29, 63
Announcing in Spanish . . . 17
Announcing, Radio & TV . . . 17
Appliance Servicing . . . 29, 46, 56, 59
Architecture . . . 29
Army Career Specialties . . . 6
Arts, Composition & Fundamental . . . 7, 29, 38
Arts, Fine and Commercial . . . 29, 38
Audio-Electronics . . . 15, 29, 32, 33, 38, 39, 46, 56, 59
Automatic Transmissions . . . 29, 38, 46, 56, 59
Automation . . . 15, 29, 46, 56, 59
Auto Mechanics . . . 29, 33, 38, 46, 56, 59, 80
Automotive Air Conditioning . . . 29, 56, 59
Automotive Work . . . 29, 32, 33, 38, 46, 56, 59

B
Banking & Finance . . . 29, 38, 39
Bee Keeping . . . 29
Bible Studies . . . 10, 35, 37, 69
Bicycle Mechanics . . . 29
Blind, Courses for the . . . 30
Blueprint Reading . . . 29, 63
Bookkeeping . . . 3, 18, 20, 22, 29, 33, 35, 63
Braille . . . 30
Broadcast Engineering . . . 15, 17, 46, 56
Broadcast Journalism . . . 17, 29, 90
Broadcasting, Radio & TV . . . 15, 17
Broadcast Time Sales . . . 17
Building Construction . . . 29, 46, 56
Building Maintenance . . . 22, 29
Business Administration . . . 29, 38, 39
Business Writing . . . 3, 29

C
Career Planning . . . 3
Carpentry . . . 29
Cartooning . . . 7, 29, 38
Catering . . . 38
CB Radio Installation & Repair . . . 46, 56
Ceramics . . . 29
Chemistry . . . 3, 29, 35
Chimney Servicing . . . 29
Civil Engineering Technology . . . 29, 39
Clerical . . . 3, 29
Clock Assembly and Repair . . . 29
Club Management . . . 29
Coast Guard Career Specialties . . . 87
College Level Subjects . . . 10, 12, 15, 22, 28, 29, 32, 35, 37, 39, 69
College Preparation . . . 3, 13, 29
Color Analysis . . . 16
Color Cosmetic Application . . . 16
Colored Stones . . . 26
Color Theory . . . 7, 16, 29
Color TV Technology . . . 15, 29, 33, 46, 56, 59
Commercial . . . 29, 38, 63
Commercial Art . . . 29, 38
Communications Technology . . . 15, 22, 29, 32, 46, 56, 59
Computer Programming . . . 4, 29, 31, 32, 33, 38
Computer Repair Technician . . . 15, 29, 32, 38, 46, 56, 59
Computer Technology . . . 28, 29
Conservation . . . 63
Construction . . . 29, 46, 56
Convention Management . . . 22
Convention Reporting . . . 72
Cooking, Gourmet . . . 38
Cosmetology . . . 29

Cost Accounting . . . 22, 29, 39
Court Reporting . . . 72

D
Data Processing . . . 29, 32
Day Care Center Faculty Training . . . 55
Deaf-Blind, Home Teaching, Pre-School Children . . . 30, 41
Deaf, Home Teaching, Pre-School Children . . . 41
Dental Office Assisting . . . 9, 29, 42, 63
Dental Office Receptionist . . . 29, 42, 63
Design in Art . . . 7, 18, 29
Diamonds . . . 19, 26
Diamontology . . . 19
Disaster Control . . . 29
Doll Hospital Operations . . . 44
Drafting . . . 3, 18, 29, 39, 63
Drawing, Freehand . . . 29, 33, 38
Dressmaking . . . 44
Drilling Technology . . . 29

E
Early Childhood Education . . . 21, 29, 55
Economics . . . 29
Education . . . 29, 35
Electricity . . . 29, 32, 33, 38, 46, 56
Electrical Engineering Technology . . . 29, 39
Electronics . . . 15, 28, 29, 32, 33, 38, 39, 46, 56, 59
Elementary School Courses . . . 35
Energy Management . . . 22, 29
Engineering, all types . . . 29, 39
Engineering Design . . . 15, 29, 38, 39
Engines & Engine Tune-Up . . . 29, 33, 38, 46, 56, 59
English . . . 3, 23, 29, 35, 40
English for Spanish-speaking People . . . 33
Estate Planning . . . 36
Esthetics . . . 29
Executive Management . . . 39
Eye Care . . . 30

F
Fashion, Introduction to . . . 7, 29, 38
Fashion Merchandising . . . 29, 38
FCC License Preparation . . . 15, 17, 46, 56
Fences & Fencing . . . 29
Fiberglass & Plastic Repair . . . 29
Fiber Optics Technology . . . 29
Fiction Writing . . . 29, 90
Financial Planning . . . 36
Finance . . . 29, 38, 39
Firearms . . . 29, 47, 63
Fire Protection and Prevention . . . 29
Fish Hatchery Technology . . . 29

CHAPTER FIFTY-FOUR

HOW TO START YOUR OWN PRIVATE SCHOOL

It may seem odd to include a section on how to start your own school in a book about learning at home. But as the Scriptures so aptly remark,

Do you see a man skilled in his work?
He will serve before kings;
he will not serve before obscure men. (Proverbs 22:29)

Some of you who read this book will thrill at the discovery that learning is *fun,* not the dry-as-dust tedium we have been trained to expect. You will scrutinize the reviews with narrowed eyes and underline the products you want to buy. You will cast caution to the winds and splurge. You will gradually buy the best teaching tools and master the best techniques. Your children will begin excelling academically. Before you know it, friends will be begging you to help *their* children!

At that point, you can either direct your friends to this book, or you can seriously consider going into the teaching business yourself.

If you love teaching, and your children love learning, chances are that you've got the beginnings of a private school.

Some other readers will get excited about giving their children a better education than they had ever previously dreamed possible. These readers, who do not consider themselves gifted with the teacherly qualities of patience and imagination, still will have strong ideas about education—ideas that the local public school will not or cannot accommodate. In this case, they will want to found a school of their own, employing others as teachers.

The moral is this: When you've got a winning idea, it's a shame to waste it. If you're developing into a great teacher, or if you at least can recognize great teaching and great educational

products when you see them, you will naturally want to give your ideas a whirl.

I firmly believe that young children belong at home. But as children get older, some parents will need to "apprentice" them to the care of a master teacher. Why not *be* that master teacher—or at least get to select the teacher?

Nobody who takes the time to become familiar with the wonderful educational products now available should have the slightest difficulty in setting up a superb program for the home *or* the classroom. And the second ingredient every school needs—teachers—is staring at you from the mirror. If you don't want to make any money and the students are already knocking at your door, you're all set. Just buy a blackboard and go to it! But if you *do* want to make some money, or if you envision a larger school than you can establish on your own, you need some help.

It just so happens that several fine books have been written to help people who want to start private schools. Here they are!

BOOKS ABOUT HOW TO START A SCHOOL

Green Hill Publishers
How to Start Your Own School. $1.95. Copyright 1973.

How to Start Your Own School by Robert Love is stoutly subtitled "How Parents Can Rescue Their Children from the Perils of Public Education." It's a quick, cheap overview of the process of starting a school and of the questions that have to be dealt with right at the beginning. Written by one of the founding parents of Wichita Collegiate School, the book contains many fascinating anecdotes about the mistakes and successes experienced by some parents who really "did it."

The book costs only $1.95, and gives suggestions on how to handle faculty, equipment, accreditation, finances, and most other nitty-gritty areas, all in a highly readable style.

Oh, since you ask—Wichita Collegiate now has over four hundred students in preschool through twelfth grade, whose College Entrance Exams score on average about 90 points above the national average. Wichita Collegiate's graduates have gone on to such schools as Oxford and Princeton.

R & E Publishers

The ABC's of Starting a Private School. $14.95. Large book. Copyright 1982.

The ABC's of Starting a Private School by Bonnie Schreiter fills in all the gaps. Based on a case study of private K to 6 schools in the Sacramento area, it contains a wealth of resources based on, in the author's words, "what is" instead of the "what should be." This book is loaded with sample forms: a sample contract for the director, sample preadmission health history, sample teacher application form. . . . You get advice on retaining an attorney and student recruitment and acquiring a facility and on and on. See how several other schools have done it.

The style is sterile, but the contents are thorough. As a handbook for prospective school founders, *The ABC's* is an invaluable reference.

R & E Publishers also carries a wide line of books about children, schooling, and learning. Their books cover such diverse topics as math instruction and cookery for the young. You might want to send for their catalog.

Arlington House

How to Start Your Own Private School—And Why You Need One by Samuel Blumenfeld should actually be entitled "Why You Need a Private School—and How to Start One." Most of this large book is devoted to describing what is bad about public education and why the system cannot be changed from the inside. This part is somewhat dated, but still interesting reading.

Follow Mr. Blumenfeld as he becomes a substitute teacher in the public schools to get a look at them from the inside. Experience the nefarious episode of the Desks Not Nailed Down and the Diligent Litterbugs. See Mr. Blumenfeld try to find out which of his students were "on the nods" and which were just faking it. You'll gain an appreciation for firsthand research, plus a whole different view of education, as Mr. Blumenfeld's belief in discipline and mental exertion confronts the sour suds of progressive education.

After his service as a sub, Mr. Blumenfeld made a personal tour of some of the new private schools started in the South right after the Supreme Court ordered integration. His discoveries about why and how these schools were started are sometimes surprising. He also looked into the old private schools and some new types of private schools, particularly the "proprietary" school which is run for profit by the founder or founders.

The book has appendices on Independent School and Accrediting Associations, Organizations of Interest to Independent Schools, Teacher Placement Agencies, Insurance Agencies Serving Independent Schools, Recommended Books, Books on the Reading Problem, and Recommended Periodicals. Some of the addresses may be out-of-date, but the lists are comprehensive and a helpful starting-place for those looking for this information.

Now, I know it is not reasonable to expect you to read three books and then leap out into the marketplace with a successful private school. You say you'd like a little more help? Here are three sources that can help Christians who are trying to establish small private schools.

Alpha Omega Publications Satellite Program

The Leadership Kit, which introduces your group to the Satellite Program and explains how the Coordinator Training Program works, is only $5. The complete training program is made up of two parts, Kit A and Kit B. Coordinator Training Kit A is $50. After your coordinator completes Kit A to his and AOP's satisfaction, he may send for Kit B, which is $350.

AOP offers to help you set up your own Homeschool Satellite Program, operating as a ministry of your church or school or as a tutorial program under a qualified teacher. I've seen the materials, and recommend AOP's approach wholeheartedly. AOP's training enables a qualified individual to oversee the Satellite Program in a professional manner. Parent Kits, assistance to coordinators from AOP's staff via a toll-free number, access to AOP training sessions, and a 20 percent discount on AOP materials are also available through the Satellite Program. *You may enroll in the Satellite training program even if you do not plan to use AOP materials,* although you would be wise to at least start with them.

AOP also sells films, videos, cassettes, books, and other materials designed to help your church see its responsibility for Christian education and to help parents discover their responsibility for the moral training of their children.

Alpha Omega is also in the business of setting up regular Christian day schools, and will be more than happy to assist you with your plans. AOP offers regular training sessions for Chritian school administrators, including a special session for those who want to start a school. Contact them for details.

Christian Liberty Academy
Starter Kit, $70.

Christian Liberty Academy's *Starter Kit for Christian Schools* will tell you everything you need to know about how to start a traditional Christian school, a satellite or umbrella school ministry to home schoolers, or an independent home school. At least that's what the folks at the Academy say, and they've never misled me before!

Your packet includes sample school forms, school handbooks, certificates, diplomas, financial and legal information, addresses of recommended publishers, information about publishers, including catalogs, sources, and advice on purchasing K-12 curricula. In addition, the packet contains advice on developing a school schedule, discipline, record-keeping, counseling, and "helpful suggestions for administrators." Anyone can buy the pack, including non-Christians who will probably find most of the info meets many of their needs.

Thoburn Press
How to Establish and Operate a Successful Christian School, $125 plus 10 percent shipping.

I know nothing at all about Robert Thoburn's package on *How to Establish and Operate a Successful Christian School,* since I found out about it only as this book was in the final editing stages. I do know, however, that Mr. Thoburn has actually done what he is writing about. Fairfax Christian School in Fairfax, Virginia, is one of the most outstanding examples of a Christian school that made it in the face of numerous obstacles. None of Thoburn Press's other books or products are overpriced, so this package is presumably worth it. Call or write Thoburn Press to find out more.

BASIC CATALOGS FOR STARTING A PRIVATE SCHOOL

Finally, you will need to order books, equipment, and supplies. You can, of course, just read through this book and pick out what you want. In order to make life easier, though, I have added this list of "must" catalogs. These companies, between them, carry all the items you will need to get started. They were chosen for their good selection and reasonable prices.

Art—send for the NASCO Art catalog.

Language lab—International Linguistics and Regents Publishing Company.

Math lab—NASCO Math catalog.

Music—Ability Development or Shar for teachers' books, Suzuki method, instruments and cassettes. Rhythm Band for classroom instruments and more music instruction materials. Kimbo Educational for children's recordings.

Physical education—Hoover Brothers has indoor gym equipment. For outdoor gyms or phys ed courses, see the Phys Ed chapter.

School Supplies—ABC School Supply and Lakeshore will do the job. So will your local school supply store, if you prefer to deal locally. Many schools try to deal with a local store or a mail-order supplier in their geographical region, to save on shipping costs. If you're starting a Christian school, Christian Light Education and Alpha Omega Publications both can supply you with classroom forms and record sheets.

Science equipment—NASCO Science catalog.

Textbooks—Choose the ones you want out of the selection in the Textbooks section. Personally, I would like to see more private schools that use few or no textbooks. A good encyclopedia, library books, and school supply kits and games should be enough for an excellent educational program. An exception is the area of math, where a good textbook can make teaching much easier.

Why don't you try using phonics records for phonics, storytelling and source documents for history, globes and atlases for geography, science kits for science, outdoor walks and zoo trips for nature study, and Bible reading for Bible? Let the teacher *teach,* instead of testing and giving busywork all the time! Children should spend a lot of time reading and a good amount of time writing, and you might consider devoting a large part of your school day to these activities. As for required homework, I am adamantly against it. If a school does its job, children shouldn't need to spend sixty hours a week on school and homework. Neither should parents be drafted to do the drillwork that they are paying teachers to do.

Samuel Blumenfeld has come out strongly in favor of the "proprietary" school, one that charges a fair market price and makes a profit for its owner. While not settling the issue of profit verses nonprofit schools, I have had plenty of exposure to schools that offer reduced tuition and then guilt-trip the parents into making donations and spending hours on school fund-raising. If you want to irritate your customers and unfairly burden the generous while subsidizing the rest, this is the way to go.

To my mind, the whole your-tuition-was-subsidized-so-you-owe-us routine lacks dignity. What I'd do is charge the market price and give wealthy individuals the option of providing scholarships for indigent pupils *of their selection,* instead of spreading donations across the board to all students. Our welfare system may throw its money at anyone who "needs" it, regardless of how responsible or irresponsible that individual has shown himself, but private schools have no good reason to emulate Uncle Sam.

Starting a private school is not really that hard. Just get in touch with the people above who can help you; read a few books; get a good lawyer and accountant; send for a few catalogs; print up some brochures; hold a meeting; and see what happens!

FOOTNOTES

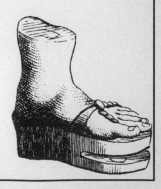

Chapter 2

[1]"The Department of Education estimates that there are 24 million functional illiterates in the United States, *virtually all of whom have had from eight to twelve years of compulsory public schooling.* Contrast this with the figures for illiteracy in 1910 issued by the U.S. Bureau of Education and quoted in the January 30, 1915 issue of James McKeen Cattell's own weekly publication, *School and Society:*

> Statistics compiled by the Bureau of Education for use at the Panama-Pacific Exposition, show that of children from 10 to 14 years of age there were in 1910 only 22 out of every 1,000 who could neither read nor write. . . . The following states report only 1 child in 1,000 between the ages of 10 and 14 as illiterate: Connecticut, District of Columbia, Massachusetts, Minnesota, Montana, New Hampshire, North Dakota, Oregon, Utah, and Washington.

"So apparently they knew how to teach children to read in 1910. Also, there was no such thing as 'functional illiteracy,' that is, a kind of low, inadequate reading ability which is the product of faulty teaching methodscin our schools. The illiteracy of 1910 was the result of some children having no schooling. Functional illiteracy is the result of the way we actually teach children to read in our schools. . . ." Samuel Blumenfeld, *NEA: Trojan Horse in American Education* (Phoenix: Paradigm Company, 1984), pp. 102, 103.

[2]John Holt tells about his friend Bill Hull's experience with the attribute blocks he invented:

> They found a very interesting thing about the way children reacted to these materials. If, when a child came in for the first time, they tried to get him "to work" right away, to play some of their games and solve some of their puzzles, they got nowhere. . . . But if at first they let the child alone for a while, let him play with the materials in his own way, they got very different results. . . . When, through such play and fantasy, the children had taken those materials into their minds, mentally swallowed and digested them, so to speak, they were then ready and willing to play very complicated games, that in the more organized and businesslike situation had left other children completely baffled. This proved to be so consistently true that the experimenters made it a rule always to let children have a period of completely free play with the materials, before asking them to do directed work with them. John Holt, *How Children Learn,* rev. ed. (New York: Dell Publishing Company, 1983), pp. 218, 219.

Holt goes on for five more pages, citing his own experience and also quoting in detail an article called "Messing About in Science," which appeared in the February 1965 issue of *Science and Children,* and also in the June 1966 quarterly report of Educational Services, Inc. The author, Dr. David Hawkins, also had observed the phenomenon of children needing a play, or "messing about," period in order to become comfortable with new concepts.

Chapter 3

[1]The following comments on modalities are loosely adapted and enlarged from a xeroxed set of sheets I received in the mail. The source was not given, so I can't credit it properly, but the person who sent them believes they were part of a handout for a college course.

Chapter 4

[1]From an Associated Press story of July 1985, quoted in *Growing Without Schooling,* Issue 46, p. 5.

[2]Ishmael has received national TV attention and has been written up in several magazines, including *Growing Without Schooling.* For the full story of this home schooling miracle, see his mother Nancy Wallace's book *Better Than School* (Burdett, N.Y.: Larson Publications, 1983), reviewed in Chapter 5.

[3]*The Boston Globe.* August 20, 1983, front page. The Harvard admissions officer who interviewed young Colfax told the Associated Press, "The young man struck me as someone who really enjoyed the learning process. It was refreshing to see." In case you're wondering, Grant Colfax ended up picking Harvard. Grant's *adopted* brothers (one is Eskimo) are now showing the same academic excellence.

[4]See Samuel Blumenfeld, *Is Public Education Necessary?* (Old Greenwich, Conn.: Devin-Adair, 1981) for faultless documentation of the charge that public education was *never* necessary, including details of how children received fine educations before public education was established.

Blumenfeld's new book, *NEA: Trojan Horse in American Education,* also has a condensed section on life in the USA before public education. Worthwhile reading.

[5]This, and the following Montessori quotes, are culled from a very excellent summation of the Montessori method by Lee Havis, published in *The Montessori Observer,* May 1985. The quotes are directly from Montessori's work. I have given the sources in the same form that they were listed in the article.

Although I have read several works by Montessori, Lee Havis did such a fine job that I can't improve on it, which is why I didn't put the extra effort into foraging for my own quotes.

The first Montessori quote was from Maria Montessori, *The Child,* pp. 23, 24.

[6]Montessori, *Spontaneous Activity in Education,* p. 131.

[7]Montessori, *Discovery of the Child,* p. 153.

[8]*How Children Learn,* p. 21.

[9]Bulletin from Hewitt Research Foundation, January 1, 1984.

[10]Dorothy L. Sayers, "The Lost Tools of Learning?," *A Matter of Eternity* (Grand Rapids, Mich.: William B. Eerdmans Publishing Company, 1973).

Chapter 5

[1]Sayers, "Lost Tools of Learning," *A Matter of Eternity.*

Chapter 16

[1]Note these figures from the Chicago school system, reported by a children's advocacy group called Design for Change:

> Of the 39,500 students who entered Chicago public high schools in the fall of 1980, only 18,500 were graduated in 1984. Of those who did graduate, only 6,000 had 12th grade reading ability while 5,000 others had only 8th grade reading skills or less.

So *less than one-sixth* of those high-school students left school with reading ability that, by today's watered-down standards, would be *normal* to expect at their age!

The reason for this abysmal performance? "The proven best method of teaching reading—PHONICS IN THE FIRST GRADE—is not used in 85% of U.S. public schools."

Above statistics from *The Phyllis Schlafly Report,* September 1985, p. 1.

[2]"Statistics compiled by the Bureau of Education for use at the Panama-Pacific Exposition, show that of children from 10 to 14 years of age there were in 1910 only 22 out of every 1,000 who could neither read nor write. . . . The following states [in 1910] report only 1 child in 1,000 between the ages of 10 and 14 as illiterate: Connecticut, District of Columbia, Massachusetts, Minnesota, Montana, New Hampshire, North Dakota, Oregon, Utah, and Washington."

Blumenfeld, *NEA: Trojan Horse,* p. 102.

[3]"In his March 1985 address to the Reading Reform Foundation meeting in Washington, Mike Brunner expressed the view that, 'The reasons vary, but the most compelling explanation is provided by those who argue that it is the financial vested interest of those associated with the reading establishment, excluding teachers, who prohibit reform. *Too many people are profiting from illiteracy*—over $3 billion a year just in ECIA Chapter I funds alone.'

"This point is made by Mary Johnson in her 1971 book, *Programmed Illiteracy in Our Schools:*

> I . . . multiplied the annual cost of the basal series workbooks by the primary grades' enrollment and found that the annual expenditure of the workbooks was more than four times greater than that on hard-cover readers. (The workbooks have to be replaced each year because the children write in them.)
>
> Thus workbooks in a sight method basal series soon become superfluous whenever phonics is taught by a direct method. This is why articulated phonics is a serious threat to any publishing company which has invested heavily in the project of a basal series. The size of this investment is much greater than most people would imagine.

"Brunner declares, 'It is certainly clear that more money is to be made from illiteracy than from literacy. . . . The economics of phonics instruction provides a different picture.

" 'For example, in Benjamin Franklin Elementary School, Mesa, Ariz., $23.42 per student was spent on reading materials in 1978. In the same year teachers were trained in phonics. By 1981 student expenditures for reading materials had dropped to $8.50, and in that year the weighted mean achievement scores had surpassed the national, state, and district norms in language skills as well.' "

Allan C. Brownfeld, "Why Are Our Schools Producing Illiterates?" *Human Events.* August 17, 1985, p. 14.

[4]Brownfeld, p. 13.

Chapter 22
[1]Bryan Griffin, *Panic Among the Philistines* (Chicago: Regnery Gateway, 1983), p. 44.

[2]*Ibid.,* p. 69.

Chapter 33
[1]*Mother Earth News,* #87, May/June 1984, "The Marvelous Mountain Gorillas," p. 67, 68.

[2]*Rand McNally Family World Atlas* (Chicago: Rand McNally & Co., 1984), "World Political Information Table," p. 93.

[3]World population as of January 1, 1984 is estimated to be 4,733,000,000. World population density is only 82 per square mile. Each square mile contains 640 acres. An acre is the area a horse can plow in one day. Right now the world contains approximately eight land acres, including inland water, for every man, woman, and child. Each family of four, in other words, would have thirty-two acres of its own if we all spread out evenly across the face of the earth. Since in fact most people have always preferred to live in cities, vast portions of the earth's surface are practically unpeopled even now. See, for instance, Iowa. Or Nebraska. Or Montana. Or Wyoming. Or South Dakota. Etc.

Wealthy and sophisticated people voluntarily live in cities whose population density is several times the density we would obtain if the whole planet moved to Texas. The Principality of Monaco, for example, lately presided over by Princess Grace, has a population density of 46,667 per square mile, *three times as great* as the one we would achieve if the whole world moved to Texas!

Figures obtained from the *Rand McNally Family World Atlas,* quoted above.

Chapter 34
[1]*The Apocalyptics: How Environmental Politics Controls What We Know About Cancer* (New York: Simon and Schuster, 1984), pp. 9, 10.

Chapter 36
[1]Neil Postman, *The Disappearance of Childhood* (New York: Delacorte Press, 1982), p. 134; cited by John W. Whitehead, *The Stealing of America* (Westchester, Ill.: Crossway Books, 1983), p. 68.

[2]*Ibid.,* cited in *Stealing of America,* footnote, p. 137.

[3]*Ibid.,* cited in *Stealing of America,* p. 68.

Chapter 42
[1]Bruce McIntyre, *Drawing Textbook: The Teaching and Utilization of Drawing for Educational Purposes* (Santa Ana, Calif.: Audio-Visual Drawing Program, 1985), pp. 7-9.

Chapter 43
[1]Laszlo Eosze, *Zoltan Kodaly: His Life and Work* (Boston: Crescendo Publishing Company, 1962), p. 79.

[2]*Ibid.,* p. 73.

[3]*Ibid.,* p. 78.

[4]*Ibid.*

Chapter 45
[1]"Phonics—The Key to Reading," *The Phyllis Schlafly Report.* September 1985, p. 2.

Chapter 46
[1]"By early 1975, more than 30 states, under pressure from the federal government (which has threatened to make funds for the handicapped contingent on screening), had passed laws

requiring local school districts to conduct such tests. In most they cover not only the familiar categories ('learning disabled,' MBD, 'emotionally handicapped,' 'visually handicapped') but also include scales rating children for 'impulse control,' 'intellectuality,' 'withdrawal' and 'social behavior.' The specific applications and consequences of these texts vary from state to state, but the objectives are similar. *There is money for special education,* for the handicapped and for other categories of disability (real or imagined): *the more clients a system can create for such programs, the more special funds it can claim* from state and federal agencies. . . . No one knows how many children have been assigned to special classes as a result of those screens or how many have been properly placed. What is certain is that since the end of the sixties, the number of special education programs, including LD classes, has mushroomed, that available funds have tripled, and that, given the vagueness of the proliferating categories and the lack of effective techniques for remediation, there is no conceivable way that most of the screen can lead to proper placements. In Washington, court-ordered testing of 'special' track children revealed that *two-thirds had been mislabeled and misplaced and should have been in regular classes.* Similar results have been reported in Philadelphia, San Francisco and other cities." (Emphasis mine)

Peter Schrag and Diane Divoky, *The Myth of the Hyperactive Child And Other Means of Child Control* (New York: Pantheon Books/Random House, 1975), pp. 116, 117. Also see the entire chapter, "Screening for Deviance and Other Diseases," which proves that the supposedly objective screening tests are, in fact, unscientific.

To give school districts extra money for every child who they manage to label is an outrageous conflict of interest that should be stopped at once.

[2]The NEA is constantly fighting to abolish *objective* tests from the schools. If they succeed, children who *want* to demonstrate what they know will be deprived of a chance to show it.

[3]Excerpts from "Standards for Educational and Psychological Tests," American Psychological Association, 1974, cited in CTB/ McGraw-Hill 1985 catalog, p. 205.

Chapter 50
[1]Question included in a Marriage and Family Living Course: "In my opinion, sex is? (a) love itself (b) a way of expressing feelings of love (c) an enduring personal commitment (d) a casual pleasure with no strings attached (e) a prelude to marriage." As the mother noted who had objected to this and questions like it, "A child who believes sex is just for marriage would have to write in the answer himself."

Phyllis Schlafly, ed., *Child Abuse in the Classroom* (Westchester, Ill.: Crossway Books, 1984), p. 116.

[2]"On Labor Day, September 7, 1981, our 22-year-old son, Joe, committed suicide. He had used marijuana since junior high. . . . He went into deep depression and took his own life by carbon monoxide poisoning. He left a note saying, 'I did it because I couldn't think or nothing.' . . .

"Two weeks after his death, when we were going through his belongings, I found some English papers he had written four years earlier when he was a senior.

"In all of them, he had written about using pot, and the

teacher had corrected them with written comments in the margins. . . . At the time I wondered why the teacher hadn't called us to let us know of his great obsession with marijuana. A year later, when I found out that Values Clarification was used in his unit in the 8th grade physical education class, I knew then why she hadn't called us. The course objective stated: 'We will attempt to teach the different categories of drugs, their effect and, hopefully, how to make a knowledgeable choice using your own individual value system.' "

Testimony of Flora Rettig from Center Line, Michigan, *Child Abuse in the Classroom,* pp. 140, 141.

[3]William Bowen, *Globalism: America's Demise* (Maryland: Huntington House, Inc., 1984), passim.

[4]Michael Levin, a professor of philosophy at City College of New York, writes,

One of the most extensive thought-control campaigns in American education history has gone completely ignored. I am referring to the transformation, in the name of "sex fairness," of textbooks and curricula at all educational levels, with the aim of convincing children that boys and girls are the same.

. . .

Thus, Macmillan advocates acceptance of the deviant; "It is unrealistic and unfair to imply that all one-parent homes are 'broken' homes"—but demands falsification of the norm: "[W]e are more interested in emphasizing what we can be, rather than the negatives that still exist. . . ." South-Western is as explicit as these euphemistic documents ever get: "Emphasis is on what can be and should be rather than mirroring what the society is." . . . "Textbooks which avoid male and female stereotyping will more accurately represent reality." The question of whether there might be some *truth* to these so-called "stereotypes" is simply dismissed. . . . All that is offered is dogma—"Women and girls should be shown as having the same abilities, interests, and ambitions as men" (McGraw-Hill).

"Feminism and Thought Control," *Commentary,* June 1982, pp. 40-44. Cited in *Book Burning* by Cal Thomas (Westchester, Ill.: Crossway, 1983), pp. 63, 64.

Is this dishonest or what? And what is all this propaganda for? To track little girls into enslaving corporate-industrial employment, as well as training them to despise their grandmothers and homeworking mothers.

[5]*Typical Course of Study,* an outline of school curriculum prepared directly from the courses actually used in public schools across the nation, lists jobs and careers as one of the areas of study in grades K-4 and 7-9 in the social studies curriculum. "Careers in science" becomes a part of the science curriculum in grade 9 and continues through grade 12. "Role of women in today's society" is a theme in social studies for grades 10 to 12. Naturally, this role is interpreted to mean careerism. Public education, with its attending bureaucracy, is eulogized in grade 11. Union bureaucracies, international bureaucracies, and our own governmental bureaucracy are explicitly praised in grade 12. William H. Nault, *Typical Course of Study* (New York: World Book, Inc., 1984), passim.

[6]Another textbook murder:

We had an English course in the 7th grade junior high school whose title was Death Education. In the manual, 73 out of 80 stories had to do with death, dying, killing, murder, suicide, and what you want written on your tombstone. One of the girls, a 9th grader, blew her brains out after having written a note on her front door that said what she wanted on her tombstone.

Testimony of Jayne Schindler from Denver, Colorado, in *Child Abuse in the Classroom*, p. 282.

The testimonies contain too many incidents of suicide caused by school courses to list here. The above is just one example of dozens.

"A government-funded study of textbooks concludes that many are biased against religion . . .

"Paul Vitz, a New York University psychology professor, reviewed dozens of books commonly found in America's public schools under a $73,445 contract from the National Institute of Education, part of the U.S. Department of Education.

" 'Public school textbooks present a very biased representation of both religion and of many traditional values,' wrote Vitz . . .

"Among 40 social studies textbooks for grades 1-4, *'not one . . . had one word of text that referred to any religious activity representative of contemporary American life,'* the report said. [Ellipses in the original newspaper article.]

"There were some uncaptioned pictures, such as a scene showing a priest talking to children or a Jewish family lighting Sabbath candles, but *the text did not mention 'any present day American who prayed or participated in worship,'* the study said." (Emphasis mine).

"Survey finds textbooks short on religion, long on liberals," *San Diego Tribune,* October 2, 1985, page A-24. An Associated Press article out of Washington.

[7]Just one example of dozens that show how public schools are used to deliberately teach antireligion. A teacher is speaking:

The student counselors this time came and they announced they would like to have a 45-minute rap session with the class students. . . .

They began this session by presenting a large chart, about a two and one-half by three foot rectangular chart, that had various pictures and writings on it. It was obvious that it was a Values Clarification chart. The different things on the chart were to be given to the children, valued by their size.

In other words, the larger the things on the chart, the more important it was. The smaller, the less important it was. . . . The two smallest things on the chart were two circles. . . . One was a circle with a little red dot in it, and the other was a circle with a Jewish six-pointed star. . . .

They lavishly complimented the kids who brought this to

their attention and said, "You are very perceptive and have done a good job of discerning; what does that tell you?" They said, "They are real small."

The counselors commented, "That is good. What does it mean?" The children said, "Does that mean it is not very important?"

Of course that is what the counselors were shooting at. And they said, "Yes, this is true. Christianity once served our country in a positive way, but now students today should seek other forms of religion to study and learn from."

Then the counselor suggested yoga and meditation, and some of the Eastern Mystic religions. *Child Abuse in the Classroom,* pp. 213, 214.

So much for pluralism and religious neutrality. This is a pretty blatant example, but the very same sort of *attitudes* those NEA-trained counselors were bringing into that public school classroom are fostered in public-school texts. One common vehicle for breaking down children's religious values is the great deference paid to primitive religions. Reading courses include long excerpts from tribal mythology. Social studies courses ask, "How can we learn something from the religion of the [name your tribe or country]?" Bit by bit, children are battered with the idea that all religions are essentially alike (*not* true: Christians and Jews don't feed the rats and let their children starve) and that the sophisticated thing to do is become either a pantheist or an atheist.

[8]"My first example was an exercise used in a high school Health class in which the teacher taught the normalcy of hating your parents. At the beginning of the unit, she asked, "How many of you hate your parents?," and about thee students indicated that they did. At the end of her very effective presentation, she asked the question again, and all but three students then raised their hands."

Testimony of Ann McClellan from Tuscon, Arizona, in *Child Abuse in the Classroom,* p. 244.

The so-called Child Abuse Prevention curricula are even more dangerous than this. Children are taught to suspect their own parents of incestuous intentions, and led to understand that anytime they want, they can get their parents in *real* trouble by lying about them. At the same time, these children will become the first generation of Americans to have incest constantly on their minds. Anyone but an idiot can see that this kind of training will *cause* incest, as boys start eyeing their sisters and, eventually, daughters as potential sexual objects. You and I never thought such thoughts when *we* were growing up; our children won't be allowed *not* to think these thoughts, if the NEA and social work bureaucracies have their way.

[9]Cited in Blumenfeld, *NEA: Trojan Horse,* p. 209.

INDEX OF SUPPLIERS

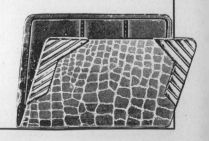

This index was designed both to give you the necessary information to order products and catalogs, and to give you an idea of each company's services. Besides addresses, the index contains telephone numbers, types of payment accepted, price of catalog or brochure (if any), refund policy, a general description of the company, and a listing of the areas under which the supplier's products are reviewed.

The subject listings are abbreviated as follows:

Key to Subject Abbreviations

Key	Chapter or Section
Ad/Voc	Adult/Vocational
Art	Art
Bible	Bible
Book	Basic Books for Home-Schoolers
Cat	Catalogs and Paraphernalia
Char	Character Education
Comp	Computers
Curric	Curriculum Buyers' Guide
Ec	Economics
Geog	Geography
Govt	Government
Gramm	Grammar
Hand	Handwriting
Health	Health
Hist	History
Lang	Foreign Languages
Legal	Legal Helps
Lit	Literature
Mag	Magazines and Journals
Math	Mathematics
Music	Music
Nat	Nature Study
P/L	Parent and Leadership Training
Phys	Physical Education
Pre	Preschool
Priv	How to Start Your Own Private School
Read	Reading
Sch	School Supplies
Sci	Science
Spec	Special Education
Speech	Speaking Skills
Spell	Spelling
Soc	Society and Culture
Supp	Supplemental and Enrichment
T & G	Toys and Games
Test	Testing
Text	Textbooks
Write	Writing and Composition

HOW TO BE A PERFECT CUSTOMER

First, please *do not call a toll-free number except to order*, unless the index entry specifically says that the supplier is willing to use his toll-free line for inquiries. Each call on an 800 number costs the supplier a substantial amount, and it is frustrating to have callers rack up your phone bill for questions that could have been answered just as well by letter. Also, companies that reserve their toll-free numbers for orders usually will not give out information to callers who use that number. This is sound business practice and should not cause any hard feelings.

It is always wise to first get the supplier's catalog or brochure before ordering, unless you absolutely *must* have the product immediately. Prices change, and so do refund policies, and you are less likely to be disappointed if you carefully check these out before ordering.

When requesting information by letter, an SASE (self-addressed stamped envelope) is always appreciated. This does not apply to requests for free catalogs, because these seldom fit in a standard envelope.

Companies that offer free catalogs do so in the hope that we will become interested enough in their products to buy from them. It is very expensive to print and mail catalogs. By all means, send for any catalogs you think you might find useful. But let's respect those who send us free literature and give them a fair chance to sell us something. We want to encourage suppliers to continue to be willing to sell to individuals, not just to institutions, and we can best do this by not abusing our requests for free services.

A Beka Book Publications
Box 18000
Pensacola, FL 32523-9160
(904) 478-8933
Check or M.O. Free order form.
Christian texts and supplies.
Hand, Health, Hist, Lit, Math, Read, Text, Write.

A Beka Christian Correspondence School
Box 18000
Pensacola, FL 32523-9160
(904) 478-8480 X 311 8-4:30 M-Fri CST/CDT
No refunds.
Home school program.
Curr.

A Beka Video School
Pensacola Christian College
Box 18000
Pensacola, FL 32523-9160
(904) 478-8480 ext. 311 8-4:30 M-Fri
Home school video program.
Curr.

A+
P.O. Box 2965
Boulder, CO 80322
(303) 447-9330
$24.97 one year (reg. price), $12 additional Can./foreign
$19.97 one year (new subscr), $6 additional Can./foreign
VISA, MC, AMEX, Bill.
Comp.

ABC School Supply
P.O. Box 4750
Norcross, GA 30091
(404) 447-5000 weekdays.
MC, VISA. Free catalog.
Returns within 30 days. $15 service charge if company not at fault.
School supplies pre-K-6.
Art, Pre, Priv, Sch.

Abilities Research Associates
Anaheim Foundation School
2650 W. Trojan Pl.
Anaheim, CA 92804
(714) 995-6059
Cathy Levesque, Director
Home school program.
Curr.

Ability Development
Box 4260
Athens, OH 45701-4260
1-800-221-9254 OH: (614) 594-3547
VISA, MC. COD. Free catalog.
"The Suzuki Place."
Music, Priv.

Achievement Basics
800 South Fenton Street
Denver, CO 80226
(303) 935-6343
Check or M.O. Free brochures.
Junior Business and speaking.
Ec, Speech.

Activity Resources
Box 4875
Hayward, CA 94540
(415) 782-1300
Check or M.O. Free catalog.
Math books and manipulatives.
Math.

Addison-Wesley Publishing Co.
2725 Sand Hill Road
Menlo Park, CA 94025
1-800-447-2244 CA: (415) 854-0300
MC, Visa. Free catalogs.
Full service text supplier.
Ec, Hist, Lang, Math, Text.

Adler's Foreign Books, Inc.
28 W. 25th St.
New York, NY 10010
(212) 691-5151
Check or M.O. Free catalogs.
Foreign language books.
Lang.

Advance Memory Research, Inc. (AMR)
4825-C 140th Avenue North
Clearwater, FL 33520
1-800-323-2500 FL: (813) 539-6555
MC, VISA, Am Ex, D Club, C Blanche.
Free brochure. Call toll-free for info.
Foreign language and speaking courses.
Lang, Speech.

Advanced Training Institute of America
Box 1
Oak Brook, IL 60521
Home school program.
Char, Curr.

Aletheia Publishers
P.O. Box 1437
Tempe, AZ 85281
Check or M.O. Free brochure.
Child training book.
P/L.

Alpha Omega Publications
P.O. Box 3153
Tempe, AZ 85281
1-800-821-4443. Ask for Home-School Customer Service consultant.
Free brochure. No returns allowed.
Christian curriculum. Home school program.
Art, Bible, Gramm, Lang, Math, Phys, Priv, Text, Write, Curr.

America's Future
514 Main Street
New Rochelle, NY 10801
Textbook reviews.
Text.

American Bible Society
1865 Broadway
New York, NY 10023
(212) 581-7400 24hrs., 7 days.
1-800-543-8000 Op. 312. Credit Card orders only.
$20 minimum.
Handling charge on credit card orders $1.95.
Visa, MC.
Foreign language Bibles.
Lang.

American Christian Academy
P.O. Box 1776
Colleyville, TX 76034
(214) 434-1776
Annual, semiannual, or quarterly payments.
Check, MC, VISA.
Good refund policy.
Home schooling program.
Curr.

American Christian History Institute
1093 Beechwood Street
Camarillo, CA 93010
(805) 987-1887
Principle Approach materials.
P/L.

American College Testing Program (ACT)
2201 N. Dodge St.
P.O. Box 168
Iowa City, IA 52243
(319) 337-1429
Check or M.O.
Tests and college entrance books.
Adult, Test.

American Guidance Service
Publishers' Building
Circle Pines, MN 55014
1-800-328-2560 MN: (612) 786-4343 collect
Returns for one year of resaleable items with
permission.
Visa, MC. Free catalog.
School courses.
Comp, Hand, Math, Read, Test.

American Map Corporation
46-35 54th Rd.
Maspeth, NY 11378
(718) 784-0055 9-5 EST weekdays.
Visa, MC, AmX. Free catalogs.
30-day money back on language materials
only.
Maps. Language courses. Anatomy manual.
Health, Lang, Geog.

American Museum of Natural History
Central Park West
New York, NY 10024
Natural history, magazine.
Nature.

American Reformation Movement (ARM)
Independence Square, Suite 106, Box 138
7341 Clairmont Mesa Blvd.
San Diego, CA 92111
(619) 298-8607
On Teaching newsletter
Char, Mag.

American School
850 East Fifty-Eighth St.
Chicago, IL 60637
(312) 947-3300
Payment plan.
High school correspondence program.
Curr.

American Vision
P.O. Box 720515
Atlanta, GA 30328
(404) 256-3978
Check or M.O. or COD.
Free brochure and subscription to quarterly
magazine.
Biblical world view.
Govt.

Ampersand Press
691 26th St.
Oakland, CA 94612
(415) 832-6669
Check or M.O. Free brochure.
Science games.
Nat, Sci, T & G.

AMSCO School Publications
315 Hudson St.
New York, NY 10013
(212) 675-7005
School books.
Lang, Lit, Text, Write.

Animal Town Game Company
P.O. Box 2002
Santa Barbara, CA 93120
(805) 962-8368 for info.
Check or M.O. Free catalog.
Returns accepted.
Creative family entertainment.
Music, T & G.

Arlington House Publishers
333 Port Road West
Westport, CT 06881
Grow or Die! Other useful books.
Nat.

Art Extension Press
Box 389
Westport, CT 06881
(203) 531-7400
Visa, MC. Free brochure.
Art history and appreciation.
Art.

Ascension Designs
6108 N. Western
Oklahoma City, OK 73118
(405) 848-5773
Software.
Bible.

Ashley's Home Tutor Kits
P.O. Box 958
Beaverton, OR 97005
Check or M.O. Free brochure.
Tutor kits.
Math, Read.

Associated Christian Schools
Home School Division
P.O. Box 27115
Indianapolis, IN 46227
(317) 782-3695
Free brochure.
Full service Christian worktext supplier.
Text.

Audio Forum
On-The-Green
Guilford, CT 06437
1-800-243-1234 CT, AK, HI: (203) 453-9794
Visa, MC, AmX, DC, CB. Free catalogs.
Returns within three weeks, full refund.
Spoken-word cassettes.
Lang, Speech.

Audio Visual Drawing Program
1014 N. Wright St.
Santa Ana, CA 92701
Drawing text.
Art.

Backyard Scientists
P.O. Box 16966
Irvine, CA 92713
(714) 551-2392
Check or M.O. Brochure w/SASE.
Book of science experiments.
Sci.

Baker Book House
P.O. Box 6287
Grand Rapids, MI 49506
(616) 957-3110 Ask for bargain department.
Visa, MC. Free newsprint catalog.
Christian book publisher.
Bible.

Virginia Birt Baker
P.O. Box 1237
Quitman, TX 75783
Check or M.O.
Book on home teaching.
Book.

Barnes & Noble Bookstores, Inc.
126 Fifth Ave.
New York, NY 10011
1-800-228-3535 NY: 1-800-642-9606
Visa, MC, AmX, DC. Free catalog.
Min order $15. 30-day money back.
Discount mail-order books.
Cat.

Basic Education
P.O. Box 610589
D./F.W. Airport, TX 75261-0589
(214) 462-1909
Full-service Christian worktext supplier.
Home school program.
Curr, Text.

BCM Publications
237 Fairfield Ave.
Upper Darby, PA 19082
(416) 549-9810
798 Main St. E.
Hamilton, Ontario, CANADA L8M 1L4
Check or M.O. Free catalogs.
Bible courses and visuals.
Bible.

Beacon Enterprises, Inc.
609 River St.
Santa Cruz, CA 95060
(408) 427-1766
Check or M.O. Free brochures.
Returns: permission, resaleable. 10 percent handling.
Self-pronouncing alphabet.
Bible, Pre, Read.

Berlitz
866 Third Ave.
New York, NY 10022
1-800-223-1814 NY: (212) 702-2000
Great Britain: 0323-638221
Foreign language courses and accessories.
Lang.

Bible Games, Inc.
4500 Airwest, S.E.
Grand Rapids, MI 49508
(800) 437-4337 weekdays.
Visa, MC. Free brochure.
Info on toll-free line.
Bible games and dolls.
Bible, Char, T & G.

Bible Lovers Correspondence School
P.O. Box 1448
Camrose, Alberta, CANADA T4V 1X4
Check or M.O. Free brochure.
Bible correspondence courses (Church of God).
Bible.

Bible Visuals
Box 4842
Lancaster, PA 17604
(717) 569-7800
Check or M.O. Free catalog.
Visualized Bible lessons.
Bible.

Birch Tree Group Ltd.
Divisions: Suzuki™ Method International
Summy Birchard Music
Box 2072
Princeton, NJ 08540
Educational music publishers, including the Suzuki Method, Frances Clark Piano Method.
Sold at music dealers.
Music.

Basil Blackwell, Inc.
432 Park Avenue South, Suite 1505
New York, NY 10016
Also: Basil Blackwell Publisher Limited
108 Cowley Road, Oxford 0X4 1J5
ENGLAND
Publisher.
Nat.

Dick Blick: 5 mail-order addresses.
Send order to the one closest to you.
Dick Blick West
P.O. Box 521
Henderson, NV 89015

Central: P.O. Box 1267
Galesburg, IL 61401

East: P.O. Box 26
Allentown, PA 18105

Georgia: 1117 Alpharetta St.
Roswell, GA 30075

Connecticut: P.O. Box 330
Farmington, CT 06032
1-800-447-8192 IL: 1-800-322-8183
MC, Visa, AmEx, COD. Catalog $2.
Art and craft supplies.
Art.

Bob Jones University Press
Customer Services
Greenville, SC 29614
1-800-845-5731 weekdays.
MC, Visa, COD. Free catalog.
Info on toll-free line.
Returns: resaleable, permission, 60 days.
Christian texts and school supplies.
Bible, Math, Sci, Text.

Bowmar/Noble Publishers
(see Economy Company)

Brainstorms
7851 E. Lake Rd.
Erie, PA 16511
454-6869 or 899-1833, Erie area customers only.
Check or M.O. Free brochure.
Returns: 10 days.
Distributor of open-ended home school materials.
Cat.

Broderbund Software
17 Paul Dr.
San Rafael, CA 94903-2101
(415) 479-1170
Software. *Bank Street Writer.*
Comp, Write.

Brook Farm Books
Glassville, New Brunswick
CANADA E0J 1L0
Catalog of home school supplies.
Cat.

Buck Hill Associates
129 Garnet Lake Rd.
Johnsburg, NY 12843
Check or M.O. Catalog $1.
Repros of historical documents.
Hist, Lit.

Builder Books and Home-Grown Kids
705 Rita St.
Redondo Beach, CA 90277
(213) 316-2483. Free brochure.
Check or M.O.
Fine assortment of home school materials.
Christian emphasis.
Cat.

Caedmon Tapes
1995 Broadway
New York, NY 10023
1-800-223-0420 NY: (212) 580-3400
Visa, MC. Free 94-pp. catalog.
Spoken-word recordings.
Hist, Lang, Lit, Speech.

California Test Bureau (CTB)
McGraw-Hill
Del Monte Research Park
Monterey, CA 93940
Testing materials.
Current offerings not suitable for home use.
Test.

Calvert School
Tuscany Road
Baltimore, MD 21210
(301) 243-6030
Free brochure with detailed outline of subjects and topics.
Home school program.
Curr.

Capper's Books
616 Jefferson
Topeka, KS 66607
(913) 295-1107
Visa, MC. Free brochure.
Authentic pioneer, old-timey stories.
Hist, Lit.

Carolina Biological Supply
2705 York Rd.
Burlington, NC 27215
Visa, MC, AmX. Huge color catalog $10.95.
Science teaching supplies and equipment.
Health, Nat.

Carollie Company
P.O. Box 99053
Tacoma, WA 98499
Check or M.O. Free brochure.
Preschool activity paks.
Pre.

Century Gospel Film Library
P.O. Box 101
Louderton, PA 18964
1-800-523-6748 PA: 1-800-492-2030
Christian films.
Bible.

Chart Your Course
P.O. Box 6448
Mobile, AL 36660-0448
(800) 824-7888 Op 50
HI, AK (800) 824-7919 Op 50. 24 hours.
MC, Visa. $2.50 sample copy.
Mag by/for talented kids.
Supp.

Chasselle, Inc.
9645 Gerwig Lane
Columbia, MD 21046
Free catalog.
School supplies.
Art, Sch.

Child Evangelism Fellowship Press
Box 348
Warrenton, MO 63383
(314) 456-4321
MC, Visa. Free catalog.
Multimedia evangelism and teaching.
Bible.

Childcraft Education Corp.
20 Kilmer Rd.
Edison, NJ 08818
1-800-631-5657 NJ: 1-800-624-0840
9-6 EST M-Fri. Visa, MC, AmX.
Free color catalog.
Returns w/permission, 30 days unused.
Educational furniture, toys, and games.
Phys, T & G.

Child Life Play Specialties
55 Whitney St.
Holliston, MA 01746
1-800-462-4445 MA: 1-429-4639
Visa, MC. Free catalog.
Replace transit-damaged parts.
Wood outdoor gyms (swing sets, etc.)
Phys, T & G.

Children's Bible Hour
Box 1
Grand Rapids, MI 49501
Christian tapes, mags for kids.
Char.

Christian Book Distributors
Box 3687
Peabody, MA 01961-3687
(617) 535-6400
Visa, MC. Membership, $3/yr.
No returns except for shipping mistakes.
Discount Christian and liberal books.
Bible.

Christian Character Concepts
508 S. Spring Ave.
Tyler, TX 75701
(214) 597-6408
Check or M.O. Free brochure.
Character curriculum. Spanish.
Char, Lang.

Christian Computer Users Association
1145 Alexander S.E.
Grand Rapids, MI 49507
(616) 241-0368
Newsletter for the industry. Other resources
available. $15.00/yr.
Bible.

Christian Curriculum
Fleming H. Revell Company
Old Tappan, NJ 07675
Sunday School materials, most not suited to
home study. Revell is a Christian book
publisher.
Char.

Christian Curriculum Project
2006 Flat Creek
Richardson, TX 75080
Check or M.O. Free brochure.
Innovative subject curricula.
Math, Music.

Christian Education Music Publishers
2285 West 185th Place
Lansing, IL 60438
(312) 895-3322
Check or M.O. Free catalog.
Refunds only for defective materials.
Music reading course.
Music.

Christian Family Educational Services
P.O. Box 47159
Phoenix, AZ 85068
(602) 272-8449
Info clearinghouse, consultations, AZ only.
P/L.

Christian Heritage Studies
5346 Cherry Ridge
Camarillo, CA 93010
(805) 484-5745
Seminars on American Christian history.
P/L.

Christian Home Schools
8731 N.E. Everett St.
Portland, OR 97220
(503) 253-9633
Check or M.O.
Home school books and magazine.
Mag.

Christian Homesteading Movement
RD #2
Oxford, NY 13830
Check or M.O. Free brochure.
Home education workshops and
minicourses.
P/L.

Christian Liberty Academy
502 W. Euclid Ave.
Arlington Heights, IL 60004
(312) 259-8736
Full-service Christian correspondence
program.
Legal manual, directory of attorneys and
organizations.
Curr, Legal, Priv.

Christian Life Workshops, Inc.
180 S.E. Kane Rd.
Gresham, OR 97030
(503) 667-3942
Check only. Brochure with SASE.
100 percent refund, except shipping and
handling.
Home school workshops on tape. Books.
Organizer. Seminars.
Cat, P/L.

Christian Light Education
1066 Chicago Ave.
P.O. Box 1126
Harrisonburg, VA 22801-1126
(703) 434-0750
Home school program and supplies.
Mennonite.
Curr, Priv.

Christian Light Publications
 (see Christian Light Education)
Check or M.O. Free catalog.
Sci equipment for AOP, school supplies,
Mennonite-approved books.
Lit, Sch, Sci.

Christian Schools International
3350 E. Paris Ave., S.E.
Grand Rapids, MI 49508
(616) 957-1070
Check or M.O. Free catalog.
60-day examination privilege for approved
accounts.
Textbooks for Christian schools.
Spell, Text, Write.

Classical Calliope
(see Cobblestone Publishing)
Kid's classical studies mag.
Lit.

CMG Productions, Inc.
Christian Mother Goose series.
Distributed by Fleming Revell,
Old Tappan, NJ 07675
Char.

Cobblestone Publishing
20 Grove St.
Peterborough, NH 03458
(603) 924-7209
Visa, MC. $10 minimum.
Children's magazines.
Hist, Lit, Soc.

The College Board
888 Seventh Ave.
New York, NY 10106
(212) 582-6210
Check or M.O. Free catalog.
Returns: Saleable, in print, 1 year.
College tests and prep.
Test.

Collier/Macmillan
866 Third Ave.
New York, NY 10022
(212) 935-2111
Publisher. *Italic Way.*
Hand.

Community Playthings
Route 213
Rifton, NY 12471
(914) 658-3141
Check or M.O. Free catalog.
Returns, 10 percent handling charge.
Play furniture and equipment.
Phys.

Computer Literacy Bookshop
520 Lawrence Expressway
Sunnyvale, CA 94086
(408) 730-9957 9:30-8 PST M-Fr, 10-6 PST
Sat-Sun.
Visa, MC., AMEX.
Computer books.
Comp.

Computer Software Store
2549 Cleveland
Granite City, IL 62040
1-800-851-8791 IL: (618) 876-2155
Visa, MC, COD.
Free catalogs Apple, IBM, Commodore
(specify which computer).
Discount software.
Comp.

Conservative Book Club
15 Oakland Ave.
Harrison, NY 10528
Check or M.O. Monthly reviews to members.
Discount book club.
Cat, Ec, Govt, Text.

Constructive Playthings
1227 E. 199th St.
Grandview, MO 64030
1-800-255-6124 MO: (816) 761-5900
Visa, MC. Free home catalog.
Play furniture, toys, and school supplies pre-
K-3. Free toy guide for parents. Free catalog
of Jewish educational materials.
Char, Phys, Sch, T & G.

Contemporary Books
180 N. Michigan Ave.
Chicago, IL 60601
(312) 782-9181
Publisher. GED Prep book.
Health, Test.

Continental Press
Elizabethtown, PA 17022
1-800-233-0759 PA: (717) 367-1836 collect.
Visa, MC. Free catalogs.
Workbooks, all subjects. Software.
Text.

Conversa-phone Institute, Inc.
One Lomac Loop
Ronkonkoma, NY 11779
(516) 467-0600
Check or M.O. Sells through distributors.
Recorded courses, self-help.
Lang, Speech.

Cornerstone Ministry
3248 Cahaba Heights Rd.
P.O. Box 43189
Birmingham, AL 35243
1-800-633-4369 AL: 1-800-633-3918
Birmingham: 967-6076
Christian films and filmstrips.
Bible.

Corvallis Open School Extended Program
960 S.W. Jefferson Ave.
Corvallis, OR 97333
The school has no phone. Call the director,
Kathleen Bottero, at home
(503) 753-6094, evenings.
Checks only.
Prorated refunds.
Alternative home school program.
Curr.

Creation's Child
1150 NW Alder Creek Dr.
Corvallis, OR 97330
(503) 745-7658
Check or M.O. Free brochure.
Home school supplies.
Cat, Hist, Read.

**Creation Life Publications—Master Book
Division**
P.O. Box 1606
El Cajon, CA 92022
(619) 448-1121
Check, M.O., COD.
Creation Science Resources. Books, video.
Sci.

Creation-Science Research Center
P.O. Box 23195
San Diego, CA 92123
(714) 569-8673
Check or M.O. Free brochure.
Science and creationism supplies.
Sci.

Creative Christian Education Service
Box K
Angwin, CA 94508
(707) 965-3004 or 3414
Mrs. Joyce George, Administrator
Registration fee of 25 percent not
refundable.
No refunds after processing.
Home school program.
Curr.

Creative Learning Service, Inc.
102 Grenoble Place
Hopatcong, NJ 07843
(201) 398-6060
Visa, MC. $20 minimum
Returns: 30 days.
Books and learning aids for preschool.
Pre.

Creative Publications
1101 San Antonio Road, Suite 101
Mountain View, CA 94043
Visa, MC. Catalog $2.00
Math, Supp.

Crestwood House, Inc.
Box 3427
Highway 66 South
Mankato, MN 56002-3427
(507) 388-1616 collect.
Visa, MC. Free catalog.
Books for reluctant readers.
Lit, Sci.

CRICKET
Box 300
Peru, IL 61354
1-800-435-6850 IL: 1-800-892-6831
Check or M.O. or they'll bill you.
Magazine for children.
Lit.

Crossway Books
9825 W. Roosevelt Rd.
Westchester, IL 60153
(312) 345-7474
Publisher.
Book, Lit, Nat, Text.

CTB/McGraw-Hill
(See California Test Bureau)

Cuisenaire Company of America
12 Church Street, Box D
New Rochelle, NY 10805
(914) 235-0900
Check or M.O. Free catalog.
Math manipulatives.
Math.

Curriculum Development Centre
229 College St.
Toronto, Ontario
CANADA M5T 1R4
Home school curricula.
Curr.

Curriculum Resources
Box 923
Fairfield, CT 06430
1-800-243-2874 CT: 576-0714
Visa/Bank Am, MC. Catalog, 50¢.
Craft kits and supplies.
Art.

*Cursive Italic News, the Barchowsky Report
on Handwriting*
P.O. Box 92
Aberdeen, MD 21001
Check or M.O.
Magazine about handwriting.
Hand.

Daybreak Software
1951 Grand Ave.
Baldwin, NY 11510
1-800-645-3739 NY, AK, HI: (516) 223-4666
Visa, MC. Free color brochure.
Educational software.
Comp, Geog, Math.

Derek Prince Ministries
P.O. Box 300
Fort Lauderdale, FL 33480
(305) 763-5202
Charismatic, premil. Bible teaching.
Bible.

Developmental Learning Materials (DLM)
Teaching Resources
One DLM Park
Allen, TX 75002
1-800-527-4747 TX: 1-800-442-4711
8-5 Central Time weekdays.
Minimum order $15.
School programs and texts.
Comp, Geog, Hand, Speech,
Test, Text, T & G.

DIDAX, Inc.
6 Doulton Place
Peabody, MA 01960
(617) 535-4757/4758
Check or M.O. Free catalog.
Art, Lit, Math, Read, Sci.

Kathryn Diehl
554 N. McDonel St.
Lima, OH 45801
Johnny Still Can't Read
Check or M.O.
Book.

Discovery Christian Schools
5547 Alabama Dr.
Concord, CA 94521
(415) 672-5670
Patrick D. Clifford, Superintendent
Home school program.
Curr.

Discovery Toys
P.O. Box 232008
Pleasant Hill, CA 94523
(415) 827-4663 for referral info only.
Home distributors, party plan.
Toys with "educational play value."
T & G.

Distar
Science Research Associates, Inc.
155 N. Wacker Dr.
Chicago, Il 60606
Public school courses with "direct
instruction" method.
Math, Read, Spell.

Dr. Drew's Toys, Inc.
P.O. Box 1003, Dept. H
Boston, MA 02205
Check or M.O. Free flier.
Thin rectangular wooden blocks.
T & G.

Doubleday & Company
Garden City, NY 11530
Major book publisher.
Comp, various other categories.

Dover Publications
31 East 2nd St.
Mineola, NY 11501
No phone orders.
Check or M.O. Free catalogs.
Return in 10 days for full refund.
Reprint bookseller. Good selection.
Art, Cat, Supp.

Eagle Forum Education Fund
Alton, IL 62002
(618) 462-5415
Check or M.O.
Free brochure lists items, prices only.
Phonics kits.
Read.

Eagle Systems International
5600 N. University
P.O. Box 508
Provo, UT 84603-0508
(801) 225-9000
Check, M.O., or they bill you.
Subscriptions: P.O. Box 902
Farmingdale, NY 11737-9802
Happy Times kid character mag.
Free sample copy.
Char.

Eastern Mennonite Publications
Route 2, Box 532
Ephrata, PA 17522
(717) 733-8913
Check or M.O. Free info with SASE.
Beginning reading program.
Read.

Easy Education
P.O. Box 4082
Malibu, CA 90265
(213) 457-5334
Check or M.O. Free brochure.
Basic educational products.
Pre.

Easy Reading Kit
P.O. Box 8724
Stockton, CA 95208-0724
No phone orders. Check or M.O.
Nobody's ever wanted a refund.
Beginning reading kit.
Read.

Economy Company and Bowmar/Noble Pub's
1901 N. Walnut
P.O. Box 25308
Oklahoma City, OK 73125
1-800-654-8608
Check or M.O. Free catalog.
Returns up to a year.
Full-service public school textbook company.
Supp, Text.

Edmund Scientific Company
101 East Gloucester Pike
Barrington, NJ 08007
1-800-222-0224 NJ: (609) 547-3488
Visa, MC, AmX, DC. Free catalog.
Science supplies and widgets.
Sci.

Educational Book Distributors
P.O. Box 551
San Mateo, CA 94401
(415) 344-8458
Distributor of small educational publishers.
Pre, Soc, Supp.

Educational Design, Inc.
47 W. 13th St.
New York, NY 10011
1-800-221-9372 NY: (212) 255-7900
Returns: 30 days.
"Skilbooks," various subjects. Mini-Labs.
Ec, Sci, Test, Text.

Educational Insights
19560 Rancho Way
Dominguez Hills, CA 90220
(213) 637-2131, (213) 979-1955, or 1-800-367-5713
Visa, MC. Free color catalog.
School supplies.
Geog, Health, Lit, Math, Nat, Pre, Read, Sch, Sci, Supp.

Educators Publishing Service
75 Moulton St.
Cambridge, MA 02238-9101
(617) 547-6706
No phone orders.
Check or M.O. Free home school brochure.
Language arts and parent helps.
Gramm, Read, Spec, Spell.

EduSoft
P.O. Box 2560
Berkeley, CA 94702
1-800-EDUSOFT CA, AK, HI: (415) 548-4304
Visa, MC. Free catalog.
Educational software.
Comp, Math, Music.

ESP Inc.
1201 E. Johnson
P.O. Drawer 5037
Jonesboro, AR 72403-5037
1-800-643-0280 AR: (501) 935-3533
Visa. Free catalog.
Full refund if not satisfied.
School workbooks, minicourses.
Comp, Lang, Music, Supp.

Evangelizing Today's Child
Warrenton, MO 63383
(314) 456-4321
Visa, MC.
Christian teaching magazine.
Char.

Everett/Edwards Cassette Curriculum
P.O. Box 1060
Deland, FL 32720
(904) 734-7458
Visa, MC. Free newspaper catalog.
Critics on cassette.
Lit.

Every Day Is Special
1602 Naco Place
Hacienda Heights, CA 91745
Check or M.O.
Activity calendar. Unique!
Cat.

FACE
(see Foundation for American Christian Education)

FACES magazine
(see Cobblestone Publishing)
Anthropology for kids.
Soc.

Families That Play Together
P.O. Box B-1
Sarcoxie, MO 64862
(417) 548-7672
Check or M.O. Free catalog.
Creative activities.
T & G.

Family-Centered Learning Alternatives
H.C.R. 63, Box 713
Naselle, WA 98638
(206) 484-3252
Home school magazine and resources.
Mag.

Family-Centered Learning Alternatives
H.C.R. 63, Box 713
Naselle, WA 98638
(206) 484-3252
Debra Stewart, Administrator
Contact your Center for fee structure and refund policy.
Home school program.
Curr.

Family Life Institute
P.O. Box 234
Norland, WA 98358-0234
Check or M.O. Club plan.
Bible story cassettes.
Bible.

Family Pastimes Games
R.R. 4
Perth, Ont., CANADA K7H 3C6
(613) 267-4819
Check or M.O. Newsprint catalog 25¢
Board and action games.
T & G.

Family Restoration International
180 S.E. Kane Ave
Gresham, OR 97030
(503) 667-3942
Check only. Brochure with SASE.
100 percent refund, except shipping and handling.
Home school workshops on tape. Books.
Organizer.
Cat, P/L.

Fellowship of Christian Magicians
P.O. Box 385
Connerville, IN 47331
Check or M.O. No phone orders.
Christian Conjurer magazine, conferences
Membership organization.
Char.

Fellowship of Christian Puppeteers
P.O. Box 708
Ignacio, CO 81137
Check or M.O. No phone orders.
Membership organization.
Char.

Fleming H. Revell Co.
184 Central Ave.
Old Tappan, NJ 07675
Check or M.O. 6 percent p & h.
Christian publisher.
Char.

Food for Thot
132 Carter
Sulphur Springs, TX 75482
Check or M.O.
Books and *Loaves and Fishes* magazine.
Book, Lit.

Foundation for American Christian Education (FACE)
Box 27035
San Francisco, CA 94127
Check or M.O. or they'll bill you.
Principle Approach to America's Christian history.
Govt, Hist, Lit, P/L, Speech.

Foundation for Economic Education
Irvington-on-Hudson, NY 10533
(914) 591-7230
Check or M.O. Some free material.
Free enterprise literature.
Ec.

Free Ed Guide
502 Woodside Ave.
Narberth, PA 19072
No phone orders.
Check or P.O.
Quarterly guide to freebies.
Cat.

Mel and Norma Gabler
P.O. Box 7518
Longview, TX 75607
(214) 753-5993
Check or M.O. Donation for materials.
Textbook analysts.
Text.

GCT Publishing Co.
P.O. Box 6448
Mobile, AL 36660-0448
1-800-824-7888 HI, AK: 1-800-824-7919
Ask for Operator 50, 24 hours.
Visa, MC. No free samples. Free catalog.
Gift/talent magazines and resources.
Supp.

Gazelle Publications
318 N. Lincoln Ave.
Liberal, KS 67901
100 percent satisfaction guaranteed.
Home school books.
Book, Cat.

General Services Administration
National Archives and Records Service
National Audiovisual Center
Washington, DC 20409
1-800-638-1300
Visa, MC. Free catalogs.
Foreign language courses.
Lang.

Ginn and Company
P.O. Box 573
Lexington, MA 02173
1-800-848-9500
Returns: 6 months, permission.
Schoolbook supplier.
Hand, Text.

Global Visuals
Box 281-B
Wadsworth, OH 44281
(216) 336-5450
Visualized Bible lessons.
Bible.

God's World Publications
P.O. Box 2330
Asheville, NC 28802
(704) 253-8063
Check only. Satisfaction guaranteed.
Kids' Christian newspapers.
Char, Soc.

Good Things Company
Drawer N
Norman, OK 73070-70130
(405) 329-7797

P.O. Box 4313
Englewood, CO 80155-4313
(303) 796-8990
Check or M.O. Free brochure.
"Adam and Eve Family Tree."
Bible.

Gospel Films
P.O. Box 455
Muskegon, MI 49443
1-800-253-0413
Christian films.
Hist.

Gospel Mission
Box M
Choteau, MT 59422
(406) 466-2311
Visa, MC. Free catalog.
No returns for properly filled orders.
Wholesale Christian book outlet.
30 percent off retail.
Char.

Grassdale Publishers
1002 Lincoln Green
Norman, OK 73069
Order from Thompson Depository.
Free brochure with SASE.
Math and algebra texts.
Math.

Green Hill and Jameson Books
722 Columbus St.
Ottawa, IL 61350
(813) 434-7905
Check or M.O. Free catalog.
Publisher.
Govt, Nat, Priv.

Grolier Enterprises
Sherman Turnpike
Danbury, CT 06810
Club plan.
Beginner Books for kids.
Lit.

Growing Child
P.O. Box 620
Lafayette, IN 47902-1100
(317) 423-2624
Visa, MC, AmX. Catalog $1.
100 pecent satisfaction guaranteed.
Developmental toys, kid's books and records.
T & G.

Growing Without Schooling
729 Boylston St.
Boston, MA 02116
(617) 437-1550
Check or M.O.
Sample issue, $2.50. Subscription $15.00.
Home school magazine.
Art, Mag.

Guidance Associates of Delaware, Inc.
(See Jastak Associates)
Test provider.
Test.

Hammond, Inc.
515 Valley St.
Maplewood, NJ 07040
1-800-526-4953 NJ: (201) 763-6000
Check or M.O. Returns with permission.
Geography and other school supplies.
Geog, Lang.

Happy Times magazine
(See Eagle Systems International)
Character magazine for kids.
Char.

Harcourt Brace Jovanovich
6277 Sea Harbor Drive
Orlando, FL 32821
(305) 345-3800
Check or M.O. Free catalogs (K-8, 9-12).
Public school texts.
Gramm, Text.

Harper & Row, Publishers
10 East 53rd St.
New York, NY 10022
Large publisher. Sells through stores.
Ec, Nat, Write.

Burt Harrison & Company
P.O. Box 732
Weston, MA 02193-0732
(617) 647-0674
Check or M.O. Catalog $2 refund with first order.
Math and science manipulatives.
Math, Sci.

Harvest House Publishers
1075 Arrowsmith
Eugene, OR 97402-9197
1-800-547-8979 OR: (503) 343-0123
Christian publisher.
Char.

Hearth Song
2211 Blucher Valley Rd.
Sebastopol, CA 95472
(707) 829-0900
Visa, MC. Free catalog.
"A catalog for families."
Art, Cat, T & G.

Heathkit
Heath Company
Hilltop Road
St. Joseph, MI 49085
1-800-253-0570 MI, AK: (616) 982-3411
Visa, MC, C.O.D. Charge acct.
Electronics courses, items, kits.
Sci.

Herald Press
Scottdale, PA 15683
   or
Kitchener, Ont., Canada N2G 4M5
Mennonite publisher.
Health.

Heritage Education and Review Organization (HERO)
P.O. Box 202
Jarrettsville, MD 21084
Check or M.O. Free brochure.
Materials on globalism, humanism, New Age, etc.
Govt, P/L, Text.

Heritage Foundation
214 Mass Ave., N.E.
Washington, DC 20002
(202) 546-4400
Visa, MC, AmX, $15 minimum.
Materials examining public policies.
Govt.

Hewitt Research Foundation (or Home Grown Kids)
P.O. Box 9
Washougal, WA 98671
Check or M.O. Free catalog.
Innovative home school materials.
Book, Cat, Gramm, Lit, Math, Sci.

Hewitt-Moore Child Development Center
P.O. Box 9
Washougal, WA 98671-0009
(206) 835-8708
Check only. 10 percent of tuition nonrefundable.
Exchange or refund, resaleable books, 2 weeks.
Home school program.
Curr.

Holt Associates
729 Boylston St.
Boston, MA 02116
(617) 437-1550
Check or M.O. Catalog w/SASE.
Books of interest to home schoolers.
Music and art supplies.
Cat, Music, Supp.

Holt, Rinehart, and Winston
383 Madison Avenue
New York, NY 10017
Public school textbooks.
Text.

Home Education Magazine
P.O. Box 218
Tonasket, WA 98855
(509) 486-2449
Check or M.O.
Home schoolers' magazine.
Mag.

Home Grown Kids
   (see Hewitt Research)

Home Life
P.O. Box 16202
Clayton, MO 63105
Check or M.O.
Refunds: 30 days.
Christian action books.
Bible.

Home School Headquarters
P.O. Box 366
Fremont, NE 68025
Resource guide for home schoolers.
P/L, Spec.

Home School Journal
P.O. Box 1245
Columbus, NE 68601
Scrappy home school magazine.
Mag.

Home School Legal Defense Association
P.O. Box 2091
Washington, DC 20013
(202) 737-0030
Check or M.O. Free brochure.
Home school legal insurance.
Legal.

Home Study International
6940 Carroll Ave.
Takoma Park, MD 20912
(202) 722-6570 general info.
(202) 722-6579 enrollment info.
M-Th 8:30-12, 1-5:30
Check or M.O.
Monthly payment plans, grade 7-12 only.
Good refund policy.
Home school program.
Curr.

Homespun Tapes, Ltd.
Box 694
Woodstock, NY 12498
(914) 679-7832
Visa, MC, COD (USA only).
Catalog $1; free with order.
Musicianship tapes.
Music.

Hoover Brothers Educational Equipment and Supplies
1511 Baltimore
P.O. Box 1009
Kansas City, MO 64141
(816) 221-7663
MC, COD. Free catalog.
School supplies.
Art, Priv, Sch.

Houghton Mifflin
Two Park St.
Boston, MA 02107
(617) 725-5000
Publisher.
Art.

Hubbard Company
P.O. Box 104
Northbrook, IL 60062
1-800-323-8368 IL: (312) 272-7810
Visa, MC, AmX. Free catalogs.
Raised relief maps. Science supplies.
Geog, Health, Nat, Sci.

ICER Press Bookstore
P.O. Box 877
Claremont, CA 91711
School At Home book.
Book.

Ideal School Supply Company
11000 S. Lavergne Ave.
Oak Lawn, IL 60453
(312) 425-0800
Order from school suppliers.
Health, Govt, Sch.

The Implanted Word
P.O. Box 3247
Tulsa, OK 74101
Check or M.O. Brochure with SASE.
Scripture memory, birth to 8.
Bible.

Independent School Press
51 River St.
Wellesley Hills, MA 02181
(617) 237-2591
Check or M.O.
Return: 9 months, permission.
Supplementary public school texts.
Gramm, Lang, Text.

Institute for Christian Economics
P.O. Box 8000
Tyler, TX 75711
Reconstructionist economics books.
Ec.

Institute for Creation Research
10946 Woodside Ave. N.
Santee, CA 92071
(619) 448-0900
Check or M.O. Free brochure.
Science books, videos, and filmstrips.
Sci.

Instructor and Teacher
P.O. Box 6099
Duluth, MN 55806-9799
(218) 723-9200
Check or M.O.
Teacher's magazine. Activity resources
catalog.
Cat, Mag.

The Instrument Workshop
8023 Forest Dr. N.E.
Seattle, WA 98115
(206) 523-6129 6-7 AM, 7-9 PM Pacific Time
Visa, MC. Free list of catalogs.
Old-time keyboard instrument kits, plans,
tools.
Music.

International Institute
P.O. Box 99
Park Ridge, IL 60068
(312) 823-7416
Full refund on undesired books.
Home school program.
Curr.

International Linguistics
401 W. 89th St.
Kansas City, MO 64114
(816) 941-9797
Returns: 30 days.
Foreign language courses.
Lang, Priv.

International Montessori Society
912 Thayer Ave.
Silver Spring, MD 20910
(301) 589-1127
Check or M.O. Free brochure.
Montessori books, course, and newsletter.
P/L, Music, Pre.

International Reading Association
800 Barksdale Rd.
P.O. Box 8139
Newark, DE 19714-8139
(302) 731-1600
Visa, MC. $10 minimum.
Establishment reading organization.
Read.

Interpersonal Communications Services, Inc.
7052 West Lane
Eden, NY 14057
(716) 649-3493
Check or M.O.
Liberal parent/child resources.
P/L.

InterVarsity Press
5206 Main Street
Downers Grove, IL 60515
Check or M.O.
Christian publisher.
Publishes *Escape From Reason,* mentioned
in Ch. 2.

Into the Wind
2047 Broadway
Boulder, CO 80302
(303) 449-5356 M-Sat 10-6, for credit card
orders only.
Visa, MC, AmX.
100 percent refund or exchange. You return
prepaid and insured.
Kites and accessories.
T & G.

Janzen Specialties
1381 S.E. Godsey Rd.
Dallas, OR 97338
(503) 623-4144
Check or M.O. or bill you.
Flannel backgrounds for Bible stories.
Bible.

Jastak Associates, Inc.
1526 Gilpin Ave.
Wilmington, DE 19806
1-800-221-WRAT
Check or M.O. Free catalog.
WRAT tests.
Test.

Jerryco, Inc.
601 Linden Place
Evanston, IL 60202
(312) 475-8440
Visa (Bank Am), MC. Cat $1.
$10 minimum.
Refund on saleable stuff, doesn't include
S & H.
Surplus stuff described with wit.
Sci.

Jewish Museum Shop
1109 Fifth Ave.
New York, NY 10028
(212) 860-1895
Visa, MC, AmX. $20 minimum.
Returns: 30 days, you pay postage.
Jewish supplies.
Char.

The Jibber-Jabber
Laura Duncan, editor
R.D. #2, Box 413
Halifax, PA 17032
Donation. Cash or checks O.K. Make checks
out to Laura Duncan.
Kid's mag entirely by/for young kids.
Write.

Johnny STILL Can't Read book
  see Kathryn Diehl

Just for Kids
Winterbrook Way
Meredith, NH 03253
Toys and games. Expensive.
T & G.

Kathy Kolbe Concept
P.O. Box 15050
Phoenix, AZ 85060
(602) 840-9770
Visa, MC. $20 minimum. Distributors.
Resources for the gifted.
Supp.

Kentuckiana Music Supply
138 E. Wellington Ave.
Louisville, KY
Music.

Kerr Publishing Co.
P.O. Box 1053
La Habra, CA 90633-1053
(212) 691-7676
Cashier's check or M.O.
Free brochure.
"Sound-Links" reading program.
Read.

Key Curriculum Project
P.O. Box 2304
Berkeley, CA 94702
1-800-338-7638 CA, AK, HI: (415) 548-2304
Visa, MC. Free catalog.
"Key to" math workbooks.
Math.

Kimbo Educational
P.O. Box 477
Long Branch, NJ 07740
1-800-631-2187 NJ: (201) 229-4949
Visa, MC. Free color catalog.
Records, cassettes, filmstrips, especially early
childhood and movement.
Music, Phys, Pre, Priv.

KONOS
P.O. Box 1534
Richardson, TX 75083
(214) 699-3555
Check or M.O.
Home school seminars. Character program.
Curr.

Konos Curriculum
P.O. Box 1534
Richardson, TX 75083
(214) 669-8337 or 238-1552
Check or M.O. Free brochure.
Christian character curriculum. Time line.
Char, Hist.

Laidlaw Brothers
Thatcher and Madison
River Forest, IL 60305
(312) 366-5320
C.O.D. Free catalog.
Returns: 10 months, permission.
Public school textbooks.
Text.

Laissez Faire Books
Institute for Humane Studies
Box 1149
Menlo Park, CA 94025
Libertarian bookseller.
Ec, Govt.

David S. Lake Publishers
A Division of Pitman Learning
19 Davis Drive
Belmont, CA 94002
(415) 592-7810
Visa, MC. Free catalog.
Sells through bookstores.
Art, Pre.

Lakeshore Curriculum Material Center
P.O. Box 6261
Carson, CA 90749
1-800-421-5334 CA: 1-800-262-1777
Info: (213) 537-8600
Visa, MC, AmX. Free catalog.
Returns: 30 days, unused goods.
School supplies pre-K-3, special ed.
Art, Pre, Priv, Sch.

Larson Publications
4936 Route 414
Burdett, NY 14818
(607) 546-9342
Check or M.O.
Better Than School,
The Complete Home Educator.
Book, Comp.

Latebloomers Educational Consulting Svc.
P.O. Box 2647
Berkeley, CA 94702
(415) 849-1430
Check or M.O. Free materials list.
Help for parents with kids labelled learning
disabled.
Spec.

Lauri, Inc.
P.O. Box F-2
Phillips-Avon, ME 04966
Crepe rubber products.
Geog, Pre.

Learning at Home
P.O. Box 270
Honaunau, HI 96726
(808) 328-9669
Check or M.O. Free brochure.
K-12 books and workbooks.
Curriculum and teaching guides.
Cat, Curr, Test.

The Learning Company
545 Middlefield Rd., Suite 170
Menlo Park, CA 94025
1-800-852-2255 CA: 1-800-852-7256
or (415) 328-5410
Refunds: 30-day money-back or exchange for
another TLC program.
Innovative educational software.
Comp.

The Learning Connection
635 Barbara Dr.
Grants Pass, OR 97526
(503) 476-5686
Jane M. Joyce, Director.
Home school program.
Curr.

Learning Every Day
Rt. 1, Box 5
Fairfield, WA 99012
(509) 291-3024
Returns: 30 days
Check or M.O.
Small home school catalog.
Cat.

Learning Systems Corporation
60 Connolly Parkway
Hamden, CT 06514
(203) 288-8807
Visa, MC. Catalog, 50¢.
All sales are final.
Miniworkbooks, Skillforms.
Comp, Math, Read, Supp.

Learning Technologies
4225 LBJ Freeway, Suite 131
Dallas, TX 75244
1-800-238-4277 TX: (214) 991-4958
$19.95 Educational Software
Refunds: one year.
Comp.

Hank Lee's Magic Catalog
24 Lincoln St.
Boston, MA 02111
(617) 482-8749 24 hours, 7 days.
Visa, MC, AmX. Catalog $5, or $8.95 with
binder.
Professional magic apparatus, wholesale/
retail.
T & G.

Leonardo Press
Box 403
Yorktown Heights, NY 10598
(914) 962-7856 or 962-5890
Check or M.O. Free catalog.
Spelling and math programs. School-tested.
Math, Spell.

Life for Little Learners
P.O. Box 701616
Tulsa, OK 74170
Check or M.O. Free brochure.
Variety of home school materials.
Bible, Comp, Read, Supp.

Lifeway Christian School Curriculum
Scripture Press Publishers
1825 College Ave.
Wheaton, IL 60187
1-800-323-9409 IL: (312) 668-6000
Visa, MC. Free catalog.
Christian school supplier.
Bible.

J. B. Lippincott Company
Educational Publishing Division
E. Washington Square
Philadelphia, PA 19105
Public school texts.
Read, Text.

Literacy Press
280 Pine St.
Madison, GA 30650
(404) 342-4062
MC, Visa. Large SASE for catalog.
Quantity discount to schools.
Phonics program.
Read.

The Literary Guild
Garden City, NY 11530
Best-seller book club.
Cat.

Little, Brown and Company
34 Beacon St.
Boston, MA 02106
(617) 890-0250
Publisher.
Gramm.

Living Heritage Academy
2600 Ace Lane
P.O. Box 1438
Lewisville, TX 75067-1438
(214) 462-1776
Installment plan.
No refunds once program opened.
Home school program.
Curr.

Living Scriptures
4357 S. Airport Park
Ogden, UT 84403
(801) 627-2000
Visa, MC. Payment plan for set commits you
to paying entire purchase price even if you
decide to cancel.
Cassette tape series. Bible, American history.
Bible, Hist.

Living Stories
Milford, KS 66514
(913) 463-5427
Visualized Christian stories. Over 40 years.
Char.

Loaves and Fishes
(Division of Food For Thot)
132 Carter
Sulphur Springs, TX 75482
Check or M.O. Free brochure.
Christian mag by/for children.
Write.

Love Publishing Co.
1777 S. Bellaire St.
Denver, CO 80222
(303) 757-2579
Check or M.O. Free catalog.
School texts, workbooks, supplies.
Comp, Spec.

Maher
P.O. Box 420
Littleton, CO 80160
(303) 798-6830
Visa, MC. Free catalog.
Ventriloquism and other entertainment
supplies.
Char.

Maher Workshops
P.O. Box 1466
Cedar Ridge, CA 95924
(916) 273-0176
Check or M.O. $2, info pak.
Ventriloquism and other entertainment
supplies.
Char.

Mandolin Brothers, Ltd.
629 Forest Ave.
Staten Island, NY 10310
(718) 981-3226
Visa, MC, AmX. Free catalog.
Minimum credit card order, $50.
Refund: 3 days, original carton, new
condition.
Stringed instruments and books.
Music.

Margwen Products
382 34th St. SE
Cedar Rapids, IA 52403
(319) 365-6398
No phone orders. Brochure w/SASE.
"Match-A-Fact" math games.
Math.

Master Books
(see Creation-Life Publications-Master Book
Division)

Math by Mail
P.O. Box 50279
Dallas, TX 75250
Uncopyrighted math materials.
Math.

Math Mouse Games
Cathy Duffy
12531 Aristocrat Ave.
Garden Grove, CA 92641
No phone orders. Brochure w/ SASE.
Make check out to Cathy Duffy.
"Math Mouse" games.
Math.

Mayflower Institute
P.O. Box 50218
Santa Barbara, CA 93150
Check or M.O. Free brochure.
Christian history and politics.
Govt, Hist.

McDougal, Littell & Company
P.O. Box 1667
Evanston, IL 60204
1-800-323-5435 IL: (312) 967-0900 collect
8:30-4:30 weekdays Central Time.
Returns: 6 months, permission.
Public school texts.
Text.

McGraw-Hill Book Company
1221 Avenue of the Americas
New York, NY 10020
Public school texts.
Text.

McGuffey Writer
400 McGuffey Hall
Miami University
Oxford, OH 45056
Check or M.O.
Lit mag by/for kids.
Write.

Medical Self-Care
P.O. Box 1000
Point Reyes, CA 94956
Health resources. New Age.
Health.

Merck & Company
P.O. Box 2000
Rahway, NJ 07065
(201) 574-5403
Doctor's diagnostic manual.
Health.

Merrill Publishing Co.
1300 Alum Creek Drive
Columbus, OH 43216
1-800-848-6205 OH: (614) 258-8441 collect
Returns: 30 days, permission.
Public school books, pre-K-12.
Text.

Message of Life Publications
58607 Rd. 601
Ahwahnee, CA 93601
(209) 683-7028
Phone orders accepted. No collect calls.
Check or M.O. Free brochure.
"Krata-Kraft" visualized Bible lessons.
Bible.

Midwest Publications
P.O. Box 448
Pacific Grove, CA 93950
(408) 375-2455
Check or M.O. Free catalog.
Classroom materials for thinking skills.
Supp.

Mile Hi Publishers
980 South Upham
Denver, CO 80226
(303) 922-5833 or 1557
Check or M.O. Free brochure.
Christian language series.
Text.

Milliken Publishing Company
1100 Research Blvd.
St. Louis, MO 63132-0579
(314) 991-4220
Visa, MC, COD. Free catalog.
Home workbooks and software.
Comp, Health, Supp, Write.

Milton Bradley/Playskool Supplies
(see any school supply house)
Flash cards, games, learning activities.
Geog, Pre, Sch.

The Mind's Eye
P.O. Box 6727
San Francisco, CA 94120
1-800-227-2020 CA: (415) 883-7701
Visa, MC, AmX. Free gorgeous catalog.
Stories on tape.
Lit.

Mini-Labs
(See Educational Design, Inc.)
Inexpensive science kits.
Sci.

Modern Curriculum Press, Inc.
13900 Prospect Rd.
Cleveland, OH 44136
1-800-321-3106 OH: (216) 328-2222 collect
Check or M.O.
Workbooks.
Text.

Montessori Services
816 King St.
Santa Rosa, CA 95404
(707) 579-3003
Visa, MC, COD. Free newsprint catalog.
Montessori supplies and books.
Phys, Pre.

Montessori World Educational Institute
P.O. Box 3808
San Luis Obispo, CA 93403
(805) 541-3100
Visa, MC. Free catalog.
Montessori supplies.
Pre.

Moody Bible Institute Correspondence School
820 N. LaSalle St.
Chicago, IL 60610
1-800-621-7105 IL: (312) 274-2549
Visa, MC. Free catalog.
15-day free trial.
Self-study adult Bible courses.
Dispensational.
Bible.

Moody Monthly
2101 W. Howard St.
Chicago, IL 60645
Christian family magazine.
Ad/Voc.

Barbara M. Morris Report
P.O. Box 756
Upland, CA 91785
Check or M.O.
Newsletter, books.
Book, Text.

William Morrow and Company
105 Madison Ave.
New York, NY 10016
(212) 889-3050
Publisher.
Hand, Read.

Mother's Bookshelf
P.O. Box 70
Hendersonville, NC 28791
1-800-438-0238 NC: (704) 693-0238
Visa, MC. Free catalog.
Returns: 10 days, undamaged.
Self-reliance books source.
Ec, Nat.

Motivational Art Training
9300 Beecher Rd.
Pittsford, MI 49271
No phone orders. Check or M.O.
Christian Art Manual.
Art.

Mott Media
1000 E. Huron St.
Milford, MI 48042
1-800-521-4350 MI: (313) 685-8773
Visa, MC. Free catalog.
Classic texts, McGuffeys, Christian character training.
Book, Hand, Lit, Math, Text.

Mountain Craft Shop
American Ridge Rd., Route 1
New Martinsville, WV 26155
(304) 455-3570
Check or M.O. Free catalog.
$15 minimum order.
Returns must be authorized in writing.
Backlog of orders, so order early.
Folk toys and reprints of old books.
Hist, T & G.

Moving and Learning
109 Berry River Rd.
Rochester, NH 03867
(603) 332-6917
Visa, MC. Free brochure.
Returns: 30 days.
Developmental exercise program.
Phys.

Museum of the American Indian
3753 Broadway
New York, NY 10032
(212) 283-2420
Check or M.O.
Free list of Museum publications.
Resources concerning Indians.
Soc.

My Big Backyard
(See National Wildlife Federation)
Preschooler's nature magazine.
Pre.

INDEX OF SUPPLIERS

NASCO
901 Janesville Ave.
Fort Atkinson, WI 53538
1-800-558-9595
Visa, MC, AmX. Free color catalog.
Art and craft supplies.
Art, Math, Priv, Sch, Sci.

National Academy of Child Development
(NACD)
112 First St.
Redlands, CA 92373
(714) 798-3028
Therapy and behavior modification programs
for the home.
Spec.

National Association for the Legal Support of
Alternative Schools
P.O. Box 2823
Santa Fe, NM 87501
(505) 471-6928
Resources for alternative schoolers.
Insurance fund.
Curr.

National Audubon Expedition Institute
Northeast Audubon Center
Sharon, CT 06069
(203) 364-0522
"Wild America Is Our Campus." New Age
treks about America for college credit.
Nature.

National Geographic Society
P.O. Box 2330
Washington, DC 20013
Geographic and cultural resources, secular.
Geog, Soc.

National Geographic *World*
P.O. Box 230
Washington, DC 20013-9865
Picture mag for kids.
Nature.

National Teaching Aids, Inc.
1845 Highland Ave.
New Hyde Park, NY 11040
(516) 326-2555
Check or M.O. Returns: 60 days, permission.
Photomicrographs and viewer.
Sci.

National Wildlife Federation
1412 16th St. NW
Washington, DC 20036
Check or M.O.
Nature magazines and resources.
Nature.

Nature Friend Magazine
P.O. Box 73
Goshen, IN 46526
Check or M.O.
Christian nature magazine.
Nature.

NavPress/The Navigators
P.O. Box 6000
Colorado Springs, CO 80934
1-800-525-7151
Visa, MC. Minimum phone order $20.
Adult self-study Bible courses.
Bible.

North Dakota State University
Division of Independent Study
Box 5036
State University Station
Fargo, ND 58105
(701) 237-7102
Check or M.O. No payment plan.
Refunds: First two weeks. Processing fee of
$5 retained.
High school correspondence program.
Curr.

Jeffrey Norton Publishers
On-The-Green
Guilford, CT 06437
(203) 453-9794
Visa, MC, AmX, DC, C Blanche.
Returns: 3 weeks, unconditional.
Educational and self-help cassettes.
Ec, Hist, Lang, Lit.

Oak Meadow Publications
P.O. Box G
Ojai, CA 93023
(805) 646-4510
Visa, MC. Free brochure.
New Age home-study booklets and curric.
Curr.

Oak Meadow School
P.O. Box G
Ojai, CA 92023
(805) 646-4510
Visa, MC. Monthly payments possible for
credit card holders.
No refunds if withdrawing for legal reasons.
Other refunds considered on individual
basis
Home school program.
Curr.

Michael Olaf
4284 Gilbert St.
Oakland, CA 94611
Check and M.O. Catalog, $1.
"The Montessori Shop."
Pre, Supp.

Hugh O'Neill and Associates
Box 1297
Nevada City, CA 95959
Check or M.O. Nice people.
Big yellow drawing book.
Art.

Open Connections
312 Byrn Mawr Ave.
Bryn Mawr, PA 19010
(215) 527-1504
Check or M.O.
Workshops and books for home schoolers.
P/L.

Open Court Publishing Company
1058 8th St.
P.O. Box 599
LaSalle, IL 61301
1-800-435-6850 IL: 1-800-892-6831
Visa, MC, AmX. Free catalog.
Returns: 90 days, resaleable, permission.
Texts for creative learning.
Comp, Lit, Math, Read.

Optasia Fine Art Designs
P.O. Box 369
Fruitport, MI 49415
(616) 865-3148
Check or M.O.
Beautiful postcards, note cards, to color.
Art.

Orion Telescope Center
P.O. Box 1158-S
Santa Cruz, CA 95061
1-800-447-1001 CA: 1-800-443-1001
Free catalog.
Astronomy supermarket.
Nat.

Orton Dyslexia Society
724 York Rd.
Baltimore, MD 21204
(301) 296-0232
Help for dyslexics.
Read, Spec.

Our Christian Heritage
7923 W. 62nd Way
Arvada, CO 80004
(303) 421-0444 or (303) 232-2313
Check or M.O. Free brochure.
Christian workbooks.
Hist, Soc.

Our Lady of Victory School
14412 San Jose St.
P.O. Box 5181
Mission Hills, CA 91345
(818) 897-1116
Checks only. Repurchase option. Quarterly payment plan. No refunds on registration. Home school program.
Curr.

Pacific Cascade Records
47534 McKenzie Highway
Vida, OR 97488-9707
(503) 896-3290
Visa, MC. Free catalog.
Returns: Defective materials only.
Music and folksongs for kids.
Phys.

Palmer Method Handwriting
A. N. Palmer Co.
1720 W. Irving Park Rd.
Schaumburg, IL 60193
(312) 894-4300
Handwriting supplies and courses.
Hand.

Pecci Educational Publishers
440 Davis Court #405
San Francisco, CA 94111
(415) 391-8579
Check or M.O. Free brochure.
Reading program and Super Seatwork.
Art, Book, Pre, Read, Supp.

Penny Power
P.O. Box 2480
Boulder, CO 80321
Check, M.O., or they bill you.
Kid's consumer magazine.
Ec.

Pensacola Christian Correspondence School
 (See A Beka Christian Correspondence School)

Perception Publications
1814 W. Seldon Lane
Phoenix, AZ 85021
(602) 997-2292
Check or M.O. or order from school supply house.
Readiness workbook series.
Pre.

Peregrine Software
1160 Appleseed Lane
St. Louis, MO 63132
(314) 997-2369 (Accept collect calls for orders)
Check, M.O., VISA, or MC.
Powerful software for Apples.
Comp.

Phonetic Spelling Lab Learning Network
31960 S.E. Chin St.
Boring, OR 97009
(503) 663-5153
Check or M.O.
Brochure with SASE. Sample pages $1.
Spelling program, including limericks.
Spell.

Pinkerton Marketing Inc.
209 Change St.
New Bern, NC 28560
Check, M.O., MC, VISA.
"The Great Book of Catalogs."
Cat.

Play 'n Talk
7105 Manzanita St.
Carlsbad, CA 92008
(619) 438-4330 7 A.M.—10 P.M. M-Sat PST.
Visa, MC, or post-dated checks for total price.
Total language arts program.
Read, Spell, Speech.

Playing for Knowledge, Inc.
4 Poplar Run
East Windsor, NJ 08520
(609) 448-8443
Check or M.O.
Large newsprint catalog $1 refundable on first order.
Distributor of gifted/talented materials.
Supp.

Playthinks
P.O. Box 2628
Setauket, NY 11733
(516) 751-2421
Visa, MC. Color catalog, $2.
Returns: 30 days, intact.
Kits for learning through play.
Supp.

Plough Publishing House
Route 213
Rifton, NY 12471
(914) 658-3141
Hutterite books, songs about/for children.
Pre.

Plymouth Rock Foundation
6 McKinley Circle
Marlborough, NH 03455-0425
(603) 876-4685
Invoice—30 days billing.
Books on Christian world view.
Govt.

Portland State University
Division of Continuing Education
Box 1394
Portland, OR 97207
1-800-547-8887 X 4891
In OR: 1-800-452-4909 X 4891.
Visa, MC. Free brochure.
Italic handwriting series.
Hand.

Praise Unlimited
1747 Cattlemen Rd.
Sarasota, FL 33582
(813) 377-3895
Christian dolls.
T & G.

Pratte Religious and Educational Supplies
7021 Omaha Ct.
Fort Wayne, IN 46804
Check or M.O. Free list.
Home school resources.
Cat.

Princeton University Press
41 William St.
Princeton, NJ 08544
(609) 452-3215
Publisher.
Nat.

Publishers Central Bureau
One Champion Ave.
P.O. Box 1262
Newark, NJ 07101
Visa, MC, AmX. $10 minimum.
Discount books.
Art, Cat.

Puritan-Reformed Discount Book Service
1319 Newport Gap Pike
P.O. Box 3499
Wilmington, DE 19804
1-800-441-7596 AK, DE, HI, Canada: (302) 999-0595
Discount Christian books.
Membership $5/year U.S., $8 Canada, $12 overseas.
Periodic membership extension specials.
Life membership is worth it.
Bible, Cat, Health, Nat.

Quality Paperback Book Club
Middletown, PA 17057
Book-of-the-Month subsidiary.
They bill you.
Cat.

Quest Academy
P.O. Box 20587
Phoenix, AZ 85036
(602) 966-6040
Dr. Rudolf Moore, administrator.
Prorated refunds on tuition only.
Home school program.
Curr.

R & E Publishers
P.O. Box 2008
Saratoga, CA 95070
(415) 494-1112
VISA, MC. Free catalog.
Books about children and schooling.
Priv.

R. S. Publications
P.O. Box 2245
Sedona, AZ 86336
Check or M.O. Free brochures.
Discovery Spanish, social studies.
Lang, Soc.

Rand McNally & Company
P.O. Box 7600
Chicago, IL 60680
East and Midwest: 1-800-245-1647
West and West Coast: 1-800-323-1887
Order small quantities through bookstores.
Atlases.
Geog.

Reading Reform Foundation
7054 E. Indian School Rd.
Scottsdale, AZ 85251
(602) 946-3567 NY chapter: (212) 307-7320
Check or M.O. Free list.
Resources on reading debate. Prophonics.
Read.

Recorded Books
P.O. Box 79
Charlotte Hall, MD 20622
1-800-638-1304
Visa, MC. Free catalog.
Current and classic fiction recorded.
Lit.

Reformed Presbyterian Church of North America Board of Education and Publication
7418 Penn Ave.
Pittsburgh, PA 15208
Check or M.O.
Psalms for Singing.
Bible.

Regents Publishing Company
2 Park Avenue
New York, NY 10016
1-800-822-8202 NY: (212) 889-2780 Op. 81
Visa, MC. Free catalog.
ESL and foreign languages.
Lang, Priv.

Regnery Gateway
950 North Shore Drive
Lake Bluff, IL 60044
(312) 295-8088
Publisher.
Lit, Nat.

Research Publications
P.O. Box 39850
Phoenix, AZ 85069
1-800-528-0559 AZ: 1-252-4777 collect.
Business hours only.
Visa, MC. Discounts for bulk orders.
Sam Blumenfeld's NEA exposé.
Book, Read.

Resources for the Gifted, Inc.
3421 N. 44th St.
Phoenix, AZ 85018
Touchtone phone: 950-1088, wait for tone,
then press 664066 for toll-free ordering.
(602) 840-9770, inquiries and customer
service.
Visa, MC. Free catalog.
Returns: 60 days, resaleable, you pay
postage.
Kathy Kolbe Thinkercise materials.
Govt, Sci, Supp.

Rhythm Band, Inc.
P.O. Box 126
Fort Worth, TX 76101
(817) 335-2561
Visa, MC, DC. Free color catalog.
Musical instruments for children.
Music, Priv.

Rifton: Equipment for the Handicapped
Rt. 213
Rifton, NY 12471
(914) 658-3141, (914) 658-3143
Check or M.O. Free catalog.
Returns: Allowed on some items. 10 percent
handling.
Exercise equipment for the handicapped.
Phys, Spec.

Rinehart Incorporated Handwriting System
South Street
Barre, MA 01005
(617) 355-2727
Check or M.O. Free brochure.
Handwriting correspondence courses.
Hand.

Rod and Staff Publishers
Crockett, KY 41413
(606) 522-4348
Check or M.O. Free brochure listing texts.
Returns: permission, 10 percent handling.
Christian schoolbooks. Mennonite.
Text.

Rodale Press
33 E. Minor St.
Emmaus, PA 18049
(215) 967-5171
Publisher. Self-help, health, organic.
Health, Nat.

Roper Press
915 Dragon St.
Dallas, TX 75207
(214) 742-6696
Check only. Brochure w/SASE.
Sample kit $15.95, returnable.
Through the Bible study program for
children.
Dawson McAllister youth Bible studies.
Since 1935.
Bible.

Rubberstampede
P.O. Box 1105
Berkeley, CA 94701
(415) 843-8910 10-4 M-F Pacific Time
Visa, MC. Free catalog.
Rubber stamps, of course!
T & G.

Rutherford Institute
P.O. Box 510
Manassas, VA 22110
Free newsletter. Donations welcome. Worthy
group.
Nonprofit legal association, defends religious
liberties.
Legal.

Saint Ursula Academy (S.U.A.)
1339 E. McMillan St.
Cincinnati, OH 45306
(513) 961-4877 or 961-3410
Check or M.O. Free brochure.
"Professor Phonics" reading program.
Read.

Santa Fe Community School
P.O. Box 2241
Santa Fe, NM 87501
(505) 471-9977
Home school program.
Curr.

SBI Publishers in Sound
Willow St.
South Lee, MA 01260
(413) 243-3235
Visa, MC. Free catalog.
Classics on tape. Some slow-playback.
Lit.

Scarborough Systems
25 N. Broadway
Tarrytown, NY 10591
Software.
Comp.

Scholastic Software
730 Broadway
New York, NY 10003
(212) 505-3000
Educational software.
Comp.

Scholastic Testing Service
480 Meyer Rd.
Bensenville, IL 60106
(312) 766-7150
Test.

School at Home
(see ICER Press)
Home school book.
Book.

School of Home Learning
P.O. Box 92
Escondido, CA 92025
(619) 749-1522
John A. Boston, educational administrator.
Home-centered learning program.
Curr.

School of Statesmanship
Route 5, Box 513
Manheim, PA 17545
Videos and cassettes on Constitution and the erosion thereof. How to get back our rights.
Free literature.
30-day money-back guarantee.
Govt.

School Supply Room
Gordonville Print Shop
3121 Irishtown Rd.
Gordonville, PA 17529
Check or M.O. List of texts, send SASE.
Mennonite texts.
Text.

School Zone Publishing Company
1819 Industrial Drive
P.O. Box 692
Grand Haven, MI 49417
(616) 846-5030
Check or M.O. Free catalog.
Home learning workbooks, flash cards, puzzles, video & audio cassettes, readers, pre-K-6.
Preschool software.
Supp.

Science Research Associates (SRA)
155 N. Wacker Dr.
Chicago, IL 60606
1-800-621-0476 IL: (312) 984-7000
Public school materials.
Math, Read, Test.

Scope City
679 Easy St.
Simi Valley, CA 93065
(805) 522-6646
Visa, MC. Free catalog.
Astronomy supermarket.
Nat.

Scott, Foresman & Company
1900 E. Lake Ave.
Glenview, IL 60025
CA: 1-800-437-6767
AK, AR, HI, ID, MT, NV, OR, UT, WA: 1-800-554-4411
Otherwise: (312) 729-3000
Public school textbooks.
Hand, Text.

Scribner Educational Publishers
866 Third Ave.
New York, NY 10022
(212) 702-9813
Check or M.O. Free catalog.
Public school textbook supplier.
Text.

Sculpture Associates
40 E. 19th St.
New York, NY 10003
(212) 777-2400
Visa, MC, AmX. $25 minimum.
Everything for the sculptor.
Art.

Sentinel Teacher Supply
1200 W. Evans
Denver, CO 80223
Sunday School and school supplies.
Free catalogs.
Bible, Sch.

Sesame Street
P.O. Box 2805
Boulder, CO 80321
They bill you.
Free sample issue.
Preschool magazine.
Pre.

Seton Home Study School
One Kidd Lane
Front Royal, VA 22630
(703) 636-9990
Mary Kay Clark, director.
Home school program.
Curr.

Shakean Stations, Inc.
P.O. Box 68
Farley, IA 52046
(319) 744-3307
Visa, MC. Free 8-page color brochure.
Inexpensive file folder games.
Supp, T & G.

Shar Products
P.O. Box 1411
Ann Arbor, MI 48106
(313) 665-7711
Visa, MC, C.O.D. Free B & W catalog.
Stringed instruments, accessories, supplies.
Suzuki materials. Huge list of sheet music for strings.
Music.

Silver Burdett Company
250 James St., CN 1918
Morristown, NJ 07960-1918
1-800-631-8081 NJ: (201) 285-7700 collect.
Returns: 1 year, permission.
Public school materials.
Lit, Music, Phys, Sci, Text.

Simon & Schuster
1230 Avenue of the Americas
New York, NY 10020
(212) 245-6400
Publisher.
Ec, Nature.

Sing, Spell, Read & Write
CBNU Extended University
Virginia Beach, VA 23463
1-800-446-READ or (804) 424-7000
Visa, MC. Free color brochure.
Total language arts K-3.
Gramm, Pre, Read.

Sky and Telescope Magazine
49 Bay St. Rd.
Cambridge, MA 02138
(617) 864-7360
Magazine and astronomy resources.
Sci.

Son Shine Puppet Company
P.O. Box 6203
Rockford, IL 61125
(815) 885-3709
Check or M.O. COD to institutions.
Free catalog.
Returns must be authorized.
Puppets, costumes, accessories.
Char.

Southwestern Stringed Instruments
1228 East Prince Rd.
Tuscon, AZ 85719
Music.

Sparrow Distribution
8025 Deering Ave.
Canoga Park, CA 91304
Christian character materials sold in stores.
Char.

Spinnaker Software
One Kendall Square
Cambridge, MA 02139
(617) 494-1200
Software for fun and learning.
Comp.

Springboard Software
7807 Creekridge Circle
Minneapolis, MN 55435
(612) 944-3912
Software for fun and learning.
Comp.

Standard Publishing
8121 Hamilton Ave.
Cincinnati, OH 54231
1-800-543-1353 OH: 1-800-582-1385
Visa, MC. Free catalog.
Bible-centered everything.
Bible.

Stay-Homish Trading Post
P.O. Box 436
Snohomish, WA 98290
Check or M.O.
Home school trade/ad magazine.
Mag.

Steck-Vaughn Company
807 Brazos
P.O. Box 2028
Austin, TX 78768
1-800-531-5015 TX: 1-800-252-9317
Check or M.O. Free catalog.
Full-service textbook company.
Text.

Stone Soup
P.O. Box 83
Santa Cruz, CA 95063
Check or M.O.
Secular literary mag by/for kids.
Write.

Stork—The Magazine for Nursery Dwellers
P.O. Box 10681
Des Moines, IA 50381
(515) 284-2194
"Health" mag for tiny tots. Colorful.
Pre.

Summer Institute of Linguistics
International Linguistics Center
7500 Camp Wisdom Road
Dallas, TX 75236
(214) 298-2436
Check or M.O. No returns without permission.
Resources for linguistics scholars.
Lang.

Summit Christian Academy
13789 Noel Road, Suite 100
Dallas, TX 75240
1-800-362-9180 for enrollments.
VISA, MC.
(214) 239-7433 for inquiries.
No payment plan.
Home school program.
Curr.

Summy-Birchard Co.
  (see Birch Tree Group Ltd.)

Sunburst Communications, Inc.
39 Washington Ave.
Pleasantville, NY 10570
1-800-431-1934 AK, HI, NY, Canada: (914) 769-5030 collect.
Call toll-free number for free catalog.
Specify Home Market Brochure or school catalog.
Visa, MC, COD.
Customer satisfaction guaranteed.
Lifetime replacement of defective parts.
Creative educational software.
Comp.

Sycamore Tree
2179 Meyer Place
Costa Mesa, CA 92627
(714) 650-4466
Check or M.O.
Catalog $2, comes with $2 coupon good toward first purchase.
Full service home school supplier.
Home school program.
Art, Bible, Cat, Curr, Health, Phys, Sci.

Louis Tannen Magic, Inc.
6 West 32nd St., Fourth Floor
New York, NY 10001
(212) 239-8383
Visa, MC, AmX. $15 minimum.
800-page hardbound catalog, $6, plus $5 UPS.
Magic tricks, supplies, books. Magic mag.
T & G.

The Teaching Home
Christian Home Schools
8731 N.E. Everett St.
Portland, OR 97220
(503) 253-9633
Home schooling mag. Christian. State editions co-published in thirteen states (as of 11/85).
Mag.

Ten Speed Press
P.O. Box 7123
Berkeley, CA 94707
(415) 845-8414
Check or M.O.
Publisher, nonfiction of all kinds.
Ad/Voc, Comp.

Textbooks for Parents
P.O. Box 209
Kendrick, Idaho 83537
(208) 276-4721
Check or M.O. Free brochure.
Public school texts.
Text.

Things of Science
814 Washington Crossing Rd.
Newtown, PA 18940
Check or M.O.
Miniscience kits. Secular.
Sci.

Thoburn Press
Fairfax Christian Bookstore
P.O. Box 6941
Tyler, TX 75711
(214) 581-0677
Check or M.O.
Returns discouraged. With permission,
resaleable condition.
10 percent returns charge plus postage,
return UPS, no returns over $35.
Publishes revised *McGuffeys.*
Also Christian books and texts.
Lit, Hand, Math, Priv, Text.

Thompson's Book Depository
P.O. Box 53158
Oklahoma City, OK 73152
(405) 525-9458
Sells Saxon's algebra and other school texts.
Math.

Toad's Tools
P.O. Box 173
Oberlin, OH 44074
Visa, MC, COD. Catalog, $1. Applied to
order.
Returns: 30 days.
Topnotch kids' tools. Expensive.
T & G.

Toastmasters International
World Headquarters
2200 N. Grand Ave.
P.O. Box 10400
Santa Ana, CA 92711
Public speaking club. Area chapters.
Worldwide. Write for info on chapter near
you.
Speech.

The Toy Factory
88878 Highway 101
Florence, OR 97439
(503) 997-8604
Visa, MC. SASE for catalog.
Minimum orders: $8 check, $15 charge.
Toys, games, books, toymaking supplies.
T & G.

Toys to Grow On
P.O. Box 17
Long Beach, CA 90801
Visa, MC, AmX. $10 minimum. Free catalog.
(213) 603-8890 6-6 M-Sat PST, orders and
questions.
(516) 794-5340 24 hours, 7 days, orders only.
Returns: 30 days.
Gift wrap, $2.
Music, T & G.

Treehouse Publishing Company
P.O. Box 35461
Phoenix, AZ 85069
Check or M.O. Free catalogs.
Publishes variety of school stuff.
Comp, Supp, T & G.

TREND Enterprises, Inc.
P.O. Box 64073
St. Paul, MN 55164-0073
1-800-328-0818 MN: (612) 631-2850
Stickers, wipe-off books, more.
Hand, Pre.

Tyndale House
336 Gundersen Dr.
P.O. Box 80
Wheaton, IL 60189
Christian publisher.
Publishes *L'Abri* mentioned in Ch. 2.

United States Government Printing Office
Superintendent of Documents
Washington, DC 20402
(202) 783-3238 8-4 M-F EST.
Visa, MC. Free catalog.
Books on wide variety of subjects.
Cat.

University of Nebraska-Lincoln
Division of Continuing Studies
Lincoln, NE 68583-0900
(402) 472-1926
Full service H.S. diploma course.
Science equipment, courses.
Curr, Sci.

Victory Drill Book
19300 Redwood Road
Castro Valley, CA 94546
(415) 889-7526
Check or M.O. Free brochure.
Speed drill, phonics.
Read.

Visual Education Corporation
14 Washington Rd.
Box 2321
Princeton, NJ 08540
(609) 799-9200 Call collect for orders only.
Cassette series.
Ec, Govt, Hist, Soc.

Warner Books
75 Rockefeller Plaza
New York, NY 10019
(212) 484-8000
Publisher.
Health.

Weekly Reader Books
  (see Xerox Educational Publications)
Summer skills library.
Supp.

Weekly Reader Family Software
  (see Xerox Educational Publications)
Educational software.
Comp.

Western Publishing Company, Inc.
1220 Mound Avenue
Racine, WI 53404
Workbooks, kids' books.
Supp.

WFF 'n PROOF Learning Games
1490 South Blvd.
Ann Arbor, MI 48104-4699
(313) 665-2269
Visa, MC, COD. Free catalog.
Games for school subjects.
Comp, Gramm, Govt, Lang, Math, Sci,
T & G.

Whole Earth Software Review
P.O. Box 27956
San Diego, CA 92128
1-800-354-8400
Visa, MC.
Software/hardware/firmware/anyware
reviews.
Comp.

World of the Gifted
  (see Treehouse Publishing)

Word DMS Inc.
P.O. Box 2560
Waco, TX 76702-2560
They bill you.
Survival Series: training for kids.
Char.

World Book/Childcraft International
Educational Service Department
Merchandise Mart Plaza
Chicago, IL 60654
(312) 245-3456
Check or M.O. Orders over $25 may be
billed.
Encyclopedia. Workbooks. Learning aids.
Supp.

World Wide Games
Box 450 BB
Delaware, OH 43015
(614) 369-9631
Visa, MC, C.O.D. Free catalog.
Satisfaction guaranteed.
Wooden games.
T & G.

Xerox Educational Publications
WeeklyaReader
245 Long Hill Road
Middletown, CT 06457
1-800-824-7888, Operator 426 for skill library.
AK, HI: 1-800-824-7919, Op 426 for skills lib.
Visa, MC. Free brochure.
Returns: 15 days, they pay fourth class postage.
Software, Summer Skills library.
Comp, Supp.

Young Companion
Pathway Publishers
Route 4
Aylmer, Ontario, CANADA N5H 2R3
Mennonite kids' mag.
Char.

Young Pilot
Prairie Bible Institute
Box 9
Three Hills, Alberta
CANADA T0M 2A0
Christian magazine for kids.
Char.

Young Writers Club
P.O. Box 216
Newburyport, MA 01950
(617) 462-7944
Check or M.O.
"Wordworks" mag by/for kids.
Write.

Zaner-Bloser
2300 Fifth Avenue
P.O. Box 16764
Columbus, OH 43216-6764
(614) 486-0221
Visa, MC. Free catalog.
Full-service spelling and handwriting supplier.
Hand, Read, Spell, Text.

Zondervan Publishing House
1415 Lake Drive, S.E.
Grand Rapids, MI 49506
1-800-253-1309 MI: 1-800-253-4475
Large Christian publisher.
Lit.

Zoobooks/Wildlife Education
930 W. Washington St.
San Diego, CA 92103
Booklets about animals.
Nature.